From Guano to Gold

*Dedicated to the memory of our friend
Peter Macdonald
who saved this diary from extinction*

From Guano to Gold

The Diary and Letters of Vicary Gibbs
from 1883-5

Edited and researched by Shirley Hinkly

Published by Crawcour Books
3 Harding Close
Selsey
CHICHESTER
PO20 0FG
United Kingdom

© Shirley Hinkly, 2014
GibbsDiary@hinkly.net

From Guano to Gold: The Diary and Letters of Vicary Gibbs from 1883-5
Edited and researched by Shirley Hinkly

ISBN 978-0-9928720-0-7

Front cover:
1. Background: detail from Map of Sydney circa 1922, showing the Gibbs, Bright & Co. wharf near the north-west inlet of Sydney Cove. From U.S. Library of Congress.
2. Foster and Martin portrait photo of Vicary Gibbs in Melbourne (1882). Courtesy of Lord Aldenham and David Hogg.

Back cover:
1. Passengers on board the Wairarapa, with Vicary Glbbs standing in the centre of the second row from back wearing a large beret. Photograph taken by Burton Brothers. Courtesy of the Alexander Turnbull Library, Wellington, New Zealand, Parliamentary Library: Photograph albums. Ref: PA1-f-178-48-1. http://natlib.govt.nz/records/22891805

Contents

Table of Pictures vii
Preface xi
Introduction 1
   The Gibbs' Family Tree 14
Diary 17
   18/08/1883: Aboard the S.S. Gallia 17
   28/08/1883: New York 24
   01/09/1883: Great Western of Canada Line and Northern Pacific Railway ... 27
   13/09/1883: S.S. Queen of the Pacific 37
   18/09/1883: San Francisco 40
   22/09/1883: S.S. City of New York 44
   21/10/1883: Sydney (1) 53
   27/10/1883: S.S. John Elder 60
   31/10/1883: Melbourne (1) 62
   30/11/1883: S.S. Sorata 76
   02/12/1883: Adelaide 77
   09/12/1883: S.S. Shannon 82
   11/12/1883: Melbourne (2) 84
   12/02/1884: S.S. Tarawera (1) 104
   20/02/1884: Dunedin 109
   28/02/1884: Christchurch 113
   01/03/1884: Tour of the West Coast of South Island, New Zealand 116
   12/03/1884: Tour of North Island, New Zealand from Wellington to Auckland 124
   02/04/1884: S.S. Tarawera (2) 135
   08/04/1884: Sydney (2) 137
   23/04/1884: East coast of Australia to Queensland 144
   01/05/1884: Brisbane 148
   28/05/1884: S.S. Ly-ee-moon 156
   31/05/1884: Sydney (3) 157
   05/06/1884: Melbourne (3) 159
   27/06/1884: S.S. Wairoa 164
   02/07/1884: Auckland 165
   07/07/1884: S.S. Wairarapa – South Sea Islands cruise; Auckland; Dunedin 166
   14/08/1884: Melbourne (4) 182
   20/11/1884: S.S. Carthage 206
   19/12/1884: Colombo 210
   17/02/1885: S.S. Brindisi 229
   04/03/1885: S.S. Mongolia 234
   08/03/1885: Florence, Italy 236
   13/03/1885: London, via Paris 239
Letters 241
   Henry Hucks Gibbs to Tyndall Bright (08/11/1880) 242
   Angus McPherson (Amby) to Bright, Chrystal & Co. (Melbourne) 243
   Letter #1 from Vicary Gibbs (Sydney) to his brother Alban (23/10/1883) ... 245
   Letter #2 from Vicary Gibbs (Sydney) to his brother Alban (24/10/1883) ... 246
   Letter #3 from Vicary Gibbs (Melbourne) to his brother Alban (02/11/1883) 250
   Letter #4 from Vicary Gibbs (Melbourne) to his brother Alban (16/11/1883) 253
   Vicary Gibbs (Sydney) to Charles Bright (24/10/1883) 256
   Frank Keating (Brisbane) to Vicary Gibbs (26/10/1883) 257
   Vicary Gibbs (Melbourne) to Frank Keating (01/11/1883) 258
   George Merivale (Sydney) to Vicary Gibbs (Melbourne) (26/11/1883) 259
   Vicary Gibbs (Melbourne) to George Merivale (Sydney) (27/12/1883) 262
   Vicary Gibbs (Adelaide) to Charles Bright (04/12/1883) 264
   Vicary Gibbs (Adelaide) to Charles Bright (07/12/1883) 268

Charles Bright (aboard S.S. Rome) to his brother Regi (Melbourne) (01/01/1884) 270
Letter #6 from Vicary Gibbs (Melbourne) to his brother Alban (12/12/1883) 272
Letter #7 from Vicary Gibbs (Melbourne) to his brother Alban (19/12/1883) 275
Letter #8 from Vicary Gibbs (Melbourne) to his brother Alban (28/12/1883) 286
Letter #9 from Vicary Gibbs (Melbourne) to his brother Alban (02/01/1884) 288
Telegram: Angus MacPherson (Echuca), to D. Chrystal (Torrumbarry) (07/02/1884) ..289
Letter #11 from Vicary Gibbs (Melbourne) to his brother Alban (24/01/1884) 289
Letter #12 from Vicary Gibbs (Melbourne) to his brother Alban (30/01/1884) 293
Letter #13 from Vicary Gibbs (Melbourne) to his brother Alban (06/02/1884) 298
Letter #14 from Vicary Gibbs (Melbourne) to his brother Alban (11/02/1884) 301
Letter #15 from Vicary Gibbs (Christchurch, NZ) to his brother Alban (01/03/1884) ...303
Letter #16 from Vicary Gibbs (Auckland, NZ) to his brother Alban (30/03/1884) 308
Letter #17 from Vicary Gibbs (Sydney) to his brother Alban (09/04/1884) 310
Letter(1) from Vicary Gibbs (Sydney) to his father Henry Hucks Gibbs (10/04/1884) ..316
Letter(2) from Vicary Gibbs (Sydney) to his father Henry Hucks Gibbs (19/04/1884) ..320
Letter #18 from Vicary Gibbs (Sydney) to his brother Alban (17/04/1884) 321
Letter #19 from Vicary Gibbs (Sydney) to his brother Alban (21/04/1884) 323
Letter #20 from Vicary Gibbs (Brisbane) to his brother Alban (08/05/1884) 324
Letter #22 from Vicary Gibbs (Sydney) to his brother Alban (02/06/1884) 327
Vicary Gibbs (Brisbane) to George Merivale (Sydney) (05/05/1884) 330
Reginald Bright (Melbourne) to Vicary Gibbs (Brisbane) (12/05/1884).......................330
Vicary Gibbs (Brisbane) to William Murray (19/05/1884) 331
Vicary Gibbs (Brisbane) to Reginald Bright (Melbourne) (19/05/1884).......................332
Vicary Gibbs (Brisbane) to Frank Keating (20/05/1884)...333
Vicary Gibbs (Brisbane) to Reginald Bright (20/05/1884)..334
Vicary Gibbs (Brisbane) to Reginald Bright (28/05/1884)..337
Vicary Gibbs (Brisbane) to Johnny Gibbs (Liverpool) (20/05/1884)............................338
Despatch Note for Amby Downs Wool to GB&Co. (Brisbane) (01/03/1884)................340
Gibbs, Bright & Co. (Brisbane) to Antony Gibbs & Sons (London) (11/09/1884).........341
Angus MacPherson to D. Chrystal (01/10/1884)...342
Frank Keating (Melbourne) to Reginald Bright (Sydney) (12/05/1885) 344
Frank Keating (Melbourne) to Reginald Bright (Sydney) (14/05/1885) 346
Epilogue..349
Indexes...355
  Index of People...355
  Index of Locations 371
  Hierarchical List of Locations 379
  Index of Books..389

Table of Pictures

1. Sketch portrait of Vicary Gibbs (1882) – courtesy of Lord Aldenham x
2. Rear view of Pytte House (present day) – courtesy of Peter Hinkly 1
3. Tyntesfield, Wraxall (present day) – courtesy of Claire Walters 4
4. Aldenham House (present day) – courtesy of Peter Hinkly 6
5. SS Gallia (1890s) – by John S. Johnston, from U.S. Library of Congress Prints and Photographs Division, Washington D.C., LC-D4-22365. 17
6. Statue of Sir Henry Edwards, MP, in Weymouth – By Shirley Hinkly 22
7. New York and Brooklyn Bridge (C1889) – by Albertype Co., from U.S. Library of Congress Prints and Photographs Division, Washington D.C., LC-USZ62-22027 25
8. Sitting Bull (at Bismarck, North Dakota) (1885) – by David Frances Barry, from U.S. Library of Congress Prints and Photographs Division, Washington D.C., LC-USZ62-111147 31
9. Northern Pacific Railway – Villard 'Gold Spike' Excursion (1883) – by Frank Jay Haynes, from Washington State Historical Society. http://digitum.washingtonhistory.org/cdm/search/searchterm/S1991.38.9 33
10. Northern Pacific Railway (present day) – courtesy of Phil Phillips 35
11. Donald Mackinnon on his way back from Oxford via U.S.A. (c1883-5) – by Isaiah West Taber (1830-1912), from State Library of Victoria, H83.47/21. http://handle.slv.gov.au/10381/85320 42
12. Cliff House, San Francisco (c1902) – by Detroit Publishing Co., from U.S. Library of Congress Prints and Photographs Division, Washington D.C., LC-USZ62-77079. http://www.loc.gov/pictures/item/2002699470 43
13. Engine 15 Firehouse and fire engine, San Francisco (1894) – By W. Cathcart, from U.S. Library of Congress Prints and Photographs Division, Washington D.C., HABS CAL,38-SANFRA,72—3. http://www.loc.gov/pictures/item/ca0639.photos.016955p/ 43
14. Members of the Northern Club, Auckland leaving by carriage from outside the club building in Princes Street for the races at Ellerslie (1880s) – from the Sir George Grey Special Collections, Auckland Libraries, ref. 7-A642 51
15. Mort & Co., wool store and the Customs House at Circular Quay, Sydney (c1885) – by Charles Bayliss (1850-1897), from Collection of photographs of New South Wales, ca. 1876-1897, from National Library of Australia, nla.pic-vn5779292 53
16. Royal Yacht Squadron – afternoon gathering (c1884-1917) – from the Tyrell Photographic Collection, Powerhouse Museum. http://www.powerhousemuseum.com/collection/database/?irn=28821 53
17. Union Club, Sydney (c1894-5) – From Album of the Boileau family's voyage from England to Australia in 1894-1895, from National Library of Australia, nla.pic-an3366506-s66 58
18. Union Bank of Australia and Gibbs, Shallard &Co., Printers, Pitt Street, Sydney (1873-80) – by Charles Bayliss (1850-1897), from the B.O. Holtermann Archive of Merlin and Bayliss photographic prints of New South Wales and Victoria, National Library of Australia, nla.pic-vn4704183 59
19. Watercolour of St. Leonards – Courtesy of Charles and Primrose Bright of Melbourne, Australia 61
20. Gibbs Bright Offices Melbourne, Flinders Lane and Bond St junction (c1880) – from State Library of Victoria, H4563. http://handle.slv.vic.gov.au/10381/69592 62
21. Gibbs Bright Offices Melbourne (detail showing Orient agency sign) (c1880) – from State Library of Victoria, H4563 (detail) 62
22. Washing Wool (c1884-1917) – from the Tyrrel Photographic Collection, Powerhouse Museum. http://www.powerhousemuseum.com/collection/database/?irn=27991 63
23. Bullock team carting wool bales (c1880) – from Scenes of Australian landscapes, Aboriginal people, wool transport and farm houses, ca. 1880, from National Library of Australia, nla.pic-vn3550658 63
24. Reginald Bright – by Tom Roberts, courtesy of Charles and Primrose Bright of Melbourne, Australia 64

25. Charles Edward Bright, by Tennyson Cole, courtesy of Charles and Primrose Bright of Melbourne, Australia 65
26. Greek text from 1 November 1883 – scanned from the diary of Vicary Gibbs 67
27. Reginald Bright as a young man – one of the 'dancing men' to whom Gibbs refers (c1873-8) – by Maull & Co., from State Library of Victoria, H2011.176/25. http://handle.slv.vic.gov.au/10381/165874 72
28. Greek text from 27 November 1883 – scanned from the diary of Vicary Gibbs 75
29. King William Street, Adelaide (c1880) – from State Library of South Australia, B62414/1/22 80
30. Jennie Lee (with J.P. Burnett?) (1885) – from State Library of Victoria, H10157. http://www.slv.vic.gov.au/miscpics/gid/slv-pic-aab24818 81
31. Circular Quay, showing wool stores including Dalgety & Co. (c1900) – from the Tyrrell Photographic Collection, Powerhouse Museum. http://www.powerhousemuseum.com/collection/database/?irn=29627 92
32. Marida Yallock (c1915-18) – by Romney, from State Library of Victoria, H83.47/33a. http://handle.slv.vic.gov.au/10381/71300 97
33. Rosa Lewis, aged 28 (1865) – courtesy of Dr Mimi Colligan of Monash University 102
34. Milford Sound, Pembroke Peak, NZ (1895) – from Album of the Boileau family's voyage from Engalnd to Australia in 1894-1895, National Library of Australia, nla.pic-an3366506-a28-a1 107
35. Donald Sutherland, Milford Sound (1911) – by Norman Cathcart Deck, from National Library of Australia, nla.pic-an11236269-8 107
36. Grand Hotel, Dunedin (c1880) – Hocken Collections, Uare Taoke o Hakena, University of Otago, 81-3783, ref S11-082a 109
37. Crawford Street, Dunedin – from Hocken Collections, Uare Taoke o Hakena, University of Otago, 81-3738, ref S11-082a 109
38. Judge Sir Joshua Strange Williams – from Hocken Collections, Uare Taoke o Hakena, University of Otago, c/n E3466/4, ref S11-082a 111
39. Canterbury Club, Christchurch, New Zealand (c1878-79) – from My Tour, 1878-79, Vol. 1. Some of the photographs in this album have been attributed to Alfred Winter, John Paine, Charles Nettleton and D. McDonald. From National Library of Australia, nla.pic-vn3916401-s97 115
41. Cashel Street bridge over the River Avon in winter, Christchurch, New Zealand (c1878-79) – from My Tour, 1878-79, Vol. 1. Some of the photographs in this album have been attributed to Alfred Winter, John Paine, Charles Nettleton and D. McDonald. From National Library of Australia, nla.pic-vn3916401-s100 116
40. Cathedral Square, Christchurch, New Zealand (1894) – from Album of the Boileau family's voyage from England to Australia in 1894-1895. From National Library of Australia, nla.pic-an3366506-s34-a1 116
42. Ivo Bligh, Lord Darnley, recipient of The Ashes Urn in 1883 (c1890) – from Wikimedia Commons, http://commons.wikimedia.org/wiki/File:Ivo_Bligh_circa_1890.jpg 126
43. Florence, Countess of Darnley, wife of Ivo Bligh (c1890) – from Wikimedia Commons, http://commons.wikimedia.org/wiki/File:Florence_Countess_of_Darnley_circa_1890.jpg 126
44. Maori King & Queen – from Sir George Grey Special Collections, Auckland Libraries, ref. 589-4 135
45. Botanical Gardens, Sydney (c1885) – from Album of photographs of Sydney and Queensland Botanic Gardens, ca. 1885. From National Library of Australia, nla.pic-vn3996427 139
46. Sydney Harbour Bridge, Southern Approach, showing Campbell's Cove front left including wool stores and Gibbs' warehouse – from State Records NSW (New South Wales, Australia). Southern Approach, from Series 12685 – Sydney Harbour Bridge Photographs. Digital ID: 12685_a007_a00704_8728000157r.jpg 142
47. Brisbane wharves from Kangaroo Point, Brisbane (1878) – from the John Oxley Library, State Library of Queensland, http://hdl.handle.net/10462/deriv/111653 143
48. SS Orient in Circular Quay (c1880-1900) – from the Tyrrell Photographic Collection, Powerhouse Museum. http://www.powerhousemuseum.com/collection/database/?irn=30835 144

Table of Pictures

49. Front entrance to the Amby Downs homestead near Charleville, Queensland (c1877) – from the John Oxley Library, State Library of Queensland. http://hdl.handle.net/10462/deriv/3751 151
50. Melbourne (1880s?) – from Album of photographs of Melbourne, Victoria, Sydney, Brisbane, Nudgee, Launceston, New Zealand and Europe 1880-1889, from National Library of Australia, nla.pic-an10638277-43.. 159
51. Collins St., Melbourne, showing Foster & Martin photographers (c1890) – from Album of photographs of views in Australia, Ceylon and Scotland. From National Library of Australia, nla.pic-an10642263-30... 162
52. Greek text from 26 June 1884 – scanned from the diary of Vicary Gibbs................. 164
53. Passengers on board the Wairarapa (July 1884), with Vicary Gibbs shown in the centre of the second row from the back wearing a beret, with his thumb hooked in his jacket. Photograph taken by Burton Brothers. From Parliamentary Library: Photograph albums. Ref: PA1-f-178-48-1, Alexander Turnbull Library, Wellington, New Zealand. http://natlib.govt.nz/records/22891805... 166
54. Gibbs' sketch of the Tongatapu Pyramid – scanned from the diary of Vicary Gibbs .. 177
55. Haamonga-A-Maui, Tongatapu, Tonga (present day) – photo by Tony Bowden. From Wikimedia Commons. http://commons.wikimedia.org/wiki/File:Haamonga-A-Maui.jpg 179
56. Melbourne Club (1880-9) – from Album of photographs of Melbourne, Victoria, Sydney, Brisbane, Nudgee, Launceston, New Zealand and Europe 1880-1889, from National Library of Australia, nla.pic-an10638277-44.. 182
57. Greek text from 16 August 1884 – scanned from the diary of Vicary Gibbs............. 183
58. Rebecca Ada Crawcour (1864-1967) – courtesy of Patrick Coppel......................... 187
59. Donald Mackinnon and Hilda Bunny wedding (1891) – by Foster & Martin, from the Mackinnon Collection, State Library of Victoria, H84.437. http://handle.slv.vic.gov.au/10381/71297 192
60. Hilda and Donald Mackinnon (c1890s) – by Mendelssohn & Co., from State Library of Victoria, H83.47/19. http://handle.slv.vic.gov.au/10381/85296................................. 192
61. Government House, Melbourne (1880-9) – from Album of photographs of Melbourne, Victoria, Sydney, Brisbane, Nudgee, Launceston, New Zealand and Europe 1880-1889, from National Library of Australia, nla.pic-an10638277-33... 200
62. James Blackett – courtesy of Robert Wilson 214
63. Greek text from 27 December 1884 – scanned from the diary of Vicary Gibbs......... 216
64. Paul Friedrich, Duke of Mecklenburg – from Wikimedia Commons, http://en.wikipedia.org/wiki/File:Paul_Friedrich_Herzog_zu_Mecklenburg.jpg 226
65. Princess Marie of Windisch-Graetz (wife of Paul Friedrich, Duke of Mecklenburg) – from Wikimedia Commons, http://en.wikipedia.org/wiki/File:1856_Marie.jpg 226
66. Don Carlos – from Wikimedia Commons, http://en.wikipedia.org/wiki/File:S.M.F._El-Rei_D._Carlos_I_de_Portugal.jpg 228
67. John Gibbs & family (1872) – courtesy of Charles and Primrose Bright of Melbourne, Australia 237
68. Circular Quay, Sydney (1880-1910) – by Charles Henry Kelly. From National Library of Australia, nla.pic-vn3700021 247
69. An 1888 lithograph of the 1883 eruption of Krakatoa – from Wikimedia Commons, http://commons.wikimedia.org/wiki/File:Krakatoa_eruption_lithograph.jpg 271
70. Gibbs' Plan of the Sydney Premises – recreated from Gibbs' original sketch by Adam Hinkly 279
71. Messrs. Gibbs, Bright and Co.'s New Offices, Pitt Street, Sydney – from the Illustrated Sydney News, 10 January 1886, http://trove.nla.gov.au/ndp/del/page/5788187 280
72. Model of the SS Great Britain – courtesy of the Port Stanley Museum, Falkland Islands. Photo by Edel, staff photographer on the Saga Ruby. 311
73. Shipping Wool, Circular Quay (c1879-1917) – from the Tyrrell Photographic Collection, Powerhouse Museum. http://www.powerhousemuseum.com/collection/database/?irn=27982 316
74. Amby Downs Despatch Note – courtesy of Peter Hinkly 340
75. Portrait of Vicary Gibbs – courtesy of Lord Aldenham... 348

1. Sketch portrait of Vicary Gibbs (1882)
Courtesy of Lord Aldenham

Preface

In the early 1980s an old friend of my husband's and mine, the now late Peter Macdonald - an administrative manager for the Merchant Bankers, Antony Gibbs and Sons - was supervising the disposal of a large quantity of paperwork left redundant by the HSBC take-over. In the City of London vaults of AG&S he came across a pile of notebooks destined for destruction. One of those notebooks was a small handwritten diary belonging to one Vicary Gibbs describing a business trip he made to America, Australia, New Zealand, and Ceylon (Sri Lanka).

Knowing my interest in the diary form, and being unwilling to consign this part of Vicary Gibbs' life to the skip, Peter lent me the diary to read – and I became so enthralled by its social and economic history that I spent the next few years researching it in more detail. Following Peter's death in December 2005, his wife Zena encouraged my wish to buy and accepted my offer for it. I hope that Peter would have been pleased to see his find researched, amplified and printed so that anyone interested could enjoy this unique time-travel experience.

The diary is presented here unedited, except to correct the spelling and to insert punctuation (which Gibbs almost exclusively omitted). Some of the names of people and places - especially in Ceylon - are very hard to decipher and I have shown in the diary text the names that Gibbs seems to have written, and noted in a footnote possible actual place names. At the end of the book is a selection of business letters of the time (many to or from Vicary Gibbs), which help to provide background information.

Gibbs occasionally used words or expressed thoughts that nowadays would be considered offensive. I have not edited these at all as they demonstrate the conventions or norms of the time rather than any intolerance on his part specifically, and I hope that no-one will be offended either by the original text or by any footnote I may have added.

This book is not intended to be an academic tract, but as an aid to reading and understanding it I have added numerous footnotes to explain words, phrases, or references which may have been commonplace in the late 19th century but are no longer, and to give a brief biography (where I can) of those people he meets on his travels, whether on board ship or in the course of business. These biographical footnotes usually appear on the first occurrence of the relevant person, and can be located via the Index of People where the page number will be shown in bold type. The footnotes are generally compiled from information in the public domain, and no specific source is shown - they are given merely for background and to provide a starting point if you are interested enough to research some aspect further.

Most of the photographs used in this book are taken from archives that generously make their collections available for little or no charge. A brief citation showing the source of each photo is shown beneath it, but there is usually some additional information shown in the Table of Pictures at the front of the book which should be enough to enable you to hunt down the original picture and view it in more detail online. Many individuals also kindly allowed me to use photographs from their own collections; my thanks to all of them - they are listed later.

There are many places where I have drawn a blank in my research, and if you see a name which means something to you or about which you can offer insight but do not see a footnote, please let me know - my postal and email addresses are shown on the copyright page. Working on this diary has been a labour of love for me, and I should be delighted to hear from you too if you find yourself similarly touched.

An undertaking of this kind depends on the collaboration of many others. I would like to offer my grateful thanks to the following people and institutions for their generously offered help with my research. Without them, this book would not have been possible.

The present day Vicary Gibbs, the 6th Baron Aldenham, and his wife Lady Aldenham, gave me permission to publish the Journal - of which they too have a manuscript copy - and helped me by answering questions about Antony Gibbs and Sons, and also by kindly arranging free access to the collection of Gibbs' records and letters held in the Guildhall Achive. With those documents, and from many others held in libraries and archives in Australia and New Zealand, I have been able to understand the part played by AG&S in the growth of trade between Great Britain and her new colonies in the 19th and 20th centuries.

I am especially grateful to Charles and Primrose Bright of Melbourne, members of the same Bright family who were friends and partners of Gibbs over 200 years, for their help in selecting pictures from their family photograph album in the Bright Archive of Melbourne University. Their encouraging emails have also been very welcome.

My delighted thanks to Dr. Mimi Colligan of Monash University, Australia, for her interest, information, and the Carte de Visite of Rosa Lewis, née Dunn.

Robert Wilson of 'Ceylon' Tea solved and explained some of the puzzles about coffee blight and the location of Gibbs' Tea Gardens in Ceylon, as well as identifying some of the leading players of the time, with a photograph of one, his own ancestor.

Preface

Professor Sybil Jack-Ungar, an old school friend of mine, and formerly on the History Faculty of Sydney University, has been my encouragement from the start. She provided me with clues and contacts which pointed me in the right direction, and being so conveniently placed in Sydney she was able to identify Gibbs Bright offices, wharves and warehouses during the period of the diary. I hope I have followed Sybil's injunction to 'research properly'.

I must not forget our visits to 'Tyntesfield', the William Gibbs home in Somerset, now part of our National Trust, and Pytte, Gibbs' fascinating house in their early Exeter days. In both we found people most helpful, particularly the Tyntesfield volunteer and writer David J. Hogg, another devotee who is the author of several interesting books about the family. Mrs Tiffany Turner was welcoming and informative when, at the start of my journey, we visited Pytte. She took us around the garden and into the house to explain its modern conversion into separate, yet attached, houses; it may be unique in its development.

When I wished to research people and places in the Southern Hemisphere myself, Saga Holidays handily produced an itinerary for their 2011 World Cruise which allowed me to follow Vicary Gibbs on some of his epic journey of 1883-5. They made it so easy and comfortable for my husband, Peter, and me to visit the Cities of Adelaide, Melbourne, Sydney, and Newcastle in Australia, and Dunedin, Wellington, and Auckland in New Zealand, as well as their Universities and Libraries - while enjoying the luxury of a good holiday.

The picture of the display model of SS Great Britain from Port Stanley Museum was taken in the Falkland Islands and presented to me by the 'Saga Ruby' staff photographer, Edel, with the kind permission of the Museum's Curator. The Islanders retain their affection for Brunel's great ship, and have followed her progress to restoration in Bristol Docks. Among artefacts connected with the ship and retained in Port Stanley are her anchor and Main Mast, between the War Memorial and the water's edge.

I discovered that the mother of a friend in the nearby village of Sidlesham was the grand-daughter of one of Vicary Gibbs' head gardeners, and had grown up in Elstree. I shall not forget the enjoyable afternoon I spent with Mrs Doris McBride listening to the memories of her and her sister's childhood there, and of Vicary in his garden at Aldenham House. Mrs McBride's happy afternoons walking and playing in the garden added much warmth and colour to my view of Vicary as an older man.

Mrs Elizabeth Varvill, of West Wittering, is a direct descendant of Vicary's youngest brother, Henry Lloyd Gibbs, and his wife Alice Mary Crutchley.

She kindly lent me the family history which disclosed the relationship of some of the names mentioned without explanation in the diary. It appears that other members of the family recall Vicary as somewhat reserved, comfortable with his books, in his garden, or with his own company. His creation at Aldenham was an outstanding masterpiece of garden design, highly praised by 'Country Life'.

Our friend, Adrian Harland, and also Dr. Nicholas Sturt, were invaluable when we were faced with quotations written in ancient Greek, or passages in a not-quite-Latin possibly known only to Vicary Gibbs.

Jay Dinnick of Selsey, Elizabeth Griffin of Chichester, Douglas Wood of Highleigh, and Ronald Pearson of Guildford, all gave their time and attention to reading and commenting most readily.

Mr and Mrs Roope of Sidlesham kindly pointed me in the direction of their particular interest, Brunel's SS Great Britain, now restored to her fine lines in Bristol Docks.

I must not forget to mention members of my own family who have been so much help to me: my husband, Peter Hinkly, who has been a willing and patient travelling companion, photographer, and tea-maker; our daughter Lucy Beale, now well trained as a proof-reader and index checker, and her husband Gary who designed our flier; our son Adam, a meticulous editor and publisher, with software at his fingertips. Adam also carried out a quantity of deep research where I had drawn a blank and came up with relevant gems to reward the reader, generated the indexes, and designed the website which I am hoping will shortly be available to my readers. In Auckland, New Zealand, my brother John Wilson and his daughter Michele Cain were also both most helpful.

I would also like to offer my grateful thanks to the representatives of the following institutions or individuals for their help with my research:

- Tyntesfield National Trust
- Haberdashers Aske's Boys' School, Elstree
- London Metropolitan Library, housing the Antony Gibbs & Sons Guildhall Archive
- Seonaid Lewis of the Central City Library, Auckland, New Zealand
- Alexander Turnbull Library, Wellington, New Zealand; particularly Ms Goodwin, Ms Chalmers, and their colleagues
- Staff of the Hocken Collections, Uare Taoke o Hakena, University of Otago, Dunedin, New Zealand
- Baillieu University Library, Melbourne, Australia; particularly Katie Wood and the other archivists
- The State Library of New South Wales, Sydney

- Sir George Grey Special Collections, Auckland Libraries
- United States Library of Congress, Prints and Photographs Division, Washington, D.C.
- National Library of Australia
- Powerhouse Museum, Sydney
- State Library of Queensland
- State Library of South Australia
- State Library of Victoria
- Washington State Historical Society, especially Fred Poyner
- Wikimedia Commons
- Phil Phillips, for his modern-day photograph of the Northern Pacific Railway
- Patrick Coppel, for the photograph of Rebecca Crawcour
- Claire Walters, for her photograph of Tyntesfield
- My husband Peter Hinkly (again), for his photographs of Pytte, Aldenham, and various letters and documents from the Guildhall

The following books were not only invaluable for my research, but were excellent reading in their own right:

- 'The history of Antony and Dorothea Gibbs and their contemporary relatives, including the history of the origin and early years of the House of Antony Gibbs and Sons', by John Arthur Gibbs, St Catherine Press 1922
- 'Diaries of Tyntesfield', by David John Hogg
- 'My Dear Uncle William - Tyntesfield Letters', by David John Hogg
- 'Fragile Fortunes: The origins of a Great British Merchant Family', by Elizabeth Neill
- 'Fertile Fortune: The Story of Tyntesfield', by James Miller
- 'Anchored in a Small Cove: A History and Archaeology of the Rocks, Sydney', by Max Kelly
- 'Presenting New Zealand, an Illustrated History', by Dr. Philip Temple
- 'The City of London', Vols. I, II & III, by David Kynaston
- 'City Bankers, 1890-1914', by Youssef Cassis, translated by Margaret Rocques
- 'Antony Gibbs & Sons Limited: Merchants and Bankers: a brief record of Antony Gibbs & Sons and its Associated Houses' business during 150 years, 1808-1958', by Wilfred Maude and Antony Gibbs & Sons
- 'The House of Gibbs and the Peruvian Guano Monopoly', by W.M. Matthew (Royal Historical Society Studies in History)
- The essay 'Charles and Reginald Bright', by Greg Whitwell

I found David Kynaston's 'City of London' a particularly enjoyable read, and I should also like to thank him for his permission to repeat below the quotation from the opening volume.

My own family's connection with guano, the 'South American gold', still figured largely in the 1930s and 40s. My father's eldest brother, barrister Eric Crawcour Wilson, killed in WWI, had been the Anglo-South American Bank's legal adviser in its Paris branch; his youngest brother, Richard, had been stationed in the bank in Bogota until its crash in 1936. My grandfather, William Wilson, had also been bankrupted by this crash. I now understand why we heard the oft-repeated rhyme: "William Gibbs made his dibs selling the turds of foreign birds".

Vicary went to Australia as the family envoy to discover what could replace the firm's earlier success with South American guano as the reach of their company extended and changed its influence 'from Guano to Gold'.

Shirley Hinkly
February 2014

By their own words and deeds these practical men are to be judged.

- from "The City of London", by David Kynaston.

From Guano to Gold

The Diary and Letters of Vicary Gibbs
from 1883-5

Edited and researched by Shirley Hinkly

Introduction

2. Rear view of Pytte House (present day)
Courtesy of Peter Hinkly

Pytte, the Gibbs' family estate near Exeter in Devon, had belonged to Vicary Gibbs' ancestors since 1560. By the 18th century, the family would have been considered 'landed gentry', like the characters familiar to us from the novels of Jane Austen. Indeed, it has been suggested that Jane Austen knew the Gibbs and may have gathered material for one of her books while staying with them.

Vicary Gibbs' great-great-grandfather, George Abraham Gibbs (1718–1794), was a man of enterprise, energy and ambition, and apparently free from social prejudice. In 1747 he married the daughter of Antony Vicary, Anne, and proved himself to be an enlightened family man with a modern view of the opportunities available to his sons. A highly successful surgeon, he practised at the Royal Devon and Exeter Hospital.

The eldest son of the marriage, Vicary (1751–1820), won a scholarship to Eton and subsequently studied at King's College, Cambridge. His appointment as Solicitor General to the Prince of Wales, and knighthood, was as much a reward for his legal wisdom and expertise as it was for achieving the royally-approved acquittal of Thomas Hardy, John Horne Tooke, and John Thelwall in the famous treason trial of 1794.

George Abraham's second son, also George (1753–1818), was eventually content to leave Exeter for Bristol at his father's bidding to join his mother's cousin Samuel Munckley in his successful House of 'West India' merchants. He was the only one of the brothers to retain the original Presbyterian faith of the family, and settled happily into Bristol life with a group of firmly-founded friendships made in the non-conformist meeting house. There he met and married Etty Farr and started his own family. Etty died eleven years later, probably after the birth of another child, leaving her husband with her surviving children: Joanna, aged twelve; a ten-year-old George; and baby Anne, aged only two-and-a-half. Despite his own family difficulties George Gibbs never lost contact with his Exeter family, helping them through the years of financial uncertainty whenever he could. He was also a scrupulously careful father, and would no doubt have been assisted himself by sympathetic relatives offering whatever support they could to the motherless children.

Later, his son George made an early marriage to Salvina Hendy, a very pretty but frail young woman. She and George were childless when she died of consumption in 1809. In 1814 he married Harriet Gibbs, the daughter of his father's brother Antony. The Gibbs were always a closely interconnected group, and this was one of several first cousin marriages in the family's history. Sadly, this second marriage too was childless.

There were also marital connections to other well-known families: the fourth of George Abraham's eleven children, Mary (1759–1819), was to marry the Reverend Charles Crawley[1] in 1784, creating links to the Crawley-Boevey and Yonge families.

The third son, Antony (1756–1815), was also apprenticed to Trade; in his case the West Country cloth trade was chosen, and thus the family direction for the next 200 years was decided. In 1788, when Antony had completed his apprenticeship to the Exeter cloth merchant, he was able to think of establishing his own business. His father was persuaded to invest a large amount of his own fortune in this venture; the export of fine Devon woollen cloth was planned, with a return trade of wines, merino wool, citrus fruit and other luxuries from Spain. Trade between the small port of Topsham, near Exeter, and Europe flourished in the early 18th century, both that officially known to the 'Revenue' and the smugglers' trade. Antony and his father were determined that their business would always remain legitimate, but their honesty had chosen a testing moment: towards the century's end the once thriving Devon woollen trade collapsed.

Antony had not only put his own capital into the business but had also financed his projects with investments from his circle of friends and family. His optimism was misplaced, and his funds were over-stretched to the point of failure. Bankruptcy forced his father, acting as guarantor, to sell both his Exeter house and contents and his country estate of Pytte. Antony's strong sense of personal responsibility made him resolve to right all the wrongs he felt he had committed and vow to pay all his debts as soon as possible. He was a determined young man who took his task seriously, but 'as soon as possible' stretched to many years; his vow was passed on to his sons. The success of his second chance would seem to show that the early failure had been unlucky and a question of bad timing – due to inexperience rather than recklessness. Subsequent action by the businessmen of the family showed an instinctive understanding of risk and an ability to grasp the moment, timing which helped them to profit handsomely for over a century.

---

[1] Reverend Charles Crawley (1756-1849), son of Thomas Crawley-Boevey (1709-1769) and Susanna Lloyd.

Antony Gibbs learned from his mistakes. He made a modest but sound success of his later venture in spite of the political problems of Napoleonic times, being energetic, adaptable and - above all - impressing clients with great moral integrity. His first move was back to Spain to act as the local agent for any British merchants wishing to do business with the country. His wife, Dorothea Barnetta Hucks (1760–1820), joined him in Madrid with their first two children, George Henry (1785–1842) – known as Henry - and Harriett (1786–1865), and a second son, William (1790–1875), was subsequently born in Spain.

There were dangerous times ahead for the British and their allies, and moments of high risk for the future of Gibbs. The British blockade of Cadiz in 1805 - in reply to Napoleon's acceleration of hostilities - preceded the Battle of Trafalgar and the land-based Peninsular War. At the start of the blockade it looked as if valuable cargo would have to remain tied up there, but Sir Vicary Gibbs, now Solicitor General, was persuaded to come to the rescue of his younger brother. His influential position allowed a carefully planned operation to take place with the willing cooperation of their Spanish friends. Cargo was off-loaded and secretly transferred to the 'Hermosa Mexicana' under the Spanish flag; it sailed out of Cadiz on its way to Peru, while the British fleet looked the other way. Antony was able to return to London to prepare for his own change of direction. The modest profits from the sale of the goods in Lima, Peru, together with the encouragement of Sir Vicary and the support of the rest of the family, established the firm of Antony Gibbs and Sons in the City of London in 1808. This was the right moment; at almost the same time the fortunes of the British, Spanish and Portuguese in the Peninsular War changed for the better at last. The first of their links with South America had been forged, the seas should now be safer, and the time was ripe for Gibbs to expand their trade.

The family motto of these pioneer 'Merchant Venturers' was 'tenax propositi': loosely, 'stick to it', or more correctly, 'strength of purpose'. It was an appropriate motto for Antony's two sons, Henry and William. The brothers had promised their father to remain dedicated to the challenge of his debts of honour when they took over the business on his death in 1815. The intention was to wipe out this blot on the family reputation by payments out of personal profit into a specified savings fund, but fluctuating profits meant that another 25 years passed before they were able to satisfy their consciences. George Abraham's old home, Pytte, finally returned to family ownership in 1859.

The business apprenticeship continued from generation to generation, and although some lessons were only learned painfully they added the qualities of care and honesty to the character of one of an exclusive group of Merchant Bankers. These people mixed socially by choice almost as much as they favoured each other in business. They were men of like mind who came together at this time for a variety of reasons. In earlier days, much of the finance for foreign trade had come from the Low Countries. From the mid-15th century onward Amsterdam had developed into an international money market. This was enhanced by its central position, the trade in gemstones, the flourishing expertise in money-lending brought by Sephardi Jews from Italy and Spain, and - in the 17th century - the achievements of the Dutch East India Company. The success of Amsterdam and the Low Countries gradually attracted French and Flemish Huguenot weavers and wool traders, and - much later - Ashkenazi 'bankers' from Prussia, Eastern Europe, and Russia. In the 18th century, religious intolerance had begun to threaten both the Jews and Protestants all over continental Europe and many were forced to flee. German settlers like the Barings followed the weavers to Devon where the home-grown merchants such as Antony Gibbs and his sons were ready to share some of their forward-looking ideas. The Baring and Gibbs families were friends and colleagues long before they met on equal terms in the City of London. The Barings had even made their home in a property originally owned by the Gibbs. Another embryonic group of investment bankers arrived in the City to join the 'club': the experienced and well-disciplined economists of the time, the Quakers.

3. Tyntesfield, Wraxall (present day)
Courtesy of Claire Walters

William Gibbs, Antony's second son, was educated at Blundell's School, Tiverton, in Devon. His business skills had been gained in the Bristol office of his uncle, George Abraham - by then expanded into Gibbs, Bright and Gibbs – before he returned to help his father in Spain. The instability of the situation in Spain was later useful for the brothers in their need to deal with the South American temperament and politics, as was their fluency in Spanish. Both William and Henry were interested in the revolutionary innovations of their time. Henry's enthusiasm turned to Brunel and his rapidly developing advance in transport conceived as the Great Western Railway. As Britain became industrialised, more of her products were of interest to Europe and to the developing colonies. The Spanish territories made their own decisions, and the City of London was alerted to many new markets. Finance was needed for the export of ideas, too: for new infrastructures such as railways, bridges and road construction. In the second half of the 19th century India, Australia, South America, and the United States, among others, turned to British expertise in civil engineering and investment for advice. As sail gave way to steam there were other members of the Gibbs family and their associates acting as shipping agents in Bristol and Liverpool who were ready to serve when the time came. Although William returned to the London office in the 1820s, he was still emotionally attached to Spain. Those early years formed his taste for most things Spanish. His later creation, Tyntesfield, at Wraxall, south of Bristol, is filled with the warmth, colour, and art of Spain. Antony Gibbs and Sons were well established in Lima before moving south and setting up Houses in Santiago and Valparaiso. In Peru, Bolivia, and Chile their honest and open style of operating impressed, and they learned to negotiate the complexities of South American political ambition without compromising themselves, deserving the respect they received on the Pacific coast.

By 1842 it had been proposed by the Chilean House that guano be imported into Britain on a long-term contract between Gibbs and the relevant governments. Apprehension on the part of the London end of the business was inevitable, and William was clearly pessimistic when responding in letters to his brother Henry. (See 'My Dear Uncle William' - The Tyntesfield Letters, edited by David Hogg, 2011). It had been considered before, but the market had resisted. Guano is formed from the droppings of sea birds, matured over centuries on small rocky out-crops such as the Chincha Islands off the coast of Peru. There were still huge mounds of the nitrate-rich organic fertilizer in spite of it having been plundered by local coastal farmers for years. A pamphlet was published with reports of trials on Gibbs' own land at Wraxall. This time, British agriculture listened; this was early in the age of scientific farming, when the nutrient depletion of soil was beginning to be analysed. Farm labourers had migrated from country to town in the hope of better pay. Fewer workers were left on the farms, but there was greater need of increased production as the hungry population in the cities grew. In spite of the reality of poverty and poor working conditions, some higher standards of living were becoming available to industrial workers who made their way up the economic scale when talent and social mobility allowed. There were also periods of depression when series of cold summers and bad harvests hit the poorest hardest. Potato blight not only meant starvation in Ireland but an influx of Irish labourers to England looking for work and food, followed by their desperate families.

The Corn Laws, which had protected the domestic product, were finally repealed in 1846 and the increased production of grain and other crops was imperative. The bird manure had been proved to be highly effective and economical in use. Thanks to the long-term contracts negotiated, the Gibbs family fortune was made. It had never been a question of unscrupulous profiteering, but those on the spot in Chile were convinced of the value of this natural product of consistently high quality; available in large quantities, guano was soon in great demand in Britain and all over Europe. Sadly, at their moment of success, George Henry Gibbs – never in robust health - died while recuperating in Italy, aged only 57. William had lost his brother and business partner and was now head of the company. His nephew, Henry Hucks Gibbs, would have to step into his father's shoes.

In the early 1860s, the first deposits of guano began to be exhausted in Bolivia, and soon the levels of those in the Chincha Islands were dropping. Other nitrate sources were needed, and Gibbs were ready to supply their prospecting skills in the hope of being given European sales rights. Substantial deposits were found inland where organic nitrates and other useful minerals could be economically extracted. This time the South American governments were more aware of the value of retaining their rights to a monopoly on excavation and to their own sales authority. William and his colleagues negotiated their own version of Fair Trade by becoming agents appointed to deal with the growing European demand at a price they thought fit. William's firm religious convictions directed him in ways relatively rare at that time.

However, efficiency of handling provided profit margins from guano with which Gibbs would expand their business into the Australian colonies as early as the 1850s, when an office was opened in Melbourne. Attention had been drawn to Southern Australia by the Gold Rush, and Gibbs made sure that their shipping interests were quickly involved in carrying 'diggers' out to Victoria and the gold fields. As merchants, the transport of goods, services, and passengers was always of importance to them. Gold was just another commodity in which to deal, and the rush of emigrants too would expand the market for services of all kinds. Antony Gibbs and Sons acquired Brunel's famed ship the S.S.'Great Britain', rescuing it from the beach where it had languished since being grounded off the coast of Ireland. Their shipping agents refitted this masterpiece of marine engineering in some style and comfort, adding an extra deck to carry a complement of 720 passengers on the long Australian run.

4. Aldenham House (present day)
Courtesy of Peter Hinkly

Public recognition followed Gibbs' immense new wealth; later, there would be the honour of elevation to the Peerage for some members of the family and even Tory political success in the Commons with evidence of substance in the ownership of large country estates. William Gibbs turned Tyntes Place, a modest Georgian house at Wraxall, into a neo-gothic retreat to suit the spiritual needs of him and his family, and at last felt able to become the philanthropist he had hoped was his destiny. Henry Hucks Gibbs succeeded to Aldenham House, an elegant mansion in large grounds at Elstree in Hertfortshire. He had received the second name, Hucks, from his paternal grandmother Dorothea Barnetta Hucks, and Aldenham came to Henry via the Hucks ancestry. In 1839, Henry married Louisa Anne Adams, six of their children surviving to maturity.

In 1839, Henry's uncle William had married his cousin Matilda Blanche Crawley-Boevey (1817-1887), 27 years his junior, after a final break with his Spanish fiancée and much heart-searching. By the 1850s they had decided to move from their large town houses in London – such as their first home at 16 Hyde Park Gardens - and settle at Tyntesfield where the children would enjoy more freedom and a healthier life. Here, the house was no longer merely a holiday home, and William and Blanche would continue their plans for its transformation. The external decoration and the interior furnishings were inspired by the high Victorian Gothic style of Barry and Pugin, who were responsible for the Palace of Westminster, and their disciple the architect John Norton of Bristol. Much of the interior work was carried out by the fashionable decorator and furniture designer, John G. Crace of Wigmore Street, London, with the specialist skills of Warwickshire cabinet makers Collier and Plucknett. Eventually a large, highly decorated chapel was attached to the house for the use of the whole family. There was something of the Baronial about William's taste, and a hint of Sir Walter Scott's influence - particularly in the romanticism of an entrance to the chapel from the upper floor, although this was clearly dictated by the levels of the site. If Jane Austen had really been able to study local colour when staying with an earlier Gibbs generation in Devon, Charlotte Yonge (1823–1901), another novelist and cousin of William and his wife, felt able to draw on the home life she saw when staying at Tyntesfield. The middle class and religious values of her very popular and moralising fiction may well be a reflection of the Gibbs family life.

Although the sons of the house were expected to play their part in the business, William and Blanche were careful to know and understand their children and to observe their strengths and weaknesses. Other relations, too, were expected to express their career preferences without fear. Henry Hucks' generation produced at least one cousin who clearly preferred the life of the Church to the materialism of merchant banking. Henry himself had moments of self-doubt in the early days but marriage, a family, and a gradual improvement in his health helped him find his true talent as a banker in spite of his inability to conform exactly to Uncle William's expectation. William's eldest son, Antony (1841–1907), was a quiet, gentle man, unsuited to the often ruthless tactics of big business. He was encouraged by his parents to pursue an artistic, philanthropic and benevolent life in the mould of the best of Victorian country gentlemen. The atmosphere at Tyntesfield was feudal but benign. Antony and his father managed the estate and farms with the help of chosen experts. It was another apprenticeship where they learned on the job as they laid down rules and concerned themselves with the physical and spiritual welfare of the family, household staff and the estate workers. Writing his journal in Melbourne, Vicary Gibbs described meeting a former coachman from Tyntesfield who had been advised by his employer and the Gibbs family doctor that the sea voyage out to Victoria and the climate there would restore his fragile health. At his employer's cost, he did make a full recovery in the colony and did not forget to thank him for his generosity.

In 1872, Antony married Janet Louisa Merivale (1850–1909), a daughter of John Lewis Merivale, close friend of Anthony Trollope. Trollope's elder son received his middle name, Merivale, from this friendship. In his novel of the 1880s, 'Ayala's Angel', Trollope enjoys himself describing the merchant banker's method of teaching his son to toe the line by sending him on a tour of foreign houses to bring home ideas for new markets. In Australia, Vicary Gibbs knew he was there for exactly that purpose, and while there he made a friend of another Merivale who figured prominently in the life of Gibbs' Australian House - many other friends and family connections had followed the firm in its extension to the other side of the world. Vicary met young George Merivale in Sydney, and later his wife and new baby, Angel - is that another Trollope-inspired name, perhaps? George Merivale accompanied Vicary on his trip to New Zealand and must have helped relieve some of those moments along the way otherwise marred by painful attacks of gout.

Janet and Antony had ten children; their eldest son, George (1873–1931) was a friend and near-contemporary of Vicary Gibbs, although a family generation nominally separated them. He was elected to Parliament in 1906 as a member for West Bristol, and in 1928 was created 1st Lord Wraxall after his second marriage, to Ursula Mary Lawley (1888–1979). George and his first wife, Victoria de Burgh Long (1880–1920), had been married 19 years and had only one surviving child, Doreen Albinia, born in 1913. In 1927, seven years after Via's (Victoria's) death, George married for the second time. Ursula Mary was the daughter of Sir Arthur and Lady Lawley, who had been a member of the Cunard family. They had two sons, Richard and Eustace. It was after the death of Richard, who remained single and was by then 2nd Lord Wraxall, that Tyntesfield died as a private house, re-emerging as a 'National Treasure' in the care of the National Trust.

The senior branch of the family, the descendents of William's elder brother George Henry, had moved to London where Gibbs' Head Office was established in the City. Henry Hucks - Governor of the Bank of England from 1875 to 1877 - and his wife Louisa made their home at Frognal in Hampstead where their first child, Alban George, was born in 1846. His sister Edith Caroline followed in 1848, and a second son Walter Antony was born in 1850 but died at the age of eight. Vicary was born on 12th May 1853, and was close in both age and temperament to his brother,

Herbert Cokayne, who arrived a year later in 1854. Herbert was a self-confident businessman, widely respected in the City of London. During the First World War, Herbert was appointed Director of Purchases of Nitrate of Soda for the Allied Powers. His success in banking and in this strategic political role earned him a peerage in 1923 when he was created 1st Baron Hunsdon. The last two sons were Kenneth Francis in 1856 and the youngest, Henry Lloyd, in 1861. Kenneth Francis entered the Church and was in later life the Venerable Hon. Kenneth Gibbs. Four of these brothers were to play their part in Antony Gibbs and Sons when Public School and University days were over, each bringing his own personal skills and experience to the business. The First World War saw nitrate demand increase with greater profitability for the traditional producers and importers, but in the 1920s and '30s another marked decline was followed by an ill-timed speculation causing pressure on the South American banking structure created to deal with the original boom. This was the Bank of Tarapaca, conceived in 1888 by John North, an investor and speculator and a syndicate of similarly involved financier friends, and it later became the Anglo-South American Bank. Banking operations continued in connection with the nitrate industry until it collapsed and was liquidated in 1936. What remained of the structure was then taken over by the Bank of London and South America, but not before considerable sums of money had been lost by investors.

The author of this diary, Vicary Gibbs (1853-1932), was the second surviving son of Henry Hucks Gibbs and Louisa Anne Adams. In early August 1871, following his Eton education and before we went to Oxford, the 18-year-old Vicary travelled with his father and his sister Edith on a modest 'Grand Tour' of Europe. This was not only an educational and cultural tour to add social polish to a young man, but an important part of his training in recorded information for his future life of commerce in the City. Henry Hucks was a regular diarist himself and it was his opinion that the ability to keep a diary record was an essential skill in business life. As Vicary wrote to one of his nephews years later, younger members of the family were expected to master the same clerical duties as any other junior employee before arriving at management level, including periods of exile to far-flung offices around the world.

The hand writing in the slim black notebook he used as his journal is as neat, mature and legible as it is in the one presented here, written twelve years later on the far longer journey to the United States of America, Australia, New Zealand, Ceylon, and home to England by way of Egypt, Italy and France. The spelling is still as erratic in the later diary, but both accounts are written in relaxed style, often sharply observant and sometimes with humour.

After the European tour, Vicary studied at Christ Church, Oxford, and was awarded a third class degree in Classical Moderations. This modest result belies evidence of his sustained interest in the Classics in his Colonial journal. He read Classical poetry for pleasure, and reverted easily to ancient Greek and to Latin for 'le mot juste' – so important to the legally trained mind.. He was called to the Bar at Lincoln's Inn in 1880 at the relatively late age of 27, but here, as elsewhere in his career, there may have been interruptions caused by periods of ill health. This account of his time away from home is punctuated by frequent bouts of a rheumatic condition described as severe gout. It is apparent from his father's journals and letters that he too was sometimes attacked by gout, as well as episodes of tachycardia. Both conditions may have been passed down through the family. Disability and damage to joints caused by this painful disease is corroborated by my interview with Mrs McBride, a member of the family of professional gardeners, two generations of whom lived and worked at Aldenham. Her memories of the house and grounds, and of the 'Hon. Vicary' himself, have helped me visualise his life there in the late 1920s. The days must have been busy and rewarded by his wide interests and continued involvement with the business. There were also the demands of other directorships and family interests on the boards of railway, shipping and trade concerns at home and abroad.

An experiment with political life failed rather painfully for Vicary Gibbs, who had entered Parliament as a Conservative member for St. Albans in 1892. He and his brother Alban were made to resign their seats when they were barred by The Contractors Act of 1872 from accepting, on the part of Antony Gibbs and Sons, an Admiralty contract. They had hoped to simplify a situation between a South American government and the British where an order had been revoked at a later date. After a by-election Alban was returned, but Vicary was defeated. He was again unsuccessful when he stood for Bradford Central in 1906.

Aldenham House at Elstree became Vicary's home by family agreement. Vicary remained a bachelor and the heir, Alban, preferred to live on the other Hucks estate at Clifton Hampden in Oxfordshire with his wife and children. Vicary, settled in his new home, was at last able to indulge in his creative talent as a gardener. He collected rare specimens of trees and flowering shrubs from around the world. No doubt they included those he had admired in their natural habitat that were capable of surviving the climate and soil of that part of south–east England. In his journal he had admired the thorns of the American Rockies, Australian flowering trees and shrubs, and the ferns and flaxes of New Zealand: as always, the observant 'plantsman'.

Aldenham became a garden of world-wide interest where Vicary and a team of gardeners, headed by the famous Edwin Beckett, worked on their chosen combination of Art and Science. Hybrids were developed in a converted building known as the 'bothy'; this old Coach House became hostel, laboratory and study-centre. Mrs McBride, on her weekly walks through the Park with her mother and her younger sister, would see the students arriving from Kew for their Aldenham 'residence'. The grounds were always freely open to the villagers of Elstree on Saturday afternoons and for their own annual Agricultural Show. Tenant farmers were called upon to add their skills to the estate when they were needed. The lake, naturally fed by the original stream, was dug and shaped by Mrs McBride's grandfather, Alfred Alonda Surridge, and his brother Ephraim. The grassland was always immaculate, and the specimen trees – each named and described on a plaque – were protected within railings. At one time, Aldenham's collection of plants was considered second only to Kew. Ephraim Surridge was proud to be given advanced training at Kew itself, paid for by Vicary Gibbs.

Elstree village was improved by the building of cottages in the Arts and Crafts style to house the workers. Mrs McBride, her two brothers, and her younger sister, were all born in the central cottage of a group of three. Her parents, Frederick George Purver and Ellen Blanche Purver (née Surridge), continued to occupy the house with grandfather Surridge and were eventually able to buy it from the estate for £900 in the 1930s.

Today, Haberdashers' Aske's Boys' School occupies the old Aldenham House and grounds. The House dates back to the 17th century, with later additions. The original drawing room is now part of the administration offices and is hardly recognisable; the entrance hall retains some of its elegance, and the staircase is still impressive. Casual access to the school is now only available to the administration area. The front elevation of the beautiful house is little changed, and some parts of the garden where Vicary's shrubs and trees were planted can still be identified, but his Gertrude Jekyll-inspired garden design has largely been obscured. Aldenham House is where he would have entertained his friends for summer house-parties, always appearing at the window on Saturday afternoons with a plate of chocolate cake for the Purver girls and their mother to enjoy. At Elstree, Vicary Gibbs encouraged the use of modern horticultural science, and, in the spirit of his ancestors, also championed 20th century transport by supporting the innovation of a commercial landing strip at the local airfield. This family had known the 'Age of Sail'; they had pioneered merchant banking around the world, and had foreseen and funded the use of steam in transport by sea and rail. They were broad-minded and hard-working enthusiasts who gave much to the modern world and had to fight to save the family and firm they had created at its worst moments. Nitrates, which had become their stock-in-trade as fertilizer, proved essential to the refrigeration process in the long distance transport of frozen meats by sea from Australia, New Zealand and Argentina to Europe, and were needed again and again to fuel the war machine with high explosives when Britain and her Allies were under threat. When South American countries experienced the growth of economic Nationalism, Herbert Gibbs was sent out to deal with the situation as diplomatically as he could in order to maintain Britain's source of supply as long as possible. Some delicate problems were resolved, for the time being, but the period was sometimes a lean one for Gibbs. Younger members of the family were always expected to be able to deal with sensitive issues on the spot. Vicary Gibbs' role in Australia, New Zealand and Ceylon was also one of mediation, although this is carefully disguised in this journal. We should try to read between the lines, even those deliberately coded, to discover the hidden reasons behind his long exile. There were commodities, available in the developing colonies and urgently needed by Britain; Gibbs expected to be ahead of the field. Newcastle, New South Wales, opened up to a large woollen market in the 1880s; Vicary reserved their harbour-side depot. It was fortunate for the company that the tour of 1883-5 coincided with the invitation to join the celebration of the completion of the Northern Pacific Railway in the U.S., where more profitable contacts could - and would – be made.

There was time, in later years, for Vicary Gibbs to give more attention to his other great interests. The family story had always fascinated him, and it was his uncle George Cokayne who encouraged his passion for genealogy (indeed, George Cokayne was - unusually - both Vicary's maternal and paternal uncle, being Henry Hucks Gibbs' sister's[2] husband and wife's[3] brother). Uncle George handed his life's work on the revision of Burke's Peerage to his nephew; Vicary completed the work at his own expense. The vast amount of research this must have entailed says much for lessons in time management and attention to detail learned over the years. Time had also to be found for his position as Vice President of the Royal Horticultural Society. During the London Season, home was his London house, 12 Upper Belgrave Street, when Aldenham was left under dust-sheets. He would return to his garden in the summer and drive to the local station daily for his train to the City. At the end of the 19th century Vicary was the nominal head of Antony Gibbs and Sons, faced with the great challenge of keeping the Bank profitable during one of the most economically unstable periods in history.

It seems that Vicary was a quietly sociable man rather than a gregarious one. In the journal, he seems to be amused by the uncomplicated company of an intelligent child, remembering, perhaps, family life with his own siblings. If Mrs McBride looks back fondly on her Saturday outings, it is as much for her affection for 'the Hon. Vicary' as for his chocolate cake. He enjoyed conversation, cards, music, theatre and books. Like most men of his class and time, he enjoyed what we would today term 'blood sports',

---

[2] Mary Dorothea Gibbs (1839-1906).
[3] Louisa Anne Adams (1818-1897).

but not from any cruel streak in his nature; he records with disgust the slaughter of rabbits left to remain where they lay after being culled on a Victoria sheep station. Hunting was something engendered in young men of this time and encouraged by the competitive ethos of Public School, perhaps as some preparation for army service. The excitement of the chase was certainly something he liked, but he was also happily able to spend time alone, when reading made a good substitute for company he did not always find congenial. If Vicary Gibbs felt anything like home-sickness it was more his deep affection for his family and a need, while separated from them, for regular news from home and the reassurance which came with it. His gift for friendship seemed effortless but was probably part of the social training of his class. Discretion and reticence were in his make up; true feelings were confided only to close friends or family, but he was well liked wherever he went. No matter how we react to his private prejudices we should remember that they were those of his time, possibly less marked in him than in many others, and were the result of a far narrower set of social rules. A closer look helps one to see the true warmth of the individual who, if he really did inherit the sardonic wit of his 18th century's namesake, reserved it for the appropriate moment only. The Victorian education of these young men made them resourceful and self confident at best; at worst, they could be arrogant. We do have evidence from the diary and even from business letters home that Vicary and his brothers had been taught to employ a natural tact at all times and respect the opinions of others without 'losing face'; the visit to the colonies gave a refreshing opportunity to join entirely new social groups and to meet, mix with, and accept 'ordinary' people from many different backgrounds.

Although Vicary was liked by many of the women he met, and probably maintained an affectionate friendship with several of them, he never married. He became increasingly disabled by his arthritis, but kept himself occupied in a full business partnership all his working life. He died of encephalitis at his London home in 1932, and was buried in the Church at Aldenham.

From Guano to Gold: The Diary and Letters of Vicary Gibbs from 1883-5

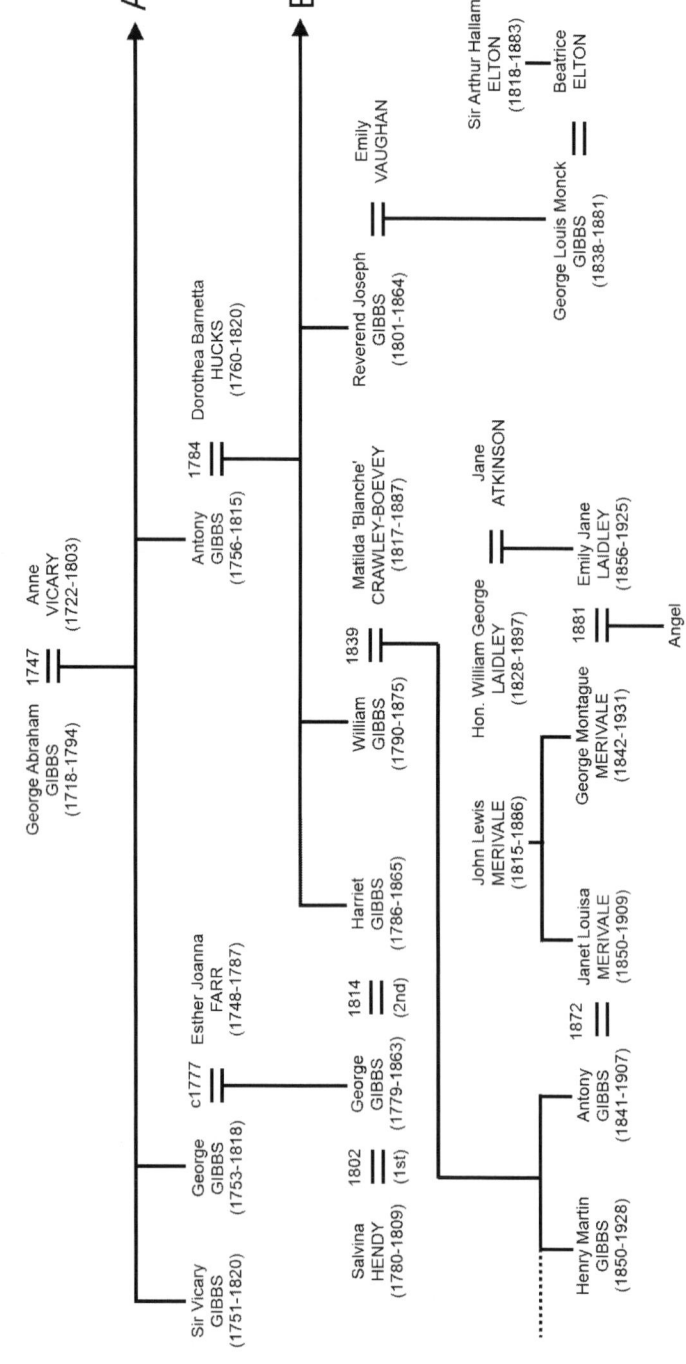

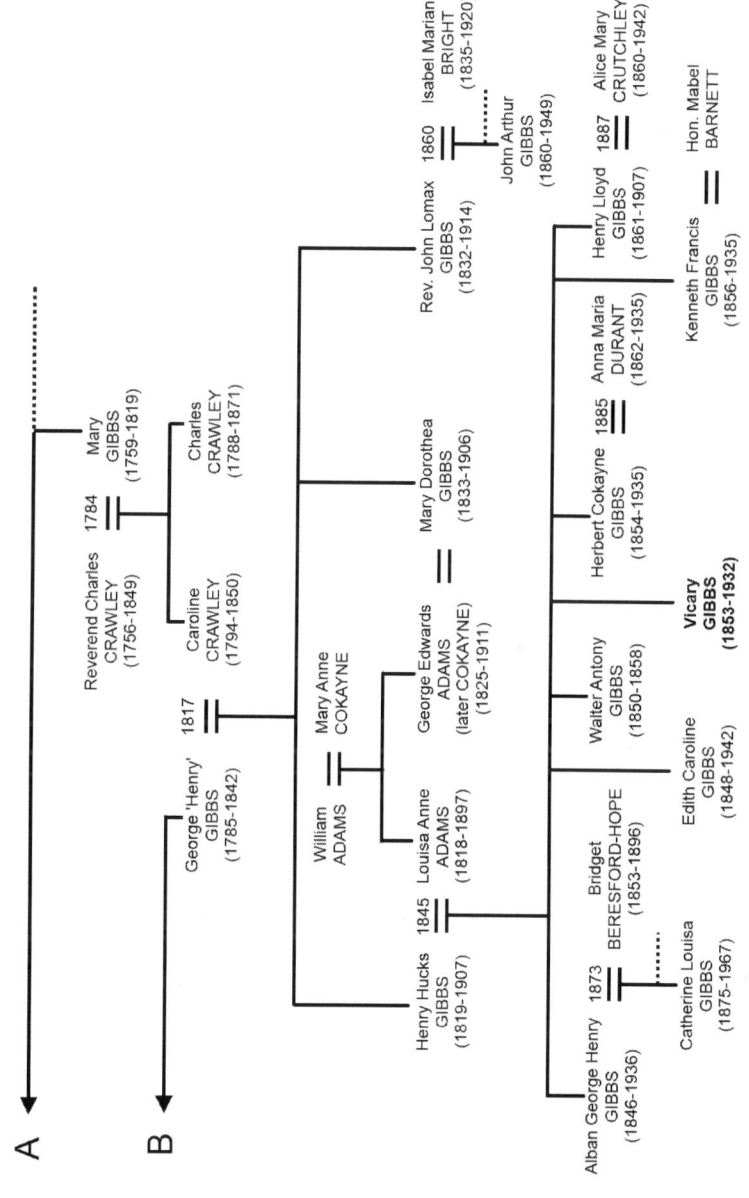

My diary will require hanging a long time before it is tender enough for public consumption. I daresay in about 300 years if a reviewer got hold of it he would work up an article out of it 'England at the end of the 19th Century' "The writer seems to have been a fair specimen of the ordinary English merchant of the time, fairly well-informed, and from internal evidence we gather that he was at Eton and Oxford. He is very careful to chronicle his ailments, and the various trashy and forgotten novels which he read and the plays which he saw, but we look in vain for the unconscious humour and simplicity of the immortal Pepys. It is instructive to notice that there is hardly any reference to public affairs beyond a few expressions of vindictive dislike to the great Gladstone and the separation of the English colonies so soon to come to pass, and which should have been clear to the shallowest mind, are unheeded or at any rate unrecorded" etc. etc.

- Vicary Gibbs' diary entry for 4th February 1885.

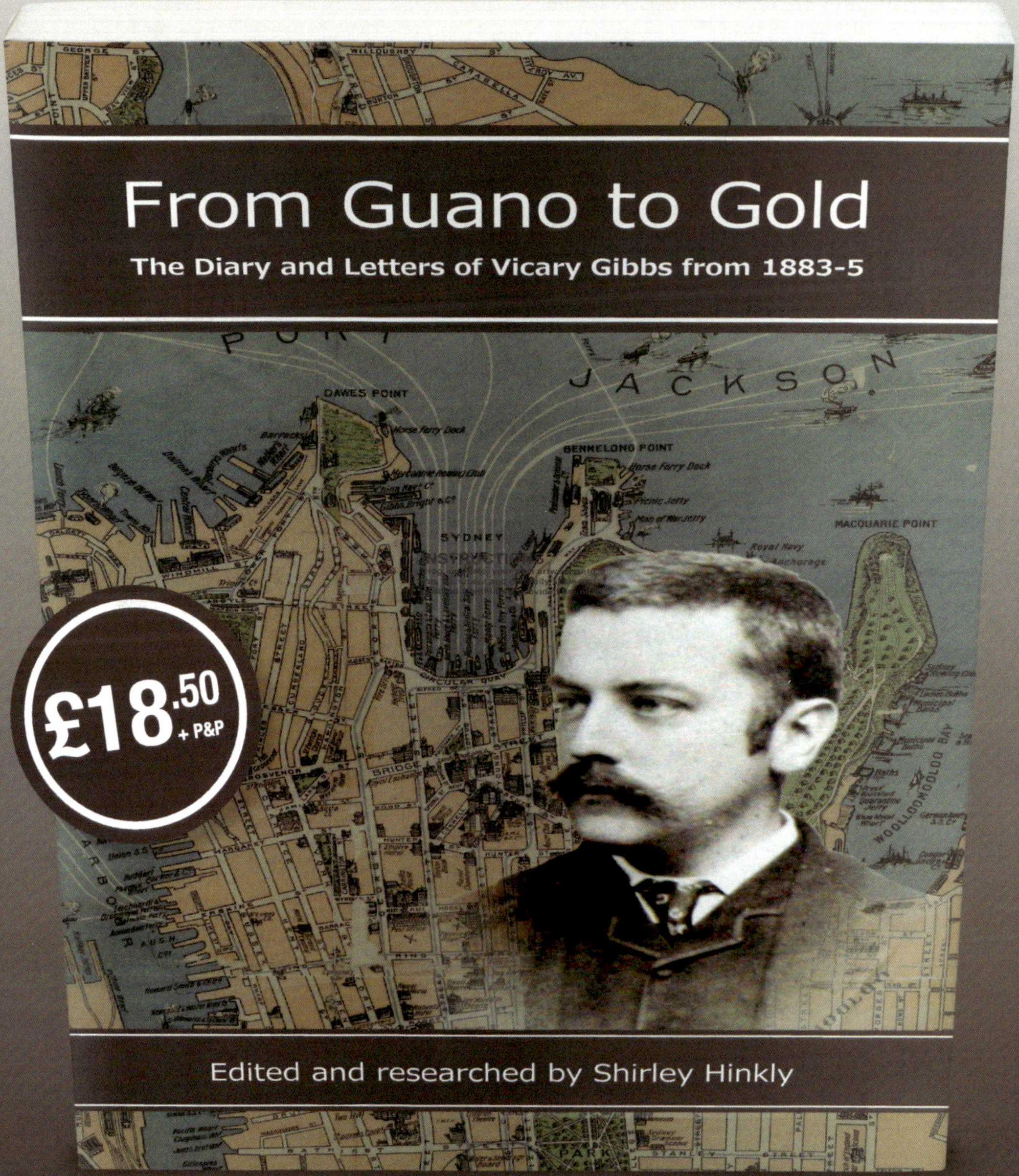

From Guano to Gold
The Diary and Letters of Vicary Gibbs from 1883-5

£18.50 + P&P

Edited and researched by Shirley Hinkly

Available now from www.lulu.com/shop

For further details or for trade enquiries please email: GibbsDiary@hinkly.net
or write to: Crawcour Books, 3 Harding Close, Selsey,
Chichester PO20 0EG, United Kingdom

From Guano to Gold
The Diary and Letters of Vicary Gibbs from 1883-5

In the early 1980s a small, battered notebook was discovered when the vaults of an old established merchant bank in the City of London were cleared. It turned out to be the handwritten diary of Vicary Gibbs (1853-1932), then a young partner in the family firm of Antony Gibbs & Sons, and later MP for St Albans.

His father, Henry Hucks Gibbs - 1st Baron Aldenham, and a former Governor of the Bank of England - sent Vicary, his second son, to the other side of the world primarily to assess the Colonial outposts of the family bank, but also to allow him to build the skills that would be required by an international financier on the lookout for new markets.

Vicary Gibbs' adventure took him to the opening of the newly-built Northern Pacific Railway in Montana, USA, and across the Pacific to New Zealand and Australia in the company of some of the most notable - and in some cases notorious - people of the time. Vicary observed and recorded the new world around him with pleasure, curiosity, and amusement, and his comments bring to life Britain's new colonies in the late Victorian period: astonishingly advanced in their development, and clearly recognisable as the nations we know today.

While the young banker discovered those promising enterprises which would produce the goods he wanted efficiently and competitively, he still found time to explore New Zealand and cruise luxuriously in the South Seas. His homeward journey by way of Ceylon (Sri Lanka) - where the company's tea-gardens were in a state of crisis - gives us clues to the Imperialist ambitions of Germany at the time.

Britain's dynamic colonialists pointed the way to power and influence with their energy and drive. Her colonies were already the envy of competitive European powers, had proved helpful in solving some of the major difficulties of rapid industrialisation, and would prove to be a part of the solution to the dramatic events of the 20th century.

This journey in time has waited for over one hundred years to be published for the enjoyment of 21st century readers, and illustrates some of the chain of events that have enabled the southern hemisphere to become a bigger player in the guidance and development of world events today.

Aboard the S.S. Gallia

5. SS Gallia (1890s)
U.S. Library of Congress, LC-D4-22365

Vicary's planned voyage to the other side of the world had fortuitously coincided with an invitation from Mr Henry Villard of the Northern Pacific Company to Antony Gibbs and Sons to join a select party of influential people and potential investors in witnessing the opening ceremony of the Northern Pacific Railway on 8th September 1883. The railway had been built in two sections, east from Portland, Oregon and west from St. Paul, Minnesota, and now the two parts were to be joined by the driving of a final Gold Spike in Gold Creek, Montana.

Henry Villard was an ambitious Bavarian American who encouraged European speculation in the railroad. Through his associates in the European Creditors Holding Company he was able to obtain control of the N.P.R., and was pushing for both early completion and increased funds. The four trains he chartered for his guests to bring them from St. Paul to Gold Creek, in luxuriant style and lavish hospitality, were an extravagant publicity stunt to encourage investment, but did not entirely pay off. The guests – many of whom were either existing or potential shareholders in the company - included British Members of Parliament and Peers, as well as members of the British and American judiciary, diplomats, and representatives of the major universities. Also present were other major investors, including Barings Bank. Antony Gibbs and Sons had only ever expressed modest interest in the scheme as their railway ambitions lay elsewhere, but Villard was always hopeful.

After the initial investor excitement caused by the grand excursion and the driving of the final spike, however, N.P.R. stock began to lose value when it was realised that the line could, at that time, only promise limited business. Villard suffered a nervous break-down and went to Germany to recover. He handed his role to Robert Harris, a real railroad man, who modified some of the tributary lines to reduce cost. When Villard returned to his post in 1887 the future of the line, although uncertain, seemed viable as the settlements along its route grew.

For Antony Gibbs and Sons, the trip to America had provided them with the opportunity to look for a New York office to handle future trade between the Chilean House and the United States and to promote their nitrate sales, which had seriously diminished in recent years.

On the night before leaving for Liverpool to board the S.S. Gallia to New York, Vicary Gibbs dined with his brother Herbert at the Carlton Club in London. At the time, much business would be proposed and discussed in one's preferred 'gentleman's Club'. By the late 19th century more bankers belonged to the Carlton then to any other. It was something of a second-home-cum-office for the Tory City gentleman; many final plans were made in those discreet surroundings. Vicary then travelled by overnight train, breakfasted with colleagues from the Liverpool office and boarded the 'Gallia' to begin his 19 months away from home. As the firm's representative he was no doubt armed with a portmanteau of instructions on the need for useful contacts, potential markets and company interests in any new and promising commodity. Vicary knew he was expected to resolve any problems that had come to light in the Houses of Gibbs, Bright and Co. since its take-over by the London head Office in 1881.

18 August 1883 - Saturday

I dined at the Carlton[4] with Herbert[5] last night, and came down to Liverpool by the midnight train. Breakfasted with John Arthur[6] at his

---

[4] The Carlton Club was founded in 1832 as a Tory party political organisation. Originally located in Charles II Street off St. James's Square in London, it moved to larger purpose-built premises on Pall Mall in 1835. The Pall Mall building was destroyed by an air raid during the Second World War.
[5] Herbert Cokayne Gibbs (1854-1935), 1st Baron Hunsdon of Hunsdon, and Vicary's younger brother.
[6] Probably John Arthur Gibbs (1860-1949), son of Reverend John Lomax Gibbs and Isabel Marianne Bright, which would make him Vicary Gibbs' first cousin, and probably the same "Johnny" with whom Gibbs corresponds by letter later. He was educated at Winchester,

lodgings, and then came down to the office where I found Tyndall[7]. He and William S. Crawley[8] and John[9] and Herbert Crawley[10] were on the landing stage to see me off. I have a pretty good cabin about the middle of the ship, and share it with Horace Davey QC MP[11] who seems a very good sort. The weather very fine and calm. I have some very pleasant neighbours at dinner: Tom Baring[12] and his brother Colonel Robert[13]; a young Lowther[14]; James Bryce[15]; Lord Carrington[16]; and one of the Mildmays[17]. After dinner, a cheerful rubber; but the play rather poor. Albert Grey, MP[18]; Robert Benson[19] whom I remember at Eton and Oxford; A. Bryce[20] who is a partner in Wallace Bros[21]. I lost 3 rubbers.

---

and Keble College Oxford. He would have been about 23 at this time, and had been working for AG&S since 1882 (later becoming a partner, in 1897). We know - from a letter Gibbs writes to him - that he is working at the Liverpool office at this time.

[7] Tyndall Bright, head of Liverpool House, and brother of Charles and Reginald Bright.

[8] Possibly William Savage Crawley (1823-?), distantly related to Gibbs.

[9] Possibly John Dennil Maddock Crawley (1861-1932), one of the five children of William Savage Crawley.

[10] Possibly Francis Herbert Maddock Crawley (1865-1916), one of the five children of William Savage Crawley.

[11] Horace Davey QC MP (1833-1907). Rugby; Oxford. Barrister. QC, 1875. Liberal MP for Christchurch, 1880-85. Solicitor General, 1886. MP Stockton, 1888-92. Privy Councillor, 1893. Lord Justice of Appeal, 1893-4. Lord of Appeal in Ordinary, 1894-1907. Created Baron Davey of Fernhurst in Sussex, 1894.

[12] Thomas Baring (1839-1923). Married Constance Barron, 1901. The Barings, a well-known Banking family, were originally Geman, moving to Devon in the 18th Century.

[13] Col. Robert Baring (1833-1915). Son of Henry Baring and Cecilia Anne Windham. Served in 19th Hussars.

[14] Lowther. Possibly one of the Westmorland family, powerful and influential merchants and politicians.

[15] Viscount James Bryce (1838-1922). Jurist historian. Ambassador to USA, 1907-13. An archive of his letters is at Princeton.

[16] Charles Robert Wynn Carrington (1843-1928). 3rd baron Carrington and MP High Wycombe, 1865-8. Governor of NSW, 1885-90. Member of Liberal cabinet after 1905.

[17] Fred Mildmay. Son of Henry Mildmay, a director of Barings from 1856.

[18] Albert Grey MP (1851-1917). Liberal MP for South Northumberland from 1880, then Tyneside. Later, Governor General of Canada. Succeeded his uncle as 4th earl Grey in 1894.

[19] Robert Henry Benson (1850–1929), merchant banker and art collector, was educated at Eton College and at Balliol College, Oxford. He was the brother-in-law of Albert Grey, MP, who is also aboard. Following his father's sudden death in 1875, Benson and his brother Constantine became partners in the banking firm Robert Benson & Co., but discovered that the firm had been badly run and was soon to fail, wiping out much of their inheritance. With the help of the banker John Cross they were able to set up the new firm of Cross, Benson and Co., and made a large personal fortune by financing railways in the American west. At the time Gibbs meets him, Cross has just retired from the company which has changed name to Robert Henry Benson & Co., and the following year would change again to Robert Benson & Co.

[20] (John) Annan Bryce (1843-1923), the younger brother of James Bryce who is also aboard The Gallia, joined Wallace Brothers in 1875.

[21] Wallace Bros., general merchants; originally India merchants.

19 August 1883 - Sunday

Reached Queenstown[22] about 5 in the morning. The harbour is certainly very pretty. Robert Fitzgerald's[23] house was pointed out to me; it is very well situated. I went on shore with several fellow passengers; we strolled about and looked in the R.C. Cathedral[24], a handsome white stone building but unfinished. There is among the passengers a man named Granville Milner[25]; a weak, dissipated, amiable fellow like Heathcote Long to look at, he is a brother of Sir F. Milner[26] and is going to some ranch[27]. Also Albert Pell[28], who is a jolly old chap; he was at school with father[29]. Also Sir Lepel Griffin[30], an oiled and curled Assyrian bull who fancies himself as a fearful thing among the ladies. He was a great supporter of Lord Lytton and ratted when the present Government came in, and has an important district in central India.

20 August 1883 - Monday

It blew hard all night and today most people have been ill. Poor Davey in a wretched state of collapse: unable to leave his berth, and very sick. The sea was breaking all over the fore part of the ship and I saw a sailor washed off his legs and carried half down the deck. Very few people at dinner. After dinner I felt bad for half an hour but soon got right and played whist with Grey, Colonel Baring and Macleod[31] of Macleod, a military man who has served in India; a pleasant and gentlemanly fair whist player, brother of the man who married Miss Northcote. I lost 2 rubbers. I was introduced

---

[22] Queenstown: the Irish town of Cobh renamed for Queen Victoria after her visit in 1849.
[23] Possibly Sir Robert Uniacke Penrose Fitzgerald (1839–1919), later 1st Baronet of Corkbeg and Lisquinlan, who became a Conservative MP in the 1885 general election. Although supposedly he did not adopt the name Uniacke-Penrose-Fitzgerald until 1896, he is recorded as a magistrate in the Cork County Directory of 1862.
[24] St. Colman's Cathedral in Cobh, built in French Gothic style by Edward Welby Pugin and George Ashlin. Construction began in 1867 and was not finished until 1915.
[25] Granville Henry Milner (1852-1911).
[26] Sir Frederick George Milner, 7th Baronet (1849-1931), was MP for York from 1883 to 1885, then MP for Bassetlaw from 1890 to 1906.
[27] This was probably Morton Frewen's ranch, on which Milner wrote a report. In 1882, Moreton Frewen bought out his brother Richard's share of an earlier company and reorganized it as the Powder River Cattle Company Ltd., with an English board of directors. Frewen served as manager of the company until 1886, and it was eventually dissolved in 1889.
[28] Possibly (based only on being born within the same school year as Henry Hucks Gibbs) Albert Pell (1820-1907), an English solicitor and Conservative Party politician. He was educated at Rugby School (as was Henry Hucks Gibbs) and Trinity College, Cambridge.
[29] Henry Hucks Gibbs, 1st Baron Aldenham MA BA FGS FSA (1819-1907). He was a senior partner in Antony Gibbs and Sons, Director of the Bank of England from 1853-1901, and its Governor from 1875-1877. He was also briefly Conservative MP for the City of London from 1891-1892, when Vicary Gibbs' eldest brother Alban was elected in his place.
[30] Sir Lepel Griffin (1838-1908). Indian civil sevice. Chief secretary of the Punjab, 1880. Writer.
[31] Norman Macleod (1812-1895). 25th chief of the clan Macleod. Served in India, and then as political agent in the Transvaal.

to Slingsby Bethell[32] today – son of old Lord Westbury – a very rum looking chap; also to Sam Rathbone[33], who seems decidedly a good sort.

21 August 1883 - Tuesday

Weather calmer and more people showing up. Made acquaintance with Major General Hutchinson[34], who is sent by the Board of Trade. He is a colleague of Tyler's[35], and reports on railway accidents; a gentlemanly old fellow. Young Milner has been in Valparaiso some time with Sir Horace Rumbold[36]. Read 'La Bouche de Madame X' by Adolph Belot, a blackguard book but rather amusing; played 6 rubbers and won 5. There is a man named Douglas[37] on board, a Scotchman living in Melbourne, a pretty wife[38] with him; seems a pleasant fellow, says he knows the Brights and that Eurella[39] belongs to him – which adjoins Amby[40]. He will go from 'Frisco[41] on the 22nd September and be my companion unless I miss it. R. Benson is amiable, but a little bit of a bore.

22 August 1883 - Wednesday

Very wet and nothing to do but play whist. I won 6 rubbers and lost 7. I read 'Reata' by Miss Gerard[42]; very pretty Polish story, the heroine very attractive – something like Hildegarde in 'The Initials'[43]. I have been

---

[32] Slingsby Bethell (1831-1896).
[33] Samuel Greg Rathbone JP (1823-1903). Second son of William Rathbone, a Liverpool merchant. Partner in Rathbone Bros. & Co. Opened offices in New York and London for the expanding China trade in tea and silk.
[34] Major General C S Hutchinson RE (1826-1912). Sent as an engineering observer by the Board of Trade to witness the completion of the North American Pacific railway. In 1889, he reported on the Tay Bridge disaster, and was still an advisor on major accidents in 1899, although he retired in 1895.
[35] John Chatfield Tyler, who married Frederic Hart's sister Fanny Mary Hart in Melbourne in 1861.
[36] Sir Horace Rumbold (1829-1913). 8th Baronet. A long-serving diplomat who left two volumes of discreet reminiscences that mention Milner.
[37] Charles Hill Douglas (1842-1898) was born in Edinburgh, emigrating to Victoria in 1859. By 1863 he had purchased two cattle stations, "Gelam" and "Budgee-Budgee", in partnership with his brother Henry, and Archibald Menzies. The brothers (sometimes along with Archibald Menzies, R. H. Kinnear, and T. Nicoll) then bought and sold sheep and cattle station over the years, amongst them the "Bringenbrong", "Khancobin", and "Indi" stations, all adjoining each other on the Upper Murray, "North Yanko" sheep station, "Walla Walla" near Albury, New South Wales, and "Eurella". Eurella was managed by Douglas' cousins, Fred and Rob Dunsmere, as Gibbs reports later. Douglas was a well-known figure in Melbourne, and was much liked and highly respected by all who came into contact with him.
[38] Henrietta Douglas (née Chapman), daughter of William Chapman, of "Lumley Park," Bungonia, New South Wales.
[39] Eurella Station, in Eurella, Queensland.
[40] Amby Downs Sheep Station, Queensland, which had been acquired by Gibbs Bright as part of their entry into the wool trade. In an area prone to drought it was precarious at times and gave much anxiety. Chrystal remained to manage it.
[41] San Francisco.
[42] Dorothea and Emily Gerard jointly published Reata in 1880.
[43] 'The Initials', by Baroness Jemima Montgomery Tautphoeus, published 1850.

talking to Francis Buxton[44], MP for Andover, and like him; also very friendly to Lord Carrington: a good chap, fair abilities, and no by God nonsense about him. Next to me at dinner is a young George Holford[45], a very handsome ingenuous youth in the Guards, I think; not very clever but nice. He is brother-in-law to Albert Grey, a much cleverer and more amusing man, with whom I have political jaws. He is a regular Whig, with a veneration for Free Trade and abhorrence of Radicals. The Americans on board are a very shimmy, poker-playing, drinking lot; hardly a decent gentlemanly man among them. There are no pretty women, but one fetching little fair-haired girl age about 9.

23 August 1883 - Thursday

Read a most horrible, powerful, realistic French novel in the Zola style by Maupassant; full of gloomy obscenity. Called "La Vie", the most ghastly scene is where the heroine, while sitting by her mother's corpse, opens and reads her mother's old love-letters and thus discovers that she had had *'un amant'*. Played whist as usual; won 4 and lost 5 rubbers. Talked to Edwards[46], MP for Weymouth; gossipy, cheerful, rather inferior man, like Greenwood[47] of the St. James[48] to look at. I believe he is noted for giving good dinners. Evicted the sitting tenant from my chair, an old woman who has been there ever since we started – very difficult job. She lied like a goodun, and swore she had hired it from the deck steward. Bought a ticket in the lottery for the ships run, and only missed winning it by 2; worth £30.

6. Statue of Sir Henry Edwards, MP, in Weymouth
by Shirley Hinkly

24 August 1883 - Friday

Tired of whist – the men play so badly – and have taken instead to piquet with the Barings. Carrington told me that for a Sir Joshua of Mrs Abingdon the actress[49], for which he had got the bill for £15 paid by one of his

---

[44] Francis William Buxton MP (1847-1911). Barrister, liberal party politician and MP for Andover.
[45] Sir George Lindsay Holford (1860-1926). 1st Life Guards, 1880-1908. Equerry to Duke of Clarence, to King Edward, to Queen Alexandra and to George V. Noted for his singular personal charm, discretion and loyalty of character. He was one of the most successful amateur gardeners of his time.
[46] Sir Henry Edwards MP (1820-1897). MP for Weymouth and Melcombe Regis, 1867-1885. A noted philanthropist. His statue can still be seen in Weymouth Old Town.
[47] Frederick Greenwood, the first editor of the St. James's Gazette.
[48] St. James's Gazette, a London evening newspaper founded by Henry Hucks Gibbs (Vicary's father) in 1880 and owned by him until 1888. It was published until 1905 when it amalgamated with the Evening Standard.
[49] Sir Joshua Reynolds (1723-1792), a famous portrait painter, painted the actress (and ex-prostitute) Frances Abington (1737-1815) several times.

ancestors, he had refused £4000 and £5000 offered by two different people. Also that, being hard up, he sold 2 or 3 years ago 3 Sevres vases for £8000, for which his father had given £500. Old Sir Sydney Waterlow[50] came and asked me to give a recitation tomorrow at some entertainment he is getting up. He is a genial old cad, with a youngish wife. Young Holford was telling me a lot about his father's pictures, those he had got and those he had missed. He had the Francia 'Pieta', now in the National Gallery, for 3 weeks in his drawing room and couldn't make up his mind to buy it. I shall go and see his pictures when I get back.

25 August 1883 - Saturday

Couldn't find anything in the ship's library to recite except Shakespeare, so I committed to memory King Lear 'Blow, winds' to 'Show the Heavens more just' and did that. I remembered it better than I expected and it went off fairly, but a saloon is a horrid place to speak in: so low, and ram full with 300 people in it. Bethell did the 'vulgar little boy' very well; the rest was singing and playing. Young Fred Mildmay is the eldest son of the partner in Barings and will, I believe, be enormously rich. He has just left Cambridge; a nice quiet lad, his father has a beautiful place in Devonshire. Colonel Baring has a very dry manner and discontented face, but he is very amusing when you get to know him – though without any of the bonhomie of Ned or Tom.

26 August 1883 - Sunday

Carrington told me some very amusing stories of his youthful escapades – how he had heard the chimes at midnight[51] – and showed me a very pretty miniature of his wife by a man named Taylor. A lovely day: just enough wind to ruffle the water and do away with the monotony, and bright sun. We have had good weather all through, except Monday when it certainly blew hard. Sir William Gurdon KCB[52] is, I think, the least popular of our party. I think he expects more consideration than he gets, and is rather huffy at having a poor cabin and not dining at our table; he is a bit of a grumbler. He went to South Africa twice and, being Gladstone's secretary, got a KCB for rather unimportant service. He is the man who went to Paris with Father as secretary to the Monetary conference, and is civil enough to me.

---

[50] Sir Sydney Waterlow (1822-1906). A philanthropist, owned a large printing firm. A director of the Union Bank of London. Liberal MP for Dumfriesshire (1868-9), Maidstone (1874-80), and Gravesend (1880-5).
[51] From Shakespeare's Henry IV, part 2, Act 3, Scene 2. Falstaff says, "We have heard the chimes at midnight, Master Shallow". Falstaff and Shallow are reminiscing about their youth – only those out drinking or up to no good would hear the clock strike midnight.
[52] Sir William Gurdon (1840-1910). MP for North Norfolk, 1899-1910.

27 August 1883 - Monday

We took the pilot on board late last night. I hear old Edwards is familiarly known as 'Count Linseed' having made his fortune in that article during the Crimean War. It is hot and I find the nuisance of being on the lower deck is I can never have my port open. We sighted land about 5pm and lay to for the night off Staten Island. Talked to Horace White[53], who is editor of the Evening Post – one of the most respectable New York papers; a very well-informed, intelligent, but common-looking man. Mr Steinthal[54], a Unitarian minister from Manchester, is going the trip with us. Altogether it has been a pleasant voyage and I have made several nice acquaintances, I like especially Buxton, Grey, Carrington and the elder Bryce. Davey is rather dull, and Edwards too vulgar. Gurdon too stuck up.

New York

28 August 1883 - Tuesday

Breakfasted on board at 6 and after making our affidavits that we had no 'dutiable' articles, we landed. Our goods were passed through the customs without examination and we were put into comfortable carriages and driven to the Windsor, which is a very large and handsome hotel somewhat out of the town. Here we had a second breakfast. Canteloupe, blue fish, fried clams, corn fritters, etc. All the cakes, rolls and breadstuff are most particularly good here. Called at Richard Irvine and saw the son, who was very friendly and took me to the top of a place called Mills Buildings where one gets a magnificent view of New York; then we went and looked down on the Stock Exchange, a fine hall with a fearful Babel going on. Went and called on the Coghills[55], but they were out of town as everyone almost is during August as the heat is very oppressive generally – though we are having charming weather. Dined with Grey and Holford. Corn soup, soft-shelled crabs and other local dainties. Everything very good except the Champagne, which was poisonously sweet and quite unfit to drink. Afterwards we went to the Madison Square theatre; a pretty little house, beautifully cool; but the play and acting only moderate, owing

---

[53] Horace White (1834-1916). Close friend and collaborator of Henry Villard, journalist and President of the Northern Pacific Railway. Villard was now proprietor of the New York Evening Post, of which White had became editor.

[54] Rev. Samuel Alfred Steinthal (1826-1910). A leading social reformer in Manchester. His interests extended to the abolition of slavery, and the improvement of conditions for workers in the Southern states of the U.S.

[55] Coghills: POSSIBLY Mr and Mrs James Henry Coghill, and Miss Coghill. Their names are mentioned in newspapers of the time at social events in New York and therefore would be the kind of people Gibbs might call on. J[ames] Henry Coghill published a book in 1868(?) called "Abroad: Journal of a tour through Great Britain and on the Continent" - a journal of a family trip. Or possibly Howard Coghill (some relation, sometimes mentioned at the same events). He married Miss Edith Dunbar (daughter of James M. Dunbar) in 1888. There is also a Miss Ella Virginia Coghill (daughter of the late - in 1886 - Frederick W. Coghill) who married Levin Joynes in 1886.

no doubt to it being the slack time of the year. We were joined by Carrington and went in to Hoffmans Restaurant, a gorgeous place with magnificent pictures in it; one by Bougereau very fine, and another by Corregio. Travelled by the elevated railway: quick, convenient and hideous thing which has depreciated the value of the house property which it passes by one half.

29 August 1883 - Wednesday

7. New York and Brooklyn Bridge (c1889)
U.S. Library of Congress, LC-USZ62-22027

After breakfast we were driven to the Quay and taken up the Hudson to West Point where we had a big lunch. The scenery very grand, something like the better part of the Rhine; the basaltic rocks are fine – they are called the 'Palisades'. Saw the place where André[56] was caught and shot. Came back and steamed round New York under the splendid Brooklyn Bridge[57]. When we landed, found carriages ready to take us where we liked; and the party broke up all going different ways to see whatever sights they most fancied. Sam Rathbone and I drove over the Brooklyn Bridge – more than a mile long! – into Brooklyn and then back for a drive in the Central Park. I dined with Irvine at the Union: a most comfortable and admirably-arranged club. After dinner we went to the Casino: a very handsome theatre in Moorish style. Between the acts one can go on the roof which is laid out as a garden restaurant; very pleasant. The piece was an Opera Bouffe answering to the pieces at the 'Gaiety' with a good topical song. The papers are full of our party, criticisms on our dress and appearance; the interviewers are continually getting hold of one or other. A man buttonholed me in the Hall the other day and one of our party has seen the account in "The Star" but I have not. Pell told one of the reporters that he had come over in the same cabin with Carrington and for a dollar he would tell about a mole which C. had and where it was. Have just met

---

[56] Major John André (1750-1780). A British army officer hanged as a spy during the American Revolution.
[57] The Brooklyn Bridge had only opened on 24th May 1883. A week later, a rumour that the bridge was about to collapse caused a stampede which crushed and killed at least 12 people.

L.J. Bowen[58]; very civil, tells me Coleridge[59] is being taken about by very third-rate shady people – it's a pity.

30 August 1883 - Thursday

Called on Brown Bros.[60] and found Mr. B. very gentlemanly and civil. He gave me a letter to Corner Bros. and I called on them to talk about New Zealand business, but there was no partner in. Went to see Bowers of the Guardian, who is a rare good sort; he gave me and General Hutchinson a capital lunch: clams, raw Pompano – which is a very good fish, etc. After that he arranged a fire brigade performance and I went and fetched the rest of our party who were keen to see it, and we all went off with the American equivalent of Captain Shaw[61]. It was certainly most wonderful. I had no conception of it from the description; it is quite impossible to realise it without seeing it. It quite took my breath away. We were driven full gallop down Broadway on the fire engine.

31 August 1883 - Friday

Left New York at 8 last night and have got a separate compartment of the car with Grey, Holford and Benson which is very pleasant. We have come by the Erie[62] and Great Western of Canada[63] line, and consequently had the opportunity of getting a fair view of the falls and rapids at Niagara. There is a Mr Stackpoole[64] of Boston, a barrister and very pleasant man; also a Mr Wells[65] who is a great statistician and economist – I believe the principal free trade man in US; he knows father and is interested in the

---

[58] Lord Justice Sir Charles Bowen (1835-1894), who was one of the guests at the opening ceremony of the Northern Pacific Railway. As a lawyer, Bowen had been involved in the famous Tichborne case of the 1860s and '70s (which Gibbs mentions in passing later - see 22 December 1884). In 1879 he became a High Court judge, and in 1882 he was raised to the Court of Appeal, becoming a Lord Justice of Appeal. He became Baron Bowen in 1893.
[59] John Duke Coleridge, 1st Baron Coleridge (1820–1894), a British lawyer, judge and Liberal politician. In 1871 he was Attorney-General, and heavily involved in the Tichborne case. In 1880 he was made Lord Chief Justice of England.
[60] One of the oldest private banks in the USA which started in 1818 as an importer of linen but later concentrated on currency exchange and international trade. The New York office was opened in 1825 by James Brown.
[61] Captain Sir Eyre Massey Shaw (1830-1908) was Superintendant of the London Fire Brigade - Gibbs was the guest of the New York equivalent.
[62] The Erie Railroad, which connected New York and Lake Erie.
[63] The Great Western Railway, Ontario.
[64] Possibly J. L. Stackpoole, a member of the board of directors of the Northern Pacific Railway.
[65] David Ames Wells (1818-1898). Professor at Harvard. Established the Bureau of Statistics in 1866. Charles Russell MP (who was also on the Northern Pacific Railway trip - see 9 September 1883) also kept a diary of the trip, and quotes Wells' insight into the future of China: "David A. Wells (the celebrated leader of the Free Trade Party) thinks the future of the Chinese nation the most important factor in the future of the world....What, he asks, will be the effect upon the world when this great mass of industrious humanity works with all the best appliances which human science and ingenuity can contrive?"

bimetallic controversy[66]. General Grant[67] is playing poker in the next car. I had a look at him: a heavy, uninteresting man. It is hot and dusty work travelling, but we are a very cheerful, pleasant party. Samuelson MP and his wife are in the train, rather second-rate looking people. Introduced to General Newton, who is a great military Engineering swell at West Point.

Great Western of Canada Line and Northern Pacific Railway

1 September 1883 - Saturday

Reached Chicago about 11 and went to the enormous Palace Hotel, and had a warm bath – very delightful after so many hours travelling. Then drove with Stackpoole and a young Swedish diplomat to see the stock yards and the pig-killing business: pretty disgusting, the most remarkable thing was the machine for getting the bristles off. The sun was tremendously hot and I did not feel equal to seeing the bullocks slaughtered. Came back to a big lunch at the hotel. Mr Evarts[68], who was counsel for the States at Geneva and for President Johnson when he was impeached and is about their best known lawyer, asked to be introduced to me and said he had met Father at Paris. He was very friendly and asked me to sit next to him; he seems a witty, sarcastic old chap, sneering first at our country and then at this own. I was interviewed again by the reporter of the Chicago Times and my views on Free Trade, American securities, Pullman cars etc. elicited for the edification of the Chicago people. This place has, I believe, doubled the population since last census.

2 September 1883 - Sunday

Left Chicago yesterday in the afternoon, and reached St. Paul about 7 this morning; a wonderful change in the temperature, being now quite cool. St. Paul and Minneapolis are two cities about 10 miles apart on the Mississippi. 25 years ago they had each about 6,000 population, and are now estimated each 80,000. About 15 miles beyond is the enormous

---

[66] The bimetallic controversy refers to the debate - which went on for many years - about whether America's currency should be linked to the gold or silver standard. The issue had started because of a change to the composition of the dollar coin in 1853, and the later discovery of large silver deposits in the Western United States. The debate continued until the gold standard was formally adopted in 1900.

[67] Former President Ulysses S. Grant (1882-1885). 18th President of the United States (from 1869 to 1877). He was promoted to a newly-created rank, General of the Army of the United States, in 1866 at the end of the Civil War. He was given the honour of driving in the final "golden spike" of the Northern Pacific Railway in central Montana (see 8th September). He died in 1885 following financial ruin by the partners in his Bank.

[68] William Maxwell Evarts (1818-1901). Lawyer, statesman, and government counsel who became a Republican in 1868. Attorney-General Secretary of state from 1877 to 1881, and New York senator from 1885 to 1891. He was noted as a public speaker.

Hotel Lafayette[69] on Lake Minnetonka, which we have reached about 10 in the morning. Went out in a sailing boat with some of the party[70], preferring it to a large steamer excursion. We bathed and landed on one of the islands, and had a very pleasant time. The lake is immense in size and very much broken up with creeks and inlets, and the shores well wooded. We were to have gone out duck shooting in the evening, but the guns were not to be found.

3 September 1883 - Monday

We got up early and all went into St. Paul, which was decorated with arches and all in gala style. Tremendous crowds in the streets. We witnessed a long procession of Indians, agricultural industries machinery and every sort of thing to illustrate the growth and products of the country, such as specimens of the old post office box, the old schooner[71] or emigrants' wagon, and a mixture of advertisements and tableaux; very curious and many of them well got up. General Grant, President Arthur[72], General Sheridan and other swells were present. We then went to Minneapolis where just the same sort of thing went on, only more so. Then we were driven to a lovely lake – Lake Lyndale[73] – where a big lunch was given, and

---

[69] The Hotel Lafayette was built by James Jerome Hill (1838-1916), a prominent businessman and Great Northern Railroad chief executive officer known as "The Empire Builder", who chose Minnetonka Beach as the site of the Great Northern Railroad's first great summer resort. The hotel had its grand opening in 1882. The area was inaccessible in winter until a road was built in 1887, at which point its popularity as a resort area for the rich and famous was enhanced. It was destroyed by fire in 1897, then in 1899 the Minnetonka Club, later renamed the Lafayette Club, was built on the site.

[70] The members of the party were the guests of Henry Villard, who had been attempting to establish a monopoly of rail transport in the north-west of the USA, especially Oregon, for some years with the help of his European connections. He had raised $8M from his associates by persuading them to invest in a "blind pool" - in other words, investing without knowing what they were investing in. This enabled him to obtain a majority share-holding of the Northern Pacific Railway. In order to encourage further investment, he chartered 4 trains to carry his guests, as well as existing and potential financiers - Gibbs amongst them, from the east of the USA to witness the driving of the final "Golden Spike" in Gold Creek, Central Montana, by General (and former president) Ulysses S. Grant on 8 September 1883. Unfortunately for Villard, the vast expense of completing the railroad at breakneck speed (a mile-and-a-half a day in 1883) and the view in the stock market that there would not be sufficient passenger income to cover those costs caused the share value of the company to fall, and Villard suffered a nervous breakdown. He resigned as president soon after the driving of the Golden Spike (although he rejoined the company later). Barings continued their involvement in the company but Gibbs and Sons remained aloof.

[71] Also known as Prairie Schooners or "covered wagons".

[72] President Chester A. Arthur (1829-1886), 21st President of the United States (from 1881 to 1885).

[73] There doesn't seem to be a Lake Lyndale in the Minneapolis area now, so it is unclear whether Gibbs got the name wrong or whether the lake has since disappeared. The name certainly lives on in the districts of Lyn-Lake and Lyndale, and in street names such as Lake Street and Lyndale Avenue. The pamphlet "Grand Opening of the North Pacific Railway", which describes the opening ceremony in some detail, seems to indicate that the lake in question is Lake Minnetonka, about 20 miles from Minneapolis, but Gibbs refers to Lake Minnetonka the previous day and is clearly talking about a different lake here.

speeches. One of the Bunsens[74] made a good but heavy speech and Evarts made one of the wittiest speeches I ever heard, making fun of everything, chaffing the Western people and Villard[75] and the English, and sailing as near the wind as possible without giving offence; he said in returning thanks for the guests, 'I am glad that this task has fallen on a cold-blooded New Englander; your modesty would have shrunk from it, you would have shown the only modesty I have ever known you to show, the best sort of modesty – you would have blushed unseen'. He spoke of the proud English and metaphysical Germans – ended with apologising for not having been able to say anything which could add to the Western men's opinion of themselves. He also contrasted Villard's enterprise with the first explorer who had crossed the Pacific through all the Indian tribes by means of a few simples and eye- water, but Villard had been more fortunate, - he had kept the eye-water for himself, found a great many simples and had roped the Capitalists into a blind pool. We trained back to Minnetonka where there was an enormous banquet given us by the citizens of St. Paul at 15 dollars a head: bear's hams, and other fancy dishes. Lord Onslow[76] has given great offence to both English and Americans by his rudeness: to begin with, he called on Villard in New York in a flannel shirt, a shooting coat, and invited himself and wife to join the party; and as this caused us to be much crowded Bryce sent over to say that some of us would join his car. This was refused, and soon after he sent his valet and lady's maid to dine with us! Carrington – who is a cousin of Lady Onslow – spoke to him, and the next day he made some lying excuses to Bryce and asked B. to apologise to us. B. said he could not undertake to do so, and told O. he had better do so himself and try to remove the painful impression he had undoubtedly created. I had a specimen of his manners yesterday: having ordered breakfast and taken two places by putting hats on the chairs for self and old Pell, we went out to wash our hands and on my return found O. seated opposite. I bowed quite civilly before sitting down; he simply stared and then said, "My party is four". I replied, 'Oh', in a tone which conveyed the notion of, 'So glad'. He said with some heat, 'I tell you, you can't sit there; my party is four'. I said, "I understand your party is a large one, but it won't interfere with me. I shall breakfast here; waiter, my breakfast". After his unsuccessful attempt to get the waiters to remove me, the noble Earl retreated to another table.

---

[74] Baron Georg von Bunsen, LL.D.(1824-1896), member of the reichstag (German Parliament).
[75] Henry Villard (1835-1900), born Ferdinand Heinrich Gustav Hilgard in Bavaria before emigrating to the USA as a teenager without his parents' knowledge and changing his name. Originally a journalist, he became president of the Northern Pacific Railway, the grand opening of which Gibbs is attending here. He resigned as president in January 1884 after the collapse of the company. He was also the owner of the New York Evening Post (from 1881).
[76] Sir William Hillier, Lord Onslow, 4th Earl (1853-1911) was to have a distinguished career as Governor of New Zealand after 1889 and later in the English government. At this time he had been Lord in Waiting to Queen Victoria and Under-Secretary of State for the Colonies.

4 September 1883 - Tuesday

We left at 12 last night, and have been travelling through the wheat country of Dakota. Our engine broke down, and we were delayed a couple of hours. I went out on the prairie with young Burns[77] – the son of the man who owns the chief part of the Cunard Co.'s shares – who had a gun; we put up a grey heron which B. missed clean with both barrels, so I returned as I felt it was no use going on if he couldn't hit a thing like a haystack at 20 yards. All the prominent Americans to whom I talk look on the Annexation of Mexico as certain and probably soon, though they mostly regret it and anticipate heavy fighting. Evarts took me into Grant's car and introduced me; a sodden fellow with cold-boiled eyes, very dull and uninteresting, but a good-shaped square head. They say he plays poker well, which explains his military success; he is supposed to be running again for a 3rd term, but has no chance.

5 September 1883 - Wednesday

We reached Bismarck early this morning: a go-ahead, flourishing, wooden-build place like all these Western towns. As one goes along the line one can see them in every stage of development, and can pretty well tell by looking at them how long they have been built. At Bismarck the usual speechifying and glorification took place, but the great feature was the appearance of 'Sitting Bull'[78], the famous Sioux chieftain who defeated and massacred General Custer and every man that was with him but one, after which he escaped into Canada with 6000 followers all of whom ultimately surrendered unconditionally. He now lives here with 200 personal followers under a sort of surveillance; the rest of his tribe are an immense way off and have settled down quietly as teamsters which they do very well. The Apaches are the only tribe that give any trouble – the rest are pretty well played out. Sitting Bull looks like an old woman; he was put upon the platform to speak and, as a preliminary, he blew his nose in a highly primitive manner; this caused me to decline the honour of shaking hands with the noble savage. He sold his autograph to a lot of people for a dollar and a half. Altogether I should think he was a degraded beast. In the evening we got to a place called Badlands: a most extraordinary place all covered with volcanic-looking cone-shaped hills of every size, and large bluffs of flat-shaped mountains with sheer sides and

---

[77] The father is Sir George Burns, 1st Baronet (1795-1890), a Scottish shipping magnate. Burns consolidated a number of companies, including the British and North American Royal Mail Steam Packet Company (which owned The Gallia, amongst other ships), into the Cunard Line (established by Sir Samuel Cunard) in 1840. His eldest son, John Burns (1829-1901), succeeded his father in the baronetcy and later became head of the Cunard Company. It is this son whom Gibbs meets.

[78] Sitting Bull (1831-1890) was once a powerful opponent who had defeated and massacred General Custer and his men. After exile in Canada, he was now living in Bismarck (Tatanka Yotanka, Little Missouri) with 200 personal followers. He said, at the opening of the Northern Pacific Railway, "I hate all white people; you are thieves and liars. You have taken away our land and made us outcasts".

covered with rich buffalo grass. There is a Marquis de Mores[79] who has started a large cattle place there; he is a son of the Duke of Vallombrosa whom 'Truth' libelled the other day. He told us he was coming to England in the fall to flog Labouchère[80], and I should think he would do it very well; he had about 20 horses up to the cars and we all went for a ride; very pleasant. The Marquis had just been tried for murder in Bismarck and acquitted under the following circumstances: he came in May last and, having bought his holding, proceeded to fence it in; this led to a dispute about boundaries, and a notice was posted that certain men meant to kill him. One evening a little way from his own house he met 3 men drawn up on horseback, armed with Winchesters. He had a 500 Express with an expanding bullet; he dismounted and lay flat and so did they, about 70 yards off. They shot his horse and put a bullet through the brim of his hat. He killed one man dead and broke the second's leg; the third threw his hands up and caved in. This last fellow had made friends with the Marquis since and was holding some of the ponies for us. We saw the tomb of the first. Altogether, it seemed a very good example of Western life. The inn-keeper told one of our party that the Marquis was perfectly safe now, having shown he could shoot.

8. Sitting Bull (at Bismarck, North Dakota) (1885)
U.S. Library of Congress, LC-USZ62-111147

6 September 1883 - Thursday

Came to a place called Billings about noon; named after a man[81] who was on board with us, and who had been President of the Line. The best part of the day we were travelling through the Territory reserved for the Crow Indians – who number 5 or 6,000, I believe. It is soon to be taken from them, as they don't cultivate it and it is too fertile. About 4, we reached the Indian camp where about 3,000 were assembled: all the braves in their war paint and formed into a great circle with the squaws and children

---

[79] Marquis de Mores was killed by his escort in 1906 while crossing the Sahara to help the Khalifa against the British.
[80] Henry Du Pré Labouchère (1831-1912). He had served as an MP, but was at this time a journalist who had founded the Truth in 1877: a weekly journal often sued for libel.
[81] Frederick H. Billings (1823-1890). First Treasurer and President of the Northern Pacific Railway of the 1870s. The railroad town of Billings, Montana, established in 1882, was named after him.

outside and a fire in the centre. They gave us a great war dance, and I bought a pair of moccasins for a dollar and swapped my braces for another pair. I suppose very few people will ever see so large a tribe in such perfection again, as they are being hustled about and broken up and are dying out. We had a lot of horse-racing bare-back as there were droves of Indian horses about: I had a most exciting race with an Indian – my knees and his were knocking together as we finished, but he just did me by a head. The Indians all draw rations from the Government, and their reservation is really a vast 'poor house' – they are not citizens and not subject to law for what they do to one another so long as they don't meddle with white men. The Crows still fight a little with the Sioux, but they are a weaker and more degraded tribe. At night we reached Livingston, a place of 3,000 inhabitants, and find ourselves in Montana and in a mining as well as agricultural district: we saw 2 wagons, each drawn by 16 bullocks, loaded with silver bars. We went to the 'Opera House', which was a sort of penny gaff. The performance was dull and decorous, though the audience was neither one nor the other. We also went into a gambling saloon where we were told poker went on all the day including Sunday and almost all night.

7 September 1883 - Friday

Read 'Altiora Peto': a very amusing satire on English Society by Lawrence Oliphant[82]. Began the ascent of the Rockies and went up one tremendous gradient of 1-in-23 with a couple of engines: this will be altered and a tunnel made. Saw some prairie dog: a funny little rodent like a marmot. Decidedly disappointed with the mountain scenery, which is not nearly as grand as I expected. Stopped at noon at a rather pretty little place called Bozeman. The inhabitants took us for a drive in their carriages; the man who drove me with a beautiful pair of horses had been a common miner in England. Reached Helena about 5, which is the capital of Montana with nothing particular in it worthy of notice, and after half-an-hour continued our journey over the Rockies. The country is much burnt up and dusty, but it is fairly cool. There has been a great prairie fire near here, which makes everything very foggy.

8 September 1883 – Saturday

At half past nine last night the couplers broke going down hill on the first section of our train, and they put on the brakes too sharp which caused the rear part to rush in the first and telescope half of a Pullman: no one was injured, as the part destroyed was given up to kitchen. Our minister,

---

[82] 'Altiora Peto', by Laurence Oliphant, the son of Sir Anthony Oliphant who originally owned the Oliphant Tea Estate that Gibbs visits whilst in Ceylon (see 6 January 1885). Laurence himself had been tutored in Ceylon. Margaret Oliphant, another author that Gibbs reads on this trip (see 9 December 1883), was his cousin.

West[83], however, had a narrow escape of his life. There was an enormous crowd of excursionists and people from Oregon to see the last spike driven. The sight was very fine: a great plateau with the mountains rising up all round. The Rockies however, are disappointing – in this part of them at any rate: they are not well-wooded, at least not on the Eastern slope, and the rise is very gradual and the hills rounded, not sheer and rugged.

9. Northern Pacific Railway - Villard "Gold Spike" Excursion (1883)
Washington State Historical Society

There were a great many speeches, but they were all in proof and the orators had to refer at intervals to their slips: this, while it helped the inferior men through, seemed to cripple and trammel Evarts completely and he made a dull speech, though spoken with great facility. Sir Jas Hannen[84] made a most pleasing and polished little speech, though somewhat wanting in fire and go. One self-made man named Billings made a most effective speech, and the rest had much better have been 'silence'[85]. However, we did have all the Governors of the States through which the line passes: a set of dull, conceited asses, each coming forward

---

[83] Hon. Lionel Sackville-West, 2nd Baron Sackville GCMG (1827-1908), a British diplomat. At the time he was Envoy Extraordinary and Minister Plenipotentiary to the United States. Although he never married, Lord Sackville had several children by a Spanish dancer, Josefa de la Oliva (known as Pepita). He is travelling here with his daughter, Victoria Josefa Dolores Catalina Sackville-West (1862–1936), the future mother of the writer, poet and gardener Victoria ('Vita') Mary Sackville-West (1892-1962).
[84] Sir James Hannen (1821-1894). A distinguished barrister whose dicta on marriage and wills are still quoted. He was a divorce lawyer, and was known as "the great unmarrier".
[85] Reference to a Hamlet quotation: "The rest is silence."

and blowing his own trumpet like the characters in La Belle Helene[86]. Someone said to me we ought to have the Governors of North Carolina and South Carolina too, and as I evidently did not understand he explained that it is a way in the States of asking a man to drink to say, "Have you heard what the Governor of North Carolina said to the Governor of South Carolina?" The navvies laid about ¼ of a mile of track at an enormous pace, each party racing against the other to reach the point where the last spike was to be driven, and then two trains covered with flags and decorations came puffing and met the men who were on the engines, shaking hands with one another amid tremendous shouting and cheering. The finest bit of scenery we have seen was the Great Divide[87] which separates the Atlantic waters from the waters of the Pacific. It would have been a curious parallel to Huskisson's[88] death at the opening of the Liverpool & Manchester if they had killed West at this.

9 September 1883 - Sunday

We travelled most of the day along the Pacific slope of the Rockies which is much better wooded than the other side. Part of the way the forest was on fire which had a fine effect. About 4 we reached Lake Pend d'Oreille[89] which is, I believe, very grand; unfortunately, it was so drizzly and misty that one could get no fair idea of the scenery. There was a steamer ready to take us an excursion, but under the circumstances I preferred borrowing Pell's gun and going off with a native to try and shoot wild geese. I had, however, no luck. Wells told me he had Thorold Rogers[90] to stay with him, but had not liked him at all; he had made Mrs. W. as 'mad as thunder' by coming down to dinner in a flannel shirt, and by bringing with him an uninvited Englishman who was as deaf as a post. Charles Russell MP[91] joined us en route: I knew him before in Liverpool; he is rather a bully, but not at all unpleasant; he is very fond of cards. He is accompanied by a quiet civil Irish member named Martin[92]. I like Gurdon better than I did;

---

[86] Jacques Offenbach's operetta "La belle Hélène" first performed in 1864.
[87] The Great Divide (properly known as the Continental Divide of the Americas) is the continental divide that separates river systems that drain into the Pacific Ocean from those that drain into the Atlantic Ocean, Gulf of Mexico, and Caribbean Sea.
[88] At the opening of the Liverpool & Manchester railway on 15th September 1830, attended by the Prime Minister, the Duke of Wellington, and a large number of important people, the Liverpool MP William Huskisson was knocked down by George Stephenson's Rocket and died later that day.
[89] Lake Pend Oreille (pronounced pond-o-ray), Idaho.
[90] James Edwin Thorold Rogers (1823-1890). MP for Southwark from 1880 to 1885; political economist and historian; a free trader. An Academic at Oxford until he legally withdrew from his clerical vows in 1870.
[91] Charles Arthur Russell, Baron Russell of Killowen (1832-1900). Catholic, several times Liberal member for Dundalk from 1880. Attorney General, 1892. Lord Chief Justice, 1894 – the first Catholic to hold the office for centuries. In 1883 he was crossing the continent to visit Mother Mary Baptist Russell of San Francisco, who with two others of his sisters had entered the order of Mercy. The Diary of the visit to the US was published in 1910 by the US Catholic Historical Society.
[92] Patrick Martin (1830-1895), elected Member of Parliament for County Kilkenny in 1874 and held the seat until the constituency was divided for the 1885 General Election.

he is a thorough gentleman, though very grumbly and discontented. Edwards MP is a greedy, selfish fellow, though not bad-hearted; he started lunch before anyone the other day, and eat all a dish of tomatoes; for this, the younger Bryce remonstrated with him, and a very fine row followed. Last night he forced himself into our rubber by asking to cut in though the rubber was made up, and to prevent any unpleasantness I got up and said I was tired and gave up my place without cutting out. This morning, to my great surprise, as Holford and I were still in our berths, I above him, about 9 o'clock, old Edwards arrived and apologised most humbly, saying he had no business to have done it and it was very good of me to let him and so on for a long while.

10. Northern Pacific Railway (present day)
Courtesy of Phil Phillips

10 September 1883 - Monday

We passed Spokane Falls last night, which the first train were in time to see. In the morning we reached a place called Ainsworth[93] where we were to cross the Snake River (which flows into the Columbia River) by a ferry as the bridge is not completed. Here an accident happened to the car in which we were – West and his daughter[94], Carrington, Bowen, Hannen and others. Fortunately not a serious one, but which narrowly missed being a frightful one. The locomotive and two cars were being backed down the incline onto the ferry boat when the couplings broke, and the car dashed

---

[93] The completion of the bridge a mile upstream from Ainsworth in 1884 meant that shortly afterwards Ainsworth became a ghost town.
[94] Victoria Josefa Dolores Catalina Sackville-West (1862–1936), the future mother of the writer, poet and gardener Victoria ('Vita') Mary Sackville-West (1892-1962).

full speed without any brake into the boat and was brought up by the engine of the boat. If it had carried away a car – which it very nearly did – it would have gone slap into the river; as it was, Carrington had a severe scalp wound, and Bowen and Hannen were a good deal bruised and shaken. The rest got off all right. Several times the couplings have broken on this trip, and they must be defective in quality or design. We were delayed a long time by this crossing of the ferry, and I filled up the time by bathing and going with Benson and Gurdon after jack rabbit in the prairie: we got 3. They are very like our blue hare. The land over here is sandy desert, covered with sage scrub, and the journey through it has been most disagreeable as the heat and dust have been awful. Food and everything hot and gritty, the milk bad, and provisions beginning to run out. About nightfall, however, it got cool, and, there being a fine moon, we saw some of the splendid Columbia River scenery with high sheer basalt cliffs towering right over the train on one side and the river rolling underneath on the other: the best thing we have seen yet.

11 September 1883 - Tuesday

We reached our journey's end last night but slept on board, and crossed over on the ferry this morning, and excellent breakfast was prepared on the boat; and afterwards we were driven to our respective places. The hotels are small and bad, so most are billeted on private citizens, but Buxton, Pell, Bryce and I are in Holton House, the chief hotel; it is not much of a place – dirty and bad attendance. The town, however, is a nice one; we went over to the Grand Stand and witnessed a procession very similar to the one at St. Paul. The town is very much decorated and hung with flags; down the principal street were hung large banners, each with the name of a guest on it. I was much amused to see a large red and white one with my name just opposite the dock where we landed. In the afternoon there was a reception and speeches which I shirked, but I believe Russell made a very good speech. Early this morning Bryce, Benson and Macleod started off with some German geologists to explore and attempt the ascent of Mt Tacoma[95] – which has, I believe, never been ascended. Bryce asked me to join them, but as there was some doubt if we should get back in time for the 'Frisco boat, and as it would have entailed missing Victoria in British Columbia which I should like to see, I refused. At night, a concert which I missed and went instead to the Chinese theatre – very curious. I made the manager's acquaintance and he explained the plot. Very handsome dresses; a frightful din with the orchestra, who sit on the stage in a semicircle behind the players. No women were active, but the men playing women's parts looked exactly like women.

---

[95] Tacoma is one of the native American names for the mountain. It is now (and probably was then) known as Mount Rainier, named by Captain George Vancouver (who reached Puget Sound in early May 1792 and became the first European to see the mountain) in honor of his friend, Rear Admiral Peter Rainier.

12 September 1883 - Wednesday

Most of the party went an excursion by rail to see the Oregon wheat lands, but I preferred joining the American party that were going in the river boat up the Columbia river; and I am very glad I did, for it is far the finest scenery I have yet seen, much grander than the Hudson, and the Yankees say better than the Hudson at its best above West Point, where I didn't go. It was a little too early for the fall colouring to be in perfection, and there was not quite enough water in the Multnomah Falls, but the general effect was superb; and the enormous firs standing up against the sky line very curious. The Yankees were very pleasant; Sturgis[96] who is vice president of the NY Stock Exchange, Morgan[97], Maxwell[98], Wells, Stackpoole and others.

S.S. Queen of the Pacific

13 September 1883 - Thursday

Last night we all went again to the Chinese theatre where there was a special performance: tumbling and conjuring. This morning I was pleased to find that the programme of the trip to Victoria had been shortened so as to get back to Portland by Saturday afternoon; this enabled me to go, and I started at 9 in company with most of the Germans and English on board the river boat. We reached Kalama about 1, where we took train through some grand forest, in the distance, Mount Adam, Mount St. Helens, then through Chehalis where there was a show of agricultural produce, and arrived at Tacoma on Puget Sound, which is a very pretty place, and there is a splendid view of a snow mountain, Mount Tacoma standing quite alone. Evidently from its shape it is an old volcano, with the light of the setting sun on it and the dark trees and sea in the foreground it is about as good as they make it anywhere; height 14,500ft. We walked through the town in a sort of procession and embarked on the ocean steamer 'Queen of the Pacific'; an uncommonly good boat, but we are pretty full. I am in a cabin on deck with Carrington.

14 September 1883 - Friday

Reached Esquimault[99] 4am; and after early breakfast drove round Victoria, a pretty place; much like the Black Mount scenery. The British Squadron

---

[96] Frank K. Sturgis was president of the Stock exchange from 1894 to 1898. A member of the banking firm Strong, Sturgis and Co., he retired from the stock exchange in 1919.
[97] John Pierpont Morgan (1837-1913). President of Drexel, Morgan & Co., and major investor in the Northern Pacific Railway.
[98] James Riddle Maxwell (1836-1912), a civil engineer from Pennsylvania, who surveyed the Northern Pacific Railway. Many of his diaries and papers are held in the University of Delaware Library.
[99] Esquimalt, British Columbia. On 27 September 1883 the Canadian government finally signed a contract to build a railway from Esquimalt to Nanaimo with Robert Dunsmuir, the

'Swiftsure', 'Heroine' and 'Sappho' were in harbour, and to my surprise and pleasure I heard that Admiral Lyons[100] was there in command: I immediately went off in a gig to see him, and found him on deck. I said, "I suppose you don't know me, Admiral". He said, "I do, perfectly: you've come to collect the 5 dollars I owe you, and which I ought to have paid you long ago!" I found that Guzman – who had taught us both Spanish on the Don, and the share of who's fee I had given Lyons – had refused to take my money, so he really did owe me some. He was very friendly, and took me all over 'Swiftsure'[101]. I also renewed my acquaintance with his secretary Liddell and Flag Lieutenant Thomas, who were pleasant and gave me a letter to a shipmate of theirs stationed in Auckland. We went on board again at noon and to Seattle for an hour, which had made great preparations to receive us; crowds of people on the docks who escorted us to a pavilion where there were a lot of sheep being roasted whole; and speeches, some very good, including an address from a young lady who was in the Seattle University. It was rather comic, and reminded me of Mrs Bancroft[102] in 'School', but she was good-looking and did it very well. Afterwards we walked about and saw some very fine furs, especially sea otter; and a lot of salmon, which are caught in enormous numbers here and tinned. The man presented me with a 28lb fish which he sent on board and for which he told me he had payed 4 cents! They are not such good eating as the English fish. The sunset on the harbour with the mountains rising up on the other side was very fine. There were some fireworks and illuminations, and we sailed about 10 for Tacoma.

15 September 1883 - Saturday

We reached Tacoma last night and were called at 6 with a 7 o'clock breakfast, after which all the party went on board the train to go back to Portland except myself and Burns, Russell, and Martin. I found that this ship was going straight down to 'Frisco so I preferred sticking to it instead of returning to Portland. I was really very sorry to leave the very pleasant party I have been with for exactly a month and feel rather dull without them, more especially Grey and Holford whom I got to like very much. Old Sir James Hannen is a nice kindly old fellow, and his son seems a good sort. After seeing them off I went back to my cabin and consoled myself by taking a nap which lasted until 3 pm and included a stoppage of an hour at Port Townsend which I knew nothing of. We have been sailing

---

coal baron, Leland Stanford and Huntington. Esquimalt was the base of the British Navy in the North Pacific and the Royal Navy dockyards.
[100] Sir Algernon McLennan Lyons (1833-1908). In 1881, Lyons was appointed Commander-in-Chief in the Pacific.
[101] 'Swiftsure': Flagship of the Pacific station
[102] Marie Effie Wilton (1840-1921) was an English actress and theatre manager. In 1867 she married Sir Squire Bancroft (1841-1926), and the couple were important in the development of Victorian theatre, making popular a genre of theatre known as 'Drawing room comedy'.

NW through Puget Sound all day, and passed Cape Flattery into the Pacific about 7. pm

16 September 1883 - Sunday

I have now had 3 Sundays on ship, and one in the Cars, and one at Minnetonka since I started. There is a pleasant American lady on board from Kentucky whose husband has come out to look at the West with a view to settling there. She has a precocious little boy who asked Russell if we had had the bounce[103] from Villard's party. Read the 'House of the 7 Gables'[104] and liked it better than the 'Scarlet Letter', though it is not so important a story. I can't quite see that Hawthorne is as big a man as the Yankees make out, 'and trust we have within our realm', etc. We keep the coast in sight all the way, and the voyage is a very pleasant and beautiful one: whales sporting away and small sharks to be seen. This ship was as nearly lost as possible last week on the bar of the Columbia[105]. No ship has ever got off before, but by jettison of nearly all the cargo, and landing passengers in boats, they managed it; weather kept quite calm, so only one life lost: a man who jumped overboard in a panic.

17 September 1883 - Monday

A splendid display of Northern lights last night[106] – the skipper[107] said he had only once seen anything like it: rose-coloured shooting lights going from the horizon to zenith. We passed through the Golden Gate into San Francisco harbour about ¼ to 7 this evening. It was indeed a fine sight: the moon rising quite crimson in front of us and the sun setting gloriously behind, with the lights twinkling in the grand harbour, made a splendid spectacle. A man told me that when he first came there 35 years ago the harbour was covered with wild fowl and hardly any town at all. I went straight to the Palace Hotel[108], the biggest in the world, I believe: the

---

[103] The 'sack'.
[104] The House of the Seven Gables, also known as the Turner-Ingersoll Mansion, was built in 1668, and is the oldest surviving 17th century wooden mansion in New England. It inspired author Nathaniel Hawthorne to write his legendary novel of the same name.
[105] The 'Queen of the Pacific' had been built in 1882. On 5 September 1883 - with many of the Villard party on board - it ran aground on the Clatsop Spit whilst trying to cross the Columbia Bar. Five tugs were involved in the difficult rescue of the ship. Newspaper reports give the captain's name as Captain Ezekiel Alexander. He had managed to ensure the transfer of all his passengers in three lifeboats to one of the rescue tugs. At the time of the accident the ship was under the charge of A. D. Wass, "a pilot of unquestioned ability".
[106] Gibbs may have been seeing an after-eruption of Krakatoa (a volcanic island in the Sunda Strait between Java and Sumatra in Indonesia). The main eruption was from 20/07/1883 to 27/08/1883, with smaller eruptions continuing to mid-October 1883 and possibly to February 1884. It caused massive tsunamis, killed over 35,000 people, destroyed two-thirds of the island, and was reported to be audible up to 3000 miles away.
[107] Presumably Captain Ezekiel Alexander, the captain at the time of the running aground on 5th September 1883.
[108] The Palace Hotel was built in 1875 and was at the time reputedly the largest and most luxurious modern hotel in the world. Its guests were carried in "rising rooms" (hydraulic lifts, an engineering marvel for the time), and had in their rooms an electric bell which

entrance like the Grand at Paris, a great hall with a band playing, and seven stories of white galleries rising up all round – really a remarkable sight. I have a very good room at the top of the house.

San Francisco

It was September 17th when, the Rocky Mountain adventure safely completed - although not without some hair-raising moments - Vicary arrived in San Francisco by sea. It was lucky for Villard that no-one had been too seriously injured in any of the accidents on the surprisingly dangerous train journey. The rate at which the track had been laid, said to have been a mile and a half of rail a day, had been risky to achieve and maintain safely. The route expected locomotives to take bends in tunnels at unprecedented speeds that were difficult for the driver to negotiate whilst maintaining the carriages firmly on the track. Villard, anxious to boost interest and investment, had planned the celebration hastily, and the guests had come desperately close to disaster several times.

The scenery in the Rockies had sometimes disappointed Vicary, who compared the journey with his first views of the Alps. He made observations with the eye of a landscape gardener, always on the look out for all that was truly dramatic in nature. The shape, height and colour of trees became a major interest of his in later life when he searched for the right specimen to display at Aldenham. Too many of the North American mountain slopes had been disappointingly barren, either north-facing or too sheer for tree cover.

San Francisco must have provided the shock of the new to the traveller's eye. In a remarkably short time, the city had grown into an efficient, modern, cosmopolitan business centre where the young man was expected to renew old contacts and see if there were any prospects for Antony Gibbs and Sons in its flourishing market. Gibbs and his companions were taken to 'inspect' and comment on the local opium dens as if they were part of a theme park. The gold mines of the United States had formed a nucleus for the immigrant Chinese labourers, as it had in other countries. Wherever they settled in some new 'Chinatown', these workers were eventually joined by their extended families and permeating culture. In hidden dens, searching for oblivion, they returned to their narcotic addictions. After this introduction to the "general squalor" of the surroundings, fastidious Vicary and his companion, Burns, spent the rest of the night in a "very good" Turkish Bath as a "precautionary measure".

Aboard the 'City of New York' bound for Australia, his first impression of his fellow passengers was not promising, apart from a young barrister,

---

allowed them to "ring" for service without leaving the comfort of the air-conditioning (another engineering marvel). It was destroyed in the 1906 earthquake and rebuilt in 1909.

Mackinnon of New College, Oxford, but as he relaxed into the ship-board routine, Vicary Gibbs began to make new friends. When his old familiar enemy, gout, returned to disable him, these kind friends proved invaluable.

The death of a passenger at sea is an event anticipated today by cruise-ship Captains just as much as it was in the old days of sail and the early steam ships, but the sudden death and burial at sea of the ship's doctor shocked the passengers on board the 'City of New York'. After saying goodbye to a man they had hoped was there to keep them fit, they slowly adapted to their life of cards, gossip and food, with amateur theatricals to enliven them and shipboard romances to add spice to the routine.

The magnificent displays of colour in the night sky – mistaken at first by Gibbs as the Northern Lights – must have continued to amaze them all. He mentions them again later, on 8th January and 27th April 1884, commenting that the English newspapers had reported them being visible nearly every night since his departure. It was a glorious, spreading, rosy light that lasted about two hours. He thought it must be some kind of aurora but had no idea what had caused it, any more than "the scientific people have any rational explanation to offer". In fact, the stunning displays were actually caused by an event that had taken place nine days after Vicary had left Liverpool on the 'Gallia': Krakatoa, the volcano in the Sunda Strait between Java and Sumatra, had erupted with an enormous explosion that sent debris 50 miles into the sky. Two thirds of the original volcanic island had eventually disappeared, with the surrounding sea, into an empty magma chamber beneath and many thousands of people on the adjacent islands had been killed, not only by falling ash and lava but also by a devastating tsunami. The wall of water caused by this vast displacement raced to Sumatra and her neighbours, destroying towns and villages over a large area. Bodies and bones were washed up on the shore of the Seychelles and the beaches of East Africa for many months afterwards. At the time of the explosion, the Norwegian artist Edvard Munch, terrified by the sudden change of the night sky to blood red, had conceived his painting 'The Scream' and its threatening sky-scape, as a response to his own shock. Perhaps in England as well as Australia the colours were predominantly beautiful, the reported blue moon seen against the rose and mauve of the sinking sun, but we know - as Vicary Gibbs did not - that the message was one of disaster.

Otherwise, the remainder of the passage to Australia was uneventful. Even the arrival in Sydney was an anti-climax: that beautiful harbour, opening before you as you pass the Heads, was unseen through the heavy rain and thick fog.

18 September 1883 - Tuesday

Walked about the town with Burns through the principal streets last night; fine handsome streets with good side walks – in fact, I like the look of the place. After breakfast I called on Thomas Bell[109]: a civil, rather senile gentleman, and found letters from mother, Mrs George Gibbs, Mr Clarke[110] and Evelyn C.[111] I then called on Falkner Bell[112], who hadn't much to say. The head partner had come over in the 'Gallia' with me, but we had not spoken to one another. Next on Wilson Meyer who were very civil Germans, and gave a pretty good account of the 'G. Britain'. After lunch I went to see White of the Fire Brigade, to whom Bowers of New York had given me an introduction. He is going to show me his men turn out tomorrow, and will evidently take me in hand and show me the various things that are to be seen here. After dinner, I sat and smoked with Mackinnon[113], a young fellow just called to the English bar

11. Donald Mackinnon on his way back from Oxford via U.S.A. (c1883-5)
State Library of Victoria

---

[109] Thomas Bell (-1892), a director of the Bank of California with mining interests. He was associated with Mary Ellen "Mammy" Pleasant, a remarkably successful woman financier of African descent. He died in 1892 leaving the family's debts in dispute and his widow implying that their first son Frederick was actually the product of her late husband's liaison with "Mammy" Pleasant.

[110] Gibbs corresponds several times with Mr. A. Clarke and his wife, and their daughter Evelyn; presumably friends from home in England.

[111] Evelyn Clarke.

[112] Falkner Bell & Co. were commission agents.

[113] Donald Mackinnon (1859–1932) was the eldest son of Daniel Mackinnon (whom Gibbs meets on 28 December 1883), and Gibbs and Donald become very good friends. He studied at Trinity College, University of Melbourne, and New College, Oxford. Whilst practising as a lawyer from 1883 onwards, he also wrote for the Melbourne Argus (Gibbs meets Sir Lauchlan Charles Mackinnon, editor of the Argus, on 7 November 1883). When his father Daniel died in 1889, Donald inherited Marida Yallock, which his brother William managed for most of his life. In 1891, Donald married Hilda Eleanor Marie Bunny, the daughter of Brice Bunny and brother of Rupert Bunny (who later painted a portrait of Mackinnon that is still at Marida Yallock). Gibbs happens to meet one of the Misses Bunny (possibly Hilda) on 26 June 1884, on a train from Melbourne to Sydney (and several times thereafter), and also meets her mother, Maria, on 4 September 1884. He mentions sharing a theatre box on 16 September 1884 with - amongst others - Mackinnon and Miss Bunny, so if the Miss Bunny mentioned is actually Hilda this could be where they met. On his

who was at New College[114]; he seems pleasant, and is going on the same steamer as myself to settle in Melbourne and practice there.

19 September 1883 - Wednesday

12. Cliff House, San Francisco (c1902)
U.S. Library of Congress, LC-USZ62-77079

13. Engine 15 Firehouse and fire engine, San Francisco (1894)
U.S. Library of Congress, HABS CAL,38-SANFRA,72--3

Got up at 6 and drove with Russell, Martin and young Evarts to the Cliff House through the Park – which, considering it was all sand hills a few years ago, and that it is 4 months since they have had a drop of rain, is wonderfully green and pretty. The Cliff House commands a good view of the Seal rock, which is a curious and interesting sight: a great number of sea lions basking and swimming and crawling about like great caterpillars. At 12, I went and saw the fire patrol turn out – not so smart as New York, and then lunched with Capt. Meyer[115] at the Union Club; a very decent little club. Wrote letters and read 'A Daughter of the Philistines' an American story, and not good at that. Dined with Marshall and a German Jewish American Baron, and was to have gone to the Chinese quarter but the beast of a detective never showed up, so went to bed.

20 September 1883 - Thursday

Drove all over the town with Capt White in his buggy. The endless cable cars look very pretty gliding up the tremendously stiff hills without any effort. Called on Landers of the Guardian, who had called on me. I shall have taken almost no expeditions and seen very little while in 'Frisco, having no one with me to make me. I am indulging in a reaction from the bustle and sight-seeing of the journey. Russell and Martin have gone to the Semite valley[116] – I shan't see them again. I like the latter: a cheerful, good-humoured, disloyal, unpractical Irishman. Wrote to Beatrice, Clarke

---

death in 1932, Donald was survived by his wife and three sons (Donald, Ewen Daniel, and Kenneth Wulsten) and two daughters.
[114] New College, Oxford.
[115] Probably of the firm Wilson Meyer.
[116] Yosemite Valley, California, usually known at the time as Yo Semite.

and Tyndall, and tried to read Lytton's 'Lucretia', but it seemed to me a sort of London journal story of aristocrats and murders and I couldn't do with it. Dined with Capt. Meyer, and played Piquet with him.

21 September 1883 - Friday

Lunched with Landers of the Guardian at the Bohemian Club. The house was full of eleven sketches and caricatures done by the members. In the evening, Marshall, Burns and I went to the Chinese quarter; the detective who accompanied us was a regular blageur and incurable liar. According to him, a man had just been shot in Chinatown 10 minutes before we arrived. *Haud credo.*[117] However, he took us into some extraordinary burrows and opium dens. It is quite incredible how close the Chinese pack one above the other on little shelves, most of them with a little tray before them with opium, a lamp and tea. In spite of the general squalor of the surroundings, the Chinese looked all very clean in their persons and linen, and I believe there are few if any epidemics break out among them. I fancy these police officers do a good deal of blackmailing among the wretched Chinese. Most of the Chinese were civil, but some rather surly; and it struck me as rather strong our going into their rooms after they had turned in. We also went behind the scenes of the theatre and saw the actors making up and cramming up their parts off a sheet hanging to a pillar, and on to the stage while the performance was going on, but neither spectators nor actors took any notice. We went to a swell Chinese restaurant, where we had some very nice green tea and sweet meats which was very refreshing after the heat, noises and stinks. Then we went to the Bella Union Theatre, which is a sort of music hall which would come very prominently under the attention of the Lord Chamberlain if it was in London. We took a box in the stalls; there was a gentleman with his coat, waistcoat and boots off stretched out sound asleep at 1 am. Burns and I adjourned to the Turkish Bath as a precautionary measure: it is a very good bath, and open all night. We slept the remainder of the night there.

S.S. City of New York

22 September 1883 - Saturday

After breakfast Carrington and Bowen arrived, and I went walking about the town with them. Wrote a line home, and came on board 'The City of New York'[118]; it is very dirty and grubby, and not much of a boat, I think. I have a large stateroom on the hurricane deck, but no bell or means of getting at the stewards, who are a long way off. They don't attempt to light the deck at night, which is beastly; altogether, for an ocean boat,

---

[117] Latin: I don't believe it.
[118] There were three boats called "The City of New York" operating out of San Francisco in 1883. This is probably the Pacific Mail Steamship Company ship, not the Inman line which was Liverpool registered.

things seem to me pretty badly managed. There is a Bishop of Ballarat[119] on board, and his wife. I am glad Mackinnon has come as the rest look anything but a lively lot. However, it's too early to say much yet.

23 September 1883 - Sunday

The Bishop and his missis performed service, and threw in some Moody & Sankey[120] hymns. The Bishop mounted his gaiters and all complete; though on weekdays he sinks the parson and sports a blue tie. There is a man named Thomas, a lawyer in Canterbury, who doesn't seem a bad sort; I asked him if he knew Cokayne[121]: at first he didn't seem to, but when I said I believed he was generally known as 'dirty Adams' he said he had known him 15 years, and gave much the same account of him as Maude did whom I knew in Barnet's chambers. He said he was honourable, straightforward and well read, spent a lot of his time in the Public Library, hated society, and never went into anyone's house, too apathetic ever to make any money or to take trouble to get more than just enough to live on. About 40 of our passengers are only going to Honolulu.

24 September 1883 - Monday

Doctor Ed Trask, surgeon of this ship, died at 11.30am quite suddenly of Apoplexy[122]; the people about me at meals are now pretending they noticed something odd in his manner last night, but I sat at the same table and there was nothing whatever. I read the English papers of the 1st, which old Bell gave me, and an amusing American book called "Peck's Bad Boy"[123].

25 September 1883 - Tuesday

Nothing of any interest. The passengers are the most dull specimens of the middle class one can possibly conceive. There is nothing the least like gentry except the little Bishop and his fat wife, to whom I have not spoken;

---

[119] Samuel Thornton DD (1835-1917). First bishop of Ballarat from 1875 to 1900, when he resigned and returned to England. He was said to be probably the best scholar on the Australian Episcopal bench, and a brilliant extempore preacher and speaker. His wife was Emily, daughter of H. T. Thornton of Devon.

[120] Dwight Lyman Moody (1837-1899) and Ira David Sankey (1840-1908) were revivalist evangelicals and missionaries whose "Sacred Songs and Solos" were published in 1876 after their visit to England.

[121] Probably George Edward Adams (1825-1911), who married Mary Dorothea Gibbs (daughter of George Henry Gibbs and Caroline Crawley) in 1856. He was Vicary Gibbs' uncle on both his mother's and his father's side. George Edward Adams changed his name by Royal License to George Edward Cokayne (his mother's maiden name) in 1873. He was the author of 'The Complete Peerage', the first edition of which was published between 1887 and 1898. Originally a lawyer and M.A., Vicary Gibbs first collaborated with him on Burke's Peerage and then took over its editing from him.

[122] Apoplexy: what is now known as a stroke.

[123] Juvenile fiction by George Wilbur Peck, who wrote several other 'bad boy' books in the late 19th century.

Mackinnon, with whom I play euchre[124]; and Mr & Mrs Douglas who are not bad, but she is stupid with her tongue too big for her mouth, though certainly pretty.

26 September 1883 - Wednesday

I got up at 6 and saw the poor old Doctor's body committed to the deep. The Service is very impressive, though the Bishop did it in a uniformly unctuous voice and no intelligent expression. There are two pleasant young American gentlemen on board who have had an university education at Yale and Harvard: one named Forbes, who is going to New Zealand on some shipping business; and the other Austin, who is going to the Sandwich Islands[125] to practise as a lawyer. They with Thomas and Clough[126], a young fellow in a wool buying business in Melbourne, are quite the pick of the passengers as far as I can judge, and they form our whist partie, and not a bad one – much better play than on the 'Gallia'. Tried to read a French novel called 'Paienne'[127], by Madam Adam: it has been a good deal talked about and supposed to be very pretty – love letters and worship of nature and so on: I couldn't do with it.

27 September 1883 - Thursday

The attendance is very bad and the food and drink dreadful; neither tea nor coffee fit to touch, and the water with a taste in it. As I am on the total abstinence lay it is pretty bad; fortunately there are plenty of limes. They have a most extraordinary rule that no one can buy less than a bottle of wine or spirits. I never heard of such a thing on a steamer before. I have been reading Alban's[128] diary on his trip, and he seems to have had a much better steamer and more lively society on this voyage than I have any prospect of. I was amused to see that I made the same mistake as he did of going all the way up to Thomas Bell's private residence in 'Frisco instead of his office. Read the sad history of the Revd. Amos Barton[129], which I had never done somehow: very pretty and touching – might have been by Mrs Gaskell instead of George Eliot.

28 September 1883 - Friday

There has been a great deal of swell in the last 3 days; always a head wind so that we couldn't get a sail set to steady her, and as there is a lot of

---

[124] Euchre is a plain-trick game for four players in fixed partnerships, partners sitting opposite. Just 5 cards are dealt to each player and the object is to win at least three of the five tricks – with an extra bonus for winning all five.
[125] The Sandwich Islands, now known as the Hawaiian Islands.
[126] From the passenger list of the 'City of New York', we know this was E. A. Clough. Clough wool warehouses had advertised in Melbourne from at least 1868.
[127] Madame Adam [Juliette Lamber Adam] (1836-1936): 'Païenne' (1883)
[128] Alban George Henry Gibbs, Vicary's eldest brother and heir to Lord Aldenham.
[129] This was George Eliot's first published work (1857), intended as the first of a series on clerical life.

machinery on deck she rolls like anything. The fiddles[130] are no use, and the plates and glasses fly around in fine style. Read 'Yolande'[131] by Black: pretty pretty, but rather maudlin and awfully inferior to the early ones; the notion of dipsomania being cured by a girl in that way is too thin altogether. This evening, while we were playing whist, the lamp came out and fell on the table: I was deluged with stinking kerosene, but luckily not burnt as it extinguished itself in falling. Have made no new acquaintance worth mentioning: all German Jews or people like English tradesmen with their families.

29 September 1883 - Saturday

Read 'Dr Claudius' by Marion Crawford – I should think, a man. I can't see why people should have cracked the book up – I didn't care for it a bit.

30 September 1883 - Sunday

We sighted Oahu about 5am, and got into Honolulu about 3pm. It is not much of a harbour: a small bay with coral reef, the place generally very much like part of Jamaica. Thomas, Forbes, Mackinnon and I chartered a carriage and drove off to a place called Pali[132]. A rough road through pretty scenery up to the top of the hills, where we got a splendid view of the sea on both sides. We gathered and eat a lot of guavas on the way: the best I have ever tasted – far superior to the W. Indian, and very juicy and good flavour. When we came back, we dined at the Hawaiian Hotel when we got a decent meal and sat smoking on the verandah till 12. When we came on board, the coaling was still going on and everything noisy, dirty, and the air swarming with mosquitoes. I remained up in my chair till 3am when we got under weigh again. The missionaries have got very severe Sabbatarian legislation in force in the Sandwich Islands, and at the hotel there was an extempore bar in a back bedroom. The Bishop was asked by the Captain[133], at the instance of some of the ladies, to forego his sermon as they wanted to look at the land, but he begged to be excused from curtailing the service of God and administered the regular 20 min. of wishy-washy platitudes to an unwilling audience. I did not call on A. Hayley, though I was shown his house in the town and hear he is much in debt; gives very good dinners, gets 'full', and uses his wife brutally. He drove her out of the house one night soon after her child was born, and she had to take refuge in an artists' named Strong. He also, I heard, insulted an American naval officer at the Club and got thrashed. I should think he will very soon have to clear out of the place.

---

[130] Fiddles were hinged table edges, designed to prevent crockery from sliding onto the floor in rough weather.
[131] William Black: 'Yolande - The story of a daughter' (1883).
[132] Nu'uanu Pali (Pali means "windward cliff" in Hawaiian) is 1,000 feet above sea level and still a favourite lookout point.
[133] William B. Cobb (from the passenger list).

1 October 1883 - Monday

We took on board a man named Raymond[134], who is correspondent for the Telegraph; he had been to see the fire lake in Hawaii. He says it is most wonderful; a stiff and long ride to get to it, but a marvellous crater: 7 or 8 acres, flames bursting up to a great height all over it, and swimming together and breaking out in new places every moment. Raymond said compared to this, Vesuvius or Etna were only places to boil a pot at. I wish I had gone in the 'Mariposa' and seen it.

2 October 1883 - Tuesday

The weather is now quite calm, and we have caught the 'Trades' which are taking us along pretty well – we did 300 miles today. We are beginning to see plenty of flying fish now.

3 October 1883 - Wednesday

Read 'Paris en Amerique'[135]: rather well done and amusing, but the praise of American institutions as compared with the old world is too much exaggerated.

4 October 1883 - Thursday

'A blank, My Lord'[136]; there is some talk of acting a play, but I doubt if it will come to anything as the young lady who wants to act is looked on rather askance by the other women, as she 'paints'[137] and flirts.

5 October 1883 - Friday

After a good deal of jaw we have decided to play 'The Day After the Wedding'[138] with this cast: Thomas – Lord Rivers; V.G.[139] – Colonel Freelove; Miss Furse, who is a very handsome, made-up 3rd rate little girl – Lady Elizabeth; Miss Macinell, a fat stupid Canadian girl – the

---

[134] It transpired later that Raymond was a swindler (see 22 December 1883). There certainly doesn't seem to be any record of him working for The Telegraph (or any other newspaper). The Telegraph had the well-known Bennet Burleigh from 1882, and during the Egyptian Campaign of 1882-3 (which Raymond claims to have been reporting - see 18 October 1883) their correspondent was Sir Godfrey Yeatman Lagden.
[135] Dr. René Lefebyre (pseudonym of Edouard Laboulaye (1811-1883)): 'Paris en Amerique' published 1863 in Paris.
[136] "A blank, my Lord": A quote from Shakespeare's Twelfth Night (said by Viola, Act 2 Scene 4).
[137] Wears make-up
[138] A very old one act interlude or farce subtitled "A Wife's First Lesson", by Marie Therese Kemble. First published in 1808.
[139] Our diary author, Vicary Gibbs, second son of the Lord Aldenham of that time. His eminent ancestor and namesake Vicary Gibbs (1751-1820), was an English Judge born in Exeter who became Solicitor General, Attorney General, and Lord Chief Justice of the Court of Common Pleas for his defence of John Horne Tooke in 1794. He was nicknamed 'Vinegar Gibbs' for his sarcastic humour, a trait we may observe in his descendant.

housekeeper; and Mackinnon for the old butler. We have taken on a new little Doctor at Honolulu.

6 October 1883 - Saturday

We crossed the line[140] last night; it is not, however, so frightfully hot as there is a nice breeze, and having got a suit of white ducks[141] and a silk shirt I am very comfortable. A deck cabin is now a great advantage – we shall be directly under the sun 2 days hence. We had a rough rehearsal which went pretty badly, the ladies having no idea of acting. The piece only takes about 25 minutes, so we shall play another also if it can be got up – probably the inevitable 'Done on Both Sides'[142] if there are enough people to get it up, but the women will prove the difficulty. I shan't take a part if I can help it as I feel rather gouty.

7 October 1883 - Sunday

They had service on deck, Mrs Douglas playing the piano inside. The singing, in consequence, went ridiculously to pieces.

8 October 1883 - Monday

Rehearsing in the Captain's cabin, and learning 'Brownjohn' in 'Done on Both Sides'. Have arranged a cast, Raymond as Whiffles; Forbes as Phibb; with Mackinnon as Mrs Whiffles; and a young fellow named Hornsby[143] – only son of the large agricultural implement maker at Grantham, who has just left Jesus at Cambridge – for Lydia: he has agreed to shave off a small blonde moustache, and ought to do very well.

9 October 1883 - Tuesday

Laid up today with a touch of gout; the heat is tremendous. Read a goodish novel by Norris called 'No New Thing'[144]. The new Doctor is an attentive, amiable, ignorant young fellow.

---

[140] The ship was crossing the equator, north to south.
[141] Ducks: European hot climate wear, especially but not exclusively on board ship. Known as 'ducks' because of the white colour.
[142] John Maddison Morton: 'Done On Both Sides', a farce first published in 1847.
[143] The firm of R Hornsby and Sons was established by Richard Hornsby (1790-1764), Agricultural Engineer. He had at least five children: Richard (1827-1864), Louisa, James (born 1836), Helen Mary Anne and William (born 1838). The eldset, Richard, took over the running of the firm from his father. After *his* death in 1864, the firm was owned by his son, also Richard. This Richard died at the early age of 50, quite suddenly, in 1877. His two brothers, James and William, jointly took over the running of the firm. We know from the passenger list of the 'City of New York' that the Hornsby Gibbs meets is J. W. Hornsby. James William Hornsby is listed as the director of Hornsby and Sons in 1899, and in the 1901 census he is aged 37, so would have been born about 1864 (which fits in with him having just left Cambridge in 1883). His wife in 1901 is Eleanor G. Hornsby.
[144] William Edward Norris (1847-1925): 'No New Thing', published in 1883. He wrote a string of novels much admired by the late Victorians.

10 October 1883 - Wednesday

In bed all day after a bad night, but getting better and will only be a slight affair, I hope. Young Hornsby seems a nice little chap. I was set against him at first as he had a fortnight's beard on and was with a horrid cad who I hear is manager of their works. Unless I get right directly, the theatricals will have to be given up as several of the troupe leave at Auckland.

11 October 1883 - Thursday

Gout much better, and I expect to be all right tomorrow. My friends on board are very good-natured, and play whist or piquet at a little table by the bed all day long: in fact Forbes, the American, is as good as a nurse, which is most fortunate as I have no bell to get at the steward.

12 October 1883 - Friday

Pretty free from gout this morning, and we were rehearsing all day. After dinner we had the acting, but unfortunately it was rough and we kept rolling about and clutching at one another, which rather spoilt the effect. 'The Day After the Wedding' went without the slightest hitch, and is a very easy piece to play, but it is too tame and too little incident. The ladies were terrible sticks. The other play made the audience laugh, though it narrowly escaped breaking down owing to not having been properly rehearsed, and to the book having been lost. Raymond – who played Whiffles – refreshed himself too freely beforehand, and though he was decidedly amusing he did not know his part at all, leaving Forbes and me to 'gag' for 10 minutes before he could be got hold of. The audience did not 'find it out'. We played in the social hall, and they made up a very fair stage, but it was a great drawback not having rehearsed in situ beforehand. The love scene with young Hornsby – who wore a dress of Mrs Douglas's, and a fringe and straw hat – was quite a hit, and produced roars of laughter. He really looked very pretty; it was a great stroke having him and Mackinnon to play the women's parts as they did them very well and it added much to the farcical character of the affair.

13 October 1883 - Saturday

A veritable '*dies non*', as we missed it out altogether and went as near as it is possible to having 2 Sundays in one week[145].

14 October 1883 - Sunday

I was a little gouty in the morning after last night's exertions, but am all right again now. Read a book of Black's called 'White Wings'[146], a yachting

---

[145] The ship was sailing across the International Date Line from East to West, so they skipped a day.
[146] William Black (1841-1898): 'White Wings'. A Glaswegian, he wrote nearly 30 novels and was immensely popular in the 19th century.

romance: very weak and poor; he has certainly quite written himself out. A man called Weaver, who came on board at Honolulu, has been paying great attentions to a sickly unattractive young girl named Chadwick: he is a tall, red-headed, goggle-eyes man, rather a cad; he never leaves her, and there has been some brisk speculation as to whether she will get him to propose. He is very well off, and has a large station in Queensland and a sheep run in the Sandwich Islands. Today he has shaved his beard off – I suppose at the lady's request – which has made a marked alteration in the betting. I think he is certainly on the job.

15 October 1883 - Monday

We ought to have reached Auckland yesterday, or at latest today, but we shan't be in till tomorrow. This evening, the stewards gave a 'nigger entertainment'[147] – some of it very well done, but too long and spun out. Far the best performer was a Frenchman who was really a very clever actor talking English perfectly and doing a mock tragic scene A.1. The Bishop did not show up either at this or the theatricals. He is a bumptious ass, and very unpopular on board. Hardly anyone will call him 'My Lord', and he will hardly answer anyone who does not give him that title.

16 October 1883 - Tuesday

14. Members of the Northern Club, Auckland leaving by carriage (1880s)
Sir George Grey Special Collections, Auckland Libraries, 7-A642

We reached Auckland about 10am. It is certainly an enormous and very beautiful harbour; the town is dull and uninteresting enough. I called on our correspondent, Cruickshank[148]: a small Scotch wine merchant, who was civil; he had already had me put down for the Northern Club[149]. To which place I went, and found it very comfortable; a nice fire burning in the reading room, which was quite welcome as the weather is quite cool. I had a good lunch, and then drove with Clough and Forbes and Mackinnon to Mt. Eden[150]; from the top we had a very fine view. After that we called on Major George and his wife, who came out in the ship with us. They were very hospitable; we had tea with them, and saw his race horses and carried off some beautiful bunches

---

[147] Probably the 'traditional sea-side show' – Nigger Minstrels were actors blacked-up.
[148] Cruickshank, Smart & Co. registered as wine and spirits merchants under the distillery act 1869.
[149] The Northern Club: In Princes Street, overlooking the Albert Barracks. Founded by a group of prominent professional and business men in 1869. The club's founders purchased a handsome four storey quarrystone building originally designed as a hotel, restructured by architect Edward Ramsey for use by the 120 founding members.
[150] One of a number of extinct volcanoes around Auckland used as pa by the Maori.

of violets and a lot of cream. We went back to the club and played Blackpool and dined, and Clough and I came back to the ship saying good-bye to Mackinnon and Forbes whom I was very sorry to part with as they are a very good sort. We sailed about 9pm: one man as near as possible missed the steamer. She had actually left the wharf, but a rope was thrown to him which he fastened round his body and jumped into the dock and was dragged on board.

17 October 1883 - Wednesday

We have taken in a lot of new people, and among others a female American doctor[151] who has been lecturing in New Zealand with her son[152]; the latter had just been fined 10/- for horse-whipping an Auckland Editor[153] for publishing some libellous attack on her.[154]

18 October 1883 - Thursday

We are making a very good passage from Auckland and did 316 today, meeting the 'City of Sydney' on her way to 'Frisco. In the evening, Raymond gave a lecture on his experiences as War Correspondent in the Egyptian campaign; it was pretty poor, but fortunately not long.

19 October 1883 - Friday

It is definitely announced that Weaver and Miss Chadwick are going to be married: it seems he proposed after he had known her a week. The purser tells me they hardly ever make a trip without an engagement coming off.

20 October 1883 - Saturday

The last day on board, as we are to be in early tomorrow. There was a sort of 'free and easy' this evening – singing, playing and reciting: it wasn't bad, and got through the evening at any rate.

---

[151] Mrs. Potts, "a lady of 50 or 60 years, who has practised medicine in Philadelphia for 30 years" and who was "like a mother" to Dr. Edward Harrison.
[152] Dr. Edward Harrison.
[153] J. D. Wickham, publisher of "Free Lance" and "Figaro" in Auckland.
[154] Harrison was fined 10 shillings plus costs for assaulting Wickham after "Figaro" published a libellous article about Mrs. Potts and Wickham refused to divulge the journalist reponsible for the article to Harrison. The sentence was reported in the Auckland newspapers of 15-16 October 1883. 10 shillings was a very small fine: on 3 November 1883, Gibbs mentions that the entry fee to the horse-racing - including access to the saddling paddocks - is 10 shillings.

Sydney (1)

15. Mort & Co., wool store and the Customs House at Circular Quay, Sydney (c1885)
National Library of Australia, nla.pic-vn5779292

16. Royal Yacht Squadron - afternoon gathering (c1884-1917)
Tyrrell Photographic Collection, Powerhouse Museum

Vicary found Petty's Hotel – supposedly the leading hotel in Sydney - intolerably dirty, so he moved instead to the city's Union Club. This was one of the private social clubs found in major cities from the 19th century onwards, where gentlemen on business could stay in relaxed surroundings and expect a good standard of service at a reasonable price, usually including temporary membership of the club. He enjoyed stretching his legs with a brisk walk through the Botanical Gardens as a welcome change from strolling around the deck, and was able to exercise his mind too in the Art Gallery before getting down to business.

The Sydney office staff - Murray, George Merivale and the others – waited, perhaps apprehensively, for their inspection: Merivale, in particular, was the newest member of staff and was unsure how his progress would be assessed by Gibbs. In addition, the office was too cramped and did not convey the firm's prestige, and if new trade were to be undertaken, more spacious accommodation with wharves and warehouses would have to be found. Vicary realised that he would need to spend more time in Sydney, but that it would have to wait until after he had established his presence in Melbourne.

Before he left for Victoria by sea aboard the 'John Elder', the importance of Vicary's visit was underlined by the presence of the Prime Minister[155] and members of his New South Wales Cabinet assembling at the Murray home in order to meet him. New South Wales had realised it was welcoming a major source of Finance, and was anxious to discover his intentions.

---

[155] Sir Alexander Stuart (1825-1886), premier of New South Wales.

At this time in Sydney, some wharves were privately owned or leased and some were owned by the Government, so any new development would be at a premium. The site for the new office was intended to be 'nearer to Circular Quay' and 'close to the Exchange', as Gibbs writes in one of his letters to the London office. Despite its proximity to the most run-down area of the city and the garbage-strewn waterfront, it extended back 130 feet, had a frontage worth £200 per foot, and it was to be designed by Wardell - the leading architect of the time. Their existing building was higher up Pitt St., alongside other prominent companies, but where there was no warehousing. In Sydney, Gibbs Bright & Co. meant to follow the example of one of the long-established and leading pioneer merchant families, the Morts. Their warehouses and wharves were clustered around Darling Harbour and backed onto Circular Quay, and were even then prepared to receive consignments of frozen meat from Mort's[156] Blue Mountain refrigeration depot.

This was a new trade already being established by the French in South America, improved upon by the Germans, and – finally - experimented with in New Zealand and Victoria. Mort himself had died in 1878 before witnessing the success of his own refrigeration technique in 1880, when Thomas McIlwraith transported a perfectly edible cargo from Sydney to London aboard the Strathleven. Further shiploads of frozen mutton and lamb, together with butter, were exported to Europe from Victoria in the following years. The earliest methods of refrigeration used were ether evaporation, air compression, and ammonia compression. In some of the earliest cargoes, the insulated chambers aboard ship were lined with clean, raw wool transported for sale at the same time. Three of the Orient Line ships were adapted for the trade, probably with the financial investment of their close associates, GB&Co.

On the 16th January 1886 the Illustrated Sydney News reported the appearance of the new GB&Co. offices in Pitt Street North, Sydney and commented that 'the firm of Gibbs, Bright, & Co. are housed in a manner worthy of their standing as a branch of the great house of Antony Gibbs & Sons, London'.

There was also an illustration of Wardell's 'freely treated' Italianate buildings on the corner of Underwood Street and Pitt Street in which the Orient Steam Navigation Co. and GB&Co. would be housed, marking with its front wall the original channel of the Old Tank Stream - that essential fresh water supply to the First Fleet in 1788. 'The proportions are excellent, and altogether the edifice is exceedingly handsome, and a credit to the city'. Vicary Gibbs' opinion would probably have been divided about the use of the local Sydney stone. He would have approved of its

---

[156] Thomas Sutcliffe Mort (1816-1878).

lower cost, but might have preferred the elegant, lighter-coloured stone from a more distant quarry.

The warehouses behind the new office must have served GB&Co's wharves further down towards Millers Point. These wharves are also mentioned in a newspaper report of December 2nd 1890 when kerosene from New York in a bonded warehouse went up in flames and caused nearly £60,000-worth of damage to a jelly used by GB&Co. Whatever the cause of the fire, it was fuelled by the inflammable material around the old harbour front and beneath the jetties, which was as much a threat to public health as it was a fire risk. It was not until much later in the development of Australia's economic career that the infrastructure of Sydney's waterfront received the clean sweep it needed. By 1900 the build up of silt and general rubbish, where the wooden piles had crumbled away over the century, had invited a rat infestation and the first cases of Bubonic plague had appeared. There had always been an effort to dredge when reconstruction was demanded and when shipping increased, but it was hampered by earlier building. At the turn of the 20th century a completely new project was carried out giving better access from sea and land that would allow – in line with the changing uses of the waterfront - more enjoyment of water sports, leisure and tourism, and the true appreciation of one of the most beautiful harbours in the world. By the 1920s some of the many detailed maps of inlets close to Circular Quay show the wharves and warehouses of GB&Co. well-placed in Campbell's Cove waiting for the arrival of the Sydney Harbour Bridge, and the time for them to move on.

21 October 1883 - Sunday

We came through the Heads about 6 am. Unfortunately, it was very wet and foggy so one couldn't do more than see how beautiful the harbour would be in better weather. We had a medical inspection, and were all assembled in the social hall. It was a great farce, but took a long while. I had omitted to telegraph from Auckland, so no one expected me. I went with the others to Petty's Hotel[157], which is said to be the best; but it is a wretched place – it was so full I couldn't get a room, but as Clough and Hornsby had got rooms I did not want to go elsewhere so ultimately I arranged to have a bed made up on the floor of Hornsby's room for tonight, and I shall move to the club or somewhere tomorrow. We had to dine in the middle of the day, and in the afternoon we went for a good walk all through the Botanical Gardens and round the quay, and Mrs

---

[157] Petty's Hotel, 1 York Street. The hotel was originally the home of John Dunmore Lang, Sydney's most famous Presbyterian minister in colonial days, who supervised the building of Scots Church nearby. He sold his house for £1,350 in 1832 to a hotel-keeper William Cummings. The hotel was bought 4 years later by Thomas Petty, who formerly had been a valet. It is interesting to note how Vicary Gibbs' critical opinion differs so greatly from the generally held late nineteenth century view of Petty's Hotel being the best hotel and select resort in Sydney.

Macquarie's Chair[158] – where there is a fine view of the shipping – and back through Woolloomooloo[159] to the hotel. We also went to the picture gallery[160] where there are several good modern pictures. 'Wedded' by Leighton[161]; 'A Jacobite Proclamation' by Gow[162]; and 'Rorkes Drift' by Neuville[163]; and others which I had seen before. I decided not to go and see Murray[164] or Merivale[165] until tomorrow. I went to the general Post Office[166] and cabled home my arrival. Then back to a sort of *table d'hote* high tea: waiting bad, and the place generally dirty and slovenly. Saw Clough off, who is going to Melbourne to attend the wool sales.

22 October 1883 - Monday

After breakfast, I walked down to the office[167] and found Murray. He was very much surprised to see me, and reproached me with not having telegraphed from Auckland that he might have come to meet me. He is a nice old chap: something like Thomas Collett Sanders to look at, only not so big headed. Hart[168] is also up here, but returns to Brisbane at the end

---

[158] Mrs Macquarie's chair was hand-carved by convicts from sandstone in 1810 for Governor Macquarie's wife.
[159] Woolloomooloo is an inner-city eastern suburb of Sydney at the head of Woolloomooloo Bay on Sydney Harbour.
[160] The Art Gallery was housed at this time in a fine arts annex built by William Wardell, the leading Australian architect, who was being considered by Gibbs Bright & Co. as the designer of their new harbour-side premises in Sydney. In 1885, the gallery was moved to its present site.
[161] 'Wedded', by Lord Frederick Leighton (1830-1896). Purchased in 1882 and still on display.
[162] 'A Jacobite Proclamation 1882', by Andrew Carrick Gow (1848-1920).
[163] 'Défense de Rorke's Drift', by Adolphe Alphonse Marie De Neuville (1835-1885), commissioned by the Fine Art Society and painted in 1880 and now in NSW Art Gallery.
[164] William Gilmour Murray (-1888), a respected senior member of Gibbs, Bright & Co., opened the Sydney office in 1875. He had arrived in Melbourne in 1853. He became seriously ill in 1886 and was given a year off work, during which time George Merivale took over management of the Sydney office.
[165] George Montague Merivale (1842-1931) was the second son of Anthony Trollope's great friend John Lewis Merivale. George's sister, Janet Louisa (1850-1909), married Antony Gibbs (1841-1907), son of William Gibbs (1790-1875) of Tyntesfield. Trollope named his own first son Henry Merivale Trollope, and 'borrowed' the young banker George as a character in his novel "Ayala's Angel" in which he is sent to the 'outposts of Empire' as part of his 'business' education. George emigrated to New South Wales, where in 1881 he married Emily Jane Laidley (1856-1925), the brother of Shepheard Edgecliff Laidley (see 30th May 1884), and settled in Sydney to bring up his family – starting with a daughter called Angel (a name possibly suggested by the Trollope novel). He joined Gibbs, Bright & Co. in their Sydney Office, later becoming a partner and presiding over the Sydney Chamber of Commerce for 2 years. George had two sons and three daughters, the elder son being killed at Gallipoli.
[166] The General Post Office was still not complete. Controversy had been created in 1883 by Thomas Sani's sculptures on the Pitt Street façade that were considered to be grotesque. James Barnet, the architect, was petitioned to have them removed.
[167] The "old" office was located at 93 Pitt Street. By 1885/6, GB&Co. were operating from their new office at 37-43 Pitt Street, nearer Circular Quay by about 300 metres.
[168] Hon. Frederic Hamilton Scott Hart, MLC (1836-1915) first went to Sydney in 1843 with his father, William Hamilton Hart, the superintendent of the Bank of Australasia. They returned to England in 1849, but returned to Australia in 1853 where they established

of the week. George Merivale looked very well, and I have come out to the Laidley's[169] house for the night. The Laidleys themselves are away, but George and his wife are there. She is expecting her confinement in December. Murray and Merivale now get on perfectly, which is a comfort. They gave me a very good dinner and a nice room. Received a friendly welcoming telegram from Charles Bright, who I am sure is sincere in his pleasure at seeing me.

23 October 1883 - Tuesday

After breakfast, drove to the office and inspected the site of the new offices[170] with Murray, and the sheds and stores[171]. A brother of Hilliard's

---

Messrs. Bright Bros. and Co. in Melbourne with Regi and Charles Bright, Frederic Hart joining the firm as junior clerk. In 1862 he was selected by Bright Bros. to manage their new branch in Brisbane. He remained with the firm until his retirement in 1898 - "one of the old guard", as Gibbs refers to him. Hart married Harriet Isabel Blanche Horsley in 1865.

[169] Hon. William George Laidley (1828-1897), and his wife Jane (née Atkinson). They had 9 children, amongst them Emily Jane (1856-1925) who married George Merivale in 1881, and Shepheard Edgecliff (1861-1945).

[170] Gibbs, Bright & Co. had been occupying offices at 93 Pitt Street since 1875 when they were opened by William Gilmour Murray. These offices were in a part of Pitt Street surrounded by other important buildings, but were some distance from Circular Quay, and were becoming too cramped for GB&Co.'s operation. In May 1884, Gibbs reports in a letter home that tenders were being invited for the construction of the "grand new house", some 300 metres lower down Pitt Street, at numbers 37-43. The land had cost £200 per foot of frontage.

In January 1886, the Illustrated Sydney News included an engraving of the new offices, and a lengthy article describing them. They were located in Pitt Street North, at the corner of Underwood Street, and consisted of two buildings. The one at the corner of Underwoood Street was occupied by Gibbs, Bright & Co. as offices, whilst the ground and basement floors of the adjoining southern building were to be occupied as offices for the Orient Steam Navigation Company. The frontage to Pitt Street was about 97ft long, and the building consisted of four stories above a basement story (which had been built out of neccessity - the old Tank Stream ran under the building and required extremely deep foundations to be dug). At the rear of the office was a spacious warehouse of 4 stories, 87ft x 30ft. The architect was W.W. Wardell, C.E., and the contractors were Messrs. Bignell and Clark (for the warehouse), and Mr. Try (for the offices). The style of architecture of the front was Italian, freely treated, and it was built in Sydney stone. "The cost of the buildings when completed, including the warehouse, will not be much less than £25,000".

It goes on to praise the building's design: "The proportions are excellent, and altogether the edifice is exceedingly handsome, and a credit to the city. The munificence which bestowed, and the taste that designed, so many splendid buildings in the old country, such as Keble College Library and Dining Hall; St. Michael's, Paddington; St. Michael's, Exeter, and a host of others, has not been at fault in Sydney, and the firm of Gibbs, Bright, & Co. are housed in a manner worthy of their standing as a branch of the great house of Anthony Gibbs & Sons, London."

[171] It is not clear which "sheds and stores" Gibbs is referring to here. The new office (at 37-43 Pitt Street, about 300m down from the current office at 93 Pitt Street) would include new warehouse space, so he may be referring to the proposed site of these. Or he may be referring to existing sheds and stores nearby - possibly at Smith's wharf, used by the Eastern and Australia Steamship Company (for whom they were agents) - or to vacant land surrounding that wharf.

called to borrow money to get back to England, but I told him I didn't know that his people would wish me to send him back, so I gave him 1 sovereign and sent him away. Got letters from Charles and Regi. B.[172] Have left the hotel and moved into the Union Club[173], which seems very comfortable. Hart seems delighted with Keating[174], and so does Mrs. Hart[175]. George M. says she wants Frank for her eldest daughter; he says he hopes Frank will settle in Brisbane altogether. These offices here are frightfully overcrowded, and there is really no private room at all – only a small space screened off.

24 October 1883 - Wednesday

17. Union Club, Sydney (c1894-5)
National Library of Australia,
nla.pic-an3366506-s66

Busy all day in the office. Took a bedroom at the Union Club: very comfortable. The head of the railway department has sent me a pass over all New South Wales' lines for the next 3 months on the strength of my being a railway director, so the 'Natal and Nova Cruz' has proved some use. I could not get a sleeping berth to Melbourne as the trains are so full of people going down for the Cup, so I have taken a cabin on the 'John Elder' leaving on Saturday, which will give me some more sea travelling – which I like.

---

[172] Reginald Arthur Bright (1833-1920), the youngest of the Bright brothers, had gone out to Melbourne as an engineer aboard the SS 'Great Britain' in 1852 to join the firm in Victoria and gain experience. He was thought to be less measured in his business decisions than his brothers and liable to take more risks; he may have felt himself inhibited by some of the senior Gibbs' management. Vicary, however, found Regi dedicated and hard-working.

[173] Union Club, which at the time was in Bligh Street. In 1884, the leading architect William Wardell - whom Gibbs meets as he is also responsible for the new Sydney offices - started a rebuilding of the club in the dignified Italianate/Palladian style then popular in similar London clubs.

[174] Francis Amboor Keating (1853-1929) was a lawyer, only son of Reverend William Keating (who had been a family friend and tutor to some of Henry Gibbs' sons). Frank Keating worked in the Liverpool office of Gibbs Bright & Co., and first went out to Australia with Alban Gibbs (probably about 1881). He married Constance Mary Prell, daughter of Friedrich Wilhelm Prell (?-1912), of Hanover and Melbourne, who was the architect who designed Felton Building, 7-9 Queen Street, Melbourne. They had one son, Harold Francis Amboor Keating, in about 1895 – he was killed in action in June 1918. In 1893, Keating was living at Punt Hill, South Yarra.

[175] Harriet Isabel Blanche Hart (née Horsley), daughter of Charles Henry Horsley, married Frederic Hart in April 1865 in Sydney.

25 October 1883 - Thursday

Wrote a long business letter to Alban. Spent some time examining Cowan's[176] premises. Dined at the Laidley's, who have returned. I like Mr. L.: very hospitable and friendly; his wife rather silly and second rate; the eldest son a handsome rather brusque young colonial. Took the steam tram[177] back to the Club.

26 October 1883 - Friday

Turned up at the office very soon after 9am, and found Murray there and all hard at work. Went with Murray round the town, inspecting the wharfs and looking at possible sites for a produce store. Hilliard turned up and paid me back the sovereign – the people for whom he has been working will advance his passage money, which is all right. I shall write to my friend and explain the circumstances. Dined with Murray – very nice, well appointed little dinner; Mrs Murray did not dine as it was a men's dinner. The party consisted entirely of the present Ministry: Stuart[178], the premier; Dalley[179], Attorney General; Dibbs[180] Col. Treasurer; Read[181],

18. Union Bank of Australia and Gibbs, Shallard & Co., Printers, Pitt Street, Sydney (1873-80)
National Library of Australia, nla.pic-vn4704183

---

[176] This is the Sydney office of the Edinburgh paper-making company, Cowan & Co., for which AG&S were responsible in Australia. The Sydney office were tea merchants (agents of the Calcutta Tea Syndicate), paper importers and publishers in the 1880s.

[177] The steam tram had only been recently established, in 1879. Trams ran to depot where the Opera House now stands, and so passed the club. A little Baldwin locomotive drew two carriages..

[178] Sir Alexander Stuart (1825-1886). Born in Edinburgh. Merchant and banker. He had defeated Sir Henry Parkes in 1882. The passage of the Land bill broke Stuart's health.

[179] William Bede Dalley (1831-1888) was born in Sydney of convict parents. He was admitted to the Bar in 1856. He contributed to the Freeman's Journal, defended the bushranger Frank Gardiner, and the man who in 1868 shot the Duke of Edinburgh. He had served as Attorney General in Robertson's ministries. He spoke up for the Chinese in 1881. He was responsible for the Criminal Law Amendment Act in 1883 and amending the Matrimonial Causes Act.

[180] Sir George Richard Dibbs (1834-1904). Born in Sydney, became a merchant, and supported free compulsory secular education. Went to jail in 1880 for a year for refusing to pay a slander judgement to a lawyer who had committed adultery with Dibbs' sister-in-law. Committed to railway building, he by-passed the problem of the suspension of land sales during the passage of the Land Bill by borrowing £14 million. In 1885 he became caretaker premier due to the ill health of Stuart, but lost the subsequent election in October 1885.

[181] Sir George Reid (1845-1918), a Scot born in Renfrewshire who became minister for Public Instruction in 1883 and was about to pass a very important Education Act. He was 12th Premier of NSW 1894-1899, and then the fourth Prime Minister in the Federal government 1904-1905.

Minister of Education. Stuart talked to me a great deal about his new Land Bill[182], the text of which is just out and is causing a great deal of comment and interest; there seems great doubt whether it will be carried. The principle is to resume ½ the squatters[183] runs, and give them security of tenure for the rest instead of being liable to free selectors. Several ladies came in after dinner, and Hart and I went back together in a hansom.

S.S. John Elder

27 October 1883 - Saturday

A busy morning talking and writing up to the last minute, and sailed at 1pm in the 'John Elder'[184] – a fine boat. Have got a very good cabin to myself. The passengers not much account: principally betting men going down for the Cup. The Captain and purser very civil and attentive.

28 October 1883 - Sunday

No service on board. It has begun to blow like fun; a head wind which will make us horribly late. Have felt rather sleepy and uncomfortable, though not actually sick – I consider I am well up to the average as a sailor.

29 October 1883 - Monday

Heavy weather continued all day, and instead of being in Melbourne in the morning we shall have to anchor outside the bay; and not alongside the wharf until tomorrow. Read a witty, cynical, rather disagreeable but decidedly amusing novel by Norris called 'Matrimony'[185], I think I remember seeing it lying about at St. Dunstans[186].

30 October 1883 - Tuesday

Arrived at 10am, and Vine – the shipping clerk – came on board and took charge of my luggage while I took the train and went up to the office[187],

---

[182] The Crown Lands Act of 1884 eventually created a new structure, introducing various new tenures not previously in existence.
[183] Squatters were settlers who claimed farming land in colonial Australia and then improved it. Prior to the Lands Act, squatters had no legal entitlement to their settlements and could have it all reallocated to other settlers who went through formal procedures to apply for land from the government.
[184] 'The John Elder': launched on 29th August 1869 by John Elder & Co., Glasgow. By 1879, she was on the London-Melbourne-Sydney run. Shipwrecked 1892.
[185] William Edward Norris (1847-1925): 'Matrimony', published 1881.
[186] St. Dunstan's was the Gibbs' London residence.
[187] The office in Melbourne at the time may have been at Little Flinders Street - that building was later (Nov 1887) sold to a Mr Henry Miller for "nearly £25,000", according to newspaper reports. New offices on the junction of Flinders Lane and Bond Street were built in about 1888.

where I found Hannay[188] – a quiet, pleasant fellow. I was surprised to find that he knows Edward Adams, and seemed to like him much. Soon the Brights came in, both looking very well, and Regi in a high white hat and short coat – very grey, and the image of Charles Matthews as 'My Awful Dad'[189]. Charles[190], on the other hand, looking intensely respectable. Went to lunch at the Melbourne Club[191] and was introduced to all sorts of people. In the evening, walked out to St. Leonards[192] with Regi, a very pretty walk through the Park, and a very snug little crib when we got there – a one storied gabled house in about 4 acres of ground. Very nicely got up inside, and full of knick-knacks and ornaments. R. has evidently taken a lot of trouble with it, and is proud of it. Charles was dining out, but R. and I had a comfortable little dinner, and afterwards sat in the drawing room and smoked over the fire (which was a most desirable addition for its beastly cold), and finally got tired of talking business and both went sound asleep in our armchairs till Charles returned from his party. I have got a very nice bedroom, and shall stay with R. – for any rate, at the present.

19. Watercolour of St. Leonards
Courtesy of Charles and Primrose Bright of Melbourne, Australia

---

[188] From a mention in the Brisbane Courier, 14 January 1887, we know that this is "Percival Ramsford Hannay (Gibbs, Bright & Co.)".
[189] Charles James Mathews (one T)(1803-1878) was a British actor. He was famous for his measured and restrained comedy. He played the lead in the play "My Awful Dad", amongst others.
[190] Charles Edward Bright (1829-1915): The elder of the two Melbourne-based Bright brothers. He had arrived in Melbourne in 1854, and left Australia aboard 'The Rome' in January 1884, returning again following Vicary Gibbs' departure for England and remaining until the 1890s.
[191] The Melbourne Club: founded in 1839, it was already the headquarters of the Melbourne Establishment. From 1858 it was situated at 36-50 Collins Street.
[192] St. Leonards is the Brights' house in Melbourne, near the Botanical Gardens. The original house no longer exists, but there is a cul-de-sac called St Leonards Court in the same location.

Melbourne (1)

20. Gibbs Bright Offices Melbourne, Flinders Lane and Bond St junction (c1880)
State Library of Victoria, H4563

21. Gibbs Bright Offices Melbourne (detail showing Orient agency sign) (c1880)
State Library of Victoria, H4563 (detail)

As early as 1880, following the takeover by Antony Gibbs and Sons of their associated House of Gibbs Bright and Co. and more than 3 years before the final decision to send Vicary to the colonial houses, it became clear that a thorough restructuring of the Australian offices was required. Gibbs Bright had been based in Bristol and Liverpool, traditional centres of the Caribbean trade, as well as in Australia. The pressure for emancipation and reform had changed public attitudes to the old trade, and the company felt morally obliged to respond appropriately. They had also seen a gradual decline in the guano trade which threatened their profitability. When a decrease in the production of sugar and the resultant higher prices destabilised the West Indian imports it was safer to turn to Australia and New Zealand where sugar growth and production were untainted by the history of slave labour. In spite of the greater distance Vicary intended to promote new business in the colonies in this and other colonial products they had not previously considered, without becoming involved in any controversy over the use of Pacific Island labour.

There was now the potential to consolidate what trade already existed in wool and timber, and investigating the possibilities of minerals such as lead and copper. The carriage of frozen meat had recently become practical and these new exports could be shipped profitably from Geelong, Newcastle, and from Sydney, where Thomas Mort had already installed his cold-store. The following newspaper advertisement summoned Queensland farmers and stockholders to a public meeting in Brisbane to discuss the formation of a 'Meat Preservation Company':

Mary Street, January 28th 1879

It has been decided to call a General Meeting of stockholders and others interested in forming a Meat Preserving Company to be held today (Wednesday January 28th) at 5pm, at the Metropolitan Hotel, to take into consideration the above question. All persons interested are particularly desired to attend.

P. C. Hawkes, Secretary

Europe need not be the only destination for some of these items; Vicary Gibbs envisaged the extension of their agency into the Asian and Japanese markets.

22. Washing Wool (c1884-1917)
Tyrrell Photographic Collection,
Powerhouse Museum

23. Bullock team carting wool bales
(c1880)
National Library of Australia,
nla.pic-vn3550658

Newcastle was fast developing as a trading port dealing in coal and steel because of the easily accessible mines, and GB&Co. saw that its proximity to the sheep stations would mean the potential for cheaper timber and wool warehousing than in Sydney. By 1885, Gibbs had acquired their own wool stores and a wool shipping company, as well as additional coastal shipping lines. In the decade up to 1880, when the new plans were already being discussed in London, GB&Co. had invested in sheep and cattle ranches in New South Wales and Queensland. Regi and Samuel Bright had acquired a considerable acreage on Amby Downs with Chrystal, and Vicary had promised to visit in order to monitor the production and quality of the wool. It was necessary to be on the spot to check that the whole ranching operation was streamlined from start to finish in order to keep the price competitive. For example, Gibbs had noted that many of the British importers would have preferred the wool to be transported unwashed, enabling them to use the lanolin acquired from the washing process themselves. He was also able to ensure investment in the ranching infrastructure: everything from the mining of metals for the manufacture of the vast amount of flexible fencing required, to the cost of labour and the acquisition of faster ships to transport the final product.

Guano, the product which had established Gibbs' success, was not forgotten: there was an opportunity to reverse the decline in its market by interesting the Australian grain producers in its benefit to their yields. With the New York office actively promoting sales in the U.S. and the Merchant Bank in London issuing loans to South America and keeping an eye on local control, it was hoped that guano would increase in profitability again.

The situation in Melbourne was a difficult one for a young man to deal with, however experienced in management or in legal argument. It was hard to come in from outside, and to interfere with decisions made by men more familiar with the area who were senior in age and previously autonomous, but Henry Hucks Gibbs had made clear his intention in his letter of 1880: they would deal with the take-over in their own way 'without any disagreement from the Brights'.

Reginald Bright, the bachelor younger brother, offered Vicary the hospitality of his own comfortable home. He had gone out to Australia as company engineer aboard the S.S. Great Britain and decided to stay. Regi, together with his elder brother Charles and younger cousin Samuel, had adapted well to Melbourne's colonial society, whereas Vicary usually preferred the company of 'the intellectual and better informed'. Many of those with useful local, political or business influence who wished to meet him belonged to a broader social group than he was used to. He, too, would learn to adapt, at the same time reserving the right to choose which invitations to accept and which to refuse. For example, Gibbs had been invited to a ball by the influential local landowner Sir William Clarke, and although reluctant to attend he did not want to step on the toes of the 'dancing Brights' - as he had dubbed them - whose enthusiasm might have been fired more by the ball than the business.

24. Reginald Bright
Courtesy of Charles and Primrose Bright of Melbourne, Australia

Charles Bright, who had been established in Melbourne for several years, quickly understood that he would disrupt Gibbs' role, and this gave him the perfect excuse to make a strategic withdrawal and a well-deserved home visit to England and his wife and family. In Australia, he had made good use of his ideas and time by taking a lead in land management issues and in local banking. He had achieved some of his best work in Melbourne as President of the Chamber of Commerce, advocating the widening of the Yarra River and the creation of the Harbour Trust on which he served as Chairman from 1879 to 1881. It was his involvement in the successful Melbourne International Trade Exhibitions that earned him his return visit to Australia in 1883 and his CMG.

25. Charles Edward Bright
Courtesy of Charles and Primrose Bright of Melbourne, Australia

While Charles may have been more interested in the economic future of the colony than his brother, the gregarious socialite Regi did become closely involved in new gold strikes - with some small success - and made another entry into the mining industry in response to the need for further smelting processes.

Vicary had arrived in Australia at a critical time for the pastoralists and it was a good moment to make excursions into the Victorian countryside and to experience some of the realities of bush life. He returned to his office desk after these visits with greater insight into their chances of diversifying the colonial business. Letters detailing the pioneering information he learned from leaders in the field of cold storage - such as George Fairbairn, owner of Lara, the 14,000-acre sheep station near Geelong - were sent back to the London headquarters with new ideas of schemes for frozen meat cargoes and other chilled produce. Fairbairn reminded Gibbs of his own father; both men 'discounted' a mere amputation of a hand, and both had a similar determination to be involved in their business plans from start to finish. He manufactured his own galvanised wire netting fences, then irrigated and rested his paddocks in rotation. Once slaughtered, the livestock would be transferred to the cold-store and packing station he had built himself. Fairbairn's enthusiasm was infectious; Vicary willingly took his advice and continued his research at the Australian Frozen Meat Export Co. of Newport, Victoria, and in Sydney.

Wool prices had declined in the 1870s, and the quantity and quality varied according to fluctuations in the weather. Producers had to operate some kind of drought-defying spread of their stations; water management was crucial, as well as the most efficient techniques of packaging, transport and storage of wool bales and carcasses of meat to ensure the arrival at their destination in a perfec

The population of Britain had grown from about 20 million in 1850, to over 35 million by 1880. In that time the price of meat in Britain had doubled; food technology was called upon to make a major leap forwards, but it was an area in which Germany was in advance of her competitors. AG&S should certainly have had their fingers on the pulse of progress as their South American nitrate would soon be in demand for its ammonia, used in one of the three new refrigeration techniques. In 1880 S.S. Strathleven, shortly followed by S.S. Protos, made the journey to Europe without any deterioration of their cargoes. Theirs was an early air compression refrigeration system created in Geelong, but it had suffered many teething problems. Shipments had had to be cancelled and sold off locally whilst modifications were made, before more meat could be bought and loaded. Occasionally, too, leakages in the pipe-work had had to be repaired en voyage. German and French refrigeration methods were more advanced and were already in use in Argentinean plants and shipping.

In Sydney, and later when he went to Newcastle and Brisbane, Vicary learned more about the firm's property and the potential of the various offices, wool stores, wharves, and other necessary installations such as preparation plants and water works. He was able to report back to his brother Alban in London where and how competitors such as Dalgety were 'doing well' in frozen meat.

Having settled in Melbourne and discovered the difficulties that faced him, Vicary turned his attention to another pressing problem. The poor trading situation in the Dunedin House remained seriously unsatisfactory and it was not long before he decided to cross the Tasman Sea with a junior manager, Merivale, as travelling companion. The mission was intended to discover from Arthur, the newly appointed senior manager, exactly what problems had been left behind by his predecessor, the disastrous Danson. Although he found Arthur's manner that of the modern, rather brash young colonial to which he was not accustomed, he felt sure that the young man's judgement was sound. Knowing the quick temper of his elder brother, and his frustration at dealing with mismanagement at a distance, Gibbs wrote to Alban at length with his findings, hoping to pre-empt a hasty response. [See Appendix Letter of 1st March 1884]. He carefully masked his own impatience with Head Office over their reluctance to give him free rein to act on Arthur's advice and local knowledge.

Melbourne (1)

31 October 1883 - Wednesday

Called at Government House, walking through the beautiful gardens that lie between it and Regi's house. I never saw such a mass of bloom as there is in his garden: all the English flowers and some semi-tropical plants – the roses particularly fine. So much flower that from a distance you could see no leaf; and scarlet geraniums 15 ft. high – a blaze of colour. Plenty of tree ferns. Heard the sad news of poor Blanchie's[193] death. Heard from Keating that he wants to come away from Brisbane on account of the heat; shall try and persuade him to stop. The streets are too fine for the buildings in Melbourne, and nature has certainly done very little for it, but it is very well laid out and the climate, I should say, far preferable to Sydney. Dined at the Club with Hannay, as the Brights were both dining out.

1 November 1883 - Thursday

Had a nice long letter from mother, but no others. Heard the sad news of poor Blanche Romanis' death in child birth. **[GREEK]**[194].

26. Greek text from 1 November 1883

2 November 1883 - Friday

Received an invitation to Sir Wm Clarke's dance – his daughter[195] is engaged to marry Sutton Tylecote[196]; also to Government House. I shall

---

[193] Blanche Dorothea Romanis (née Cokayne) (1858-1883), the daughter of George Edward Cokayne (formerly Adams) and Mary Dorothea Gibbs. She married Reverend W. F. J. Romanis on 10 August 1882, and died in childbirth on 17 September 1883.
[194] Greek: "Men in their generation are like leaves..." – Homer reflecting on mortality, from Iliad (book 6, line 146). The full quote translates something like: "A generation of men is like a generation of leaves; the wind scatters some leaves upon the ground, while others the burgeoning wood brings forth - and the season of spring comes on. So of men one generation springs forth and another ceases."
[195] This daughter is by Sir William Clarke's first wife, Mary Walker. The youngest daughter (may or may not have been this one) was Ivy Clarke.
[196] Edward Ferdinando Sutton Tylecote (1849-1938) was a cricketer playing with the English Test team in Australia in 1883. The team spent Christmas at the Clarke property, and, after the Australians lost, Lady Clarke apparently presented the captain (Ivo Bligh – also mentioned later in the diary) with a small urn containing the ashes of the stumps and announced that she would like it to be a perpetual trophy between the two teams.

go to the latter, but except these I don't mean to go out in the evening, unless to dinner: it's not good enough. Met Chrystal[197], the part owner of Amby[198]: a good, rough sort of chap in a great funk about the New South Wales Land Bill[199], which he thinks will ruin him. He has a vivid recollection of Alban's duck-shooting powers, and was anxious to know if I was equally good. The Brights very pleasant and good-natured, but like Beatrice Gibbs[200] I feel a craving for more intellectual and better-informed company; indeed it is, I feel, very unselfish of me to try and persuade Frank[201] to stay in Brisbane!

3 November 1883 - Saturday

The office shut up, and the racing carnival has begun. We three went off in a waggonette to the course, which is about 3 miles out of the town on the salt water river. A splendid course, Grandstand; and all most admirably arranged. The crowd good-tempered and well-behaved; plenty of ladies and bright dresses. 10/- admitting one to saddling paddocks and everything. The place 'takes the cake', as the Yankees say, from anything I have seen in England. The finishes were not very close and exciting. We lunched at Dr Fitzgerald's[202] carriage, and dined at the Club. I met a young Sandeman who was at Oxford with me: he is engaged to a girl here. I was introduced to a heap of people.

4 November 1883 - Sunday

A lovely day: after church we all sat and smoked, and read the 'Australian' in the St. Leonard's garden[203] – which is about as pretty, old-fashioned a flower garden as could well be imagined. I think it is a great credit to Regi:

---

[197] In the University of Melbourne archives is a document showing David Chrystal's station (Amby Creek) to be mortgaged to the Oriental Bank for £7,000 with a lien over wool, under the superintendence of A L P Cameron.
[198] Amby, originally called Amby Creek, became a township in 1883 and forms part of the eastern boundary of the Outback region, where the "grain belt" and "grazing belts" meet. Amby quarry is a lava flow, quarried for road bridge and dam construction.
[199] The New South Wales Land Bill was enacted in October 1884 as the Crown Lands Act of 1884, coming in to force on 1st January 1885. The letter from Angus MacPherson (manager of Amby Station) to Bright, Chrystal & Co. (David Chrystal, co-owner of the station with the Brights), our copy of which had no date but was presumably written in late 1884 or soon after, hints at some of the effects of the Act on the Station.
[200] Beatrice Gibbs, née Elton, daughter of Sir Arthur Hallam Elton of Clevedon Court (close to Tyntesfield). She married George, 2nd son of Reverend Joseph Gibbs of Clifton Hampden, who was William Gibbs' nephew. George entered the family firm in the London office.
[201] Frank A. Keating
[202] Sir Thomas Naghten FitzGerald (1838-1908) arrived in Melbourne in 1858 and became an honorary surgeon at most Melbourne hospitals. He was a brilliant diagnostician and immensely resourceful. In 1884 he became a clinical lecturer at Melbourne University and was idolised by generations of Melbourne's medical students. Some saw him as a genius. His wife, Margaret, was the daughter of James Robertson of Straun House, Launceston, Tasmania.
[203] It is likely that much of Regi's garden and plant collection later became incorporated in the public Park created in that part of the Melbourne suburbs.

there is a specimen of almost every common English flower and shrub, and I don't know a better place in which to enjoy, "That content surpassing wealth/ The Sage in meditation found"[204] – that is, if the worries will let you. A Mr[205] and Mrs Youl – Tasmanians: very nice, gentle people – came to dinner: the lady I should say an old flame of Regi's. Hannay also: quiet and civil, with plenty of head in spite of small weak chin – he improves on acquaintance and is, I think, a steady good fellow.

5 November 1883 - Monday

Dined at the Club at a big dinner given by the Brights: 22 to dinner, very well done on the whole. The *bêche-de-mer* soup nice, and very like turtle; also snipe good – larger than our English birds. I sat next to a Mr Molesworth Green[206], who is President of the Club: a cultivated, gentlemanly fellow of Irish descent. Though pleasant and friendly enough, I have not met any very interesting people since I came to Melbourne.

6 November 1883 - Tuesday

Cup day, and all the world going to the races. Fine weather and a tremendous crowd: the papers say that ¼ of the whole population of Victoria were on the course. A curious prophecy has been going about, and appeared in the papers **before** the races, to the effect that Martini Henry would win the Derby, that Dirk Hatteraik would win the Cup, and that the prophet would die before either event came off. Two of these events having come off, there was some excitement as to whether the Cup would fall to D.H. – however, it was won by Martini Henry. Dined at the Club.

7 November 1883 - Wednesday

Rather seedy this morning in spite of total abstinence yesterday. P&O mail went out: wrote to mother and Smeb[207]. Dined with a man named Sullivan, and met a lot of Sydney men up for the races. Sat between Mackinnon[208], Editor of the Argus, and Joseph, who is a hospitable Jewish merchant in Sydney. About 12 at dinner, and very well done.

---

[204] From Percy Bysshe Shelley: 'Stanzas Written in Dejection near Naples'.
[205] Although there is no way to be certain, it is likely that this is James Arndell Youl (1811-1904), CMG (1874), KCMG (1891), of Tasmania, brother of Dr. Richard Youl (the Victoria Coroner that Gibbs meets in Melbourne later). James Arndell Youl married the widow Charlotte Robinson (née Williams) in September 1882.
[206] Molesworth Richard Green (1827-1916), pastoralist, JP, trustee of the Melbourne Public Library, National Gallery and Museum, and president of the Melbourne Club in 1883.
[207] Smeb is obviously a nickname for a colleague or family member – possibly Samuel Bright (1843-1910), brother of Heywood Bright (see index) and cousin to Reginald, Charles Edward, and Tyndall Bright.
[208] Sir Lauchlan Charles Mackinnon (1848-1934) became general manager of the Argus in 1881.

8 November 1883 - Thursday

More racing, of which I have had nearly enough. The Oaks day very bad for backers. Dined at the Club at a large dinner given by the Melbourne Club to the Governor of Tasmania, Sir George Strahan[209], and the Governor of South Australia, Sir Will Robinson[210], and the officers of the 'Nelson'. Sat next to Robertson[211] of Colac, a very nice fellow – a large cattle breeder who was a Varsity oar; and on the other side a horrible cad, Ashbury; formerly member for Brighton. M. Green made a capital speech proposing the guests' health, and Sir W. Robinson responded also very well. After dinner, most of the party including the Brights went to a masqued ball at the Town Hall: a very gay affair from all accounts; but I had a rubber with White[212], who plays very well and is the owner of the Cup winner, and then turned in.

9 November 1883 - Friday

Went with the Brights to an Agricultural Show which is going on in the suburbs. Saw some very fine horses and sheep. We were showing a very ingenious seed-separator for taking oats, peas etc. out of wheat: it does its work beautifully. There was also a large traction engine, screaming and puffing about the ground with Gibbs Bright & Co. in large letters on it, and a large crowd following. Storey, dressed in blue stoker's dress, driving.

10 November 1883 - Saturday

It poured with rain in torrents all last night and this morning, and the 'Yarra' has overflowed its banks, so the steeplechase is put off. Went to the office and arranged for Hannay to go up to Brisbane, and Keating to come down here.

11 November 1883 - Sunday

Still very wet, but cleared up in the afternoon and took a longish walk with the Brights to St. Kilda. R.B.[213] always has someone to dine on Sunday.

---

[209] Major Sir George Cumine Strahan (1838-1887): a military Scot who had just arrived in Hobart in December 1881 and stayed until 1886.
[210] William Cleaver Francis Robinson (1834-1897) had been governor of Western Australia 1875-1877 and 1880-1883 and was governor of South Australia 1883-1889. He was also governor of the Falklands, Prince Edward Island and the Straits Settlement.
[211] William Robertson (1839-1892), a second son who was at Wadham College, Oxford, and 1861 rowed in the winning team against Cambridge. At this time the Robertsons were still the major breeders of shorthorns and Herefords, but as the price of cattle had collapsed they were about to turn to sheep farming.
[212] The Honorable James White (-1890) was the owner of the Derby winner, Martini Henry, the first New Zealand-trained horse, although James White himself had won before. He reputedly built his house - Camelot in Kirkham Land, Elderslie, NSW - on the winners from Chester in 1877. James and his brother Charles were enormously wealthy and not very scrupulous businessmen, who owned Bando Station. He was Member of the Legislative Assembly for Upper Hunter 1864-68, and Member of the Legislative Council 1874-90.
[213] Reginald Bright

Today came a Dr. Ford and his daughter[214], the latter in spectacles and engaged to Matthew Arnold's[215] son[216]; she goes home to be married in a few months. I believe neither family like the match. Also a Miss French and a Mrs Joseph and her daughter, the latter an ordinary Jew girl, but the mother a very handsome white-haired, clever old lady – knew the Laidleys well, and considered GM's[217] wife had been completely spoilt as a girl. Rather fast, and very inferior to him, but much improved since her marriage.

12 November 1883 - Monday

The steeplechases came off in spite of heavy going. After a morning in the office, Regi and I popped down by train: we just missed a railway accident which happened to the train immediately preceding ours. The steeplechase course is fearfully stiff, but quite plain – no water or bush fence or banks or doubles, but great palings, hurdles, post and rails, and log fences ranging from 3 ft 11 to 4 ft 5. There is no galloping through them, and there were several frightful spills – rather a gladiatorial exhibition.

13 November 1883 - Tuesday

We were to have gone to Colac to see a great cattle sale at Robertson's[218] – we were called at 5.30, breakfast at 6.0, and all ready to start for the 7am train; but our cab, which had been ordered, never came so we had nothing to do but walk about in the Botanical Gardens[219] till it was time to go to the office. When I got there I found the mail in, bringing me plenty of letters with lists of deaths and illnesses. Father, Mother, Alban, Miss Clarke, Edith[220] all wrote. In the evening, went to some theatricals given by the Bohemian Club[221]: 'The Squire', a very feeble play still more feebly acted – the most colourless performances I ever saw in my life; the man who played the parson was fair. I think this the very worst type of piece possible, full of drivelling sentimentality and impossible situations. Time: 1 am; scene: the heroine's bedroom, in which is the man who has bigamously married her; enter the bailiff, who kicks up a bobbery. Query from husband, "What entitles you to act as the protector of this lady?" A: "I gathered flowers with her when I was a boy." Query from bailiff, "Is she

---

[214] Frances Ford
[215] Matthew Arnold (1822-1888), the British poet and son of Thomas Arnold, the famed headmaster of Rugby School.
[216] Richard Penrose Arnold (1855-1908), the third but only surviving son. He had emigrated to Melbourne where he worked in a bank but returned to the UK to work as a factory inspector in Manchester. He was an amateur pianist and a friend of Elgar, and his 'distinctive laugh' is in the Enigma Variations.
[217] George Merivale.
[218] The Robertson cattles sales were annual events, and some of the catalogues survive.
[219] The Melbourne Botanical Gardens opened in 1846, and under William Robert Guilfoyle from 1873 had been landscaped to be picturesque as well as including non-native species.
[220] Edith Caroline Gibbs, Vicary's sister.
[221] The Bohemian Club, then in Russell Street, later in Collins Street.

your wife?" Answer, evasive and unsatisfactory, "She is my wife before God." Q. "Is she your wife before the Law?" A. "No" – "Then look out!" Double-barrel scatter gun pointed. Lady screams, faints, and the audience laugh a little and look ashamed and uncomfortable. Perhaps with real genius and delicate handling the public might stand this sort of thing, but why in thunder anyone should play them when there exist real comedies like 'London Assurance'[222] or 'The Heir at Law'[223] or 'Masks and Faces'[224] or 'The Porters Knot'[225] passes my persimmon.

14 November 1883 - Wednesday

The 'Ramsay'[226] is a total loss with all the Amby wool on board: well insured – a good thing for us – but I fear the poor Captain is lost.

15 November 1883 - Thursday

Working at the Code[227] with Hannay all day, and dined with him at the Club. Wrote to Herbert, and walked home to St. Leonards. Everybody else went to a grand ball at the Town Hall given by Sir Wm. Clarke[228]. I get a lot of invitations to dances, owing to the Brights being such dancing men. All the other colonials have now left Melbourne, and the Club has now settled down into its normal condition. I can only be an honorary member for 6 months.

27. Reginald Bright as a young man - one of the "dancing men" to whom Gibbs refers (c1873-8) *State Library of Victoria, H2011.176/25*

16 November 1883 - Friday

The mail went, and I was busy writing letters.

---

[222] 'London Assurance' by Dion Boucicault (1820-1890), first performed in 1841.
[223] 'The Heir at Law' by George Colman, first played in 1797.
[224] 'Masks and Faces' by Charles Reade (1814-1884) and Tom Taylor (1817-1880), first performed 1852.
[225] 'The Porters Knot' by John Oxenford (1812-1877), first played in 1858.
[226] Ramsay: a barque of 821 tons, owned by J. R. Harpe. Built in 1863 and registered at London on 31 October 1883. Lost off Elizabeth Reef, Coral Sea, on a voyage from Brisbane to London.
[227] The Code: a cipher used for "Private Series" (usually referred to as "PS") communications between Houses.
[228] Sir Willliam John Clarke (1831-1897), born in Tasmania. Managed his family estates in Victoria in 1874, and was the largest landowner in the colony. Encouraged scientific farming and local defence forces. He was a noted social entertainer and philanthropist, and a memorial to him was designed by sculptor Sir Bertram Mackennal in 1902 and is in the Treasury Gardens, Melbourne.

17 November 1883 - Saturday

Went to a cricket match in the afternoon with Hannay, and Portman, a young officer on the 'Nelson'. He is a nephew of Lord Portman, and knows several Dorsetshire friends of mine: Long, Paget and Floyer among others. We saw an innings of the giant Bonner[229]: he made one enormous hit on to the pavilion roof.

18 November 1883 - Sunday

The Brights left yesterday afternoon to stay till Monday with Ryan[230]. A beautiful, warm day, most of which I spent in the garden reading Froude 'Henry VIII'. Hannay dined with me and we had a pleasant evening: he related a great many of his Ceylon experiences – big game shooting, etc. – of which he has had a good deal. I like him, and shall be sorry to part with him.

19 November 1883 - Monday

Hannay left today for Sydney, en route for Brisbane.

20 November 1883 - Tuesday

Took my passage in the 'Ballarat'. Had 2 teeth stopped by a New York dentist: he appeared to do them very well. Charles Bright has decided to leave on 20th Dec for England via Calcutta.

21 November 1883 - Wednesday

Had 4 more teeth stopped, and decided to postpone my visit to Adelaide as there is some possibility of my having to go up to Brisbane to look at a site they are very anxious to buy for Wharfage accommodation.

22 November 1883 - Thursday

Just as well I put off going to Adelaide, as I have got a slight attack of gout in the right hand. Had another tooth stopped, which completes the necessary dental repairs for the present. The man charged £11, which seems a good lot, but there was a good lot to do for the money.

23 November 1883 - Friday

Another holiday: Separation Day from New South Wales – of all senseless things to rejoice at, being the opportunity of making a frontier and establishing tariffs and protective duties. I never heard of such a place as

---

[229] George John Bonnor (1855-1912). A 6'6" Australian cricketer renowned for the strength of his throwing and batting.

[230] Charles Ryan (1818-1898), an Irish overlander and one of the pastoral pioneers, who had arrived in Australia in 1840 and who had founded the stock and station firm of Ryan and Hammond at Derriweit Heights, Victoria. Gibbs later meets Ryan and some of his family.

this for holidays; they seem to be always coming. The Brights and I spent the morning in the office, but the clerks were all gone playing an annual cricket match against Henty's[231]. A man named Francis, who is an old friend of the Brights and has a son – a clerk in the office – had a paralytic stroke today in the Club. I should fear it's a bad business.

24 November 1883 - Saturday

A pleasant and grateful letter from G. Merivale, accepting the terms of a 3 years agreement which fixes him satisfactorily. Dined at the Club and played Whist.

25 November 1883 - Sunday

Have read lately a clever, posthumous work of Nathanial Hawthorne, 'Dr Grimshaws Secret', published by his son, Julian H. It is like all Hawthorne's books: full of a sort of suggestion of the supernatural. It has some very fine bits in it, and is interesting, but it is fidgeting to read, being very incompletely worked out. I have also read 'The Waters of Marah': rather clever, very cynical, immoral, disagreeable, and stuffed full of Shakespearian quotations. A Dr. Fitzgerald[232] dined here with his wife, a pleasant lady: he is the leading Doctor and Surgeon in Melbourne, and has an enormous practice – principally operations. He nearly killed his wife by injecting sulphuric acid under her skin instead of morphia when she was ill one night. Luckily for him, his practice is well-established, or such a mistake would have frightened away his clients. The Melbourne Coroner, a gentlemanly old party named Candler[233], also dined.

26 November 1883 - Monday

Absolument rien.

---

[231] James Henty and Company, of Melbourne. The firm were competitors of Gibbs Bright, but were obviously on good terms as this annual friendly cricket match shows. Much more recently, in 1981, both James Henty and Co. and Gibbs Bright were merged into HSBC.
[232] Sir Thomas Naghten FitzGerald (1838-1908). Gibbs dined in his carriage at the Melbourne races on 3rd November 1883, but this sounds like the first time he actually met him.
[233] Samuel Curtis Candler (1827-1911). Candler lived at the Melbourne Club for more than 50 years, as described in his diaries which are now in La Trobe library. He was actually coroner of Burke county in 1883, not becoming that of Melbourne until his friend and colleague Dr. Richard Youl (see 28th November 1883) died in 1897. He fathered four children from 1872-77 by Laura Kennedy, but did not marry her until 1882 when her uncle became a member of the Melbourne club. Even so, the marriage was kept secret and Laura finally went off to Rhodesia with the children and with Candler's diary, which was not returned to La Trobe until 1973.

27 November 1883 - Tuesday

The mail came in, bringing letters from Mother, Edith, Alban, Herbert and Tyndall. Deaths: Sir Arthur Elton[234], and the Romanis' baby – [GREEK][235].

28. Greek text from 27 November 1883

28 November 1883 - Wednesday

In the evening, Sir Wm. Clarke and his wife and daughter, and Dr. Youll[236] – a cynical, rather amusing old fellow – came to dinner; his daughter was married this morning. A sister of Lady Clarke's also dined, rejoicing in the euphonious name of Snodgrass. Lady C.[237] was a handsome, agreeable woman. Sir Wm. silent with a shy nervous manner as if he drank. The daughter bright and rather pretty; engaged to Sutton Tylecote[238]. Either her dress was dyed, or she would have been better for a reckless expenditure in tar soap. We had grouse for dinner, from England: just as good and fresh as any I have ever tasted; also mackerel, which I should have thought not worth the bother of sending.

---

[234] Sir Arthur Hallam Elton (1818-1883), 7th Baronet, a writer and politician (briefly Liberal MP for Bath). He lived at the family mansion of Cleveland Court in Taunton, Somerset, about 45 miles from the Gibbs' home in Tyntesfield, and was the father of Beatrice Gibbs. He died on 4th October 1883.

[235] Greek: "Death is held to be the most powerful cure for misfortunes". We could not find the source of this quotation.

[236] Dr. Richard Youl (1821-1897) was the Melbourne coroner from 1854-1897, replacing his predecessor William Byam Wilmot who had been the first ever Melbourne coroner. Born in Tasmania (Van Diemen's Land at the time), Youl had studied medicine at Paris, St. Andrews and London. He was a prominent figure in colonial society and introduced formal medico-legal procedure, including a post-mortem in every case. Youl remained in the post until a few days before his death in 1897, and was then replaced by his friend and colleague Samuel Curtis Candler. His wife Sarah Ann Jane ("Annie") (née Martin) had died of Bright's Disease in 1881.

[237] Lady Clarke (1851-1909) was born Janet Snodgrass and became Sir William Clarke's second wife in 1873. She was noted as a social hostess and for her service to the people of Melbourne, and there is a rotunda to her in the Queen Victoria gardens. She was a member of many charitable societies. She helped to organise the Women's Work Exhibition in 1907. Clarke's influence was such that she became the first president of the National Council of Women of Victoria in 1902, and of the Australian Women's National League in 1904.

[238] Tylecote did not actually marry Clarke's daughter (see later in the diary).

29 November 1883 - Thursday

Old Ryan, the station agent whose daughter[239] married Lord Charles Scott[240], dropped in to breakfast; horridly deaf, but not a bad sort otherwise. Regi has an old poodle named Mouton who has had its hind leg broken, and flaps about just like Brag does with his fore leg. Charles dined at Government House, and Regi and I decided – as nothing particular was going on – I would make another try to get down to Adelaide in the 'Sorata'[241].

S.S. Sorata

30 November 1883 - Friday

We dined at the club, and came back to the office after dinner to finish off for the Mail. At 11 o'clock, I said goodbye to the Brights and went down with the shipping clerk by train to the tender. It was a rough, dirty night and the tide – and some bad steering – got us under the quarter of a big American ship, from which he had some bother to get clear. However, in the end we reached the 'Sorata' all right, and I at once turned in.

1 December 1883 - Saturday

As everyone prognosticated very rough weather, it is pleasant to find exactly the reverse. I was kept awake a little last night by some horrid cats who had got on board at Williamstown and kept up a demoniacal caterwauling quite close to my cabin. We started about 1 am: only about 14 1st Class passengers, but there are never many going home at this time of year. I was surprised to recognise the Doctor[242] – the same who was on board the 'Galicia' when I went down to Bordeaux; he of course did not know me and stated, as his reason, that I had looked so frightfully ill then and so particularly well now! He told me a lot of curious stories about young Charles Bath, who was my fag at Yonges[243] and who went out with Charles Lambert this last time for the benefit of his health. It seems that CB remained in Santiago, while Mr. Lambert went up country and, having nothing to do and having his stomach out of order, worked himself into an hypochondriacal and partially insane state. He was under Dr. Cooper's

---

[239] Ada Mary Ryan (1855-1943), the fourth child (second daughter) of Charles Ryan. She married Admiral Lord Sir Charles Thomas Montagu Douglas Scott on 23 February 1883.
[240] Admiral Lord Sir Charles Thomas Montagu Douglas Scott (1839-1911), commander of HMS Bacchante from 1879 and HMS Agincourt from 1885. In 1889 he was made Commander of the Australia Station, the (then British) naval command responsible for the waters around Australia.
[241] 'Sorata': Built at Glasgow in 1872, she made her first appearance in Australian waters in April 1879. The ship had a history of several misadventures.
[242] It is slightly unclear whether Gibbs is meeting Dr. Black or Dr. Cooper here, but it seems more likely that it is Black (and therefore that he was the Galicia's doctor), and that a Dr. Cooper treated Charles Lambert 'up country'.
[243] Yonge's was formerly a House at Eton.

hands for some time, who vainly tried to persuade him that there was nothing the matter; he declined to eat anything, and for 4 months the resources of science were called on to keep him alive in an abnormal way. He telegraphed to Mr. L. to see if he should go home, who seems to have been sick of him and replied that he must use his own judgement – in his state of mind about the worst thing he could use. At any rate, he sailed in the 'Galicia' along with Black, and seems to have worried the Doctor's life out with his fancies and nonsense. He looked on himself as immediately about to die, and would offer to bet the doctor he wouldn't live a week. He drew up a document to this effect, "I, Charles Bath, being of sound mind (!!) and about to die, do solemnly desire that a post mortem be held on my body and that the stomach and its contents be sent to Dr Cooper and any other physicians who have attended me, to show that my view and not theirs is correct." He seems to have been convinced that all food he ate remained in him without undergoing any alteration. It must have been partly sham, for he would go to the pantry sometimes – unknown to the doctor – and eat ravenously, afterwards coming imploring for an emetic[244]. Mrs Lambert and Mrs Bath met him at Lisbon, and what state of mind and body he may be in now I don't know.

Adelaide

Adelaide pleased Vicary Gibbs as it still pleases so many visitors today. He found the use of the local white stone gave a feeling of light and space so often commented on. It was a contrast to Sydney's 'drab, brown stone' buildings closely gathered around, behind and above the water-front in those days. Vicary had found that the even darker blue-black buildings of Melbourne did not live up to the promise of the city's wide streets.

Met by the manager of the Adelaide office, Vicary Gibbs had been drawn immediately into the local situation. Alfred Meeks was keenly involved in his role. He had set up the Adelaide branch and his energy and enthusiasm already promised his future success. The diary often holds an initial critical comment, which is later set aside to make room for more mature appraisal. Meeks' education and background would seem to Vicary very different from his own, but he certainly recognised a safe pair of hands and praised them; Alfred Meeks' pleasant, deferential manner had earned him an advocate, but Vicary underestimated Meeks' business acumen.

Alfred Meeks had arrived from England as a small boy, in 1854, with his family. He first trained as book-keeper to local merchants, and in 1873 married a cousin who had also emigrated from Cheltenham in Gloucestershire. With the company of Bright Bros. he worked his way

---

[244] Bath was probably suffering from the condition now known as Bulimia.

quickly up to departmental manager and was sent from Melbourne to Adelaide to establish the new branch of Gibbs, Bright and Co. there, not long before Vicary Gibbs' visit. Alfred Meeks was able to diversify the expanded business. In a short time he had also risen to the position of Chairman of the local Chamber of Commerce. He made steady progress upwards in society and onwards into many business directorships, extending his expertise into Banking and Insurance and eventually into liberal politics. After Vicary Gibbs returned to Britain there was further reorganisation of senior management in the Australian Company. It was then, in 1888, that Alfred Meeks moved to Sydney to become the Senior Partner of GB&Co. They had found the ideal forward-looking leader for the Australian enterprise who would go on to earn his national recognition with a Knighthood in the honours of 1920. Alice Meeks shared her husband's interests and social conscience and contributed much to their partnership. The Meeks' tragedy was one they shared with so many other loyal Commonwealth citizens: their son Victor was injured at Gallipoli and died in 1926.

The report on progress in Adelaide was good. In Melbourne there was news from Sydney of the good year anticipated but also of the urgent need for more spacious accommodation; all this would be added to Meeks' achievements in Adelaide and sent back to Alban Gibbs at the London House. Frank Keating had arrived from Sydney to discuss South American business and his own future, and Murray reported on the practicalities of the overcrowded offices. There was much to occupy Vicary and it would entail serious application of his diplomatic skills. He had to juggle with personnel, depriving Hart of Keating and changing him for Hannay, knowing that the Brights had no wish to exchange Hannay for Keating. Charles Bright would have little say in the matter as he was leaving for England, but Regi would be without his brother and ally and knew that Keating was always Gibbs' man. In this atmosphere Vicary had to keep silent during an unpleasant exchange between the two brothers - who had completely different temperaments - in the knowledge that many more difficult decisions would have to be made as company restructuring continued.

Wool stores had to be inspected in Melbourne, and farmers questioned as the possibilities of increasing AG&S's share of the Australian wool trade with Europe were weighed up and conclusions shared with London.

2 December 1883 - Sunday

The Captain, Dixon by name, is a gentlemanly, pleasant chap. I had a long chat with him last night, and he gave me an excellent cigar. He told me that Capt. Brough – who took Herbert out in the 'Britannia' – had been dismissed: too much given to wine, cards and other irregularities. I have been reading Froude's 'Short Studies on Great Subjects': all very readable, and some very good – his anti-ritualistic and anti-Catholic feeling continually cropping up. Also read a great deal of Motley's 'Dutch Republic': very well written and all that, but hardly looking at it enough from the Spanish point of view, to which the Dutch must have seemed simply rebels. The cruelties of Philip and Alba become too sickening to read, even at this distance of time.

3 December 1883 - Monday

We anchored a little before 7 last night, and Meeks[245] came on board. We walked up and down the deck for an hour, talking business; he is an energetic, keen, talkative little man with pleasant manners, very fair hair and beard – about 36 years old I should say. We took the train to go from the Port to Adelaide, but Meeks was so excited relating his plans and ideas about business that he omitted to change, and as it was the last train on Sunday night we found ourselves 8 miles from the City on a little dark platform with no prospect of getting on – however, in the end we got a buggy and arrived about midnight at the Adelaide Club, where I got a bedroom all right. This morning, I had some cold wild Turkey for breakfast, which was very good – something like wild duck, only better. After breakfast, I went down to the office, which is capitally situated exactly in the heart of the city; it has the appearance of a private house outside, and indeed has been a bachelor's residence. It is comfortable, but in a short time will be too small for the business; there are four clerks. I have had a very busy day, as Meeks had been shelving several things in anticipation of my arrival, and using me as 'Jorkins'[246] – "You had better speak to our Mr Gibbs", and that sort of thing. I dined at the Club, and met two or three men whom I had seen in Melbourne. The Club is a comfortable, well-arranged house, smaller than Melbourne, but I like it as well, and the members are very sociable and the average, I think, more gentlemanly than the Melbourne men. Young Fenwick – the son of the Hertfordshire man – is staying here, and is contemplating settling in the Colonies.

---

[245] Sir Alfred William Meeks (1849-1932). Son of a shoe-maker who had emigrated to Australia in 1854. He became manager of a department of Bright Bros. and Co. after training as an accountant. In 1882, he went to Adelaide to establish a branch of Gibbs, Bright & Co. and was instrumental in expanding the business. A few years from now, in 1888, he would move to Sydney and become the senior resident partner. He was knighted in 1920.
[246] Jorkins: a reference to a character from David Copperfield by Charles Dickens.

4 December 1883 - Tuesday

29. King William Street, Adelaide (c1880)
State Library of South Australia, B62414/1/22

An exceedingly long and worrying day in business with some people called Winham[247] who have been inclined to break their agreement with us, and have got involved in temporary difficulties through speculating. I had to take them up very sharp indeed, and we had quite a breeze. I was in the office from 9.30 to 11pm, with only a short interval for dinner, and feel very gouty and knocked up. At dinner I met a man named Brown – a very nice fellow whom I knew at Christ Church[248] and have not seen since; his hair is quite grey, but then he tells me he has a wife and three children. He wanted me to go out and stay with him, and I should have liked to, but can't well spare the time. I like this place very much; King William Street, the main thoroughfare, is on the whole the finest place I have seen in the Colonies. The place has greater natural advantages than Melbourne, and finer built than Sydney. The local stone is white, which makes everything bright – and indeed glaring – and is a great contrast to the hideous blue-black of Melbourne and the brown stone of Sydney.

5 December 1883 - Wednesday

As I expected, in bed with gout in right hand after a bad night, but not much pain; awfully dull: no books but a most trashy novel by Florence Marryatt. She talks of a man being "coerced in his mind" – meaning thereby, "troubled". The secretary was civil and attentive, a retired sea-dog, having been purser on a P&O. When I asked him how he liked sea life he replied "that the man who would go to sea for pleasure would go to hell for a pastime". Meeks in and out pretty often, but I was hardly up to talking business with him to any purpose. I never saw such fine cherries in my life as they have here: perfectly beautiful to look at.

6 December 1883 - Thursday

Still in my room with gout, but it is passing off. Hart, whom I met in Melbourne when I was seedy, called and chatted for a long time very pleasantly ("may his tribe increase"). He was full of the insolence and

---

[247] There were some established Adelaide wheat and grain merchants named Winhams who are referred to in several of Gibbs' letters as causing AG&S some problems - in one letter, Gibbs reports that Winhams have run up debts and needed a loan of £8,000 from AG&S. Gibbs feels that Winhams are worthy of supporting as they have plenty of capital, albeit tied up in steamers, land, etc.
[248] Christ Church, a college in Oxford University, sometimes known as The House.

caddishness of the young Chamberlains[249]; their conduct seems to have made a great impression in Adelaide. I got hold of a copy of Bret Harte's poems – some very good, besides the well known ones. 'The Hawk's Nest', for instance; "Peter's brother leadin'" is a good touch in the account of the chase after the slayer of Monsieur Pierre. Directly he gets off life in the Western States he is feeble to a degree. The letter from the 'Belle of the Ball' is as good as anything of Mackworth Praed. Had a long go with Meeks in the evening; shall be all right tomorrow, I hope.

7 December 1883 - Friday

30. Jennie Lee (with J.P. Burnett?) (1885)
State Library of Victoria, H10157

The gout all right again for the time. Drove all round the town, and down to North Adelaide in a train after breakfast with Major Dowling – in command of the 'Nelson'[250] marines. All the 'Nelson' officers are in and out of the Club here, and very pleasant fellows most of them. I went round calling on the various bank managers and merchants with Meeks. Saw Sir Thomas Elder[251], a rum old Scotch man with dyed hair, and others. After dinner, went with Dr Nott of the 'Nelson' to see part of 'Jo'. Jenny Lee[252] as clever as ever – the other actors and actresses neither better nor worse than when I saw it in Liverpool. Afterwards, in the Club, a lot of young fellows who had been playing polo sang and played the banjo, and fooled around in the smoking room till pretty late. Very cheery chaps – much like a rowdy Oxford lot at a wine.

---

[249] We wondered at first whether this referred to the future Sir (Joseph) Austen Chamberlain (1863-1937) and his younger half-brother the future Prime Minister (Arthur) Neville Chamberlain (1869-1940). Their father, Joseph Chamberlain (1836-1914), was President of the Board of Trade in Gladstone's Second Government (1880-5). However, Neville and Austen would have been only 14 and 20 at the time (not being elected to Parliament until 1911 and 1892 respectively), so it seems unlikely.
[250] 'Nelson': One of the British navy ships stationed in Australia at that time.
[251] Sir Thomas Elder (1818-1897). Scottish by birth, he had come to Adelaide in 1854 to join the family firm and then set up a company (Elder, Stirling & Co.) with his brother-in-law Robert Barr Smith (1824-1915) and with Edward Stirling and John Taylor. They financed copper mines and built up a huge pastoral empire. He was an eccentric bachelor and a major philanthropist, and notably introduced camels and Shropshire sheep to Australia.
[252] Jennie Lee (1858-1930), an actress well-known at the time for regularly playing Jo the crossing-sweeper in "Jo", the play by her husband J.P. Burnett which he adapted from Dickens' Bleak House. Lee played Jo from 1875, and continued playing the part for 20 years. Gibbs meets Jenny Lee on his sea voyage to Ceylon later (see 24th November 1884), referring to her as 'Jo'.

8 December 1883 - Saturday

Have seen a good deal of Fenwick – not a bad sort, but rather a lout and overdressed; a case of not such a fool as he looks. I went to the office in the morning, and then Meeks and I drove to his house: a pretty little crib with a beautiful view over the hills at the back. I paid my respects to Mrs. M.[253], a vulgar little brown colonial; enquired after their little girl, and complimented them on their little boy[254], and made myself as pleasant as I could. They had asked me to dinner, but owing first to my gout and then to the illness of their little girl – who they fear may be sickening with a fever – it won't come off: which is a good thing, as it would have been a bore. Drove off with Meeks up the hills to a place called the 'Eagle on the Hill'[255] on the way to Mount Lofty; a very pretty drive through the country, though rather burnt up. Back to dinner at the Club, and played Ecarté with Le Patourel, Lord Normanby's[256] ADC; and so to bed.

S.S. Shannon

9 December 1883 - Sunday

Had a cup of tea early in my bedroom; paid bill, and took train from Victoria Square down to the harbour. Went on board the 'Shannon'[257] about 9.30 am. She is a splendid P&O boat built in '81; the saloon forward, and the whole width of the ship lined with white and grey marble – very handsome. She is cram full, as all incoming boats are at this time. I applied for a berth back directly I got to Adelaide, but was told it was quite hopeless. However, on Friday a clerk came into the office applying for an insurance place, and said he should want a week as he had taken a berth on the 'Shannon'. I got him to take my berth on the 'Iberia' 3 days later instead, as I want to get back to read my mail letters which are on board. I share my cabin with a man named Edwards[258] and a smart looking young Jew. It's no use attempting to make acquaintance with my fellow passengers, who have been together so long and whom I shall only see for 3 days. There is a Sir Edward Strickland, whom I have met before, but he is such a disgusting feeder I can't do with him. I have attacked the

---

[253] Alice Freeman (-1932), Sir Alfred Meek's cousin, was the English-born daughter of a bootmaker from Cheltenham. They were married on 14 October 1873 at Richmond. Alice died a few months after Alfred, on 21 July 1932, at their home in Darling Point.

[254] Victor, the only son of Alfred and Alice Meeks, later served with the light horse on Gallipoli and died in 1926. In 1930, Alfred and Alice gave a small hospital to the Boy Scouts' Association in his memory.

[255] 'Eagle on the Hill': Now in a quiet Adelaide suburb, but at the time the hotel was well known.

[256] Lord Normanby: His Excellency the Marquis of Normanby, Governor of Victoria.

[257] The 'Shannon': She made regular trips from London to India until 1901 when she was scrapped in Bombay.

[258] Probably Frederick Lewis Edwards (1828-1906), a law stationer and book-seller who joined forces with Philip Dunlop to form Edwards, Dunlop & Co. Ltd., paper merchants and wholesale stationers. Gibbs is to shortly find out that Edwards is a competitor.

ship's library, which is above the average. Read Froude's book on Bunyan in the Morley series: rather interesting, as I knew next to nothing about the life of 'Mr Badman' or the 'Holy War'. I also read a feeble life of Voltaire by Mrs Oliphant[259]: nothing in it worth reading which is not in Carlyle. This led me to read again his Miscellaneous Essays: Burns, German playwrights, Voltaire etc. published about 1821. I like them very much, far better than his later work when he had his head and free rein to play what cantrips[260], as to matter and manner, he liked. The table is very good on board – my waiter a Portuguese coolie from Goa.

10 December 1883 - Monday

Weather very calm. The man, Edwards, in my cabin is a sort of religious fanatic who has put on the whole armour of low church controversial works. He rather fastened on me; a vulgar dog, he is our principal opponent in Sydney in the wholesale paper business. He has been spending his time on the voyage in the unprofitable task of trying to convert the little Jew boy. I read about ¼ of 'The Cloister and the Hearth': the 15th century seen through Reade's 19th century spectacles is too thin. A Burgundian soldier expressing the modern views on bleeding etc., and the impertinent and continued introduction of Ch. Reade's own personality, are too much. It wants Scott or G. Eliot to make antique historical romance anything better than a masquerade. And even then, 'Jeanie Deans'[261] and 'Adam Bede'[262] are miles in front of 'Ivanhoe'[263] and 'Romola'[264]. It's the last night on board, and people are in the usual effusive state after a 7 weeks voyage. There was a presentation of a purse and testimonial to the Captain after dinner, and a fearfully bad speech to which the nautical hero replied in a very manly sensible fashion. Health drinking and general enthusiasm to finish.

---

[259] Margaret Oliphant (née Wilson) (1828-1897), born near Edinburgh. She married her cousin Francis Oliphant, an artist. When he died in 1859, she - like several other women writers of the time - provided for her family by becoming one of the most popular and prolific novelists of the century. By 1899, the year in which she published her autobiography, she had joined other respected members of this Scottish writing family in writing many works of non-fiction, history and literary criticism. Margaret's cousin, Laurence Oliphant, is another of the authors Gibbs read on his trip (see 7 September 1883); he was the son of Sir Anthony Oliphant, whose Oliphant Tea Estate Gibbs visits whilst in Ceylon (see 6 January 1885).
[260] Cantrips: magic spells, chanting, etc.
[261] Jeanie Deans is a character in "The Heart of Midlothian" by Sir Walter Scott.
[262] "Adam Bede", the first novel by George Eliot (the pseudonym of Mary Ann Evans).
[263] "Ivanhoe", by Sir Walter Scott.
[264] "Romola", by George Eliot.

Melbourne (2)

11 December 1883 - Tuesday

Went through the heads at daylight, and alongside the wharf about 7, but were kept messing about for 3 hours – the hawser breaking and so on. I went straight to the office and found Keating, who had arrived by sea from Sydney the day before; he looked brown and thin, but otherwise all right. He dined with Merivale and found him very pleasant, but thought his wife a 'spoilt child' and didn't care for her. Talking all day about Brisbane and Adelaide business. Regi dined out, and Keating came to dinner. Charles in high good humour at the near prospect of his return to *placens uxor*[265]. Heard from Father, Mother, Herbert and Alban: pretty good accounts.

12 December 1883 - Wednesday

Began a long letter to Alban. Murray turned up, and we talked over Sydney premises. They are going to have a good year in Sydney. After business, I walked a long time in the gardens with Frank, and back to St. Leonards where Murray came to dinner: very amusing and naïve, giving us his account of how he had been promised by the premier a seat in the Legislative Council and then been passed over – the premier insinuating, whether truly or not, that his name had been dropped out at the instance of the Governor, who was offended with Murray. I expect Murray's support of that blackguard Thersites McElhone[266] stood in his way.

13 December 1883 - Thursday

Woke up feeling gouty in the left foot. Read some odes of Horace before breakfast, which I have taken to doing lately but have got pretty rusty. I drove into the office instead of walking; had a long jaw with Given, and finished letter to Alban. Walked with Keats and hobbled back. Regi had a dinner party – Dr Ryan[267] and Mrs R.[268] The former had been through the Russo-Turkish campaign, and distinguished himself; his wife very nearly very handsome, – but fainted during dinner in consequence of the jessamine smell. Robert Power[269], a stock and station agent, and his

---

[265] *Placens Uxor* (Latin): The comfort of his wife.
[266] Thersites McElhone (1833-1898), MP for Upper Hunter, known at the time as a political maverick.
[267] Although Gibbs may not have been aware of it, this is very probably Major General Sir Charles Snodgrass Ryan (1853-1926), the second son and third child of Charles Ryan (station agent of Derriweit Heights, Victoria) and his wife Marian. Sir Charles Ryan is known to have served in the Russo-Turkish campaign of 1877-78, as Gibbs mentions. He later went on to become a surgeon for the Royal Melbourne Hospital from 1878 to 1913.
[268] Alice Elfrida Ryan (née Sumner), whom Sir Charles Snodgrass Ryan married on 5th July 1883.
[269] Robert Power (1834-1914), born in Ireland, founded Powers Rutherford and Co. Also one of the original founders of the Victoria Racing Club, and was himself an amateur rider – once rode in the Melbourne steeplechase. He married twice. The name of the first wife is

wife[270] – both agreeable; and a Mr Lumley Hill[271], a Queensland man, a connection of the Miles Tyndalls and Tom Hill. He told us an extraordinary story of one of his men being cut off by the floods, and being 10 days up a tree without food! I was so seedy with gout I could barely get through dinner, and as soon as Mrs Power joined the faint heart in the drawing room I retired to delight myself with bicarb., blue pill, etc. in my bedroom, greatly fearing for the morrow – which is mail day.

14 December 1883 - Friday

The 'Orient'[272] Mail went today. Dined at the Club with Keating, Westby, and Forrest[273], who was formerly a partner in Moreheads, Brisbane, – a pleasant chap. Went back to the office after dinner with K. to finish the 'Cuzcos'[274] business; the Brights dined out.

15 December 1883 - Saturday

Walked to St. Kilda with K., and spent afternoon sitting on the sea shore eating cherries. Dined at the Club, and had a rubber with Sullivan[,] Greig and Lumley Hill.

16 December 1883 - Sunday

Keating and Storey came to dinner: it's a pity the latter is so uneducated – or rather, not educated at all; his spelling and writing are about on a par with Spacey's. Otherwise, he is gentlemanly enough, and very hard-working. Read 'Through One Administration'[275]: I like it well enough, and it is clever, but not so attractive as 'That Lass o' Lowries', and 'Louisiana'. I bought two cockatoos, Corellas, the same breed as the dear departed at St. Dunstans[276], to replace him. They are very tame but no conversation as yet. I shall get them home in a sailing ship.

---

unknown, but produced two daughters: Mary Elizabeth (who married Captain Alan Thomas of the Royal Navy) and Kathleen Maud (who married Archibald (Archie) Campbell MacLaren, the English cricketer, in 1898). The second marriage was to Harret Maria Ffrench (1847-1938), daughter of Mr. Acheson Ffrench, a station owner in the western district. That marriage produced a single child, Herbert.

[270] This could be either the first or the second Mrs Power.
[271] Charles Lumley Hill (1840-1909), often referred to as Mr Lumley Hill, migrated to Australia in 1863. He managed and owned several sheep stations. He was prominent in measures to suppress the aboriginal population. He later became a politician in Australia.
[272] The 'Orient': The Orient Line was a British-owned shipping line which AG&S were seriously interested in obtaining.
[273] William Forrest (1805-1903), was born in Ireland and emigrated to Australia in 1853. Forrest knew Frederic Hart and his brother Graham Lloyd Hart, the solicitor, at whose funeral he is listed in the congregation in 1897.
[274] Gibbs presumably means Cusco (or Cuzco), Peru: and therefore this must be some reference to AG&S's South American business.
[275] Through One Administration (1881). A novel by Frances Hodgson Burnett
[276] St. Dunstan's, Regents Park. The London residence of the Gibbs family.

17 December 1883 - Monday

Two letters came from Herbert and Mother, which have been to 'Frisco, Auckland, Dunedin, Melbourne, Adelaide and back, having taken 75 days getting to me. Nothing very important except the suggestion of my visiting Mexico, which I should have much liked. Hart writes, grumbling at Hannay being substituted for Keating, and the Brights are equally discontented at having K. instead of H.; however it can't be helped. The wife of the Captain of the 'John O'Gaunt' has promised to take charge of the Cockies.

18 December 1883 - Tuesday

Talked to a man named Christison[277] nearly all day about Frozen Meat. Dined at a little French eating house called 'The Maison Dorée' with F.A.K.[278] Very nice light dinner.

19 December 1883 - Wednesday

Went out in the afternoon to see a large traction engine of ours perform before some people who are thinking of buying it: it did its work very well, but twice set the grass on fire which is a serious drawback – they will have to make some wire gauze receiver for catching the sparks. Dined again at the 'Maison Dorée' with Keats[279], and afterwards in the Club where they were playing whist. They disputed about some point of a card being dropped, and appealed to me to decide, agreeing that what I said should be final. I tried to get out of arbitrating, but couldn't. A man named Webster, who I decided against, was extraordinarily insolent, and afterwards sent me a written apology!

20 December 1883 - Thursday

Charles Bright left this morning in the 'Rome'. Went to the Public Gallery again, and had a good look at their pictures: they have a lovely large sea piece of 'Rotterdam' by James Webb[280], and E. Long's 'Esther'[281] is very beautiful and grows on one. There is also a clever picture by a Frenchman[282] 'Le Dernier Etape de Coco': a cheap jack's horse having fallen

---

[277] Robert Christison (1837-1915), a Scottish migrant. In 1881, Christison became interested in the frozen meat trade and went to London to form the Australian Company Limited, which was granted a lease at Poole Island near Bowen in northern Queensland. In 1883, frozen meat export was a very recent development, and this was the first company to export from Queensland. However, a cyclone devastated the area on 30 January 1884 and the company did not recover.
[278] Frank A. Keating
[279] Frank A. Keating
[280] James Webb (1825-1895)
[281] Edwin Long (1829-1891). The painting of Queen Esther is still in the National Gallery of Victoria.
[282] Pierre-Marie Beyle (1838-1902). "La Derniere Étape de Coco" (The last resting place of Coco) was painted in 1878.

dead, the woman on her knees, and the dog thoughtfully smelling him – clever. A very powerful picture, also by a Frenchman, represents an old ewe bleating and standing over a dead lamb in the snow with a ring of old crows all round, waiting to eat it. It is painful but the colours are wonderfully managed; there is nothing but whites and blacks yet it is not staring.

21 December 1883 - Friday

Up to Club for lunch. Dined alone with Reg. – both of us overslept in our chairs after dinner till 3am. Very stormy weather; Charles will have a rough time down to Adelaide. FAK and RB[283] don't get on at all cordially in business; they are very uncongenial, and RB's cheery and boisterous, not to say blatant, insistence on the shallowest worldly maxims – such as that 'everybody is actuated by self interest alone' – irritate K. to frenzy. R.B. is like T.B.[284], only untempered by the sweet uses of adversity. He was very rude – indeed unwarrantably so – to K. in my presence the other day, but I kept still silence, though it was pain and grief to me; no doubt I shook my head paralytically. I believe it to be a Bright effort to protect himself from any interference now Charles has gone.

22 December 1883 - Saturday

I had hoped to have got away for 3 days' rabbiting, but it has fallen through. Lunched with Clough, who was on the 'City of New York' with me: quiet, pleasant fellow. He tells me that Raymond, who was on the steamer, has turned out a regular swindler: borrowing money right and left, cashing cheques with no effects, and has now bolted with the detectives after him. It's a wonder he didn't let me in, for I saw a lot of him on board. Dined at the Club and went with Regi to Lecoq's 'Manola'. Too much talking, too little singing and dancing. The birdsong pretty, and one or two good jokes and puns: 'not really true, only a Venetian blind', 'digest it and digest after it', and so on. Had a couple of rubbers at the Club, and walked home by moonlight.

23 December 1883 - Sunday

Walked over to the Club after breakfast. Read part of a vulgar, trashy book: 'Court Life Below Stairs'[285], Georgian times Had read pretty well all before, better told, in Walpole, Hervey, Johnson etc. Went for a walk with Keats in South Yarra[286] to call on a man named Strahan who was out, and then to Tyler[,][287] Hart's brother-in-law, and found him at dinner. F.A.K. dined at St. Leonards; Regi very pleasant in his own house. He told us that New

---

[283] Reginald Bright
[284] Tyndall Bright
[285] J. F. Molloy:Court Life Below Stairs, or London Under the First Georges 1714-1760
[286] South Yarra is a suburb of Melbourne.
[287] There is no comma in the manuscript, but Gibbs often left out punctuation. This seems to refer to someone named Tyler who was the brother-in-law of Frederic Hart.

Guinea had been discovered 200 years before Christ by a Portuguese, Don Fulano – a time when 'wild in the woods the noble Portugee ran!' I could hardly keep my countenance, but said I should have thought the Phoenicians would have been more active in naval enterprise at that time. The 'Age'[288] yesterday had something about Fox's invectives against Sir Robert Peel, which is not much better.

24 December 1883 - Monday

A public holiday; Keats, Regi and I at the office. Hart has, I am sorry to say, had a very sharp attack of dysentery. I feel anxious about him; his loss would be an unmixed evil.

25 December 1883 - Tuesday

Keats came to lunch, and we three went for a walk to St. Kilda[289]. A perfect day: bright sun, and delicious cool air off the sea. Hundreds of children paddling in the water, and a bright, pretty scene altogether. Reg dined out, and K. and I at the Club, where a fat Englishman lectured Keats and me on the observance of Sunday in England, under the impression that we were Colonials born.

26 December 1883 - Wednesday

Another holiday. Three mails are in, so we came down and spent the morning reading letters; heard from Mother, E.[290] and Herbert. Then Reg went off to the Caulfield Races, and K. and I to see the Cricket match – Victoria v. New South Wales. Murdoch[291] played a splendid innings of 158. Dined at the Club, and read Balzac[292] and watched some fellows playing poker.

27 December 1883 - Thursday

Mackinnon – who came from 'Frisco with me – called. He was very pleasant, and asked me to come up to his father's place for some shooting. Meeks turned up from Adelaide, his little girl having got over her illness (which turned out to be very bad measles). Capt. Conran to dinner: a pleasant, gentlemanly Irishman; he knew poor George[293] and all the West Coast[294] people. An old fellow called Burston also dined, and Meeks – who

---

[288] The Age was a Melbourne newspaper, established in 1854 and still published today.
[289] St. Kilda is a seaside suburb of Melbourne.
[290] "E." is probably Edith Caroline Gibbs, Vicary's sister.
[291] William (Billy) Lloyd Murdoch (1854-1911) was an Australian cricketer. He also captained the Australian team in England in 1880, 1882 and 1884.
[292] Honoré de Balzac (1799-1850)
[293] George Gibbs (1827-1846), son of George Henry Gibbs (1785-1842) and Caroline Crawley, drowned in the River Isis at Cambridge. 'Poor George' was therefore Vicary's uncle.
[294] The family of another branch of the Gibbs who lived around Exeter and Bristol.

behaved well and sustained an unequal conflict with his H's and plurals very nobly.

28 December 1883 - Friday

Candler walked over to breakfast, being led thereto by his devotion to Regi's mulberries, which are very fine. He was full of a row at the Club: the head housemaid, who has been sacked, having made a lot of charges of peculation against the secretary; apparently a true bill, though coming from a very suspected quarter. Mackinnon's father[295] called to see me in the office, but he never said who he was and began at once about shifting a 'Dr. Somebody's' berth from the 'Liguria' to the 'Iberia'; so I, being very busy, asked him to speak to the shipping clerk; he then said the Dr. was 'off his head'. Regi burst in saying he couldn't have any madmen, and asked him if he was the Dr., which suggestion he indignantly rejected. When he was gone one of the clerks told me he was the father of my friend.

29 December 1883 - Saturday

Lunched at the Club after business, and then took the train with Keats to Lillydale, 30 miles up country: a rough, bare township something like a town in the Western States; not very much to look at – a horrible, dusty, hot day with the hot wind blowing very badly. Going down the Domain Road in the morning it was so bad that we had to pull the cab-horse up and walk. There was a perfect wall of dust, so that one couldn't see to drive. After a rough meal, we went out for a walk, and back to our rooms which we had secured in advance because of the crush of holidaymakers.

30 December 1883 - Sunday

Horribly bitten by bugs last night; I remonstrated with the landlady, who first said there were none, and – when I produced an enormous specimen in a tumbler – that I had 'brought them with me'! Finding that the coach did not go, we joined with a man and his wife and took a private carriage through the Yarra flats to Fernshaw, getting there in time for the midday dinner – a heap of people, and a great scramble for bad food. A lovely place, however, with beautiful tree ferns, and well worth coming to see. We walked along the banks of the River Watts and loafed about, as it was pretty hot. After tea, we went a regular walk along a fine gully where we saw the celebrated high trees ranging from 250 to 400 ft high: not at all pretty timber; but the general effect is fine, especially by moonlight, and with the jackasses laughing and screaming, very different to any thing I

---

[295] Daniel Mackinnon (1818-1889), father of Donald Mackinnon, had been born in the Isle of Arran and had made Marida Yallock one of the most famous fattening properties producing shorthorn cattle, hacks and carriage horses. He had Queensland and New Zealand properties. His letters, including some from his sons Donald and James Mackinnon whilst at Oxford and Cambridge, are in the State Library of Victoria.

had seen. When we came back the landlord insisted on smoking his pipe and drinking his whiskey with us. He was screwed, and very amusing. He talked about Shakespeare, sailing ships, his losses, better days, and so on, in a wild jumble. Evidently a clever, well-educated man, but his brain softened by drink. K. and I slept in a sort of bothy[296] – clean and rough.

31 December 1883 - Monday

Our drunken landlord came to our door after we were in bed, proposing that he should come and smoke another pipe with us. I declined with some vigour, and he retired. This morning we were late for the general scramble breakfast, so I had an interview with the pretty daughter of the house in the kitchen, the result of which was a comfortable private meal of fish, eggs and mulberry jam. We walked off to see the raspberry gardens: acres of splendid fruit being gathered and packed in long barrels to send in to Melbourne for jam and vinegar. We were at liberty to eat as many as we liked *gratis*, but having no gaiters[297] did not go in, for fear of black snakes which are numerous and dangerous in the ranges. Then we went on on the coach, in company with an artist and government surveyor named Hall – a well-informed and interesting companion. The scenery was magnificent over the hills to 'Narbethong' (Starvation), but after that – and when the great divide was crossed – it was not so good, as a different variety of gum tree – the Messmate – does not run so big. The drive was a tremendous pull for the horses, and we got out and walked several times – and I was not sorry, as it was very bumpy going over the sleeper laid roads, which they call 'corduroy'. We got to Marysville – about 60 miles from Melbourne – at tea time (everyone dines at the middle of the day up country); it is not so taking a place as Fernshaw, but still very fine; the hotel cram full. K. and I got a little bedroom together, which was really two corners of the veranda boarded up into a room, and immediately adjoining the wall of the public parlour. We turned in about 10pm, and were both woke up about 11pm by a horrid piano which might just as well have been in our bedroom. I sallied off in my pyjamas and attacked the landlord, and with some difficulty got the instrument silenced. The culprits were a middle-aged couple who ought to have learnt *'sic utere tuo ut alienum non lædas'*.[298]

1 January 1884 - Tuesday

We got up at 6, hired a couple of horses, and rode to a waterfall. Not a great fall: sheer, but very pretty, and a pleasant ride through the woods.

---

[296] A bothy is a small hut or cottage, typically provided for workers on an estate, or as mountain refuges for travellers.
[297] Gaiters are a leather or cloth covering for the lower leg.
[298] Latin: "use [what is] yours so as not to harm [what is] of others". Or "use your property in such a way that you do not damage others'". A legal maxim related to property ownership laws, often shortened to simply *sic utere* ("use it thus").

We saw a native bear[299] up a gum tree. They are harmless beasts; I believe only one has ever been got to England. They will only live on gum leaves and tea leaves, and are a sort of small sloth. A capital outdoor bath when we got back. A magpie hanging up outside who did the 'cooy', and whistled the Quaker's Wife – very well. It's a bigger bird; not so handsome as the English one. After breakfast, we started in the coach and I had a considerable row with a man who tried to take K's place, K. being as always not in time to start. He told me I had no soul to be saved, whereupon I threatened personal violence and he collapsed. Drove back through the same scenery again; beautiful weather. Dined at Fernshaw. We saw a black snake crossing the road, and our driver got down and killed it with his whip. Got back to Melbourne about 9 and had some supper at the Club, and find Regi there. Drove back to St. Leonard's with him.

2 January 1884 - Wednesday

Dined with Keating and met Curtayne, the manager of the Union bank – too much jewellery and hair dye – and a man named Strahan; a pleasant evening.

Many new contacts were made as much 'out of hours' at the Club, or on the country estate, or even at dinner or the theatre, as they were within the office environment. There are sometimes hints and suggestions in the Diary that Gibbs preferred to conduct many of his business or administrative meetings informally, often whilst strolling through some art gallery or botanic garden. However, the cables and ciphered 'post-scripts' were usually the safest place for ideas arising, and the future plans for GB&S.

London hoped that Australia would prove to be a source of commodities to equal their successes in guano and iodine from Peru. But there were serious competitors, usually established Australians themselves, jostling for wool cargoes, wheat, sugar, and – increasingly - mineral ores. The much earlier discovery of coal within Sydney harbour itself had alerted the young government to the potential of mining reserves. Wool had long ago taken over from the whale oil and seal products of the Sydney and Port Jackson whalers. Vicary saw Newcastle as the fast-developing new wool port, convenient for its proximity to the Queensland squatters and the New South Wales outback sheep stations. He preferred its cheaper wharfage to Sydney's overcrowded waterfront where the old names like Dalgety, Parbury, Chapman, and Morehead held the prime positions and land came at a premium. However, in Sydney Vicary welcomed the chance to give greater prestige to the Gibbs Bright House, and at the same time relieve office overcrowding, by accepting the Bright plan to move from the upper end of Pitt Street to the lower end - closer to Circular Quay - onto land the Brights had acquired as a family investment. There was room enough for spacious offices, part of which could potentially be let to a

---
[299] Koala.

government department, and a warehouse behind with its own access road. On a 1922 map of Sydney, Gibbs Bright are shown with an extensive wharf and warehouse in Campbell's Cove adjoining what would later become the Dawes Point pier of Sydney Harbour Bridge.

31. Circular Quay, showing wool stores including Dalgety & Co. (c1900)
Tyrrell Photographic Collection, Powerhouse Museum

3 January 1884 - Thursday

I have had a rash lately so I went and saw Dr Fitzgerald. He is the swell surgeon, and makes £12,000 per annum. His room was cram full, but fortunately he was a respecter of persons and I was dodged through into the operation room and straight off and given an arsenic prescription[300]. Dined with Regi, and worked out an ingenious table for cabling.

---

[300] Arsenic was commonly used to treat a wide variety of ailments until the 1880s, but by that point most of the medical profession agreed that it had very unpleasant side effects and rarely did any good - although it carried on being prescribed regularly. Gibbs may have been prescribed some arsenic-based ointment for his skin condition, but it is also quite possible that he was being given Fowler's Solution (a solution containing potassium arsenite), used as a general tonic but also for rashes and other skin conditions.

4 January 1884 - Friday

I inspected the various wool stores with Nicholls, and started 4.30pm to go to 'Lara', Mr Fairbairn's[301] place near Geelong. We were met at the station, and found a man named Alec Murphy going there too. The house is a very comfortable one, standing on a farm of 14,000 acres. The family consists of Mr Fairbairn, a Scotch gentleman of about 65; 6 sons – 4 of whom were there, splendid athletic fellows all over 6 ft high, and 2 of them 6 ft 3. They rowed in the Cambridge eight and all that sort of thing; quiet amiable giants, and to be trusted with matches in the immediate neighbourhood of the Thames without danger. Mr. F. has lost his right hand just above the wrist, like Father. He plays billiards about equally with Father, but has quite a different plan. He uses his left arm, and has a thing like a paperweight with a rest head above it through which he slips his cue. Instead of writing with his left hand he has a pen fixed into the stump of his right arm. There is also a bright-looking, rather pretty, only daughter, about 20, who has more wit than her brethren. She will have a pot of money as he is one of the very richest men in Australia, and people here are usually guilty of the injustice of dividing their money equally between sons and daughters.

5 January 1884 - Saturday

After breakfast, the sons and Murphy and I went off in a buggy to shoot rabbits. Keating stayed with Mr. F. The place we went to was called the Anika paddock and was 3 miles square. It was something like the Beaudesert shooting, only very little bracken but piles of dead gum tree boughs lying about, out of which bolted innumerable rabbits. We walked in line; six guns, and all of them shot splendidly. I was the worst, though I

---

[301] George Fairbairn (1816-1895): a considerable personality of the period. He was an extremely wealthy self-made man who achieved efficient wool and meat production on his extensive properties. Although he doesn't mention it in his diary, Gibbs will most certainly have used this visit as an opportunity to learn from Fairbairn (and other pastoralists) the processes involved in the wool trade, from pasture to wool storage and shipping. The Australian product could be second to none, but the hazards were complex. More than in almost any other area of sheep farming, success or failure was dependent on the fluctuations of climate and the producers must have reasonably easy access to alternative pasture in times of drought or flood. Herding sheep over the vast areas of Queensland, New South Wales and Victoria in a widespread drought could decimate flocks. The early involvement with Chrystal at Amby Creek had taught them several hard lessons. There were not only water shortages to contend with but also devastating floods, plagues of rabbits, and accidental fires which cleared the grass from huge acreage. Novices overstocked, the international market prices rose and fell (as in the 1890s, to Gibbs' cost). Advances had been made on clips and on station properties, along with various other improvements - all funded by Gibbs. Wire netting and fencing were necessary when economies could be made on stockmen, but pasture also needed to be rested and irrigated. These costs were added to interest on older loans and earlier debts; commission charges always made the business of 'indenting' a risky one. However, in 1885 they acquired a wool shipping company in Newcastle, New South Wales, and were able to establish coastal shipping links. With these considerable holdings the company earned the right to be admitted into the Australian banking ring that same year at the favourable rates they had asked.

shot well up to my average. It was regular butchering business; we killed over 600 between 11 and 5pm. No one ever stopped to look at a rabbit or asked if we hit or missed; we simply stalked on, firing away, and only stopping when the barrels were too hot to hold. It seemed horrid not picking the rabbits up, and certainly lessens the sport. We killed several black rabbits, and one bright red like a fox. We saw few birds: some curlew, parrots and hawks. I brought a lot of cartridges with me, which my hosts told me is never done here as people are only too glad to provide cartridges for their guests to kill their vermin with.

6 January 1884 - Sunday

Fairbairn has quarrelled with his parson, who appears to be a brute; consequently, nobody went to church. We had some capital lawn-tennis, and drove over to tea about 3 miles off at one of the Fairbairns, who is married to a Canadian.

7 January 1884 - Monday

By the early train to Melbourne, and in the office at 10.30. Dined at St. Leonards, and nothing of any interest.

8 January 1884 - Tuesday

A reproduction of the day before except that the mail came in, bringing satisfactory home news. Letters from Father, Mother, Herbert, Smeb, Harry[302] and Wilcox[303]. A splendid light in the sky this evening[304], and I see in the papers there has been something of the kind in England; every night, nearly, since I left 'Frisco the heavens have been lit up with a glorious rosy light beginning about an hour after sundown and lasting about 2 hours. I should think it must be some kind of aurora, but I don't think the scientific people have any rational explanation to offer.

9 January 1884 - Wednesday

Attended the annual meeting of the Trust and Agency[305], and modified the vulgarity of our advertisement in the Melbourne directory.

10 January 1884 - Thursday

Busy all day writing to Alban, and in the evening read some of the 'Voyage of the Jeanette': all perished, and the diary of Captain Long[306], who was

---

[302] Probably Henry Lloyd Gibbs (1861-1907), Vicary's youngest brother.
[303] We learn later (17th February 1885) that Wilcox is a clergyman - presumably from near Tyntesfield.
[304] Continuing Krakatoa phenomenon?
[305] Trust and Agency Company of Australasia (Limited) was a finance and mortgage agency of which Gibbs Bright were managing agents.
[306] Captain George Washington De Long

the last survivor, gives one after the other the death of all his mates and is very touching. He seems to have been a nice fellow; he must have kept his diary up to within a few hours of his death.

11 January 1884 - Friday

Finished writing to Alban and wrote a few notes to the rest of the family, and started about 3pm for Echuca[307]. A lot of children in the carriage, who would show me all the objects of interest such as cows, rabbits, bridges. I couldn't help envying the intense enjoyment they extracted out of a hot, dusty, railway journey. I read 'All sorts and conditions of men' by Besant and Price. Charrington's Brewery is worked in; it is pleasant reading, but not so good as 'The Chaplain of the Fleet', and verges on silliness – being also rather boring, with its evident moral purpose. Chrystal met me at Echuca, which I reached at about 11pm. We had some supper, and then a dusty drive in splendid moonlight to his farm house 'Torrumbarry', getting there at 1. Chrystal: well-informed, clever, roughish man; a good sort, self-made and educated, and well done at that; son of a Scotch baker.

12 January 1884 - Saturday

A large family: 9 children, two grown-up girls, pleasant and plain, who prepared breakfast which, as their father remarked to me, would be convenient for their husbands – if they were lucky enough to get one. Mrs C., who is somewhat of an invalid, did not show up at breakfast. We drove about 12 miles to the swamp[308], keeping a good look-out for wild turkeys on the way, but not being lucky enough to see one. The swamp is an extraordinary place, about 15 miles of which overflows from the Murray and forms a shallow inland lake. The land has only recently been submerged, and the gum trees still stand out of the water – for the most part bare and dead; it has increased in size since Alban was there. I was greatly disappointed in the shooting after what Alban had told me. I got very little sport; I saw no wild geese or swans, and it was exceedingly difficult to get within shot of the ducks, and they were not very numerous. I was paddled about in a sort of shallow dug-out and got 2 or 3 birds; then Leach, the manager of the Gunbower station[309], turned up and sent a fellow on horseback up the creek to drive the duck down – by which means we killed a few rocketing teal, black, and wood duck. We dined, or rather, tea'd, at Leaches; and played cards and had a cheerful evening with 2 or 3 men who dropped in. Mrs Leach: a pleasant little woman. Chrystal and I slept at the house. The sun broiled down on my gun so during the day that I could hardly hold it.

---

[307] Echuca is close to the border of Victoria with New South Wales, in a pastoral and well-irrigated area on the Murray river.
[308] In Letter 14 to his brother Alban from Melbourne on 11 February 1884, Gibbs refers to this swamp as "New Swamp" and comments on the heat and bad shooting.
[309] Gunbower is a town about 170 miles north of Melbourne.

13 January 1884 - Sunday

Left after breakfast, and back to Chrystals. Heat 125 to 142 in the sun, and got to 110 in the shade. Strolled about with C. in the evening, and inspected C's mill and sheep sheds. Tipped a schoolboy Chrystal 1 sov., which was appreciated. Read some poems by a man named Gordon[310] who settled in Australia and shot himself; he must have been a very clever fellow – his 'local colouring' poems – 'Sick Stock rider', 'Ride from the wreck', etc. are as good as Bret Harte, and something like. There are also some pessimist [sic] ones strongly influenced by Swinburne, and some sporting like Whyte Melville, only infinitely better. 'How we beat the Favourite' is the best galloping account of a steeplechase I ever read; it ends thus:

'And so ends the tussle – I knew the tan muzzle'
'Was first tho' the Ringmen were yelling 'Dead Heat'.'
'A nose I could swear by, but Clark said 'the mare by'
'a short head, and that's how the favourite was beat'.

14 January 1884 - Monday

Got up early, and went out with Chrystal and a fellow on horseback to two small lagoons close to the house. In about ½ an hour I got 15 shots, all rocketers, and bagged 1 black duck, 1 shag, 1 hawk and 6 teal. I was in good form. The Chrystals altogether very hospitable, doing their utmost to make me comfortable. A curious ménage, only two servants, a slavey and stableman. Chrystal owns about £100,000-worth of land and stock (of course, heavily mortgaged) and his expenses and style not half what Selby's would be. Every squatter in Australia, almost, has his land in what an English landowner would consider a frightfully embarrassed state, and a station not heavily mortgaged to a Bank or Merchant is almost unknown. Even when the men are all very rich, the style of living is exceedingly simple. And hardly anybody has menservants in the house. Heat terrific driving in to Echuca; played 6d. nap on the journey with some men in the train, and by the time we got as far south as Kineton it was quite cool; reached Melbourne 11pm.

15 January 1884 - Tuesday

Got a letter from Herbert about finance but no news. Dined with Keats at the Maison Dorée, and read some of Trollope's autobiography; a sort of cookery recipe: how to dress and serve a novel. He must have been a regular machine: not much of the divine afflatus about him, but very conscientious and painstaking. Merivale wrote to me the other day that young Noel Fenwick left Sydney leaving his Club bill unpaid, and that M. – having proposed him – had had to pay it: did I know who or where Fenwick was now? Accordingly, I dropped on to Master F. pretty sharply,

---

[310] Adam Lindsay Gordon (1833-70) was seen by Australians as their first major poet.

and he was inclined to be bounceable and rather haw-haw about the matter, saying, "What is your friend's name? I will send him a cheque". I replied, "Your proposer's name is Mr Merivale, who knows nothing of you except that you brought a letter of introduction from our London House, and I consider you owe him a full apology for the way you have behaved: I have already had to write to him and say that I know your father, and that he will be paid. I am quite sure your father would highly disapprove of what has passed". On this, he curled up at once and promised to write properly to G.M.

16 January 1884 - Wednesday

Saw Dr Fitz[311] again and had some new medicine – rash practically gone; saw him contemplating an operation on a man for mydatids[312] in the neck while I waited in the operation room. Old Butterfield is having a row with the Melbourne authorities about the new Cathedral he is building here; they have disobeyed his instructions as to the quality of the stone they are using in some part, on the ground that their experience shows it won't stand the weather. I think they have treated him cavalierly; I like the look of the building very much as far as it has gone, but the site is as bad as possible, in a hole crowded up with common buildings and near a railway station. The Adelaide Cathedral, which is also in process of erection – Butterfield being the architect – I do not think will be attractive.

17 January 1884 - Thursday

32. Marida Yallock (c1915-18)
State Library of Victoria, H83.47/33a

Mail went; wrote to Herbert and a line to Edith, and left between 4 and 5 for Marida Yallock, the Mackinnon's place in the Western District of Victoria. It is about 150 or 160 miles from Melbourne, but the trains are very slow and I did not reach Camperdown, the terminus of the line, till after 11pm. My friend Donald Mackinnon was at the station to meet me, having been playing with his brother in a cricket match, and waited to bring me out. The brother was driving and, being called Bill and speaking with a strong native burr and being dressed in the roughest style possible, I mistook him for a groom with unusually free manners. However this did not appear, luckily. We had about 12 miles moonlight drive, and got to the house where Mr and Mrs M.[313] were up and greeted me with great

---

[311] This is Dr FitzGerald, as before.
[312] Cysts produced by growth of immature tapeworm.
[313] Jane Mackinnon, née Kinross.

friendliness. We had some supper, and I turned in to a comfortable room – for which I was quite ready.

18 January 1884 - Friday

Breakfast at 8, and plenty of porridge; everything roughish, plain and good. The family consists of the father, an old, grey-bearded highlander with strong Scotch accent – 'twa doogs'; a regular Cottars Saturday night old man, been out there 40 years; much respected, quite a gentleman. Neighbouring place called 'Mackinnons Bridge' after him and that sort of thing. His wife, a cheery, good-tempered, intelligent, lowland Scotch lady who reminded me of Mrs Brune[314]. A silent, plain daughter who had been educated in a Church of England school, and knelt at prayers when the others stood up. A younger, better-looking and cheeky girl.

The above mentioned Bill who is what they call a 'back blocker', that is he is settled on a station in the 'back blocks' of the New South Wales country, is at home for a holiday during the hot season, having got Barcoo Rot, or a sort of eczema to which most men are liable in those parts. He is rough, but a very good sort apparently. Also an overgrown lad – over 6 ft – about 17, named Jim; much like Bill, only better-looking; and an attractive little boy named Kenneth at 12. After breakfast, we had prayers and a chapter from Jeremiah about his having bought a piece of land from his first cousin who seems to have realised his real property on account of a panic about the Chaldeans. Then we played lawn tennis in a very pretty garden, and two young fellows named Black – who are owners of a fine neighbouring property – came over in their buggy, and we then drove to the forest about 4 miles, and shot bush kangaroo[315] with a heavy buck shot. I killed 6, which was a fraction over the average. They got up pretty wild and went at a great pace when alarmed, and will carry away any amount of shot unless hit in the head or hind legs. Back to dinner, whist and smoking in Donald's room.

19 January 1884 - Saturday

Donald and I rode over to the Blacks[316] who have a large, handsome country house much like an English one, but rather a steep staircase –

---

[314] Possibly mother of Beatrice Brune (see 25th May 1884 and 25th October 1884)
[315] Bush kangaroo is a term normally used for the Eastern Red Kangaroo, although as Gibbs later [21st January] describes the Forrester kangaroo - which is almost certainly the Eastern Grey (macropodeus giganteus) - as larger, it may be that he is actually shooting a type of wallaby. As there are 53 types of macropod - although not all would be found in this area - we cannot be certain.
[316] The Black papers are in the State Library of Australia. Niel Black (1804-1880) was born in Argyllshire and had been in partnership with the Finlays. The dissolution of this partnership, amid accusations of double-dealing, had seen him lose what he considered the better part of the property Glen Ormiston (a heritage station house) to Finlay (who Gibbs meets the following day) while he received Mount Noorat. Niel Black had three sons: Archibald John, Steuart Gladstone, and Niel Walter. The 'elder Black' mentioned is presumably Archibald

which is absurd where one can have any amount of land. The house at Marida Yallock is on a better plan for the country, though far less pretentious. It is one-storied, something like a barrack. You enter in the centre with sitting rooms right and left, and walk straight through to a quad with wooden veranda all round on to which all bedroom doors open; one wing, boys rooms; other wing, servants offices and rooms; other side of quad facing main building being the stables. We had lunch at the Blacks and then the elder Black (who has not long left Cambridge), DM and self went out rabbit-shooting in the bracken. I did not shoot well and the rabbits were awfully difficult to see. We killed about 120, Black killing over 50 to his own gun. We were late for dinner which annoyed old Mrs Black, an invalid. Played billiards and then Mack and I started to ride home, pitch dark – couldn't tell one end of the horse from the other, but my nose and ears told me the groom was drunk. We started, and I thought the horse went very differently from what he had in the morning: pulling, knocking me against a gate post, and having no mouth and almost unmanageable. DM laughed at my 'woah-ing' and 'steady boy' and so on, and we got on all right crossing a ford and so on, till a little way from home when he bolted and pulled up at his own stable door, when I got down and found that the bit had never been put in his mouth, so I had been guiding him by the forehead band!

20 January 1884 - Sunday

The country here is very fine and rich, and the climate very cool – more like England than any part of Australia. There are no runs and all freehold land, the paddocks being of more reasonable size. It is all valuable grazing land suitable for fatting stock, and some of it sells as high as £30 an acre against 10/- or £1 in other parts of Australia. The estates are mostly small, about 10 or 12 thousand acres, and farmed by their owners who come nearer to the English country gentleman than anyone else on this side of the globe. It is quite cool here now, fires every evening – a curious contrast to that beastly Echuca country last week. We all went to the Kirk[317] and there was a temporary parson, a fellow who looked like a city waiter in a shiny black coat and white tie and gold studs and who preached the most grotesque sermon possible, on the text of 'come over and help us'; and on the incidental mention of Troas, he proceeded to tell us the tale of Troy divine with the most ridiculous mispronunciations, Helen and Menelaus becoming 'Healin' and 'Manylaws', and the story being described as originating in Virgil's 'Oenoid'! After lunch a Mr Campbell Finlay[318] came over; he is a Scotch neighbour who lives mostly in London. He has the

---

John who would have been about 22. On the wedding photo of Donald Mackinnon and Hilda Bunny in 1891, A. J. Black is listed as the best man.
[317] Gibbs presumably refers to the church as the 'Kirk' because his hosts used that Scottish term.
[318] Campbell Finlay had the fine house of Glen Ormiston (now home to a branch of the Technical and Further Education Commission, NSW), which Niel Black had built in about 1840.

finest breeding establishment of race horses in the Colony and was very civil to me, asking me to come over, lunch, and see them. The Finlays have a fine old Scotch feud with the Blacks which they have inherited from their fathers and which is in a very healthy state, considering it is in the 2nd generation. The Mackinnons have in vain tried to bring peace, as both parties are nice, though Finlay is a bit of a *'petit maître'* and has an irritating way of laughing while he speaks. I spent the afternoon in the garden, much as I should at Aldenham, with boys and terriers: killing native cats, eating mulberries and examining the habits of bulldog ants. In the evening, hymns and laudable promptness in break-up of party. I sat in Donald's room smoking and he gave me a long German lesson translating a lot of Heine's short poems to me which are certainly very good. I was particularly fetched with one beginning with two children hiding in a hen-house.

21 January 1884 - Monday

In the morning, we went hunting the Forrester Kangaroo – a larger, lighter-coloured variety than the Bush Kangaroo[319] we were shooting on Friday. We had six greyhounds and were all well-mounted. It is very exciting galloping full pelt through cover over fallen timber, and the horses steer very cleverly. We killed 6, and young Ken and I had a splendid run together after one which got away. The reckless way in which the little beggar rode perfectly astonished me, but nothing happened to anybody and we got back to late lunch and then started off 'bees nesting'. The *modus operandi* is to saw down the gum tree and then stop up the hole of the bees nest as well as one can, and then make two cuts, with the cross cut about a quarter through the tree above and below the nest. One man then covers his head with gauze, and with the axe splits up the wood above the nest and scoops out the honey into a pail. The first tree was rotten and a weak hive so we soon put the thing through; then the Blacks joined us and we drove to another big tree where Ken had spotted a nest high up. We had a great argument, as the tree was close to a rail fence and all declared that it must fall on it – except me, and I stoutly maintained that if they would cut as I directed it would fall clear. We worked for an hour, turn and turn, with the cross cut saw and axe, and to my delight the tree fell just where I said. It may of course have been a fluke but after it, all looked on me with respect and surprise – the ingrained conviction in the young and untravelled Australian being that a recently arrived Englishman must be a fool. We returned in triumph – more or less stung – with two milk pails cram full of honey, having spent a jolly boyish sort of afternoon. In the evening I played picquet with the younger Miss Mackinnon, who is a bright little girl. To bed very stiff after hunting.

---

[319] See footnote for 18th January.

22 January 1884 - Tuesday

Played lawn tennis until driven in by the rain, and had to give up going to lunch at Glen Ormiston, the Finlay's, for the same reason; but later on we dressed up in mackintoshes and drove off to try and get some duck-shooting. No luck, however. I shot one snipe – our total bag; like an English snipe, only as big as a woodcock; plenty of fun, laughing, chaffing and horse-racing. They pressed me most warmly to stay on, but I thought I should be back in the office tomorrow, so after dinner I drove in to Camperdown to be ready for the early start. I was really sorry to go – they were all so awfully friendly and made me feel as if I had known them all my life; indeed my spirits were so good while I was there in the easy life and cool weather, they must have thought me rather a buffoon.

23 January 1884 - Wednesday

Called at 3 in the morning; still pouring in torrents and pitch dark; surly beast of a landlord having a row with a parson, but my portmanteau too heavy to lift without his assistance so couldn't afford the luxury of a row with him myself. Reached Geelong at 8am where I had breakfast, and in the office soon after 10. A busy day picking up the events of the last few days. Dined at the 'Maison Dorée' with Keats, and home to bed early – pretty tired after long journey and strong exercise at Marida Yallock. Met Robertson of Colac, and read a French novel called 'La Vie en Boheme': rather amusing. Heard there had been an attempt on the Prince of Wales' life.

24 January 1884 - Thursday

Mail in; home news all right. Wrote to Alban and Mother. Heard from them about father and Edith. Dined at the club and had a long chat with old Curtayne and others, who are agitating and conspiring to stop the high gambling at the Club. Read some of Morley's 'Diderot': his defence of D's treatment of Mrs D. is most impudent, as if a man of genius was to be absolved from all moral law and because he has married a woman beneath him in life and without education he is justified in a liaison with a woman who writes bad verses. To talk also of 'piety turning sour as piety is apt to do' because his wife (who had saved every penny to make him comfortable, and won the heart of his family who had opposed the match) resented his deserting her entirely for 3 years and living with another woman, is too thin.

25 January 1884 - Friday

'The trivial round, the common task'[320].

---

[320] Gibbs is quoting the English Anglican priest, theologian and poet John Keble (1792-1886). "The trivial round, the common task / Would furnish all we ought to ask / Room to deny ourselves, a road / To bring us, daily, nearer God."

26 January 1884 - Saturday

Got up at 5am and saw Regi off till Tuesday to the Finlays at Glen Ormiston a few miles from where I was staying with the Mackinnons.

27 January 1884 - Sunday

Read 'Othello', some of Gordon's poems, and a book about English journalism. Walked to St. Kilda with Keats and dined with him.

28-30 January 1884

Office hours 10 to 6, and nothing beyond the most ordinary routine to chronicle.

31 January 1884 - Thursday

Wrote to Alban and Edith.

1 February 1884 - Friday

Mail in with letters from Father, Mother, Alban; and Regi – tiresome in business, though private relations continue excellent; I shut the door and had it out with him – result satisfactory, he behaved beautifully as the Brights always seem to do when tackled.

2 February 1884 - Saturday

Went with Keating to tea in the afternoon with a Mrs Lewis[321] – a clever, bright little woman who has been an actress. Dined with Curtayne, a party of about 10 to Sir Wm. de Voeux[322], Governor of Fiji – a

33. Rosa Lewis, aged 28 (1865)
Courtesy of Dr Mimi Colligan of Monash University

---

[321] Rosa Lewis, née Dunn (1844-1920), daughter of John Dunn (also known as John Donaghue), a well-known and well-respected actor, and an actress in her own right. From the Sydney Mail, 11 July 1885: "Mrs. L. L. Lewis, long and favourably known to a playgoing public of 20 years ago as Rosa Dunn, at the time when Mrs. Marcus Clarke, then Marion Dunn, was also on the boards, played as one of the principal 'Bohemians', with a success that can be easily understood when we remember that it was a veteran of the stage that we were applauding". Rosa Lewis was said to have been the mistress of her brother-in-law, Marcus Clarke - the writer of the Australian Convict classic, 'For the Term of his Natural Life'. Their relationship was turbulent, possibly because of his bohemian lifestyle. He was only 35 when he died in 1881. Rosa and her husband Ludwig Lewis lived in London until the financial crash of the 1890s, when he remade his wealth in Melbourne but died shortly afterwards in 1910. Gibbs seems to have been much attracted to her.
[322] Sir George William des Voeux, GCMG (1834-1909) was a British colonial governor who served as Governor of Fiji (1880–1885), Newfoundland (1886–1887), and Hong Kong (1887–1891).

pleasant man; his secretary is Wallington, Tommy Shepherd's nephew, who was up at Oriel with me and came out here bear-leading young Callender. Also Col. Disney[323], who is in command of the defence forces here.

3 February 1884 - Sunday

Torrents of rain; Regi had a little party: Tennant of Gibb Livingstones from Foochow[324], Dr Ford, Keating and Disney – very pleasant evening. The drought has broken up all over Queensland, which is a good thing. Read some of a book called 'Klytia'[325], translated by Miss Corkran from the German (? sister of the painter). Thought it rather stiff, and not very well translated.

4 February 1884 - Monday

Nothing happened.

5 February 1884 - Tuesday

Same as 4th.

6 February 1884 - Wednesday

I had Mackinnon, Tennant and Keating to dine with me at the Maison Dorée, and we went to the Bijou Theatre and saw Byron's play of 'Our Girls'[326]. It is a poor, badly constructed piece, and the acting was not up to much except a man named Hall who did Captain Gungah very well; we had a very jolly evening.

7 February 1884 - Thursday

My three months are up at the Club, and as I can only have six as honorary member I shan't begin another month until I come back from New Zealand.

8 February 1884 - Friday

Nothing.

---

[323] Colonel Thomas Robert Disney (1842-1915), of Ireland, where he was commissioned Lieutenant in the Royal Artillery. He was Commandant of Victoria from 1883 to 1888 with the local rank of Colonel. He was later made a Lieutenant Colonel.
[324] Fuzhou (Fujian Province, China).
[325] "Klytia", by George Taylor (translated from the German by S.F. Corkran).
[326] Henry James Byron (1834-1884) was a writer of pantomime/burlesque comedy. The best, 'Our Boys', was successful and accomplished.

9 February 1884 - Saturday

George Merivale arrived, looking very jolly and bringing good accounts of his wife and daughter Angel! Regi was away for the day at Ivo Bligh's[327] wedding, and I was made very angry by telegrams coming in from Sydney and Adelaide addressed to him on our business. I will stop it for the future. GM and FAK dined with me at the Maison Dorée, and we saw a couple of acts of Byron's new play 'Our Loves' – better than 'Our Girls', at any rate.

10 February 1884 - Sunday

GM came over to breakfast, and he and Bright and I very busy talking business. I hear there is some prospect of our losing Arthur in Dunedin but hope this will end in smoke. Old Murray and Merivale now as thick as thieves, but some irritation between Murray and our Mr Reginald.

11 February 1884 - Monday

Merivale dined at St Leonards, but K and I dined together in town. The mail in with satisfactory letters from Father, Mother, Herbert and Clayton[328]. Wrote to Alban and Father. Murray has been circulating some vulgar little almanacs with our advertisements like a grocer; he will be giving away French plums to our lady customers next. Have stopped it.

S.S. Tarawera (1)

Although there was initially some opposition from London, Vicary was in favour of another Bright plan to purchase the Kangaroo Point wharf on the Brisbane river. The GB&S ownership of the wharf immediately gave the company more power and influence – and woke up the 'old guard' – and would prove to be an economy in the long run.

There were also other shipping lines that Vicary had his eye on in the competition for trade, but he was determined to shed any which had brought problems - just as he was sure that S.S. Great Britain was an expensive liability and must be sold on. He saw the Orient Line as an opening to the Indian markets once the East India Company's monopoly was no longer an impediment. If the 'Messageries' Postal service also became part of Gibbs' Agency the French would make useful partners, drawing the Japanese wool buyers into their clientèle.

---

[327] The Honourable Ivo Francis Walter Bligh (1859-1927), 8th Earl of Darnley. He was marrying Florence Rose Morphy, of Beechworth, Victoria, a music teacher, whom he had met during his visit to Australia as captain of the England cricket team two years earlier.
[328] Probably T. Clayton (Gibbs refers to him later in the diary as "T.C."), who was on the staff of the London Office of Antony Gibbs & Son.

The months in the colonies were a major assignment for a young man representing his firm. London needed to be kept fully informed, and that was Vicary Gibbs' responsibility. He had to judge the staff's reaction to change and test the opinions of colleagues before deciding upon any course of action. He certainly had his own prejudices, but we can see from his letters that he was trying to be fair whilst not sparing honest criticism of the four offices. He saw the Melbourne office as being 'well managed', and Sydney's record was one of efficiency although their results were occasionally disappointing and he found their advertising 'vulgar'. He accused the Brisbane office staff of being 'stick in the mud' and slow to act when it came to correspondence - although of course that may have been due to the high humidity of the climate. He was sure that Meeks, out on a limb in Adelaide, was an intelligent and perceptive man. He may only have had an elementary education and he expressed himself badly, but he was loyal and dedicated - instinctively a first-rate manager. Vicary and his fellow directors at head office had reluctantly to accept Bell's judgement that the Winham's wheat fiasco was merely due to bad luck.

12 February 1884 - Tuesday

Sailed about noon in the 'Tarawera' with George. FAK came down and saw us off. She is a nice boat, very well fitted up. Electric light and all the latest improvements; pretty full, but we have got a four berthed cabin to ourselves, so we shall do all right.

Old Ryan introduced me to his wife[329] and daughter[330] who are going to the hot springs. She[331] is a vulgar, scheming woman full of Lord Charles, her unfortunate son-in-law, and boasting about their place and Lady Charles' beauty – also grumbling and sneering at the other people on board, which I hate. Of course, I was perversely optimist and had a good word for everyone. She went below soon, and placed her little girl in my

---

[329] Marian Ryan, daughter of John Cotton (1802-1849). She married Charles Ryan in 1847, and the couple had 7 children: Marian Ellis Ryan (1848-1922), who married Captain Frederic Charles Rowan (c1845-1892) in 1873 and achieved fame in her own right as a botanical illustrator; Henry Ryan (1850-?), who later took over from his father in Ryan & Hammond, and married Denise Anne Nankivell (daughter of Thomas J. Nankivell, J.P.) in 1879; Major General Sir Charles Snodgrass Ryan (1853-1926), who from 1878 was a surgeon in Melbourne - and may be the Dr. Ryan that Gibbs meets in Melbourne on 13 December 1883 - who married Alice Elfrida Sumner in July 1883; Ada Mary Ryan (1855-1943), who married Admiral Lord Sir Charles Thomas Montagu Douglas Scott (1839-1911) in February 1883, becoming Lady Charles Scott; Blanche Adelaide Ryan (1859-1938), who remained unmarried until her fifties; Cecil Godfrey Ryan (1866-1954); and Mabel Hartley Ryan (1861-1914).
[330] Probably Mabel Hartley Ryan (1861-1914), the 7th child and youngest of four daughters of Charles and Marian Ryan. She would have been 22 or 23, and is most likely to be the daughter that Gibbs is meeting here - the next eldest daughter Blanche being a couple of years older.
[331] The wife

charge as she did not like to leave her alone on deck! The little girl is in the mignonne style, small with very fair hair in a towsle: very affected, "I am such an artless thing"; shrieking at the gulls and kissing both hands to Papa; she has been to a fancy dress ball as Titania and never got over it. She is 21, looks 18, and acts 14.

13 February 1884 - Wednesday

Made acquaintance of Crace[332], a man about 40 who married one of the Morts[333] of Sydney; he is a friend of G's[334] and seems a very good sort – a son of old Crace[335] of Wigmore Street. He is a large squatter in New South Wales. Also talked to his companion Murdoch[336], a successful civil engineer – a pleasant man. It was a rough night, and so continued all today; after taking bath and breakfast all right I succumbed, and was pretty bad all day – as was George. I read again 'Northanger Abbey'[337] and 'Persuasion'[338] with pleasure. Northanger Abbey is very witty – the conversation between Henry, Eleanor and Catherine when they take a walk is capital – but the story is rather faulty and the General, I think, behaves impossibly; giving such tremendous encouragement on the strength of idle gossip told him by Thorpe, and kicking her out on the same authority, without in either case making any enquiries elsewhere. Anne, in 'Persuasion', is a very nice character; but the respectable villain Mr Eliot (against whom her suspicions are raised by learning that he had travelled on a Sunday when he was young) is absurd.[339]

14 February 1884 - Thursday

Still very seedy, and sea high. Read 'Stories From Clerical Life'. There is certainly something in George Eliot far above Jane's[340] refined little Dutch realistic pictures.

---

[332] Edward Kendall Crace (1844–1892), an English-born grazier, who married Kate Marion Mort (1852-1926) - niece of T. S. Mort - in 1871. They came to Australia in 1865 on the Duncan Dunbar, surviving its shipwreck. Crace died in September 1892 when his vehicle was washed away whilst crossing Ginninderra Creek, killing him, his coachman, and one of the two horses pulling it. Crace had extensive land holdings around Canberra, and its suburb of Crace is named after him.

[333] Kate Marion Mort (1852-1926), the niece of Thomas Sutcliffe Mort (1816-1878), an industrialist responsible for improving the refrigeration of meat carcasses for export to Europe.

[334] George Merivale

[335] John Gregory Crace (1809-1889), the son of Frederick Crace (1779–1859) after whom the company was named. The firm of Crace made furniture for Gibbs' 'Tyntesfield' family and were one of the best interior decorators of the time.

[336] G. B. Murdoch.

[337] Jane Austen (1775-1817): 'Northanger Abbey' (1817, but written in 1798-9)

[338] Jane Austen (1775-1817): 'Persuasion' (1818)

[339] Gibbs has obviously missed the point of Austen's joke!

[340] Jane Austen.

15 February 1884 - Friday

Weather still rough, but I am all right; played mild 'nap' and whist, and read 'Dr Breen's Practice' by Howells; inferior – very – to any of his others that I have read – quite tiresome with its triviality; one good scene between the lady doctor and her disagreeable mother.

16 February 1884 - Saturday

Sighted New Zealand in the afternoon; grand, black, inhospitable-looking coast, very different from Australia. Just before 6pm we entered George's Sound, and, going to the end, anchored there for the night. Very pleasant to get into quiet waters and have an undisturbed sleep after the ceaseless rolling and pitching. These Sounds are very beautiful; I believe the things most like them in Europe are the Norway Fiords, but they haven't got the fine timber and foliage on the mountains. We came winding along perfectly still water with the mountains rising up sheer on either side, thickly covered with brush; it seemed like a splendid river.

17 February 1884 - Sunday

34. Milford Sound, Pembroke Peak, NZ (1895)
National Library of Australia, nla.pic-an3366506-a28-a1

35. Donald Sutherland, Milford Sound (1911)
National Library of Australia, nla.pic-an11236269-8

George and I got up about 5am and went on the bridge in our pyjamas, and the hills looked lovely in the clear morning light. We sailed about ½ an hour after, and about 9 we entered Milford Sound and went right up it. It is like George's only much more so; the enormous snow-capped mountains on both sides of all shapes, ragged and grand, covered with timber right down to the edge of the still water in which they were reflected. An immense height: to 4 or 5 thousand feet. I had never seen anything like it, and it was so grand and impressive that I felt – like the Queen of Sheba – that I had 'no heart left in me'. The steamer, as I was told it would, looked like a little boat, as there was nothing for the eye to compare it with except the mountains. On both sides there were a great number of waterfalls coming right down the side of the hills, and at the end of the Sound where it broadens into a bay there is a big waterfall and a little hut – or 'humpie' – at the foot, where lives a man named Southerdon[341], all by himself – the only inhabitant. I believe he is prospecting or exploring. He put off in his boat and rowed up to us, in company with a fellow who was taking photographs. 'The Hermit and the Photographer', like 'the Walrus and the Carpenter'; the hermit looked a dirty, uninteresting fellow and, having got ½ a sheep from the ship, went. We stayed about 2 hours, and some of the passengers landed to gather ferns. When we got outside again it was horribly rough and I was seasick again, and – the gout coming on – took to my bunk.

18 February 1884 - Monday

We reached the bluff early this morning, and we had meant to land, go up to Invercargill and thence to Lake Wakatipu and Kingston and so by coach across to Dunedin – but I could not put my foot to the ground, so we had to give this up and stick to the 'Tarawera', which was a great pity as I believe the scenery is splendid. I read a story by Shorthouse[342] called 'The Little Schoolmaster Mark': rather pretty, but not much in it – a sort of hopeless little allegory. The Prince's speech in answer to the 'Court' towards the end of the book is good.

---

[341] This is probably Gibbs mis-hearing the name of Donald Sutherland (1843/1844-1919), a Scot who fought with the British volunteers who joined the Italian patriots under Garibaldi in 1860. By 1863, after a time as a sailor in the British coastal trade, Sutherland had arrived in Dunedin and deserted from his ship to prospect for gold at Gabriels Gully, without success. He then fought with the Waikato Militia, but after deserting again joined the Armed Constabulary in 1868, reaching the rank of Corporal and eventually receiving the New Zealand War Medal. After briefly becoming a sailor again, in 1877 he left and set sail from Dunedin in a small open boat with his dog (named "Johnny Groat"). He landed at Milford Sound on 3 December 1877 and made his home there for the next 40 years, close to the Bowen Falls. He discovered the Sutherland Falls in 1880, and Sutherland Sound in 1883. During the 1880s, Sutherland lived a hermit-like existence until 1890 when he married a widow, Elizabeth Samuels. The photographer mentioned by Gibbs may have been Alfred Burton, who - with his brother - took many photographs of the Milford Sound area in 1883, as well as the cruise photos of the Wairarapa trip (including the group photo on the back cover).

[342] Joseph Henry Shorthouse. The Little Schoolmaster Mark was written in 1883, and subtitled "A Spiritual Romance".

19 February 1884 - Tuesday

We reached Port Chalmers at 8am. Arthur came on board: a quiet-mannered man; he arranged to have a first class carriage run down the wharf along side the ship, and at 4 I managed – with George's help – to dress and get hoisted in, and the Engine ran us up to the Station and the train took us about 9 miles into Dunedin. The Club was full but I got a first rate room on the first floor of a new 'Grand Hotel' just built; had some tea and went to bed.

36. Grand Hotel, Dunedin (c1880)
Hocken Collections, Uare Taoke o Hakena, University of Otago, 81-3783, ref S11-082a

Crace looked in – very friendly and obliging. There is a nice cool fresh Scotch air and appearance about everything – climate, vegetation and so on – which is refreshing after flat, arid, gum-growing Australia.

Dunedin

20 February 1884 - Wednesday

Still lame, but much better. Went down to the office[343] after breakfast in a cab. Uncommonly good offices they are; it is only a pity there is not more business to be done in them. This is a great place for hotels. Ours is a large and good one, like a continental one, and I hear there are two other big ones – very different to Sydney, where there is only that wretched hole, Petty's. The town itself is beautifully situated and well laid out; fine streets without the monotony of Melbourne.

37. Crawford Street, Dunedin
Hocken Collections, Uare Taoke o Hakena, University of Otago, 81-3738, ref S11-082a

Stayed at the office all day, talking things over with Arthur and writing to Regi. Didn't find Arthur as down in the mouth about business as I expected, though he says he would far rather have started in a completely

---

[343] The Gibbs, Bright & Co. offices in Dunedin (from newspaper advertisements in 1882) were located at 9 Bond Street.

new place than come after Danson. George went out for a drive with Crace, and in the evening Crace and Arthur came to dinner, and we played some mild nap after dinner.

21 February 1884 - Thursday

Today, a general holiday; the first day of the races, to which we went. A very pretty course about 2 miles out commanding a fine view of the town. Pretty fair racing, but the stewards must be a poor lot: all sorts of rabble seemed to get into the enclosure and the races were very unpunctual; the starter, too, was an awful duffer. I saw the Totalisator[344] working for the first time. It is an excellent plan – far better than working with Bookmakers. The Club make 10% on the investments, and the rest of the money does not leave the public. I met a fellow named Houlton who used to be my fag at Yonge's; also Forbes who was on the 'City of New York' with me. A very pleasant day, on the whole. When we got back, we went up a wire tramway (like the San Francisco ones) which they have recently started here. It took us up a lovely hill looking over the harbour. When we got to the top we went into the engine house and had a look at the machinery, and then back to the hotel where Crace and Murdoch dined with us. After dinner, Merivale and Crace went to the theatre, and Murdoch and I sat and smoked.

22 February 1884 - Friday

We found we could now get rooms at the Club, and as the hotel was very dear and we thought the Club would be more amusing we moved in there. Met Judge Williams[345], Alban's friend, who asked me and Merivale to dinner tomorrow. Spent most of the day going round with Arthur, calling on the Merchants and Wholesale Tradesmen. The Fernhill Club is very prettily situated and seems a nice little place. I saw old Danson looking very stupid and vinous, but we did not speak. Merivale went to see some people who do business with us in Sydney.

---

[344] The Totalisator was a system for calculating the odds on winners according to the extent to which they were backed. Nowadays, the term refers to automated machines which operate the system, but the first automated Totalisator was not invented until about 1915 by the Australian George Julius (later Sir) and first installed at Ellerstrie Racecourse in New Zealand in 1925.
[345] Judge Joshua Strange Williams (1837-1915) was born in London, and read Law and Mathematics at Cambridge. He was called to the Bar at Lincoln's Inn in 1859, but emigrated to New Zealand two years later for health reasons and was admitted to the New Zealand Bar at Christchurch in 1862. By 1875, despite his youth and limited experience as a barrister, he was appointed to the Supreme Court of New Zealand. He had four sons and three daughters by his first wife, Caroline, and at least two daughters by his second, Amelia.

23 February 1884 - Saturday

Pouring in torrents so did not go to the races, especially as the change in climate has made me catch cold – the first since I left England. As it was Saturday, Arthur knocked off about 2; but as there was nothing else to do I had the fire lit and stayed in writing letters till 6 when I went to the Club and dressed. Went out to the Williams, who live in a good house some way out of town on the bay. There were 13 to dinner, owing to some gentleman turning up who hadn't been asked, and it was a very pleasant evening. Mrs Williams[346] a bright, pretty little woman. I took Miss Williams into dinner, a stout, middle-aged, clever woman, and there was a lot of singing and playing after dinner, and the people were all gentry or near enough. R.B. goes out very little in Melbourne society and seems to know very few people outside the Clubman set[347], and I think anyway there doesn't seem much dinner party giving in Melbourne, so I enjoyed it for a change. My hosts were very nice and seemed to have a very friendly remembrance of Keats and Alban.

38. Judge Sir Joshua Strange Williams
Hocken Collections, Uare Taoke o Hakena, University of Otago, c/n E3466/4, ref S11-082a

24 February 1884 - Sunday

Rained all day and up to now – 10pm – since last Friday evening. Very unfortunate, as it has prevented our taking a drive and seeing something of the country. Dined in the middle of the day, at Arthur's. Mrs Arthur: very pleasant, well-behaved woman; rather his senior, I should say; a lot of plain, hearty, healthy-looking children. Mrs Murray was there, having been staying with them for a month. She is rather screwy about and affected, but clever and agreeable. Arthur himself is intelligent and well-informed, and has evidently taken a lot of pains to educate himself. It poured, so George and I stayed on smoking in the back room, and did not leave till after tea. Arthur has a comfortable house with good garden. He has been

---

[346] Amelia Durrant Williams, née Jago, was Judge Williams' second wife whom he married in 1877 following the death of his first wife, Caroline Helen Williams, née Sanctuary.
[347] The 'Clubman Set' would be a well-recognised label for 'young men about town' in the 1880s, and Gibbs is possibly implying a certain superficiality to Reginald Bright.

put on the Committee of the Club, which looks well. I fancy the firm stands well here, as Walcott, the old manager, was much respected.

25 February 1884 - Monday

Met a fellow called Anderson, son of the Head of the Orient Co.; they have lived at Frognal[348] since Father left. Danson called to see me at the office, but we only talked about general subjects. The Anglican Bishop here gets £200 per annum, so the English Church is not very flourishing. The Presbyterians have got rather a fine Cathedral. Lunched with Ritchie[349] of the National Mortgage Coy., a gentlemanly man with a very pretty place. Paid a long visit to a tallow factory which Danson has very foolishly been lending money to. Arthur dined at the Club, and we said goodbye meaning to start the first thing tomorrow for Oamaru.

26 February 1884 - Tuesday

My cold so very heavy in all my limbs that I was afraid to move lest I should lay-up at Oamaru, so I stayed in bed all day to try and give it a chance. This will necessitate our knocking Oamaru and Timaru out of our programme, and going straight to Christchurch. GM very good natured about it all.

27 February 1884 - Wednesday

Left by the 8.10am train, still feeling very seedy, but I wrapped up in my Ulster and rug and made a start. The journey was very beautiful as far as Oamaru all along the sea coast: something like the Great Western [Railway] by Dawlish, only much finer cliffs. I was too seedy to enjoy it as I should otherwise. After Oamaru it was through great rolling wheat plains with the snow-covered mountains in the distance. G.M. remained outside on the platform, and there were two schoolgirls in the carriage who amused me very much. I lay coughing away in a corner, wrapped up with rugs and reading 'Old Mortality'[350], and they took no notice of me and talked away on 'the propriety of accepting presents from gentlemen' and

---

[348] Frognal is an area of Hampstead, North West London in the London Borough of Camden.
[349] John Macfarlane Ritchie (1842-1912) went to Dunedin, New Zealand, from Orkney, Scotland in 1865, and joined the National Mortgage Association. By 1873 he had been made a partner in what became Russell, Ritchie and Co., and was the senior partner by 1884. At this time, New Zealand began to experience a steep decline in land values, and only the careful survived. Ritchie was always cautious, and adopted a policy of paying only modest dividends while continuing to make careful loans to selected, trusted clients on a long term basis. He bought into the local dairy produce and meat freezing industry, and would have been a good contact for Vicary Gibbs. On his death in 1912, Ritchie left an estate worth over £150,000; his success at a trying time was not only due to his habitual caution, but also to ethical management. The prosperous merchant became a careful owner of valuable agricultural land, an industrial developer and exporter of frozen produce whose career mirrored the stabilisation of the New Zealand rural economy.
[350] 'Old Mortality' by Sir Walter Scott.

other kindred things, just like the answers to correspondents in the London journal. At one station a young man was on the look out for one of them and she had a long titter with him through the window. This led to some delicate banter from the other damsel. We arrived at Christchurch about 8, and found a boy on the station with a letter from Crace who had taken rooms at the Club and got supper for us. I felt pretty tired and glad to get to bed.

Christchurch

Vicary Gibbs's departure from Dunedin had been delayed by a heavy cold, and he made the journey northward to Christchurch without a halt. He had hoped to stop in Oamaru, where a fact-finding mission to investigate its modern meat-packing techniques would have been immensely useful. However, he was at least able to meet Parker, a son of Lord Macclesfield, who had been his junior at Eton and was now doing well managing Dalgety's newly-developing enterprise in Christchurch. He was also introduced to Banks, the resident partner in Miles and Company. Parker and Banks were the most experienced in the present state and future promise of the frozen meat trade. It is interesting to observe how the second half of the 19th century saw a revolution in aristocratic attitudes to Trade; perhaps it was as much adventure as new wealth that these younger sons of noble families were looking for.

When on his own Antipodean mission, Alban's letters home had inspired all his younger brothers. Vicary, in particular, had been longing to see the rugged scenery of New Zealand. His knowledge and love of plants, trees, and garden design were just as important to him as the need to understand the new market opening up in the colonies.

These were early days in the supply of farm produce from the colonies to Europe, a trade that would eventually become vital to both parties. On February 15th 1882 a shipment consisting of a mixed cargo of mutton, lamb, and pork had left Port Chalmers on board the 'Dunedin' on its second attempt. It arrived in London on May 24th, with only one carcass failing the thorough fitness test. A second consignment followed aboard the 'Mataura', with further shipments leaving regularly from then onwards. As so often in human development one thing leads to another. Successful refrigeration techniques began to make sea travel more acceptable in those early days of long, slow voyages. Quite shortly after exploring New Zealand, Vicary Gibbs enjoyed the new sophistication possible to the ship's chef aboard the 'Wairarapa' as he cruised to Fiji.

A 'New Zealand Refrigeration Company' was eventually formed, and by the 1890s there were more than 20 depots established around the meat production areas. On shore and aboard ship most of the cold store technology had been a British monopoly at first, but the dedication of the Germans was superior and their determination to excel second to none. The British, as so often, failed to value their technicians adequately and eventually lost ground. The export of dairy produce followed on from meat once specialised cargo carriers had been designed and built; mechanised handling in depots and ports streamlined the operation and reduced time and cost. At the end of the century the assessed cost for meat arriving in London Docks was a mere 2d per pound.

Meat was not the only item Vicary had in mind while enjoying the scenery. The possibilities of gold were beginning to enter the sights of AG&S, wherever it would prove economically viable. His tour of the South Island by train, horse, foot and coach took in the West coast gold mining area at Kumara and Reefton, where the mining surveyor on site was very helpful. Apparently, to that date, the Grey River was the only place in the world where gold and coal were thought to have been found side by side. The coal mines already exported their 'illimitable supply of good hard gas coal' to Australia.

The New Zealand journey brought Vicary into close contact with people who considered themselves his equal in every way, regardless of any professional qualification or prestigious position. He recognised the benefit he had gained from this classless society, and thought that his 'poor Aunt Mary and others like her' could also have learned from this land of equality. Nelson turned out to be worth seeing - 'an attractive town' - but Wellington disappointed Vicary Gibbs. He was glad to move on to Napier by steamer, but unfortunately without George Merivale who had to return to his work and wife in Sydney. The hot springs of Rotorua offered Vicary the possibility of some relief from his rheumatic pain - possibly brought on by the meat-rich New Zealand diet - although it seems that the drier climate of some parts of Australia suited him better in any case.

On the way north to Auckland, the Hon. Ivo Bligh - the Captain of the first English cricket team to visit Australia – was taking his new wife on their 'Wedding Tour'. Vicary already knew and liked Bligh, although he had made an adverse comment in his diary about the sharp features of his young Australian wife. Now, however, he was won over by her unsophisticated charm, and enjoyed the couple's company, especially appreciating the offering of their more comfortable quarters when he was afflicted by gout.

By the time he reached Auckland, Vicary was beginning to tire of travelling alone. He longed for news of England and was looking forward to a return to Sydney and the challenge of work. Gout had hampered some of his tour but the scenery was memorable, the New Zealand colonists refreshing, and future business promising.

28 February 1884 - Thursday

Gout again; couldn't put my foot to the ground, so had to stay in bed. Not much pain, luckily, but cold very heavy. Read 'Old Mortality', which I have not read since I was at Brownings – nearly 20 years. I liked it very much indeed. Banks[351] – a partner in Miles'[352] House here, to whom I had letters – called on me; very civil and attentive. Also Thomas, with whom I travelled from 'Frisco. Murdoch came in the evening and played euchre. Gout not going to be much, and got through the day somehow.

29 February 1884 - Friday

39. Canterbury Club, Christchurch, New Zealand (c1878-79)
National Library of Australia, nla.pic-vn3916401-s97

Gout better, and hobbled downstairs – but did not go out as my cold is still heavy. Wrote to Mother and T.C.[353] and read some old Blackwoods[354]. My third day here, and I have seen nothing of the place whatever – or people; very unfortunate, but it can't be helped. Crace and Murdoch left for Wellington. C. sent me a lot of grapes; he is a most good-natured, liberal fellow but a terrible grumbler and very much disposed to be autocratic so he gets into frightful rows with people, especially the neighbouring selectors. Mr Banks, the resident partner of Miles and Co, called on me again to ask me to dine, but I refused – too gouty. The Club here is not a bad one – larger than the Dunedin one – but the manager is an impertinent, off-hand sort of chap. Crace complained of him to the committee.

---

[351] Mr. F. Banks (-1894), seventh son of Henry Banks of Wiltshire. He had gone out to Australia originally, in 1853, with William Mackworth-Praed and Reginald Bright, on the first voyage of the S.S. Great Britain to Australia. Having worked for Miles, Kington and Co. in Melbourne, he then went to New Zealand in 1857/8 to establish and manage the Christchurch office.
[352] Messrs. Miles & Co., originally Miles, Kington & Co., a branch of the well-established Bristol house of Miles Bros. & Co. Their premises at 208 Hereford St., Christchurch, included large offices and warehouses, and a wool and land auction room. They also owned nearby premises for storing wool and grain. They were the local agents for the Royal Fire and Life Insurance Company, and for the Australian and New Zealand Mortgage Company, and were export merchants experienced in frozen meat carcasses - a field that Gibbs Bright & Co. were trying to break in to. The Trust and Agency Company of Australasia (mentioned in several of the letters) had offices nearby at 211 Hereford Street.
[353] "T.C." is probably T. Clayton (see 11th February 1884).
[354] Blackwood's Edinburgh Magzine, published by William Blackwood. It ran (under several different names) from 1817 to 1980, and had a dedicated readership throughout the British Empire amongst those in the Colonial Service.

Tour of the West Coast of South Island, New Zealand

40. Cathedral Square, Christchurch, New Zealand (1894)
National Library of Australia,
nla.pic-an3366506-s34-a1

41. Cashel Street bridge over the River Avon in winter, Christchurch, New Zealand (c1878-79)
National Library of Australia,
nla.pic-vn3916401-s100

1 March 1884 - Saturday

Still lame, but went out after breakfast and with George's help got to Dalgetty's[355] and thanked Parker[356] for putting my name down for the Club. Parker is a son of Lord Macclesfield[357] and was at Eton with me, though junior to me; he is now Dalgetty's manager in Christchurch, and has married a Dunedin girl. I went on to the Miles' office where I wrote my letters and got them passed. They very civilly got me some lunch. Then as it was very fine I went for a drive with George in hopes to shake off my cold. The town is certainly pretty, though flat. The Avon running through it, with its clear water and willows on the banks, is pleasant, and the houses are not set close together but all detached and with pretty gardens. The English Cathedral is rather fine, but the East unfinished. There is an ecclesiastical savour about the place altogether. We drove to a Sir Cracroft Wilson's[358] place, which seemed well-planted and laid out. All the green stuffs and the ferns at the sides of the lanes looked very attractive after the wide, flat, sandy roads and split rail fences of Australia arida. Here, the hedges are quick or gorse, and grow very luxuriantly.

---

[355] Dalgety and Co. was founded by Frederick Gonnerman Dalgety, a Scot via Canada, who emigrated to Australia in 1833. By 1886, Dalgety and Co. and Gibbs, Bright and Co. were competing vigorously in the wool export trade in the Northern district.
[356] Hon. Edmund William Parker (1857-1943).
[357] Thomas Augustus Wolstenholme Parker, 6th Earl of Macclesfield (1811-1896), a British Peer who had formerly been MP for Oxfordshire.
[358] Sir John Cracroft Wilson (1808–1881) was a farmer, politician, and judge. He was well-known for spending vast amounts of money improving his estate, "Cashmere" (after which the Christchurch suburb of Cashmere was named), and for exhibiting stock - especially Lincoln sheep - at agricultural shows.

When Vicary and his holiday companion Merivale arrived in Dunedin and discovered the true extent of the difficulties of the New Zealand House, they held out little hope for its continued existence unless they felt sure that the future of the refrigerated meat trade would justify it. In the Dunedin area, Port Chalmers and Oamaru had made a courageous start, while further north Christchurch and Lyttleton were also attracting experienced workers and growing enthusiasm. The progress of each one of these centres of commerce was very much dependent on the development and example of the others.

As the 1880s progressed in Australia, the meat preparation and pioneering refrigeration processes in purpose-built depots became more streamlined in Victoria and New South Wales, and local transport by train and coastal shipping speeded up the carriage of carcases to the main ports and onward. GB&Co. found their way into as many of these and other enterprises as they were able. By 1916, the firm owned interests in a large area of productive agricultural land, and held agencies in 62 manufacturing companies, 18 financial organisations including insurance, and three shipping lines. They had also invested in several mining enterprises where they were able to install their own managers, and could thus import enough tin, copper and other good quality mineral ores to satisfy what was sometimes strong European demand. Over the turn of the 19th and 20th centuries the gold mines of Western Australia at Coolgardie and Kalgoorlie became a particular focus of the City of London – including AG&S - until the two World Wars created their havoc.

2 March 1884 - Sunday

Gout worse; in bed all day and George took my excuses to Thomas where I was engaged to dinner. Read a story called 'A Woman Hater'[359]; rather clever and amusing. Don't know when this beastly gout will stop. I shall have to give up going to Hokitiki[360] if it lasts.

3 March 1884 - Monday

A good deal better. Banks came in the afternoon and took us for a drive. We went to the Museum where we saw the skeletons of the gigantic bird of New Zealand – the Moa, or Dinornis; one was twelve feet high and the thigh bones bigger than an ox. They are not supposed to have been long extinct – only shortly after the arrival of the white man. I suppose the Kiwis and Platypus will soon become extinct too, as they belong to an earlier order of animals. We drove to the frozen meat works in which Banks is interested, and saw rows and rows of splendid sheep hanging up, and everything clean and very well kept. Also pails of kidneys, which won't

---

[359] 'A Woman Hater', by Charles Reade.
[360] Hokitika, West Coast region, South Island of New Zealand.

freeze and sell for next to nothing. A London restaurant would be very glad of them. The freezing machinery was explained to us; it is done without any chemicals, simply compressing the air and passing it through cool tubes and then letting it expand. The frozen carcases ring like iron, and are perfectly impervious to a blow. In the evening I had rubber with Houlton, and Cotton – who is master of a pack of harriers near Christchurch and comes from Derbyshire, and another man.

4 March 1884 - Tuesday

Left by the 7.30am train though I felt barely up to the journey, but I was sick of messing on. Reached Springfield, about 40 miles off, in 3 hours – a fine specimen of New Zealand railway travelling. A young fellow named Studleigh came so far. He was a very handsome ingenuous youth but not, I should say, quite a gentleman. He amused me a good bit; he came from Exeter, and knew the Buckinghams. He confided in me that he had got Molly Buckingham's photograph. George says she is a little flirt. We fooled about in Springfield for about 2 hours and got dinner, and then the coach came. There was a young married couple on their way to England, and an old Scotchman named Lorrimer[361] – a partner in Connell Hogarths[362] – and a man named Terry[363] who is a partner in D&G Fowlers[364], Meeks's hated rivals in Adelaide. We had the usual dispute about the outside places as George and I, and Terry and Lorrimer, each professed to have been promised them in Christchurch, and both sides appealed to the coach agent. However, I knew our claim wouldn't bear examination as we had only booked yesterday, so I proposed to compromise and treat the thing in a fair and sensible manner and go turn and turn instead of disputing. Old Lorrimer was inclined to be obstinate and said he should see nothing inside, to which I replied that he wouldn't see any less than I should, and public opinion being against him he gave way. We went through some fair scenery, barren hills much like the road from Tyndrum to Black Mount – certainly not better; however all the fine scenery is the other side of the range. We got to Bealey for dinner and there found a roaring wood fire, which was pleasant. The room was full of a coach load coming the other way, and among them an old fellow named Milner Stephen[365] who is a curious character. He is a brother of Sir Alfred

---

[361] John Lorimer (-1888).
[362] Connell, Hogarth, and Co.
[363] Charles Gailey Terry (c.1850-1892) had been with D. & G. Fowler's since a young man, and by 1879 he was made a partner. He came to work in the Adelaide office in 1883, only staying in Australia for a year before returning to London in 1884.
[364] David Fowler (1826-1881) and George Swan Fowler (1839-1896), wholesale grocers, who by 1881 were a major commercial house. After David Fowler's death the firm became D. & J. Fowler's.
[365] George Milner Stephen (1812-1894), born in Devon, was first educated at Honiton Gramar School but emigrated with his lawyer father to Australia. He was a brilliant scholar and a fascinating man of many talents. Stephen had a chequered career after early failures in land speculation and charges of perjury. However, he had good administrative skills and great perseverance, becoming a barrister, geologist and 'accidental faith healer'. Stephen's

Stephen[366], who is the chief justice of New South Wales. He has been a barrister, and is rather a 'Skimpole' – but a very affable old gentleman. He goes about the country working miracles, and really makes them pay very well; he does it by laying on of hands. When he was up in Brisbane – when Keating was there – the people mobbed the place where he was, to be cured, and Australia is full of stories of the wonders he has done. And he has no doubt been very successful in nervous cases. It reminded me very much of the Lourdes stories. He had just come from Greymouth and the local paper was full of his cures. I do not know if he is an enthusiast or a conscious impostor, but I do know that if I had the power I would put him in jail lest he should deceive more men. George told him I had the gout, and he offered to lay hands on me and cure me – I suppose gratis.

5 March 1884 - Wednesday

We were called about 8.30am; perfectly dark, and the first sound we heard was the rain falling in torrents on the corrugated iron roof. Pretty miserable, considering we had come for the scenery. However, there was nothing for it so we packed and squeezed into the coach, except the hardy George who preferred the box. I was opposite a sickly-looking woman with a sturdy little boy of 4 or 5 on her lap. She looked very tired so I offered to take the child – trusting, I must say, to her motherly instinct to decline – but here I was sold, for she said, "Oh, you are kind", and handed him over; and he went sound asleep holding my thumbs in his hand. About 11 we stopped at a small place to change horses, and the rain being now trifling I got out on the roof. The Otira Gorge[367] is as grand as anything in Switzerland, certainly, and the growth of timber and variety of ferns and other foliage very remarkable. We got to Kumara, a gold mining township. They have cut away the hill above the town and burrowed right underneath, and one can see the shafts below on the side of the cliff where they shoot the rubbish into the Grey River valley beneath. The place swarms with Public Houses – out of 7 houses, I counted 5 so-called 'hotels' in a row. We dined at Stewart's Hotel, which we were told was the best, and the coach went on to Hokitiki[368], but George and I and Terry decided to go to Greymouth instead as there was a better chance of catching a steamer for Nelson. Stewart was a very civil, respectable Scot. He gave us a good cigar apiece, and walked down to the tramway station for Greymouth with us. The tramway is made of wood, and the car bumps along on it through a narrow track cut straight through the forest. It reminded me exactly of the tramway through the woods to the convict

---

interests in science and geology went deep and his contribution in this field was notable. He also had talents in music and the arts. He married and had a family, but only three of his sons survived him.

[366] Sir Alfred Stephen (1802-1894) was Chief Justice of New South Wales from 1845 to 1873.

[367] The Otira Gorge is located west of Arthur's Pass National Park, and the whole area is now a popular tourist attraction.

[368] Hokitika, West Coast region, South Island of New Zealand.

station in the centre of Trinidad. It was very pretty, but the car got off the rails once and we had all to get out and hoist it on.

There was a police magistrate with us named Stratford – a gentlemanly man who had been in the Royal Navy. When we came to the Grey River we got out and were swung over in a cage. It was over 1000 ft. across, some old fellow told me. They used to cross the river at Clifton[369] in a somewhat similar fashion before the suspension bridge was put up. Earlier in the day, we crossed a strong river and passed the wreck of a coach which had been upset a fortnight before and the horses drowned, but no lives lost. There was an old Jew who was in a ghastly funk whenever we went near a steep place, holding away from the window. Also, when we got among some cattle he was very ridiculous and said in a tone of great terror to the woman, "Don't be alarmed Ma'am; it's following us" – referring to a stray bullock. We put up at Gilmer's Hotel, Greymouth, and got very comfortable rooms. The landlord, an Ulster man, came and talked to us, but we were all dog-tired and very glad to get to bed.

6 March 1884 - Thursday

Walked about and looked at the place, which is [a] flourishing, go-ahead sort of sea port – or rather, it is on the Grey River but close to the mouth. The making of the place will be the large coal mines near – which are beginning to be actively worked – where there is an illimitable supply of good, hard, gas coal. There is also a certain amount of gold mining in the neighbourhood. We had ourselves ferried over the river and took a beautiful walk of 7 miles through tree fern and lovely lanes along the river bank to Brunner[370]. Here we came across the Director of one of the mines – 'The Coal Pit Heath mine' – who offered to show us over it, which I was rather glad as I had never seen a coal mine. We went down the shaft about 3 or 400 feet, and were each provided with lighted candles. The mine is very dry, though in parts it is under the river bed. The seam of coal is extraordinarily thick, an average of 17 foot; consequently, the passages are most spacious, and there is no creeping and crouching as in most English mines. In some places the coal was all round us – floor, ceiling and walls. I saw a horse down there which had been in the mine 4 years: it looked as well as possible. We came up after inspecting the machinery and crossed the river; and back to Greymouth by train.

I should think some day Melbourne and Adelaide should get the bulk of their coal from the west coast of New Zealand. Played dummy whist in the evening with Terry and George M.

---

[369] Clifton is a suburb of Bristol, England. The Clifton Suspension Bridge, designed by Brunel and eventually completed in 1864, spans the Avon Gorge and River Avon from Clifton to Leigh Woods in North Somerset.
[370] Brunner experienced New Zealand's greatest workplace disaster when there was a mine explosion in 1896, just 12 years after Gibbs' visit, killing 65.

7 March 1884 - Friday

Had breakfast and left at 7.30 in the coach for Reeftown[371]. The scenery very fine and richly-wooded with abundance of rivers – very like Switzerland. We reached Ahaura about noon and had a meal. There was the monthly mining court being held so we looked in, and the sitting magistrate – or warden as he is called – was Stratford, whom we met on the 5th. He recognised us and sent his clerk to put us into seats. The warden's court was adjourned while we were there, and the magistrate's court opened. We saw an old fellow charged with vagrancy, and then had to run off to catch the coach. We stopped and changed horses at Nelson's Creek[372] and took up a pleasant talkative girl, the daughter of a storekeeper in Nelson. I rather like, in travelling in New Zealand, the complete absence of class distinction – and the same in Australia. Coachmen, barmaids, landlords and people in the position of gentry all dining together, and I think the average behaviour is better than it would be in England. There is no such thing as domineering or servility. One has certainly to do many more things for oneself than one would in England, and if one is waited on at all it is done as a favour. I think 6 months in New Zealand at some period of her life would have been excellent for poor Aunt Mary[373] and others like her who are always thinking that people they meet at hotels are not quite gentlemen or ladies. We reached Reeftown at 6 and had tea. It began to rain just after we got in. We found there was a travelling company of actors going to play, so we went. The piece was called 'Led Astray' – an emotional drama in six acts. It was a powerful, rather melodramatic piece adapted, I should think, from the French. The heroine, a Miss Crawford, acted admirably – though she a little overplayed it. A man named Rede, who took the part of the good-natured cousin who is everybody's friend and peacemaker, was also particularly good – but some of the others were comically bad. Hardly any of them knew their parts, and Miss Crawford had to prompt them all. She seemed very good-natured, for her best tragic scenes were quite ruined by a fool of a local amateur who played her husband. He looked like a waiter, and he tried to gag where he didn't know his part; and his own very homely language was in amusing contrast to the stilted lines of the piece. He forgot to give her his will before fighting a duel, and she had to say, loud, "Give me the will; do give it me". There was also a vulgar woman looking like a housemaid who was cast for the 'Grande Dame', and when she was asked how she liked a ball she said, "My word! I never was in sech a mob. I'm quite 'sterical", which was evidently a little thing of her own, for the Baron – who had not got his cue and didn't know what to reply – walked off the stage laughing, without making any reply at all. There was a girl, too, who played as badly as Louisa Adams – which is saying a good deal. I enjoyed the piece thoroughly, both the good and bad acting; indeed I was seldom

---

[371] Reefton, about 50 miles north-east of Greymouth.
[372] Nelson Creek, about 20 miles ENE of Greymouth.
[373] Probably Mary Dorothea Gibbs (1833-1906), Vicary's father's sister.

at a theatre where I had better money's worth for my 3/-. It must be impossible for a large company to do well on the West Coast, where travelling is so expensive. One of the actors told me they only took £15 in any one night.

8 March 1884 - Saturday

Reeftown is a biggish mining town, and not so pretty as Greymouth. Everybody one meets is more or less interested in the gold fields, and Terry – who is a mason – met a brother mason who offered to take us over the Globe gold mine, which is a particularly successful one and has paid its capital three times over in the 3 years that it has been working. We walked with him to Crushington, about 4 miles off, where this and many other mines are, and saw the crushing, and quicksilver and blanketing, and the buckets carrying the quartz, and all the rest of it. It was very interesting. Our guide was an Irishman, and had been a great deal among the Maoris. We had not been able to get a coach to go on towards Nelson, so we took a buggy for the three, and started for Lyell. There was very little flat land on the journey – almost all mountain and river. We reached Lyell at 8, our horses very tired. We crossed two big rivers in punts. We put up at a hotel kept by an Italian, and had supper. There is a mining surveyor here who has been telling me a lot about the mining. He tells me that the geological formation here has quite upset all preconceived ideas, and that this is the only place in the world where gold and coal have been found side by side.

Terry, our travelling companion, is not a bad sort, but he would not do for long – I should get tired of him. Unless we are stopped by floods we ought to get to Nelson on Monday night, but it is chancy work fording these rivers, as they swell up very quick. In most places there is a sort of light foot-suspension bridge, made very cheap for about £100 with thin boards and galvanised wire. We saw 2 or 3 Maori hens in the bush. They look like a bantam fowl in shape and size, and like a grey hen in colour. They do not fly, and have very imperfectly developed wings like lots of Australasian birds[374]. The commonest bird is the tooy[375] **[sic]**, or parson bird, which is like a blackbird or starling with two white feathers in the neck that have just the appearance of bands.

---

[374] There are no large-winged birds - the main predators of smaller birds - recorded in New Zealand archaeology, which may be one of the reasons that birds there have lost their need of, and thus ability for, winged flight.
[375] Tooy: Gibbs' misspelling of Tooey or more usually Tui, also known as the Parson Bird. It is a honey eater.

9 March 1884 - Sunday

Lyell (I suppose named after Sir Charles[376]) is a small mining town consisting of one long strip squeezed in between the mountain and river. The landlord of our Inn is an Italian named Fama. We left about 8am, our horses pretty fit, and were driving all day through a narrow wild gorge above the Buller River. At noon we stopped to bait[377] at a little roadside accommodation house kept by a Cornish man named Oxham. There was a picture of Wesley[378] hanging up inside, as might be expected of a Cornishman. There was no one in the house but Mrs Oxham, as all the men had gone into the bush. She was rather surprised at our turning up, as it is very rare for anyone to come – except the coach. However, she set to work and got us some steak, and apple pie and cream, and got us a very fair meal. We stayed 2 hours to rest the horses, Murphy and Tommy, who had had a very rough journey, and then moved on, the road getting rather worse. We were very nearly stuck up by a road-slip at a very precipitous place going downhill. I stayed in the trap to keep the break [sic] on, and a couple of miners and Terry and George hung on behind, and we just squeaked through. Our horses got awfully 'done', and it was with a shout of joy that we saw the smoke curling up from the Inn where we were going to stop for the night, having come 47 miles of very bad road.

There was only the one house, called Hope River; kept by a brawny, black-bearded Frenchman hailing from Cherbourg. There was a large family of girls crowded round a roaring wood fire and we were made very welcome; and some Irish stew and the inevitable tea – which last, appears at every meal in Australia and New Zealand up country. I chatted and smoked with some drovers, and talked French with Ribet. He told me there were a lot of wild pigs[379] in the bush, and also wild cattle; that he had killed a wild bull the other day with a military carbine. It was a fine, moonlit night and we could hear the Maori fowl calling to one another all round. Our bedrooms were tiny little cabins, but clean.

10 March 1884 - Monday

We left soon after eight and drove through forest to some flats where there was no Inn, but a little farm kept by two Buckinghamshire men, sons of a keeper at Dashwood's[380]. I talked with them about Thame and 'The

---

[376] Sir Charles Lyell (1797-1875), a British lawyer and famous geologist, and a friend of Charles Darwin.
[377] To bait: to halt on a journey for refreshment or rest.
[378] John Wesley (1703-1791), or his brother Charles Wesley (1707-1788), founders of the English Methodist movement. Cornwall particularly embraced Wesleyan Methodism.
[379] The majority of wild pigs in New Zealand are descended from the feral "Captain Cookers" breed introduced by Captain Cook when he first visited the country in 1769.
[380] Sir Francis Dashwood – founder of the notorious Hellfire Club – lived in West Wycombe Park (now National Trust), near the town of Thame. Sir Edwin Hare Dashwood (1825-1882) resigned his commission in the Indian Army and settled in 1848 in Motueka (where many

Three Pigeons', where I have been several times and which they knew. We drove on after a rest and began to get into more civilised-looking country and saw some hop gardens, of which I believe there are a lot round Nelson. We reached a little village called Belgrove about 5pm, to which place the railway comes from Nelson – and is in course of further extension[381]. But as there was no decent Inn, and no train today, we drove 2 miles further to Foxhill and put up at a house kept by a Yorkshireman named Gaukrodger. Had some dummy whist; and so to bed. The Port Darwin line has been interrupted and I see in the paper that the men sent up to repair it have discovered a man dead under the line 120 miles north of the Peake. In despair he had cut the wire hoping to bring assistance. A horse was found dead alongside the body. The nearest water 20 miles distant. What a horrible picture it calls up of the poor wretch; and an ingenious idea too.

11 March 1884 - Tuesday

Left at 7.30 by the train into Nelson, through a fertile valley. It is a very pretty town, and prosperous-looking though quiet. It has the name of 'Sleepy Hollow' and I believe a good many retired Indians are settled there. We walked up a zigzag path and got a good view of the town; afterwards called on a firm named Neale & Haddow[382] who send hops to us in Sydney. Mr Haddow insisted on us going with him to a meeting of hop growers. It was rather amusing, as the hop growers were very indignant with some Jew who had been 'bearing'[383] the hop market, and they talked some tremendous rot. At 6 o'clock we went on board the 'Wanaka', a small steamer of the Union Co. The weather calm.

Tour of North Island, New Zealand from Wellington to Auckland

12 March 1884 - Wednesday

We reached Picton[384] about 1am and stopped 2 or 3 hours, arriving at Wellington by 10 – a much larger and uglier place than Nelson. We put

---

colonial families from India retired), also having bought a successful sheep station near Blenheim. He and other later Dashwoods returned to England as members of the line died unexpectedly early and the West Wycombe estate needed heirs. Herbert Cokayne Gibbs' future wife, Anna Maria Durrant, was the daughter of Charlotte Still Dashwood, of the same family.
[381] This isolated, government-owned railway line was known as the Nelson Section, and operated from 1876 to 1955. At the time Gibbs visits, the line extended from Nelson and its port as far as Belgrove but eventually it was extended to Glenhope.
[382] Still going strong: Neale and Haddow Ltd, 52 Rutherford Street, Nelson, is an old style store and gallery that stocks tools, general hardware and DIY.
[383] Trading term, as in bear market.
[384] Picton is on the north-east coast of South Island, and Wellington on the south-west coast of North Island, with Cook Strait in between.

up at the Occidental Hotel, went to the Bank and Post Office, and then for a long walk over hilly downs and back through the Botanical Gardens which are very ill-kept. Wellington has no minerals or agricultural country near it and depends only on being the seat of Government. It is a one horse place, and far inferior in beauty to the South Island towns.

In the evening we went to see 'Youth', which was playing a long time in Drury Lane but I had never seen it. The hero was well done by a handsome young fellow named Cates[385] who was at school with G.M. The hero's father, a parson, when he catches his son in some intrigue says, "I too was not without my follies in youth, but when my family and position required it I left the woman who would have been a millstone round my neck without a moment's hesitation". This truly magnificent sentiment was cheered by the gallery!

13 March 1884 - Thursday

About 10 on Wednesday night we went through the Frenchman's Pass, which is a very narrow passage between a small island and the mainland. Through this the sea rushes like a mill race, and as it was bright moonlight we saw it very well. It is a neat piece of steering as the ship goes close enough to the land to chuck a biscuit on, and it has to alter its course sharply in the middle of the strait.

Merivale and I went for a 10 mile walk to Lower Hutt, the other end of the bay; it was the original site selected for Wellington but was given up on account of the earthquakes. After dinner, G.M. left for Sydney in the 'Wakatipu'. I was very sorry to lose him, but he had seen the Hot Lakes before and wanted to get back to his wife and work. Our trip through the South Island has been a very pleasant one on the whole, though I was seedy the first part. By going so much overland we have seen a lot of the country in a short time, and the coach travelling – though more laborious and expensive – is far more interesting than coasting steamers. I certainly like George better than ever after a month in his company, and think his wife very lucky to have such a kind, good, manly husband.

14 March 1884 - Friday

Heard to my disgust that the 'Rotoruahama' is put off and sails tomorrow, so I am stuck up for another day in Wellington with nothing to do.

Glad to see they have given Furnival a small pension. I think he deserves it. Had a look at the museum – an interesting room, fitted up with native carvings. In the evening went to a circus – pretty fair. I've only been to 3 circuses in my life: one at Whitby, one at Antwerp and one here at Wellington. Heard of the failure of Greig, whom I have often met in

---

[385] Frank Cates

Melbourne. He was about the best – and certainly the pleasantest – whist player there; he has gone for £90,000 and absconded[386].

15 March 1884 - Saturday

Went for a walk, then on board the 'Rotoruahama' which sailed at 4pm. She is a very fast ship, averaging 13 knots without using 2 of her boilers. There is a Miss Cruikshank on board, with her father[387], whose sister I met with the Laidleys. She is a pleasant, unaffected sort of girl; he rather senile and hypochondriacal. They are going to the Hot Lakes. I have a fair cabin with one other man, amidships, and the sea seems to be behaving well. The Hon. Ivo Bligh and his bride[388] are on board. She has a pretty face but will soon be 'nutcrackery'. Played 3 games of chess.

42. Ivo Bligh, Lord Darnley, recipient of the Ashes Urn in 1883 (c1890)
Wikimedia Commons

43. Florence, Countess of Darnley, wife of Ivo Bligh (c1890)
Wikimedia Commons

16 March 1884 - Sunday

Arrived after breakfast at Napier. There is no harbour, only an open roadstead. It seems a rum place to have built a town. A small steamer came and took us off, and we were landed at the back of the town and

---

[386] W.J. Greig, a well-known merchant, disappeared from Melbourne in May 1884, leaving his company W.J. Greig & Co. unable to meet its liabilities. He reappeared in June 1886 and met his creditors in an attempt to re-start his business.
[387] Possibly D. B. Cruickshank, the Director of the Mutual Assurance Society of Victoria Ltd. in the Auckland National Bank Buildings (this from an advertisement in the Waikato Times, New Zealand, from 1884). Gibbs later visits Cruickshanks on 2 August 1884 to collect his mail.
[388] Florence Rose Morphy, of Beechworth, Victoria, a music teacher.

had to drive a mile through a gorge to get to it[389]. It is the only town I have been at on this side of the globe which is on the open sea. It has a parade and beach rather like what St. Leonards must have been 50 years ago.

I met Major George, whom I saw a good deal of on the 'City of New York' and who asked me to his house in Auckland. He did not know me in the least, though he was civil enough afterwards. People are so imbecilely stupid about recognising me it makes one almost shrink from speaking, knowing that one will have to explain even if one feels sure they will be glad to see one – when they have realised that it is the same man they have been quite intimate with six weeks ago. I believe I have almost got an 'invisible' cap. The town is much crowded as the races are on tomorrow. But Terry and I have got a decent room together at the best hotel, 'Criterion'.

17 March 1884 - Monday

The coach doesn't start till tomorrow, so as there was nothing to see in Napier we took the train and went about 20 miles to Hastings where the race course is. We had very good racing, and enjoyed it. Major George's horse ran second.

In the evening we went to a Scotch entertainment of ballad singing and stories given by a family of father, son and 3 daughters, named Kennedy. The theatre was cram full. Got a letter from R.B., forwarded from Auckland, but no home letters which I had hoped for. Our hotel full of bookmakers making a beastly row; the place is used as a sort of 'rooms'.

18 March 1884 - Tuesday

Called at 5am; got a cup of tea with a raw egg in it and started in the coach – very full. A man named Smith, another[,] Ryder, and another[,] Berkeley, on the box; and inside, a Derbyshire farmer and his wife on their way back to England after a trip, a lame girl going to the baths for rheumatism, a Captain Anderson of the Constabulary,[;] an Irishman,[;] Terry and myself. At first the scenery was pretty, and when we got up into the hills, very fine. I have never travelled any road like it for steepness of hills and sharpness of curves, and the driver went an awful pace. The farmer's wife screamed and giggled, and the road being very greasy with the wet the coach skithered[390] along and jumped over the stones, shaking one to pieces.

---

[389] The difficult approach to Napier was eased significantly by a catastrophic earthquake in 1931, The Napier Earthquake (also known as the Hawke's Bay Earthquake). The rebuilding of the town, which was almost totally destroyed, took ten years. It is now an Art Deco architectural attraction.
[390] *Skither* is old Irish slang for a badly behaved child. Presumably, Gibbs doesn't mean this, but rather is conjoining two words, *skittered* and *slithered*.

They have two immensely powerful breaks[391], one which the driver puts on, and the other, the other box passenger. I don't suppose there is really any danger as long as nothing goes wrong with the tackle and there is no obstruction on the road. The road is 3 miles and a half long, average about a grade of 1 in 13 – and in parts is 1 in 5. We took 15 minutes getting to the bottom. Here we stopped for some lunch and the old fellow, Smith, had a frightful row with the driver, whom he called a maniac and said ought to be sacked. He said he wouldn't for £1,000 come down it again, and that if he had known the way the driver was going to do it he would have put him off the box and driven it himself. However, as I had heard there was another hill to come – worse than the last – I was most anxious to appease the driver, who was furious, and none of us felt inclined to trust ourselves to Mr Smith's care. The next hill was no worse but the turns were sharper. The coachman drove beautifully; quite a young chap, about twenty six. We reached Tarawera[392] about 6pm and found a rough little public kept by a civil Dane. His little girls, about 10 and 11 – rather pretty and very sharp – waited on us; the only place where the waiting has been good. Mr Smith turns out to be Tyson, the richest man south of the Line. He calls himself Smith because all sorts of people run after him to get him to buy things and invest in things, so he goes incognito. He is an illiterate old block, and got a good deal of jaw, but he seems intelligent. He had never been out of Australia before. He is unmarried and penurious[393].

19 March 1884 - Wednesday

Called at 5, but the coach rather late. Went and looked at the grave of a woman on the hillside, the only person who is known to have died in Tarawera. The first 2 hours of the drive: fine views and hilly; after that, rough-going through pumice stone country – barren and not very beautiful. The farmer's wife chatted ceaselessly and 'h'-lessly – the most infinite nothings, just for the pleasure of hearing her confounded tongue wag. Everybody was furious with her. Fortunately she over-ate herself at lunch and was sick. Berkeley gave her some brandy and she was quieter for a bit. Ryder is not a bad sort; he is a friend of old Broad, who was a clerk in No. 15[394]. There was no half-way house so we had our sandwiches at a bridge. Later on, about a mile outside Taupo, one of the leaders got his leg over the trace and set to kicking. He kicked himself clear of everything, and there was near being a general smash up, but the other horses behaved very well considering, and several of us got down and got

---

[391] An old alternative spelling of "brakes".
[392] Tarawera is now nothing but a cafe on the Napier-Taupo highway, roughly halfway between the two cities. Lake Tarawera and Mount Tarawera (a volcanic mountain, which erupted in 1886 killing 150 people and completely burying the Maori village of Te Wairoa) are roughly 75 miles north, near Rotorua.
[393] Probably in its definition of 'stingy', rather than the now more usual 'poor'.
[394] Refers to the AG&S office at 15 Bishopsgate. Antony Gibbs & Sons had been based at 13 Sherborne Lane, Lombard Street (from about 1809), 20 Great Winchester Street (1814-15), 28 Great Winchester Street (1815-26), 47 Lime Street (1826-50) and 15 Bishopsgate (from 1850) - later renumbered to 22 Bishopsgate.

to their heads. We were patched up and got into Taupo about 5 after a 50 mile drive – about the same distance as we came yesterday. Lake Taupo is an enormous lake, the biggest in New Zealand, but not so beautiful as some I have seen. It is about the middle of the North Island. We played euchre – Terry, Anderson and I.

20 March 1884 - Thursday

Left again in a new coach about 6am – at least I did not, as I got a riding horse: a very pleasant, easy, hack, but a slow walker. I enjoyed the riding very much, but it poured with rain a great part of the time. The scenery nothing particular. We should have liked to have stayed 2 days in Taupo and seen some of the springs, but we could have got no conveyance on for a week. It was a curious sight, as I rode along, seeing the puffs of steam coming up from the valley like white clouds. We had a rough lunch in a little place – tinned meat and so on. I got a rub down with a rough towel. We reached Ohinemutu[395] about 5; the air smells very strongly of sulphur, and lakes and ponds boiling up in all directions. The big lake so rough it looked like a sea. I was exceedingly glad to have a warm bath in the garden of Graham's Hotel, the land outside the bath all bubbling and steaming. In spite of a ride of 56 miles and having been up the last 3 days at 5, and travelling all day, I don't feel particularly tired. At dinner I saw Mrs & Miss Ryan, who were very friendly, and Mrs R., much better for the waters.

21 March 1884 - Friday

A pretty place, and fine view from the balcony of the Maori village below and the lake Rotorua and the mountains. We walked about in the early morning and looked into the whares[396], and watched the native children swimming and diving into the hot water. Then we went to the Government baths and took the priest's bath – which is a large, square bath capable of holding 10 or 12 people; temperature about 95° [Fahrenheit] and in the open air – it is very strong of sulphur and alum, and has some sulphuric acid. The fumes are so strong my silver chain was quite blackened by hanging up in the dressing room, and the attendant showed me his watch, quite black. The bath was pleasant and unlike an ordinary hot bath – invigorating. After lunch we started to drive to Wairoa, the party being almost the same as the coach, viz. Terry, Berkeley, Tyson and Ryder. We stopped at a village about half a mile off called Whakarewarewa[397], or some such name, where we saw some small geysers and hot springs. The air is very strongly charged with sulphur, and reminds

---

[395] Ohinemutu is a suburb situated on the North Island of New Zealand. It is located in the Waikato region. Local landmarks include Hinemoa Pool, Kuirau Park, Lake Rotorua, Ngatautara, Ngongotaha, Pohaturoa, Redwood Grove, Tangatarua.
[396] 'Whares' (pronounced similarly to 'worry') are Maori meeting houses or village halls.
[397] Whakarewarewa, or Whaka for short, is Rotorua's best-known thermal zone and a major Maori cultural area. It is a popular visitor attraction and health spa.

me of my beloved Harrogate. It's a fine drive to Wairoa, passing through some beautiful bush and by some lakes. About half way, we picked up a dead Maori. He was a young man, and could only have been dead a short time as he wasn't stiff. He had by him an empty bottle of brandy, do. [ditto] of rum, and do. of beer, with the contents of which plus exposure at night he had been killed. We reached Wairoa and put up at the smaller of the two Inns, Moncrieff's, and then walked down to see a waterfall about a mile off. After tea we went to the native meeting house to see a Haka[398], or native dance – 15 men and 15 women. They stood still and made extraordinary gestures, wriggling themselves about; it was a rum sight.

22 March 1884 - Saturday

Fortunately a fine day; about 7 we started and walked to the lake across which we were rowed in a large boat, about 8 miles, and then in a canoe to the terraces. They don't look much at first sight, but when one gets on to them they are wonderful; a sort of creamy white silicate with marvellously clear water flowing over it, and every now and then deep pools of clear milky-blue water; the water steadily increasing in heat as one goes up, till the top which is a large crater of perfectly clear boiling water throwing off steam. After this we visited the other sites: the Devil's Hole – a round hole in which was a frightful noise like the engines of a ship blowing off steam; and boiling mud caldrons and geysers, the land all about crackling and steaming and bubbling. Our guide, a Maori woman named Sophia, was intelligent and talked English very well; she told us she had had 15 children. Then we went to the Pink Terrace[399] – which is similar, but smaller – and here we all bathed, moving about into pools of various temperature as we felt disposed. Sophia bathed too.

We got back about 5 to Wairoa after a most agreeable day spent in seeing what is certainly one of the greatest 'Wonders of the World'.

After dinner we drove back 12 miles to Ohinemutu through bush which was covered with glow-worms. As we passed the meeting house, the natives were having a tangy[400] or wake over the body[401] which they had propped up in a sitting position in the centre of a circle. It rained hard as we drove back; most lucky that it did not come on before, as half the beauty of the terraces and water would have been lost without the sun.

---

[398] The Haka is a traditional Maori War Dance; it is performed in unison by a group of Maoris, with intimidating gestures, posturing and stamping and accompanied by War Cries and grimacing.
[399] The Pink and White Terraces of Wairoa were thought, until 2011, to have been completely destroyed by the eruption of Mount Tarawera on 9-10 June 1886, just over 2 years after Gibbs' visit. However, parts of the Terraces were recently rediscovered during mapping of the lake floor, and it is thought that the remainder was simply covered by sediment from the volcanic eruption rather than being destroyed.
[400] Tangi: funeral and/or wake (Maori origin)
[401] Presumably, this is the body found the previous day.

23 March 1884 - Sunday

Took a Priest's bath again; very jolly. Old Tyson left for Cambridge. Rather interesting to have met a man like that, who has lived a life of untiring industry and self-denial. This is the first holiday he has ever had; he told me he had never consulted a doctor, taken medicine, or had any kind of illness that he could remember. He has never given a bill in his life, never been in debt except for current expenses, says he can't understand what people mean by love, and is, I should think, entirely devoid of natural affection; always been perfectly upright and honest, and never thinks of or takes any interest in things except as to how they will pay. He has made the making of money an end in itself – and bringing the whole of a shrewd mind and healthy body to bear solely, entirely, and always on this one point he has succeeded marvellously. There is a Queensland Squatter here in the hotel for whom in 1846 Tyson used to herd stray cattle on the Herbert at 2/6 a head, and now, one year with another, he is said to be worth 3 to 500 thousand per annum. It is known that he offered the Queensland Government a million cash the other day for 4 million acres, and they would have taken it but for the popular outcry.

He has no education, mispronounces, drops his H's, and has great difficulty in expressing his ideas at all. He told me if those he left his money to found as much pleasure in spending as he had found in accumulating they would do very well.

Strolled about the village and read some articles of Sydney Smith[402]; one about the ballot witty, violent, and amusing now in a new way, from its unfulfilled prognostications of evils that would arise from a change that has proved of little importance.

Service in the dining room in the evening by a clergyman from Thames, and talked in the smoking room with a clever, excitable man named Haig, in the last stage of consumption. The Blighs are here, and Ivo introduced me to his wife – Miss Morphy that was. She is certainly very pretty, and has pleasing manners. She does not strike me as at all Colonial and will, I should think, go down[403] in London. She is something like Mrs Finch Hatton, Harcourt's daughter, only better-looking.

24 March 1884 - Monday

Took a sulphur bath again, and a walk with a Townsville police magistrate name Morey. He had been a squatter, but was ruined by dingoes and had to begin the world again at 42 with a wife and 3 children and not a 6d. except what he earned. Preparations going on in the village and hotel for

---
[402] Sydney Smith (1771-1845) was a highly respected Church man who was also a talented humorist - and a political thinker who fought for Catholic emancipation.
[403] We would say "go down well" nowadays - "go down" would imply the exact opposite.

receiving the Governor, Sir William Jervois[404] who is expected today. I have a letter to him, but I don't think I shall present it. Went for a walk with Terry up a neighbouring hill; when we were about 4 miles off we heard the cheering going at the Governor's arrival. We heard when we got back that he had had a great reception, and the natives had taken his horses out and drawn the carriage to the hotel. At dinner I talked to Mrs Bligh, who is very fascinating; and after dinner, began to feel gouty in the left ankle, and as it came on very fast I went to bed.

25 March 1884 - Tuesday

Rather a bad night and couldn't move my foot this morning, but very little pain. All sorts of people calling to enquire and sit with me in the most friendly way; indeed, if I had been really bad, there would have been too many. Directly after breakfast Dr Lewis, the resident Doctor who was in the Navy and is a friend of Merivale's – a very nice chap – looked in 'as a friend' with some medicine consisting of iodide of potassium, aconite and a little colchicum – it certainly was very efficient. The Bligh's sent to ask if I would move into their room as it was larger and brighter – which was very civil – and Lewis came in and smoked his pipe and spent the evening with me; also Berkeley and Mumford. I read a French novel by Alphonse Karr called 'La Famille Alain', a pretty story of Normandy fishermen – very suitable to give a girl to read. Altogether I got through the day very well, my gout getting less as it went on. I shall, however, have to give up starting for Cambridge tomorrow which is tiresome as I want to get to Auckland and read my letters – besides, I have had a long holiday. If I am well enough I shall go by Tauranga on Friday instead.

26 March 1884 - Wednesday

Terry went off via Cambridge this morning and my gout seems to have passed off as suddenly as it came. I was almost tempted to try and go too, but felt it would be too risky as I am lame still. Read some of 'Tristan Le Roux' by Dumas Fils, but could not get on with it.

27 March 1884 - Thursday

Quite well again, and a beautiful day. A man named Walters and I got up a picnic in a sailing boat to the island in the middle of the lake. It reminded me very much of going to Isola Madre, only there is no palace on the island, only a few Maori Whares. The rest of our party were Mr & Mrs Morey, Mrs & Miss Ryan, Mr & Miss Cruickshank, poor Haig, and Berkeley; we got to the island about 1 o'clock and made a fire with sticks. I was appointed cook, and with the assistance of a gridiron and frying pan managed to turn out a lot of chops and omelettes to the general satisfaction, though I have not done any since I left Eton. It was a pleasant,

---

[404] Sir William Francis Drummond Jervois, GCMG, CB (1821-1897), was Governor-General of New Zealand from 1882 to 1888.

cheerful party and nobody quarrelled. We strolled about the island and sailed back with a fair wind to dinner. In the evening I played some eccentric whist with Miss Cruikshank, Berkeley and Miss Ryan, and there was a horrid vulgar girl from London who screeched through some Scotch songs. Mrs R. entrusted me with a lot of letters to Melbourne for no possible reason that I can see except to save the postage.

28 March 1884 - Friday

Called at 5. Breakfast 5.30 and started at 6 to ride to Tauranga. I had a capital horse, a much better walker than the one I had at Taupo, which is very important in a long journey. A Scotchman named Wilson came with me, a very decent fellow; and it was fine weather and not hot. I enjoyed it immensely. We reached Tauranga at 2. 42 miles in fine weather with a mate is far preferable to 56 by oneself in pouring rain. I was not the least tired. We had 17 miles through grand bush and stopped to bait at a little roadside shanty – which was in some confusion as there had been a distress for rent; however, we got some eggs and wineglasses for eggcups. After 2 hours in Tauranga we started in the S. S. 'Wellington' for Auckland. Tauranga is a pretty place with a great rocky island standing up in the centre of the entrance to the harbour. On our road we went through the Gate Pah[405] where the British troops were massacred. As far as I can understand our gallant fellows behaved very ill, much like Majubah Hill. They first took the hill and drove the blacks out, who tried to bolt across some swampy ground below. But when headed back by another detachment of English who were stationed there to turn them, they rushed back in confusion up to the Pah, and the British troops thought they were returning of their own accord, being reinforced; so a panic took place and they fled and were cut to pieces. The Gate Pah did not strike me as being an extraordinarily strong place or particularly suited for defence. Wilson wants me to come and stay with him at Thames but I shan't have time.

29 March 1884 - Saturday

We had a fine passage and reached Auckland early in the morning. I breakfasted at a hotel with Walters and then called on Cruickshank and got a large budget of letters from home, all pretty satisfactory I am happy to say. I then went up to the Club and read and wrote letters till dinner. I played whist in the evening and afterwards watched some men playing euchre till very late. I have got a comfortable bedroom; the Club is very well managed, and the cooking is excellent. One notices it after a month of bush inns with nothing but steaks, chops and tea.

---

[405] The Gate Pa was a remarkable Maori victory achieved against tremendous odds. The battle more than any other convinced the British of the futility of assaulting a completed modern pa and undermined their will to continue the Waikato War.

30 March 1884 - Sunday

Overslept myself pretty thoroughly; my watch had gone wrong and stopped. I had no idea it was so late when I woke, and came out of my room in my pyjamas to look for the bath room and met a man who seemed amused; so I asked him the time and he said 10 minutes to 2!

At dinner I met a Colonel Reader[406], who was in the Crimea and is Secretary for Defence and Chief of the Constabulary in New Zealand. I had a long talk with him and found him very agreeable. I read the 'Fortnightly'[407] for Jan 1884, an excellent number; a most interesting article on 'The fallacy of Irish History' by Goldwin Smith, a good one on his visit to America by Lepel Griffin who went over there in the same steamer with me. A very clever dialogue on 'Life and Death' by Lilly. Two biographies of Lords Lytton and Lyndhurst; and an account of the acting of 'The Birds' at Cambridge by Jebb, an article on Hablot Browne and some verses by Swinburn, besides other articles which I did not read. A pretty good half crown's worth for anybody. Certainly Escott is an A1 Editor and if the Review is always up to this standard it is well worth taking in. We had some dotterel for dinner, a sort of large sea snipe – rather oily, not so good as a snipe and not so bad as a curlew.

31 March 1884 - Monday

Read press copies and wrote letters in the Northern Club most of the day and walked over to Oram's Hotel and had a chat with Terry.

1 April 1884 - Tuesday

Recalled to the date by 2 girls making a fool of me in the street. They stopped me with a cock and bully story to which I listened till I saw their eyes brimming over with enjoyment and they ran away shouting 'April Fool'. I was pleased at being selected as a victim as I considered it a compliment to my benevolent appearance – though at the expense of my intelligence.

The 'Tarawera's' sailing was put off until 8pm so I had time for a comfortable dinner on shore. The Bligh's are fellow passengers, of which I am glad; also the Moreys[408]. I have a small cabin to myself, but just over the propeller which is a very bad position. The flag's flying half mast for

---

[406] Lieutenant Colonel H. E. Reader, Commissioner of the New Zealand Constabulary and - as at 1880 - Under-secretary for Defence.
[407] The Fortnightly Review (established 1865), a British periodical which - despite the name - was only published monthly from 1866. The then editor to whom Gibbs refers was T. H. S. Escott.
[408] From the passenger list of the Tarawera, we know that their name was Moray rather than Morey.

poor Leopold[409]. I should fear it would have a serious effect on the Queen, her health being so queer.

S.S. Tarawera (2)

2 April 1884 - Wednesday

44. Maori King & Queen
Sir George Grey Special Collections, Auckland Libraries, ref. 589-4

The vessel is very light and she keeps getting the screw out of water, and it wakes one up with a feeling as if something had burst in one's head. Tawhiao, the King of the Maoris, is on board with his suite. He is going 'home' to complain to his sister of England[410] at the way the Maoris have been treated about the Land Question. He is a 'cheapish' sort of thing in kings, and a filthy feeder. He plays draughts very well – a game much in vogue among the Maoris. He is tattooed very elaborately on the face, the only part left clear being the cheekbones and centre of the forehead.

Most people seasick – no ladies up. I am keeping pretty well, though not exactly comfortable. Read 'Mansfield Park'[411] and liked it, but it is rather *borné*[412], and the hero and heroine are rather prigs. However, Mrs Norris, Sir Thomas and Lady Bertram are excellent. But the denouement is poorly worked out. I observe in this book Miss A. strongly advocates the necessity of a parson living in his parish. About this nothing is said in a similar case in 'Northanger Abbey'. Query as to dates of the two books.

---

[409] Queen Victoria's haemophiliac fourth and youngest son, Prince Leopold, the Duke of Albany, died suddenly in a fit at 2 o'clock on the morning of 28th March 1884 in Cannes.
[410] Gibbs is noting that Tawhiao obviously thinks of himself as an equal to the Queen of England, his adopted home.
[411] Jane Austen (1775-1817): 'Mansfield Park' (1814)
[412] French: narrow-minded

3 April 1884 - Thursday

There is an Irish gentleman on board named Lloyd. I have met him at the Melbourne Club; he is a large New South Wales Squatter and a racing man. He is pleasant company, and has lived a wild, various life; among other things cutting wood at so much a cord[413] for a steamboat on the Illinois River; shooting duck for a living in the early days of Victoria, in the diggings and so on. Read 'Dr Thorne', an agreeable story. I see from Trollope's autobiography that he thought a great deal of it himself, but it struck me as rather crude and certainly inferior to some of the clerical series which came after.

I played a little nap with some vulgar fellows whose names are of no moment. A head wind, and we don't expect to make Sydney before Monday morning.

4 April 1884 - Friday

Forgot to say that we lay to all the 2nd in the Bay of Islands, coaling. It is a beautiful bay, and if there were a town there it would be as much thought of as Sydney Harbour[414]. A concert this evening of the ordinary sea-going type – readings, recitations etc.; a girl of the barmaiden type who smelt of bad scent and sang 'Ehren on the Rhine' very ill. Albertsohn[415] and I bought a sack of oysters for 4/-, which makes an abundant daily meal for us on the voyage. Read a little of Marcus Clarke's powerful, painful story, 'His Natural Life'.

5 April 1884 - Saturday

The sailors treated us to a concert this evening, but as I had heard all their songs on the trip to Melbourne I didn't much care for it. The weather seems to be going to be stormy. A man named Campbell[416] on board, whom I knew at University, Oxford, and met at the Palace Ripon[417]; a nice fellow.

---

[413] Cord: *Noun.* a unit for measuring cut wood, equal to 128 cubic feet
[414] In fact, there *was* a town there: the original European settlement of Russell (Kororareka), New Zealand's first 'town' (now only village-sized), opposite Waitangi where the Treaty of Waitangi was signed in 1840.
[415] The only name close to this on the passenger list for this voyage of the Tarawera is a Mr. Abbotson (possibly K. Abbotson).
[416] Donald Campbell. There is a Mr Campbell shown on the passenger list, along with Mrs Campbell and an infant Campbell – although Gibbs doesn't mention the wife and child. Gibbs later goes on a trip to Fiji with Donald Campbell - this is highly likely to be the same one.
[417] Presumably Gibbs is referring to the ruins of the Palace of the Archbishop of York in Ripon (in what was formerly Yorkshire West Riding, now North Yorkshire).

6 April 1884 - Sunday

Raining hard all day and blowing, and towards evening it came on very dark, and the Captain evidently didn't quite know where we were, and couldn't sight the lights at Sydney heads so he lay to in the heavy sea which was a disappointment to those who hoped for a quiet sleep inside the heads. Some of the passengers in a panic and stayed up all night; one bothered the Captain to know if there was any chance of our getting on shore tonight, to which the Captain gruffly replied, "It will be broadside on if we do"!

7 April 1884 - Monday

Slept very well, considering the sharp squalls. We got alongside about 7am, and after breakfast and a friendly farewell to the Blighs – who go on by P&O to England – I went down to the office, and Murray soon arrived and gave me a large budget of letters; all well at home, I am happy to say. The Merivales have kindly asked me to stay with them at their little house on Darling Point, and I went there in the evening. They have made it very nice and comfortable, and Mrs M. was very pleasant and friendly. The little Angel seems a well-behaved baby, but as Keating says, "one cannot sometimes always tell", and it's a daring name to give a daughter of Eve.

Sydney (2)

8 April 1884 - Tuesday

Working hard all day reading and writing and struggling to make up arrears. Walked home; rain came on – wet through, and caught cold. Wrote to Herbert and Edith.

George's wife mending his socks. She takes a lot of trouble to make him comfortable, and seems sensible about money. She sits all the evening with her ears pricked up and the door open lest the baby should make a sound. She thinks of nothing else; it is amusing to watch her.

9 April 1884 - Wednesday

Mail day, wrote to Alban. Called in the evening on the Laidleys. Heard from Keating. Mrs. M. made me take several doses of camphor.

The dogs have been all kicked out of the house. They are supposed to give the baby fleas – this is an improvement. The M's are a happy couple.

10 April 1884 - Thursday

The Ms went off this morning – Mrs and baby for some time; George, only till Monday. I shall stay on, as it's so difficult to get a decent room on account of the races, and shall 'meal' at the Club. Read some of 'The Voyage of the Wanderer'[418]; thought it no worse than other books of travel. I consider the 'Sat. Review' was rather cruel, as it is perfectly inoffensive if rather trivial.

Went to the Union Club and met a man named Romilly who was at Eton and The House[419] with me, though I hadn't known him. We talked over a lot of common friends – 'how some beneath the Church yard lie, and some beneath the Speaker'[420]. Also met old Spiro, who told me all the Melbourne gossip – about Greig's bankruptcy and absconding.

11 April 1884 - Friday

Wrote a long letter to A. Clarke. At midday Regi arrived but I missed him, but came across two men named Berkeley and Bull whom I had met in New Zealand; they asked me to dinner. After dinner, I looked into the Club and found Bright. He walked part of the way home with me, talking business. Read 'The New Paul and Virginia!'[421]. Harry had assured me it was so amusing but I had long avoided it, suspecting I should not find it so; my worst suspicions were confirmed. I then tried some of 'Is Life Worth Living?' – better than the other, but not good enough: that fellow Mallock shot his bolt when he did the 'New Republic'. A1 at parody, but as a serious supporter of the Church against Tyndall and Huxley, *non tali auxilio*[422] is the battle to be won, and ridicule is a parlous weapon to employ in the contest. The Club is full of Melbourne men up for the week; everyone very pleasant and civil – one might as well be in Collins St[423] at once. Regi seems pleased with Keating. He advises me to go on to Queensland from here[424], so I shall go and get it done though rather loath; I am fast becoming a confirmed Victorian.

---

[418] The Voyage of the "Wanderer", by Charles J. Lambert and Mrs. S. Lambert, published 1883
[419] Christ Church, a college in Oxford University, sometimes known as The House.
[420] A slight misquote from W. M. Praed's 'School and Schoolfellows': Some lie beneath the churchyard stone, And some before the speaker.
[421] The New Paul and Virginia: Or, Positivism on an Island, by W. H. Mallock, published 1878
[422] Latin: 'not with such allies'
[423] Collins Street was the location of the Melbourne Club (see 30th October 1883).
[424] It seems that here, as elsewhere, Regi is trying tactfully to keep Vicary Gibbs at arm's length.

12 April 1884 - Saturday

Of course a holiday, but Murray, Regi and I met at the office for a palaver[425]. Then R.B. went for a walk, and we did the picture gallery. They have just purchased a large work by Luke Fildes of a cottager's sick child. It looked very well. The Botanical gardens next, where the hibiscuses and amaranthuses look gorgeous. The gardens are not so well layed out as Melbourne, but what a site; the blue harbour with the English fleet lying at anchor and the fortified island: quite a fairy scene – more brilliant than the most brilliant Claude[426]. Dined at the Club with Robertson, Sullivan and several Melbourne men, and walked back early to Darling Point.

45. Botanical Gardens, Sydney (c1885)
National Library of Australia,
nla.pic-vn3996427

13 April 1884 - Sunday

Yuill[427] gave us a picnic in a small steam boat to Middle Harbour. Very pretty scenery, but I was a little spoilt for it by my recent New Zealand trip. We were about 16 or 17 in all; started about 12.30 and got back 7.30. We had an excellent lunch and sat on the bank and ate little rock oysters with which the sides are covered. A pleasant party and I knew nearly all: Forrest, Morehead, Osbourne and others. We landed at the North Point close to the heads where there is a camp going, a pretty large affair: the officers were very civil, showed us the fortifications and gave us Brandy and Soda. Had tea at the Club with Sullivan and Robertson; and the former, who has had a very rough life prospecting for new country round the Lochlan and Barcoo in the early days, gave a lot of us some very interesting accounts of his life and adventures. He boasted of having killed only one black in all his life. Very different to most of the Queensland settlers who killed them down wholesale. All these men were saying (and they are anything but sentimentalists or Exeter Hall men), that the way the Queensland natives had been treated would always be a disgrace to Australia. White men – when few and scattered among a savage race, and without the restraint of a society – seem to me to rob and murder in the most wholesale way; at least that is on all sides the history of Queensland.

---

[425] Palaver: being used in its original sense (taken from the Portuguese for 'word') of a conversation.
[426] Claude Lorrain, usually known simply as Claude, was a French artist of the 17th Century, known for his use of colour.
[427] Probably George Skelton Yuill, the Australian manager of the Orient Company.

14 April 1884 - Monday

Regi and I went to the races. A beautiful day, and the Randwick course is very well arranged. Good racing, and the match between the two crack horses of the year – Le Grand and Martini Henry – produced extraordinary excitement. I spent most of the day with Donald Campbell, as Regi was fluttering around paying compliments to the ladies. How ill white hairs become a flirt and trifler[428]. Old Murray, in contrast, in the stand looking severely bourgeois with his wife. Dined with Palmer, Robertson and a little bank inspector who, when he was accountant aged 17 in a Melbourne Bank, behaved with great gallantry in collaring a man who presented a pistol and tried 'to stick the Bank up'. The man shot at him, missed him and he hung on until assistance came, and the man was caught and afterwards hung. 'I didn't think the little man had it in him'.

15 April 1884 - Tuesday

In the office all day, and in the evening dined with Murray, Yuill, Regi and George there. A pleasant little dinner, after which Regi and Yuill off to a big race ball – *dormitum ego*[429]. I was very much disappointed that having accepted Murray I had to refuse an invitation from James White. He is a very wealthy squatter, and his dinner is the thing of the year. I met him in Melbourne, and it was very civil of him to ask me. I saw the table which was splendidly laid out.

Old Murray is delighted with his testimonial from the E & A Company: the clock is somewhat like the one in the hall at Aldenham, and the silver tea service handsome, but too much ornate engraving. I think Mrs M. doesn't consider their present pretty little house swell enough, and means to rout him out pretty soon. He talks of wanting to pay a visit to England in 1886 – which is looking ahead with a vengeance. Young Keyser of Berkhampstead has been pilled[430] as a non-member of the Union Club here.

16 April 1884 - Wednesday

We went to the races again as it was the Sydney Cup Day, but it was dull, coldish weather and drizzling rain. I was not betting myself but all who did lost their money to the bookmakers, and consequently it was not so cheerful as Monday. In the chief race, two valuable horses were thrown down and one had to be shot, the jockey also being seriously hurt, and this threw a gloom on things.

---

[428] A deliberate misquote from Henry IV, Part 2: "How ill white hairs become a fool and jester!"
[429] Latin: I went to bed.
[430] Pilled: possibly meaning turned down or black-balled?

I lunched with some people named Griffiths who had met Antony[431] at Haxley. In the evening I dined with G.M., a barrister named Lingen, and Murdoch. We had a quiet little rubber afterwards. Butterworth, who is settled as a barrister here, wrote saying he had just seen my name as he was starting on circuit and should be very sorry to miss me. Much disappointed not to hear from home by the 'Rome'. I think Keats must be playing the fool with the letters.

17 April 1884 - Thursday

A letter from Mother to say that poor Kenneth[432] has got typhoid – happily, not very badly. Business talk all day with Regi and Murray.

The efficient integration of the widespread Gibbs Houses into an operative, profit-making whole had to be completed to everyone's satisfaction before Vicary Gibbs left the colonies. He sent some rather stiff and impersonal letters, often long-winded and repetitive, to London: those in charge at Head Office needed diplomatic persuasion to reach the conclusions he hoped for. The export of wheat had made a bad start in Adelaide, but they must persevere and hope for a steady improvement in supply. At the Brisbane House, he was confident that sugar would become a major interest as the Caribbean trade declined.

GB&Co's presence in Newcastle eventually prospered with the flourishing of the wool trade in boom times, and held its own through the down-turns. It is puzzling that today it is difficult to find any record of that presence, despite a visit to trawl expectantly through the historical archives. The handling of a large variety of sought-after commodities kept the company busy well into the 20th century as they became more involved with a range of valuable imports and exports and their onward carriage from the entrepôt ports. Wherever a GB&S office was located – Sydney, Melbourne, Adelaide or Brisbane in the south and east, or eventually Perth in the west - they all benefited from the solidly-established foundations of a trade that had been built up by a loyal and enthusiastic work force.

There were good times and bad. Other family members travelled over from the London base to make themselves known, and to experience business in the southern hemisphere. Highly skilled technicians, workers and executives, themselves born in the colonies, gradually took over

---

[431] Probably Antony Gibbs (1841-1909), eldest son of William Gibbs and Matilda Blanche Gibbs (née Crawley-Boevy), and therefore Vicary's first cousin once removed (roughly the same age as Vicary but actually from the previous generation because William Gibbs had children so late in life). Antony married Janet Louise Merivale (from the same family as George Merivale of the Sydney office) in 1872.
[432] Venerable the Hon. Kenneth Francis Gibbs (1856-1935), Vicary's brother. He was Archdeacon of St Albans from 1909 to 1933.

senior roles in all the colonial companies, both as merchants and manufacturers. GB&S played a part in this later industrial revolution, having learnt to adapt through depression and in response to changing demands. The company reached its peak during the Great War and enjoyed a period in the following years when one of their most successful commodities was the hard wood needed for European reconstruction. They were long established and respected in Sydney by the time their wharf in Campbell's Cove was wound down to make way for the wonder of the 1930s and pride of the colony, Sydney Harbour Bridge. The Gibbs and the Bright families looked back on their history as Merchant Venturers with pride, but turned to their financial expertise for the future.

46. Sydney Harbour Bridge, Southern Approach, showing Campbell's Cove front left including wool stores and Gibbs' warehouse
State Records NSW

18 April 1884 - Friday

The 'Liguria' in having made the quickest passage on record, letters delivered in Sydney in less than 34 days. Better account of K., but Herbert has had the measles.

19 April 1884 - Saturday

Another day's racing; very good sport, but I have had enough of it. Randwick is a very pretty course, sandy like Ascot, not so big or grand as

Sydney (2)

Melbourne, but capital for seeing racing. Mrs Merivale and the baby came back today.

20 April 1884 - Sunday

Called on the Laidleys in the afternoon. The house full of people, many of whom I knew. Then George and I walked on to the Whites – a splendid house with such a view of Double Bay and Rose Bay, it could not be finer. Mr White very friendly and gave us some cigars and whiskey and water.

At this point in the original diary the following cutting from The Sydney Morning Herald on 22 April 1884 has been stuck: "The first pile of Messrs. Gibbs, Bright and Co.'s extensive new warehouses at Kangaroo Point was driven today." Followed by "Queensland Telegrams" in Vicary's handwriting.[433]

47. Brisbane wharves from Kangaroo Point, Brisbane (1878)
John Oxley Library, State Library of Queensland

21 April 1884 - Monday

Regi went back to Melbourne. I wrote to Father and Alban, and heard from Keating. I have fixed to leave Sydney on Wednesday night, after a pleasant stay. The Merivales both very hospitable, and made me very comfortable.

---

[433] In 1881, Antony Gibbs & Co. absorbed two associated business houses including Gibbs Bright & Co. of Bristol.

Tower[434] came to dinner; an uncommonly nice, gentlemanly fellow certainly.

22 April 1884 - Tuesday

Called at the Orient Office and went over Cowans with young Cook and Murray. Afterwards, to the Warehouse and sample rooms with Merivale. Called on Mrs Murray, who was in; and the Griffiths, who were out. Looked through a very trashy paste and scissors book called 'The Queen and Royal Family'.

48. SS Orient in Circular Quay (c1880-1900)
Tyrrell Photographic Collection, Powerhouse Museum

East coast of Australia to Queensland

23 April 1884 - Wednesday

Lunched at the Club; called at Dalgetty's and went over their office. Heard from Keating. Went back to dine at George's and said goodbye. I have got to like Mrs Merivale, through living in the house with them; though I had not cared for her at first, she is useful, obliging and good-tempered. At 11pm, I started in the 'Kembla' with old Murray for Newcastle – a decent little cabin on the deck, for the two of us.

24 April 1884 - Thursday

A quiet passage, and reached Newcastle at 5am. Mr Brown, the colliery proprietor, had a buggy and a very handsome pair of horses to meet us. We drove up to his house, called 'The Crows Nest', on the side of a very steep hill but commanding a good view of the harbour. Mr Brown, a pleasant-looking man about my age, came out in his pyjamas to welcome us, and we were shown into two very comfortable rooms and went to bed again for 2 or 3 hours. Very preferable to the steamboat berths, even with a calm sea. After breakfast we drove about the town, calling on various constituents of the Sydney House and inspected the wool stores, landing

---

[434] Possibly Ferdinard (or Ferdinand?) Ernest Tower, who died in England in June 1891 but who is described in his obituary as being "representative of Messrs. Gibbs Bright & Co. in Adelaide".

stages, wharves and water works. Then we had lunch, and then went out sea-fishing in a small tug. It was not bad fun; we caught some small schnapper; parrot fish, which are lovely in colour; and a small shark. I had a lot of talks about Dalgetty's business who have opened a house here and done very well. After dinner Murray started back to Sydney and I, being tired, turned in.

25 April 1884 - Friday

Left at 8am in the train for the North, and reached Armidale – which is as far as the train goes at present. The greater part of the journey was through country which had suffered very much from drought, and I saw dead horses, sheep and cattle. The first two hours I had a one-legged man who smelt of whiskey in the carriage with me. He told me that he had thought he should be a success in life and do something grand, but he hadn't. After he left there was nobody till 8pm when I reached my destination. I had 'The Vicar of Wakefield' with me, which I read. Its simplicity and pathos and humour explain its success, for it strikes me as very poorly constructed, and the Vicar is very tedious at times. I had forgotten that Thornhill also abducts Sophia and think this unnecessary, unlikely and disgusting: Thornhill finishing up as the humble, homeless, dependant, playing the French Horn in his Uncle's house is absurd, and the suggestion of Olivia being reconciled to him is not satisfactory. Goldsmith deals very tenderly with the vices of the 'Quality'[435], but when all's said and done it's a delightful book. I had a letter to the contractor who is constructing the line on to Glen Innes, so as soon as I arrived I went off to the hotel where he was to look him up and find when the next engine would be starting. I found him just going to bed, and he told me the engine might come in any time and that I was welcome to a lift. It would probably start about 7 in the morning, but he would have me stirred up whenever it did start. As I walked back through the badly lit town, a man stopped me and asked me if my name was Gibbs. I expressed some surprise when he told me he had a telegram for me. It was from the Sydney House, and addressed 'V. Gibbs, passenger from Sydney to Armidale'. I thought it very sharp work that they managed to deliver it. I got some tea at my Inn, and was just beginning to undress when I heard the whistle of the ballast engine and soon found that I should have to start at once. The contractor called for me and by 9 I was off again. The rails were laid all the way to Glen Innes, though the ballasting was not quite finished. It was not such very rough travelling – only bitterly cold. I had a very thick Ulster but was glad of some sacks too. This New England climate is wonderfully keen and bracing, and the country is wild and hilly and rather picturesque. One of the roadside stations north of Armidale is called 'Mother of Ducks'. We expected to get in soon after 1am but the workmen had left a truck on the line about a mile out of the town, and it was so dark we feared we should have to wait till daylight. However, the

---

[435] The 'Quality': i.e. the upper classes.

stoker went off and returned about 3 with a cart, and before 4 I was in the Commercial Inn. There had been a big drunk [sic] on the night before, and some of the revellers were still up – including the landlord – but all quite screwed. I foraged about for myself and found a room prepared for someone else who was too drunk to go to bed, so after pushing the table against the door to bar it I turned in.

26 April 1884 - Saturday

I was woke [sic] up about 7 by the rightful owner bursting in to tell me it was his bed. I told him if he would wait another hour he could have it and he retired saying he shouldn't go to bed at all. I got up and booked my seat in the coach for Tenterfield, and walked about the place. I never saw so many sodden, drunken-looking faces anywhere. The coach started soon after 9. We were very crowded: a Gloucestershire wheelwright and his wife and little girl; a prize fighter and his two little boys; an Irish ganger; and myself; besides 4 outside on the box, and 2 on the roof. One of the roof men was drunk and wanted to fight the driver. He soon jumped off the coach and fell on his face in the road; the driver wouldn't stop for him. The scenery was not good – all dry, monotonous, gum bush. We dined at a place called Bolivia, but it was not till 9.30pm that we got to Tenterfield. I was very tired after 30 hours' rough travelling – out of 36 – but I have the satisfaction of having come from Newcastle quicker than it has ever been done yet. The people at the Inn hardly believed that I had only started yesterday morning.

27 April 1884 - Sunday

Left in the coach at 7am, and luckily got a box seat. The driver was a musical fellow and sung a lot of songs very nicely. We crossed the Queensland frontier about noon and got into Stanthorpe at 2.30 – a prettily situated village consisting of two broad streets at right angles and the hills rising up all round. A clean little Inn. The Church of England parson came in to tea. He had all the appearance of a gentlemanly young Englishman, but he told me he came from North Carolina. We had one of those gorgeous red sunsets[436] or after-glows which have not been so common lately as they were a few months back; the new moon, in the middle of the rich crimson, looking quite white – and a heavy bank of black rain clouds above had a curious effect.

---

[436] Probably the after effect of Krakatoa, as before.

28 April 1884 - Monday

I telegraphed the first thing in the morning to Mason[437][,] Fisher's Manager[,] to say I was coming to his place on the Darling Downs[438], and left by the train at 9; and reached Clifton, the railway station, about 2. I found my own telegram there which had not been delivered. But a sprung cart was there from Mason's, and I drove over in that – 7 miles. Mr Mason seems a pleasant, gentlemanly man. He has recently married; his wife[439] is Irish; there is also a young lady named Plunkett in the house. After lunch Mason took me to the stables and stock yards. They are very large and there were some splendid prize Bulls and Horses. Then we went out for a ride and had some coursing. The country would be very pretty if it were not for the drought. We played cut-throat euchre and backgammon in the evening. This station is all freehold; about 40,000 acres of as rich land for grazing as there is in the Colony. Mason had a tame dingo tied up; he is a very handsome specimen with a fine brush.

29 April 1884 - Tuesday

I read some Rabelais[440] in the morning and I can't for the life of me see what pleasure anyone can find in the beastliness. I think Montaigne is worth 50 of him. I arranged with Mason to send a consignment of tallow to AG&S[441]. Happy to see in the paper that the drought has really broken up in New South Wales. The loss of sheep there, and in Queensland, is now estimated at 15 millions. They say there has been no such drought for 34 years, in 1851. The number of people actually ruined will be fearful. Went out for a good ride through the paddocks and sheep yards. They have not lost any stock on this station yet. I put my horse, a good one, over some log fences which he negotiated very creditably.

30 April 1884 - Wednesday

Left about noon, after lunch. Mason drove me in to the station. Read 'The Caxtons'[442]; its style is a good bit copied from 'Tristram Shandy'[443], but not the wit. A good deal of maudlin sentimentality. I think the book is dull

---

[437] Maurice Charles Mason (-1886), a grazier. From newspaper announcements of the time, we know that he came up from South Australia in 1869 to establish a branch of the widely-known Fisher flock at Headington Hill station, in partnership with a Mr. G. H. Davenport. He made Headington Hill one of the chief breeding establishments on the Darling Downs by the time of his death in 1886. He was also the manager of Pilton Station, also on Darling Downs. He married Julia Elizabeth Kelly in November 1883.
[438] The Darling Downs is a vast 4,000,000-acre farming region on the western slopes of the Great Dividing Range in southern Queensland.
[439] Julia Elizabeth Kelly, the youngest daughter of Thomas Kelly, of Tyrane, County Tyrone, Ireland.
[440] Francois Rabelais (1494-1553), was a French monk who gave his name to the adjective 'rabelaisian'.
[441] Antony Gibbs & Sons
[442] The Caxtons, by Edward George Bulwer-Lytton, published 1850.
[443] The Life and Opinions of Tristram Shandy, Gentleman by Laurence Stern, published in nine volumes over ten years from 1759.

and overrated. I fancy Father thinks well of it; it bored me. Reached Brisbane a little after 10pm; pouring with rain. Hannay met me and we went to the Club where we found Hart who had kindly prepared an oyster supper. After talking British India[444] till nearly 1, I turned in.

Brisbane

1 May 1884 - Thursday

Hannay called for me and we went to the office, a curious, old-fashioned little place but with a bustling, lively view of our wharf, with the tugs 'Boko' and 'Cadell' lying alongside and the winding river and bamboos on Kangraoo point forming a pretty picture. Dined with Hart, and he and his Mrs very pleasant. He has a comfortable house with a lot of well-behaved children.

2 May 1884 - Friday

Left the Club as my bedroom was not comfortable, and moved into Portland Place where Alban was. Spent the day at the office, and dined at the Club. Dirty, slovenly dinner, badly served. The Club is not well run. Met the Murphys, Lumley Hill and others whom I have known in Melbourne.

3 May 1884 - Saturday

Letters from home – all well. In the afternoon went for a walk with Hannay and young Musgrave[445], nephew of Sir Anthony[446], the Governor here. He had been in Jamaica and we had a pleasant talk about many places and acquaintances. He told me about young Fuller who put me up at Newcastle, Jamaica, who poisoned himself – *'foemina telerrima causa mortis'*[447]. Poor Hannay seems to feel his father's loss very much. He showed me some cuttings from Scotch papers – he must have been a fine

---

[444] Whenever Gibbs mentions "British India" he is referring to the British India Steam Navigation Company, originally formed in 1856 as the Calcutta and Burmah Steam Navigation Company to carry mail between Calcutta and Rangoon, and renamed in 1862. In 1873 it became part of a new group of companies named British India Associated Steamers. This same group also formed Queensland Steam Shipping in 1881, which ran the Queensland Royal Mail line.
[445] Sir Anthony Musgrave's nephew and private secretary was also named Anthony. He later became colonial secretary of British New Guinea.
[446] Sir Anthony Musgrave KCMG (1828-1888), born in Antigua, was Governor of Queensland from 1883 to his death in Brisbane in 1888.
[447] This rather odd corrupted Latin phrase may be Gibbs hinting that Fuller had caught syphilis from some woman and had been driven to suicide. 'Femina' means woman, but the root 'foe' is an implication of foulness, and merging two Latin words or a Latin word and a Greek word was common practise among classical scholars. 'Telerrima' may be a combination of Greek and Latin, and be an implication of dirt or disease. 'Causa mortis' is 'cause of death'. Of course, this is all hypothetical: it could just be bad spelling on Gibbs' part.

old gentleman – and a very nice letter from his eldest brother saying that he considered he held the property in trust for the Hannay family.

Hannay killed a big rat in his bed last night. My lodgings are comfortable and I do not dislike Brisbane to stay in. Hannay seems quite reconciled to it now, so I suppose he will stop here.

4 May 1884 - Sunday

Dined in the middle of the day with Hart. Mrs Hart was in bed with spasms. In the afternoon went a good walk with Musgrave and Hannay. The former a good fellow but a little soupçon of official priggishness as becomes the Governor's secretary. They seem to have taken up Hannay a good bit at Government House. Lumley Hill tells me he is to be the new Postmaster General for Queensland and will get a seat in their Upper House; he will be a very poor speaker. Dined at the Club and read some of Sir William Temple's essays, and some of 'Tom Jones'[448]. It is a splendid novel, I should say; with all faults, the best that ever was written.

5 May 1884 - Monday

Heard that A.G. & S have resigned the British India, and telegraphed to them on the subject. Got a curious, civil, letter from Mrs Bell[449] – who was the George Gibbs[450] nurse from Elstree Cottage – asking me to call on her. I will do so. Smoked a pipe with Hart in the evening.

6 May 1884 - Tuesday

Busy writing in the office in the morning, and went to see Mrs Bell, now Grimes, after lunch – she is a widow and in comfortable circumstances. She wants to pay back £60 George lent her. Her husband is dead, and left her some land. Read a lot of Cowper's letters in the evening; very graceful and pleasant, but not specially amusing.

7 May 1884 - Wednesday

Walked in the botanical reserve – some beautiful varieties of amaranthus, but the gardens might be better kept. Dined with Hannay at a man named

---

[448] 'Tom Jones', by Henry Fielding, published 1749.
[449] A nurse-maid would typically be taken on when she was around the age of 15, and would stay until the last child had left for prep school or boarding school, possibly at the age of 7 or 8. George Gibb's 7 children were born in the first three decades of the 19th Century (Henry Hucks - Vicary's father - in 1819, and the youngest sibling John Lomax in 1832), so potentially Mrs Bell was working for George Gibbs until the early 1840s, and whilst we are guessing here it is possibly that she borrowed money from George Gibbs before his death in 1842 to fund her emigration to Australia where we find her now, over 40 years later, finally finding a Gibbs descendant to whom she can repay the loan (see the next day in the diary, 6th May).
[450] George Henry Gibbs, the father of Henry Hucks Gibbs and grandfather of Vicary Gibbs.

West's. He knew Uncle Charles[451] at Shanklin – described him as 'neat and fussy'. He was a pleasant chap, had lost all his money in Ceylon – poor fellow – and has now got an engineer's billet under Government. Played whist in the evening at the Club with Lumley Hill and two squatters. The first played well, but the others maddeningly slow and anything but sure.

8 May 1884 - Thursday

Saw Captain Hansard[452], who has been so troublesome here; he was scrupulously civil; also Captain Hay[453] of the 'Dorunda', from whose father Alban rents that farmhouse in Scotland. I rather like these officers – they are so cheerful. Hart too is a thorough good fellow, indeed much superior to his appearance; his wife a brisk, brown-eyed, handsome little woman who has been very bad with spasms. Brisbane is not a bad-looking town, but a good deal of it is unbuilt or has old ramshackle hovels. The river twists about through it in the most confusing way. Played whist at a whist club with Lumley Hill and a lot of 'friend and fellow townsman' sort of chaps; the play pretty good. Got back to Portland Place before 12 and found old Sandeman, a cousin of Albert S.[454], a gentlemanly old squatter but a terrible bore. He reminded me very much of the Colonel, especially when he had a young cousin fresh from Eton staying with him who laughed at him.

9 May 1884 - Friday

In the Office all day talking about British India.

10 May 1884 - Saturday

Wrote letters, and Hannay's friend West came to lunch. In the afternoon Hannay and I went by train with Musgrave to Sandgate, the neighbouring watering place, and strolled about the pier and had our evening meal there.

11 May 1884 - Sunday

Dined with Hart in the middle of the day, and as a heavy thunderstorm came on I went to the Museum instead of a walk – a very fine collection of birds.

---

[451] Lieutentant Colonel Charles Gibbs (1829-1890), brother of Henry Hucks Gibbs (Vicary's father).
[452] Captain Arthur Agar Hansard (c.1856-1913), Marine Superintendent of the Queensland Steam-shipping Co., Agent for British India Company.
[453] Captain Alexander Hay of the 'Dorunda', from London. Part of British India Steam Navigation (for which Gibbs, Bright and Co. were agents in Brisbane).
[454] Presumably Albert Sandeman, and possibly the Albert George Sandeman of Sandeman Port fame.

12 May 1884 - Monday

Hart called for me in a cab at 5am and we drove to the station; still quite dark. The train crowded; a long, tedious journey down, which I relieved by reading an inferior novel by Henry Kingsley called 'No. 17' and by playing écarté with old Hart for 'love'. I won 16 games running. The country looked very bad. We got to Roma after 10pm and secured very comfortable quarters in the Inn. No scenery en route worth speaking of except the Toowoomba ranges[455], which I thought even finer seeing them the second time – such an extensive panorama.

49. Front entrance to the Amby Downs homestead near Charleville, Queensland (c1877)
John Oxley Library, State Library of Queensland

13 May 1884 - Tuesday

We had to start at 4.30am, and by train to Amby Crossing. Macpherson[456] met us – it was bitterly cold. He, a good-looking, active man about 35. Drove in a buggy 7 miles to the head station, and very very glad of a warm fire and breakfast. His wife a pleasant woman enough with 3 little children. I started for a ride with M. while Hart rested. I shot a Kangaroo and tried

---

[455] The Toowoomba Ranges are part of the Great Dividing Range, or the Eastern Highlands, which is the third-longest mountain range in the world, stretching over 2000 miles along most of the eastern coast of Australia.
[456] Angus MacPherson (1851-1930). Managed Amby Downs, Bymount, Cornwall and Euthulla Stations for Messrs. Bright, Chrystal & Co. from 1878-1894/5.

in vain for some ducks, but knocked over a Kangaroo rat[457] among the reeds. In the afternoon we drove over four in hand[458] to Eurella – Menzies[459] and Douglas's station – and made acquaintance with Fred and Rob Dunsmere, the managers – cousins of Douglas. Drank some whiskey and asked them to come over for a Kangaroo drive.

14 May 1884 - Wednesday

My room awfully draughty – great slits in the long walls, and the washing apparatus very imperfect. The nights and early mornings are very cold here in the winter time. Watched a horse being broken in in Colonial fashion. He had only been caught that day. They tied up one leg, and while I watched they got bridle, surcingle and crupper on him and got the kick out of him. Tomorrow they will mount him, and in about a week he will be considered broken in. I also saw a couple of bullocks broken in in an adjoining yard. These bush fellows are awfully good at handling animals. I rode up a high hill at the back of the station and got a splendid view – all Amby as far as the eye could reach. Drove 4 in hand again through some rough bush, and I managed to get the leaders foul of a stump. The team had never been together before and one of the horses only twice in harness, so it was pretty hard work, twisting and turning through the trees with no regular track; and as the horses were so green I had to keep driving all the time – the horses are not, however, high-spirited like English ones so all went well. I killed a couple of plain turkeys – great fine birds with a head something like of a heron. I believe they are really a bustard – the meat is brown like a goose, but there is a slice of white meat close to the breast bone. One I killed weighed 16 ½ lbs, plucked.

15 May 1884 - Thursday

We started for a Kangaroo drive. Robert Dunsmere turned up; he has a horrid, spluttering, explosive laugh. His brother has broken his arm owing to a saddle slipping round with him. All the station hands turned out; a nice cheery lot of young fellows. Goodwin, the super, is a capital chap, and the others mostly drafts from the Melbourne office either on account of scrapes or failing health. MacPherson drove Hart in the buggy, and the rest of us scampered along on horses. There were not considered to be enough Kangaroo to make it worth while to try and drive them into a yard, so the guns were posted and we had 3 or 4 drives – but owing to the wallaby fencing, and the law giving a price of 8d. a scalp, the marsupials have been wonderfully cleared off. And over the very part where Alban saw so many 2 years ago, I don't supposed we saw more than 50 or 60 all day: this is capital for the station, but makes very poor sport. We only

---

[457] Gibbs is probably referring to the Rufous Rat-Kangaroo, a small marsupial about the size of a rabbit which is now very rare.
[458] A four-in-hand, or coach-and-four, is a team of four horses controlled by a single driver.
[459] Archibald Menzies.

killed 3 kangaroos and 2 wallaby to 5 guns. I got the wallaby, a right and left. I enjoyed the day thoroughly.

16 May 1884 - Friday

Said goodbye to Mrs Mc and started at 9 o'clock driving the 4 in hand to Roma as we thought it would be pleasanter than going by train from Amby and would enable us to see Bendango[460]. We passed 3 mobs of travelling sheep from New South Wales – walking skeletons, so weak they couldn't or wouldn't come from under the horses' feet, and the dead and dying were lying all about. One mob had only been able to travel 2 miles the day before and had lost 1,000 sheep between Mitchell and Amby, besides losing 400 merely in crossing our run[461]. As we came near Bendango there were 2 wild turkeys close to the fence. So as I was driving, MacPherson let fly at them and hit them both hard. One fell apparently dead in the paddock. I took the gun and went to get him and on the way bowled over a wallaby as he was scuttling off. We lunched with old Beddoe[462], the manager. He is about 60 and is fast drinking himself to death. He was very friendly and hospitable, quite a gentleman. He reminded me a good deal of G.S.H.[463] and is suffering bodily in the same way. He has a curious temper, and recently turned a man out of his house who was dining with him for speaking disrespectfully of some lady who B. knows. He produced all sorts of whiskey and special Madeira for us, and it was with great difficulty we could get out of the house. We got to Roma all safe about 5pm and found Fred Dunsmere there with his arm in splints, but up and about. The hotel was very full; at first we were only offered one bed between us, but ultimately got a poky little room with 2 beds.

17 May 1884 - Saturday

A frousty[464] little bedroom it was, in spite of propping the window open with a tooth mug. No trap in the morning to take us to the station, so we had to carry our things. Not nearly so cold as Amby. We left Roma at 5am and reached Brisbane at 10.30. Mrs Hart kindly sent round to Portland Place that she was expecting me to an oyster supper. Read 'Geoffrey Hamlyn' by Henry Kingsley[465] in the train. Not at all a bad story, and the Australian part very well done: it is, however, far below 'Ravenshoe'. Letters from Father, Mother and Smeb; all well, the latter 2 remembering

---

[460] Gibbs must mean the plateau of Bindango, where - despite considerable investment - sheep farming had proved problematic. As a result, the company intended parceling up the station, along with other more successful ones in areas with a more suitable climate, into a single lot to be sold in an effort to recoup some of their losses.
[461] The 'run' refers to the vast expanse of bush which the Amby station covered.
[462] George Beddoe (c.1827-1890). He died suddenly on 21 August 1890, aged 63.
[463] G.S.H. *may* refer to Hayton (see May 30th 1884), as Gibbs implies at separate times that both of these people are heavy drinkers.
[464] Frowsty (or as Gibbs spells it, frousty) means musty or stuffy.
[465] 'The Recollections of Geoffrey Hamlyn', by Henry Kinglsey

my birthday[466] – the first that I have ever passed without remembering that it was my birthday, and now I'm not sure if I'm 31 or 32.

18 May 1884 - Sunday

The Harts had a picnic down the river in the 'Boko'[467] as far as the bay. Pleasant weather and very enjoyable – some people named Roberts on board, and Hannay. In the evening Hannay and I went to tea at the Roberts's. A lot of rowdy girls singing and laughing – not bad fun.

19 May 1884 - Monday

Back at the office, and plenty of letters to write owing to my visit to Amby. Dined at the Club and smoked with Hart in the evening. They are jolly homely people, and Mrs H. is bright and cheerful. There are two sharp little boys whom I like. They make Hannay just like one of the family. Old Hart is much better than he looks. He is quite a gentleman in feeling, and during my stay I have got to like them all very much.

20 May 1884 - Tuesday

Wrote to Gray Dawes & Co.[468] resigning the British India agency in as stiff and dignified style as I could assume.[469] Took the Governor's box for the play tomorrow to take the Hart family to 'The Lights of London'.

21 May 1884 - Wednesday

Morning in the office, and then Hannay and I took a half-holiday and went with a riding party got up by Musgrave. We rode to 'Enoggera', the Brisbane reservoir; it is a beautiful lake. We had tea there and I talked to a nice old lady, Lady O'Connell[470], who drove out to meet us. There were a lot of girls; the nicest Miss Hale[471], the Bishop's[472] daughter. I had a good horse, but rather a puller. Hannay and I hurried back to go to the theatre. The play, a sentimental melodrama; I with difficulty kept awake. I don't see why it has had such a run; not so good, to my mind, as the Drury Lane pieces 'Youth' and 'The World'.

---

[466] Gibbs was born on May 12th, 1853.
[467] The Boko was a tug boat owned by the Brisbane office.
[468] Gray, Dawes & Co., an Australian firm of General Merchants and Agents from 1880 to 1973.
[469] See the letters from Gibbs to the London office for the background to the dispute with Gray Dawes & Co., and the clipping from the Brisbane Courier shown in the diary entry for 27 May 1884.
[470] Lady Eliza Emily O'Connell, widow of Sir Maurice O'Connell, Lt. General and four times Deputy Governor of Queenland.
[471] Possibly Georgina Theodosia Hale, daughter of Bishop Hale.
[472] Matthew Blagden Hale (1811-1895), the first Bishop of Perth and now (1875 to 1885) Bishop of Brisbane.

22 May 1884 - Thursday

The 'Almora' sailed today, and arranged with Captain Smith to take a king parrot and a small cockatoo, rare and pretty, home. I hope they will arrive safe.

23 May 1884 - Friday

The mail came in last night, being very late, but only brought me a note from Alban. Today is a whole holiday; Queen's birthday[473], or something of the kind. Hannay and I got up early and down to the office by 8.30, and got through at express speed a long letter to London re British India to go by the mail closing today. At 11.30 we went off in a cab to the races. Hart as usual acted as judge, and I went into the box with him to take the third horse. Exciting work when there is a close finish; unfortunately the rain came on and it got dark. It was fearfully difficult to tell the horses as the silk jackets were perfectly discoloured with mud and wet – and the horses so splashed one couldn't tell bay from chestnut. However, all went right and it was good fun in spite of the weather. One of the horses got killed in a hurdle race. Dined with the Harts afterwards.

24 May 1884 - Saturday

Another holiday, racing again. A beautiful day: I gave a big lunch in a Marquee to the Harts; Morehead[474]; Romilly[475], the Com. of the Pacific, whom I knew at The House[476]; Mansfield[477], a judge here; a friend of Keating's, and others. It went off very well. The starting was very bad and the starter was hooted. The course also was badly kept as the Police were sulky and wouldn't work. The sport however was very fair.

25 May 1884 - Sunday

Dined in the middle of the day with Morehead; his wife a stout, pleasant, party; met two Romillys, young Anderson, and Musgrave. A good house with a pretty view over the Brisbane river. Had tea and spent the evening with Lister, who was in the 71st. I knew his father and brother in Liverpool. His wife a bright, brusque, half-foreign little woman who had many relations in Genoa and knew Constance Adamoli[478]. Both Mr and Mrs L. sang beautifully, and there was a lot of it – very jolly. I liked particularly a

---

[473] Victoria Day
[474] Boyd Dunlop Morehead (1843-1905), a member of the Legislative Assembly of Queensland for the Mitchell District from 1871 to 1880 and later (1888-1890) the premier of Queensland. In 1873 he had founded B. D. Morehead and Company, general merchants and stock and station agents, with A. B. Buchanan.
[475] Hugh Hastings Romilly (1856-1892), Deputy-Commissioner for the Western Pacific.
[476] Christ Church, a college in Oxford University, sometimes known as The House.
[477] His Honour Deputy Judge Edward Mansfield (-1905). He was the father of Sir Alan James Mansfield (1902-1980), Chief Justice and Governor of Queensland.
[478] Constance Adamoli was a Gibbs cousin on the Italian branch in Genoa.

duet out of Belisario called 'Sul campo della gloria'. I also got her to sing 'La Racheline', which Beatrice Brune[479] used to sing.

26 May 1884 - Monday

I called on Captain Heath[480], R.N., the portmaster here – a relation of old Baron Heath[481]. He was very civil, and we had some talk about The British India and Hansard. Dined at the Club, which closes after today as they move into the New House. The members will certainly have a better building, and I hope for their sake it may be better managed. I bought a copy of Brunton Stephens' 'The Queensland Poet'. but I was much disappointed with him – very inferior to the Victorian, Lindsay Gordon[482].

27 May 1884 - Tuesday

Chrystal turned up from Amby. In the office all day, clearing up as Hart and I start early tomorrow for Sydney.

A cutting from the Brisbane Courier dated 21 May 1884 is attached at this point in the diary: "We are informed by Messrs Gibbs Bright & Co. that they resigned the Agency of the Queensland Royal Mail Steamer line early in April last, and are now only attending to the steamers until the company find themselves in a position to make fresh arrangements."

Had a final dinner with the Harts, and in the evening went over to call on his brother[483] the Solicitor who is just back from Melbourne.

S.S. Ly-ee-moon

28 May 1884 - Wednesday

Musgrave came to breakfast to say goodbye, and at 9.30 I went on board the 'Lyeemoon'. As I passed the Harts house Mrs H. and the children were looking out and flourishing their handkerchiefs. As we went down the river the 'Boko' dipped her flag and saluted us. The Brisbane river is very pretty. Altogether I have had a pleasant stay in Queensland and I hope it has been useful. The 'Lyeemoon' is very fast; she was one of the old opium

---

[479] Beatrice Brune: an American Soprano.
[480] Captain G. P. Heath, the Brisbane Port Master.
[481] Robert Amadeus Heath (1818-1892), 2nd Baron Heath, Italian Consul General, of Coombe Hill House in Croydon.
[482] The Victorian Poet, by Adam Lindsay Gordon.
[483] Graham Lloyd Hart (1839–1897), who lived in Brisbane. He was the son of Hamilton Hart (originally a member of Bright Bros, and Co.). In 1863, Graham Hart came to Queensland where his brother Frederick Hart was working for Gibbs, Bright and Co.

runners, and belonged to the Dents[484]. I have a comfortable cabin to myself. I turned in for a nap a little before noon.

29 May 1884 - Thursday

My nap lasted till 8 this morning when I was woke by the steward – or 20 hours, which is an extraordinarily long stretch even for me. I played nap with the Captain[485], Chrystal and Davenport – the last of these a brother of the man who married one of the Clutterbucks[486]. He is a Queensland squatter and seems a pleasant chap. He knew a lot of men that I did. I read some of 'Readiana', a collection of Charles Reade's letters on all sorts of subjects. Very clever, vigorous, crotchety stuff it is. I believe it's settled now for Bell[487] to go to Dunedin, at which I am glad[488]. The sea is calm and it is rather a pretty voyage, in sight of the coast all the way.

30 May 1884 - Friday

Arrived very early in the morning but breakfasted on board, and at the office by 9. Got my home letters – April 18th – all well. I heard that Shepherd Laidley[489] is engaged, and Miss Cruickshank is going to jilt her lover though she telegraphed for him out from England to marry her – rather rough on him. Heard from Hayton, who must be keeping wonderfully sober. The Merivales have asked me to stay with them again and I shall do so.

Sydney (3)

31 May 1884 - Saturday

Found Mrs M. very pleasant. Busy writing all the morning, and at noon Yuill brought Bell in who had come from Melbourne in consequence of my telegram. I had a good talk with him, and spent the afternoon walking with him. Murray has asked him to stay at his house. I called on Mrs

---

[484] The SS 'Ly-ee-moon' was built in 1859, and was originally owned by Dent & Co., a company involved in opium running. It was the fastest opium steamer afloat at the time. It was lost in May 1886 after running aground off Green Cape (about 350 miles south of Sydney).
[485] Captain D. Walker
[486] Presumably, and based solely on the name, Mr and Mrs Davenport had recently given birth to the future Vice Admiral Robert Clutterbuck Davenport (1882-1965).
[487] George Frederick Bell (1848-1929), the son of Father Thomas Blizzard Bell, a Free Church clergyman, and Agnes Agnew, the sister of Sir Andrew Agnew, a 'well-known landowner in Wigtownshire'. Bell is mentioned at length in Gibbs' letters to the London office.
[488] Gibbs might be 'glad' at this because Bell was Scottish, and might be more likely to fit in to a city like Dunedin, which was founded by the Scots in 1848 and known as The Edinburgh of the South.
[489] Shepheard Edgecliff Laidley, who eventually married Ethel Frances Moore and had a son Captain William Shepheard Laidley who died in action in 1918. Shepheard was the brother of Emily Jane Laidley who married George Merivale in 1881.

Murray and had a chat; she pitched in to me about wearing thin cotton socks.

1 June 1884 - Sunday

Went for a walk with Bell after church, and like him. He seems to have a good general knowledge of business, plenty of conversation, and pleasant manners and appearance. He had tea at the Merivales and we stayed smoking a long while.

2 June 1884 - Monday

Wrote to Mother, Alban, Kenneth and Smeb. Decided for Bell to come back with me to Melbourne on Wednesday instead of going up to Brisbane. Went to the Mitchells after dinner and played Black pool. I was in very good form. Young Mitchell is a good sort. There was a man named Cheyke there who didn't seem a bad fellow.

3 June 1884 - Tuesday

We had 'wongas' for dinner. They are a variety of pigeon, sent George as a present, and considered a great delicacy. The meat is white and in taste and appearance they are very like a partridge.

4 June 1884 - Wednesday

(In the train). A more eventful day in my Eton life than now[490]. Left Sydney with Hart and Bell about 5pm, Murray calling after us that 2/- was amply sufficient for the cab. Forrest of Brisbane was going down too, so we got a carriage to ourselves and played whist. Hart played ill, and Forrest got quite ludicrously angry with him so that he – F – played wrong on purpose like a child. Bell and I laughed consumedly, and F. got rather ashamed of himself. At midnight we changed to our sleeping berths.

---

[490] Gibbs is referring to the "Fourth of June" (nowadays held on the Wednesday before the first weekend in June), an Eton celebration of the birthday of its patron King George III.

Melbourne (3)

5 June 1884 - Thursday

Breakfasted at Albury and changed carriages at Wodonga on the Victoria frontier, the idiots having a different gauge in the two colonies. I read a story called Frescoes[491] by Ouida, harmless and rather pretty. We got to the office at noon and found all well, but my headache came out so badly I was obliged to go home and lie down.

50. Melbourne (1880s?)
National Library of Australia, nla.pic-an10638277-43

6 June 1884 - Friday

Back again in Regi's very comfortable quarters. His parlour-maid told me 'they were beginning to be afraid they had lost me.' Busy in the office reading up letters, and in the evening read Georges Sand's 'Fadette'. It is certainly a fetching little story, though rather 'anodyne'.

7 June 1884 - Saturday

We were robbed of our Saturday half-holiday by the 'Belgravia' going away, and we all dined at the club at 7pm as a protest against the new rule to have 6.30 o'clock dinner, which is a horrible nuisance for us as we have to dine directly we are out of the office. After dinner, Keats had a box for "La Fille de Mme Angot", and Bell and I looked in; not bad.

8 June 1884 - Sunday

Bell came to breakfast and we lunched at the Club and had a long talk with Gowan Evans[492] of the Argus, and heard of a great find of silver which has taken place[493]. In the afternoon we went to the Zoo.

---

[491] Frescoes, by Ouida (the *nom-de-plume* of Marie Louise de la Ramée).
[492] Gowen Edward Evans (1826-1897), of the Melbourne Argus. Gibbs spells Evans' first name as both Gowan and Gowen throughout his journal, and there is similar confusion in the Australian newspaper reports of the time whenever he is mentioned.
[493] Gibbs is probably referring to the discovery of the "richest silver-lead mine the world has seen" in Broken Hill, Victoria, in September 1883.

9 June 1884 - Monday

Dies carbone notanda.[494] The mail came in bringing letters from Mother, Edith, Herbert and Mrs Clarke. The Tylers[495], Hart, and his daughter[496] to dinner – the latter improved in appearance considerably in the last six months.

10 June 1884 - Tuesday

Dined at the Maison Dorée with Clough, Mackinnon, Forbes and Hornsby, all of whom were in the 'City of New York', and we had a very jolly dinner. They are very good fellows; Mc and I walked home together.

11 June 1884 - Wednesday

Regi poisoned his old three-legged poodle 'Mouton'. I found a card from young Burns at the Club whom I met on the Cunarder[497] and in 'Frisco. 'Sorry to have missed me and had met Lucy[498] while travelling in Japan – who used to edit 'Mayfair', and had asked to be remembered to me'.

12 June 1884 - Thursday

The usual routine.

13 June 1884 - Friday

Dined at the Club and played a pleasant rubber of family whist with Keats, Bell and Hart. Regi went to a Cinderella dance, over at 12! *Quot homines, tot sententiae.*[499]

14 June 1884 - Saturday

Half day at office, and off at noon by train to Mount Macedon to stay with the Ryans. R., a deaf stock and station agent, came down with me and we walked through the bush to the house which commands a grand view all round the coast; the climate quite different to Melbourne as they are a long way above the sea. The grounds are beautiful around the house, admirably planned and kept up. Tree ferns and luxuriant semi-tropical foliage mixed with every kind of English shrubs and trees, ornamental

---

[494] *Dies carbone notanda* seems to be a reference to the days becoming darker (as it was winter in the Southern Hemisphere).
[495] Fanny Mary Hart (1838-), one of Frederic Hart's sisters, and wife of John Chatfield Tyler.
[496] F.H.S. Hart had 7 children, born between 1866 and 1883. This is most likely to be his eldest daughter, Camilla Rose Hart (1866-), who would have been about 18. The second daughter Isabel Hart (1868-1941), would have been about 16.
[497] Cunarder: Gibbs is referring to the Gallia.
[498] Sir Henry William Lucy (1843-1924) founded a short-lived journal called 'Mayfair' in 1877, which collapsed two years later. Later, he wrote for the satirical magazine Punch, as "Toby M.P.".
[499] *Quot homines, tot sententiae:* "There are as many opinions as there are men". A quote from Phormio, by the Roman comic dramatist Terence (185-159 BC).

water, fancy ducks etc.; though cold and wet they are almost free from frost. Mrs. and the youngest Miss R. I had met before and they were 'the same to a surfeiting identity', one bragging, the other childish and affected. The elder girl[500] plain but sensible. At all meals the mother kept the girls continually on the move waiting on one – which was very disagreeable – no doubt to show how useful they were. A fire in my bedroom – most comfortable, and everyone very civil. Captain Rowan[501], a son-in-law, came by a late train – kindly bringing my mail letters; all well, thank goodness.

15 June 1884 - Sunday

Unfortunately, heavy mist all round. They have only Church here every other Sunday, and this was a one Sunday. I smoked a good deal and read some 'High Spirits'[502] – not bad stories, but I had read them before. We dined in the middle of the day and I puddled about the garden with old Ryan among the plants.

16 June 1884 - Monday

Left at 8 and in the office by eleven. Mail out; short walk with Keats, and dined with Regi.

17 June 1884 - Tuesday

Read 'the Godolphin Arabian' by Brunton Stephens. It is thought a lot of here, but it only seemed to me moderate.

18 June 1884 - Wednesday

Bell left for Dunedin. Dined at the Club and watched some men playing écarté, but did not play.

---

[500] This must be one of the three eldest daughters: Marian Ellis, Ada Mary, or Blanche Adelaide. It is unlikely to be Ada Mary - Gibbs is almost certain to have called her Lady Charles. Marian Ellis would have been married to Captain Rowan for over 10 years by this point, and is probably unlikely to have been pressed into waiting on Gibbs. So it is most likely to be Blanche Adelaide Ryan (1859-1938), the third daughter, still unmarried at this point and about 25 years old.
[501] Captain Frederic Charles Rowan (1844-1892), who married Marian Ellis Ryan (the eldest child) in 1873, was the nephew of Field Marshal Sir William Rowan. After training with the 59th Regiment in Aldershot as a surveyor and field sketcher in 1863, he was appointed to the 43rd Light Infantry and served in New Zealand to repress a Maori outbreak, after which Captain Rowan resigned his commision and joined the New Zealand Armed Constabulary, where he earned his captaincy. He was noted for bravery, and at one point carrying a wounded officer off the field when he was hit by a bullet which shattered his jaw. He subsequently had a prosthetic gold jaw made. He migrated to Victoria in 1877 and worked as a civil engineer.
[502] 'High Spirits: being certain stories written in them', by James Payn (published 1879).

19 June 1884 - Thursday

Knocked off at 5pm and went for a long walk with K., which made me rather late for dinner.

20 June 1884 - Friday

Had my photograph[503] taken at Foster and Martins[504].

51. Collins St., Melbourne, showing Foster & Martin photographers (c1890)
National Library of Australia, nla.pic-an10642263-30

21 June 1884 - Saturday

Lunched at the Club where they had a lot of ratting going on in the area. Then old Candler, Keats and I went to look at a big football match between Melbourne and Geelong. It was a good game but very different to English football, whether Eton or Rugby. Then we called on the Lewises[505], a Jewish broker with a very clever, pleasant, wife who was once an actress. We dined at the Club and I played Nap and won a few sous; it is a rotten game though.

---

[503] This is the photo of Gibbs that appears on the front cover.
[504] Foster and Martin's were well-known photographers of Collins Street, Melbourne.
[505] Louis Ludwig "Lucas" Lewis (abt 1834-1910). Vicary Gibbs got to know the Lewises very well, and was one of the executors of Mr. Lewis' estate. Mr. and Mrs. Lewis were a very wealthy couple who were active in raising funds for various Melbourne charities. The Lewises had just retired to Europe at the beginning of the 1890s when their fortune – largely investments in Melbourne - was wiped out by the Australian economic downturn of 1893. Mr. Lewis returned to Melbourne and went back into business, managing to rebuild his fortune.

22 June 1884 - Sunday

In the afternoon, K., Regi and I called on the Powers. He is rather a raffish fellow – great pal of Regi's. He has a very pretty wife. We found two jolly old priests there, telling stories and drinking grog. They had both travelled a great deal and were very entertaining. They might have been exhumed straight out of Charles Lever's[506] novels. Then we called on Colonel Disney, who was out, and we talked some time with Mrs. D.[507], a pleasant, handsome, stupid Irish lady – 'there were a wife if any such there were'. Two of the other English Military ladies – wives of Colonel Ind[508] and Major Brownrigg[509] – have got themselves into a frightful row by sending their ladysmaids to a charity ball instead of going themselves, and Melbourne society is convulsed with rage against the haughty English.

23 June 1884 - Monday

Young Mackinnon came in to see me and asked me to help him with a leader for the Argus on barrister's fees. I did so. Dined at the Club and played a rubber.

24 June 1884 - Tuesday

Hart left us, and K. and I went down to the train and saw him and his daughter off. He is a good, simple-minded, fellow. Just as we came into the station they were carrying out a young fellow who was out on bail for fraud and had shot himself through the body. I dined at the Lewises and had a very pleasant evening. They asked me to act in some private theatricals which are to take place when the new governor arrives. I declined.

25 June 1884 - Wednesday

Dined at the Club, and played billiards and whist. Donald Campbell very keen on my joining him for a month's trip to Fiji and Friendly Islands[510], but I don't see how I could spare the time – though it would be very interesting.

---

[506] Charles Lever was an Irish Doctor who also wrote many novels. His early works were light and amusing, but later he became more serious.
[507] Anne Eliza Disney (Colonel Disney may also have had a daughter of the same name).
[508] Actually Captain Ind, another member of the Victoria Military Force under Colonel Disney. Gibbs refers to him later as Captain Ind.
[509] Major Brownrigg was another member of the Victoria Military Force under Colonel Disney.
[510] Tonga apparently became known as the Friendly Islands because of the friendly reception accorded to Captain James Cook on his first visit there in 1773.

26 June 1884 - Thursday

Mail out, and at the last moment I decided I would go to Fiji as there was nothing particular doing and Regi pressed me very strongly to do so. I feel very much the idle apprentice. I left Melbourne at 5pm. Mrs Lewis is going too, as far as Sydney, and accompanied by a very handsome girl named Bunny[511] in the [GREEK][512] style. Her father[513] is a judge, and her mother[514] a native of Frankfurt am Oder. While the young lady was taking a nap, Mrs L. gave me her dossier in the French tongue. Supper at Albury and then sleeping car.

52. Greek text from 26 June 1884

S.S. Wairoa

27 June 1884 - Friday

Played euchre in the train with Campbell and a Scotchman named Gibson. Reached Sydney at noon and spent a few hours at the office with Hart, Murray and Merivale, all much surprised at my sudden move. Sailed by 5pm on the 'Waihora'[515] for Auckland. I have a comfortable cabin with Campbell.

28 June 1884 - Saturday

Weather roughish and I felt rather uncomfortable. Played piquet with C.

---

[511] Brice and Maria Bunny had three daughters. One of them, Hilda Eleanor Marie, married Donald Mackinnon (Gibbs' friend) in 1891 - this could be her, although we cannot be certain.
[512] Greek: A quote from Homer's Illiad (book 1, line 551) referring to Hera as "ox-eyed" (meant in a flattering way).
[513] Brice Frederick Bunny (1820-1885) emigrated to Australia in 1852 to find gold. In 1856, he married Maria Wulsten, a beautiful German woman. They had three sons and three daughters.
[514] Maria Bunny née Wulsten.
[515] Actually the S.S. Wairoa.

29 June 1884 - Sunday

There is a pleasant old Scotchman named Carnegie[516] who is going on the trip to Fiji; a brother of Lord South Esk[517], I fancy.

30 June 1884 - Monday

I rather wish I hadn't gone – it will mess away such a lot of time.

1 July 1884 - Tuesday

Nobody of any interest in the steamer. We ought to be in Auckland early tomorrow morning. The skipper[518] rather an amusing, good-natured fellow.

Auckland

2 July 1884 - Wednesday

Got in at 10 o'clock and found the Club full and the town too, the elections being on. C. and I spent about 3 hours walking about trying every hotel, public- and boarding-house before we at last persuaded someone to take us in as a favour, who didn't usually take lodgers. We got a decent room with 2 beds, and shall meal at the Northern Club where the cooking is excellent.

3 July 1884 - Thursday

Letters, billiards, walk, and then to the theatre where we saw 'Manola' very well played and sung. I had seen it not long ago, and like it very much this time.

4 July 1884 - Friday

Lost our latch-key and had to get into the house burglariously through the window, I getting onto C's shoulders and so on to the sill. Houlton, my Eton fag, burst in to the bedroom as we were dressing in the morning, having met someone who told him I was in Auckland. So he came to look me up before going to Auckland [sic]. He was very friendly, but rather airified.

5 July 1884 - Saturday

Read a lot of old fortnightlies; a couple of good articles on Lucrezia Borgia, and the first Lord Shaftesbury. Wrote to Arthur in Dunedin.

---

[516] From the passenger list, the Hon. Charles Carnegie (1833-1906).
[517] James Carnegie, 9th Earl of Southesk (1827-1905).
[518] Captain E. A. Holbeche, commander of the S.S. Wairoa from 1883 until his death at sea in 1887.

6 July 1884 - Sunday

Our lodgings are very comfortable and the landlady very civil.

S.S. Wairarapa - South Sea Islands cruise; Auckland; Dunedin

53. Passengers on board the Wairarapa (July 1884)
Alexander Turnbull Library, Wellington, New Zealand

7 July 1884 - Monday

Did some shopping – almost the first since I left England. Bought a lot of shirts and socks etc. Said goodbye to our various club acquaintances, and went on board the 'Wairarapa' at 5pm[519]. I have a comfortable, large cabin

---

[519] The passenger list for this trip lists Vicary Gibbs and his fellow travellers: Messrs C. G. de Betham, J.H. Crossman, F.V. Crossman, H. Gething, V. Gibbs, G. H. Gowring, H. McLaren, J.S. McLaren, J. Patch, F.A.L. Popham, W.H. Still, J.M. Shaw, R.F. Smith, O.G. Sanders, Rev. Canon Tebbutt, Mrs Tebbutt, Mr and Mrs C.M.C. Whatman, Hon. C. Carnegie, Messrs R. Henderson, R. Millar, T.R. Icely, Mr Mrs and Miss Kidman and child, Mr A. Kidman, Messrs. D. Campbell, R. Farie, H.F. Singleton, H. Buckland, G.R. Bloomfield, L.R. Bloomfield, J.H. Good, C.A. Harris, junr., Major Mair, W. Motion, Dr. Payne, Mrs Payne, Miss Field, Messrs P.W. Donnar, W.R. Chambers, D. Downes, W. Finlay, Mrs and Miss Hirschberg, Messrs E.W. Kane, W. Seed, W.F. Wheeler, H.D. Gardiner, W. and G. Gerard, Mrs and Miss Gerard, Messrs W. Prudhoe, R. Smith, W. Tombs, Mr and Miss Twentyman; Mr, Mrs, and Miss Wilson; Messrs A.R. Inwood, A.H. Burton, D. Drummond, Mr and Miss Ewing, Miss Forsyth, Hon. Capt. and Mrs Fraser, Dr. and Mrs Macdonald and child, Mrs George McLean, Mr. J Thompson, Miss Wilson, Mr J. T. Wright, Rev. R.S. Rishworth, Mrs A Smellie, Mr W. Inder, Miss Finlay.

amidships, shared with a Major Mair[520] – a handsome, gentlemanly-looking man about 50 who, I hear, distinguished himself in the Maori war. There is also on board an old Scotchman, Captain Fraser[521] – a cousin of Campbell's. A Mr Crossman[522] – a brewer who saw something of Father about the Brewer's Company[523] – and his son[524], who is lame – a pleasant young fellow and a good whist player. He seemed to know Harry slightly, having been at Humes[525]. We have made a capital start in calm weather.

8 July 1884 - Tuesday

There are also two young Maclarens[526][527], nice sort of chaps – cousins – and one or two travelling bear cubs[528] with their bear leaders; also old Carnegie who was on the Waihora and is, I should say, certainly a good sort. On the whole there seem to be a good lot on board, though there are more stout middle-aged women and common third-rate people than one would expect on this sort of trip.

9 July 1884 - Wednesday

A concert in the evening, and recitations rather above the average steamer performances. I gave them Gordon's 'How we beat the Favourite'[529], which is always popular with Australians[530].

10 July 1884 - Thursday

We have a very good four for a rubber: Campbell; the younger Crossman; and a Mr Wright[531], a Dunedin merchant – about the best set I ever played

---

[520] Major William Gilbert Mair (1832-1912). He would have been a useful companion as he spoke fluent Maori, having been a member of a family who were early settlers in the Bay of Islands.
[521] From the passenger list, the Hon. Captain Fraser, on board with Mrs. Fraser.
[522] James Hiscutt Crossman (1833-1899), second son of Robert Crossman, the corn and seed merchant who founded the Albion Brewery at Berwick-upon-Tweed, later Mann, Crossman & Paulin. James Crossman was a partner in the company, and in 1880 served as Master of the Worshipful Company of Brewers. His third son was also named James Hiscutt Crossman, and died in a car accident in Cannes in 1908.
[523] The Worshipful Company of Brewers, one of the City of London's Livery Companies (trade associations).
[524] F.V. Crossman, according to the passenger list. The F is possibly for Freeman, which is a common first name in the family.
[525] Humes was a house at Eton College, where Henry Lloyd Gibbs had been educated.
[526] From the passenger list, H. Maclaren.
[527] From the passenger list, J. H. Maclaren.
[528] Teenagers on a 'grand tour'.
[529] 'How We Beat the Favourite', by Adam Lindsay Gordon.
[530] Gibbs neglects to mention that he forgot his lines halfway through his recitation, but as the critic in the ship's passenger-produced newspaper, "Wairarapa Wilderness", reports: "the quality of the piece selected atoned for the defective delivery in the ears of a good natured audience". Apparently he gave two further recitations of the poem, on 10 July and 18 July, although Gibbs himself mentions neither. Most of these narrative poems would have been familiar to Victorian, and Edwardian, audiences in the English speaking world.
[531] From the passenger list, Mr J. T. Wright, a merchant, of Dunedin. John T. Wright set up business as merchants, stock and station agents and wool brokers Wright Stephenson &

with. What with bull[532] in the morning, and cards, and talking, the day passes pretty quick.

11 July 1884 - Friday

We sighted land about 7, and landed at Suva at half past two. The place has the ordinary tropical beauty which palins, crotons and hibiscuses always give, but nothing out of the common; though as one stands on the shore there is a fine range of mountains the other side of the bay, and the sunlight on the coral reefs and the change of colour in the shallow water has a pleasant effect. Campbell and I walked up to Government House to call on Sir William de Voeux, whom we knew in Melbourne, and Wallington[533], a nephew of Tommy Sheppard's who is a very pleasant fellow and was at Oxford with us both. We then watched a native eleven trained by Wallington playing cricket. They played very well, especially the fielding. We dined on shore at the hotel where we had a scrambling meal, not so good as we should have had on board, and then most people went to see an amateur performance of the 'Pirates of Penzance', but I felt sleepy, gouty and seedy so I went off to the ship and turned in. Suva is the modern capital of the Fijis and is on the biggest island of the group. The old native town where the seat of the Government was is on another island, Levuka. The native men are fine fellows, and not ill-looking. They bleach their hair with lime which turns it to various shades from straw to red, and wear it very long and standing straight out in an enormous mass all over their heads.

12 July 1884 - Saturday

When I woke up I couldn't put my feet to the ground with gout, so I took some medicine and laid up. Some of the party went in boats up the Rewa River to see a sugar mill[534], which I shouldn't have cared for as I have done that sort of thing pretty thoroughly in the West Indies. The others played a cricket match against Wallingon's eleven, and got well beaten. I was asked to dine at Government House, but of course couldn't go. And in the evening there was a grand meki meki[535], or native dance, which I was sorry to miss; only the men dance in Fiji. The Governor[536] is very unpopular

---

Co. Ltd. with Robert M. Robertson in 1861. In 1865, John Stephenson joined the partnership, and when Robertson retired in 1868 the business carried on under the name Wright, Stephenson & Co. The company was involved in livestock and wool auctioning, grain and seed merchandising and land sales. It was also involved in the development of refrigeration for the transport of meat, which would have been of interest to Gibbs, who visits Wright's house in Dunedin on 6 August 1884.

[532] Army term for cleaning routine.

[533] Wallington was William des Voeux's secretary. Gibbs met them originally on 2nd February 1884.

[534] The Colonial Sugar Refinery Co. built a sugar mill on the Rewa River in 1872, after Sugar took over from cotton as the main industry of Fiji following a slump in cotton prices in 1870. The mill survived until 1959.

[535] Meke: a Fijian national dance.

[536] Sir George William des Voeux was Governor of Fiji from 1880 to 1885.

with the white inhabitants. I read a novel by Whyte Melville called 'The Interpreter'. I fancy I have read it before; anyway, it is not worth reading once, though pleasantly written enough.

13 July 1884 - Sunday

I was all right again when I woke this morning. We left Suva about 9. There is a parson on board named Canon Tebbits[537], or some such name, who did the service. We reached Levuka, the harbour full of small craft as there are no roads and all the communications are by water. We passed close to the wreck of a large ship, 'The Syria'[538], who was lost lately on one of the many coral reefs. Levuka is a far prettier place than Suva, and the two Maclarens and I walked through the town and up a high hill whence we got a very fine view of the bay. On going back to the ship I found a very civil letter from Henry Cave[539], with whom we do business here, asking me to stop with him during our stay in Levuka, so I put a few things into my handbag and went off to his house which I had some difficulty in finding as it was getting dark and the road steep and slippery. Cave is a gentlemanly fellow about 36, with a nice-looking pleasant wife. I have a comfortable bedroom, which will be cooler and airier than the cabin.

14 July 1884 - Monday

Up at 7, and after a cup of coffee we rode up a gorge – a beautiful ride to a waterfall, and there bathed in a deliciously cool pool. As we swam about we could look right down on the harbour and sea 3 or 4 miles away. The Caves went on board the Wairarapa to lunch, and then I bought some good photos of the natives, and went for another ride with Cave along the coast to a native village. Here we went into the chief's house and sat down and smoked some of the native cigarettes which are rolled up in dry banana leaves instead of paper. I also tasted their native grog, which tasted like soapy water. It has the peculiarity if taken in excess of affecting the legs but not the senses. I also bought some of their tappa[540], or native cloth, made out of tree fibre – rather pretty. Cave talks Fijian very fluently so we got on very well. In riding back, Cave's horses cannoned him against a coconut tree and nearly unseated him. Before he could recover himself the beast set to kicking, and set him flying over his head. He was cut and bruised but not much hurt, but he lost his ring. Campbell came to dinner, as he had known Mrs Cave when she was a girl in Melbourne. We had a

---

[537] From the passenger list, the Rev. Canon Tebbutt of Lincoln, England, on board with Mrs. Tebbutt.
[538] The Syria was an iron sailing ship which ran aground in the Nasilai Reef, four miles from shore, on 11th May 1884 with the loss of 59 lives, whilst sailing from Calcutta to Fiji.
[539] Henry Cave, of Cave and Co., merchants, of Levuka. He was a resident of Levuka from 1872 until at least 1890. The Cave family were originally connected socially and in business with Bright and Gibbs in Bristol, where they cooperated in the West Indian trade and in the establishment of the Great Western Railway.
[540] Tapa

pleasant dinner, and after I went on board with him as we sail early tomorrow.

15 July 1884 - Tuesday

We reached Taviuna[541], another island in the Fiji group – and not a particularly pretty or interesting one, about 2.30. There is only an open roadstead and nothing worth seeing unless a large sugar mill, to which everybody went. The sugar looked to me badly made – small crystals, dull and off colour – and the canes were in very bad order and condition; over-ripe and flowering. There were some cars running on a tramway with a small engine for bringing down the cane, and on these most of the party went the round of the estate. But I didn't see the joke of being jolted around like a lot of cattle with black smoke blowing in your face looking at a lot of cane pieces each just like the other. So I walked by myself and saw the canes, and then lay on the beach and watched the bright sea breaking over the reef till the people came back grumbling. I don't know why we touched at Taviuna – it certainly was not worthwhile.

16 July 1884 - Wednesday

At the Caves they had a lot of native vegetables cooked for us to try. The usual sweet potatoes and yams; also taro, a big root with a leaf like a water lily which the natives grow in irrigated terraces like water cress, keeping the plant always flooded. When cooked it tastes something between a chestnut and a Jerusalem artichoke. There was also Mummy apple, or Papau[542] as it is called in the West Indies. It is insipid as a raw fruit much like a melon, but when gathered unripe and boiled it is like a very good vegetable marrow. There were also some nuts and other vegetables, breadfruit, etc. I thought it good-natured of Mrs Cave to have taken the trouble to get them. Today we reached the small island of Mango[543] about noon. It is an open roadstead, but the island looks very pretty from the sea. We landed and walked through some large cocoa nut[544] plantations, and saw large quantities of copra. And then to some cotton fields, which I had never seen growing before. The plant is about as big as a gooseberry bush and has a pretty yellow flower like a half-blown tea rose. This island was originally taken up for growing cotton when it was so dear. Now it doesn't pay, and sugar has pretty well replaced it. Mango has been sold three times, first for £50, then for £300, and last for £30,000. It is now for

---

[541] Taveuni Island
[542] Gibbs probably means Pawpaw (also known as papaya and Mummy apple, amongst other things).
[543] Mago (pronounced Mango) Island is a volcanic island, 8.4 square miles in area, located about 170 miles to the ENE of Suva. In th 1860s the Ryder brothers of Australia had established a cotton plantation on the island, but by the time of Gibbs' visit it would largely have been turned over to a sugar cane plantation and sugar mill, which closed in 1895. The island is now privately owned.
[544] Because of the reference to copra, Gibbs must be referring to coconut here (something which would not have been overly familiar to an Englishman at the time).

sale for £50,000. A lot of money has now been spent on it, fitting up elaborate sugar machinery and vacuum pans, centrifugals etc. A great part of the land has been cleared and cultivated, and it is a very pretty place – though perhaps a little 'out of the world'. We visited the sugar mill and were hospitably entertained by the manager, and then Carnegie, Campbell and I walked across the middle of the island – about 6 miles – to a beautiful land-locked lagoon. The hills rose all round it, richly clothed, and one break about 60 yards wide where the hills were cut straight and clean away as if with a knife, making an entrance for small craft. Through this, one could see the sea breaking outside on the reef. The lagoon looked an ideal place for one of Marryatt's pirates[545] to run into for shelter. We were much tempted to bathe, but forbore for fear of sharks. After rowing on the lagoon in a boat for a bit we walked up some hills to a coffee plantation. The plants were neither in flower nor cherry, and had suffered from leaf disease[546], but there was a fine view from the planter's house, where we got some lime drinks and then made our way to beach and so to the ship after a long and very pleasant day.

17 July 1884 - Thursday

Left before daylight, and – the sea being rough – a great many people ill. I had no feeling of discomfort. I never do, if I can get through the first three days. There is a chess tournament going on, on the American system. Some pretty good players. My score at present is 4 lost and 7 won. Read Shakespeare in the evening, Crossman being too seedy for the rubber.

18 July 1884 - Friday

There is rather a nice young fellow on board named Still[547], descendant of the bibulous Bishop of Bath and Wells[548]. Passed Hope Island[549] about half way to the Samoan group. Read 'The Haworths'[550] by the authoress of 'That Lass o' Lowries': I liked it least of any of hers that I have read; rather unnatural and disagreeable, but powerful in parts.

---

[545] Gibbs is referring to the swashbuckling books of Captain Frederick Marryatt, with which he would have been familiar from his childhood.
[546] This is a problem which Gibbs meets again later in Ceylon.
[547] From the ship-board passenger newspaper, W. T. Still (although given as W. H. Still in some Australian newspaper reports of the passengers). He appears in the passenger photograph on the back cover, second from right with a pipe.
[548] John Still (c.1543-c.1607).
[549] Niuafo'ou ("many new coconuts"), the most northerly island in the kingdom of Tonga, is also known as Good Hope Island or Tin Can Island. It is formed from a volcanic rim, so consists of a circle of land with water within. The name Tin Can Island supposedly came about because of the method of mail delivery used in the 19th century, called Tin Can Mail, involved passing ships throwing mail sealed in biscuit tins over the side as the island did not have a harbour.
[550] "The Haworths", by Frances Hodgson Burnett.

19 July 1884 - Saturday

We reached Apia[551], the chief town of the Samoan group, on the island of Upolu. It is the most beautiful place we have been to yet, and far the wildest and most primitive. The Germans are supposed to have the most influence and to be jealous of English interference. There are several largish German stores, and a good bit of German shipping in the port, but there was a decided preponderance of English among the few Europeans, and all the natives spoke English who spoke anything besides their own tongue. The native language is considered prettier here than in any other of the islands. About 10am, Campbell and I landed and called on the English Consul[552] to whom we had letters from Sir William de Voeux. He was very friendly and civil: then we strolled into town and bought some tappa, the native cloth. They had a lot of clubs, but all new and made to sell, so we did not think them good enough to bother with. The natives are very handsome – especially the men, but some of the women have beautiful eyes. I bought some photos of them. We rode in the afternoon to a place called the Sliding rock, with a deep pool of water at the bottom, and running at an angle of about 45°. We bathed, and sat on top of the incline and slid down a great pace about 30 ft into the water. We came back and went to take Kava, or ava, as they call it here, at the Consul's. He has a young native girl who comes in every afternoon to make it for him. The natives are very fond of this drink, but only the men are supposed to take it. They have some dark wooden bowls on 3 legs, which the Kava gradually covers with a beautiful pale blue enamel. The process is this: the girl sits down cross-legged by the bowl and takes a lot of bits of Kava root in her mouth till it gets to a pulp like putty. Then she puts it in the bowl, and cold water is poured onto it. Then the stuff is all strained through hibiscus fibre till it is quite clear, and drunk in polished halves of coconut which also get a beautiful enamel from the ava juice. The making of the drink is not a pretty sight, but people get accustomed to it, and all the whites drink it. It is very refreshing and I have got to like it, though I didn't care for it the first time. We dined on board, and went to a wild native dance by torch light in the open air afterwards.

20 July 1884 - Sunday

We had meant to ride inland to see some curious large carved stones, something like Stonehenge only more elaborate, which are supposed to mark some ancient civilisation previous altogether to the present inhabitants. It was, however, so awfully hot that we gave it up. We bathed

---

[551] Apia is the capital and the largest city of Samoa, located on the central north coast of Upolu, Samoa's second largest island. Its exposed harbour was badly hit by a cyclone in March 1889, just 5 years after Gibbs' visit, which wrecked the three U.S. and three German warships which had been in a tense standoff in the harbour for several months during the Samoan Crisis. The single British warship, H.M.S. Calliope, survived.

[552] Although there is some confusion over his name, the British Consul to Samoa - based in Apia - at this time was probably William B. Churchward.

in the afternoon, and saw the Consul again. He told us anyone can get married for 4 dollars or divorced for 20d. by the American Consul[553] in Apia. A large school of native boys came on board with their master, a French priest, and sung a lot of native songs and some Catholic Church music – Gloria tibi Domine. Old Carnegie told me that in their native music the notes were the black notes of the piano, or those of the bagpipe – it certainly had the drone of the bagpipe. We called in the afternoon – that is Major Mair and self – on a chief of the neighbouring island of Tutuila. He was living in the guest house of Apia. He had recently been at war with his cousin – some quarrel about a name – and a good many lives had been lost, so our English man-of-war had gone there and fetched them both away to Apia to live there till things had cooled down. He was very civil to us, and we drank Kava and discoursed him for a long time.

21 July 1884 - Monday

Whatman[554], Campbell and I rowed out in a boat to the reef at low tide and walked about on it. It was very beautiful, the coral being mostly brown with a violet crown, and far down in the still deep water one could see the red bits. There were some small fish swimming about in the pools like carp – a brilliant, vivid ultramarine blue in colour, with scarlet dorsal fins. Then there was a native lunch, entirely composed of native dishes, at the International Hotel. It reminded me of the feast after the manner of the Ancients in 'Peregrine Pickle'[555]. Strange and *nauséabond*[556]-looking innards, and crustaceans of all kinds – octopus etc. – requiring a high courage and strong stomach. On the ship in the afternoon there were any amount of natives crowding and jabbering and trying to sell things. We sailed at 4pm.

22 July 1884 - Tuesday

We reached the harbour of Paugo Paugo[557] in Tutuila at 8am. There are no white people, but two native villages. The harbour[558] is a fine one with thick, steep, wooded sides, something like the New Zealand sounds except for the presence of coconuts[559] and absence of snow. Some of us went for a picnic in one of the ship's boats, climbed up a hill, bathed, and visited a native village. A very pleasant day – after dinner on board we went off in a war canoe to see a native dance. It was far the best I have seen yet, and there was a rude attempt at a sort of dramatic performance of the pantomime kind. Two or three girls, decidedly handsome. One like

---

[553] Possibly Theodore Canisius.
[554] According to the passenger list, this is Mr. C.M.C. Whatman from England. He is travelling with Mrs. Whatman.
[555] "The Adventures of Peregrine Pickle", by Tobias Smollett.
[556] French: 'sickening'
[557] Pago Pago, Tutuila Island.
[558] Pago Pago Harbor is a large natural inlet in the central south coast of the island.
[559] Gibbs appears to have learned to spell this now.

Cleopatra dressed in a stove ornament of dried grasses. It was a wild orgy, and the noble savage ran wild in the woods in his best style.

23 July 1884 - Wednesday

We started again about 10; a great number of natives around the ship in their curious double canoes. Rather an amusing incident took place – there had been an exceedingly pretty girl on board (I never saw such long eyelashes in my life), and one or two of the young fellows had been very spoony, giving her necklaces and so on; after the natives had cleared out of the ship and were paddling round, someone threw a shilling into the water, and in the bustle, diving after it, this girl's canoe was upset and a large cabinet photo of a young passenger sent floating face upwards on the sea, amid shouts of chaff and laughter.

24 July 1884 - Thursday

A good deal of pitching and tossing. Most passengers sea sick, and I rather gouty. A headwind; we reached the island of Vavau[560] in the Tongan group before night, but too late to go in. The stewards and sailors gave us a Christy Minstrel[561] entertainment, which was pretty good except for some vulgar stupidities.

25 July 1884 - Friday

Entered the long winding harbour[562], very fine – as good as Sydney – and the colours on the water splendid. We were ordered to lie off and hoist the yellow flag as measles was supposed to exist in Samoa. We had got a clean bill of health thence so there ought to have been no difficulty, but Tonga is completely under the control of a beast of a Wesleyan missionary named Baker[563] who has got the ear of the King[564] and calls himself 'premier'. He is making a pot of money out of the place, and his game is to keep away white people – especially English – as much as possible. He has passed – and enforces – the most absurd tyrannous and grandmotherly laws. A man is fined for chewing Cava, fined for not wearing a shirt, – and other offences, not recognised as such in England, are punished by 12 mo. imprisonment. As this arbitrary gent had kept the 'Wairarapa' away the last trip, the general opinion was that he would do so again, but after keeping us waiting his pleasure, during six hours, he

---

[560] Vava'u, Tonga
[561] Christy Minstrels were blacked up travelling players who provided beach entertainment to holiday makers.
[562] Port of Refuge is a deep-water harbour on the south coast of Vava'u. The capital, Neiafu, is situated next to the harbour.
[563] Reverend Shirley Waldemar Baker (1836-1903), was born in London, England, but stowed away to Australia in 1852. He became a missionary in 1860 and was ordained and sent to Tonga, where he became influential with King George Tupou I and was made his Prime Minister. The oppressive form of Methodism he instituted caused civil unrest, and there was an attempt on his life in 1887. He was deported to Auckland in 1890.
[564] King George Tupou I of Tonga (1797-1893).

fortunately allowed us to land. We went on shore; the town[565] not very pretty, but splendid orange groves loaded with fruit, with which last we all fell to pelting one another like a lot of schoolboys. The place is spoilt by corrugated iron, wooden houses, Manchester soft goods, imitations of civilised life, and the bastard form of intolerant priest-craft introduced by Reverend Baker.

Next we went off in the boats to visit some caves[566] which were beautiful, the finest about 70 ft every way and very deep, intensely blue, clear water. At the bottom bits of broken stalactite could be clearly seen, and at the back by climbing up the rocks one could go along a long tunnel about 200 yards, with a large natural shaft going up to the open air through the hill. Over this opening the convolvulus vines were growing and interlacing – and looking up it was exceedingly beautiful out of the dark cavern. The floor was a mass of fine soil with a slight ammoniacal smell; no doubt a sort of guano[567]. The stalactites were poor – very inferior to Cheddar, for instance – but the cave itself, with rich green and blood red colours on the rocks, and marvellous blue of the water, quite unbeatable. Those who had seen both said it was much superior to the blue grotto at Capri. Some of us stayed and bathed, and then visited another cave where another man and I caught a splendid water snake about 3 ft long, in bright black and silver bands. The other man jabbed a boat hook into it or against it as it glided along a flat rock, and then I passed a boot lace over its head and with a noose drew it tight; and fastening the other end of the lace to the boat hook brought him safely along. He turned out to have no fangs, so I put him into a bottle of gin and will give him to the Auckland museum. Went on shore in the evening, and sat on the beach with Campbell and smoked.

26 July 1884 - Saturday

Having heard of some wonderful accounts of a submarine cave[568] about 15 miles up the harbour on the coast, Campbell, Still, a pleasant chap named Chambers[569], and myself hired a native guide and a boat and went to it. It was represented to us as a most wonderful sight, and is described somewhere by Byron[570]. Only one Englishman is known to have gone into

---

[565] Neiafu, the capital.
[566] Probably Swallow's Cave on Vava'u.
[567] The smell of guano would have been familiar to Gibbs, of course, because it was the source of the family wealth.
[568] Mariner's Cave, first described in Mariner's "Tonga" (published 1802).
[569] William Knox Chambers (1850-1938), from Gisborne, was born in South Australia. He moved with parents to Hawkes Bay, New Zealand, where the family were sheep farmers. He was chairman of Gisborne Authority, Cook County, North Island, New Zealand from 1882 to 1884.
[570] Mariner's Cave is supposedly described by Byron in his poem "The Island", although he takes the liberty of shifting the cave's location to a different island.

it – a Captain Luce[571] – and he cut his back and head frightfully against the rocks at the top of the passage owing to having no guides. The mouth of the cave is barely 6 ft. below water at low tide, and then the passage into the cave is about 15 ft. The natives go in and out with perfect ease, and when you get in there is really nothing to see after rising to the surface except an ordinary smallish cave dimly lighted by the sun through the water. It is a funking sort of thing, but the only risk is rising too soon and cutting oneself against the sharp coral and then losing your head. The niggers[572], however, look after this – pushing and pulling you, and making you know when it is time to rise. While we were seeing this cave, most people went to a large island cave 15 ft deep with water at the bottom but with no specially interesting features that I could learn. In the evening, the Governor of Vavau – Wellington G. Tubou Malohi[573], the King's grandson – came to dinner. He is a stout, pleasant man, under 40. Pleasant in manner and speaking English well, he made a good speech, partly in English and partly in Tongan, interpreted by Baker who accompanied him. He has been extravagant, and has been put under Baker's thumb through money difficulties. Baker made a vulgar, ostentatious speech – without h's – informing us that he was invincible and would resist annexation with all his powers. I should think there is little doubt that sooner or later the Tongan group will come under English rule[574].

27 July 1884 - Sunday

A very tiring and oppressively hot day. We left Vavau at 7am. Service in the Saloon. Canon Tebbit read, and a dissenting man preached. I was very gouty all day, and couldn't use one hand. We passed an active volcano in the distance. We could just see the smoke rising and a curious conical mount – Kao[575], 5,000 ft high. We lay to off a small island at nightfall, the navigation being too dangerous and uncertain to proceed: the coral reefs are fearfully numerous in these parts, and during the trip we have seen ever so many wrecks – the ribs of old ships, sticking up against the sky like the one in the 'Ancient Mariner'[576], giving a ghostly effect.

---

[571] Luce was the captain of HMS Esk. He lacerated his back so badly in the accident that he died a few days later.
[572] This word would not have been considered offensive in Gibbs' day, of course.
[573] Wellington Gu Tubou Malohi (-1885), Crown Prince of Tonga, son of Tevita Uga and grandson of King George Tupou I of Tonga. He died aged just 31 in 1885, 8 years before his grandfather the King.
[574] Tonga actually became a British protectorate on 18th May 1900, until 1970 when it joined the Commonwealth with its own autonomous Monarch.
[575] At 1125 metres, Kao is the highest and most spectacular volcano in Tonga. The lower slopes of the volcano are covered in jungle.
[576] "The Rime of the Ancient Mariner", a poem by Samuel Taylor Coleridge, published in 1798.

28 July 1884 - Monday

We reached Tonga Tabu[577] at 9am – a flat, low coast; the ugliest place we have touched at. Campbell and I went on shore and called on the English Consul, Symonds[578], to whom we brought a despatch from Sir William de Voeux. He has a beautiful house built in the native fashion of reeds and thatch roof over a frame of very handsome beams, or rather poles braided with fibre; the two ends of the building screened off to form a bedroom and writing room, the offices being outside. The walls were hung with Tappa and covered with a very fine collection of barbaric weapons, canoe models, etc. An open doorway in the middle looks into a small, well-kept garden with close-trimmed hibiscus hedge all round and a blaze of colour from poinsettias, oleanders and crotons. A little monkey nibbling a bit of coconut, and some lovely doves, grey with rose and green breasts, completed the picture and made me quite inclined to settle in the tropics. How much more sensible to live in that fashion than as most Europeans, in a frousty, bad English house with corrugated iron roof to draw the heat, 2 stories, and every feature hideous and unsuited to the climate. There were some of the women passengers calling on Symonds, so after 10 min. we cleared out and went on to the German Consul's, who most kindly got a couple of horses for us, and taking Carnegie in his buggy with him we all started off inland to visit the wonderful monumental stones. The ride was rather monotonous and it rained most of the way, but as we had very little on it didn't much matter – though a wetting of that kind in the West Indies would almost inevitably lay one up with intermittent fever. We first visited a banyan tree said to be 120 ft. round and the biggest in the Southern Pacific, then to some stones called the Pyramids which are burial places of great antiquity. They consist of 3 tiers of large slabs of coralline stone about 20 ft by 12, and one ft. through, set on their sides, the soil being mounded up inside – something in this shape:

54. Gibbs' sketch of the Tongatapu Pyramid

The place is so overgrown with thick brush that it is impossible to get a general view of these tumuli – of which there are three pretty close

---

[577] Tongatapu
[578] Henry Francis Symonds (1855-1887). British vice-Consul in Tonga from August 1880 to October 1886, when he was transferred to Samoa. He died of tuberculosis shortly afterwards at the age of 32.

together. In Tonga there are many tumuli still used for burial, only without these slabs – merely large, earth mounds with flat tops spread over with fine-pounded white coral gravel – the places of the graves being marked with small, round, bluish greenstones. After riding on for some time and passing two native villages with earthwork fortifications round and then some way further, about 50 yards off the road on a green plot in the bush, we came to the curious Stonehenge-type monument called Koe Ha Amoga A maui[579][580]. The natives have no traditions about it and there

---

[579] It is interesting to note that the Easter Island monuments in the shape of figures are also called Maui.

[580] An article in New Zealand's Evening Post on 2 June 1909:

THE ANTIQUITIES OF TONGATABU - THE TRILITHOX AND THE PYRAMID TOMBS

Last week a correspondent enquired through our columns for detailed information concerning a remarkable ancient trilithon in the island of Tongatabu, brief reference to which is made in the Encyclopedia Britannica. The required particulars were supplied by Mr. E. Tregear in a letter which we published, and Mr. W. G. Lodder sent us a copy of a very rare privately-printed pamphlet containing a detailed account of the interesting monument. The pamphlet is called "The Wairarapa Wilderness," "in which," it is added, "will be found the wanderings of the passengers of the second cruise of the S.S. Wairarapa from Auckland to the South Sea Islands and back during the month of July, 1884". It contains the logbook of the voyage, list of passengers and crew, and a reprint of the newspaper written by the passengers during the trip. The article from which we make extracts is headed "Description of Ancient Stones near Village of Kologo Tonga, called Koe ha Amoga a Maui". The site is located as "near the village of Kologo, which is situated about fifteen miles from Nukualofa, the principal town in the island."

"The monument consists of three large blocks of stone composed of a limestone conglomerate, in which may be seen much fossil coral and many coral shells. At first sight it might appear that the upper stone was not of quite the same nature as the lower ones, but careful examination led all our party to conclude that it really was of the same nature, only less weatherworn and more dressed by hand. The shape of the monument at first sight appears to be identical with the form so well known at Stonehenge: two upright stones, with a third one lying across the top of them; but a moment's observation shows a very marked diiference. Instead of the upper stone being merely superimposed, in this case it is carefully inserted into the other two; a groove about two feet wide has been cut in each upright stone, and the upper stone, which has been carefully cut to the right size, has been placed in it so that the ends are about flush wiih the outside of the perpendicular stones, whilst the top is about flush with the top of the stones, though owing to the easternmost stone being a little lower than tho other one, probably from breakage, it rises a little above it on that side. The horizontal stone lies east and west, and it is noticeable that either by accident or design there is a slight though perceptible inclination of the faces of the perpendicular stone: towards the north — that is to say, the north end of the opening between the stones is slightly narrower than the south. "On the centre of the top of the horizontal stone a hollow has bsen scooped out, about the size of a coconut shell, and about an inch and a half deep. Whether this hollow has been part of the original design or has been made at a subsequent period, it is impossible to say. Owing to the pressure of time and the absence of any correct tape or ruler, the measurements must be considered to be approximate; they are, however, roughly as follows: — Height of perpendicular stones, 14 to 15ft; depth of horizontal stone, 4ft 6in; distance between perpendicular stones, lOft; base of perpendicular stones, north-east side, 4ft; base of perpendicular stones, north-west side, about 12ft, probably less; breadth of perpendicular stones at the top of east and west sides, about 7ft, probably more. It will thus be seen that the space contained between the three stones is nearly a square, if not absolutely so, as possibly accurate measurement would find it to be".

seems to be no doubt it is the work of some earlier race. The stone is of a rough, coralline conglomerate, in which fossils of all kinds can be plainly seen. The two square pillars are much broken and weather-worn, and so full of holes that I was able without much difficulty to climb up one and examine the top stone, which is 2 ft across with a cup-shaped hollow scooped out in the middle. The pillars had a lot of scrub stuff growing on them which gave them almost the appearance of old trunks of trees. They were about 4 ft square and 16 ft. high, narrowing somewhat towards the top. The lateral stone, instead of being layed on them as at Stonehenge, was cut down into them its own depth – about 4 ft ½ – so that it was flush. The length of the top stone was about 20 ft. It was a very interesting thing to see altogether. We stopped our horses and had tea and eggs at a hospitable German's, and then rode back. My horse got very tired, and I could hardly kick him along; the distance altogether about 36 miles. We had supper on board at 9 and I turned in soon after, having had a pretty long day.

55. Haamonga-A-Maui, Tongatapu, Tonga (present day)
Photo by Tony Bowden, from Wikimedia Commons

29 July 1884 - Tuesday

Sloped about the village to see if there were any curios worth buying, but got nothing. All the best things are in Samoa; the Tongans make, and have, very little. We left about 3pm, after a very pleasant trip. Samoa is far the most worth seeing of the three groups.

30 July 1884 - Wednesday

Getting rapidly cooler. Read an amazingly schoolboy sort of novel called 'Charlie Thornhill'[581] and 'M or N'[582] by Whyte Melville.

---

[581] Charlie Thornhill; or, The Dunce of the Family (1863), by Charles Clarke (aka Charles Carlos-Clarke).
[582] M. or N. "Similia similibus curantur." by G.J. Whyte-Melville

31 July 1884 - Thursday

Played chess and whist. The nicest people on board, and those I would like to see again, are: the two Maclarens – the elder of whom has a face like the priest in 'Une Bonne Histoire'[583]; Mrs Fraser[584], a very charming old lady; old Carnegie; a young fellow called Chambers; besides many more very decent and passable, young Popham[585], a good boy.

1 August 1884 - Friday

Nothing.

2 August 1884 - Saturday

We reached Auckland at 11 o'clock. It looked bare and bleak after the rich foliage of the tropics. I hurried off to Cruikshanks to get my letters, and was disgusted to find none. Some stupid mistake, I suppose, though I particularly asked for them to be forwarded here. On going to the Union Company[586] I found there was no steamer going to Sydney for a week, so I shall stick to this boat which sails today for Melbourne via Dunedin. This will enable me to look Bell up, and I shall be in Melbourne by 13th. Lunched at the Northern Club, and played skittles with the Maclarens and Campbell. We sailed at 6; a great many came to see us off, and a lot of cheering and good-byeing and 'he's a jolly good fellow' sort of conviviality. I forgot to mention that we had a very wet last night in the Smoking room. Singing and drinking kept up till a very late hour. I was in the chair, and collected the fines for swearing etc. which went towards drinks.

3 August 1884 - Sunday

The ship seems very dull and empty; the skipper[587], who had been rough and surly all the trip, came into the smoking room and was, for him, quite civil. He had been so rude that Captain Fraser, Whatman, Campbell and self left the saloon when his health was drunk.

4 August 1884 - Monday

The sea has got up very much, and at intervals last night in the cabin next me I could hear a new arrival pitiably ill. It is fearfully cold, and all the hills covered with snow along the coast. So the change is very sharp after the tropical heat of only a few days ago.

---

[583] 'Une Bonne Histoire' is a painting from 1853 by Leo Hermann. A Catholic priest roars with laughter after enjoying a few drinks and 'A Good Story' with a colleague.
[584] From the passenger list, the wife of the Hon. Captain Fraser, an influential merchant from Dunedin, New Zealand.
[585] From the passenger list, F.A.L. Popham, from England.
[586] Union Steam Ship Company of New Zealand, founded in 1875.
[587] Captain H. W. H Chatfield.

5 August 1884 - Tuesday

We came alongside the wharf at Port Chalmers at 10 o'clock last night, but it was so cold and miserable that Campbell and I decided to sleep on board and come up to town by an early train this morning. Bell met us at the station and I walked over to the office with him and talked over things which are as dull and unpromising as possible; played billiards and whist in the evening, and dined at the club.

6 August 1884 - Wednesday

The office in the morning, and note to Alban. Went for a walk in the afternoon beyond the race course, and on the beach watching a high sea coming in. Fine rollers and gray sea, with the sand hills and gorse – very like an English coast scene. Dined with Wright who has a fine house, formerly the Bishop's Palace. Played whist till very late – a good rubber. I think, from all I can hear, New Zealand is in a bad way financially. An immense amount of borrowed money has been spent with great extravagance.

7 August 1884 - Thursday

Rough weather and very cold. I have a comfortable cabin to myself, however.

8 August 1884 - Friday

Nobody interesting on board. The skipper much more friendly than he was on the trip.

9 August 1884 - Saturday

We are not going to call at Hobart[588] but go straight, which is unusual. I am rather sorry, as I should have liked to see the harbour.

10 August 1884 - Sunday

The sea-sick people beginning to reappear. We stopped at the Bluff[589], but I did not go up to Invercargill. The Bluff is a most forsaken-looking place.

11-12 August 1884

Nothing to 'Chronicle'.

---

[588] Hobart, Tasmania.
[589] The bluff (a high, steep bank by the sea, or a cliff with a broad face) was known by sailors as Old Man's Bluff. The town by the bluff, about 20 miles from Invercargill, had been called Campbelltown since 1856, and was renamed Bluff in 1917. The bluff itself is now called Bluff Hill.

13 August 1884 - Wednesday

Read 'Samuel Brohl et Cie' by Victor Cherbuliez, and liked it. A very clever idea: an adventurer passing himself off as a Polish noble who had died, and so learning the past as to acquire some of the fine nature of the dead man. Reached Sandridge[590] at 9.30pm and Campbell knowing the Custom House Officer he took us off in the boat at once, and we went to the Melbourne Club – of which place I found I had become a member, having been elected in my absence; everybody very friendly. I meant to have slept there but, Bright dropping in from the theatre, I walked back with him to St. Leonards.

56. Melbourne Club (1880-9)
National Library of Australia,
nla.pic-an10638277-44

Melbourne (4)

14 August 1884 - Thursday

Heaps of letters accumulated – from the family. Nothing particular gone wrong I am thankful to say. In the evening, to private theatricals by the Bohemian Club at a theatre. The Governor[591] and all the fashion of Melbourne there – a very full house. The stage very nicely set and all well turned out; beautiful play bill and so on, but no first class acting, though a very level, fair, performance. The first piece, 'Leap Year' by Buckstone, was well played. I was rather interested to see the part of Captain Mouser, as I had been offered it. It is a rather good, low, comedy, one of the fortune-hunting kind. The 2nd piece was 'Woodcocks Little Game'. It was not so good as the other, and dragged. As far as I can remember, not so well done as a St Dunstans – the present exponent of Woodcock very inferior to Gerald Young.

15 August 1884 - Friday

Dined with Regi, and we both resumed our habit of going to sleep instantly after dinner till about 1. I never want to sleep anywhere else, but I find no difficulty to adapting myself to his ways in that respect. He is cheerful enough but does not care for conversation on any subject, and after a long day in the office and a walk back to his house, then a good

---

[590] Sandridge is now known as Port Melbourne, Victoria.
[591] The Governor of Victoria from July 1884 to November 1889 was The Rt Hon. Lord Loch, GCMG KCB.

dinner, a warm room, a comfortable arm chair and a pipe, it seems natural to sleep.

16 August 1884 - Saturday

Lunched at the Club and walked with Gowen Evans and Miller[592] – the Manager of the New South Wales Bank – to a man named Strachan's[593], who hospitably entertained us with Brandy and Sodas and cigars. Dined at the Lewis's, and met the handsome [GREEK][594] Miss Bunny [GREEK][595]. She'd do for a model of Germania on the Rhine.

57. Greek text from 16 August 1884

17 August 1884 - Sunday

Wretched cold wet weather. The winters here are not so much better than England, and the summers far worse. Bright away for Saturday to Monday with the Clarkes. I dined with Evans – a swell dinner at the Grand Hotel, very well served – to meet Miss Genevieve Ward[596], who is playing here in Lady Macbeth. A clever woman with a powerful Gorgon face, but not a good expression.

18 August 1884 - Monday

Campbell asked Regi and me to dine at the 'Maison Dorée', but the temptation to go home and sleep after dinner too strong for us both so we declined.

---

[592] Possibly George Miller (known to be the General Manager of the Bank of New South Wales in 1891).
[593] Possibly Hugh Murray Strachan (1851-1933), a financier, merchant, and wool-broker, who had invested in sugar in the past.
[594] Greek: Gibbs' formation of his Greek characters is hard to decipher, but this phrase seems to be "deep bay" which may code for "full-breasted".
[595] Greek: A quote from Homer's Illiad (book 1, line 551) referring to Hera as "ox-eyed" (meant in a flattering way). This is a repeat of the quote from 26th June.
[596] Lucy Genevieve Theresa Ward (1837-1922) was an American-born British actress who had first become famous as an operatic soprano. She married a Russian nobleman, becoming Madame La Comtesse De Guerbel. She performed under the stage names of Madame Guerabella and Genevieve Ward. As an actress she was famous for her portrayal of Lady Macbeth. Whilst on one of her visits to Melbourne she organised a charity benefit for the Women's Hospital, the proceeds of which went towards a new 'Genevieve Ward Wing'. She was created a Dame Commander of the Order of the British Empire (DBE) on her birthday in 1921.

19 August 1884 - Tuesday

Dined at the Lewises again; very pleasant. Met the Leishmans, and a man named Haggett from Adelaide. Mrs L. very bright and lively.

20 August 1884 - Wednesday

Dined at the Club with Regi, and Howard – a fortune-hunting young officer in the Defense Force. He proposed to Miss Fairbairn the other day, but she very sensibly refused him. Afterwards, we went to see Macbeth. Miss Ward not bad, but very inferior to Ristori. Vernon[597] execrable as Macbeth and the rest, of course, nothing. Well put on, and good scenery, but too much singing, and witch pantomime interfering horribly with the action of the drama.

21 August 1884 - Thursday

Have been reading lately a novel called 'Sarah Barnum'[598]: a stupid, gross, vulgar, spiteful attack on Sarah Bernhardt[599]. It seems to have made a good deal of talk – Lord knows why.

22 August 1884 - Friday

Nothing.

23 August 1884 - Saturday

Went over to the Lewises in the afternoon to some lawn tennis, but did not play as I felt gouty. Bright had several people to dinner: the Clarkes and Powers – Miss Power[600] has been jilted by Lucas[601], the Cricketer, one of the Contractor family[602], I believe.

24 August 1884 - Sunday

Lunch with Strachan, and then walked over to call on the Simpsons, very wealthy Scotch people living in a large tasteless mansion. Keats is thinking

---

[597] Howard Vernon, part of the same dramatic troupe as Miss Genevieve Ward.
[598] 'Sarah Barnum', by Marie Colombier.
[599] Sarah Bernhardt (1844-1923) was a world famous French actress who suffered a great deal of anti-Semitic prejudice.
[600] Miss Power must be one of the two daughters of Robert Power and his first wife (name unknown): either Mary Elizabeth Power(who married Captain Alan Thomas of the Royal Navy), or Kathleen Maud Power (who married Archibald (Archie) Campbell MacLaren, the English cricketer, in 1898).
[601] Lucas: possibly either Charles Frank Lucas (1843-1919), or his cousin Alfred Perry "Bunny" Lucas (1857-1923). However, Charles Frank Lucas had already married Helen Bionda Carlyon (1850-1926) in 1878, so it is more likely to be A.P. Lucas (who never married).
[602] Gibbs is presumably referring to the well-known Public Works contractors from Norfolk, the Lucas brothers: Charles Thomas Lucas (1820-1895) and Sir Thomas Lucas (1822-1902).

perhaps of marrying one of the girls[603]. They will each have £40,000 apiece. I don't think it will come to anything. Coming back, I got wet through and rather tired. Laing[604], of the Ducal Line, came to dinner – a shrewd, gentlemanly, pleasant, young fellow, but I think humbugging us. My gout came on very fast in my left ankle which was swollen up as if I had elephantiasis, and I could feel it in every joint. No doubt the result of chill. Felt very seedy.

25 August 1884 - Monday

Gout pretty bad, but not much pain. In bed all day, and read 'Sappho'[605] by Alphonse Daudet. Not so nice a book as the 'Nabab'[606] or his others that I have read, but clever. It is dedicated, "To my sons when they shall have reached 20". I don't think it would be very profitable reading for them. Also read a lot of Horace and some of the 'Diable boiteux'[607].

26 August 1884 - Tuesday

Still in bed during day, but up in evening and hobbled into sitting room. Lewis, who had heard I was down, had called very kindly for a chat, as did also Strachan. Read a very pleasant, amusing, little American book – rather farcical – called 'Rudder Grange'[608]; also 'Les Fortunes de Rongon', a very painful story by Emile Zola about the Coup d'Etat. He has a good wholesome hatred of Napoleon III.

27 August 1884 - Wednesday

Bad weather, so I didn't attempt to leave the house. Read a rum little old book professing to be a life of Bedloe[609], of Popish Plot celebrity, written soon after his death[610]. Really nothing more than a blackguard, lying, little anti-Popish novel, making out Bedloe rather a hero than otherwise. Tried

---

[603] Frank Keating presumably didn't marry one of the Simpson girls - he married Constance Mary Prell.
[604] A report on the wrecking of the "Duke of Westminster" in 1884 mentions a "Mr. Laing" as appearing "for the owners" – who were the Eastern Steam Ship Company Ltd. (trading as the Ducal Line). However, we were unable to find any more information about this Laing. There was a shipuilding company based in Sunderland, called James Laing, and several Laings were serving as Directors: possibly James Laing Snr., Philip Laing Snr., James Laing Jnr., and Hugh Laing. These may or may not be relevant: however, the shipbuilders did build some ships for the Ducal Line, so there may be a link.
[605] 'Sappho', by Alphonse Daudet, published 1884.
[606] 'Nabab', by Alphonse Daudet, published 1877.
[607] 'Le Diable Boiteux' (The Lame Devil), by Alain René Lesage, published 1707.
[608] 'Rudder Grange', by Frank Richard Stockton (1834-1902). A middle-American comic novel.
[609] William Bedloe (1650-1680) was an English fraudster. In 1679, he wrote "Narrative and impartial discovery of the horrid Popish Plot" which was considered totally untrustworthy.
[610] Probably "The Life and Death of Captain William Bedloe, One of the Chief Discoverers of the Horrid Popish Plot. Wherein all his more Eminent Cheats and whatever is remarkable of him, both Good and Bad, is Impartially Discover'd", by John Hancock and Enoch Prosser.

to read 'Lady Grizzel'[611], a historical novel by Lewis Wingfield, but I prefer getting court gossip and Duchess of Kingston's case neat in Hervey's memoirs[612] on state trials to having them diluted into a novel form. Gowen Evans came in to see me – also, later on, young Mackinnon.

28 August 1884 - Thursday

My gout well enough to let me go to town, and Regi off to Sydney for the races; rather late in the office and dined at the Club, where I am going to stay for a bit. Keating to theatre, and I sat talking with Mackinnon.

29 August 1884 - Friday

Met old Mackinnon, who asked me to stay with them again in the western district. I declined; too busy just now. Read some of Hawthorne's 'Twice Told Tales'[613] – 'The Rill from the Town Pump' very neat and pretty. Tylecote just come out to marry Miss Clarke – wedding fixed in a month's time.

30 August 1884 - Saturday

Went for a walk with Evans, and called on the Mackinnons and Fairbairns– both out. Hot wind clouds of dust, very disagreeable. Played whist at the Club.

31 August 1884 - Sunday

Went to the Lewises in the afternoon and tried to play lawn tennis on their asphalt court, but the gout came on directly in the right hand so I had to give it up. Had high tea there.

---

[611] 'Lady Grizel', by Lewis Strange Wingfield.
[612] John Hervey, 2nd Baron Hervey (known as Lord Hervey after the death of his half-brother in 1723). His somewhat outspoken memoirs were published posthumeously in 1848.
[613] 'Twice Told Tales, by Nathaniel Hawthorne.

1 September 1884 - Monday

58. Rebecca Ada Crawcour (1864-1967)
Courtesy of Patrick Coppel

Dined at Club. Keating had a party to the theatre, consisting of Evans, self and Captain Dobie[614], R.A., from India – a very nice fellow, nephew of the Poetaster[615] Locker[616]. Also Miss Croker[617], who is considered a beauty; and Miss Bunny, who is one, with Mrs Lewis as chaperone. It was an amateur company, the women's parts being taken by professionals; the play an emotional one called 'Black Sheep', the acting ludicrously bad except one lad who played the larrikin[618] part admirably, and brought down the house again and again; altogether, a very pleasant evening.

2 September 1884 - Tuesday

Read a long Quarterly[619] article in the evening contrasting the 'Adonais', 'Lycidas' and 'In Memoriam'; a good idea to compare the three, but very heavy and feeble in execution. Heard that Miss Clarke has jilted Tylecote and he is going back next boat. Pretty rough on him to make such a fool of him, corresponding for a year and bringing him out from England with the Wedding Day fixed, and Sir William having withdrawn 'all opposition,' – his dear girl's happiness being the first consideration, etc.

---

[614] Captain Dobie was an officer in the Royal Horse Artillery, with a younger brother (Stanley Locker Dobie) also in the army as a surgeon, and another (Herbert Dobie) working in the Railway Department of Auckland. He also had three sisters: one married in England, one (Bertha Dobie) married to a Major Goring, and a third and youngest daughter who was murdered in New Zealand in 1880. The children's mother was the brother of Frederick Locker (later Locker-Lampson) (1821-1895), a poet, and of Arthur Locker (1828-1893) (novelist, and editor of *Graphic*).
[615] Poetaster was a derogatory term for a bad poet. The word was popularised by Ben Jonson's play of the same name, first performed in 1601.
[616] Frederick Locker (1821-1895), later Frederick Locker-Lampson when he added his second wife's surname.
[617] There were certainly Crokers in Melbourne at the time, the most well-known being William H Croker, an influential local solicitor specialising in maritime law, who built a mansion named 'Maritimo' in the Williamstown suburb in 1885 of which only the 'Maritimo Fence' now remains. However, there is a possibility that Gibbs misheard the name of Miss Crawcour (1862-1966), a young Jewish woman well-known in 1880s Melbourne as "the beautiful Miss Crawcour" (possibly with reference to the character in "Somebody's Luggage" by Charles Dickens). Gibbs may have mistakenly attributed the name Croker from the painting by Sir Thomas Lawrence, "The Beautiful Miss Croker". I rather favour this explanation, as Rebecca Crawcour was a cousin and direct contemporary of my own grandmother, Elizabeth Emily Crawcour.
[618] Larrikin means clownish or high-spirited.
[619] The Quarterly Review was a literary and political periodical published from 1809 to 1967.

3 September 1884 - Wednesday

Dined at Club and played billiards with Captain Thomas[620], an interesting man who has seen and done a lot. Read the 2nd series of Henry Greville's Memoirs; rather flat after Charles'[621] – a stupid thing to have a woman edit that sort of book.[622] Some interesting stories about Napoleon III.

4 September 1884 - Thursday

A dinner party at the Lewises. Met a Mr Travers, a squatter, and his wife, Mrs Bunny – a clever old German lady from Frankfurt an der Oder, furiously anti-French ('that miserable nation'). I took her in to dinner. The dodge in Australia is for the servant who takes your hat in the hall to give you a slip of paper with the name of the woman you are to take in. It saves a lot of chattering with the host, who probably forgets or tells you wrong. There was also Mr Cornish and wife, who acted well in 'Leap Year' – decidedly pretty but powdered – and 5 or 6 others; a good party. The white soup was coconut, which I had never tasted before – not bad.

5 September 1884 - Friday

Went all over the new E&A[623] boat, the 'Guthrie', with Captain Craig[624]. She is well arranged, and the passengers accommodation good – except the bathrooms, which are wretched for a ship running in hot seas. A party of discontented steerage passengers, headed by a regular beast of a sea lawyer, invaded my office to complain of their fare and treatment on the 'Liguria'[625]. They claimed return of passage money, and threatened proceedings and tried to bully me into saying off-hand if their claim would be met or refused. I would say nothing but that it would be forwarded to

---

[620] Thomas was Captain of the S.S. Nelson, which belonged to Patrick Henderson and Company.
[621] Charles Cavendish Fulke Greville (1794-1865) was Clerk of the Council for forty years from 1821 under George IV, William IV, and Victoria, during which time he kept journals. These were posthumously published in several parts: A Journal of the Reigns of King George IV and King William IV; A Journal of the Reign of Queen Victoria from 1837 to 1852; and A Journal of the Reign of Queen Victoria from 1852 to 1860, each in several volumes, starting in 1875. They caused so much outrage that an attempt was made to recall them. His brother, Henry Grenville (1801-1872) was attaché to the British Embassy in Paris from 1834 to 1844 and also kept a journal, part of which was published as "Leaves from the Diary of Henry Greville" in 1883-4.
[622] Quel prejudis!
[623] Eastern and Australian Steam Navigation Company.
[624] Captain Hugh Craig, commander of the S.S. Guthrie. Later, in 1896, he was awarded the Knighthood of the Royal Military Order of Our Lord Jesus Christ by Charles (Carlos) I, King of Portugal (whom Gibbs meets in February 1885, before he was King) for services rendered in relation to the transport of troops and officials during the Timor Rebellion whilst he was commander of the S.S. Menmuir (also of the Eastern and Australia Steamship Company).
[625] The 'Liguria' was an Orient Line ship. The exact date that Gibbs Bright & Co. became agents for the Orient Line is not known, but a photograph of their Sydney office shows a sign above the door saying they are agents: unfortunately the exact date of the photo is not known, but seems to be from around 1880. However, a letter from Gibbs to his brother Alban implies that they were still hoping to "get" the Orient Line agency in March 1884.

the head office and considered. Dined alone, as Keating had to go down to the office after dinner to sign the 'Soratas' papers – who goes away at midnight.

Began to read Cesar Birotteau[626] by de Balzac. Met young Conran, a son of Colonel Conran[627] of Geelong. I am much worried about our wool liens[628]. R.B. is so secretive when anything is wrong.

6 September 1884 - Saturday

Lunched at Club, and went down to Mount Macedon. Found buggy to meet me, and got to the Ryan's a little before dinner. A Miss Bell, an artist, staying there. A clever woman who had lived a good deal in Germany and travelled about. Also a younger sister who would have been pretty in the Lady Hamilton style, but very bad teeth. She wore her hair slightly powdered, which gave her an odd, made-up look. There was also a Miss le Soeuf[629] – a very handsome, shy, silent girl about 19. Her mother[630] had become a Plymouth Sister[631] or something, and will hardly let her go anywhere.

7 September 1884 - Sunday

No service. Pottered about the garden with old Ryan – the violets and primroses magnificent. Mrs. R. very full of *l'affaire* Clarke-Tylecote. Midday dinner and high tea; smoked a great deal, rather bored. Had to take some tickets for some *tableaux vivants*[632] which Mrs R. is getting up for a charity.

---

[626] Honoré de Balzac (1799-1850): 'Grandeur et décadence de César Birotteau' (1837), part of La Comédie Humaine
[627] Lieutenant-Colonel Lewis Charles Conran (1821-1893). Cape Conran near Marlo in East Gippsland, Victoria, is named after him. He lived in Highton, near Geelong. He had 6 sons, of whom only the first 4 were born by 1884: Thomas Wills Conran (1850-1915); Henry Lewis (Harry) Conran (1851-1924); Charles James Curtis Conran (b. 1854); and Marcell Conran (1855-1935).
[628] Liens: for the French, meaning "connections".
[629] Caroline Lilian Le Souef (1863-1939). The Le Souef family were particularly talented in the world of ornithology, zoology, veterinary science, and in art and design.
[630] Caroline Le Soeuf (née Cotton) (1834-1915) was the sister of Marian Ryan. She married Albert Alexander Cochrane Le Soeuf (1828-1902) in 1853. Albert Le Soeuf is one of 713 people who appear in The Explorers and Early Colonists of Victoria, a historical photographic montage of 1872 by Thomas Foster Chuck (1826-1898). It shows that he arrived in Victoria in 1840. Two other members of his family (Charles, arrived 1838, and William, arrived 1840) are also shown. Albert Le Soeuf became director of the Zoological Gardens in Melbourne in 1882.
[631] The Plymouth Brethren were (and still are) a strict Christian sect.
[632] *Tableaux vivant* ("living pictures") were popular in the Victorian era, before the advent of film. They consisted of static scenes in which actors posed, sometimes to represent a painting or theme, or - more usually in theatres - to tell a story through a series of snapshots. Mrs. Ryan's *tableaux* are presented at the Melbourne Athenaeum on 9th October - Gibbs is in the audience.

8 September 1884 - Monday

Early breakfast – cooking really infernal, worse than a bush Inn. Mrs R. told me cook under notice to leave. In the office by 11. Another mail out today; the Ryans having kindly given me an enormous nosegay of violets, I sent them over to Mrs Lewis. Dined there in the evening again, and met the Leishmans. Mrs L.[633] very bright and lively – a most pleasant evening. Went and slept at St. Leonards to see how it was going on.

9 September 1884 - Tuesday

Walked in by the river – the willows have all come into leaf the last week, and make the bonny braes[634] of Yarra very pretty. Dined at the Club with Evans, and billiards with Captain Thomas. Met Wardell[635], the architect's son – a gentlemanly fellow, a Roman Catholic.

10 September 1884 - Wednesday

Nothing of interest; dined with Keats, the 'Mignonette'[636] seems to be a regular case of guzzling Jack and gorging Jimmy[637]: very horrible. We have had a most sensational account of the fire on board the 'Orient' ship, 'Lusitania'[638]; sixty men insensible at one time from the fumes of charcoal and burning meat. Everybody behaved admirably; unless the letter is grossly exaggerated, it must have been a fearful scene; hitherto it has been kept out of the papers.

---

[633] Mrs. L. is probably Mrs. Lewis rather than Mrs. Leishman – Gibbs was always most attentive to Mrs. Lewis.
[634] Bonny (or bonnie) is Scottish dialect for beautiful, pretty or attractive. Brae is Scottish dialect for a slope or hillside, especially the sloping bank of a river valley. Gibbs is probably quoting from the traditional Scottish song, 'The Bonnie Banks o' Loch Lomond', which starts with the line, "By yon bonnie banks an' by yon bonnie braes".
[635] This is one of the six sons of Gibbs Bright's Sydney architect, William Wilkinson Wardell, whom Gibbs meets on 29 December 1884.
[636] Not, as we originally thought, the name of an inferior restaurant or sauce for serving with oysters, but a reference to the gruesome events that took place on the English yacht 'Mignonette' which set sail from Sydney to Southampton in May 1884 and sank in a gale on 5th July. The crew of four – Tom Dudley, the captain, Edwin Stephens, Edmund Brooks, and Richard Parker, the cabin boy – managed to lower the lifeboat and get away with only two tins of turnips for food but no fresh water. After about two weeks, Richard Parker – already ill – was killed by the others and eaten.
[637] This is a quote from "Little Billee", by William Makepeace Thackeray (1811-1863), about three sailors who ran out of food. Two of the sailors plan to eat Little Billee – although in the end his fate is somewhat more fortunate than Richard Parker!
[638] From the Hobart Mercury, 13th September 1884: "FIRE ABOARD THE S.S. LUSITANIA: A fire, which burned for several hours, occurred in the refrigeration chamber of the Orient steamer Lusitania when in the Indian Ocean. Two hundred and fifty carcasses of frozen meat were jettisoned."

11 September 1884 - Thursday

Mrs Ryan asks me to take part in some *tableaux vivants*; offer declined with thanks. I consider 'paying-up' quite sufficient without having to make a fool of myself too.

12 September 1884 - Friday

Dined at the Lewises and played penny Loo.

13 September 1884 - Saturday

Dined with Robertson, who had a dinner party at the Club; afterwards to his box at the theatre to see Miss Reid[639], who is supposed to have an English reputation, as Juliet[640]. She was pretty, and the scenery and dresses good, being hired from Irving[641], and the same as used in the Lyceum performance. The acting was very poor except Mercutio, who was admirable though rather a weak voice. Darley[642] was his name. I left after 2 acts, as I have to see it again on Tuesday. Played whist at the Club and won a few pounds.

14 September 1884 - Sunday

In the afternoon played lawn tennis at the Lewises, and dined with Regi. A horrible young Liverpool cad there with a provincial swagger. He spoke of Tyndall Bright as Brindle Tight before Regi! R. went to sleep after dinner, and I had to talk to him. Most thankful I was when the beast at last went. I strongly recommended him to go to Sydney.

15 September 1884 - Monday

Read a book called 'My Enemy's Daughter' by Justin Macarthy[643], very deficient in incident, and not specially interesting.

---

[639] Fanny Reid.
[640] Romeo was played by Frank Cates.
[641] Henry Irving, an actor-manager responsible for the original Lyceum production in 1882.
[642] Brian Darley.
[643] My Enemy's Daughter, by Justin McCarthy (published 1869)

16 September 1884 - Tuesday

59. Donald Mackinnon and Hilda Bunny wedding (1891)
State Library of Victoria, H84.437

60. Hilda and Donald Mackinnon (c1890s)
State Library of Victoria, H83.47/19

Had a box at the theatre: the Lewises, Miss Bunny, Strachan, Mackinnon, F.A.K. and Captain Thomas. We had very good fun – a lively party. Cates, whom I met in New Zealand, played Romeo very ill, working his neck up and down like a gander going in to a barn.

17 September 1884 - Wednesday

Finished off my mail letters yesterday, and slept at the Club. Starting at 5.30am for Camperdown to have a couple of days' shooting. Arrived at 1, and coached 8 or 9 miles to Cobden where I was met by a buggy, and drove to the hut in the Otway Forest[644] where I found my host – young Clough, who came from 'Frisco with me. There was also a pleasant fellow named Buckley. We went out for a couple of hours shooting rabbits. I was in very good form. Played cut throat Euchre for 1/- a game in the evening. Macknickel, the boundary rider whose hut we are in, seems a sodden, drunken brute.

18 September 1884 - Thursday

Last night between 12 and 1, after we were in bed, some fellow tried to break into the house at my bedroom window. I got my gun and run out, and he got on his horse and galloped off. I holloaed to Macknickel, but he didn't come till all was over. I believe it was a put up thing, and he was in it. If the man hadn't had a light I shouldn't have woke, but I had an idea the place was on fire. We killed several big forester kangaroo, and I shot a poor native bear[645] with a pea rifle.

---

[644] The Otway Forest area is now a protected environment and a highly significant fossil-find location.
[645] Koala

19 September 1884 - Friday

Rather better sport than yesterday, but most of the bush kangaroo have been poisoned by phosphorized oats. We tried some fillets of kangaroo for dinner instead of our corned beef. It was not bad – like tasteless mutton.

20 September 1884 - Saturday

Pouring with rain, so we decided to go back to Melbourne. All this country looks very pretty with its English grasses, quite unlike Australia. I got a telegram from old Mr Mackinnon who had heard I was in the neighbourhood and asked me to come and stay with them. Very kind of him, but there is a mail out on Monday. Reached the Club at 9pm, had some poached egg and tea and a rubber, and slept at the Club.

21 September 1884 - Sunday

Walked with Hogg[646] and Robinson[647] to the Lewises and played lawn tennis. Had supper there and went back to Bright's, whom I found asleep in his armchair.

22 September 1884 - Monday

Regi had a row with his maids who have been out till 4am at dancing saloons, so he has given them the sack. Read a book by James Payne called 'Thicker Than Water'[648]. Rather too much effort to be funny, and too melodramatic, but on the whole a clever amusing story.

---

[646] This is presumably William E. ("Willy") Hogg (?-?), son of Francis Henry Hogg (abt 1814-1883) who was the wine merchant who set up the original Hogg Robinson partnership with Augustus Octavius Robinson (?-1895) in 1845. This is a reasonable assumption, as it is known that a subsidiary of the Hogg Robinson Company was set up by W. E. Hogg and Augustus Frederick Robinson in 1895 in Sydney and Melbourne, called Hogg Robinson and Co. Property Ltd, and we know that the Robinson that Gibbs meets is indeed Augustus Frederick Robinson (see below). Francis Henry Hogg, the father and founder of the parent company, married his business partner's sister Ellen. The activities of Hogg and Robinson were of interest to Gibbs Bright who maintained their close business connections and personal friendship with them as they moved into Newcastle Wool-warehousing and shipping in their footsteps, as part of the necessary progress into their own acceptance on the Wool Exchange.

[647] Augustus Frederick Robinson (1851-1931), originally of Greta House, Leigham Court Road, Streatham Hill, London, was the son of Augustus Octavius Robinson (?-1895). Although Gibbs never mentions him as anything but "Robinson", we know (from entries on 16th November 1884 and 2nd March 1885) that Robinson married a widow named Parbury. This marriage, which took place on 19th January 1885, was announced in the newspapers of the time, including the Brisbane Courier and the Queenslander. Augustus Octavius Robinson, the father and founder of the parent company, also married the other business partner's sister - Frances.

[648] "Thicker than Water", by James Payn (no E).

23 September 1884 - Tuesday

I was invited to give evidence before the Commission which is sitting to consider about the advisability of amalgamating the two branches of the legal profession[649]. It is curious they should have asked me.

24 September 1884 - Wednesday

Keating and I had a box together for Henry VIII[650]: the doctor[651]; his wife[652] and mother[653]; the Lewises; and Colonel Rede[654], the sheriff, a nice old fellow. We had supper afterwards at the Headleys. It is a dull, stupid play to see acted, whoever wrote it. Just a string of historical scenes with one great *'purpurens pannus'*[655] about Wolsey's disgrace. Miss Ward and Vernon were both good, far better than in 'Macbeth', and the two Cardinals in their scarlet, lace and white hair made a beautiful stage picture.

25 September 1884 - Thursday

Dined at the Club. Regi went to 'Fun on the Bristol'[656], but I was too lazy – played billiards, and slept at the Club.

---

[649] There had been several attempts to introduce legislation to amalgamate the two halves of the legal profession, solicitors (attorneys) and barristers, starting in 1846. This particular commission was probably related to the attempt to introduce The Legal Profession Practice Bill of 1884 in Victoria, which failed by a slim margin. Legislation was eventually introduced with The Legal Profession Practice Act of 1891.
[650] "The Famous History of the Life of Henry VIII", also known as "All Is True", is a lesser-known play by William Shakespeare. There is some disagreement as to how much collaboration there was with John Fletcher (hence Gibbs' comment, "whoever wrote it").
[651] This is probably Sir Thomas Naghten FitzGerald, who treated Gibbs in Melbourne earlier in the year.
[652] Assuming the Doctor is indeed Fitzgerald, this is his wife Margaret, the daughter of James Robertson of Straun House, Launceston, Tasmania.
[653] Assuming the Doctor is indeed Fitzgerald, this is his mother Catherine Naghten FitzGerald (née Higgins), wife of John Fitzgerald.
[654] Robert William Rede (1815-1904) had caused some controversy for his handling of the Eureka gold mining rebellion of 1854, but was nevertheless appointed deputy-sheriff of Geelong in 1855, then sheriff in 1857, sheriff of Ballarat in 1868 and of Melbourne in 1877. He also became a major and then a colonel of various volunteer detachments as Australia began to establish their own militia independent of colonial rule.
[655] Latin: "purple patch", a phrase coined by the poet Horace in his *Ars Poetica* (c. 20 BC). Whilst nowadays it is often used to describe a period of notable success or good luck, that sense did not really begin to appear until the twentieth century. At the time Gibbs was writing, he would be using its original sense as an overly elaborate or effusive piece of writing.
[656] 'Fun on the Bristol, or A Night At Sea', was a farce produced by Henry C. Jarrett. The author is unknown. This was its second season in Melbourne, and was playing at the Bijou Theatre, performed by John F. Sheridan and company.

26 September 1884 - Friday

Hardly any use keeping a diary, there is so little worth noting. A new and most hideous maid came to Regi's. She won't get many partners at dancing saloons.

27 September 1884 - Saturday

Went to the tennis court and saw a very good match played. It is a pretty game to watch, but I don't quite understand it. Dined at the Lewises; Robinson and Keating there.

28 September 1884 - Sunday

Played lawn tennis in the afternoon at the Lewises, and had supper there. Captain and Mrs Ind there. She is very pretty, but a fearful chatterbox and silly '*a faire peur*'[657]. It is becoming a regular institution for Keating and me to practically spend Saturday to Monday at the Lewises. Gowan Evans says we are in receipt of outdoor relief!

29 September 1884 - Monday

Played Patience in the evening, and read the 'Midsummer's Night Dream'[658]. The first part seems to me the most beautiful.

30 September - 1 October 1884

Nothing

2 October 1884 - Thursday

The Nankivell's[659] dance, to which Regi and Keating went. I dined at the Club and played whist with Colonel Sullivan, Aleck Sullivan and Creswick[660]. The play very bad; I won some money.

3 October 1884 - Friday

I dined with Captain Thomas on board the 'Nelson'. He has very nice quarters there. Gill and Ryan also there; a pleasant evening.

---

[657] French: "To make one afraid", i.e. she is 'frightfully' silly.
[658] A Midsummer Night's Dream, by William Shakespeare.
[659] Possibly Thomas J. Nankivell, the father of Denise Anne Nankivell (who married Henry Ryan, eldest son of the station agent Charles Ryan mentioned elsewhere). Thomas J. Nankivell was a partner in Fanning, Nankivell and Co., which invested in Queensland sugar. It might also refer to his son, George Nankivell.
[660] Possibly one of (or a son of one of) the three brothers, Henry, Charles and John Creswick, who founded a sheep station in 1842 at what is now known as Creswick, Victoria (80 miles NW of Melbourne).

4 October 1884 - Saturday

Lunched with the Lewises and played lawn tennis. A Miss Hutton and Miss Cunningham[661] there. Nearly everybody in Melbourne gone to Caulfield races. Dined with the Lewises; Robinson and Keating there; played 1d. loo[662].

5 October 1884 - Sunday

After church, lunch at Lewises and played lawn tennis. Coldham[663] and Weigall[664] [and] Sturgis there, all excellent players, and I had some very hard games. Dined with Bright. Yuill[665] and Candler, the two coroners, there - both clever old fellows; the former a very bitter tongue. They argued about *locomotor ataxy*[666]; an interesting evening.

6 October 1884 - Monday

Watt[667], our salesman, has presented me with a stuffed owl. It is a very rare and beautiful bird but, of course, I didn't want it. It is meant as a peace offering in gratitude for my not sacking him – which I nearly did after a tremendous jobation 2 or 3 months ago. Keating and I dined at St. Leonards to avoid having to assist Mrs Ryan with a rehearsal of her *tableaux*.

7 October 1884 - Tuesday

Heard of Heywood Bright's[668] approaching marriage. Lord William Neville[669] has got himself engaged to Miss Fairbairn; she refused young Howard of the Defence Force, who was also after the ducats and the daughter. Old Fairbairn has declined to allow the engagement – very sensibly, I think, as the lover is a vacuous, idle, bejewelled young man – and madness on both sides does not make the prospect a bright one.

---

[661] Possibly May Constance Cunningham, who marries Arthur Ranken Blackwood (see 12th October 1884) in 1885.
[662] Loo: once the most popular card game in England. Here it is being played for penny stakes.
[663] Possibly Walter Timon Coldham (1860-1908), barrister and sportsman, who played tennis for Victoria in 1885-7.
[664] Possibly Theyre à Beckett Weigall (1860–1926), barrister, judge, and keen tennis player (and was President of the Lawn Tennis Association of Victoria, 1909-1926).
[665] Actually Dr. Richard Youl (1821-1897), whom Gibbs had already met earlier.
[666] *Locomotor ataxia* – the inability to precisely control one's own bodily movements.
[667] We know (from the letter Gibbs sends to his brother Alban on 6th February 1884) that Watt the salesman "is not altogether satisfactory", had replaced Meeks in Melbourne, "is clever and sharp but hasty, scatter-brained and, I think, untruthful; he is young, about 27 [in 1884]".
[668] Heywood Bright (1836-1897), son of Samuel Bright (1799-1870), and first cousin of Reginald, Charles Edward, and Tyndall Bright.
[669] Lord William Nevill (no E) (1860-?). Fourth son of the Marquis of Abergavenny. Gibbs' view of Lord William Nevill proved to be justified: he was imprisoned on several occasions from 1889 onwards for various offences including fraud.

8 October 1884 - Wednesday

Old Carnegie, who was on our South sea trip, has turned up in Melbourne and dined with me this evening at the Club. I like the old boy.

9 October 1884 - Thursday

Dinner at the Club, and went afterwards to the *tableaux* at the Athenæum[670]. They were not bad, and – as I got a seat between Mrs Lewis and Mrs Leishman – I enjoyed myself. A crowd of men around Mrs L[671]. all the time, and Regi making broad jokes, rather unpleasant – and Mrs L. very angry with him.

10 October 1884 - Friday

Dined with Strachan; old Colonel Rede, the Sheriff, a nice old man; and Haddon[672], Editor of the Argus, an '*homme solide*', my convives; a very pleasant evening.

11 October 1884 - Saturday

Lunched at the Club, pouring rain. Played whist in the afternoon. Dined at the Lewises – G. Evans there, just back from Sydney, and the usual set. A very cheerful party.

12 October 1884 - Sunday

Tennis at the Lewises in the afternoon, and dined at St. Leonards. Carnegie, Arthur Blackwood[673], James White[674] of Sydney, and Keating there. The talk principally of racing and cricket. The evening went off well.

13 October 1884 - Monday

English mail in – all well. Dined at the Lewises.

---

[670] The Melbourne Athenaeum at 188 Collins Street, Melbourne, was completed in 1842. Originally called the Melbourne Mechanics' Institute, it was renamed to the Melbourne Mechanics' Institution and School of Arts in 1846, and to the Melbourne Athenaeum in 1873. It is one of the oldest public institutions in Victoria.

[671] As before, Mrs. L. is probably Mrs. Lewis rather than Mrs. Leishman – Gibbs was always most attentive to Mrs. Lewis.

[672] Frederick William Haddon (1839-1906). Editor of the Melbourne Argus from 1867 to 1898.

[673] Probably Arthur Ranken Blackwood (1850-1905), who became joint managing director (with James Aitken) of Dalgety, Blackwood & Co. in 1884. See reference to Dalgety's on 1st March 1884. Arthur Blackwood was a member of the Melbourne Club and chairman of the Victoria Amateur Turf Club in 1884-5. He married May Constance Cunningham in 1885 – Gibbs mentions a Miss Cunningham on 4th October 1884 (that could be a completely different person, of course).

[674] James White (1828-1890), pastoralist and racehorse breeder and owner.

14 October 1884 - Tuesday

Dined with Bright. Learnt *'Otium Divos rogat in patente'*[675] by heart and then played patience – and went to sleep over it as usual.

15 October 1884 - Wednesday

Went to see Mackinnon at his chambers in the Melbourne temple and had a look at the Supreme Court[676], library etc. Dined at the Club. Played billiards with Captain Thomas and talked to Gowan Evans.

16 October 1884 - Thursday

My cabman today informed me that he had been second coachman at Tyntesfield[677], and had been sent out by Martin[678] for his health. He asked a lot of questions and seemed grateful.

17 October 1884 - Friday

Nothing.

18 October 1884 - Saturday

Went with Regi to Caulfield races; a cold wind, and I was rather bored. Mrs Ind there, looking extraordinarily pretty. Dined with the Lewises. Heard that that ass Mattheson[679] has married a Miss Money[680]. It is only a few days since Miss Bailey broke off her engagement, so I suppose he must have been determined to go back to England married to somebody.

---

[675] Horace, Ode 2.16: *Otium diuos rogat in patenti prensus Aegaeo, simul atra nubes condidit lunam n eque certa fulgent sidera nautis.* (The man caught in the open Aegean sea asks the gods for peace, as soon as a dark cloud has hidden the moon, and the stars with sure light don't gleam for sailors).
[676] The Supreme Court of Victoria, located at 192 William Street, Melbourne. It would have been a relatively new building at the time Gibbs visited, construction having only been completed in 1882.
[677] Tyntesfield was the Somerset home of the other branch of the Gibbs family and is now in the ownership of the National Trust.
[678] 'Martin' may refer to a family doctor, or possibly to Henry Martin Gibbs (one of the 3 surviving children of William and Matilda Blanche Gibbs), who was himself sent out to Peru for his health in the 1870s. He was referred to as 'Martin' on occasion, and may well have been helping his brother Antony with management of the Tyntesfield Estate at the time that the cabman was sent out to Australia. The Gibbs family would almost certainly have paid for the cabman's trip, hence his gratitude.
[679] Sir Alexander Perceval Matheson, 3rd Baronet of Lochalsh (1861-1929) migrated to Australia in 1894, becoming a commercial agent and company manager on the goldfields, and later a politician.
[680] Eleanor Money (?-1959) was the daughter of Reverend Kyrle Ernle Aubrey Money. She married Sir Alexander Matheson on 18th October 1884. They were divorced in 1925.

19 October 1884 - Sunday

Read Horace, and played with the tame magpie in the garden – which now looks very pretty. In the afternoon, had some capital lawn tennis at the Lewises. Dined with Regi who went to sleep, and I played Patience.

20 October 1884 - Monday

K. and R. went to a ball. I walked over to the Lewises in the evening. Mrs L. had been having a vapour bath, and was playing écarté with her husband. She was in great deshabille, with her hair all untidy, and in a sort of red flannel petticoat. As the parlour maid observed it, "it was that stupid of Mr Lewis to walk Mr Gibbs straight into the room". It was very funny; of course, I went on talking and tried to look as if [she] was in her usual costume, but she got scarlet in the face and kept her head at right angles to me with her chair drawn close under the table. At last she said, "Mr Gibbs, look the other way directly while I go upstairs and put my dress on". They had been always telling me to drop in any evening, so there was a good deal of laughing at the result of my first visit.

21 October 1884 - Tuesday

Very seedy with headache, and eat [sic] nothing all day after breakfast.

22 October 1884 - Wednesday

All right again. Certainly my health has been wonderfully good in Australia on the whole. Spent the evening at the Lewises. Regi at a ball. The season of Melbourne 'Gaiety'[681] has regularly begun, and the old Adonis Evergreen[682] is very much to the front.

23 October 1884 - Thursday

Played whist at the Club.

24 October 1884 - Friday

Nothing particular.

25 October 1884 - Saturday

I went to see some athletic sports on the Melbourne cricket ground with young Mackinnon, and had a long talk with him about the doctrine of constructive murder. Dined with Evans at the Headley's, and went with them to the 'Cloches de Corneville'[683]. It wasn't badly done and I rather

---

[681] Melbourne 'Gaiety': i.e. the social season.
[682] This is a gently sarcastic remark about Regi.
[683] "Les Cloches de Corneville", an operetta by Robert Planquette known in English as "The Chimes of Normandy" or "The Bells of Corneville" and first performed in 1877 in Paris. The air Gibbs refers to is actually "From Pallid Cheek".

like it, especially the song 'By Pallid Cheek' that Beatrice Brune used to sing. The theatre, however, was so hot that I kept going to sleep, so I left before the end.

26 October 1884 - Sunday

The usual thing in the afternoon. Some capital lawn tennis. Miss Croker and the Inds there: Keating and I dined with Regi who went to sleep the instant after dinner, and K. and I read Horace's Epistles.

27 October 1884 - Monday

Dined with the Lewises. Mrs L. very sad at her pet dog having died in a fit.

28 October 1884 - Tuesday

Garden Party at Government House. I shirked going.

29 October 1884 - Wednesday

61. Government House, Melbourne (1880-9)
National Library of Australia, nla.pic-an10638277-33

Dined with Mackinnon, Editor of Argus. Took in a Miss Campbell, who lives near Crace; a pleasant New South Wales girl. After dinner – which was rather dull (all Scotch people except Gowan Evans, who was at the other end of the room) – the Taylors drove me in their carriage to [the] Government House reception – a fine house for a crush. After talking to a lot of people for an hour, the Lewises drove me home in their Brougham[684].

30 October 1884 - Thursday

I went up to the Lewises in the afternoon and dressed up in the Dragomans[685] which they lent me, and then to the Club where 30 of us dined together in fancy costume. A very bright amusing sight; handsome dresses, and a good deal of chaff and fun. Then to the Town Hall to the dance which was given by Sir William and Lady Clarke; the room beautifully decorated with roses in profusion, and, there being a large

---

[684] A brougham (pronounced "broom") was a light, horse-drawn carriage with an enclosed body and two doors, usually seating two people inside (sometimes with drop-down seats for additional passengers). The driver, and sometimes another passenger, sat on a box seat in front.
[685] A Dragoman was an interpreter from the Ottoman Empire who translated between Turkish, Arabic and Persian, and wore a traditional elaborate red gown.

gallery all round, one could walk about and watch the people. I enjoyed it very much, infinitely more than I expected. I was, as nearly as possible, not going. Slept at the Club.

31 October 1884 - Friday

Dined at the Lewises to meet Sir William Robinson, the Governor of South Australia – a regular swagger dinner, well turned out. I sat between a Mrs Rowe[686] and a Miss Wittie. A very musical evening, as the Governor a great performer.

1 November 1884 - Saturday

On reaching the office, found a telegram telling me to go at once to Ceylon. Very much worried, both at having to go and at the cause, as I fear there must be some serious trouble there. This is the first day of the annual races, so after cabling home that I could start on the 20th but didn't want to, Regi, Keating and I and a beastly cad of a ship-owner went off in a jingle to the races. Taylor talked the whole way about his money and what people were worth, and what they would cut up for when they died, in a way that was perfectly sickening. Keats had a headache and was very gloomy at my approaching departure, so I had to answer him. I did not enjoy the races, but mooned about and caught a chill. Dined at the Club and played whist. Ingles[687], the owner of 'Malua'[688] – the favourite for the Cup, drove home with me. He tells me he can hardly lose, and advised me to put something on. I may perhaps put a pound or two.

2 November 1884 - Sunday

Overslept myself until very late, and feel gouty and out of sorts. Lunched at the Lewises and spent the afternoon there. Two pretty little Miss Robertsons[689] called. Dined with Regi, Hill, Hamilton, Osborne, Maclaine, and Howard[690] – Robinson's ADC – at dinner. Rather a pleasant evening. Lumley Hill fell asleep during dinner, and when the potatoes were handed

---

[686] Mrs. Rowe is probably the wife of the Rowe whom Gibbs meets in Ceylon. It is possible that the husband is Charles James Rowe and his wife is Annie Rowe née Gray. Gibbs says, on 5 January 1885, that Mrs. Rowe knew all his Melbourne friends.
[687] J. O. Inglis was the owner (and sometimes jockey) of Malua.
[688] Malua was apparently the most versatile thoroughbred racehorse in history. He was originally called 'Bagot' – Inglis changed his name when he purchased him as a two-year-old colt.
[689] Presumably the daughters of William Robertson, the cattle breeder of Colac, whom Gibbs first meets on 8 November 1883. If that is the case, then one of these sisters would have been Elise Christian Margaret Robertson (1866-1939), the eldest daughter of William and Martha Robertson. Elise, known as Dolly to her family, was the subject of an 1885/6 painting, "Miss Robertson of Colac (Dolly)", by Robert Downling, which is now held in the National Gallery of Australia.
[690] Ernest William Howard (?-1915) was the Private Secretary and head of the official staff of Sir William Robinson. He married Miss Phillips of "an old South Australian family", but they had no children. She survived him. His younger brother Charlie was Western Australia's Chief Inspector of Police.

to him his beard was hanging down his shirt and he was gently snoring. Everybody was laughing, but he never moved until I shook him and told him he wasn't in the bush. I fell asleep twice after dinner in the drawing room, as of course did Regi at intervals, so we were a lively family. I like Hill – he has been very friendly.

3 November 1884 - Monday

A nasty cold in my throat. At the office, but nothing doing in business on account of the race carnival. I was engaged to dine with Hogg and Robinson at St. Kilda and should have liked to cut it, but ended by going in a Hansom with Keats and left at 10 o'clock.

4 November 1884 - Tuesday

Cup day. General holiday, beautiful weather. No telegram from home. I felt better. The Club crammed full of people, almost all of whom I knew. I went to the races with Maclaren[691], whom I knew up at Exeter[692]. He is a brother of the Maclaren who was on the South Sea trip with me. A great crowd on the course, and the Cup proved an exciting race. 'Malua' won – Lumley Hill and I had a modest fiver on between us, otherwise I didn't bet. I talked to a Miss Carter, a handsome, attractive woman about 30. She was engaged to Lord Canterbury[693], who jilted her. Mrs Lewis told me she once said to her, "I know, my dear, he hasn't got two ideas to rattle together on a tombstone, but he was the only man I ever cared about". I dined with Sullivan at the Club. About 15 to dinner, all racing men except myself. Played a couple of rubbers with Donald Campbell, James White, Lumley Hill; but my voice quite gone so cleared off early to bed in a close cab.

5 November 1884 - Wednesday

Laid up with heavy cold, sort of bronchitis and gout. Beastly seedy, and heard that I must be off on the 20th. Just about time to get well in, I calculate. Read a book called 'The Leavenworth Case'[694], sent to Regi by Mrs Dick Bright[695]. Just what one might have expected – a vulgarly written murder case in the style of Gaboriau[696], but far inferior.

---

[691] Gibbs met two cousins, H. Maclaren and J. H. Maclaren, on the South Sea trip - he doesn't specify of which this is the brother.
[692] "Up at Exeter" refers to Exeter College, Oxford, of which the Gibbs family were the main benefactors.
[693] Henry Charles Manners-Sutton, 4th Viscount Canterbury (1839-1914). His sister, Anna Maria Georgiana Manners-Sutton, married Charles Edward Bright (Regi's brother) in 1868.
[694] The Leavenworth Case, by Anna Katharine Green.
[695] Emma Katherine Bright, née Wolley, wife of Richard Bright (1822-1878) (Regi's eldest brother).
[696] Émile Gaboriau (1832-1873), a French writer who created the detective Monsieur Lecoq.

6 November 1884 - Thursday

Cold better and gout worse, but not very painful. Read through 'Judges', 'Samuel' and 'Kings'; and a novel called 'Jill'[697], describing the adventures of a lying, dishonest, unamiable girl, daughter of a baronet who runs away from home and goes into service as a travelling lady's maid. I was not pleased with it, and the grammar and tone were alike: inferior.

7 November 1884 - Friday

Gout pretty bad. Mrs L. sent me over Taine's history of English Literature[698] in 4 stout volumes. I liked it, and think it very well done on the whole, and certainly wonderful for a foreigner.

8 November 1884 - Saturday

Sluggish gout all through my right foot and ankle. Read a novel called 'Lancelot Ward MP'[699]. Not very bad or very good, and the hero ends most unnecessarily by cutting his throat on the day after he is married.

9 November 1884 - Sunday

Cold gone, and gout getting better. Read the Bible, Shakespeare, and played Patience.

10 November 1884 - Monday

Up to breakfast, and feeling nearly right. Another Public holiday – Prince of Wales' birthday. A lawn tennis tournament at the Lewises in which I had been going to play. Keating called after breakfast and persuaded me to drive over and have a look at it. I went. K. won, as he had a splendid partner. The Lewises live only about ¼ of a mile off and I kept my leg up all the time, but I got overtired and felt the worse for it instead of the better.

11 November 1884 - Tuesday

Had a bad night, and consequently not so well again. It is very inconvenient not being able to get about as my time in Australia is so rapidly coming to an end.

12 November 1884 - Wednesday

Better. Up in the afternoon, and wrote letters to Merivale, Murray and others to say goodbye. Donald Campbell came to see me and play piquet.

---

[697] Jill, by Elizabeth Amy Dillwyn (published 1884).
[698] *Histoire de la littérature anglaise*, by the French writer and historian Hippolyte Adolphe Taine (1828-1893).
[699] "Lancelot Ward, MP – A Love-Story", by George Temple.

13 November 1884 - Thursday

Much better; up to breakfast, but kept quiet all day that I may be fit to go into town tomorrow. Old Candler walked over to see me and stayed an hour or more; then Strachan came, and lastly Keating who had been kept at the office. As it is a good 2 miles from Melbourne it is very kind of them to take the trouble. Regi dined at home, and afterwards he to a ball and *dormitum ego*[700].

14 November 1884 - Friday

Mail day. Went down to the office in a cab and a cloth boot, working up my arrears and hard at it all day, talking and writing. Lewis drove me out in his trap to his house where I shall stay till Monday. I have for a long while promised to stay there, so it is now or never. I wish I was fitter.

15 November 1884 - Saturday

Not worth going to the office for half a day, and not feeling very grand so stayed at home and wrote – and talked to Mrs. L. Keating telephoned[701] up to me that Merivale had arrived from Sydney to see me and say goodbye; very good of him. Lewis back to lunch, and I found he had most kindly asked Merivale to come up with Keating in the afternoon to play lawn tennis and stay to dinner. This will enable me to talk to George comfortably.

16 November 1884 - Sunday

I have a very nice room here[702] and everything as jolly as can be, but I can't get rid of gout. Hogg, Robinson and Merivale came to lunch. I sat in the garden and watched them playing lawn tennis. Robinson told us he was engaged to Mrs Parbury[703], a pretty young widow from Sydney. K., M. and I dined with Regi, who was unusually wakeful. I went back early, to bed, in a cab. I can't walk yet. George tells me old Laidley[704] is seriously ill.

---

[700] *dormitum ego*. Latin for "I went to sleep".
[701] The telephone was invented around 1876, and was in use in England by about 1880. The first telephone system in Australia was a private system connecting the offices of Robinson brothers in Melbourne and South Melbourne in 1879. The first Australian telephone exchange was opened in Collins Street, Melbourne, in 1880. At that stage there were only enough subscribers to fill a single page. By 1887, 8000 calls a day were being made, mostly during business hours as the early subscribers were mainly the wealthier businesses. It is interesting that although in 1884 this must have been a relative novelty, Gibbs mentions it only in passing. This is the only mention of a telephone call in the entire diary. Gibbs were innovators wherever possible, and their new office were one of the first in Sydney to have a lift installed.
[702] At the Lewis house.
[703] Clemence L. Parbury (née Lamb), widow of B. P. Parbury, married Augustus Frederick Robinson on 19th January 1885.
[704] 'Old Laidley' is the Hon. William George Laidley, George Merivale's father-in-law. He survives for another 13 years.

17 November 1884 - Monday

Drove in with K. to the office, and in the evening Lewis drove me out. Merivale to dinner, and we played 1d. loo. Certainly no people have been kinder to me than the Lewises, and I feel very grateful to them for contributing so much to make my stay in Melbourne pleasant.

18 November 1884 - Tuesday

Called for Regi in my cab – down to the office with him, where I have been all day clearing up. Saw Merivale off again to Sydney, and sorry to see his back. Had meant to dine at the Club, but feeling my gout rather worse again I had tea with Dr Wilkie[705] and Donald Campbell instead and we studied all the Drs. book on elephantiasis[706], of which D.C. and I saw a lot in the South Seas. Then I played a couple of rubbers and, feeling very seedy, cleared off to St. Leonards in a cab.

19 November 1884 - Wednesday

I had a bad night, and quite made up my mind I shouldn't be able to leave my bed this morning or to sail tomorrow. I am a little better today, and able to get to the office, but very lame with gout in tendon Achilles. Mrs Lewis came down to her husband's office to wish me goodbye, and gave me a German dictionary and a copy of Heine's poems to improve my mind on the voyage. In the evening, to the Club where Candler, Hill, Robertson, Campbell and others gave me a dinner. It was a very good one, the table very pretty with flowers – but rather a 'feast of Tantalus'[707] in my Goutish state. Old Candler made a moving speech, and I replied. Played 2 or 3 rubbers, and home early.

---

[705] Possibly Dr. David Elliot Wilkie (1818-1885). Born in Scotland, he moved to Adelaide in 1838 and to Melbourne in 1839. He specialized in diseases of women and children, and was an honorary physician to the Melbourne Hospital for many years. He retired in 1881, and died unexpectedly in France in 1885.

[706] Elephantiasis – the coarsening of the skin, particularly in the legs and genitals – is a horrifying symptom of Filariasis, an infectious tropical disease caused by parasites. Gibbs would have seen victims of this in the South Sea Islands.

[707] Tantalus was the son of Zeus and the king of Sipylos. Invited by the Gods to eat nectar and ambrosia at their table, Tantalus asked them in return to a banquet on the summit of Mount Sipylos. Each guest was to bring a contribution to the feast. For the final course, Tantalus served his contribution, intended as a sacrifice to the Gods: the flesh of his son Pelops, diced and boiled in a cauldron. Demeter, goddess of the harvest, was the only one to eat the flesh. When Zeus saw this, he ordered that the flesh be put back in the cauldron and the bite-sized chunk of the child's shoulder replaced with Ivory. Zeus destroyed Mount Sipylos in punishment, and sent Tantalus to Tarturus where he was condemned to stand in a pool of water under luscious fruit trees. The water receded whenever he stooped to drink, and the fruit was out of reach. The English word tantalise is derived from the name Tantalus.

S.S. Carthage

20 November 1884 - Thursday

Finished my packing, and down to the office by 10. Mackinnon, Ryan, Robertson called to say goodbye; M. kindly bringing some French novels. Received an absurdly gushing letter from Mrs Ryan to the effect that she likes and esteems me. Strachan, Bell, Hogg, Watson and MacPherson, beside Keating and Bright, came down to the steamer. Old Watson introduced me to the skipper, Captain Hector[708] – which has led to my being placed close to him at table. I have a good cabin to myself, forward of the engines; the ship is not at all full. We sailed about 1.30 and I, feeling tired and gouty, lay down and slept away the time till dinner. I am in no pain, but continue perfectly lame. There is no one on board that I know except Jennie Lee, the actress.

21 November 1884 - Friday

Cold, wet and rough. Quite half the people seasick, but I was quite free from it. There is a Captain Morland[709] on one side of me at dinner who is harbour master at Bombay, and his wife[710] opposite who was a singer named Carandini – very second-rate people. A nice little naval man named Captain Coghlan[711], who is head of the Marine Survey Department in Western Australia. Unfortunately, he doesn't go any further than King George's Sound. Also a young man named Berthon-Preston[712] – a young fellow in a Dragoon Regiment who has married a woman named Miss Le Brere[713], who is acting at the Bijou in Melbourne. Altogether, I was never on a steamer with a less promising lot in my life. There are two theatrical girls, rather pretty, with bleached hair. One of them is going to Calcutta to marry somebody.

---

[708] Captain G. N. Hector of the R.M.S. Carthage.
[709] Sir Henry Morland (1837-1891), of the Indian Navy. At the time was dock and signal master of Bombay, but later went on to become President of the Board of Marine Examiners.
[710] This was Henry Morland's second wife, Fanny Helen Hannah Carandini, an opera singer trained by her mother, Countess Marie Carandini (née Burgess) – born in Brixton, London - who married Count Gerome Carandini (who died in 1870). Madame Marie Carandini and her daughters were a famed singing group travelling throughout Australia and overseas to perform.
[711] Captain J. E. Coghlan had recently returned from a surveying expedition to the Cambridge Gulf, east of Darwin, in command of the 'Meda'. He is shown on the passenger list as Staff Commander Coghlan, aged 44.
[712] Captain George Berthon Preston (c1859-1940), in the 2nd Dragoon Guards. Son of Robert Berthon Preston and Eleanor Leonora Preston née Rogers, but in the census of 1871 his mother has changed her name to Eleanor Leonora Berthon and he has a step-father, Alderson Berthon. Whilst a Lieutenant in 1882, he married Miss Ellen Washington Knox (better known by her name on stage, Miss Marie de Gray). By the time Gibbs meets him in 1884 he appears to have been promoted to Captain.
[713] Miss Ellen Washington Knox (better known by her name on stage, Miss Marie de Gray).

22 November 1884 - Saturday

We arrived early at Glenelg[714], and after breakfast I went on shore. On the jetty I met the Judge's Associate[715], who told me the Chief Justice[716] had sent him down to say he hoped I would be his guest for the day and come up to his house. I arranged to go to the office first and go up to lunch after. I found Meeks very busy and flourishing. I had a long talk with him and went to see the new offices, which are an improvement. Mrs Meeks called in to say goodbye. After writing to F.A.K. and Mrs Lewis, a couple of goodbyes; and, settling some business, I went off to the Judge's house – whom I found most pleasant; a little man with false teeth, and fair hair standing up all over his head. His house was done up with great taste, and a lovely garden full of birds. Curlews, gulls and jackasses walking about, besides a great variety in aviaries. He had a very good library which he showed me, and we had a little lunch. Then he gave me a lot of little American books to read on the voyage, and took me out for a drive in his carriage, and we had a long legal-mercantile discussion as to when a buyer is justified in rejecting a whole contract for wrong delivery of a part, and when he should only be allowed to sue for damages. Afterwards we had dinner, about 5, to which came – Sir Thomas Elder and Captain Hector. And then the Chief Justice finished up his civilities by driving me down himself to Port Adelaide. Evidently the Lewises must have recommended me very strongly to him.

23 November 1884 - Sunday

We sailed about midnight, and in the morning a tallow-faced, red-bearded, blue-ribboned parson read the service very affectedly. I read 'All in a Garden Fair'[717], by Besant. Rather pretty, but with a weak, improbable plot, and beaten out very thin. I also spelt out a good bit of Heine – with frequent reference to the Dictionary.

24 November 1884 - Monday

Played chess with a Dutch Jew named Snyder[718], and had some talk with 'Jo'[719] who doesn't seem a bad sort.

---

[714] Glenelg is a suburb (and port) of the South Australian capital, Adelaide.
[715] Cecil James Sharp (1859-1924) was associate to the Chief Justice (Sir Samuel James Way) from April 1884 until 1889.
[716] Sir Samuel James Way, 1st Baronet (1836-1916) was the Chief Justice of South Australia from 1876-1916.
[717] "All in a Garden Fair", by Sir Walter Bessant.
[718] The passenger list shows a J Sniders, aged 50.
[719] 'Jo' – the crossing-sweeper played by Jennie Lee.

25 November 1884 - Tuesday

Read 'Halves'[720] by James Payne – not at all a bad story; also some Heine, which begins to get easier. Some of the lyrics are very fetching. I think, judging from this small experience, that German poetry is much easier for an Englishman than French. The musical talent is extremely strong on board. The Doctor is a great violinist, and there is a Madame Elmblad[721] who is a professional musician; and Mrs Morland has a grand voice like Antoinette Sterling[722]. Before her marriage, Miss Carandini, she was a shining light in India and Australia. Captain Preston[723] also sings very well. Except for this good feature, the company is socially far below steamer average – at any rate, of P&O.

There are 2 young girls going alone under the skipper's charge to marry men in Calcutta, so if there were any eligible young men on board there would be some desperate flirting. When Captain Coghlan goes tomorrow I shall have nobody, as far as I can see, to talk to.

26 November 1884 - Wednesday

Reached King George's sound about 10 o'clock am, and went on shore. The sound is fine, though the coast is barren looking. Albany looks a forsaken little town, but I am told land there is going up tremendously in price. The Captain got up a little picnic, to which he asked me and two or three more, and we climbed up Mount Clarence and got a fine view of the harbour. We started about 4pm, and when we were about 25 miles out we found that we had left three people behind – a Mrs and Miss Baker of Adelaide: I believe very agreeable, but who has been so sea-sick I had seen nothing of them. Also a boy who was apparently dying of consumption. It is incredible that people can be so foolish as to run the risk of being deprived of all their effects, and spending a fortnight in Albany.

27 November 1884 - Thursday

Passed the Lewin[724] with a fair wind. Read some of 'Natural Law in the Spiritual World'[725]. Funny of the little bigoted Bedford to scream blasphemy and ram his ostrich head in the sand. Played backgammon

---

[720] "Halves", by James Payn (no E).
[721] Madame Maggie Elmblad (née Menzies) (c.1845-1887), a professional pianist and organist, was the eldest daughter of Mr. A. Menzies of Menzies' Hotel. In 1878 she married Johannes Wilhelm Samuel Elmblad, a famous Swedish bass. The couple were friends of Clara Schumann (Robert Schumann's wife), Arthur Rubinstein, Johannes Brahms and Richard Wagner. Madame Elmblad committed suicide in Switzerland on 8th August 1887. The passenger list shows Madam Elmblad aged 39.
[722] Antoinette Sterling (1850-1904), an American, was known for her rendition of 'The Lost Chord', a popular sentimental song of the period.
[723] Captain George Berthon Preston.
[724] Gibbs must mean Cape Leeuwin on the south-western tip of Australia. A lighthouse had been planned there since 1881 but was not actually built until 1895.
[725] 'Natural Law in the Spirtiual World', by Henry Drummond (1851-1897), published 1883.

with the Captain after dinner and talked to Miss Edwards[726], a cleverish, well-informed, strong-minded, not particularly amiable woman, given up, I believe, to good works.

28 November 1884 - Friday

Had tea in the skipper's cabin and played chess with him; a good sort of man, but rather a prig. I have now settled down to the voyage, and as usual it is not disagreeable: though the people are not interesting, still they are very friendly. Jenny Lee is too boisterously vulgar to suit me, though I believe she is a good-hearted, hard-working little creature. Gowan Evans is devoted to her, which is funny as he is so particular. Her husband[727] seems a civil, harmless fellow.

29 November 1884 - Saturday

It is beginning to get hot, and we have awnings up for the first time. The steering gear broke early in the morning, and proved rather a nasty accident – injuring the fourth officer and a couple of Lascars[728]. I find Preston was at Eton with me.

30 November 1884 - Sunday

Played cricket on deck and had some very good fun, but it made me fearfully hot. The skipper is very unpopular with his officers, though very pleasant to me. 4 o'clock tea in his cabin is rather a pleasant affair and helps to put by the day.

1 December 1884 - Monday

We had a very good concert yesterday, some beautiful singing and playing, and Jenny Lee gave a recitation from 'Joe' which she did very well. Mrs Morland has a lovely voice, and the Doctor is a wonderful fiddler. It is very rare to get on shipboard such a collection of high class talent, and I enjoyed it very much as far as I could understand it.

[The section of the diary from 2nd to 18th December 1884 is missing]

---

[726] The passenger list shows a Miss Edwards, aged 18.
[727] Jennie Lee's husband was J. P. Burnett, who wrote the play "Jo" (adapted from Dickens' Bleak House) in which Jennie Lee played Jo the crossing-sweeper. The passenger list shows Mr Burnett (38), Mrs Burnett (36), two Burnett children aged 4 and 10, and a nurse aged 19 travelling with them.
[728] A Lascar was a sailor or militiaman from the Indian Subcontinent or other countries east of the Cape of Good Hope, employed on European ships from the 16th century until the beginning of the 20th century.

Colombo

By October 1884, Vicary Gibbs felt that he had successfully carried out the work which had been required of him in the Colonial Houses. He had made connections which not only gave him a better understanding of the state of the economies in New Zealand and Australia, but allowed him a foot in the door of the most potentially thriving businesses – including being appointed to the London Board of the Queensland National Bank. He was looking forward to the respite of the long cruise home, but instead received a telegram from GB&Co. on 1st November telling him to go at once to Ceylon.

From a few comments made earlier in the diary, it seems that Vicary had been worried by the developments there already and had considered sending Bell to assess the situation, but was beginning to realise that the crises in the estates and tea gardens were more serious than he had originally thought. On the day he received the telegram, he reports in his diary that he was "worried, as I fear there must be some serious trouble there" – but he was probably also annoyed by the interference to his plans. Indeed, the uncertainty of the situation seems to have triggered another attack of gout, and the time he was to spend in Colombo may have had a further detrimental effect on both his health and his morale.

GB&Co. must have known for some time that their investments were at risk in Ceylon. They, and other growers, had expended large sums of money on the production of coffee and tea, the extraction of vegetable oils, and more recently the distillation of quinine from cinchona bark.

They had been anticipating a good return on all these investments, but now the income from coffee was being threatened by the coffee blight, and the other profits were being put at risk by one or two of their superintendents whose heavy drinking led to careless discipline.

Unfortunately, we don't know the exact details of these problems because not only were the GB&Co. confidential telegrams so cleverly coded that even today their meaning is unknown, but there are 17 missing days from Vicary's diary on the voyage to Colombo at about the time he may have been describing the situation he faced. This is probably just an accident, although there is the slight possibility that he later removed the pages because they contained information too sensitive to release. However, from the few remarks Gibbs makes in the diary it would seem likely that not only was there mismanagement on the estates, but there may also have been financial irregularities. A radical reorganisation of the senior staff was going to be required; the names Leechman and Downall are particularly singled out for mention by Gibbs.

It is interesting to see that Vicary Gibbs is shortly befriended by the Imperial German Consul in Colombo, a man called Freudenberg. Germany felt so strongly that she had lagged behind Britain in Colonial possessions that she created outposts in many of the Asian and African colonies where it was felt that opportunities to step into British shoes may present themselves. Many years later, GB&Co.'s valuable oil mills and other Ceylon interests were taken over by German enterprises, including Freudenberg's own company.

19 December 1884 - Friday

Left Colombo at 6am with Howell[729] and Porter. I was very lame with gout, and should not have gone except that it would have been very inconvenient to do otherwise. Reached some unspellable station about 11, and then a drive in coach to a village where Jardine[730], the Superintendent[731], met us. A strong, silent man of 50 who seemed to know his work. Then about 7 miles to the foot of the estate, Rock Cave. I could only hobble very little, so they rigged up a chair on bamboos and 4 coolies[732] carried me. The estate very pretty, and a beautiful view from the top. Had a good tiffin[733] in the bungalow, but I felt exhausted and seedy. The place is planted with cocoa and Liberian coffee, but very little of the former is yet in bearing, and I almost think the place had better be abandoned. We went back to the station, and Howell returned to Colombo so as to be on the spot if there was any telegraphing to be done while Porter and I travelled on through Kandy to a place called Matale[734], where we arrived at 8pm and slept the night. In the rest house I found Antony Crawley Boevey[735], and he supped with us; a terrible stammer, but I rather liked what I saw of him. The rats made a frightful row in my bedroom at night.

20 December 1884 - Saturday

Up very early, and gout better. Drove to within 2 miles of Ellagalla[736] and walked to the estate. The superintendent a quiet, sensible, young man

---

[729] Alfred Howell. Howell worked for Anthony Gibbs & Sons.

[730] Jardine is possibly related in some way to Jardine, Matheson and Co. who were involved in the development of tea in South East Asia, although there doesn't seem to be any direct link between the company and tea plantations in Ceylon.

[731] The Superintendent of one of their estates would often be an Englishman employed by Gibbs Bright to go out and manage it.

[732] Coolie: a manual labourer or porter.

[733] Tiffin is lunch, or any light meal, a word originating in British India.

[734] The town of Matale is in Central Province, about 16 miles from Kandy and 90 miles from Colombo.

[735] Antony Page Crawley-Boevey (1855-1924). In 1889 he married the daughter of Sir Samuel White Baker (1821-1893), who had established his own prosperous plantations in Ceylon before returning to England.

[736] There is an Ellagala (three Ls rather than 4) in Central Province, near the south-east coast. However, it is about 150 miles from Matale so Gibbs could not have got there and

about 30, named Peto. The place seemed in very good order. The cinchona[737], tea and cardamoms looked very healthy, and what coffee remained in an awful state. I begged them to spend no more money on it. A grand extended view all round, and much healthier feeling in the air than Rock Cave. Back to supper and early bed at the rest house.

21 December 1884 - Sunday

Porter is a dull dog, but respectable and knows his work. He seems to look sharply after the superintendents. Took the early train to Kandy, which we reached about 9am. It is a beautiful city – a lovely lake with a drive all round it, and the hills rising up close by on every side. There is also a very fine Singhalese Temple with curious frescoes representing the sort of hell tortures that await various breaches of Buddhist Law. The carvings too were extremely rich and quaint, somewhat like the Moorish. Heavy, elaborate and rounded arches; in short, I was much struck by it. We breakfasted at the Club, then I took a nap, read the magazines, and wrote to Edith until it got cool. Then Porter and I drove out 2 or 3 miles to the Botanical Gardens of Peradeniya; in their way I should think the most lovely in the world. Not well kept up, and little or no flowers. But such foliage, and the giant bamboos by the riverside as high as a house, waving and crackling in the wind. I enjoyed them thoroughly – and back to dinner at the Club where there was a young Kay Shuttleworth[738], brother of our friend. I did not speak to him. I believe he has been swindled into buying a coffee estate for a lot of money, which is not worth anything. Read an article on Madame du Barrie[739]; and so to bed.

22 December 1884 - Monday

Left Kandy early by train via Gampola(?)[740] for Nawalapitya[741], and there we hired a carriage and drove to our estate of Honoocutua[742]. We were met by the Superintendent, one Paxton: a superior, respectable

---

back in a day. There is an Ulagalla, which is just under 50 miles north of Matale - still not likely in a day.

[737] Cinchona: an evergreen, the bark containing quinine

[738] One of the sons of Sir James Kay-Shuttleworth (1804-1877) (born James Kay, but added his wife's surname when he married Lady Janet Shuttleworth in 1842). One of his sons was Ughtred James Kay-Shuttleworth (1844-1939), MP for Hastings until 1880 and later Under-Secretary of State for India.

[739] Madame du Barry: Jeanne Bécu, comtesse du Barry (1743-1793) was the last Maîtresse-en-titre of Louis XV of France and one of the victims of the Reign of Terror during the French Revolution.

[740] This name is illegible in the diary manuscript, but looks like Guinfuila or Guinguila (possibly without the first U in both cases). The first letter could possibly be J or Y instead of G. There don't seem to be any actual place with a name like that: the nearest found was Gurugalla, which is about the same distance west of Nawalapitiya as Kandy is north-east of it and therefore seems unlikely. Based on the current railway route, it is possible that Gibbs is referring to Gampola (about halfway between Kandy and Nawalapitiya), although the name doesn't really look like that.

[741] Nawalapitiya, about 40 miles from Kandy.

[742] Hunukotuwa estate, Nawalapitiya.

Scotchman. I should judge his age to be about the same as mine. Went over a good bit of the land; the young tea coming on well, and generally I thought better of the place than Ellagalla. The coffee, of course, is doomed. I read in the train a novel by James Payne[743]. It is not uninteresting, but is little more than a *rechauffee*[744] of the Tichbourne case[745] and there is an intertwined effort to be funny which is tiresome. Porter thinks very well of Paxton, and is going to put the adjoining estate of Hennewelle under his charge.

23 December 1884 - Tuesday

Heard from Howell; up very early and walked over to Hennewelle, not so valuable or so well kept up as the other. The manager is under notice to leave. His face looked rather 'drinky', but I believe he has done his work well. After spending the whole day inspecting and talking tea and cinchona and cardamoms and pretending to examine his accounts, back very tired to Honookootua to sup and bed.

24 December 1884 - Wednesday

Drove away early to Nawalapitiya where I parted from Porter, he going back by train to Colombo and I driving on another ten miles to Banagalla where Blackett[746] met me. Had a cup of tea at Smith's[747], the Superintendent of Banagalla, and then rode with Blackett to his estate of Penylan and had breakfast with his Superintendent Crowther, who lives

---
[743] "Lost Sir Massingbird" (published 1864), by James Payn (1830-1898).
[744] Réchauffée: French, meaning "reheated".
[745] The Tichborne case was a famous court case of the 1860s and 1870s. Sir Roger Charles Tichborne, heir to the Tichborne baronetcy, had been a passenger on a ship which had been lost at sea. His mother, believing her son to still be alive, advertised in newspapers around the world, hoping to find him. A butcher from Wagga Wagga, New South Wales, who called himself Thomas Castro (although it later turned out he might have been an Englishman called Arthur Orton), saw the advertisements and replied, claiming to be Tichborne. With his wife, Mary Ann Bryant, he travelled to England at Lady Tichborne's request. Castro and Bryant stop to re-marry on the way, using the name Tichborne. Once in England, Lady Tichborne believed that Castro was indeed her missing son, but the rest of the family did not. A court case later found that Castro/Orton was an impostor and sentenced him to a long prison sentence for perjury.
[746] James Blackett Jr. (1831-1893), son of James Blackett Sr. and Mary Blackett (née Brown). In 1846, Blackett (Sr?) was planting experimental tea bushes, Hemilia Vastatrix, on the land he was managing, and reports from the time indicate that although coffee was widely damaged by blight, these new tea bushes were healthy and productive. James Blackett Jr. is recorded as Resident Manager of Paroogalle Coffee Estate in the District of Udepalate (owned by A. Stephens) in 1854. He was married to Katherine Blackett (née Russell Scott) (1842-1893) in 1863, and they had a son Major Walter Scott Blackett in 1867, by which time they were at Pen-Y-Lan. His son Walter and his future son-in-law Robert Wilson (1868-1952) - married to Alice George Blackett (1870-1915) in 1896 - continued planting in neighbouring estates for many years. In 1885, Gibbs sees James Blackett Jr's estate as the 'one bright spot' in Ceylon. Other records from 1885 show that tea had now taken over from coffee as the main harvest and was flourishing.
[747] Possibly William Smith, tea planter, recorded as having a bungalow at Mattakelle in the Kandy district which was visited in 1872 by the Governor of Ceylon, Sir William Gregory (1817-1892).

there. Mrs C. a nice little woman, whom I found to be a sister of a lady whom I dined with and saw something of in Trinidad – and she is married to the head of the police in Port of Spain. The tea on Penylan is splendid, a large amount in full bearing; the machinery in the tea houses good and elaborate; in fact, the estate is valuable and well cared for – the first bright spot and I fear the last in Ceylon. Our money is safe here in Ceylon unless anything happens to Blackett. In the evening we rode on to Dotyloyan[748] where Blackett lives, and there we had a Christmas dinner party – 5 or 6 planters coming over from the neighbouring places, nearly all ruined and the cause of ruin to others, but none the less festive and even rowdy. One man told me that he had just bought at auction his own estate on which there had been a debt of £15,000, for 12 rupees or say 1 sou[749]. The whole of the island is rotten. The men have been ruined by great prosperity followed by great adversity, and they have no conception for the most part of common honesty in commercial dealings. The evening was kept up very late. Old Blackett danced a reel, and the whole lot (except myself, who totally abstained) *tho' no that fou were just a wee drap i' the ee*[750].

62. James Blackett
Courtesy of Robert Wilson

25 December 1884 - Thursday

A beautiful Christmas Day; up early with Blackett riding over the estate, which is large and fine with a great deal of forest land which could be brought under cultivation. There is a lot of succirubra[751] fit to cut, and I am very pleased... oh, *si sic omnia*[752]. Rode over in the evening to spend Xmas with the Smiths; any amount of children at dinner, and two or three planters. I played blind man's buff, and there was a lot of crackers and very innocent foolery – not unpleasant.

---

[748] Doteloya Estate.
[749] 1 sou - from a historic French coin worth very little, and thus "practically nothing".
[750] This is possibly a quote from Robbie Burns: "For though they were na very fou, That wicked wee drap in the e'e has done its turn...". Gibbs means that everyone present was somewhat merry, but not outrageously drunk.
[751] "Cinchona succirubra" is quinine bark powder.
[752] Latin: "Would that everything had been done thus".

26 December 1884 - Friday

Up early, and had a game of lawn tennis and the barbecue. Had a look at the teahouse – machinery etc. on a much smaller scale than Blacketts. Left about 11am; a magnificent drive through the hills to Nawalapitya. The scenery almost, if not quite, surpasses Jamaica. Took the train there to Colombo; arrived between 6 and 7 – met by Howell at the station with two telegrams from London in his hand. After dinner at the Club[753], sat late talking and arguing about business and decided that H. should put off going to Downall's[754] till Sunday. In the train I read a French story by Victor Cherbuliez called 'Meta Holdenis'[755], by no means unamusing but inferior to 'Sam Brohl et Cie'. My servant[756] all through has come in very handy, and they give no trouble like Europeans would to one's host, for they keep themselves on their bhatta, or rice, require no room of any kind, and sleep outside their master's room on a mat which they carry with them. I feel quite inclined to bring my man home; he is so clean, quiet, attentive, respectful and picturesque. He is always in waiting, which an English servant never is; however, no doubt, he would lose all his virtues in England.

27 December 1884 - Saturday

Mail arrived; heard of poor Arnold Dent's[757] sudden death; how often he and Edward Stubbs and I have been in the same room together – how odd it seems they should both have ceased, *et mihi forsan*[758] etc.

I wonder how Edward is: perhaps he too is among the [GREEK]; well if it is not now it will be hereafter, if it is now it will not be to come, the ripeness is all[759].

---

[753] The Colombo Club was founded in 1871, "for the promotion of social intercourse among gentlemen residing in Ceylon". G. B. Leechman ("Sangsue", whom Gibbs meets later) and his brother were two of the 23 original members.
[754] Reginald Beauchamp Downall (1843-1888), who had arrived in Ceylon to grow coffee in 1863. He had good years followed by coffee blight and ruin.
[755] Published New York D. Appleton & Co. 1877
[756] Gibbs calls his servant 'Sinnatambi'. When I visited Colombo during the researching of the diary I asked two young men in the street if Sinnatambi was a common name; they found my question hilarious, saying it was a pet name meaning 'little brother'. Sinnathambi (with an H) certainly means 'little brother' or 'younger brother' in Tamil ('thambi' means brother).
[757] Arnold Robarts Dent (1856-3 Dec 1884, aged 28). The son of Thomas Dent (1796-1872), the founder and head of Thomas Dent and Co., China tea and opium merchants, and the second largest English firm on the China coast and Canton area after Jardines.
[758] Latin: And to me, perhaps
[759] This is a misquote of a line from Hamlet: "If it be now, 'tis not to come. If it be not to come, it will be now. If it be not now, yet it will come. The readiness is all". Gibbs might be confusing "ripeness" with "readiness" because of another Shakespeare quote, this time from King Lear: "What, in ill thoughts again? Men must endure Their going hence, even as their coming hither; Ripeness is all: come on."

Sent a long telegram home and spent the day dictating to Howell a rather washy, unsubstantial [sic] letter. I think I shall probably get away in less than 4 weeks, but H. will have to stay much longer from his *'domus et placens uxor'*[760], which he hates, but sees the necessity of. He will prove, I am sure, a great acquisition, and I think he was an A1 selection.

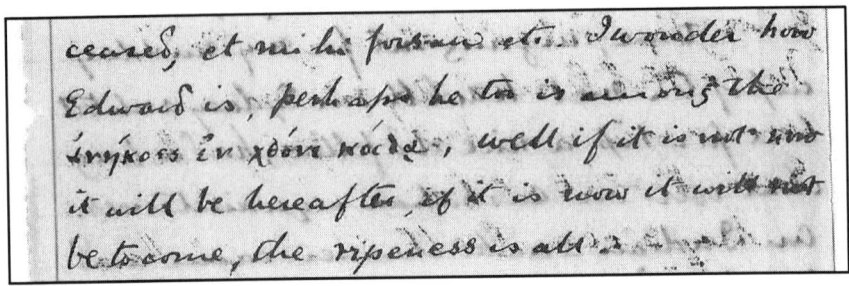

63. Greek text from 27 December 1884

28 December 1884 - Sunday

Had to keep the office open while I wrote letters all the morning. Later on I took a drive with Freudenberg[761], an intelligent German merchant, and sucked his brains about Ceylon. He thinks that tea, too, will be overdone[762].

29 December 1884 - Monday

Gouty again, in the left foot this time. In going out for my midday cup of tea met Wardell[763], our Sydney architect, here for a trip – a nice old fellow. Had a long chat over our Australian acquaintances. And an Indian snake charmer came and performed to us most marvellously. He did the mangoe [sic] trick[764] *'a faire peur'*[765]. It is almost impossible to believe that such things are not supernatural, and shows what sleight of hand will do. He worked the cobra into fury with one stick, and paralysed him instantly

---

[760] Latin: Home and the good wife.
[761] Philipp Freudenberg (1843-1911), Imperial German Consul to Ceylon from 1876 to 1906. Founded Freudenberg & Co. in 1883. Freudenberg takes over the lease of to the Hultsdorf coconut oil mills from G. B. Leechman in 1886 (see 9th January 1885).
[762] The implication being that tea will suffer the same fate as the coffee crops, and fail.
[763] William Wilkinson Wardell (1823-1899), Gibbs Bright's Sydney architect, and the most famous of his day having designed several Australian Cathedrals, the Art Gallery and the University of Sydney, amongst many other buildings. He had been a close friend and pupil of Pugin and also a friend of John Henry Newman; these friends persuaded him, after his own careful thought, to convert to Roman Catholicism. He had married in England before emigrating to Australia for his health and had four daughters and six sons, one of whom Gibbs met on 9 September 1884.
[764] Better known as the Indian Mango Trick. The performer places a mango seed in an empty pot, waters it, and covers it with a cloth. The mango plant appears to grow under the cloth, and eventually ripe mangoes start dropping out. When the cloth is finally removed, a fully-grown mango tree laden with fruit is revealed.
[765] French: "To make one afraid", i.e. he did the trick 'frightfully' well.

at the sight of another. Since I have been here I have seen two or three Australians '*en passant*': Mrs Hogg, to whom her husband charged me with messages (she was a Miss Elder), and Molesworth Green, who cross-examined me about all the Melbourne Club gossip

30 December 1884 - Tuesday

[No entry]

31 December 1884 - Wednesday

Left Colombo at 7am. Hot, dull journey; slept a great deal, and picked up Blackett at Nawalapitya, and together as far as the terminus where we took the coach for 20 miles to Newera Eliya[766] – a sort of health resort. A great change in the climate from the sluggish heat of Colombo, to cold nights, blankets and fires. We put up at Barnes Hall[767], Downall's, or rather our property, now a hotel – and a very expensive one. We got there in time for a 'baddish' dinner, and a horrid fellow sucked his teeth next to me all through.

1 January 1885 - Thursday

Left early and drove to Newabudde[768] to breakfast, and had a look at a native coffee garden. Rode thence to Moonerackanda[769] where Downall and Howell met us. I had to walk the latter part as my horse cast a shoe and went lame. It was dark when we got in but a coolie met us with a lantern. As I expected the coffee looks well, but – if one examines closely – the traces of disease are clear enough. Like its master, the coffee is intent on preserving appearances but does not bear fruit.

2 January 1885 - Friday

Busy during the morning, writing for the mail. Had a talk with Downall, who behaved as well as could be expected. But there is much shallowness and silliness to be observed in the way of clothes, and dogs, and servants – 'scratch my head, Mustardseed'[770]. A fellow came solemnly in to light his pipe; a heap of servile Indians is very demoralising. The view from the

---

[766] Nuwara Eliya: a town in the central highlands of Sri Lanka (Ceylon), important for tea production.
[767] Barnes Hall was the former Hill Country mansion of Sir Edward Barnes, governor of Sri Lanka from 1830 to 1850.
[768] This name is illegible, but appears to be Newabedde - but there is no place with that name. Gibbs might be referring to Nayabedde, which is about 4 miles north of Monarakande Estate. However, he says that he stops at this place for breakfast after leaving Barnes Hall in Nuwara Eliya early morning, so it seems more likely that he is referring to a place reasonably close to Nuwara Eliya and not 35 miles away.
[769] Monarakande Estate, slightly over 40 miles south-east of Nuwara Eliya.
[770] Actually the quote from Midsummer Night's Dream is "Scratch my head Peaseblossom." Mustardseed is a different character in the same scene. The implication is 'brainless but used to power'.

bungalow veranda is splendid over the rolling patnas and forest, but I daresay it would become monotonous. There is a beautifully-kept little garden. In the afternoon I walked about the estate and saw some very bad cinchonas.

3 January 1885 - Saturday

Visited Lamostotte[771], the next estate of D's. I didn't take much to the Superintendent; he smelt of whiskey. He had rather a nice wife, and the most gigantic baby I ever saw. There is a tramway aerial for carrying up manure. I daresay it may be useful, but it is not yet paid for. Everything is done as if everybody was rolling in money instead of bankrupt. *Oh genus improvidens agricolarum!*[772] My servant Sinnatambi ('little brother') has been gradually shrivelling up like a fly in the cold weather. I think he would die if he stayed here long. He has neuralgia and a touch of fever. He came to me today crying, "Please, master, do something for me. Look at my eye." I gave him some quinine and some pills, and a flannel coat, and told him to lie down and keep warm. They are very like dogs or obedient children, gentle and trustful, or untruthful and ungrateful. I like them infinitely better than Negroes. My boy certainly doesn't steal anything, which is good of him, and he watches my room like a cat so that no one else steals.

4 January 1885 - Sunday

Rode to Dambetenne, the 3rd Estate of the Group, and breakfasted with Chamberlain; a pleasant fellow, and seems to know his work. In the evening, the Super on Moonerakanda came to dinner – a great elephant shot. Downall said 'my first idea is to have gentlemen', a speech reminding me of GSH[773]. My first idea would be to have men who knew their work and stuck to it, the rest is all but 'leather and prunella'[774].

5 January 1885 - Monday

Left at 8. I fear Blackett's estimate of these properties will be very low. Rode to Hiragalla, one of Duff's estates on which a great red-bearded man named Orchard is Super – *'Cerrepu dosé'* (Fire master), the coolies call him.

---

[771] Llaymostatte Estate, near Haputale in Uva Province.
[772] Latin: Gibbs meant, "Oh, the wastefulness of farmers".
[773] G.S.H. may refer to Hayton (see May 30th 1884), as Gibbs implies at separate times that both of these people are heavy drinkers.
[774] "It is all leather or prunella". Nothing of any moment, all rubbish. Prunella is a woollen stuff, used for the uppers of ladies' boots and shoes.

I breakfasted here and met Rowe[775], a nephew of James Hayne[776]. He lives on an estate near and does nothing but write long letters to the papers, signed 'outcast'. His wife was there too, an Australian who knew all my Melbourne friends, and we had a great confab. I liked the female outcast particularly, and was sorry when we had to ride away. After a journey of 20 miles we reached Wilson's[777] bungalow where we dined and slept. Howell had to pay 6 rupees for breaking the lamp globe, which made him more bitter against Ceylon than ever. A long day.

6 January 1885 - Tuesday

Drove to Newera Elya, about 12 miles – pouring with rain. Played draughts, beastly game – H. beat me every time. In the afternoon, visited the Oliphant tea estate[778] belonging to Brook's[779]; Aitken manager.

7 January 1885 - Wednesday

Howell left for Colombo before I woke, taking Sinnatambi with him as he was too seedy to be any use. I meant to have gone to Maha Uva, but found I was too gouty to put my foot to the ground; so stayed in bed and read 'The Improvisatore'[780] by Hans Anderson, a sort of biography in story form. I rather liked it. Blackett came back at 10pm with Whiteford, the Maha Uva manager.

8 January 1885 - Thursday

Blackett came in at 5am – I was still very lame, but he persuaded me to try and get down to Colombo. I was carried to the coach, and managed the

---

[775] Rowe was one of the children of James Charles Hayne's wife's sister. James Charles Hayne married Caroline Winifred Grimanese Pfeiffer, and her sister was Sarah Amelia Pfeiffer, who married a Charles Rowe in 1841. They had 6 children; the male children were Charles Rowe (-), George Rowe (-), and Arthur Rowe (1853-1906). The most likely seems to be Charles (James) Rowe - he married an Australian, Annie Gray of Nareeb Nareeb, Victoria, in 1881, and he is said to be of Hiralourah (or Hiraleurah), Haputale, Ceylon. Haputale is about 50km from Nuwara Eliya. Rowe's wife might be the same Mrs. Rowe Gibbs met in Melbourne on 31 October 1884.

[776] James Charles Hayne (c1829-1886), one of the partners in AG&S from 1880 until his retirement at the end of 1886. In 1855, at the age of 26 and working for the company in Lima, he married Caroline Winifred Grimanese Pfeiffer, 22, of Lima. The couple gave birth to a daughter, Caroline Maria, there in 1856, and another, Amelia Sarah, in 1857. Hayne lived in South America from 1849-1879, being made a partner on his return. He was the nephew of John Hayne (-1864), who had helped establish the company in Peru and was a partner from 1848 to 1859 after he left South America in 1846.

[777] David Wilson. He was the father of Robert Wilson (1868-1952) who married Alice George Blackett (daughter of James Blackett, Jr.) in 1896.

[778] Hon. Sir Anthony Oliphant (1793-1859) was a British Lawyer who was appointed Chief Justice of Ceylon in 1830. His tea estate, the Oliphant Estate, was situated in Nuwara Eliya and was the first estate to grow tea in Ceylon, originally using tea plants smuggled from China. His son, Laurence Oliphant, is one of the authors Gibbs read on his trip (see 7 September 1883) - and Laurence's cousin Margaret was another (see 9 December 1883).

[779] Possibly Arthur Brooke, founder of Brooke Bond & Co. in 1869.

[780] Hans Christian Anderson (1805-1875): 'The Improvisatore: or, Life in Italy' (1869)

journey somehow with cushions. Talked to Whiteford, who came with us part of the way – he seemed sensible and quiet. Read 'La vie de Boheme'[781] by Henri Murger; found I had read it before, but some of it is very amusing, and the story about the muff is really pretty, though *'assurement je ne donnerais pas cette histoire à ma fille*[782]. Howell met me in Colombo with the carriage, and I heard from him of Herbert's engagement to Anna Durant[783] – *sit felix*[784].

9 January 1885 - Friday

Gout better; in the office writing mail letters, and wired home congratulations to Herbert, and 100 ton **[Unreadable]** list of losses on various accounts. How ineffably rotten all this Ceylon business is. Had Leechman[785] on the operating table for some time. 'Oh for an ounce of civet, good apothecary'[786].

10 January 1885 - Saturday

Busy writing – mail off. Bought an enormous Pith hat; very light, shady and comfortable.

11 January 1885 - Sunday

Wrote, read, and drove symptoms of returning gout away. I believe the dry climate of Australia is the cure, certainly – nowhere have I been so long free.

---

[781] Scènes De La Vie De Bohème, by (Louis) Henri Murger (1822-1861)
[782] French: "I would definitely not give this story to my daughter".
[783] Anna Maria Durant, daughter of Richard Durant and Charlotte Still Dashwood. Married Herbert Cokayne Gibbs on 12 February 1885 at Shenley, Hertfordshire, England.
[784] Latin: "Be happy" (or "Rejoice!").
[785] Gibbs mentions his initials later: this is G. B. Leechman, founder of Messrs. Leechman & Co. in 1864 when coffee was the principal product of Ceylon before its failure about 10 years later due to leaf disease. Subsequently, the company was among the first to branch into cinchona and tea production, and later into rubber production. In 1866, G. B. Leechman also founded another firm, G. and W. Leechman, with his brother William Carey Leechman, leasing and operating the Hultsdorf Coconut Oil Mills (producing coconut oil and soap) after the original owners went into liquidation. In 1886, Philipp Freudenburg took over the lease of the Hultsdorf Mills. The Leechman brothers were also among the 23 original members of the Colombo Club, founded in 1871, "for the promotion of social intercourse among gentlemen residing in Ceylon".
[786] Shakespeare's King Lear says 'Give me an ounce of civet, good apothecary, to sweeten my imagination'. Gibbs might be saying he is depressed by the Ceylon business, with the same sarcastic use of 'civet' as Shakespeare. Civet is a yellowish, fatty substance with a musk-like scent, secreted by a gland near the genitals of the civet cat and used in making some perfumes. But pure civet is foul-smelling.

12 January 1885 - Monday

Engaged to lunch at Mount Lavinia[787] with Law – rough but not unpleasant merchant here. Had to go, but hardly up to it. Met Commissary General Tayler, a very handsome man something like Garnet Wolsey[788]; a good deal of the 'fat' about him. Gout getting rapidly worse, returned to Club Chambers and straight to bed. Telegram in from London approving of ringing[789] up Bell from Dunedin. Perhaps it is the best, but it seems an awful fuss and disturbance to be making.

13 January 1885 - Tuesday

One of my awful nights, simple agony. Luckily I had ordered Sinnatimbi to sleep in the passage and he kept up hot fomentations and behaved well, gentle and careful. Early this morning, pain being bad and not having closed my eyes, sent for Dr. White[790] who injected morphia. In 15 minutes, pain dulled and state of heavenly semi-stupefaction for 4 or 5 hours. Then pain better, but too bad to read or do anything.

14 January 1885 - Wednesday

Bed, chess, business jaw, and read Cromwell's letters ed. Carlyle[791].

15 January 1885 - Thursday

Bed, chess, more jaw, less Gout, read old Illustrated News[792].

16 January 1885 - Friday

Same, and endless jaw, dreary bed. Wired home, postponing return; could not be well enough to go on 20th. Up on a sofa in the evening.

17 January 1885 - Saturday

Up for first time, and took a drive. Saw giant tortoise at Duncan's[793]: supposed to be 120 years old – 3 men can stand on his back at once! A very disturbing telegram from London. They seem to think Sangsue[794] should be got rid of. I must take some decisive measure. [There is a short

---

[787] Mount Lavinia: now part of Dehiwala-Mount Lavinia, a newly created city immediately south of Colombo. Then, Mount Lavinia was a town famed for its beaches.
[788] Field Marshall Sir Garnet Wolseley, 1st Viscount Wolseley (1833-1913).
[789] A joke?
[790] Possibly one of the sons of Dr Abraham White of Ceylon (1787-1818).
[791] "Oliver Cromwell's Letters and Speeches – with Elucidations", edited by Thomas Carlyle.
[792] The Illustrated London News, the world's first illustrated weekly newspaper, was published weekly from 1842 until 1971, then less frequently thereafter until it ceased publication in 2003.
[793] Although this is the only mention of Duncan in the diary, J. Duncan was one of the founding members of the Colombo Club.
[794] Referring to Leechman. 'Sangsue' is French for 'leech'. Later, Gibbs refers to Leechman's children as "the little leeches".

illegible sentence here, which looks like "2 to her 8th." or "Q to her 8th."] Howell or I must go home[795] and talk it over. What a worry it all is.

18 January 1885 - Sunday

Write to Alban; being Sunday, Howell to Cathedral[796]. Lunched at Freudenberg's[797], and then back to office to go on writing to AG&S, discussing and arguing as to return. I can't possibly go this steamer – I am much too seedy, and H. thinks he or I should go at once. If so it must be he, but I don't like the idea of sticking here. Told H. the story of the goat and the fox in the well![798]

19 January 1885 - Monday

Decided reluctantly to stay and wired home to that effect, giving AG&S the opportunity of stopping H. at Aden, if they wish.

20 January 1885 - Tuesday

More trouble with Downall – rows and recriminations. He has quietened down, however, and become amenable. Gout rather worse, but sluggish and painless. Howell left at 3pm – I suppose it is the best. Dined solo at the Club. I must get to know some people, but when one is ill and lame it is difficult.

21 January 1885 - Wednesday

Freudenberg has asked me to come and live in his house. He is a clever, well-informed German. I think I shall very likely go if he will agree to my paying my share of expenses. Spent the day at the office, and played chess in the evening with an old judge whom I beat. He was not of the premiere force, and the Muzio gambit was too much for him.

22 January 1885 - Thursday

Wrote and read and hobbled about. Moved to the Freudenberg's house in Cinnamon Gardens, taking Sinnatambi. Rather glad to leave the club; being ill in a place makes one hate it. Drove for the first time in a jinrickshaw – a sort of two-wheeled light bath chair, drawn by a coolie who

---

[795] i.e. to the UK
[796] St. Lucia's Roman Catholic Cathedral in Colombo.
[797] Freudenberg's house was called Glen Esk, presumably named after the mountain valley ("glen") of the River North Esk in Angus and Abderdeenshire, Scotland.
[798] One of Aesop's Fables, "The fox and the goat in the well", the lesson being that as soon as someone clever gets into trouble, he tries to find a way out at someone else's expense. A fox had unwittingly fallen down a well and found herself trapped inside its high walls. Meanwhile, a thirsty goat had made his way to that same place and asked the fox whether the water was fresh and plentiful. The fox set about laying her trap. 'Come down, my friend', said the fox. 'The water is so good that I cannot get enough of it myself!' The bearded billy-goat lowered himself into the well, whereupon that little vixen leaped up on his lofty horns and emerged from the hole, leaving the goat stuck inside the watery prison.

runs between the shafts. They are very comfortable, and go as fast as an ordinary fly, but I could not help feeling rather ashamed at lying back, smoking my manilla, while a fellow creature was rattling along like a beast of burden. One hasn't a whip, but otherwise it is driving a man instead of a horse.

23 January 1885 - Friday

4 o'clock tea at Mrs Leechman's – the little Leeches rather pretty, fair-haired animals. Played a rubber – the average Club play better than Melbourne. I can't yet get a boot on. I am comfortable at Glen Esk[799].

24 January 1885 - Saturday

Up at 5 o'clock. Smoked and played chess with F. There is a splendid Bougainvillea growing along the veranda. I shall find England a great change from this; query if it's not more comfortable to be always warm as in the tropics. A long visit from Bosanquet[800] who talked about Australian business, and in the evening to see the gymkhana – a race meeting which took place outside the Club on the Green – not bad fun. Pony race, hack race, dog race, tandem race – riding one pony and driving another, riding at the ring, tent-pegging etc. A man named Delinage came in in the evening, a vulgar, bragging beast – and I should say an unmitigated liar.

25 January 1885 - Sunday

Smoked, played chess, read German. Went for a drive. Got a telegram saying AG&S approved of Howell going home.

26 January 1885 - Monday

Had some business talk with Freudenberg, who wants to draw on us against produce with documents attached. The mail in but of course nothing for me, and only a short note from AG&S for Howell. Whist at Club; gout nearly well, but still cloth boot.

27 January 1885 - Tuesday

Wrote to Frank and Regi, and took a little walk.

28 January 1885 - Wednesday

Nothing to chronicle.

---

[799] Freudenberg's house.
[800] There isn't enough information to track down exactly which Bosanquet is meant here, but the family is of Huguenot origin and throughout the last two centuries has been well known in many fields of expertise. Some family members were much involved in British India and the Indian Army. They also seem to have played several roles in commerce and as Eastern Merchants, including dealing in various commodities in Ceylon. Gibbs would almost certainly have known several members of the family both in business and socially.

29 January 1885 - Thursday

English mail in, and long letter from AG&S to Howell. I see they think Sangsue should be done away with, and I shall offer no opposition. Very sorry to learn that Herbert has had an accident, but no particulars given.

30 January 1885 - Friday

Gout again, so did not go out; read some German, and some 'Artemus Ward'[801] – which bore re-reading better than I expected, and is really very amusing. Also a lot of Macaulay's essays[802]. Very fascinating style, no doubt, but I get very tired of him and prefer Gibbon's[803] pomp to his tinsel.

31 January 1885 - Saturday

Had a horrible night; a great pain, but that subsided in the morning. Lay all day on a couch in the veranda. A Mr[804] & Mrs Tetley to tiffin. She, a very fine voice, and sung from the Messiah. Also a Mr Walker, with whom I played chess. Read 'La Vie de Renan'[805]; he must have been in many respects very attractive, and the affectionate picture he draws of St. Sulpice[806] is very pretty; for an absolute infidel, he is significantly free from all bitterness against Christianity. Read a horrible book by Adolphe Belot called 'Helene et Mathilde', a real French plot.

1-2 February 1885

Heard from Melbourne by Cable that Bell does not leave before 26th of this month, so I shall be stranded here for Lord knows how long. Gout better; read a trifling, harmless story called 'Folies Amoureuses'[807].

3 February 1885 - Tuesday

In the office again. Mail to England. Wrote Mother, Alban, Downall, Bosanquet, etc.

4 February 1885 - Wednesday

Read some of Lord Malmesbury's Memoirs – decidedly amusing. My diary will require hanging a long time before it is tender enough for public

---

[801] Artemus Ward was the *nom de plume* of Charles Farrar Browne (1834-1867).
[802] Thomas Babington Macaulay, 1st Baron Macaulay (1800–1859), a British historian, Whig politician, and prolific essayist.
[803] Edward Gibbon (1737–1794), an English historian and MP. He is best known for "The History of the Decline and Fall of the Roman Empire".
[804] No doubt related to Tetley Tea in some way.
[805] 'La Vie de Renan' is presumably a joke: Joseph Erust Renan wrote a book called 'La Viè de Jésus' (which Gibbs reads later), but also wrote an autobiography called 'Souvenirs d'enfance et jeunesse' (Recollections of my youth).
[806] Église Saint-Sulpice is a Roman Catholic church in Paris, the second largest church in the city.
[807] "Folies Amoureuses", by Catulle Mendès (edited by E. Rouveyre and G. Blond).

consumption. I daresay in about 300 years if a reviewer got hold of it he would work up an article out of it 'England at the end of the 19th Century' "The writer seems to have been a fair specimen of the ordinary English merchant of the time, fairly well-informed, and from internal evidence we gather that he was at Eton and Oxford. He is very careful to chronicle his ailments, and the various trashy and forgotten novels which he read and the plays which he saw, but we look in vain for the unconscious humour and simplicity of the immortal Pepys. It is instructive to notice that there is hardly any reference to public affairs beyond a few expressions of vindictive dislike to the great Gladstone and the separation of the English colonies so soon to come to pass, and which should have been clear to the shallowest mind, are unheeded or at any rate unrecorded" etc. etc.

5 February 1885 - Thursday

I wish I were well enough to travel, or free to go home or back to Australia or something. I am sick and silly of fooling away my time and brains here. Worked away and got through 4 pages of 'Die verlorene handschrift'[808], but it is uphill work, and I don't know that there is any special object in my knowing German. The combined absence of work friends and amusement *friget toedet poeintet*[809] and so on. I am led into smoking too many Manillas. 10 fell victims yesterday to my *desoeuvrement - es ist zu viel...*[810]

6 February 1885 - Friday

Read some of 'Our Old Actors'[811]. It interested me. What a nasty woman Mrs Siddons[812] must have been, hated by other actors and actresses, certainly chaste; but after all, that is not the conclusion of the whole matter, even in a woman. All the law and the prophets don't hang on that. Bracegirdle[813] and Kitty Clive[814] were just as virtuous.

---

[808] 'Die verlorene Handschrift' (The Lost Manuscript), by Gustav Freyatg (1816-1895), published 1864. Freytag was a German novelist, dramatist, and critic, and was perhaps Germany's most popular author from 1850 to 1870. He portrayed the struggles and triumphs of the rising middle class with engaging realism.
[809] This is very unclear, but could be "friget" (=it is cold) or "piget" (=it irks, or it's a shame), then possibly "toedet" (?) or "taedet" (=tired/bored/tedious), then "poeintet" (?) or "pocintet" (?) or "pociutet" (?) (="rather" or "preferably"?).
[810] '*Desoeuvrement*' is French for 'idleness'; '*es ist zu viel*' is German for 'it is too much'.
[811] "Our Old Actors", by Henry Barton Baker.
[812] Sarah Siddons (1755-1831), a Welsh actress, who was most famous for portraying Shakespeare's Lady Macbeth.
[813] Anne Bracegirdle (c.1671-1748), an English actress, widely rumoured to have been the mistress (or even secret wife) of the English dramatist William Congreve (1670-1729).
[814] Catherine "Kitty" Clive (née Raftor) (1711–1785), a British actress.

7 February 1885 - Saturday

64. Paul Friedrich, Duke of Mecklenburg
Wikimedia Commons

65. Princess Marie of Windisch-Graetz (wife of Paul Friedrich, Duke of Mecklenburg)
Wikimedia Commons

Freudenberg got a telegram from Duke Paul of Mecklenberg[815] 'Komme Mit Hezogin[816] und Don Carlos[817]. Tibre.'[818] It seems his brother stayed with Freudenberg 2 years ago and enjoyed himself. After a council of war we decided it would be quite impossible to put up the Duchess, so F. took rooms for the lot at the Grand Hotel, and looked out his store clothes and had his Black Eagle of Mecklenburg – or White Rabbit or whatever the 'order' is -- cleaned up for the arrival. Wrote to AG&S, and by a piece of foolery missed the mail. Dined at the Club with Walker, and played whist. Home in a jinrickshaw by 12. Heard of the fall of Khartoum, and fear Gordon[819] must be killed. If England stands that, she deserves all she gets. It makes me mad. I hope Gladstone's Government will be held responsible

---

[815] Duke Paul Friedrich of Mecklenberg (1852–1923), of the House of Mecklenburg-Schwerin. He married the Duchess (his cousin, the Austrian-born Princess Marie of Windisch-Graetz) in 1881.
[816] Herzogin (with an R) means Duchess. The Duchess, Princess Marie of Windisch-Graetz, the daughter of Prince Hugo of Windisch-Graetz and his wife Duchess Louise of Mecklenburg-Schwerin.
[817] Carlos the Diplomat (also known as the Martyr) (1863-1908), who became Carlos I, King of Portugal and the Algarves in 1889.
[818] German: "I'm coming with the Duchess and Don Carlos. Tibre.". The S.S. Tibre was a Messageries Co. steamer that sailed to Colombo.
[819] Major-General Charles George Gordon, CB (1833–1885), nicknamed Gordon of Khartoum, was a British army officer. He was indeed killed - on 26 January - during the Madhist Revolt, whilst trying to defend Khartoum.

for his blood. I wish Gladstone and Gordon could change places – so would it be better for England.

8 February 1885 - Sunday

Read 'Les Filles de John Bull'[820] – very amusing, but not so good as 'John Bull et son Ile'[821]. This is a little indecent, and makes one inclined to say d----d Frenchman in good old British style. He is, however, a very friendly critic, and has a great deal of humour. I feel I have resisted all 'temptations to belong to other nations'[822]. The 'swells'[823] dropped in to tea and buns, and behaved very well for people in their station of life. The Duchess speaks English fairly well, and I found my French fluent enough. Don Carlos has entirely lost his voice. He remembered going round the 'Bank of England', and referred to his having been hissed. He says those sort of demonstrations are arranged by the Spanish Ambassador. The Duke, a stoutish, good-natured fellow. Rather glad when they went away. The *Altesse royale*[824] business soon becomes a bore.

9 February 1885 - Monday

Gout, I may almost say, is well. Took a short walk – my first for a long while – in the Cinnamon Gardens, and read 'Mons. Camors'[825] by Octave Feuillet, a very painful, rather powerful story. I missed yesterday's English mail, thinking it closed today.

10 February 1885 - Tuesday

Duke Paul rode with Freudenberg before breakfast, and having gulled his royal person came in about 6 o'clock unexpected, as I was sitting on the veranda smoking a cigar in my pyjamas. He sent for his things, and stayed to breakfast. He was apparently glad to get away from the Duchess, and he made himself very jolly, and related an improper Berlin story to show there was no ill-feeling, and we had some bother to get rid of him by eleven o'clock.

11 February 1885 - Wednesday

Another mail in from England, and this time bringing me letters. Old T.C.[826] seems wild with delight at the prospect of my return. Am reading

---

[820] 'Les Filles de John Bull', by Max O'Rell, the pseudonym of Léon Paul Blouet (1847-1903), a French journalist, lecturer and critic.
[821] 'John Bull et son Ile', by Max O'Rell.
[822] A quote from Gilbert and Sullivan's H.M.S. Pinafore (written in 1878): "But in spite of all temptations / To belong to other nations / He remains an Englishman!".
[823] Referring to the Duke and Duchess, and Don Carlos.
[824] French: "His Royal Highness".
[825] "Monsiuer Camors", by Octave Feuillet.
[826] "Old T.C." is probably T. Clayton (see 11th February 1884).

'Sans Famille'[827] by Hector Malot; a very pleasing story, and fit for an English girl to read.

12 February 1885 - Thursday

Busy telegraphing to London, and writing to R.B. I hope I may get away from here next week, but I hardly expect it. Today, bar accidents[828], Herbert and Anna have been married, *sint terque quaterque beati*[829]. A pleasant letter from H. yesterday in which he says Anna has always liked me!!! Don Carlos, the Duke, Freudenberg and I dined at the Club, an appalling long *sederunt*[830]; nothing could have been more easy or pleasant than the Grandees, but they kept it up without moving till 1.30am, and Don Carlos has a most filthy mind, and his manners in some respects in spitting and eating, very bad. His extreme confidences to me, both on public and private life were, I take it, more prompted by the flowing bowl than by anything especially attractive in me. I suppose one must make allowances for him as one of the Latin race, but certainly no English gentleman would be tolerated who talks and acts as he does.

66. Don Carlos
Wikimedia Commons

It is curious to see, mixed up with so much that is contemptible, such devotion to certain fixed principles. He told me Prim[831] offered him the Crown of Spain if he would take it as elected, and not as his right. Also Alfonso[832] has recently offered him the command of the Army and any title or position he likes in Spain, if he will recognise the present dynasty.

---

[827] 'Sans Famille (Nobody's Boy)', by Hector Malot.
[828] Possibly an allusion to Herbert's unspecified accident that Gibbs refers to on 29 January 1885.
[829] Latin: "There are three and four times blessed". Possibly a quote from Virgil's Aeneid: Aeneas's first scene in the poem features him wishing he was dead. His words speak loudly for all people having a rough time: " o terque quaterque beati, / quis ante ora partum Troiae sub moenibus altis / contigit oppetere!" His situation seemed so hopeless for him, that he wished for death.
[830] Sederunt: Latin, '(they were) sitting'; a long discussion or session, originally a session of court.
[831] General Juan Prim, 1st Marquis of los Castillejos (1814-1870).
[832] Alfonso XII (1857-1885), King of Spain from 1874 to 1885.

13 February 1885 - Friday

The Duke again invited himself to breakfast; he brought with him a large photo on which he wrote his name, and today he and his Duchess went to Madras, and F. and I dined with Don Carlos – whom I liked better at the Hotel. Yesterday, I telegraphed suggesting I should leave here by next mail and not wait for Bell. Bought some rather pretty Indian mats.

14 February 1885 - Saturday

Busy fixing up at the office in case I should go, and took a berth on the Brindisi provisionally. Dined at the Club and played whist. Finished 'Sans Famille', and like it very much. The account of the inundation in the mine is admirable.

15 February 1885 - Sunday

Went to the office after breakfast, and got a telegram telling me to use my own judgement. I shall go. The Hatterods of Trieste came to lunch. A very pleasant young couple, friends of the F's. Played a very long game of chess for about 3 hours with a man named Green, and just beat him.

16 February 1885 - Monday

I have handed my servant over to the Hatterods. Busy all day in the office, principally writing to Australia. Called on Don Carlos, who was very civil and asked me to dine, but I excused myself as I was engaged to Leechman. Freudenberg, Christopher L., Bosanquet and self were the party. Rather a bore, and B. especially I found to be an ass. Should have much preferred to dine at home with the F's, but it had to be done, and it went off all right and makes a proper finish.

S.S. Brindisi

17 February 1885 - Tuesday

Superintended packing till 11, then to office and wrote to AG&S. My share of rent, wages, expenses of all kinds for the month is 93R plus my servant's wages 15T = £9 =£108 P.A. So it is clear I could live in Colombo comfortably for £200 per annum.

I have got quite accustomed to the F's, and our living together has answered admirably, and I daresay if I had gone on living with them I should have picked up German.

A final talk with G.B.Leechman and Porter, and I went on board the steamer at 4 o'clock. F. came to see me off. I have a fair cabin to myself on deck, which I prefer to being below. There seem about 40 first class, and the ship is by no means full. At dinner, sat next to a Mr Bryans, a clergyman travelling for his health: curiously enough, I have been in his house, as his is the next parish to Wilcox, and I walked over there when W. took his service for him. W. told me in a letter of him, which I got at Colombo. He seems a very pleasant, cheerful man. I knew his brother in college at Eton.

18 February 1885 - Wednesday

Played chess with B. and beat him; and made acquaintance with a pretty little woman, very lively and full of fun; married to an old Dr Smith, who is going home having got an appointment at Southampton. I don't think the people on board look a very bright lot. The weather is perfectly calm. Read the 'Vie de Jesu' by Renan[833], which belongs to Howell. It is pleasingly written, and not calculated to offend people unnecessarily. There is an old chancery barrister on board named Caldecott, who seems not a bad sort.

19 February 1885 - Thursday

A beast of a Lascar dropped block of holystone on to my head through the skylight this morning and hurt me. There is a Miss Jackson on board who had been to Penang to marry a man who had engaged himself to her saying he was a solor[834], but when she got there she found he was only a solor's clerk, so she came back single. There is a stout, vulgar woman named Halford, whose call Mrs Smith did not return in Calcutta. So the two are at daggers drawn, and no doubt they will play '*le diable*' and quake in the course of the voyage. There was some fearful singing this evening.

20 February 1885 - Friday

Read 'Grandeur et Decadence de Cesar Birottean'[835] by Balzac. Good, but heavy and not very interesting. Rather rough today and a good many people seedy. Did not affect me beyond making me very sleepy.

21 February 1885 - Saturday

The following question was put to me: A swindler buys a pair of boots, price and value £1; gives a £5 note in payment. The boot-maker, having no change, cashes the note at a neighbour's, and gives the swindler his £4 change. The next day the neighbour, having found the note to be bad, makes the boot-maker refund his £5. How much does the boot-maker lose? I found no difficulty but it is surprising how many give £9 as the answer.

---

[833] La Viè de Jésus, by Joseph Erust Renan.
[834] Solor is legal slang for a solicitor.
[835] Honoré de Balzac (1799-1850): 'Grandeur et décadence de César Birotteau' (1837), part of La Comédie Humaine

22 February 1885 - Sunday

Bryans did the service, giving no sermon. There is a missionary on board from Amoy[836]: not a bad sort, but with a sickly wife and 3 children! A fine assistance to missionary effort. The protestant notion of missionary life is too contemptibly ridiculous compared with the way the Catholics go to work.

23 February 1885 - Monday

Read 'L'allemagne amoureuse' by Tissot. Gossiping trash, and full of spite against the victors of Sedan. The steamer is very quiet and we are spared all concerts, entertainments, sports and pleasures of that kind.

24 February 1885 - Tuesday

Reached the barren Isle of Aden[837] between 5 and 6pm. I did not go ashore as I was told there was nothing to see. The usual crowd of boys diving for 6d. pieces, and rascally Arabs trying to sell ostrich feathers, coral and suchlike rubbish. We were several hours coaling, and the ship in an awful mess. My cabin being forward on deck, I got a good benefit of coal dust, and could not go to bed until after midnight. No letters from home, but a note from Howell dated Alexandria the 3rd inst.

25 February 1885 - Wednesday

Howard Vincent[838] – who was head of the detective department in London and was, I think, *congédié*[839]- joined us at Aden together with his wife; rather a pretty little woman. He looks an ass; he has been and is going wherever the British flag flies, and has got the 'Imperial' stop on full pressure. I should say he is preparing to stand somewhere in the Conservative interest. I saw him in Melbourne and heard of him in India; he will be a fine bore.

Saw the home papers, and in the 'Colonial Mail' of the 6th, among the forthcoming fashionable marriages, was Herbert's.

---

[836] Amoy (also known as Xiamen) is a city on the south-east coast of China.
[837] Aden: now part of the Republic of Yemen, but prior to 1937 it was governed as part of British India and, after the opening of the Suez Canal in 1869, an important coaling station. It is not an island.
[838] Colonel Sir Charles Edward Howard Vincent KCMG CB DL (1849-1908), known as Howard Vincent, was a soldier, barrister, police official, and Conservative MP from 1885 to 1908. Following the Trial of the Detectives of 1877, when three senior Scotland Yard officers were imprisoned for corruption, Howard Vincent founded the Criminal Investigations Department (CID) in 1878 as the successor to the Detective Branch.
[839] Dismissed

26 February 1885 - Thursday

Read 'La Fille aux yeux d'or'[840] by Balzac, a horrible story. B. is very long-winded, though clever.

27 February 1885 - Friday

We are having a delightful passage through the Red Sea. A pleasant breeze, and just the perfection of temperature and the moon being about full makes the nights lovely. Life on board is very comfortable, if rather monotonous.

28 February 1885 - Saturday

Chess and whist most of the day, and I won 10 rubbers out of 11! I held 9 trumps in one hand!

1 March 1885 - Sunday

Quite cold, but bright and fine. I have to put on my cloth things again. Alas, no more white 'ducks' for many a long day. I do not like the return to an English climate after having been quite warm for 18 months or so. About 10am we sighted a Messageries[841] steamer coming up in our track, and gaining on us at a great pace with her yards squared and the sun glistening on her and on the track we had left. It was an extremely pretty sight. She proved to be the 'Yarra'. She passed us just before service quite close to starboard, within hail, dipping her flag, and the people waving their handkerchiefs. A short service, and no sermon. About 5pm, into Suez harbour and got 2 letters. Kind one from Uncle[842] asking me to stop and see him on my way through Italy, and a short note from Alban saying he had no news! but that I should probably change my plan of going to Marseilles when I heard that Herbert was in Italy. From this I infer that H. has been married as arranged.

I immediately decided to change my route, and wired home that I was going to Brindisi. I had very little time, but I saw the P&O agent and got leave to change my route; and packed up, sending most of my luggage on in the 'Brindisi' to London, and then turned in as I shall have to make very early start tomorrow.

---

[840] Honoré de Balzac (1799-1850): 'La Fille aux Yeux d'Or', part of La Comédie Humaine
[841] The *Compagnie des Messageries Maritimes* was the state-owned French steamship service, established in 1835 to run between Marseilles and the Levant. By 1881 it had expanded dramatically and had started to run a service between Marseille and Adelaide, Melbourne and Sydney. The Yarra had been built in 1883.
[842] Reverend John Lomax Gibbs (1832-1914) ("Uncle John"), husband of Isabel Marianne Bright (1835-1920). At this time he was a vicar in Devon.

2 March 1885 - Monday

After I was asleep last night a lot of fellows came back from the shore, partly screwed, and started singing a drinking toddy in the next cabin, and nothing would satisfy them but I must join them. One tried to climb the wall of my cabin and get down through the skylight, but his friends pulled him down by the legs. It was no use being angry, so I had to get up and go in and talk to them for a bit, and I ultimately persuaded them to go to their respective berths. I was soon asleep again: at 4.30am had to get up, and after a cup of tea went on shore in the steam launch with the Vincents, Isaacson, Wilson and others bound for Cairo and Alexandria. We waited in the open shed of a station till 8, very cold, and nothing to do but smoke. We saw evident signs of our being at war in the tents and stores which were scattered about, and in 2,000 camels who were all about the shore, standing out against the horizon in the clear air as if they were cut out in cardboard. The drivers were ruffians and half-castes of every description. Half an hour's train took us in to Suez town itself – an ugly, forsaken sort of place – and we got a scrambling snatch of a breakfast at the hotel. I sat next to a couple of officers who were off to the front that day; they told me the place was cram full – two generals in one room the night before, and so on. Started again at 9 – the first part of the way sandy desert, and we recognised the masts of the 'Yarra' and 'Brindisi' in the canal. In my carriage was Ormond[843], a vulgar, enormously wealthy, well-known Melbourne man and his two nieces – one very pretty, and both great chatterboxes. I learnt from one of them that my friend Robinson and his newly married wife were on the Yarra. Very sorry I missed them. There was also Mrs Vincent, who chirrups incessantly like a grasshopper. Her husband having a swaggering match with Ormond, and implying that his presence was necessary in England at this crisis. Isaacson, the most boring type of silly, restless, empty, magpie undergraduate. Wilson was the last, a dry, silent, intelligent Yankee. After some howls, he and I found the company intolerable, and at Zagzig[844], he having 'guessed' that he would rather walk than have any more of it (as he liked to hear people talk where one could get something out of it) and he 'reckoned' there was nothing of that sort there, we moved into a second class carriage – empty – and – starting our cigars – were happy. Said goodbye to Caldecott, who was going to Cairo. I liked him one of the best on the 'Brindisi', except Bryans and the Smiths. Mrs S. gave me a pretty photo of herself, but she had to make out that her husband would object to her giving it – which was silly.

The country changed quite suddenly to be very fertile. I saw a man ploughing with a buffalo and a camel. I believe there is no scriptural

---

[843] Possibly Francis Ormond (1829-1889), son of a Scottish mariner who emigrated to Australia and became a grazier. From humble beginnings as a stable-boy, Francis Ormond learnt to manage his father's land and quickly became successful - and very rich - himself. A great philanthropist, he donated much of his money to educational and religious causes both during his life and in his will. A suburb of Melbourne is named after him.
[844] Zagazig, a town in lower Egypt.

prohibition of that combination. Wilson and I had a light Arab lunch – very nice – hard-boiled eggs, dates and pistachio nuts, with some excellent coffee.

A French man got into the carriage who was better at eating eggs than anyone I have ever seen. He eat 4 hard-boiled straight off as hard as he could go, and then sucked 3 raw rather like a weasel. We had 3 changes and it was a very dusty, tiring journey. Two men got in, named Smith and Heriot, with whom we played whist till dusk. At 9 we reached Alexandria and went to the Hotel Abbat where, after most needful ablutions, a welcome supper and bed. I saw a bug on the window blind, but was too much tired to care. I forgot to say that just before starting I got from the P&O clerk a long, bright, amusing letter from Brien giving me a full account of Herbert's marriage: very kind of him to take the trouble.

3 March 1885 - Tuesday

Hired a dragoman after breakfast, and Wilson and I went round the town looking through the bazaars. The town has been terribly injured by the bombardment and fires, and many parts are still in ruins. There is a very Frenchified air about the buildings and the principal Place, which is well laid out with a very good bronze equestrian statue of Mehemet Ali[845]. We went to the forts and saw the effect of the heavy shells, which was interesting; then to the principal Mosque, and out to see Pompey's Pillar which is a fine granite column with base and capitol standing on a good site of high tableland overlooking the town.

Went on board the 'Mongolia' at six to dinner, and have a good cabin to myself on the hurricane deck. After dinner the chief steward told me he had letters for me sent on from Suez, but it turned out they had been stupidly sent back to the office. I told them to send up to the town for them and, as I was going to turn in, to wake me up when they came as I might have to telegraph.

S.S. Mongolia

4 March 1885 - Wednesday

At 3am I was woke up by a letter from Herbert, just as our ship was getting under way. He proposes my meeting him at Bologna, but I shall wire to him from Brindisi to come on to Venice as I shall leave the steamer there. At 10 o'clock the third officer gave me a large business letter from AG&S which had been on board all the time, and contained letters from Alban, Howell and Mother. Apparently there is one missing from Edith, but otherwise I have at last got all. Glad to learn that the London jewellers

---

[845] Muhammad Ali Pasha (or Mehmet Ali Paşa) (c.1769-1848), the founder of modern Egypt.

think so well of the sapphires[846] - they seem to be a bargain pecuniarily, as well as giving satisfaction to H. & A. Late last night a lot of passengers came on board from the Bombay mail, and we are about 50 all told. Played chess and whist.

5 March 1885 - Thursday

A strong headwind and sea, some people ill. I am all right. Passed along the barren coast of Gavdo[847], an island south of Crete, during the morning.

Wrote to Howell, Alban and Brien. We ought to be in Brindisi very early the day after tomorrow. Began to read a new book of Emile Zola: 'Nais Micoulin' – rather a relief after the grind of reading Balzac's disquisitions.

6 March 1885 - Friday

A glorious sunny day and the wind has dropped; passing along the coast of various islands in calm water. Had a good deal of talk with a Colonel Swaine[848], Military Secretary to Lord Wolseley. He gave me some very interesting particulars of the breaking of the English Square, Burnaby's[849] death, etc.

7 March 1885 - Saturday

Found ourselves alongside at Brindisi between 3 and 4, and my steward brought in letters from Herbert, Uncle John and Howell, learning from there that all my relations have accumulated in Florence. I decided not to go to Venice as that would bring H. and A. north again, which would be a mistake in this cold weather. I therefore packed up at once, had breakfast, and got my things passed through the Customs without much bother. Got a corner seat in a 1st Class, from which the *chef du gare* turned me out to make way for an Australian family. Read 'Nais Micoulin' and other stories by Zola; clever, and decidedly worth reading. Played piquet with a Frenchman. Dined at Ancona, and reached Bologna after midnight. Had a cup of coffee and slept soundly in the waiting room till 3.30 when I went on to Florence, reaching there about 7am.

---

[846] The sapphires were Vicary Gibbs' wedding present to Herbert and Anna.
[847] Gavdos, the southernmost Greek island which lies south of Crete.
[848] Colonel (later Sir) Leopold V. Swaine, of the Rifle Brigade.
[849] Colonel Frederick Gustavus Burnaby (1842-1885) was an English traveller and soldier. He died on 17 January 1885 in the hand-to-hand fighting of the Battle of Abu Klea, during the Sudan Campaign to rescue General Charles Gordon from Khartoum, of which Lord Wolsely was in charge.

Florence, Italy

8 March 1885 - Sunday

Herbert met me at the station. I could see no difference in him from when I went away, but he is very happy and looked delighted. We went to the Hotel Grande Bretagne. Anna met us in the doorway, looking fresh and nice. Bathed and changed and breakfast, then a short walk with Herbert in the bright sun, and looked at the grand Palazzo Vecchio, and its beautifully decorated columns inside. Saw the fine Loggia dei Lanzi with the admirable Perseus by Benvenuto Cellini, and the pretty Judith by Donatello. Then a glance at the Duomo[850], and Herbert took Anna to Church while I went off to the Uffizzi[851]. Very cold and damp like a tomb. I wandered rather aimlessly about feeling a little disappointed. So long and straggling a gallery, and so ill-adapted for pictures; very badly lighted, and badly arranged. The swell room, the Tribune answering to the Salon Carre of the Louvre, has several uninteresting and to my mind inferior pictures; a really poor Corregio Holy Family, and an academical Raphael of St. John Baptist, besides Riberas and such cattle. The Titians recumbent Venuses were also inferior to those I have seen in Germany. Nor do I care for the weak and feminine statue of Apollo. On the other side, the Wrestlers, the 'Slave Sharpening a Knife' and the Venus de Medici. The Fornarina and the big Andrea del Sarto and the Corregio Madonna praying over the sleeping child are beyond praise. After lunch we all three went to S.M.M. di Puzzi[852] and looked for a long while at the lovely fresco by Perugino of the Crucifixion, of which I have an Arundel copy over the bed in the Lavender room. Then to S. Croce[853] which has a modern, inferior West End of marble. The Campanile I like, but I believe it is not considered very good. Some very good monuments in the Church. Then we walked to S. Miniato[854] where you get a splendid view of Florence, and we saw the David of Michelangelo which I admired, but it seemed too weak in the hips and too fine below the knee. A good pavement in Church and splendid square marble pulpit. Went to dine with Uncle John and Party at their pension. Found them very pleasant and affectionate, but the two elder girls[855][856] have got very plain and carty[857].

---

[850] The Basilica di Santa Maria del Fiore, usually down as The Duomo or Florence Cathedral, is the main church of Florence.
[851] The Uffizi Gallery in Florence is one of the oldest and most famous art museums of the Western world.
[852] Santa Maria Maddalena dei Pazzi, a religious complex in central Florence.
[853] The Basilica di Santa Croce, the largest Franciscan church in the world.
[854] San Miniato al Monte (St. Minias on the Mountain), a basilica in Florence.
[855] The eldest daughter of the Reverend John Lomax Gibbs (1832-1914) ("Uncle John") and Isabel Marianne Bright (1835-1920) was Caroline Blanche Gibbs (1861-1945).
[856] The second eldest daughter was Isabel Alice Gibbs (1862-1942).
[857] He implies 'heavy'.

9 March 1885 - Monday

Went to the Boboli gardens and walked about there some time. There are some fine ilex avenues, but the hilly ground is not suited for the formal French gardening. Then to the Pitti, which I liked better than the Uffizi – so much less trouble to see – handsome rooms opening one out of the other. Two good Raphaels of a Pope and a Cardinal, but it is a ridiculous waste to have a portrait by R. which Rubens or Vandyke would have done at least as well. A delicious little baby by Tiberio Titi and a luminous portrait in armour by Sustemans. Raphaels Madonna del Granduca seemed to me really divine and I liked it far better than the Seggiola or Cardellino, however *securus judicat orbis terrarium*[858]. A perfectly gorgeous Cristofero Allori of 'Judith' in an orange brocade, and the blackhaired head plastered against it. Went to S Maria Novella; a fine Cinnabue and frescoes by Giotto and others. I was interested in the Duomo after knowing Louis Hague's picture. Herbert lost his cane, and we went for a drive in the Cascine – not particularly beautiful.

10 March 1885 - Tuesday

67. John Gibbs & family (1872)
Courtesy of Charles and Primrose Bright of Melbourne, Australia

Went to the Uffizzi in the morning with the others, and enjoyed it much more. My eye having become more educated, I presume, in the last two days. A perfectly lovely Sodoma[859] of St Sebastian in a greyish tone, and a very heavenly Fra Angelico of 'The Virgins Coronation'. One realises here

---
[858] Latin: "Easy to judge the earth for".
[859] The Italian Mannerist painter Giovanni Antonio Bazzi (1477-1549), known as Il Sodoma.

how good Botticelli, Angelico and, in his way, Andrea del Sarto are. Called on the J. Gibbs party, and they talked to me for a long while about Francis[860]. Then Uncle J, Isabel and Francis and I went out for a walk and saw the Baptistry thoroughly with its beautiful gates and frescoes, then the duomo which is undergoing extensive restoration; internally very disappointing, and not worth going into except for the rich old stained glass. Next we went to the Piazza S. Annunciata, and in the Foundling Hospital Chapel saw a splendid altar piece of Don Ghirlandajo – two lovely little holy-innocents adoring the infant Jesus, the colouring extremely rich.

11 March 1885 - Wednesday

St Marks in the morning – a good painted crucifix by Giotto in the Church; in the monastery, a very large crucifixion fresco by Fra Angelico and an interesting 'Last Supper' fresco by Ghirlandajo – especially St. Peter's face, very good. A great many small frescoes by Fra Angelico. Next, to the Capella Ricardi; rich and brilliant decorative frescoes by Benozzo Gozzoli. In the afternoon, again to the Uffizzi and had a good look at the Niobe – a pity the group is broken up. I was delighted to see how well the three modern English portraits – Watts, Millais and Leighton – stood out; to my mind, first-rate works for any age. A very fine portrait of an old man by Carracci and a full length by Moroni with a Latin motto struck me especially. The colouring of some of Filippino Lippi's is very gorgeous, but not half the feeling of Fillippo.

Tea at the John Gibbs in the evening; took them some sweets, tipped Francis, and said goodbye.

12 March 1885 - Thursday

Looked into a lot of shops but didn't buy anything. Saw the Medicean Chapel[861] – heavy, coloured marble, good proportions – but didn't much care for it. In adjoining chapel, fine statue of a soldier 'Il pensiero' by Michel Angelo. Then to the Pitti[862] again, which I do like. Had a long look at the Seggiola, and the Murillo 'Madonna and Child', and at a splendid Rubens portrait of Duke of Buckingham. Herbert tried to pass off a large Salvator Roas as a Claude on me; it was very bright and clean, and the finest S.R. I have ever seen. It is good, but it is too much like S.R. – which gave me some kudos. After lunch we went to the Academia degli belle arte[863] where there is Michel Angelo's David and some important pictures

---

[860] Francis Lomax Gibbs (1869-1943), 6th child (4th son) of Reverend John Lomax Gibbs ("Uncle John") and Isabel Marianne Bright.
[861] The Medici Chapels are two structures at the Basilica of San Lorenzo, Florence, built in the 16th and 17th centuries to celebrate the Medici family, patrons of the church and Grand Dukes of Tuscany.
[862] The Palazzo Pitti is a very large mainly Renaissance palace in Florence, situated on the south side of the River Arno.
[863] The Accademia di Belle Arti ("Academy of Fine Arts") is an art academy in Florence.

of Botticelli, Lippo Lippi and Fra Angelico. I enjoyed it very much. We all dined at the restaurant at 6, and left together about 7.30.

London, via Paris

13 March 1885 - Friday

Reached Bologna last night at 12, and said goodbye to Herbert and Anna. Had some *café au lait*, and started again. No sleeping berth, but got through the night pretty comfortably. Travelling all day, and read a beastly realistic novel 'Fille de Fille'[864].

14 March 1885 - Saturday

Reached Paris 8am, and not finding myself tired in spite of continuous travelling decided after Breakfast to go on to Calais. Read Professor Seeley's 'Expansion of England'[865], and found it very interesting and instructive, written in a tone of cold good sense, no enthusiasm at all, but very timely warning that we cannot stand still but must go forward or back. A roughish passage – I wasn't ill. Reached London 6pm, and I am thankful to say found Father, Mother, and the rest, well.

Here ends 19 months' diary. I shall now be too busy to keep one.

---

[864] 'Fille de Fille', by Jules Guérin.
[865] 'Expansion of England', by Professor John Robert Seeley, published 1883.

From Guano to Gold: The Diary and Letters of Vicary Gibbs from 1883-5

Letters

When Antony Gibbs & Sons were eventually taken over by HSBC in the late 20th century, the vaults of its London office were cleared of piles of documents and boxes of old, hand-written business letters. A few records were scattered and lost to researchers hoping to make sense of the forces driving the new economies of early British colonial development, but fortunately many valuable documents did find their way to the Gibbs' archive in London's Guildhall, and others were copied and given to Melbourne University for their Bright family collection.

These letters had originally been sent between the colonial Houses and the London head office. Among others of interest was a comprehensive correspondence between Vicary Gibbs and his eldest brother and senior partner Alban Gibbs, written while Vicary was in Australia from October 1883 until November 1884, after which he left for England by way of the coffee-blight crisis in Ceylon. Our better understanding of company plans for future growth and the solution to the Ceylon problem would have been helped by later 'copy book' letters which presumably existed, but I was unable to find them. We can only hope that they may still be carefully kept somewhere.

At least we do now have a clearer idea of the time Vicary spent scrutinising the management and operation of each business in the colonial houses of the 1880s, a decade marred in Australia by periods of economic depression. Read alone, the Diary is an enjoyable and informative account: a good 'cover' for the complex purposes of his visit. Social contacts were made, and interesting personalities revealed. If an acquaintance was of use as a source of business or information, Vicary and his colleagues assessed his value. Success in commerce was an all-important background for a young man with ambition in those early days, all the more so if he appeared to be gentlemanly. When read in conjunction with these letters the journal does help to explain some of the influences already present which drove economic development. They were often a by-product of the ambition to create, by supply and demand, more comfortable middle-class living standards in the new Australia.

Henry Hucks Gibbs to Tyndall Bright

In 1880, Antony Gibbs & Sons took over Bright's Liverpool business and wrote to Tyndall, the senior partner, to explain and confirm their future policy for the 'new' partnership.

Private

Nov. 8th, 1880

My dear Tyndall,

I now send you a memorandum of the basis on which we may carry out your proposal that we should take over and absorb your House and its branches.

You will think that they look very tyrannical and dreadful when set out in black and white, but we find, and you will find, that a benevolent despotism is, in practice, a very tolerable sort of government to live under. But as it is apt to be supportable just in proper time as its authority is understood and recognised, it is better to set it out squarely before people who are not bound to live under its splendour unless they please.

Such as it is, we have all lived under it. My Uncle Charles Crawley[866], Hayne, Davy[867], myself, George and Sillem[868] and all our partners on this Coast and very pleasant living we have found it. Of course there will BE a regular Partnership deed, and there will be also many things to settle which I have not particularised in setting down.

[Remainder of letter missing]

---

[866] Charles Crawley (1788-1871), one of the eight children of Reverend Charles Crawley and Mary Gibbs, and brother of Henry Hucks Gibbs' mother, Caroline Crawley. He was a partner in Antony Gibbs & Sons from 1820 to 1838.
[867] Possibly George Thomas Davy. A man of that name is mentioned as one of the defendants (along with William Gibbs, Henry Hucks Gibbs, George Louis Monck Gibbs, Charles Edward Stubbs, Augustus Sillem and George Baden Crawley) in the 1868 case "Ross v Gibbs".
[868] Augustus (Charles Herman?) Sillem: a partner in Antony Gibbs & Sons.

Angus McPherson (Amby) to Bright, Chrystal & Co. (Melbourne)

This business-like letter from Angus MacPherson was a late arrival among photocopies to be transcribed. Although we are only able to make an educated guess as to its date, there are several interesting points covered, including the impact of the 1884 Land Act on Run holders. Severe weather conditions such as drought and flood impacted on costs - the need for substitute fodder, for example - and had to be factored into the economic plans made by estate owners and managers. Government inspectors had to be accommodated and dealt with diplomatically, and the professional skills of the superintendent were the best advertisement for the quality product in animal husbandry.

[Unknown date][869]

Messrs. Bright, Chrystal & Co., Melbourne

Gentlemen,

Enclosed please find forms of application to bring Runs under the provisions of the Crown Lands Act of 1884.

I wrote to Messrs. Gibbs, Bright & Co. of Brisbane for these forms intending to have sent them in myself, but they advise me that unless I hold a power from you to sign them that it would be as well to fill them in and send them to you for signature and thus as there is no time to lose I send them to you at once, as I am further advised that as it is proposed to get Parliament to alter some of the conditions it is advisable to put in our application at once.

Messrs. Gibbs, Bright further say that Messrs. Morehead & Co. advise your saying nothing about how you wish the Run divided in your application.

They say that when the commissioner visits us, to see how we propose to divide them, if his idea coincides with ours well and good but if not, then to do our best to get them to alter his idea - it to assimilate as near ours as possible.

---

[869] The date of this letter is unknown, but must have been 1884 or later (as it refers to the Crown Lands Act of 1884).

I have fastened each of the sets of application together as I would like you to apply for them as three different runs, as I think we would do best by doing this.

Bullocks[870]

I wired you the other day that Messrs. Bell and Dangar had bought our bullocks and that I intended starting to muster at once.

It will take us four or five weeks to [get] the bullocks together, but I hope we will be able to make a good muster of them.

It is fortunate that such a strong firm as Messrs. Bell and Dangar have bought the bullocks as there need be no fear about the bill although I have written to Morehead and told them that the bill must be remitted to Messrs. Gibbs, Bright and Co. of Brisbane for approval.

Other matters on the station go on much in the same way as when I wrote you, there is no grass for the horses and therefore we are compelled to feed all those we are working, and the myall is keeping the sheep all right.

Yours faithfully,

(Sgd)

Angus McPherson.

I forgot to say that the forms will have to be signed before a J.P. of Queensland.

---

[870] Four years later, an article from the Western Star and Roma Advertiser (28 July 1888) reports on a cattle show: "The cattle sections were not so well filled, those that were shown did not appear in very good showing condition, although the breeding was quite up to the mark. The champion bull shown by Messrs. Bright Chrystal &c. of Amby Downs was a fine beast and no exception could have been taken to the award of the judges in this class. In the Durhams, for the best three heifers Messrs Bright Chrystal and Co. of Amby were the fortunate victors, beating Messrs Elliot Lethbridge and Elliot's which were also a very nice lot of cattle. This is the first year Amby Downs has shown these cattle, and Mr. McPherson's present success should certainly induce him to exhibit more largely in the cattle sections next year."

Letter #1 from Vicary Gibbs (Sydney) to his brother Alban

Vicary Gibbs was sent to Australia and New Zealand in 1883 by the partners to inspect their Houses in the various, established, centres of trade. He communicated by letter with his brother Alban in the City of London office and by cable, using a pre-arranged code as was the practice in those days. For future reference, Vicary numbered his letters to Alban and to his father Henry Hucks Gibbs, but some of these numbered letters were missing from the copies I was able to read. Some, too, were damaged or smudged by the copying process, and have been difficult to decipher. Vicary wrote letters #1 and #2 to Alban on his arrival first in Sydney, and then in Melbourne, with the later letters #3 and #4 outlining the business situation and giving his preliminary impressions.

23rd October 1883 - Sydney

No. 1

My dear Alban,

I arrived here on Sunday 21st. and take the opportunity of the P&O Mail going out today and write you a line although naturally I have not much to tell you about business at present.

They were all much surprised to see me here, as they thought I was quite decided to go through New Zealand. I had better have telegraphed from Auckland, however it is of no consequence.

I was under the impression that I had left it quite open before leaving England as to which I should do. It was not good enough to knock about seeing scenery by myself and I found no suitable person disposed to accompany me, also I thought Charles Bright would be very glad of my early appearance.

I have received very kind letters from him and Regi, and the latter has asked me to stay with him at St. Leonards. I shall leave here on Monday next for Melbourne.

Mr Hart is here just now but returns to Brisbane at the end of the week. He expects a very good clip from Amby and says they have got through their shearing without rain and have since had some nice rains. He speaks in highest terms of Keating and to the way he has managed in his absence; he seems to have acted with great tact and firmness, and Hart is very anxious to keep him permanently in Brisbane but I fear F.A.K. won't stand a Queensland summer.

They are frightfully overcrowded in these premises; I have seen the new site which is a very fine one but I have no time to write at large on this or any other matter today but I will put a regular letter on the stocks tomorrow and hope to write you fully and regularly while in the Colonies. I will send copies to Tyndall. I should like to hear about Strauss & copper. They are getting hold of a capital sugar business here, getting large quantities and selling it freely. I am very much pleased to see it.

Your affect. brother Vicary Gibbs.

Letter #2 from Vicary Gibbs (Sydney) to his brother Alban

24th, 25th, 26th October 1883 - Sydney

No. 2

My dear Alban,

I last wrote to you yesterday No. 1.

Tower. He seems a very pleasant gentlemanly fellow and Murray is very well satisfied with him. He was I hear quite indignant at some suggestion which was made a little while back to move him to one of the other Houses. I daresay you were surprised at my using S.A. code[871] to cable my arrival in good health but as I had it in my trunk and it was Sunday I made use of it not wishing to delay till I could get the other. From what Hart says I believe that all the Amby wool is coming forward washed which is a pity as if I remember right you wanted some of it at any rate, 'in the grease'.

New Premises. The site is a very good one nearer the Circular Quay than this and very close to the Exchange. I should think quite a picked place for a House of Business though at present most of the important buildings are higher up Pitt St. and round about our present site. There are still some mean little two storied shops and houses about the new site owing

---

[871] S.A. - probably "South Australia". The "code" is mentioned several times in the letters and diary with no explanation. It is presumably either a relatively simple letter substitution cipher, or a more complex code using for example numbers for key phrases. It is not known whether Gibbs' code was to reduce the length of expensive telegraph messages, or for security (or both).

to some difficulty about Trust Estates but these must very soon disappear. Of course the price paid is very high – £200 a foot frontage but there is a very good depth, 130ft. and though we may see a temporary depreciation in value at some time, I have no doubt the purchase is all right. I believe land in George St. has been sold as high as £900 a foot frontage.

I have seen the architect who has prepared various designs; the one he recommended is a little like Baring's new office. It is in brown Sydney stone for the ground floor and red brick above, 4 stories, long windows, and the building relieved by flat pillars running down; it has a large gable something like the building on the Embankment just west of the Temple so that you can't see the roof from the street. It is proposed to build on the land that Regi has bought at the same time and in the same style which would very much improve the appearance and would save expense in the party wall. The building is not very beautiful but it is plain and not meretricious or in bad taste and would, I believe, be reasonably cheap. It has not however found favour at all with the Brights who for some reason desire stucco which would be more expensive, liable to require repair and generally undesirable to my mind. At their request Mr Wardell has prepared two beastly pseudo classic plans for a stucco front which I shall try and persuade them to give up. It seems possible there may be some little difficulty in getting good foundations as an old stream[872] used to run under part of the building.

68. Circular Quay, Sydney (1880-1910)
National Library of Australia, nla.pic-vn3700021

Of course it will be desirable to start the new building as soon as possible and I hope to see it up before I leave Australia. I don't suppose you will require to have the plans sent over for your approval as it would cause 3 months delay.

Sugar business. They seem to have worked up quite a large business in this by sending Medcalf round on that touting tour in the Clarence and Richmond districts; only in one case have they advanced against growing crop; in every other case no money is advanced until the sugar is lodged in our warehouse. They have engaged a sharp sugar clerk and have been obtaining very good prices from the up country growers. In fact it is worked on precisely the same basis as the flour which as you know

---

[872] The old 'Tank Stream'.

Arthur[873] started and has proved a success. Of course a certain number of bad debts are made especially among the bakers but this is well covered by debenture and as they have about 200 baker constituents the risk is well distributed: they estimate that in the first half of this year they sold more than 1/4 of all the flour sold in Sydney and the suburbs. Medcalf has again made a second trip among the sugar planters and is now engaged in it. He is at the same time endeavouring to get maize sent down to us in Sydney for sale in the same way; this is principally used for horse feed.

When the new premises are built I suppose this branch will be employing about £80,000 capital. I see Cave of Fiji account is down to £2000 and I understand in a few months it will be down to £1,500, which was the amount of indebtedness he was to be allowed.

Young George Arthur is a very ordinary young fellow with no presence or manner tho' I daresay a very good clerk. Hart tells me that Ch. Bright suggested G.A. going up to Brisbane but Hart declined as he did not consider him competent to talk to and receive people properly; very likely as he gets older he will improve in this.

Hart seems a jolly old fellow and has got over his dangerous illness wonderfully, and at the same time he seems very anxious to have a competent second who would be ultimately fit to take his place. He says that Southerden would never do for this as though very good and faithful he is too blunt in his manner and cranky. I think you could not do wrong to lay down another young fellow for if he is any good he is sure to be able to be used at once. Perhaps it might be well to look at that young fellow Balteel whom Tom Baring recommended, and if you liked him, have him trained.

Merivale seems to be taking an active interest in the business and to be thinking a great deal how to open or develop our trade in the staple products of the colony, wheat, flour, maize, copper, coal, which are certainly much more worthy of attention than the cedar pencil and cigar holder sort of thing.

In all probability within 2 years N.S.Wales will be exporting wheat and it will be most desirable to get hold of that business. Our present large and increasing connection with the millers whose flour we now sell will give us an excellent start in getting hold of it[874].

---

[873] This Mr. Arthur is probably the same one who Gibbs meets later in the Dunedin office. He is probably related to (probably the father or uncle of) "young George Arthur" mentioned later in this letter.
[874] It is interesting that this drive increasing the export of grain gives lie to the prediction by Major Sir George Gipps (1791-1847), governor of New South Wales from 1838 to 1846, in

Wine business. The salesman has just sold a lot of Hart's Port which has caused me to have a talk about this and the beer and spirits. As you know we don't do very much in them and indeed it is impossible to do so unless we engaged an expert who really knew and understood the difference between good and bad liquor, and who would go about among the hotels and public houses and get in with them. We have I fancy a reputation in Sydney for selling rather rubbish in some of these lines and it is not likely that we can really compete well with wine merchants who devote their whole attention and knowledge to the matter. There are still several lots of whiskey belonging to Bright Bros. unsold and which is almost impossible to clear. It is impossible to do every kind of business and there are so many other kinds more pleasant and satisfactory to develop that I do not see any object in pushing wine and spirits.

Mr Ronald. He appears a nice intelligent young Scotchman. He is, you will remember Bow McLochlan's[875] salesman. He is said however to be almost entirely without business experience. He has been travelling in northern N.S.Wales and Queensland and obtained a few small orders. He considers there is a prospect of doing business in time but the older and better sugar machinery firms are well represented so it is uphill work.

During the first 8 months of this year Boko[876] has netted £3000; the Cadell, £1000, and the Wharf £1,500, and the other Brisbane accounts look well so far as can be seen at present. That branch should do at least as well this year as last. Young Cook has now recovered his health and is working Cowan's business well and to Murray's satisfaction. He seems intelligent and without his brother's[877] bumptious assurance. The old stocks are gradually being worked off but the Sydney buyers are not speculative and it is not easy to get them to take more than they want for immediate requirements even if a considerable discount is offered.

New South Wales Copper. I am going to look very closely into this and report to you about the mines, production, quality. etc. It would I think be very desirable business for this branch to get copper for shipment. Under advance and with this object it might be well to put Merivale on the board of one of the mines. The Sydney House might find the money for the Director's qualification and I do not see any objection to such a course

---

the 1830s that Australia would soon be unable to produce adequate food for its own growing population let alone the export market.
[875] From newspaper adverts of 1884 we know that Gibbs, Bright, & Co. were agents for Bow, McLachlan & Co. who sold sugar-making machinery and marine engines.
[876] Boko and Cadell were Gibbs Bright river tugs in Brisbane.
[877] James Cook.

provided there was no liability beyond the few shares that had to be bought.[878]

Tallow. Could you give orders in London for this? The Sydney House is very well in with the men who control the tallow here. Please look into this.

'Flotilla Australia'. E. & A. Co. Line[879]. I have been over this wharf and premises today and found everything in very good order and well kept, the ships stores no more than enough for absolute requirements and everything looking all right in the engine room. The recent accident to the 'Catterthun'[880] seems to have satisfied Murray that the iron of which the Coy's Ships have been built is not of good quality. As the same builders are being employed for the new ones it might be well to give Tideman a jog on this point.

I am leaving Sydney today Oct.27th.Saturday and will therefore finish my letter today relating to Sydney matters and begin another when I get to Melbourne.

Your affectionate brother, Vicary Gibbs.

Letter #3 from Vicary Gibbs (Melbourne) to his brother Alban

2nd November 1883 - Melbourne

36 Flinders Lane West

No. 3

My dear Alban,

I last wrote to you from Sydney, No. 2. Oct. 24th. I arrived here on Tuesday the 30th. of Oct. and find everything going on satisfactorily.

Melbourne Premises. The offices here strike one as dark and clumsily built, great heavy upright timbers like the 'tween decks in a sailing ship. The first floor has all been remodelled to give further office accommodation and the books have been moved up there, while the

---

[878] At this time Antony Gibbs and Sons had 'lost' their share of copper from South American mines.
[879] Eastern and Australian Steamship Company Ltd., formerly known as the E&A Line.
[880] The S.S. Catterthun, which steamed for Sydney on 6th. August 1880 with 99 passengers and mixed cargo, hit a reef at 2.25am at full speed. 55 people died.

samples have retreated to the 3rd. floor. Reg. wants to add a 4th. story and no doubt with reason tho' I have not gone into this question yet or understood why it is immediately requisite. A new staircase has been added to connect the first and ground floor.

I have been talking a great deal about a permanent second in Brisbane and enclose you copy of a letter I have written to Keating on the subject. I do not see how we can well fill the place on this side as Keating and Hannay are wanted here. Merivale is doing very well in Sydney where I think he is very useful and neither Lorimer or Tower have at present shown sufficient ability. This disposes of the new entries and to put any of the clerks from here or Sydney over Southerden's head would cause jealousy and ill feeling. Hart mentioned to me that Hannay had told him of a man who he thought would do. As I have had a chat with Hannay on the subject the following are the particulars. The man's name is Bell; he is a Scotchman, a gentleman by birth and education. His father[881] was a Free Church clergyman and his Uncle on the mother's[882] side is a Sir Andrew Agnew[883] who is I understand a well-known landowner in Wigtownshire. He is aged about 36. He was a partner in J.M.Robertson & Co., Colombo, Baring's agents, when Hannay was manager under him. He was no relation of any member of the firm and had his own way to make there; before he had an interest in the profits they paid him £1000 p.a.[884] so they must have thought him a valuable man. Hannay says he has any amount of work in him and he considered him about the best businessman in Ceylon. He is now in Colombo but under notice to leave under the circumstances mentioned in his letter to Hannay, which you will find enclosed. The Barings know about him especially Edward but he has rather swaggering haw-haw sort of manner which Hannay fancies may have set Ed. Baring rather against him.

The above account seemed to me on the whole to be so satisfactory that I told Hannay he might reply to Bell to this effect: that if he was coming to London of his own accord he might call on you who would see him; and if enquiries about him proved satisfactory and he was prepared to accept a modest salary to begin with you could engage him to come out here to the Colonies for whichever of our Houses he might be wanted for. I told Hannay to add that there was a risk of your having filled up the vacancy in the mean time, but all the same there is such a demand for good men

---

[881] Reverend Thomas Blizzard Bell (1815-1866).
[882] Agnes Agnew (1825-1893).
[883] Sir Andrew Agnew, 8th Baronet (1818–1892) was appointed Deputy Lieutenant of Wigtownshire in 1843 and Vice Lord Lieutenant in 1852. From 1856 to 1868 he was the MP for Wigtownshire. One of his sisters was Agnes Agnew (1825-1893) who married Reverend Thomas Blizzard Bell and had five children, the second of whom was George Frederick Bell.
[884] Using cost of living comparison based on the Retail Price Index, £1000 in 1883 would be worth slightly over £80,000 today.

that if he turns up and you like him I could engage him anyway, put him through the same sort of course as Hannay and send him out.

Of course I have been very careful not to compromise you in the least, but Hannay is so strong about Bell's good tone and capability, that I shall be pleased if he does go to London and give you the chance of getting him. I don't know what his views about salary may be but if you could engage him on a 3 years agreement, - 6, 7, or 800 p.a. - I should say that would be very good.

Mr Murray Robertson, Director of the Chartered Mercantile Bank knows Bell, but as you will see from Bell's letter he does not wish his affairs talked about so you would not speak to Robertson until you had seen Bell.

Previous to going to Ceylon Bell was seven years in Manchester and must therefore have a good knowledge of soft goods. I send you a press copy of the letter which Hannay has written to Bell and hope you will approve. Of course I talked the matter over thoroughly with the Brights.

London Directory. If you have got a couple of decent Directories in the London office not required, send them out here; there is nothing in this office since 1860.

Charles Bright has not yet fixed anything about his time for leaving, but of course he quite understands that he is at liberty to do so as soon as ever he thinks it desirable, and no doubt he will be off before long.

Adelaide. Meeks seems to be doing exceedingly well and I shall probably pay him a visit in about a fortnight's time.

Nicholls has been buying a certain amount of wool at the Sales: in a letter of the 21st. of Aug. to me Herbert complains to me that Nicholls did not know the charges on wool between London and Roubaix[885] though he had booked an order on a fixed limit. I spoke to N. about this and he says that he knows them now that they are 25/6 per ton.

Mexican Railway. I should like to hear about this; also general information about stocks and shares in which we are interested.

Telegrams re Fisher's[886] Loan. I am rather surprised that you did not understand 'with money in hand' to mean that they had become possessed of fresh funds since their previous statement that the Tool

---

[885] Roubaix, a town in the north-east of France about 10 miles north-east of Lille.
[886] Charles Brown Fisher (1818-1908), a grazier who became one of the biggest pastoralists in Australia.

funds were exhausted: I certainly don't think "Robertson £10,000" was sufficiently clear.

I hope you sold the 'Great Britain' cargo to arrive soon after you had bought it.

I remain your affect, brother, Vicary Gibbs.

Enclosures: Bell to Hannay. Press copies Keating to me, Self to Keating, Murray to me, Hannay to Bell, Merivale to me, Charles Bright to me.

P.S. As the Pacific Co. have sold their boats to the Orient Co. there no longer seems any special reason for the Lpool House holding the P.C. shares and if it is true as reported here that they have had a sharp rise they might as well be sold.

Letter #4 from Vicary Gibbs (Melbourne) to his brother Alban

16th November 1883 - Melbourne

No. 4

My dear Alban,

My last letter to you No. 3. was dated Nov. 2nd. and I have since received yours of Oct. 5th.

I think the Sydney land will be a capital speculation and as the Brights borrowed the money on Mortgage at 6% and as I understood Catty Bright and Antony have both put money into it, it won't be such a heavy lock-up of the House capital. My idea is to build a good four-storied building on the whole frontage capable of being separated or used together and then we can either sell half right out or - what I should like better - let on a 21 years lease to Government the 3rd. and 4th. stories of both buildings for their clerks and writers and the Ground and First floor of the Brights half to another merchant for 3 years or on a yearly agreement. I think this would be quite feasible for I believe the Government are very much in want of offices, and it would enable us, if the Sydney business extends, to get suitable premises. There is no doubt that we shall be able to let at a respectable profit on our outlay and we shall have as good merchants offices as anybody in Sydney, and as you know it is very hard to get offices there.

Bell. You will have been amused at the coincidence of our both having been laying for the same man from different quarters of the globe. I see you say Keating would not be such a fool as to think that Bell could be obtained for much less than £800, £900 and £1000 but you will see from my letter that I was such a fool and Hannay and the Brights fall under the same condemnation. As Merivale, Hannay and Keating are all now doing so very well I was anxious if possible not to put any one distinctly over their head and thought you might certainly have tried 6, 7, and 8. If you have not fixed anything definitely before receipt of this or committed yourself in any way I hope you will try and get him on a 3 years agreement for £800 p.a. without any advance being promised during that time. I feel that since he is entirely out of employment he will not refuse this.

You will see from the enclosed correspondence that Keating can't stand the Brisbane heat any more for the present, so Hannay will start on Monday to relieve him, and though H. only goes nominally for 3 months, my idea is that if he settles down well there and Hart keeps his health, to leave him there and take Bell in here rather than make a fresh shuffle on Bell's arrival. You will of course impress on Bell that he is only coming to Melbourne for orders and not to a direct post.

Ships to load. What does Tyndall mean by saying "We carefully avoided any guarantee as regards the 'Winifred'; there was no objection to your loading a ship between the 'Holmesdale' and her"? The facts were that the 'Winifred' was such a long while out at sea that we had loaded the 'Holmesdale' and were badly in want of another ship and had a lot of our own wool to go which we were obliged to give to other ships; for instance we gave 1000 bales to the 'Normanton' and 1700 bales to the 'South Australia'. On the 21st Aug. we asked by cable if we might fix a ship between the 'Holmesdale' and 'Winifred' and on Sept. 3rd received answer "Must not do so unless despatched before arrival 'Winifred'". This is wretched management, we were prevented from taking up a ship, as if we had we should have run a risk of a repetition of the 'Soukar'. It is far better to leave us to take up all the ships on this side than to make such arrangements as they have done in this case.

Fisher. I am sorry you advanced that extra £15,000 to Fisher as we had got all his wool already but I suppose you did not understand this.

Ellis. I am glad you did not take up this business.

Ciphers for shipping sovereigns. This is attended to in a telegraph letter going forward by this mail.

Brisbane Wharf new purchase. I have carefully read the correspondence and had a talk with Hart when in Sydney, but not knowing the spot my opinion is of little value; I feel however strongly disposed in favour of a scheme which Hart, Keating and the Brights are all equally anxious to see carried out, and as they seem to consider it essential for the keeping together and development of our Brisbane shipping business, I do not think we ought to refuse it owing to the outlay of £15,000 which will be required in all. We are expecting a cable from you on this subject and should it be in the negative I shall at once run down to Brisbane and personally inspect the place. I see however in the Liverpool letter that we have permission to spend £5000 on this project so I hardly suppose the other £10,000 will make any difference.

Charles says nothing about his return but he fully understands that you are anxious to have him as soon as he can get away.

Lpool P.S. no. 65 Sydney Premises. I see Tyndall speaks of our sending plans home of the 3rd. story for you to decide whether you should have one but I feel so certain that this ought to be that I don't want to make a certain loss of money by delaying making the contract for the building for three months unnecessarily; as I said before offices are let in Sydney as fast as they can be built.

Barnard Lee. You will find him a prosy bore but an anxious, hard working, methodical man.

Copper from Sydney. I do not know of course how you had been getting rid of your old stocks or what humour you have been in for speculating and as it seemed a particularly favourable moment for buying in Sydney I sent you a cable. The mine were asking for tenders. The last successful tender had been £60.5.0, a drop of £2.5.0 on the tender before and we were able to get nominal freight The Sydney calculation was that buying at £60.5.0 we could lay down in London at £62.0.0. Chile bars at the same time being quoted at £65.4.0. If you had given us authority we should have tendered somewhere under the last tender say £60.0.0 and the copper would have stood you in very cheap. As it happened the mine did not accept any of the tenders so I suppose they were very low. Please let us know, or rather let Sydney know, if it is worth while for them to cable you on this subject when they can get cheap freight and there seems a good opportunity to buy for any other London firm when you are not in the market.

Your affectionate brother, Vicary Gibbs.

Enclosures: Letter F.A.K. to me.
Copy letter self to F.A.K.

Copy letter by Vicary Gibbs: [illegible word] and Great Britain [illegible word]. Must call to mind any money of importance which can be said to be sunk. I don't know any investment in Australia since I came into business that, up to the present date, has turned out ill. We cabled you that I could easily go to Brisbane and inspect and cable you a report but personally I do not suppose you would care for my opinion having all the facts put most fully before you.

I am very much interested from Herbert the new arrangements for working the SA[887] business and await the news as to how the parties affected take your decision.

Since writing the above we have had your cable which says that the Kangaroo proposal is absolutely declined either by you or the British India[888] with a proposition for them to buy a wharf as it would have been suicidal having regard to our interests as Eagle St. wharfingers.

Vicary Gibbs (Sydney) to Charles Bright

Vicary Gibbs announces his arrival in Sydney to Charles Bright in the Melbourne office.

24th October 1883 - Sydney

My dear Charles,

I arrived yesterday morning after a very pleasant journey and today in the middle of a long talk with Murray and Hart your kind and welcoming telegram arrived.

My present idea is to stay here a week and reach Melbourne on Tuesday but I shall hear from you what you think best and will do whatever you wish. I am looking forward to shaking hands with you and Regi.

Yours very sincerely, Vicary Gibbs.

Everything seems brisk, busy and satisfactory in this office. I am much pleased with the new site.

---

[887] South American.
[888] British-India Steam Navigation Company.

Frank Keating (Brisbane) to Vicary Gibbs

Frank Keating, in Brisbane, is surprised to hear of Vicary's 'early' arrival, and welcomes him to Australia.

26th October 1883 - Brisbane

My dear Vicary,

You astonish me. I pictured you about now, smoking cigarettes in the hot springs of Rotorua. Have you passed by N.Z. and come straight on to Sydney? Anyway I am delighted you are here. Hart writes that he will be back on Monday (the 29th) and I think soon after that I may get south again. I've been up here 5 months now and it's getting most infernally hot. I shan't be keen on remaining longer than my services are required. I am very glad Hart expresses himself satisfied with my performance. He's such a thoroughly good fellow it's a pleasure to have anything to do with him.

It's 'Chip' who writes to you. He is perfectly mad, poor devil, and in the worst stage of Syphilis which he refuses to treat. He has written me a series of perfectly insane letters. H[889] couldn't afford to buy his passage[?][890] and if you feel inclined I will go halves with you in giving him a £20 passage home.

What do you think of Sydney? I think it far and away the finest city in Australia. Melbourne is so very unequal and the streets are far too wide for the buildings while this place is simply a big village. However the Club at Melbourne is first rate and you will find yourself thoroughly comfortable there. You will just be in time for the grand festive season of Australia which culminates in the Melbourne Cup. I don't think I should back 'Le Grand' if I were you. There is a Ball at Government House Melbourne on Saturday 10th and no end of private entertainments.

I shall be thundering glad to see you again. Till which time I remain your affectionate FAK.
P.S. I would suggest merely a free passage for Chip. If he has money he will merely dissipate it and not go home at all. I have given him money and he merely spends it at once and demands more.

---

[889] Hart, presumably.
[890] The words "afford to buy his passage" are a guess, as the text of the original letter is unreadable.

Vicary Gibbs (Melbourne) to Frank Keating

Vicary Gibbs' reply, from Melbourne, to Keating, whose letter had eventually been forwarded from Sydney.

1st November 1883 - Melbourne

My dear Frank,

Many thanks for your letter of 26th Oct. I came straight on to Sydney as I was tired of knocking about by myself and wanted to get back to work. I hope to be on this side of the globe for at least 18 months so I shall have plenty of time to visit New Zealand later on.

Your letter was forwarded on to me here as I left Sydney last Saturday by the 'John Elder'.

'Chip' I am happy to say got his passage money lent to him or given by somebody else, which relieves us from any responsibility in the matter. I asked Murray to try and get some employment for the younger brother, who looked a steady, healthy young man, or something of the kind. I also wrote to Cocky[891] telling him what had passed. Hart as you know is very anxious to keep you in Brisbane which is no doubt flattering but no one would wish you to run any risk of injuring your health and as soon as you find the heat too much you must come down south here. The fact is I have been talking a good deal with Hart and the Brights about who should help H. in Brisbane as it is essential there should be someone. Hannay's name has been mentioned but he is just getting hold of the Melbourne work and Reg Bright does not want to let him go if he can help it. I have heard a very good account of a Ceylon man[892] who I think would be just the thing and I am writing to the London office suggesting him[?][893] or someone else, but of course this will take time as even if he were immediately engaged he would have to be a couple of months in L'pool to see the view of the business. What therefore I want you to do is to be as much in Brisbane as you can for the next 9 months until we get a man to replace you which we will endeavour to do as quickly as possible.

---

[891] Probably George Edward Cokayne (originally George Edward Adams), mentioned elsewhere in the diary.
[892] Bell.
[893] The words "office suggesting him" are a guess, as the text of the original letter is unreadable.

You see I don't see anyone to fill the gap except you and Hannay, and as you have picked up knowledge of the shipping business and been very successful with it, you seem much the more suitable.

You understand my proposal:- come away when you find it too hot, stay over 2 months or whatever is requisite to set you up here and recruit you and then go back till we replace you, - or this at any rate would be best for the business, but you must be the judge as to how far you can stand a tropical climate. Let me hear from you soon about this and any other matter of business interest,

and believe me, Yours affectionately,

Vicary Gibbs.

George Merivale (Sydney) to Vicary Gibbs (Melbourne)

George Merivale, recently married (and related to Gibbs by his sister's Tyntesfield marriage), wrote to Vicary in Melbourne to report on his assessment of the Sydney House.

26th November 1883 - Sydney

My dear Vicary,

I have not written for some time on general subjects. Simpson has been away unwell for some days and I have had as much as I could do to keep up with the work without looking much ahead. Everything goes on satisfactorily and I have not many suggestions to offer.

Copper. I am sorry the London House could not do anything in this and am afraid if they do begin trying Australian Copper, it will be with the S.A.[894] brands, Wallaroo and Parrearra[895][?].

Cobar[896] is chiefly known in Calcutta. In this latter business we are much hampered by the difficulty of getting through freight per P.&O. with trans shipment at Colombo. I have therefore proposed to S.A. that they should allow us to ship <u>via</u> London and have been sounding the P.&O. agent here as to whether his company will name through rates in this way for regular

---

[894] South Australian.
[895] The name of this copper mine is hard to read, but is most likely to be Parrearra.
[896] Cobar: probably refers to the Great Cobar Copper Mining Company Ltd., established in 1878 after copper was discovered in the Cobar area in 1870.

shipments or from time to time. At present they have made contracts with regular shippers of tin and copper here and are much in their hands but the agent thought it would be quite possible when these contracts fall through and they are able to make other arrangements. You might I think manage something of the sort with the Orient Company and some Calcutta line, or the command of a cheap freight would materially assist you in getting consignments of copper and tin from the companies for sale in London.

Sugar. This is doing well and will be, if we manage well, a permanent business. At present we are much assisted by having plenty of money. Our rivals have to pay them 10% to the bank mostly and so cannot compete on equal terms. But next season we shall no doubt have a rigorous apportion added. I have been thinking it might be a good thing to have some man from the West Indies who thoroughly understands the trade as carried on there and also the manufacture of sugar. Most of the clients are men who have been created by sugar growing. They don't know much about it and it would create a good effect to send a man from time to time travelling among them who could advise them as to making the most of their cane etc.etc. Our present man, Pearson, who is a capital man but he is well acquainted with all the other branches of the sales and there is no doubt that Simpson is overworked and wants his assistance, while at present the sugar takes up the whole of his time. We must increase our sales room staff, and by a good man, so why not have a man from an old sugar country who can teach us something. I have not spoken of this to Murray. You know the West Indian mode of their business and can advise whether it would be a good thing to import it. I am also a little afraid that the sugar business will require a bolder line of action than we are likely to take. The season has been good and in consequence many growers are talking of putting up mills either singly or in clubs. They are seen to come to us for advances on the machinery to enable them to put it up. If they don't get it from us they will get it from the Banks or elsewhere and we shall lose the sugar.

However this won't crop up for a month or two, I think; 'sufficient for the day etc' but it might be useful to you to look ahead and give the Sydney House encouragement to do this business, or not, as you think fit. I doubt whether Murray would do it unless he was directly backed up by the higher prices. We are delighted to have a near prospect of storage at any rate, which will repay itself. In fact a proper store of 3 or 4 stories ought to pay a good rent for the whole premises. I calculate our storage expenses (paid that is by our constituents) will be about £1000 this year and we could easily increase our sum by letting room which we did not want.

Woolpacks etc. Supposing a parcel ordered from G.A. & Co.[897] is thrown up for some <u>fault of ours</u>, and resold at a considerable profit, does this profit belong entirely to us or must we share it with G.A.&Co.? Again, supposing we order cornsacks at their quotation, and see an opportunity of selling at a much more favourable price than we anticipated when we sent the order.

We naturally accept the unexpectedly good offer, and cable for more at the same price to supply our original want. Is this extra profit to be divided with Gillanders or do we get it all and merely send them their 1% com. The case has occurred and wants thinking over though for my own part I don't see any difficulty. G.A.&Co. send us consignments on their own a/c and for all the profit so I see no reason why we should not make all the profit of an order from us. It becomes our adventure and stands on the same footing as their consignments. At the same time this is not the business G.A.&Co. contemplated when they arranged to do it for a small commission. In other words our agreement with them prohibits over-ordering as a rule on our own account or else we shall be reaping the advantages of their cutting price down to a much greater extent than they and perhaps spoiling the trade we eventually hope to make by not giving the full advantage of the low price. And though in the case mentioned I think the profit should belong to us because it is unexpected and out of the normal run of business there is I think no doubt but that we should together take advantage of the present state of things and obtain what firm orders we can at 8/- or over for cornsacks, place them at Calcutta at G.A.'s quotation of 6/2 and divide the profit.

No doubt the Melbourne people understand all this thoroughly but there seems a little haziness here as to how far our agreement with G.A.&Co. to act on joint a/c as to commission lines us in transactions out of the regular groove.

I like Hannay very much and we had a good deal of talk together over business in general. The system of advancing on plantations etc. in Ceylon strikes me as much more risky than the plans pursued here.

How about starting a tame auctioneer. I don't think we could keep him at work here <u>as yet</u>, but if produce is sold at auction with you in Melbourne as I believe it is, we might help you with N.S.W. commodities.

Affectionately, George Merivale.

---

[897] Gillanders, Arbuthnot & Co.

Vicary Gibbs (Melbourne) to George Merivale (Sydney)

Vicary Gibbs replies to two letters he had had from George Merivale.

27th December 1883 - Melbourne

My dear George,

Thank you for your two letters of the 19th and 22nd. We are all in confusion with these blessed holidays and three mails, - Orient, Frisco, and P.&O. - to read today.

Cowans. The reason for insisting on charging them 2½% for the advance was that you had to make the advance at a time when we particularly wanted the money for another purpose; also they treated us very shabbily for not bearing their share of the 20% we had to pay to Cook. Both the Mr Brights are very strong about not charging less than 2½% and under the circumstances I don't know that it is particularly out of the way. As to altering the £400, £500 or £600 which you are to have, into £500 all round, I don't suppose that as you make an official application to that effect that there is any reason to suppose that it could not be emended. I have not said anything to R.B. about it and if you take my advice you will leave it alone.

Our position with regard to the different roles in the Sydney office is perfectly well established and I think it foolish to compare in your own mind this retainer with yours or to trouble your head whether they do so or not. All you have got to consider is that you have worked creditably and to the satisfaction of all concerned and are now in a position of trust and responsibility. I cannot think that asking the alteration you suggest would strengthen it – indeed that it needs any strengthening. I would gladly endeavour to have it made – I am perfectly aware, as you say, that it is not a question of money, only I think you would do well to follow the legal maxim *'de minimis non curat lex* [?]*'*[898].

Wharfage. I note what you say and am glad to learn that you will have ample means for using the new warehouse. I was only anxious to build mainly what was needful for our own requirements. As to your remark about the policy of building warehouses worth from £100 to £200 per foot, I can only say I fully agree with you, only we never dreamt of doing anything of the kind. Lot 3, on which it is proposed to build the warehouse

---

[898] The last two words of this Latin phrase are unclear, but presumably it reads "De minimis non curat lex" ("The law does not concern itself with trifles").

was at £88 a foot at auction, and I may remind you that the lots immediately behind it are invested to precisely the same purpose by Wilson's, as a company speculation. Of course if Murray's idea of bringing Cowans next door shall be carried out, it would be capital, but I much doubt our being able to arrange it.

Wheat. No doubt when Charles Bright gets to London he will see what can be done in the way of getting you orders for this and other colonial produce.

Irvings. Personally I agree with what you say about this firm and several times put the matter before the home houses. No doubt some day we shall do this work ourselves. I don't suppose with a new arrangement we shall lose the Chip's business as Irvings would still get his return commission.

E&A. It is certainly unfortunate that we can't do better for them in Melbourne but we can't quote to the consignees and if Butterfield and Swire[899] decide cutting like anything on the other side and [illegible word], also undertake to deliver at the wharf which suits consignees as it saves them [illegible word] and they don't get their chests pushed about. Our ships on the other hand are too big to come up the river.

Gibb Livingstone would I believe be willing enough to arrange this if you could satisfy them that it would pay in spite of the somewhat sharp tone you wrote to them about the E&A business.

British India. I think is shown by their pushing the buyer business monthly. I will write home however suggesting that one of the partners should call on Gray Dawes. But of course if you can't do a satisfactory business it's no use keeping the agency. It would not I presume be possible to make any arrangements with a man to try to sell and get orders for you and divide commission.

Wishing your wife and baby well,

I remain yours affectionately, Vicary Gibbs.

---

[899] John Swire and Sons, a Liverpool import-export company, began to trade with China in the 1860s, and in 1866 established Butterfield and Swire (in Shanghai and later Hong Kong) in partnership with R. S. Butterfield. The Swire Group still trades today.

Vicary Gibbs (Adelaide) to Charles Bright

On a visit to Adelaide to assess business and to meet Alfred Meeks, Vicary wrote at length about the venture into wheat and flour, but his letter had to be concluded by Meeks when Gibbs' gout confined him to bed briefly.

4th December 1883 - Adelaide

My dear Charles,

I arrived here all right after a calm passage and have been thinking of and talking about nothing but Winham's ever since. I feel a good deal worried about them, - they are very speculative people. They have sold a large quantity of flour for delivery during the next 5 months and they sold a lot of wheat some time back both [illegible word] being at prices which will in all probability bring them out all right or leave them a profit; but it is not satisfactory to see them gambling right and left. Winham also bought a large quantity of corn sacks both from us and from others on which he will unquestionably make a loss. Yesterday he did not meet his bill which came due in part payment for the corn sacks we sold him and for this we are at the moment unsecured; he told us yesterday that the Bank of Adelaide would find the money if we held over the bill for a day, but when he went to see them the Bank declined to allow him to increase his overdraft.

He has of course a large quantity of capital but it is all locked up in steamers, land, Bank shares, Steam Co. shares etc. and is not available. Last night he put before us a proposal to advance him £30,000[?] against these various properties to enable him to meet his bills to us and to Fannings[900] for corn sacks roughly speaking about £15,000 and pay off or at any rate reduce his banking account. This we should of course have declined but when he came this morning he said he had thought it over and did not consider it would be necessary and proposed that we should advance him £16,000, that is to say 8 more than the little which he has not got[?], he depositing 2,200 bales of corn sacks, which would secure us if they had to be sold as low as 6/1¼ net. I asked him what reason he had to suppose the Bank would not press him to reduce his overdraft in which case we should be having him coming again for further advances; he said there was no chance of this, but I pressed him to go and see the Bank Manager and come to some clear understanding with him on the point and then come and see us again. Meeks and I then went round and saw the Bank Manager and had a confidential talk with him. He repeated his

---

[900] Fanning's - possibly Fanning, Nankivell & Co. (see index entry and footnotes for "Nankivell").

statement that he considered Winham's honesty worth £50,000 but at the same time he seemed cross and discontented with them.

This overdraft is £23,500, - that is £15,000 John Winham & Sons and £8,500 W. Winham & McEllister, - this last account the Manager said the Bank meant to make them pay off though he admitted that the Bank was fully secured for the amount and said the Bank was quite willing to surrender securities fully equal to the value of £8,500. I am afraid it may be necessary for Gibbs Bright & Co to make this further advance of £8000 to Winham's to secure them from loss on the bill which should have been paid yesterday, and as we shall take full powers to sell the corn sacks whenever we think fit, we cannot be out of the £8000 more than 2 months at the outside. Meeks will not have to draw on more than the £6000 already arranged as he has plenty of his bills coming in this month which he can discount. Of course we shall make a small profit in interest on the transaction, and standing by itself I consider it quite a safe one, but I need not say I should not have dreamt of entering into it except that it seemed the only way to secure us from loss on £5,200 till overdue and to keep up Messrs Winham for the moment.

Thinking what was best to be done in this matter has given me a great deal of anxiety and from what I have heard and seen I am quite satisfied that Winham and McEllister are not people with whom it is desirable to do business on so large a scale; at the same time the Bank reports were so favourable that they quite justified Meeks going into the business with them. Indeed they have plenty of money and were it not for over-trading and speculating in produce and sacks they would be in no difficulty whatever as to financing. I don't want to fidget you needlessly and hope it will all come out right and that the London and Adelaide House will make a good commission out of selling the wheat. At the same time I don't like having to make further advances to them, and only sanction it because I feel it would be an awful blow to the Liverpool chartering business if Winhams couldn't load these vessels they have fixed.

As matters stand I have seen Simon our lawyer here and ordered him to draw up the most stringent undertaking possible for Winhams to sign to the effect that in consideration of our advancing £[illegible],000 they will pay for[? or transfer?] the[?] rate the 22,000 bales and order Dunn to pay all money coming to him for wheat through our hands instead of direct to Winhams. This agreement was to have been ready by four this afternoon, and Winham and McEllister were to come in and sign it and were to bring the holding orders for 22,000 bales. When they came I told them the agreement was not ready, but they might as well give us a holding order for 1000 bales as security for the £5,250 bill which he had not met, and which of course I was awfully anxious to get hold of. McEllister said, "I shall give up nothing till you have signed the agreement (for advancing

£8,000 more). If you don't give us the money we can get it elsewhere and I don't know why Mr Winham puts up with this sort of thing; I never saw so many difficulties raised in business," and more in the same style. I said difficulties are sure to arise in business when people don't pay their bills when they fall due and I wired in at him pretty stiffly, insisting on his handing up the holding order. He turned to Winham and said, "Shall I do it?", and Winham said, "Yes". He then gave up a holding order for 394 bales, said he couldn't find the other, but of course saying he would bring them tomorrow and with this I had to be content.

Our position at the moment therefore is that we are secured for £2,500 out of the bill for £5,200 and that we have had drawn up an agreement under which we should advance £8000 more; now my idea is this: that as it is to be exceedingly stringent, they, Winhams, will perhaps kick at something, in which case I shall back out and say I must refer to you before advancing any more. You will understand that I think it is the right thing to make this further advance but I don't like taking the responsibility on myself alone of making it, and would prefer to rest content with having bettered our position by getting security for £2,500 and leave Winhams to get out of their hole how they can. At the same time if Winhams agree to sign the agreement without raising any objection we shall have to make the advance. I omitted to mention that when Winham's came in this afternoon they informed us that they had carried out our suggestion and seen the Bank Manager, and he had said he should require account 'Winham & McEllister' reduced by £2,500. This of course is only the beginning as he told us he meant to get it in altogether. I forgot also to give you an account of my first interview with Winham's before I knew they were in any financial difficulties. Winham asked me if I could reduce our selling commission as he said other houses were ready to do it for 2½% including exchange. Something was said by either me or Meeks to the effect that he was bound to send all wheat shipped by him this season to our House for sale. He did not exactly deny this but said he would bring McEllister round who would give us his views. McE. arrived in due course, – a noisy, blustering cad, - and said that the agreement only bound them to ship wheat equal in amount to what they had to receive under the liens, and that for the remainder they could send it where they liked but that they would let us have it if we would do the business for 2½% including exchange which was the same as they were offered by others. I replied that the agreement was perfectly clear that unless they rechartered they were bound to ship all their wheat to us but that they were bound not to recharter more than would leave wheat equal in amount to what they had to receive under the liens. I also said that before going any further I must insist on this view of the agreement being admitted before I said a word one way or the other about reducing commissions. McEllister replied, "Oh, if you choose, Mr Gibbs, to stick to your strict legal rights and can't give Mr Winham any financial assistance, he can't carry the matter through. Besides it would be easy enough by a subterfuge for Winham to nominally recharter". I said it would be easy enough for Mr Winham to act dishonestly but I have no reason to apprehend he will do so, and I added if Mr Winham agrees with you and considers he is free to put part of this wheat in other hands why doesn't he say so instead of leaving all the talking to you. Winham then rather to my surprise said plainly that he considers he was bound to put all the wheat in our hands for sale, on which McEllister said, "Then I have nothing more to say". I then told them that we couldn't cut the commission below 3% but that we would undertake that exchange should not amount to more than ¼ with which they must be satisfied.

Winham at a later interview told me that F A Woods[? name unclear] in London had telegraphed to him that he could have a credit on the Chartered Mercantile Bank for £30,000 if he deposited securities (which as we know he could easily do) and put the balance of the wheat through their hands for sale. This business has been pressed on him by a man named Lord, and as the advance would have enabled him to pay off his Bank and pay for the corn sacks and the rate of corn exchange - 2½ in all - was low he had gone to McEllister who had persuaded him to try it on us as a lever to get us to reduce commissions.

I relate all this so fully because although we knocked it on the head when Winhams tried it on, yet there is nothing to prevent us consenting to it; if you are in a funk about the business, it would mean us leaving about 5 ship loads of wheat to sell in London instead of 25 and it would be a great pity to do it unless absolutely necessary. I have written this letter without consulting Meeks or sending his House PS[901] that you may have the opportunity of getting 2 independent accounts of a rather confused and intricate matter. This letter may help you to understand the other. Unfortunately my right hand is gouty which makes me write worse than usual and with difficulty.

5th December. Mr Gibbs is unfortunately laid up in bed this morning with the flu so he is unable to write further and finish this letter but the later points in concern will be found in the House P.S.

(signed) Alfred Meeks.

---

[901] House PS: although it is nearly always referred to as PS or P.S., the full name "Private Series" is mentioned once in a single letter from Gibbs, Bright & Co. Brisbane to Antony Gibbs & Sons London. It is not clear whether P.S. was telegraphed or sent by the postal system, or whether the "Code" that is sometimes referred to is a system of encrypting communications, or is used simply to reduce the length of telegraphic transmissions.

Vicary Gibbs (Adelaide) to Charles Bright

The previous letter to Charles Bright in Melbourne was later continued on the theme of wheat and Winhams by Vicary himself once his gout had subsided.

7th December 1883 - Adelaide

My dear Charles,

I have got over my gout for the time at any rate and am up and about again.

Winhams. I think this will all go straight now, indeed there never should have been any anxiety or bother at all if they had sold their bags a month ago as they ought to have done instead of staying on this track[?] finding the money to meet the bills with in the event of bags not going up in price. As it is they have injured their market a great deal and frightened a good many people by showing themselves as just speculators; and of course it is in the interests of other charterers, Darlings, the Milling Co. and Allens with whose business Winhams have **[10 words illegible]** and pointed out to him the mischief he was doing himself by branching out into all these specs at once and putting it in his Bankers power to put him in such a hole[?]. He admitted that he had acted very foolishly and promised faithfully not to go into any other speculation of any kind till this wheat business was through.

I could not get a berth by the P&O so I shall wait and return by the Iberia. No doubt you were very much pleased to get leave to 'insufflate' Kangaroo Point[902] and I hope its acquisition will lead to as great a development of the Brisbane business as you anticipate.

---

[902] Kangaroo Point is a peninsula in Brisbane, around which the River Brisbane flows. Gibbs, Bright & Co. had originally operated from wharves in Eagle Street, on the opposite northern side of the river, but the increaasing number and size of steamers was becoming more and more difficult to handle because of the restricted wharf space. The Australasian Steam Navigation Company had relatively new wharves on Kangaroo Point, opposite Mary Street. In February 1884, GB&Co purchased a 350ft length of river frontage further down Kangaroo Point, opposite Creek Street and alongside the vehicular ferry, and in March 1884 newspaper advertisements invited tenders for the building of the wharf, boundary fences, caretaker's cottage and office, with plans and specifications available for viewing at the offices of F.D.G. Stanley, the architect, in George Street. The contractors chosen were Robert Porter and Co., with McFarlane and Co. for the shed. The first pile for the new wharf was driven on 20th April 1884, and by November 1884 the newspapers were reporting the wharf "nearly finished". The first ship to utilise the completed wharf was the British India steamer R.M.S. Chyebassa on or about 17th January 1885. Later, in February 1893, the River

The bookkeeper and salesmen here seem pleasant, intelligent young fellows and since I arrived Mr Meeks has engaged a new insurance clerk.

I missed seeing Charnock[903] who went home in the Sorata which has been the cause of all his troubles. Many people here think he was ill-directed to fight the Government on the Barge question and I hope he has gone home to try and get the Pacific Company to pay up: and the [illegible] solicitor to [illegible] who appeared for the Government in the Court [illegible] says he has no legal claim [illegible] against the Pacific. If this is so I don't see how the P&O having regard to the interests of their shareholders can possibly pay up to Charnock. Now I am told if they do not meet him he means to bring an action against them, and if he does this I suppose he must lose his agency, that is if the P&O retain their interest in the Australian Line. If he loses his Agency I suppose we are pretty safe to get it. Everyone here cordially believes we are going to have it. Someone very indiscreetly said to me in the Club before several men, "I hear, Mr Gibbs, that your firm are going to have the Orient Agency here". I said, "Well I have heard nothing about it and I believe our friends Messrs Stilling[904] have charge of it". I went all over Stilling's offices and stores at Port Adelaide yesterday, - splendid premises – but not half full and too large by far for the business he is doing. I should think he must be making a heavy loss on them and I hope Charnock will call on the London House: if he does, Alban could see something of him and perhaps if he is really thinking of exiting from business he might be got to make some proposition for parting with the good will. You see he might very likely even if he were contemplating retirement put the matter in the first instance before Dalgetty's who are his London agents and whom it would, I should think, suit very well and whom it would be a pity to see starting here.

Yours very sincerely,

Vicary Gibbs.

Brisbane flooded, costing many lives and destroying many of the wharves and warehouses on Kangaroo Point. Large sheds on GB&Co.'s wharf partly collapsed, but were presumably rebuilt as much later newspaper articles (1931) are still referring to the Gibbs, Bright wharf.
[903] William Henry Charnock (c1823-1903), head of the shipping firm Messrs. Joseph Stilling & Co. with E. P. Sabine. He lived in Australia from 1849. He was at various times the Adelaide representative of the Orient Steam Navigation Company, director of the Adelaide Steamship Company (with G. Anderson), chairman of the Chamber of Commerce, chairman of the Port Adelaide Sailors' Home, a director of the old Talisker mine, and was associated for some years with Messrs. George Wills & Co.
[904] Messrs. Joseph Stilling & Co.

Charles Bright (aboard S.S. Rome) to his brother Regi (Melbourne)

On his way home to England aboard the S.S. Rome, this letter from Charles Bright to his brother Reginald - holding the Bright fort in Melbourne - was his last word for the time. He found himself back in Melbourne at the opening of its next great trade exhibition, the Centennial in 1888, so much of which he had himself made possible.

1st January 1884 - Tuesday - 'Rome'

My dear Reginald,

Many happy New Years to you. It is a roaster today and no mistake and likely to be so until we pan the Line[905], and probably then head winds to Colombo where we expect to be Monday next at day break. Fancy, no lemons or lime juice on board. They don't take fruit from Australia, - they are only put on board at Colombo. Tell Milo[name unclear] it might be a good subject for an advertisement.

This is a slow boat and rolls, certainly, without any apparent cause – in a smooth sea.

She is comfortably roomy and airy. Capt. Cater is a capital fellow, the Commodore of the fleet; been with this Coy. about 33 years. Officers good, quick and keep to their work. Stewards extraordinarily good. Food fair enough, but the refrigerator being too small they have to take live stock on board as well. This is a [illegible word] as you will suppose. Our runs[906] have been: 224, 248, Adelaide, 138 - 12 hours, 276, 298, 302, King George's Sound, 179 - 12 hours, 282, 313, 313, 287. We had all head winds till late last Saturday.

I wrote to you from Adelaide as well as King George's Sound – and hope you got my letters.

We have a nice lot of people on board - very agreeable I think – but slow. This certainly due to the weather that has not been favourable for

---

[905] Pan the Line - i.e. cross the equator.
[906] On board ship, the number of nautical miles travelled in the last 24 hours would be announced each noon. Passengers would often bet on the number of miles that would be announced each day.

amusements, singing etc. There is an old fellow on board who bought the [illegible to end of paragraph].

I think I told you that Mann from Adelaide was on board – I believe he is going to Calcutta to see if anything can be done about a horse breeding establishment in South Australia for the [2 words illegible].

The 'Punkahs'[907] are just put up today which will be an advantage. I believe the 'Kuiru i Huid'[name unclear] is the boat from Colombo to Bombay. She will leave about 24 hours after our arrival. About half the passengers leave this boat at Colombo. I will finish this before arrival there and then post it. Pray wish Vicary and Keats many happy New Years from me.

Jan 4, 84

I will continue my voyage, Jan.1: 299, 287, 289, 280. [2 words illegible]

It is very hot disagreeable weather but a smooth calm sea. We are not going very fast but slowing to get to Colombo on Monday morning early. The voyage from Melbourne can easily be made in 3 days less time. We have been passing through a good deal of scoria[908]. Capt. Cater says he passed through a great deal on the voyage down. The disaster[909] at the Straits of Sunda[910] took place after he passed it. It is to be supposed there must have been some great submarine eruption about here.

I think I forgot to mention that I left most of my Melbourne bills unpaid – please have them settled up. For food; Milton[name unclear] - Ogg[name unclear] - Haigh Bros[911]: Mun & Dennerd[name unclear], McGuigan[name unclear] - might be a few

69. An 1888 lithograph of the 1883 eruption of Krakatoa
Wikimedia Commons

---

[907] Punkahs: large fans hung from the ceiling and operated by a servant pulling on a rope.
[908] Scoria: a geological term meaning large masses of rock formed by solidified lava.
[909] The eruption of Krakatoa, as observed by Vicary Gibbs in the diary on 17 September 1883.
[910] The Sunda Strait, between Java and Sumatra, linking the Java Sea to the Indian Ocean. The disaster referred to is the eruption of Krakatoa in 1883, which killed over 35,000 people.
[911] Haigh Bros., Collins Street, Melbourne.

shillings on the Club but I don't think so and don't think I owed any more [illegible word] bills.

Bye the bye, you remember hearing that Tower in the Sydney Office was engaged to be married to a girl there. Curious enough she is on board with her father going to England. Mr Backhaus, her father, is a Sydney Architect. Not a bad kind of girl, I should say. She told me yesterday of her engagement. She is going to stay with the Tower Family in Bath. The family of Keating and Tower are most friendly. If there was any chance of pushing him on[912] I am sure I would do so. The father and daughter are going to travel and then return to Sydney – some months yet. I wonder if Tower is of any good at all. If Danson is out of Dunedin would he do for that place. They have written – from Home, if you remember, pointing out the young clan of clerks in that place – among other things perhaps you would bear this matter in mind. I have been having a talk with a young fellow on board, Mr Turner, a squatter in Queensland.

[Remainder of letter missing]

Letter #6 from Vicary Gibbs (Melbourne) to his brother Alban

Letters ##6-9 to his brother Alban were all written from Melbourne before Vicary left for his journey through New Zealand. The price of land, new supplies of tin and copper, the wheat market, and the possibility of gaining control of shipping lines were discussed at this level; and the brothers exchanged views on various experiences with new sugar producers, without forgetting the more familiar Australian commodity, wool. All these points were certainly more confidentially expanded in cable code. Letter #7 is an extended description of Gibbs' ambitions for the Sydney House and its transfer to a new, more prestigious site with warehousing nearer to Circular Quay. Equally ambitious was the Kangaroo Point project in Brisbane referred to in letter #8.

12th December 1883 - Melbourne

No. 6

Dear Alban,

I last wrote to you on the 27th Nov. No. 5 and since then I have to acknowledge your note of Nov. 2nd which is now before me.

---

[912] "Pushing him on" - referring to his career in the company.

I am glad to hear that affairs are looking better in the City and hope they will continue on the up line down to the 31st of this month.

With regard to your enquiries about Amby; your views as to the property selling at a profit are quite understood and concurred in, both here and at Brisbane. In the present however there is no prospect of selling a highly improved and, therefore, expensive station and you must therefore make up your minds to hold for some time.

Money is very tight in Queensland and 7% and 8% are being obtained on first class freehold mortgage. The only way to get out of Amby would be to choose a time when money was cheap in the London market and then for A.G.& S. to bring out a pastural company onto which we could throw Amby, taking shares to the amount of its value. Of course on this side we would arrange with 5 or 6 large squatters to put their estates in, selecting properties in various parts of Australia so as to make the best insurance possible against drought.

Nymagee Copper. This is a new mine and the copper is about equal to Cobar, rather better because more malleable. Hitherto their stocks have been consigned to a London House, MacEwans, under advance; I believe £59 was the amount advanced but of course that must have been when copper was much higher. Would it suit to A.G.&S. to advance against this in consideration of getting the sale, at the London rate of interest? The Nymagee people are very much dissatisfied with MacEwans. I think of going to the manager and having a chat with him. I don't understand how the essaying would be arranged, whether it would be safe to take the mine's guarantee of the copper being usual quality of output, how far copper varies or in fact anything about mineralogy or mines, but supposing such points to be satisfactory, it appears to me if I could get the Nymagee people to consign to you it would be a good thing.

Tin. This house has received Henry Bath's order for tin and is trying to execute. The tin market here is a very close borough and worked in a very unsatisfactory way. There are a lot of small mines all of which sell their ore to a man named Kelly who has the only considerable smelting works in the colony and he thus rules the tin market. His system is to make intending buyers quote a price at which they will buy and Kelly himself acts as the agent for buyers in London and in Calcutta and is therefore both buyer and seller; it is open to him at any time to sell the tin to whom he likes and he could favour his own principals. He proposes to act perfectly honestly, but how shall a 'huckster escape sin' when he can earn a commission. Yesterday we had a long interview with him and he stated that he had 50 tons of tin for sale. We tendered for it at £80.10.0. This morning he sent round to say the tin was sold at £80.15.0. Merivale went to see him and offered to buy another 50 tons at that price of £80.15.0., which [3 words illegible] and a little commission, to which he declined on the ground that he had no more tin to sell at present. He told Merivale that 'Gilchrist Watt' had bought the tin and showed him their offer; he said he had had one other offer at £80.0.0. Gilchrist Watt are the agents for your friend Strauss who is the principal buyer of tin in this market. Gilchrist Watt are an old rich firm whose business has fallen off and both the partners are in England. If anything happened to make Strauss suspend them this house could buy his tin for him if you thought well. I don't think however this tin business will ever be satisfactorily worked unless Kelly's monopoly is broken down. Could not Baths make arrangements to smelt the ore at home and we could buy the new material straight from the mines and ship it home to London[?] as ballast by May next. Let me know what you think of this.

If allowance is made for the [illegible word] which Tyndall has shifted off L'pool's book onto Melbourne's, what was the British [illegible word] for 1883?

Caernarvon Castle[913]. L'pool should not have fixed her without authority from Adelaide. I suppose it was a bit 'over zeal' in Richards the shipping clerk and will not wear; there will be a loss in rechartering.

Wheat advances. You may have been annoyed at the delay in replying to the London cable of Jan.23rd on this subject, but we did not understand it. When however Adelaide telegraphed to us a somewhat similar message which they had got from L'pool and asked us what they were to do, I telegraphed you what had been drawn on the current year on you for Adelaide business, and today we have instructed Adelaide to tell L'pool the amount they are advancing or have advanced per quarter (which is a matter of fact not 'opinion'). I hope somehow we have told you what you want to know.

Ramsay. I am glad to see you recovered the money all right.

China Traders. As we shall lose this agency we are now withdrawing to obtain the North China Insurance Agency which we hear is a better company. We are writing by this mail to China applying for it and Remnant, of Gibb Livingston, have written recommending us. We are trying to get the Union of Canton for Dunedin.

Banks buying out of Parbury's. I hear they are going to 2% dividend. I don't know where Exchange is going to.

---

[913] S.S. Caernarvon (or Caernarfon) Castle.

As to D's[914] impertinent suggestion of taking over our business, I should simply ignore it and say "at present we have come to no decision as to the future of the Dunedin Branch".

British India. It is not to my mind a question of their making other arrangements not so convenient for them as those they had with us: for the life of me I can't see how they are to make arrangements at all. I do hope that if the London House have definitely broken with them there will be no lack of energy in the home houses setting to work to persuade Andersons[915] or someone else to go into the trade.

I have also to acknowledge your note of the 23rd enclosing press copy re Winham, but this I have not yet had time to read.

As far as I can make out there won't be D.[916] for the Adelaide House out of the sale of Young; I feel it is a bad business.

Yours very sincerely, Vicary Gibbs.

Letter #7 from Vicary Gibbs (Melbourne) to his brother Alban

19th December 1883 - Melbourne

No. 7

My dear Alban,

I last wrote to you on the 12th and have nothing since from you. I wrote to Herbert on the 17th a letter about Keating, Hannay and Bell discussing where they had better reside and other business matters.

My present idea is to go down to Dunedin towards the end of next February, through New Zealand, and back to Sydney, spend a fortnight there which will bring me to early May. I then propose for Keating to join me in Sydney and we should go up together to Brisbane. Hannay would then return to Melbourne. Keating would take charge in Brisbane and Hart

---

[914] D's: possibly Danson or Dawes.
[915] Possibly related to Anderson, Head of the Orient Company? (see diary entry 25/02/1884).
[916] Presumably this is a person "D." rather than some other form of abbreviation, and if so then it is probably the same person "D." referred to earlier in the letter.

(according to the wishes he has expressed) would accompany me on a visit of inspection to the northern Queensland parts.

Of course the above is subject to all sorts of modification as chance and time determine.

Messageries Coy. We have been trying to get this Agency for our Adelaide House and there seems a fair prospect of success; it would not be a paying affair for the present. Indeed it is doubtful if we should not be out of pocket at first as we should have to engage a French clerk. Morgans are giving up the Agency on this account. My idea would be to raise only a small amount of share capital and get the rest by 4% debentures as the Trust and Agency Co.[917] have done. This plan commends itself very much to me and I hope you will give it your serious consideration and confer with Charles Bright on his return. Should it meet your approval it would be well to think out and arrange every detail beforehand, so as to be ready to avail oneself of a favourable moment in the London market.

B. D. Morehead stand in just the position to the Scottish Investment Co. whose largest station is Mount Abundance as we should do to the proposed company. You must remember that the sale of the wool would by no means represent the total advantages to our various houses of such an arrangement. The wool shipping would add greatly to our power and importance, and the supply of station requisites, wire etc. greatly to our profit.

Manners Sutton[918]. With regard to Tyndall's suggestion, I don't know exactly what to say. Altho' there is no doubt that Charles will be of immediate use to you himself in the London management of Australian business, yet I don't know exactly what staff he will require at first, or whether he could find employment for a man like M.S. No doubt a regular Australian department will have to be organised but this must be done gradually after Charles is there. I am quite satisfied that M.S. should be engaged if it should be found that his services could be made use of. He is very amiable, [has] good abilities, and can work hard and with intelligence; at the same time he got heavily in to debt in L'pool and under the pressures of difficulties incurred owing to his own self indulgence and

---

[917] The Trust and Agency Company of Australasia had offices at 211 Hereford Street, Christchurch. In 1883, its General Manager was a Mr James Hora. A Mr Charles Robert Blakiston managed the business for Gibbs, Bright and Co. who were the Managing Agents. Miles & Co. (mentioned in the diary on 28th February 1884) had nearby offices at 208 Hereford Street.

[918] Possibly the son or nephew of Henry Charles Manners-Sutton, 4th Viscount Canterbury, the brother-in-law of Charles Bright (see diary entry for 4 November 1884), or possibly John Manners-Sutton, 3rd Baron Manners (1852-1927) who would have been about 31 years old.

without as far as I can see any special cause he behaved rather dishonourably in borrowing money from clerks and other people who were not in a position to afford it.

Personally I like him and think him in many ways a good clerk; I really think I should leave it to Charles to engage him or recommend him for engagement after he is with you, at the same time if it were known that it rested with Charles to take him or not it would put Charles in a very invidious position as he might have a delicacy in putting him forward, - and on the other hand the M.S. family might think it hard if he didn't get J.M.S. employment when in his power to do so.

George Bell. I am very glad to hear he has accepted your offer and hope he will answer to the high account we have of him.

Adelaide. I returned from this place yesterday morning and found Keating here who had just come back from Sydney. He is looking very thin but otherwise well enough.

I was just a week in Adelaide and was very much pleased with the place though the enjoyment of my visit was rather interfered with by the worry of Brisbane business which laid me up with 2 days gout: however on the whole I am very glad I was there as it would have been a great responsibility for Meeks alone and I was able to talk over every item of his business with him.

I consider him a very sharp, garrulous, pleasant fellow with very good manners and he seems to be on very friendly terms with the people of the place.

Winham's Business. You will find this is so fully dealt with in my letter to Charles and the Adelaide P.S., copies of which went to you by last mail, that it is unnecessary for me to go through all the matter again, more especially as everything has now come right and there is no reason to apprehend any further trouble. Indeed, yesterday we got a telegram that the advance of £8000[?] which we agreed to make some time back will not be required, so I have no doubt that Winhams have got their account taken up by another Bank. Indeed I consider their position so sound that I am at a loss to understand the action of the Bank of Adelaide except on the hypothesis that some of the Directors (which is quite on the cards) had a personal interest in cornering Winham and putting him in a hole, with the object of getting hold of the ships he had chartered at a much lower rate. There is an immense quantity of wheat to be shipped from S.A. and not too much tonnage; I shall be very much surprised if we don't see freights higher and wheat lower in February-March.

Winham and McEllister told Meeks after I was gone that I was a very outspoken gentleman but they did not dislike me!

Waterhouse the bookkeeper is a very intelligent young fellow and writes a beautiful, clear hand as you will notice in the Adelaide letters to London. Wilson the salesman is also a superior young man; he has been at the Cape, ostrich farming and is shaping well. A new insurance clerk has also just been engaged to look after the business of the New Zealand Coy., which business, as we shall have the Insurance of Winham's ships, will more than pay his salary. Meeks pays them each £150. p.a. and this is cheap as colonial salaries go. There is also an office boy and a porter and Cowan's new man sent out by J. Cook, which comprise the present staff.

Cowan's man has at present only booked a few orders but he seemed to know his business and had had most of the tradesmen in to inspect his samples and expects to do good business. He is being much pressed to keep stock in Adelaide and we shall have to see about this when Cook comes out. We shall very likely send our hardware and soft goods salesman from this office down to Adelaide for a fortnight to help Meeks to make a start in those lines.

Meeks himself is coming up here for a visit about Xmas time which will do good. I pressed on him the necessity of acting with caution and not being too ambitious to do a big business at once, but I feel very confident myself that we shall do a large and satisfactory business there in time. They will not do more than pay their expenses for the first eight months ending Dec.31st but this is owing to none of the commissions on the chartering business coming into the current year's accounts.

Ad.[919] premises are in an admirable position in the heart of the business quarter, but they have the disadvantage of being upstairs, and not being specially suited for offices, they are small and it is very unlikely they will answer our purpose longer than - if so long as - the three years for which they were originally taken.

Stilling's business. You will note my remarks on this subject in a letter to Charles of which you have a copy; it is an old fashioned, very well established business, the best wool connection in Adelaide and a good shipping and general mercantile connection, but it is very little pushed and I should think rather falling off than advancing. Charnock, the head of it, has, I believe, good private means and has no partner. There seems a general idea in Adelaide that he would be disposed to retire or make some new arrangement about his business. He has gone home in the 'Sorata' to press his claims on the Pacific Company for the loss of the barge

---

[919] Adelaide.

at the time the 'Sorata' went ashore. He is an obstinate man and if he litigates I presume he must lose the Orient Agency; he has been very friendly to Meeks and to the Adelaide House and he is, I believe, quite a gentleman. It is possible that he may be going home with the idea of offering his business to some London firm as well as settling his claims against the Pacific. I think it would be very desirable that you should have him to dinner and see something of him, and the same thing applies to Tyndall in L'pool if Charnock stops there. He may possibly put some proposal before you, and at any rate you may learn the truth as to his views and ideas. Should any open rupture occur between him and the Pacific you would be ready to use your influence to get us the Orient Agency in Adelaide. I do not know his exact London address but you can get it from Elder[920] whom Sillem or you know personally and who is Charnock's London agent.

Murray arrived here yesterday and has been talking over Sydney business, which seems to be going on very satisfactorily. They ought to make £12,000. profit at that branch this year.

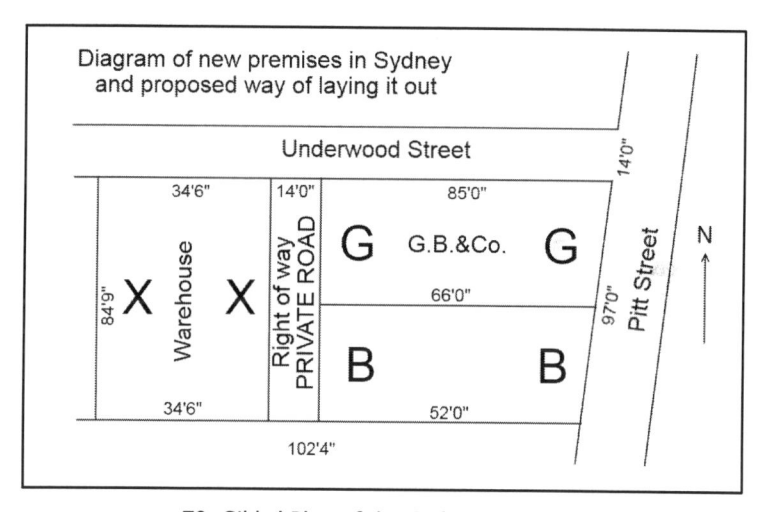

70. Gibbs' Plan of the Sydney Premises

Sydney Premises. I have been thinking a great deal about these and talking with Murray. I enclose a plan of the site showing the way in which we have decided to lay it out. We propose to make a private road as shown to give light to the back of the offices and front of the warehouse. I find that so much money is spent at present by the Sydney House in storage in various warehouses about the city that it will amply pay us to retain the whole of X and build on it a perfectly plain brick two storied warehouse sufficiently strong to carry two stories more should it be found necessary to add them. You will readily see the advantage for supervision

---

[920] Probably related to Sir Thomas Elder.

and convenience of having the stores adjoining the offices, being close to the Quay and under Murray's eye.

I have told Murray to try and get a private offer for block B. which we value at £6000 and should he get a reasonable one we shall accept it, knowing that this course would meet your views. Of course if it would facilitate a sale we would make arrangements with the purchasers of B. to leave him a portion of the warehouse on X. Should however no proper offer for block B. be forthcoming at the moment, I do not think we should let it lie or delay to build on it simultaneously with G.

71. Messrs. Gibbs, Bright and Co.'s New Offices, Pitt Street, Sydney
Illustrated Sydney News, 10 January 1886

As to the style of building, we have had a great many discussions and have ultimately fixed on a plain four storied building of red brick with brown stone dressing as plain and inexpensive as we could possibly arrange it considering that the façade is to the principal street in Sydney. I hope the architect[921] will send you a copy by this mail. We gave up an architecturally far handsomer plan partly on the score of expense and partly because we did not think the rooms would divide up so manageably in any other fashion than that of a square building with square ordinary sized windows.

The cost of building the two blocks G. and B. with the warehouse on X. will be £20,000; this is a lot of money but we can borrow ¾ of the whole cost, being that of building, from the insurance Co. on mortgage at 6% and there seems no doubt in anyone's mind that we can Let to return us 9%.

---

[921] William Wilkinson Wardell.

As mentioned in a previous letter there would be a considerable saving on building the two blocks, G. and B., simultaneously.

My idea is to at once set about building the warehouse, which will cost £2000 and would I believe be anybody's money either to rent or buy. If on receipt of this letter you cable the word 'iota' we shall consider that, in the event of our being unable to get a fair price for B., we are at liberty, if we think it advisable, to build on B. and G. together. If you send us 'kappa' we shall know that in no case are we to build on B., but only on G. and X.

Murray suggests that Cowans should sell Winyard Square[922] premises and either buy or lease B. for their joint business. This would be a capital arrangement if it were feasible. Cowans are so suspicious that they would immediately think we were going to take an advantage over them. It would bring everything together under Murray, and the paper business could sit at a cheaper rate than it does now. I think there would be a fair prospect of selling Cowans present premises for £20,000 or £21,000. I really don't know if it would be worth while broaching this idea to Cowans, but if you did and if they entertained it you might send us the word 'gamma', by which we should understand that we were at liberty to offer Winyard Square premises at £21,000. The new site and building on B. would cost Cowans say about £13,000., against £20,000 or a saving of £7000.

Cowans business in New Zealand We have had Given here today and gone fully into matters with him. He seems a pleasant, intelligent little man, and Cowan's, Edinboro' have a very good opinion of him. He has hitherto been in Sydney receiving £500 p.a.. We have now arranged for him to take up his quarters in Dunedin, where he will have an office under our roof there and room in our warehouse for his stock. He is to be entirely under Arthur in all matters of giving credit etc. and he will travel in the island to get orders. I have sketched out a circular to be sent to the New Zealand customers to the effect that Cowan & Co., Edinboro' have decided at once to open a branch in Dunedin under the management of Mr Given who has a thorough knowledge of the paper business and that all letters are to be addressed to him c/o G.B. & Co., Dunedin etc.

We shall have to give him £600 the first year and £650 the next too, but he is a thorough expert and I believe worth the money.

---

[922] Wynyard Square, Sydney. Presumably the Cowan premises surrounded the Wynyard Square Recreation Park, a fenced off open space available for use to an exclusive membership until 1887 when it became the public Wynyard Park. It is about 500 yards - a 5-minute walk - from Underwood Street and Pitt Street, the proposed location of the new premises.

We do not expect the paper business in New Zealand to cover the expenses the first year but after that I would hope to do a good business there. I expect our own business in Dunedin to be a few hundred pounds to the bad this year but this was anticipated as it had to bear Arthur's and Danson's salaries.

Cadell. The valuation of this tug is exactly £3000. I presume that must have given the valuer an idea of the value he (Hart) put on it himself. Subject therefore to the approval of yourself and the parties interested in England, I suppose the new firm will take it over as from 1st January next. I do not however, nor does Charles, consider it worth one penny more than the above price. There are however advantages in taking it over, shutting out competition etc. which make it worth while to buy it at this price.

Boko. I see there is a mistake of £100 in your calculation in the London account of depreciation on machinery of this tug.

E. & A. Co. The prospects of this company don't look so bright as they did a year ago in consequence of the heavy competition. I don't know whether you have taken your seat at the Board or not? I confess I was surprised to see a telegram from the Sec.[923] to Sydney about the Adelaide Agency to the effect that if Morgan's declined the joint Agency we were to reappoint them sole Agents. If this was done without consulting you and getting your consent it seems to me cool not to say audacious, having regard to the large amount of money we put in on the distinct understanding that we were to have the Adelaide Agency.

However we are very friendly with Morgan's and there is no reason whatever to suppose they will object to the joint Agency. Hitherto, all the work has been done by Morgan's and they have returned us half the commission earned. What I should like to see next year would be for our house to do all the work in Adelaide and Morgan's to do all the work at the port and we make them a return of say a % of the commission. This would retain Morgan's services which are of advantage to the Coy., and by bringing passengers and shippers into our town office would make our firm better and more widely known.

It is the custom in Adelaide for all Houses of any importance to have a branch house and stores at the Port, which is about 12 miles from the City. Of course we want to avoid opening an office at the port as long as possible but if we had the sole Agency of the E. & A. we should have to do so.

---

[923] The Company Secretary of the Eastern and Australian Steamship Company Ltd.

Another telegram has come from the Sec. to Sydney to say that the Co. can't allow 5% to the Adelaide agents. I hope indeed this only means that they can't allow 5% to Morgan's and 5% to us, for they certainly ought to allow 5% in all.

Gillanders and Arbuthnot. Continued complaints keep coming in from various indentors about the quality and weight of these shipments, and as we told Mr Moore when he was here, unless they give greater satisfaction this business will come to an end altogether. It is a great pity for if G. & A. had shipped right weight we should have had the whole of this trade and a most profitable business to them and us.

T. Irving and Co. When Charles gets home you will have to seriously consider whether it would not be advisable to terminate our arrangements with this firm and have the work they do at present done by chartering and forwarding clerks under Charles. The reason for keeping our arrangement with them - that they got us ships for consignment - has almost ceased to exist owing to the falling off of sailing ships and to the fact that those that do come, come under a hard and fast rule of the amount of cargo given to the ships, and not through 'free from favour or affection'. Of course they could continue to jackal for us and bring us any business they liked and we would make a fair return of commission, and even in this I don't approve of present arrangements and would suggest in future that we should never return *com in perpetuo* except to a firm who is going to do a portion of the proposed business or take a proportion of the risk. Take for example Hang's timber business in which we make heavy advances. This was originally put before the old firm by Irving's; nothing came of it and the matter dropped for 5 years after which Hang wrote direct to us and we made arrangements for advancing against cargoes. Irving's then running no risk and having no trouble, claim and receive in perpetuity a full return commission of 7%. I told Stubbs[924] before leaving that this was not fair and that their com[mission] ought to come to an end at a fixed time. Personally I would much rather make a large return to a firm introducing business for 2 or 3 years than a small one for an indefinite time.

Sydney and Adelaide both complain of Irving's and in all our houses there is a strong feeling of dissatisfaction against them, and I know the clerks would work more cordially if they thought the commissions were being divided with you than with an outside house especially one which they, one and all, think get the best of us.

---

[924] Possibly Gibbs' friend Edward Stubbs (about whom he reminisces on the 27 Dec 1884 diary entry - although it is not clear from that entry whether Edward Stubbs is still living).

In fact I come back to 'Delenda est Carthago'[925], which is the song I have been singing the last two years and to this completion it must come sooner or later. I have talked the matter well over to Charles and think he more than half agrees with me. When you see him you will no doubt look closely into it and perhaps do a half measure of taking away the chartering and leaving the forwarding for the present?

Kangaroo Point. No sign of your telegram. Hart was advised of its contents and asked whether he was still perfectly satisfied of the desirability of this purchase and he replied, "more than ever"; it has therefore been bought.

This was a case where, I think, we were bound to be guided by the local opinion and Hart was so strong about the advisability of the purchase, both as an investment and for the good of the business. Mr McIlwraith[926], the ex-premier of Queensland was in this office yesterday and seemed to think we had made a very good buy. You must remember Hart is supposed to err on the side of caution and inactivity, and not at all fond of new ventures and developments.

We received L'pool's P.S. No. 68, after the time for the purchase had expired, but I don't think it would have affected the result had it come before. I understand now that the British India have declined to go to the other side of the river, but if we bear the cost of transporting the goods I don't see how it matters to them which side they go. As to their getting Howard Smith's[927] wharf it is to the last degree unlikely that this wealthy firm who are doing a large business and have just transferred themselves into a Limited Coy. with a million capital, would take the suicidal step of allowing themselves to be outbid for possession of their present wharf. Again the British India can't afford to split with us as long as our alliance with Parbury Lamb and B. D. Morehead continues as ¾ of the wool shipped from Brisbane comes through our, or their, hands; and we could if forced to it make arrangements with the E.& A. or Orient or some other line to load them and drive the British India out of the field. At the same time we are not anxious to keep in with the B.India both because of the present business in Brisbane and because of further developments of which we hear. McIlwraith tells us that he has had an official application from Dawes for a subsidy for a direct line from Calcutta calling at Brisbane,

---

[925] Delenda est Carthago: Latin for 'Carthage must be destroyed', which comes to mean 'that which stands in our way must go'.
[926] Sir Thomas McIlwraith (1835-1900), premier of Queensland from 1879-1883, and again in 1888 and 1893.
[927] William Howard Smith (1814–1890), known as Howard Smith. He formed a partnership with L. J. L. Burke, who had a large coal business in Melbourne, later acquiring the firm and making it one of Melbourne's largest and most efficient coal importers. In 1883 it was incorporated to form William Howard Smith and Sons Ltd., and in 1884 Howard Smith retired from active management and the company was taken over by his sons Walter S. and Arthur Bruce.

Sydney and Melbourne. This was refused but Dawes wrote again to say the B.I. intended to go on with the project. Now we are open for and shall be delighted to undertake the Agency in all three plans, and I hope you will do your very best to try and secure it. The B.I. connection is so valuable that it is worth while putting up with a little rudeness from Dawes. I enclose press copies of two letters from Keating to that which will help to enlighten you on the Kangaroo Point. You see we now move to sell all the land on the north side except what is absolutely required for offices, and build our stores on the cheap (by comparison) Kangaroo land.

Machinery. This department has not been well attended to in L'pool; questions have not been answered and there has been great neglect in not letting us know the discounts which we could deduct from the Davey Paxman[928] engines. This is very hard on Storey; we were blaming him for not making sales and beginning to think he was no good. It now turns out that he has actually refused offers which he could have accepted had he been in possession of information he got last mail. This is a very important department and if undertaken at all must be very well looked after. The stock is bulky and costs a lot to store and runs into a lot of money. I see the machinery letters have been written lately by Johnny[929], [illegible name] and James[930]. They must be fuller and replies must be made to all queries or reasons given for not doing so; - don't know if James is to blame, but no doubt you will look into this and read him these remarks.

Charles Charles desired me to say he hoped you would settle all matters about his signature and anything else relating to his position in the London Office before his arrival.

I am afraid I have written you an awfully long letter and fear you may rather shy at it, but I think most of it is to the point and I have had no time to make it any shorter. I suppose when Charles goes I shall put most of this into P.S. and relieve you from personal infliction of my views.

I hope you and all your household are well, and remain your affectionate brother, Vicary Gibbs.

Sir Thomas McIlwraith goes home in the Cuzco. You will remember you dined with him in Brisbane. He has great influence with the British India

---

[928] Davey, Paxman & Davey, Engineers, founded in Colchester in 1865. At this time they were general engineers and ironworkers, manufacturing steam engines, boilers, agricultural machinery, and mill gearing, and supplying machinery to the Kimberley diamond mines in South Africa. They are still trading today as diesel engine manufacturers under the name Paxman.

[929] Probably John Arthur Gibbs, Vicary Gibbs' first cousin, known as Johnny.

[930] 'James' is probably a first name rather than a surname - Gibbs seems to be referring to junior clerks who were probably members of the Gibbs or Bright families.

and is safe to be Premier again at the next turn of the wheel. Hart has always been a staunch supporter of his. You can get his address from the Agent [illegible word] and have him to dine. Lady M.[931] is with him.

Letter #8 from Vicary Gibbs (Melbourne) to his brother Alban

28th December 1883 - Melbourne

No. 8

My dear Alban,

I last wrote to you on the 19th and have not heard from you since.

Messageries Coy. I feel pretty confident we shall get this agency; I had a talk with George Morgan, Sir William's[932] brother, who was up here the other day in the Club. He blackguarded the Agency a good deal and wished us joy of it if we got it, saying it gave endless trouble, there were incessant complaints, and they hardly ever got any space to speak of left in Adelaide, it being all taken up in Melbourne. However when I asked him point blank if he would have given up the Agency had he been carrying on business on his own account, he said "No". There is always a chance of an Agency of this kind assuming important proportions at any time and I am sure it would help Meeks to get it.

Old Danson wrote a very proper, nicely expressed letter to the House thanking for past kindness and expressing regret at the termination of the connection.

Kangaroo Point. I am sorry Dawes has shown himself so obstinate about this, but as far as I can gather there is no chance whatever of his securing the Corporation Wharves. There is some possibility of a free Government ferry across the river from Kangaroo. The objection to renting Brown's was the high price £750, and the fact that at the end of five years we should have been completely at Brown's mercy, he having bought Barker's, so I think it would have been a short sighted arrangement. For Kangaroo we

---

[931] Lady Harriette Ann (née Mosman) McIlwraith, who married Sir Thomas McIlwraith in 1879 after the death of his first wife Margaret (née Whannell).
[932] Sir William Morgan (1828-Nov.1883), premier of South Australia from 1871-81. Founded William Morgan & Co, and in 1865 the Bank of Adelaide. Retired in 1881, returned to England in May 1883 and died there in November 1883. Knighted in May 1883.

sit at a rent of £900 as against £500 Barker's and £750 Brown's, or £1250 together.

Finance. The L'pool House wrote saying we should have discounted rather than sold our drafts on you in order to remit £30,000 some time back, but we should have lost money had we done so. They are quite alive here to remitting in the cheapest way, but it is impossible for you to know on your side of the world what we can sell our drafts on London at, as the current rate is no guide. Turner and Saurey in this office - whose positions answer roughly to those of Lowrey and Langley - are dull dogs, especially the latter, but Brown the head bookkeeper is clever and intelligent and these sort of questions are talked over with him.

Amby. In consequence of the drought and the tightness of money in Brisbane, I should think it would be quite impossible to sell this property just now except at a sacrifice; however it is paying a good interest, and should any chance of getting out at a profit of any kind arise we will avail ourselves of it.

Winham's Business. The original advance of £12,000 was certainly against growing crop but there was the personal security of the two men which after careful enquiry was estimated at from £60,000 to £100,000. Meeks is up here now and I read him the passage in the London P.S. No.23, expressing your strong disapproval of advances against growing crops.

Our wool telegram Nov. 5th. This would have been clearer if the order of the words had been transposed, but your explanation that the return of 38% to 44% was in reference only to 'greasy', was of course correct, and if old Bywater knew anything about wool he would have understood it so. The L'pool House had better in future submit the proof of their circulars to their wool brokers for correction.

Private Code. I have no copy of this and therefore we don't send the cipher 'Cacaohulse'[933]. I hope Irvings will soon send out the new chartering Code as I can't get on with the rearrangement of our general Australian Code till I see what language the ciphers are in etc.

I send you a capital table for quoting for wheat, barley etc. by means of figures. It is very simple and the most comprehensive I ever saw.

I am, my dear Alban

---

[933] Cacaohulse: possibly referring to the cacao bean? Could be the name of the code, or possibly just an allusion to the double shell of the bean?

Your very affectionate brother,

Vicary Gibbs

I have spoken about our remittance letters only containing for the future bald statements of fact; any remarks to go in P.S.

Letter #9 from Vicary Gibbs (Melbourne) to his brother Alban

2nd January 1884 - Melbourne

No. 9

My dear Alban,

I last wrote to you on the 28th of Dec. and have not heard from you since. I have very little to say this time, and the P.S. of today to L'pool goes fully into all matters of interest.

Sydney Sales. You will be pleased to see from the clear and statistical letter P.S. from Sydney this mail that their increase in sales is so good, roughly speaking £40,000 advance in House produce and £30,000 in Colonial; I did not expect the former would have been nearly so much.

British India. Reading Tyndall's account of his interview with Gray Dawes is rather irritating as their complaints are unreasonable, and if their Brisbane Superintendent told them we sent the 'Boko' out unnecessarily, he is a liar, for it is never sent out without his (Hansard's) approval. I should be glad if you would read again the clear and full letter P.S. from Brisbane to L'pool No.29, which practically disposes of these complaints beforehand. What they want us to do is reduce our wharfage and tug rates below market rates for their benefit, and this we can't do.

Hart writes a points note evidently finding Murray more useful as he gets into the work.

I am my dear Alban, yours affectionately,

Vicary Gibbs

Telegram: Angus MacPherson (Echuca), to D. Chrystal (Torrumbarry)

Telegram from Angus MacPherson, Echuca, for D. Chrystal Esq., Torrumbarry Station with reference to the breaking of the 1884 drought.

Telegram Feb 7th 1884 Echuca for D. Chrystal Esq., Torrumbarry Station[934]

Letter received plenty rain things all right now

Angus MacPherson[935]

Letter #11 from Vicary Gibbs (Melbourne) to his brother Alban

Letters ##11-14, from Vicary Gibbs to his brother Alban. There is a surprise comment by Vicary referring to S.S. Great Britain in terms which point to the once ignominious end of that great ship. I have been able to witness her gradual restoration several times and can only feel Vicary's verdict was entirely driven by what he saw as the huge liability competing with his business itself.

24th January 1884 - Melbourne

No. 11

My dear Alban,

Many thanks for your letter of Dec. 13th & 14th. It is not at all my idea that you should be at the trouble of keeping up a series, or answering my letters either fully or regularly. Indeed, my remarks are not meant specially for you but are written as to the L'pool House, Tyndall receiving copies; I merely select you as a victim instead of writing P.S. as it puts one in a position of greater freedom and less responsibility.

We had your telegram about not advancing against sugar machinery and this no doubt referred to a remark of mine in a letter to G. Merivale of

---

[934] Torrumbarry is about about 160 miles north of Melbourne in Victoria. Echuca is about 10 miles to its south-east.
[935] The clerk receiving the telegram has spelled the name "McPherson", but obituaries in the Australian press from 1930 spell it "MacPherson" or "Macpherson".

which you may have disapproved (I may mention that I showed the letter to R. Bright before sending it). You will see in enclosed correspondence between the junior manager G.M. and self some more remarks on this subject. I have endeavoured to send you all correspondence between the junior managers as the remarks are often valuable in themselves and help you to form a clear idea of the character and abilities of the writers. I know the objections that have been urged against this sort of correspondence going on at all, but so long as great care is taken to stop all bickering or disloyalty to heads of Houses, I consider the objections are outweighed by the advantage of practising the younger hands in what are practically P.S. and of stimulating their general interest in the business. I want to give you a general caution not to comment on any of this class of correspondence in P.S. as if it were in P.S. from us. Thus supposing letters to be on the way from you to Sydney saying, "We should not at all like advances against sugar machinery and consider them most undesirable", Murray might say, "I should never think of doing so", and might arrive at the correct conclusion that this idea emanated from G. Merivale, and be irritated thereat.

Sydney Premises. I have quite subordinated my Queen Anne[936] feelings to the idea of making such a building as would most readily let and sell. There seems to be so much delay in getting to work that you will have the façade in time to telegraph should you disapprove.

Bell. I am glad you approved of Hannay's letter to Bell; I arranged it with him. It was not on the score of cheapness only that I wanted a lower salary than you offered but principally because he would be easier to handle in conjunction with Hannay and Keating.

[Page 3 of this 7-page letter is missing]

[Page 4 starts] is very heavy indeed; there is all the unimportant detail of L'pool besides a continuous amount of anxious and responsible new business cropping up, people incessantly seeing one besides the noises incident to a shipping office which can hardly be realised by those living in the quiet Bank-like dignity of No. 15[937]. I can only say I have never worked harder or indeed so hard in my life since I have been in Australia and I have taken several days' holiday whereas Regi has never been away for a business day since I came; he sticks very closely to work. I am sure you will bear all this in mind whenever you have occasion to complain of

---

[936] The Queen Anne style of architecture can refer to either the English Baroque style approximately of the reign of Queen Anne (1702–1714), or to a revived form that was popular in the late 19th and early 20th century.
[937] Refers to 15 Bishopsgate - see the footnote in the diary entry for 19th March 1884.

any laches[938] or errors of judgement which must occur when men are working at high pressure.

Nicholls. A new wool code, or rather, table, has been prepared by Keating. I consider it a triumph of comprehensive ingenuity, and with the most ordinary care (intelligence not required) no mistakes can occur in issuing circulars on your side while the remarks will be fuller than hitherto. Next mail they will be sent to you.

Great Britain. I am very sorry you did not sell her cargo directly after buying; I quite counted on that. Tyndall is *muy porfiado*[939] about this ship. His brothers dislike her as much as I do which is saying a great deal. I hope when Charles gets home you will seriously consider the propriety of slaughtering her. She will be a running issue of money.

I have not had time to look at the *verbosa et grandis epistola*[940] from our Prior[941], but after the mail Regi and I will go most thoroughly into it. I am glad to see the moderate tone of your remarks re Finance as I was getting rather panicky.

You will have realised that in the present state of the Exchange market it is next to impossible for us to sell drafts on now, but we will remit all money we can and try and circumscribe Winham's business about which I write in P.S. to Adelaide today.

I am glad to see you have had some good shooting; I had a capital day Kangaroo hunting in the western district this week.

Your letter has been delivered so late, only 24 hours before the out-going steamer, that I have had no time to write to you fully and fear I may miss some subjects altogether.

Jules Presse. We have made a new agreement with, guaranteeing £600 for the current year but reducing his share of commission from 50% to 25%. We also paid him £400 p.a. on his second year though we had not undertaken to make up his commission to that amount. We have acted very generously to him, as he feels, and perhaps more than Tyndall may approve, but I felt it desirable to satisfy him if possible, if the business was

---

[938] Laches: in law, an unreasonable delay pursuing a right or claim in a way that prejudices the opposing party.
[939] *Muy porfiado*. Spanish: very stubborn.
[940] *Verbosa et grandis epistola*. Latin: Wordy and long letter.
[941] The Prior: an echo of the early days of AG&S when William Gibbs was at the head and was always known as 'The Prior', in line with his firm religious principles; it must refer to Henry Hucks Gibbs at this stage.

to go on, and he has no doubt worked hard, inaugurated a good business, and I really believe been out of pocket.

James Cook. We have not yet entered on terms with, but I think all will go smoothly. He seemed at first to resent our having made an arrangement with Given in his absence, but Regi was pretty firm. With regard to our general agreement with Cowan to embrace all our Australian joint business and to supersede previous agents, Cook the other day to our great astonishment sent in to Regi for his perusal a letter dated London Dec. 1st, 1883 signed Cowan and Co. and written, as Cook informed us, by Jas John Cowan empowering Cook to act on Cowan's behalf in the arrangement of the terms of the new agreement. Of this letter you will receive a Copy. I consider the impropriety of such a course as Cowans have taken more extreme and we certainly shall not discuss with Cook, our joint servant, the arrangements we make with Cowans, but in preference shall send out views to L'pool for them to make the new agreement with Cowans at home. I am determined not to let Cook get any further out of his proper place than he has already, and if he is not to be the employee of G.B.&Co. he had better go. I am not going to have him used by Cowans as the man who is to protect their interests with us, or we shall have as much trouble as Brisbane has with the British India Superintendant, Hansard.

London Directory. Don't forget to send us your old copy of this.

I remain your affectionate brother Vicary Gibbs.

P.S. I have received press copy of Herbert's letter to us of Dec. 7th.

Enclosures –
Press copy Self to Herbert 15th Jan. 1884
Press copy Self to Merivale 24th Jan. 1884
Press copy Self to Keating & Hannay 22nd Jan. 1884
Original Hannay to Keating 14th Jan. 1884
Original Merivale to self 17th Jan. 1884

Letter #12 from Vicary Gibbs (Melbourne) to his brother Alban

30th January 1884 - 36 Flinders Lane West, Melbourne

No. 12

Dear Alban,

I last wrote to you on the 24th and since then we have not heard from England as the 'Garonne' is rather late and her mails won't be delivered till tomorrow.

Winham's Business. We have not been able to get a positive answer from Adelaide as to whether they will load any more ships for him or not, but I feel almost sure they will not, in sight of my last P.S. to them. Meanwhile we are unable to reply to the London House cable of 22nd Jan., "Give us your opinion by telegraph regarding minimum advances required wheat?" which we understood as asking us how much we shall have to draw on you to meet advances to Winham on his wheat. If this is right I think the cable very vaguely worded, and indeed I feel no security as to what you do mean.

I have read very carefully Father's letter (to Charles, Dec.12th) and it is very clear and interesting:-

Page 1. Statement of Capital drawn up by Tyndall. We have not had a copy of this which I should have liked to have seen.

Page 2. Gibbs Bright & Co. Melbourne owed to other persons on the 31st of Dec. last about £34,000 or credit balances in ledger £33,000 and one bill payable, since paid. I assume he means advances to consignors by AGS & Co not advances by G B & Co as it is written in the last line.

Page 3. Your having some document before you which I have not seen puts me at a great disadvantage in examining the figures. Father says, "Melbourne appeared to be using £260,628 besides indents and advances". How and where does this appear. I have before me our trial balance sheet, 30th June, from which I suppose Tyndall compiled his figures but I only make out that Melbourne were employing £113,000 or £146,000 owing to Dunedin and London, plus profits made by commissions etc. £9000 - £42,500 owing from the Brisbane and other Colonial Houses.

Page 4. Goods sold but not paid for £52,171 are both goods invoiced to indentors and consigned goods sold, that is they are open accounts for which we hold no bills - we do deliver goods without receiving cash or bills, taking the ordinary trade risk, making the most careful enquiries from Banks and other sources, and trusting none but first rate firms except for small sums and short periods.

Of course, a certain amount of bad debts are made, especially by the Sydney House, but I do not consider the risk is great or more than our *del credere*[942] fairly covers. There are also a fair amount of indents rejected, either through blunders in the execution or other causes but these we sometimes sell at a profit, and sometimes recover from the manufacturer, and allowing for all these, the business can be shown to be a very profitable one, with its risks well divided.

Page 5. Father says the indents business, though comparatively safe with a small circle of indentors for limited sums might not be so when the indentors are large and widely scattered and the sums large. I cannot see at all how the risk is increased by spreading the risks over a larger number of indentors; I should have thought if anything we would insure the other and it would be lessened. Of course, where the sums are large the risk is greater unless we are dealing with people whose credit is proportionately better.

Executive Documents Father speaks with great respect of these, and lays much force on our always having them. I know, having had a legal education, I ought to be able to say what are the great advantages of taking a man's promissory note, but for the life of me I can't do so beyond the fact that you can sue him on it under the Bills of Exchange Act instead of the ordinary way. Surely he has no priority over unsecured creditors, at least I never heard anything about such a priority in my life. There appear to me to be only 3 courses: Cash, Credit or Security. But Bills can only be valuable as a means of raising money yourself and preventing discussions about 'act current'[?].

My contention is that even if you do hold the executive document "you have no security except the faith of the indentor and your share of his assets in case of failure". If my view is wrong or the law has recently been altered let me know, otherwise it is no use attaching superstitious value to notes and bills.

I think the indent business is a good one for the merchant and very profitable, and that others think so is shown by its being keenly competed

---

[942] *Del credere.* Italian: of belief or trust. A *del credere* agency is one which guarantees (for a commision) to the firm whose services or products it is selling on credit that the purchaser is solvent.

for and the Australian Banks will do all the financing part free of commission; that is to say they will pay for the goods in England, on receipt of b/l[943] & Accts[944] and get repaid here 60 days after sight of docts[945], and as to the buying for him, some of the New Zealand Banks even do that.

I don't quite see what is meant by "if the indentor knew how good"- he surely must know exactly the pull he gets.

Page 6. Our System of Sale. Our general practice with regard to indents is as follows: We take an indent here for say £1000, and send it for execution to Liverpool. L'pool pay the £1000 a <u>fortnight</u> after they have got the goods and despatched documents to us. Sixty days after sight of documents (which always come by steamer) we receive from our indentor £1000 plus Bank Exchange (which represents the price which must be added to a b.o.d.'s[946] bill in Australia) to net for it if discounted in London £1000) at 4% = £40 plus our commission say 5% = £50 - or in all our indentor pays to us here £1090, 100 days or thereabouts after £1000 has been paid by AG&S and Co in L'pool. We have then of course to remit back to England the £1000 and we can do this by a gold remittance or sight Bank Bill in about 50 days or by a 60 d.s bill in say 180[?] days. So to take Father's example, if Liverpool paid the money on the 1st Jan. they would have sent the documents about a fortnight before and you would be in funds again 40 days + 60 days + 50 days after a fortnight before the 1st of Jan or the 21st of May. This of course is supposing it to fit exactly and is the very quickest time in which the money could be turned over.

You could however take it for granted that we could always remit you back by June 9th if we shipped gold or by Aug.8th if we sent 60 days bank bills.

Four months is a most inordinate time for father to calculate on a sailing vessel taking; 90 days is the usual calculation, but this becomes unimportant when you understand that the 60 days run from receipt of documents by steamer not from receipt of goods.

It is true that we very frequently give to our indentors further credit, say 3 months after the period of 60 days from sighting docts., but when we do this we always take a bill or p.u.[947] and charge 8 or 9% interest. These bills we can, if it is thought desirable, always discount so that they do not at all necessarily, or unless we choose, increase the period during which money is locked up in indent transactions. Of course there is another method

---

[943] b/l: abbreviation of 'bill of lading'.
[944] Accts: abbreviation of 'accounts'.
[945] docts: abbreviation of 'documents'.
[946] b.o.d.: abbreviation of 'bill of distribution'.
[947] p.u. = per unit??

and a very simple one by which any cash advances in England on indent account might be avoided. L'pool might draw on us at 60 days for all indents paid for by them and might sell such drafts to the English Banks for cash at current bank Exchange. This in fact is the operation for which our indentors are charged (in lieu of interest) so that we should be in no way out of pocket and should merely forego the profit on Bank Exchange, gaining instead exemption from the interest we are now charged while you are out of the money.

The gain to us by sticking to the present system would be about 1%, but this would be far better than having the business restricted. As to such a plan affecting your English credit, I should like to have your views also as to the relative effect of this plan or of the L'pool House not paying cash.

Shipment of Produce from Australia. I do not propose to say anything about, as Father practically waives all objections and allows of indefinite extension of this branch for the present.

Page 9. Bank deposits. I should have thought myself an average of £4000 for each House would have been enough. Here, directly we get the chance, we reduce our balance to the lowest sum decency permits, and pop it into the sugar company who allow us 5% for it on call.

Sundries and Ships. It is very hard to find out what this is composed of and therefore whether it can be retrenched. We have no debits on ships here as we are always in funds for disbursements, but on the 30th June last I fancy there was the Killarney in Sydney whose owners failed, and the account may include advances made in L'pool; against ships to come out for sale here such as the 'Sharpshooter'.

Page 10. Dunedin Exchange Account. It is of course gone. The statements which Father wants I have instructed our bookkeeper to prepare, and will do the same to the other Houses. In case we don't do it quite right, please send a proforma statement as the Valparaiso House furnishes you.

Page 11. The London Assurance Co. is not represented and has no Agency here otherwise; we would gladly have given them our reinsurances.

Page 8. Fixed Capital Premises etc. Would it not be well to Mortgage all or any of these as opportunity occurs to 2/3 of their value, and so liberate a little more money.

Page 9. Father says the Australian business should not owe at any one time more than £250,000 on 5 specified items. Did they do so on the

Dec.31st last? I shall be surprised if they did, at any rate I see no reason why for the future we should not keep well within these limits.

As to the amount of AG&S's capital employed on Dec.31st 1882 by Melbourne I would refer you to the statement of the <u>Amount of employment of Capital</u> in the last annual accounts. This statement shows as you will see the sum of £21,579. 6. 2. as the real capital employed here; it seems monstrous different to the huge sum Father states we appear to be using only 6 mo. after, viz £260,628. 0. 0.

I know this letter is very scrappy, jerky and slovenly, but it is mostly facts and I feel I am not replying to it formally but merely furnishing notes for brief for our counsel in Bishopsgate St. I will perhaps return to the matter again but I have been much pressed with other business and it is now 8.0 pm and I am hungry.

Goodbye, my dear Alban,

Your affect. Brother, Vicary Gibbs.

Enclosures.
Duplicate of my No. 11.

P.S. On 31st Dec. 1883 I observe Sydney owed London £52,000, Brisbane were in Credit, Adelaide, and Dunedin I presume trifling tho I have not their accounts. Melbourne, omitting produce, scarcely if at all more than Sydney. Say £100,000 for all Colonial Houses exclusive of advances against produce and fixed Capital: this is no more than a rough estimate and there may be some error, but I will look into it more closely when I have got all the ledger balances.

If it is anything like correct, Father's letter authorising indebtedness on 5 items of £250,000 is a permission to extend rather than instructions to curtail business. VG.

Letter #13 from Vicary Gibbs (Melbourne) to his brother Alban

6th February 1884 - Melbourne

No. 13

Dear Alban,

I last wrote to you No.12 on the 30th Jan. and since then have a note from you of Dec.21st and a letter from Herbert dated 28th Dec. replying to my No. 4 to you.

Ships to load. How is it that Tyndall does not see that when he cables to us forbidding us to load a ship between the Holmesdale and Winifred, it is from our point of view the same as if there was a guarantee that we should not load a ship, and yet he writes in P.S.74 to us that he had made no guarantee, but cabled to us not to load a ship to avoid any dispute!

Ceylon Business. Please let me know how this is going on?

Wool. It will be well when all this business is moved to London; at present people have sometimes to correspond with 3 Houses - Liverpool, London and Melbourne - at various stages of the same transaction.

Produce Code. We are sending by this mail an additional list of lines in which we hope to do a firm order business in the English Markets. It is desirable that James or some new man should keep a sharp look out for cheap lines for which there is a constant demand in this market, and of which we will now have a full list; by use of the table he can cheaply and comprehensively send us quotations or firm orders, where he thinks the lines are unduly depressed in your markets by a bankruptcy, over production or other causes.

Sydney. Murray's fault is being a little too greedy to swell the profits of his particular branch; he argues and jaws very fully about bearing the cost of various items.

Cadell. Tyndall writes "looking at what she now earns" she is worth more than £3000. This however is not the way one should look at it, but to consider that it is a rapidly depreciating property for which it is impossible to find a buyer.

Orient Co. I do not think there is much fear of their starting an office of their own, at any rate for some time to come.

Kangaroo Point. I see from the Garonne's letters that you have realised at home our motives and ideas in pressing this purchase on you.

Gray Dawes & Co. I am glad to see Brisbane have begun sending you copies of their letters to this firm. It should have been done before.

Ramsay. Prom. Note. The only difficulty I can see as likely to arise is that Harper's should object to so long an exchange being charged when they have to pay so soon but in this you might meet them and it would not touch the outlay of the security. The legal position is surely just the same as an unaccepted Captain's draft, and there is no reason why, if they would have been willing to accept the one, they should refuse to pay the other. In either case they might act dishonestly and be compelled by law to disgorge. We will endeavour for the future to obtain a promissory note as collateral security to the draft on owners.

Money shipped from London. Your telegrams about this were unnecessary as in both cases the news had been in the Australian papers of the day before. I think you may take it for granted that we are always in possession of any news of public interest; the newspapers are so enterprising and well posted.

China Traders, Melbourne. The enclosed press copy will show you that we have doubled this company's business in the last year, and today we get the disgusting news that we have done so well for them that they will take their business from us and open an office here on their own account. They offer us 5% com. for the 1st year, 4% for the 2nd, and 3% for the 3rd. if we don't take another Insurance office during that time.

Mason Bros. Limited. You will see in the Sydney P.S. to us about this firm a good example of successful Colonial overtrading with very little capital.

Meeks. Owing I think to deficient education his letters are often confused and rather badly expressed, though he is clever and energetic.

Watt. The salesman here is not altogether satisfactory. He is in a very responsible place having replaced Meeks. He is clever and sharp but hasty, scatter-brained and, I think, untruthful; he is young, about 27.

Tennant, the Foochow partner of Gibb Livingston is here; he is a nice gentlemanly fellow. He seemed very sore at the way Tideman wrote and complained to them and expressed his pleasure at there being a sensible man on the board now, meaning you. He said that if they had been allowed to charter during the last 12 mo. and keep the trade together Swires[name unclear] could never have got a chance to start.

I somehow don't feel sanguine about the E.&A.'s prospects, but I hope I am wrong.

Nicholls said some time ago that he thought we might get orders for buying wool in Japan and asked if we had any correspondents there; I asked Tennant to tell us the names of some respectable firms and he mentioned:

Macpherson & Marshall, Yokohama
Fearon & Low, Kobe
Fraser & Co., Nagasaki
Maryllan & Harriman[name unclear], Kobe
Alt & Co.

The first three Gibb Livingston had other business with and knew to be respectable and of good means. You might enquire which of these would be a good firm for us to correspond with. I daresay the Dents could tell you. I believe Fearon of Fearon & Low is now in Melbourne.

Bell. I hope very much that you will say or do nothing on your side to define his position as over Keating or Hannay for the present. It seems to me quite sufficient that he should be under Regi and nothing but time can show who is the best man on this side to be the ultimate head at some future time.

I am my dear Alban,

Your very affectionate brother,

Vicary Gibbs.

Letter #14 from Vicary Gibbs (Melbourne) to his brother Alban

11th February 1884 - Melbourne

No. 14

Dear Alban,

I have today received your note of Jan.4th and as I am off to New Zealand tomorrow I will reply to it today though I have very little to say, having last written to you on the 6th.

Fisher £15,000. I have no doubt you only did this to develop the wool business and your energy with the T&A is quite appreciated: if you happen to see Horn or any of the directors of the T&A you can tell them I am quite convinced that it would be in their interest to extend the limit of £30,000 which may be advanced to any one person or squatter, although it might be well not to allow more than £30,000 advanced against any one station; but where a man like Sir William Clarke wants an advance of £60,000, his security is far better than a little man like Chrystal say can offer for £15,000. Of course too the rule can be practically marched around by sticking in dummies of cousins and nephews, and this is what Fisher has done. The only real result is that it is possible our rule may send away a first rate borrower in a huff.

I quite recognise the propriety of not advancing too heavily on any one station or indeed district but where a man wants a block loan on a station in Victoria I don't see that his position is affected by his having had a loan on a Queensland property.

New Swamp[948] be blowed, I went there, the thermometer 140[949], and about as much wild duck shooting as Elstree Reservoir.

E&A Co. There seems an idea in the Sydney House that this Company's interests are not well looked after by Brisbane and that they are too much put aside and subordinated here in Melbourne to those of the Orient which monopolises the attention of the shipping department. It might be well if a P.S. from England said that the home House was so much

---

[948] Gibbs records his visit to this swamp - whilst visiting Echuca in Victoria - in the 12 January 1884 diary entry.
[949] 140°F is 60°C. Gibbs is either exaggerating, or referring to the temperature in the sun rather than the shade.

interested in this company that they wished it to receive more attention than the profits to any individual branch might possibly repay, but as their business is merely being worked by the Executors no doubt they have to look exclusively to immediate results. The business would be desirable for us in many ways. It would add to the importance of the Adelaide branch, bring us into contact with French merchants, making our name known in France, make it easier for us to get tallow freight and help J. Presse in his touting. Of course should we get the Orient Agency we should at once give up the 'Messageries'.

We have a telegram from Meeks to the effect that "Morgans will keep the Messageries Agency up to the middle of February next, that Conil the head manager of the M. Coy. has written to his directors on the subject of what new agents shall be appointed & that he, Conil, will recommend us but that we must apply too".

We have instructed Meeks to make a formal application but should be glad if you would make an application on behalf of your Adelaide branch setting forth our experience and competence to attend to the Coy's business.

I am my dear Alban, your affect. brother,

Vicary Gibbs

Letter #15 from Vicary Gibbs (Christchurch, NZ) to his brother Alban

Letter #15 from Vicary to Alban, on his arrival in Christchurch. This letter is of great interest, giving the first picture of the different atmosphere of business life in New Zealand. Immigration to Australia had begun at an earlier stage, bringing with it much of the speed of change of Victorian industrial growth to meet a new land soon promising potential for a richly mixed economy. Both Australia and New Zealand would need home-produced food, but New Zealand's was the more obviously agricultural economy by virtue of its temperate climate. At first, it seemed that mineral resources would enter into the account there too, but there turned out to be only limited supplies, whereas the hidden stores of Australia's coal and mineral ores are still in vast reserves, some as yet untouched. It was in New Zealand that Gibbs began to see the extent of the future transport of frozen meat carcasses to Britain, and the start of what became a traditional supply of chilled dairy produce to the old country.

1st March 1884 - Christchurch

No. 15

My dear Alban,

I last wrote to you on the 11th Feb. and since then I have your note of the 11th Jan.

Kangaroo Point. I was absent when they sent you the telegram about "disastrous to our business"; it was a strong expression to employ, but I don't think you will ever regret the purchase.

Gray Dawes are very cheeky and offensive; they are not the sort people it is any use knuckling down to, the more we stick out a certain part of our person the more they will kick it.

E&A Co. I am glad to hear they will pay a dividend. I am not sanguine as to their prospects; it will require exceedingly careful management to make them pay against the opposition they will meet.

Melbourne Club. Thanks for your suggestion, but I think I shall very likely become a member; that is if they don't pill[950] me.

Bellasyse Estate. What have you done about this; I suppose refused it as you wouldn't want to be locking up money just now. From what I remember there was a prospect of satisfactory proposals to do their business. I like the Barbados business because we have such good men to work it.

I found when I got to Dunedin that Arthur was sore about the Brisbane House, who had neglected some consignment of flour which had been sent from N.Z. He also complained of the way letters were answered. No doubt he inherits this feeling of soreness from Sydney, who have long been dissatisfied with Brisbane, but after looking over the correspondence I felt satisfied that the Sales department in Brisbane had not been all that could be wished so I wrote the enclosed note to Hannay. The enclosed note from Hannay to Merivale shows that my view of the matter was correct and also that Hannay is doing his best to set it right.

The Dunedin Offices are excellent, large, bright, admirably situated and cheap.

Arthur is rough, brusque and Colonial and has a horrid habit of introducing quotations followed by, "as Lord Macauley[951] said" like a sort of literary Sam Weller[952]. He is however frank and straightforward, clear headed and energetic, and seems to have got on very well with the people of the town.

I observed that he was on the House committee of the Fernhill Club. I dined with him on Sunday; he has a wife and large family; his age is 38. I heard before I went to Dunedin that he had had an offer of a partnership in Sydney and had written to Murray to ask his advice: so I thought it possible that he might take the opportunity of my coming down to give us warning, however nothing of the kind occurred, but in the course of conversation about the results of last year's N.Z. business, prospects for next and so on, he said, "I tell you frankly Mr Gibbs that I doubt if this business can bear my salary, and I almost think you ought to look for a cheaper man. If you think so, I hope you will tell me for I don't want to hang on to the skirts of the firm unless I can be of use". I replied that we had no thought of making any change, and that whatever we might feel

---

[950] Pill (historical): To reject or exclude by ballot someone from membership of a club or society; to blackball.
[951] Thomas Babington Macaulay, 1st Baron Macaulay (1800-1859). British historian and politician, famous for his political writings.
[952] Sam Weller: a humorous character in Charles Dickens' Pickwick Papers who frequently quotes (or misquotes) others - "wellerism".

about Dunedin we were quite satisfied with him. He then said, "Don't think I want to leave the firm. I like it and want to work for it, and if you open a House anywhere else or think I should be of more use in any of your other Houses I shall be glad to go." He is not a man in whom the bump of reverence is particularly developed, and he criticized and commented on the way in which our business is conducted in several points with more freedom and vigour than one would have expected. He seemed to consider we were particularly weak at home in the matter of securing agencies and consignments, and mentioned many instances of far inferior Houses in every respect in Sydney and Dunedin having secured good agencies during the last few years: whereas what we had were saddled with return commissions. In this relation he said to me that if we liked he should be very glad to travel for us in England in general goods as Coles does in soft goods. I thanked him for his offer and said I should think the matter over. I am not at all sure that James is man enough, and believe it would pay to have a man travelling in England of Arthur's stamp who thoroughly knew the Colonies, but I am blocked by not knowing how far you wish to develop this part of our business and I feel how impossible it is to keep a business like ours stationary. It must either develop extraordinarily as it has done in Sydney under able men like Murray and Arthur, or dwindle to nothing like Dunedin under Walcott and Danson. Several people in Dunedin spoke in high terms of Walcott as a man, though they evidently looked on him as feeble in business. Nobody mentioned Danson to me. I am convinced that another year of Danson would have let us in for some heavy losses. It is extraordinary to me how little control or watchfulness was exercised over him considering how entirely unfit he was to manage our business. Of course there were no inter-colonial P.S. till the other day but my impression is he wrote very little about what he was doing.

The following transactions will illustrate what I have been saying: Just before Arthur came down to Dunedin, Danson lent £700 on some scrip of the Cromwell Gold Mine, which at the time might have realised about that amount but since have become absolutely worthless, and the borrower has bolted. Now about this transaction he said, I believe, nothing to Charles and certainly nothing to Arthur who did not find it out until the balance sheet was got out. As far as I can learn there was no prospect of inducing business and Danson was merely doing an exceedingly bad banking transaction without consulting anyone.

The other affair is not so bad in character but worse in result. Some years ago a small man of the labouring class started tallow making on a small scale outside Dunedin and from time to time Walcott used to advance him £30 or £40 against tallow for sale, which was all right. Danson however gave him money, practically as much as he wanted, which he expended in solid brick buildings, machinery, unnecessarily good stables, and actually I believe part in buying a private house for himself while he put a man into his old cottage by the works. Soon after Arthur got to N.Z. he asked Danson about this and suggested that the tallow manufacturer, Mr Durston, should be asked to reduce his account.

Danson replied, "If you go pressing him or prying about his place, he will just take his account away altogether." This stopped Arthur for the time, but of course he soon looked into it and this is the position. Durston is in our debt for £2,500 against which we have security over 2 acres in another suburb value £150 otherwise we are entirely unsecured. If we were to sell him up at once we should lose £1,500.

Somebody else has a 1st mortgage over the land and buildings £1000 and it is not supposed the land would fetch more at a forced sale. However I told Arthur to get a 2nd mortgage, and also a bill of sale over the machinery. I spent an hour or more at the works with the man; he seemed a steady hard working fellow, he had kept no books but said he was making £600 a year profit, which is exceedingly improbable: £400 is about the mark, however the tallow can be sold faster than he can make it at good prices in the local market. I spoke very plainly to the man about reducing his account, and said he must observe the strictest economy, but I was afraid to say much as if he thought we were going to sell him up he might sell all his bone dust off his place and cheat us that way. I settled with Arthur that the man was to keep a set of books, but he was to be told to sell his house and go back to the cottage and that we would keep him going for 12 months on the understanding that his account was at no time to be increased by a penny, and that unless at the end of that time he could show a fair profit on working and reduce the account by something he must be sold up. I told Arthur he must write off £500 in 1883 on this account, so that with Cromwell Scrip makes £1800 loss, so you must make up your minds for losing £2000 last year in Dunedin. Of course the amount isn't much, but if Danson had been dealing with big sums instead of 2d.1/2[953] ones, what a spanker he would have eventuated.

Trust and Agency Coy. Arthur is very keen to get some of this company's business, and he is anxious to know if there is any chance of our being made agents for the company in the province of Otago, leaving Mr Blakiston Canterbury. The latter recently returned his credits and they were sent on to us in Melbourne. He could not find investments for his money, and yet I believe he made no attempt to make enquiries in Otago, where Arthur would have found no difficulty in finding a safe outlet for at any rate some of the money. The T.A. is practically unknown in Otago; there is I believe an idea that applications for loans should be made through our Dunedin House, but no business has ever resulted as Blakiston, I presume to avoid a return commission, has always taken care

---

[953] i.e. tuppenny-ha'penny, the implication being a negligible amount.

to refuse. At this moment I believe the T. & A. have no money lent out in Otago.

Given. Cowan's business. N.Z. I refer you to my remarks on this subject to Regi, press copy enclosed. I think now it would have been better policy to have taken N.Z. clean away from Cook and given him no share of the corn, leaving the management of the business to Given under Arthur as far as giving credit was concerned. Cook may be a clever fellow but he can't really look after N.Z. or know much about its requirements.

T. Irving & Co. Arthur is more violent against this firm than our other managers. He says they play into the hands of the brokers and never get us an advantage in freight.

The rate paid by the Dunedin Iron and Woodware Coy. for cement per Fenstanton, which left London last December was 4/- Irvings paid for 500 casks. Gostlings cement per same vessel 5/- & 10%; how can we compete against people who get such a pull in freight. What is the explanation?

Morewoods too the other day shipped gal[954] iron at 42/6 and 10% per Fenstanton, though we had advised them that the market was flat. Their last lot before was shipped per sailer[955] at 30/-. Of course this per Fenstanton S.S. will leave a heavy loss. I don't know if Irvings had anything to do with engaging freight for them.

Business is in a very bad state in Dunedin. Almost all the firms are insolvent except Briscoes[956] and ours and one or two more. They are all kept up by the Banks, and the Bank of N.Zealand is actually obliged to run on its own account a large ironmongery and furnishing business. I fancy people in England have a very exaggerated value of securities in N.Zealand and the failure of a Bank or Loan Coy. would cause an awful bust-up and exposure. Most of the private firms are being driven out of trade by these big companies to whom the confiding[957] AR[?][958] lend money at 4% as much as they want.

Goodbye, my dear Alban,

Your affectionate brother, Vicary Gibbs.

---

[954] gal: abbreviation of galvanised.
[955] sailer: a sailing ship (as opposed to a Steam Ship).
[956] Arthur Briscoe & Co. opening in 1863, an offshoot of the Melbourne firm Messrs. Briscoe & Co. established in 1854, which was itself an offshoot of a company based in Staffordshire sometime around 1750. Arthur Briscoe & Co. were mainly wholesale ironmongers and hardware merchants with some limited retail trade.
[957] confiding = confident (now obsolete).
[958] Unreadable - possibly "AR".

Letter #16 from Vicary Gibbs (Auckland, NZ) to his brother Alban

Vicary Gibbs' mind was already on the various Australian projects by the time he wrote letter #16 to Alban from Auckland, but was enlightened by much of his experience; in particular, by his meeting with Tyson (alias Smith), one of the wealthiest Australian 'squatters' of the late 19th century.

30th March 1884 - Northern Club, Auckland

No. 16

My dear Alban,

I last wrote to you on the 1st of this month (copy enclosed) and on arriving here yesterday found yours of the 18th & 25th Jan. and 1st Feb. for which I am much obliged. I am very sorry to see from your letters that Mr Hayne has been ill and worried. Pray remember me very kindly to him.

It also vexes me very much to see my dear Alban from the tone of your epistles that you have had a lot to bother you. I can't help saying again that the Australian business is rather the scapegoat than the cause of your anxieties. Of course the close cross examination to which it has been and is being subjected is excellent and I have no doubt some weak points will be disclosed.

I am very glad you write so warmly of Keating's value. I feel he was my selection, and feel proud of it. I consider he has developed into an A1 businessman. The only difficulty about arranging for K. and Hannay to be in Melbourne and Bell in Brisbane is that it would not have the approval of Reg. and Ch. Bright, at least I don't think so. Also it would be saddling the Brisbane office with a very heavy salary.

Amby Downs. I meant to say that improved stations the size of Amby, which are worth a lot of money, are very difficult of sale when money is tight. Fisher and men like him have made money by taking large runs of back country, spending as little money as possible on them and selling them as the rest of the world came after them, in fact acting as auctioneers. Fisher is a very speculative man, and always in want of money although he has these large concessions, and is very heavily involved.

I have been travelling lately in Tyson's company, the richest man in Australia, and another N.S.W. squatter told him that he had recently sold

Fisher up and taken his bill at 3 months for £9000. He said he was very nervous till the bill matured, and Tyson evidently took the same view. I give you this for what it is worth; it serves to show Fisher's position is not as undoubted in some folks' minds as I for one had thought.

I was talking to a young fellow the other day who had been much in Spain and knew the Rio Tinto and Mason & Barry Mines well. He said the latter was beginning to be worked out and if he had some shares now he should sell them for what he could get. No doubt you have better means of information, - still you might make some fresh enquiries.

Hopcraft's scheme for consigning the Lamoi Produce[? or **Purchase**] to you sounds very good and I hope it will go through.

Manners Sutton. I think we are better off without him. I fancy Charles Bright has had to pay a lot of money for him.

Winham, Adelaide. I feel nervous about this a little, but I won't say anything until I get back to business for which I feel quite ready; indeed I am rather ashamed of having taken this long trip to N.Z. when I didn't particularly want a holiday, - gout has done much to spoil it, but it is a glorious country.

Messageries Agency. I do not see that having this will the least interfere with our giving it up if we get the chance of the Orient.

I leave for Sydney on the first and shall stay there probably for a fortnight. I can't make up my mind whether I shall go from there to Brisbane, or back to Melbourne, but I think the latter; things centre there and one gets out of it anywhere else. Of course I mustn't put off my visit to Brisbane too late but take advantage of the cool weather.

I have sent no copy of this to Tyndall so you can read or send him extracts.

Your most affect. Brother,

Vicary Gibbs.

Love to Bride[959].

---

[959] Alban's wife, Bridget Gibbs (née Beresford-Hope).

Letter #17 from Vicary Gibbs (Sydney) to his brother Alban

Back in Sydney, and able to catch up with the news on the ground as well as replies from London, Vicary put Alban in the picture in his letter #17, before getting down to dealing with some of the points raised by his father, Henry Hucks Gibbs, in two replies to him.

9th April 1884 - Sydney

No. 17

Dear Alban,

I last wrote to you on 30th March (copy enclosed) and since then I have received yours of the 8th, 14th, 23rd (also points note 22nd and 29th of Feb.), for which I am duly grateful.

I am sorry to hear of your headaches; I hope now Charles is home you have taken a well-earned holiday. You must have had a great deal to think of, so much overhauling of and discussion of Australian business as has been going on in addition to your regular work.

Merivale is perfectly happy and contented and working most satisfactorily, and is now, I consider and so does Murray, a valuable man whom it would not be easy to replace at short notice. Murray just now, of his own accord said to me, "I am impressed at the improvement he has shown; I have the greatest confidence in him". As you saw from my letter I took advantage of my intimacy with him, to write pretty sharply about that nonsense of his 'position' and when I saw him he mentioned the subject saying I was quite right.

Of course you got angry at not receiving an answer to your telegram about wheat on 22nd Jan. and I myself was fidgety about it and suggested that some sort of reply should be sent though either Keats Regi or I could answer. I thought that if I had been 'managing the shops' alone you would have had one. When Adelaide received Tyndall's cable, they wired to us for instructions, and Regi happening to be absent for the day, Keating and I prepared an answer which we sent, and the next day instructed Adelaide to send another, feeling sure that the two together would tell you what you wanted to know.

I am ashamed of myself that I did not look into the question of the amount advanced to Winham, but I took for granted that it had been arranged between Charles Bright, Adelaide and the home houses that the advance was to be such an amount less than the market price for the time being. However, I plead guilty to a want of thoroughness in the matter and am rather disgusted about it.

Eggert. Correspondence received and will speak to Murray and see what can be done. I have not yet had time to read more than that it's about a nephew.

Great Britain. I am sure that you would like her to look at; her lines are beautiful but they don't seem to have fallen in the pleasant places.

72. Model of the SS Great Britain
Courtesy of the Port Stanley Museum, Falkland Islands. Photo by Edel, staff photographer on the Saga Ruby.

Liverpool. I am glad you liked your visit there and thought the office going on well. I always considered Carruthers very intelligent but my faith in him is shaken now you tell me he says my calculations about drawing and remitting were wrong.

I am very sorry to learn that Katie[960] has been out of health. I hope next mail will bring news of her being all right again.

Small dividend. Please find enclosed.

British India. Their complaints are irritating and their tone offensive and such as the Brisbane House does right to resent, but I cannot but think from other things which have come to my knowledge that there is a dilatoriness and want of push about Hart, Southerden and the old blood in Brisbane; though both Keating and Hannay have as far as I can judge been very active there: it shall go hard but I wake them up when I go North; I wish if possible that Hannay should not have left when I get up there and I know he will tell me all his impressions.

My views about Brisbane are formed from what I have heard in our other branches, and also from such conversations as the following: I met a large Queensland squatter in New Zealand; he asked me if I had anything to do with G.B. & Co., Brisbane and then said "very respectable, very well thought of; I like Mr Hart – purely a shipping business, I think," and then, "oh, indeed, well, I understood they had quite given up their store business, at any rate they don't attempt to push it; I used to get all my stores from them but now I go to so-and-so".

I had to write a line to Hannay about their salesman's letters as I found Dunedin were sore and he took it as more personal to himself and more to heart than I meant. You shall have the letters next mail but you will see from the end of his private note to G.M. enclosed, with some amusement, that he thought I was disgusted with Dunedin, that the House there would be shut up and some of our staff reduced, and that I was seeking occasion to slay him.

E&A. I think will probably not get the tender which was at a farthing per trip and lower of course than the other two, but the Govt. want to bind us in a penalty of £200 though they pay no subsidy, and to this, Murray will not agree. He says make the subsidy as low or as high as you like and let the penalty be double the subsidy, which one would have thought reasonable enough to satisfy even a S.A. Government.

My No. 10. I am much gratified that you all find this long yarn interesting. I think it was about the longest letter I ever wrote, and it is very ingenious of you to have induced our Prior[961] to interest himself in Australian matters and to reply so fully as he has done. You must make my apologies to him

---

[960] Catherine Louisa Gibbs (1875-1967), Alban's daughter.
[961] Our Prior: Gibbs' father, Henry Hucks Gibbs.

as I have no hope of answering his numerous and copious letters this mail, though I do hope to write a line or so acknowledging them.

Frank[962] is quite lean; I don't know what his object was in representing himself to you as otherwise.

I am much pleased to see the new plan adopted for press copies by Liverpool House; it is not as good as a good press copy but far better than a bad one. I will give your message to the Adelaide House and suggestions; their copies are vile and so is Meek's writing.

Silver Cres. I note what you say as to the difficulty of getting a fair sample.

Winham's business. I shall be relieved if we get out of this without loss.

Yours of Feb. 29th. I quite agree with what you write in the first 2 pages, but it calls for no reply beyond what you will see in mine to Herbert going forward by this mail.

Kangaroo Mortgage to Keating. I am not sure if you look at this in quite the proper light. In the first place from his point of view, he is living in a country where first class mortgages are readily obtainable at 6%. Indeed as I told you the former owner of Kangaroo paid 7%. He is naturally anxious to get the benefit of this rate and naturally enquires if we should like his money before he puts it elsewhere. Then from our point, it does not suit us to lock up our money unless certainly it would pay us 9% as we could make more money by trading with it, and I therefore look upon it as clear gain to set free this £10,000 which would be locked up in Kangaroo.

If any of your home depositors desired to invest money in first class mortgage in Australia they would obtain 6% less merchants' commissions and cost of remitting. Of course you don't want to disturb your depositors, I know that very well, but supposing at any time, any friends desired to invest in Australian first class town mortgages it would pay these houses very well to do the business, which I learnt from Bankers of Ch.ch., N.Z., that Miles & Co. do to a very large extent in N.Z.

We should net the investor say 5. 1/2 % payable by you in London.

Mackinnon. I am glad to see you have seen, and shall wait with interest the result of your field day. I should be very sorry to lose the British India Agency.

---

[962] Frank Keating.

N.Zealand. I did enjoy thoroughly; it is a grand country for holiday making, - very different to this machine-made continent, but very inferior for making money in.

North China Coy. I am very pleased at getting this in Melbourne, it will be such a sell for the China Traders and serve them right for throwing us over. I sincerely hope they will find that they have reckoned without their host and that it is our connection not their connection that is valuable.

I suppose we are safe to get the N.C. in Dunedin also.

Fels & Co. Partnrs[name unclear] Now they have thrown us over here it is worth while taking some trouble at home to try and learn if there is another respectable Patnas[?] house with whom we could do business.

The drought has been awful here in N.S.Wales and 2/3 of the colony are still suffering; the remainder has had recent and abundant rain. I do not know if you will be frightened at the deficits on liens. I do not feel so myself only we must watch it with extreme closeness next season; of course we have had a very exceptional season.

Keating's letters to you of March 20th and April 2nd. Press copies are before me which I have read with great interest, but as he deals very fully and clearly with most important matters it is no use my going through them again as any knowledge at the moment owing to my holiday is very inferior to his.

I am disgusted to see how ill he anticipates the Melbourne and Adelaide results will show. I see nothing to dissent from in anything he writes, and indeed on the principal of constant dripping wearing away a stone I add my humble petition to his that you will disestablish and disendow Irving & Co. and rise in strength and smite them in the hinder part and put them to perpetual shame; I am sick of their grasping ways and want to be shot[963] of them.

Sydney premises. There is not sufficient 'bond' to build these in brick and stone so they will be all in brown stone.

Sugar advances. This is a fine business for the Sydney House and I don't want to see them lose it if it can possibly be helped: the sort of advances against machinery would, if done at all, be to a very limited extent and would mean 2 or 3 hundred pound to help a constituent to put up a vacuum pan, a sort of thing which as far as I know you wouldn't hesitate

---

[963] Although Gibbs apparently uses the word "shut" rather than "shot" - a possible archaic version?

to do in Barbados, and which if done here would mean a large increase in the amount of sugar coming to this branch for sale. Of course there would be no idea of finding the money for people to put up new plant on new ground, and I think in this matter you may fairly trust us not to make extensive or imprudent advances of any kind, and to obtain the security of the sugar land as well as machinery. Please let me have your views.

This branch has been discounting heavily lately at the request of the Melbourne house and to enable them to carry on their wheat racket, over 50 thousand in the last six weeks. Of course this means a loss of say £75 to this branch.

I don't suppose one can regulate that sort of thing, only some day it might give an unfair idea as to how the different houses were doing: though of course it is quite right to look to the thing as a whole.

Merivale to Herbert by this mail. Please read what M. says by this mail about sugar machinery.

Messageries Coy. I am sorry we did not get this as I hear Yuill is disposed to have his own agency in Adelaide if there is any change from Stillings; perhaps he means to job his brothers in. I do not consider there would have been anything unfair to the French Co. in taking their Agency *pro tem*. They would know perfectly well that no house would retain it as it has no money value if it could get the Orient.

Union S.S.C.[964]. I see you say in P.S.30 to Melbourne that this company needs a competitor. I can only say that my impression after knocking about a bit in their vessels is of a very full service very well conducted.

Amby.. I dare say my suggestions about making this into a Coy. were crude and wrong but I will come back to the charge some time when I have thought the matter out.

No time for more but I will write you again next week and wipe up anything forgotten and neglected.

Best love to Bride[965], from your very affectionate brother, Vicary Gibbs.

(No time for a word to father).

P.S. My own wish, as before said, is that Bell should go to Brisbane but I must see what Regi thinks, and fear that he will want it different. Keating

---

[964] Union Steam Ship Company of New Zealand, founded in 1875.
[965] Alban's wife, Bridget Gibbs (née Beresford-Hope).

and Hannay are both very keen for Melbourne and my own feeling is that other things being equal they ought to have the pull over the newcomer.

Letter(1) from Vicary Gibbs (Sydney) to his father Henry Hucks Gibbs

10th April 1884 - Sydney

My dear Father,

I am shocked to see that I have six letters from you to answer dated Jan. 9, 18 and 25, and Feb. 8 and 21. Although this seems a terribly long list, yet a great deal of the matter has been either replied to in anticipation or in my letters to Alban and Herbert, or in Keating's and the Melbourne House letters.

It was useless my attempting to write on the subjects you discussed when I was travelling about N. Zealand and without anyone to consult, and indeed there was nothing immediately pressing in what you wrote.

73. Shipping Wool, Circular Quay (c1879-1917)
Tyrrell Photographic Collection, Powerhouse Museum

Yours of Jan. 9th. What you say on pages 1 and 2 on the perils that do environ the making of liens on wool is quite correct. I see in my last to you of Feb. 12th I say something of the same kind. This branch of our business is in fact undergoing a severe trial. The awful drought which still continues over a large portion of N.S.W. and Queensland has hit the squatters very hard. I hear of 8 million sheep dead in the former and 5 in the latter country. It strikes me as appalling. Of course a succession of such seasons is undoubtedly conceivable and would mean the ruin of half Australia; everybody knows that drought is the great risk which those interested in this continent have to face. At the present moment in our books the deficits on lien accounts amount to £10,000, and though we shall of course restrict our advances on next clip as much as possible yet this season having been bad will make the squatters more clamorous for money while we are more loath to fork out.

I believe I have already said in a letter to Alban that I consider the wool business the most risky in which these Houses are engaged in, so much as the advance is not on bill of lading but on a future growth. Still spite of all these drawbacks and dangers which it is a folly not to admit I look on the business taking one consideration with another as a very lucrative one: and it is in its favour that it can only be undertaken by large companies or very strong private Firms.

There has been an enormous increase in the World's production of wool and I expect prices will gradually fall, and this should be kept in view.

Although I said that we should be able to largely increase our number of liens, I am far from feeling anxious to do so hurriedly and 'piano' shall be our motto.

Remember that there is a strong competition for this wool business among big houses, and this - though not proof - is evidence of its being sound. Recent letters will have explained to you how the finance of advances is managed between the period when they are first made and the actual shipment of the wool – advances on ensuing clip are often applied for and granted almost immediately after the shipment of the preceding year's clip. The Squatter supplying gives his bill at 3 months for the amount and at the same time his cheque for interest for the same period. We then discount his bill and retire it at maturity taking a new bill which is treated in the same way, and so on till shipment. In this way, so long as the Banks will discount, - in doing which at present they have shown no hesitation - there is no necessity for our drawing on you or being out of pocket until the wool is actually shipped. The advance of £10,000 made to Robertson in Jan. is being financed in this way.

Of course, as soon as the wool is actually shipped - or in our hands for shipment - we are really out of funds and must then draw on you. A bill on you at 60 days should in most cases not mature until after the wool has arrived, and were the wool always shipped by steamer this would invariably be the case. Besides, we could always send 'executive documents' such as b/l[966] and policies which would be in your hands before maturity of the bills. We shall probably discontinue bills at longer usance than 60 days, but you should bear in mind that it is only our strong financial position that enables us to negotiate such instruments at all and

---

[966] b/l = Bill of Lading

unless a regular custom of longer usance should grow up, our weaker rivals to whom you refer would not be able to negotiate them.

Sugar machinery. What you say is no doubt quite true, but you have somewhat misapprehended the object and extent of proposed advances. Given a respectable man engaged in cultivating a sugar plantation, the interest being thoroughly proved and established in the country, the capability of production and the ready sale of the product being an established fact: why should the advance of a few hundreds to him to enable him to improve his appliances and increase his produce coming to us for sale shock you so much that you telegraph to forbid it? - when the same thing has been done as a matter of course in the West Indies as for example the advance to the Revd. North Pinder[967]. I fully agree in disallowing any extensive advance on machinery, as for instance helping a man to put up new plant on new land. But if you mean that the Sydney House is not to assist a man who has been consigning regularly, - to put up a vacuum pan, say - making arrangements for yearly reduction of the debt: when a refusal would probably mean not merely losing that man's sugar but possibly throwing all the sugar growers into the hands of 'The Sugar Company'[968], a powerful and wealthy body on whom we have got the bulge and who are trying all they can to get the sugar growers into their hands again, I can only say (to bring this intolerable long sentence to an end) that I think it a great pity.

The case I have stated is not a mere hypothetical 'if your uncle was your aunt' sort of affair, but has very nearly if not quite arisen and will have to be decided off hand. You must remember we got the whole of these sugar growers in a body and shall lose them in a body if they think that they can't depend on us for proper support. Of course you must do what you think best, *vous êtes bien les maîtres*[969], only I think a little latitude would be advisable and I am loath to lose a very good business which we got by great luck.

Insurance of Gold per Sorata. Yes, this was all done in one Company (The China Traders) but they only retained £12,000, the balance being reinsured. Of the fact of the reinsurances we of course were aware as we effected them ourselves. I do not know how the law stands supposing the Sorata to have been lost and the China Traders simultaneously to have gone bankrupt. Could we have recovered the reinsurances in full: or, would the amounts due from the other Companies [have] been ordinary

---

[967] A Reverend North Pinder (1828-?) inherited Hothersal Plantation in Barbados from his brother Francis Ford Pinder in 1869.
[968] 'The Sugar Company' possibly refers to the Colonial Sugar Refining Company, a company formed in 1855 following the dissolution of the original Australian Sugar Company (established in 1842).
[969] *Vous êtes bien les maîtres.* (French) You're the boss, after all!

assets of the bankrupt Company. I should say the latter and in that case there is certainly a small risk in giving so large a line to one Company.

Yours of Jan. 18th. You must be sick of reading about Gold shipments from this side, the explanation after all was simple enough: the Banks had miscalculated their requirements and uprated[?] too freely; a good deal of nonsense seems to have been written in the English newspapers.

I still feel rather nervous as to what the result of this wheat business in Adelaide will be and my attitude is rather hope than confidence with regard to it.

Yours of Jan. 25th. As far as it relates to business does not seem to me to call for any reply and the same as to yours of Feb. 1st and Feb. 8th.

Yours of Feb. 21st. The law is extremely severe and a Squatter can be put in prison if he does not consign his wool where he has got an advance, and the merchant granting the lien can follow the wool into the hands of a bona fide holder for value. This is a protection to the Merchant of a substantial kind.

Indent Business Page 5 of Regi's capital report on the annual accounts for 1883 showing the very small amount of money lost in compulsory adventures through rejected indents is satisfactory. I have not your letter to Charles before me, but I have already done my best to answer it in Melbourne.

I do not think there is any likelihood of our really being admitted into any banking ring: it would undoubtedly hamper us for they wouldn't keep their engagements as to rates whereas we should continue to act honestly; I merely mentioned Parkes' speech as showing the estimation in which he professed to hold our House. I think if an exchange operation was profitable to us we should not scruple to do it though it might not appear so, people can hardly criticize and analyse our business as closely as that comes to.

Ever your affectionate son,

Vicary Gibbs

Letter(2) from Vicary Gibbs (Sydney) to his father Henry Hucks Gibbs

Via: P&O Valetta
Our last: 15th April 1884
Your last: 14th March 1884
19th April 1884 - Sydney

Dear Father,

Many thanks for yours as above.

You are guilty of representing me as saying something I did not say and telling me I am wrong in doing so. I am much obliged to you for explaining the advantages of holding executive docs. which were already known to me. I should never have been so foolish as to say that "holding them carried no advantage". I specially mentioned to you that you could sue the buyer under the Bills of Exchange Act and that it prevented him from opening up accounts for discussion. What I did say was that by taking a man's bill you had no security beyond the buyer's good faith and your share of his assets in the event of failure; after reading your answer I cannot see that you have.

You say that if you take a man's bill the money becomes due on a certain day - so it does, surely, if you sell him goods; by law the money is due the moment the goods are delivered unless a future time is fixed in which case it is due then.

[A largely illegible paragraph has been omitted here]

Alban doesn't consider my remarks worth more answer than to crush me "by dint o' Greek"[970].

I am very much pleased to hear that the New Library and other alterations at Aldenham are improvements; I hope it won't have changed any more before I get back except in being tidy. Mother had not mentioned Maxwell's marriage; "it was time" as old Nap.[971] said. Please ask Herbert or Harry to get him a wedding present – 5 or 6 £ - and debit my account.

---

[970] "By dint o' Greek" - a quote from "Epistle To J. Lapraik" by Robert Burns.
[971] Napolean.

Clayton sends me a capital article of his in the St. J.[972] on "Thoughts on Shakespeare" by Canning[973]. It is a frightful hammering. Did you see it?

To return for a moment to the executive docs. – I quite see the stimulus they give to make the debtor pay, and the advantage for simplicity when he goes bankrupt, only if you *can* prove the debt without holding paper, you are in just as good a position as if you held paper. Reginald returns to Melbourne on the 21st and I go north to Brisbane a little later in the week, stopping on the way with Murray to have a look at Newcastle. I should like to see the new premises up in Sydney before I leave Australia. I believe in 5 years' time we shall be doing a bigger business here than in Melbourne.

Your affectionate son,

Vicary Gibbs.

Letter #18 from Vicary Gibbs (Sydney) to his brother Alban

In letters ##18-22 (of which #21 is missing), Vicary Gibbs reviews many of the points discussed by the brothers before, and refers to London for approval as he goes north from Sydney to Brisbane to check for loose ends he may need to examine before leaving, as well as to assess progress.

17th April 1884 - Sydney

No. 18

My dear Alban,

I last wrote to you on the 9th and since then have nothing from you and indeed from anyone, my own per S.S. Rome not having come to hand which puzzles me. On this account and also because I have written to Father on business and because the week has been cut to pieces with holidays and races I have almost nothing to say, but enclose a large number of enclosures of various importance which speak for themselves.

---

[972] St. James's Gazette, a London evening newspaper founded by Henry Hucks Gibbs (Vicary's father) in 1880 and owned by him until 1888. It was published until 1905 when it amalgamated with the Evening Standard. The first editor was Frederick Greenwood.
[973] "Thoughts on Shakespeare's Historical Plays" (1884), by Hon. Albert Stratford George Canning (1832-1916).

Smeb's nephew. I have read the correspondence; yours and his first letters might be printed as samples of letters from people not knowing the Colonies. As you know the market for anything in the shape of clerks or semi-genteel indoor town employments is fearfully unstructured, but I have spoken to Murray, and wherever or whenever the young fellow turns up we will do the best we can.

Sugar advances. The planter who largely assisted us in getting hold of this business has applied for assistance in increasing his plant, and we should have been glad if it had been possible to meet his views, but after going into it thoroughly with Regi and Murray we considered the security far from satisfactory or sufficient so have refused.

From all I can hear I anticipate hard times for N.S.W. during the next few months; the area over which rain has fallen is gradually extending but the drought can not be said to have broken up and of course the sheep are dying every day.

Bell. Regi seems disposed to send him to Brisbane and have Hart and Hannay in Melbourne; this I should like tho' I feel Bell's salary is too high for them in Brisbane and Hart may remonstrate at this besides not liking another when he has got accustomed to Hannay. Anyway we will have Bell in Melbourne for a bit to see what he is like.

Enclosed find list of shareholders of <u>Pacific Fire and Marine Insurance Co.</u> I understand that the [illegible word] action of the London board which was causing alarm has been stopped by the head office. The liability of shareholders is unlimited and those ticked in pencil are known to be all men of substance and some very rich; of course, since publication of this list many may have sold their shares.

Leighton in this office appears to be in much better health and is doing his ordinary work again.

Statement showing the position of the accounts of the various branches. I attach this to this letter. We have obtained it by telegram from each House - deducting £60,000 advanced against produce to your consignment of £10,000 advanced by the other branches; it would appear that we are employing at the moment about £100,000 of your money out of the £280,000 allowed to us but of course something must be added on for what Liverpool is in debt to you for indents purchased.

Melbourne Results 1883. I cannot help being disappointed with these, even when all allowance is made for the mess which Tyndall has shifted off L'pool's back onto Melbourne's.

What was the result of the British holdings[?] for 1883?

Yours affectionately, Vicary Gibbs.

Letter #19 from Vicary Gibbs (Sydney) to his brother Alban

Via: S.S. P&O Valetta
Our Last: 17th April 1884
Your Last: 14th March 1884
21st April 1884 - Sydney

No. 19

My dear Alban,

Many thanks for yours as above. I am sorry you did not like the numerical cipher system. I should have thought with ordinary care it would have worked admirably; Lenders have used it for some time. Of course if the telegraph authorities won't send the figures correctly it must be given up.

Lenders. I do not understand how it was that you at home twice informed us that this firm was undoubted, and now Tyndall coolly writes that they are worth nothing. I wonder you did not ask them for a Bank Credit which they used to be willing to give for a small charge, which charge we could calculate in our quotations. I don't want to stop this business if you can make it right on your side as to Lenders financial position, for they are sharp and active and we can put business through on their offers which we have not been able to do with the offers from our own Houses.

I am sorry you have been bothered by remarks in my letters which should have been in P.S. but the fault lies with the P.S. for omitting them. My letters have not been meant to take the place of the Melbourne P.S.; they have however related almost entirely to Australian business and in every case Tyndall has had a copy by same mail. My impression was that you would have filed them with the P.S. of same date, and so had no difficulty in reference.

British India. I am very sorry to hear that this is gone and shall anxiously await particulars.

Bata[974]. Who are your agents or correspondents there; a good bit of Australian wool was bought there last season, and if we had some good people there we might get a share of it.

I leave here on Wednesday night in Murray's company for Newcastle on my way north. You remember Merivale has often written about Newcastle of which he had a high opinion. Last season Dalgety's opened a branch there for wool shipping, and the result was very successful. They get a lot of fresh wool which used to go down here as squatters were very glad to save the additional journey and Sydney charges.

A considerable quantity of rain has fallen in different places, but the drought still continues [illegible word - possibly a short place name] way, and it is not safe yet to say that it has actually broken up though it may be hoped so.

I send a few unimportant enclosures and with nothing particularly interesting to tell you this time I remain,

Your affectionate brother, Vicary Gibbs.

Letter #20 from Vicary Gibbs (Brisbane) to his brother Alban

8th May 1884 - Brisbane
No. 20
My dear Alban,

I last wrote to you from Sydney on April 21st and since then I have received yours of 21st March forwarded to me from Melbourne.

Winham. I am glad to hear the prospects for the crop are good this season. I learnt yesterday that the long anticipated stoppage of the Oriental Bank has at last come; I suppose it is no concern of ours.

Meeks. I think you will come to my opinion of his letters, - they are diffuse, illegible and rather unintelligible. Have been much worried about this Winhams business, and don't think its conduct reflects much credit on Meeks' thoroughness of thought.

---

[974] This word (almost illegible) appears to be "Bata". If that is the case, it is unknown whether it refers to Bata (in Equitorial Guinea) or is an abbreviation of Batavia (the former name of Jakarta), or something else.

North China Co. Melbourne are endeavouring to get their Agency for this branch. I forget why the Union of Canton was applied for for Dunedin, but I believe we have now got the North China there.

Bell, George. I am very glad to read what you said to him. I have no doubt I shall like him and that he will be a valuable acquisition.

Melbourne Accounts. I will speak about these being carefully made up.

Charles Bright. I hope he will prove a success. The account of him was very good; - if you are sure that you want such a man in London at present.

I left Sydney on the night of the 23rd April with Murray for **Newcastle**, and spent a day there looking over the wharves and calling on people. You will see that the result has been that Murray suggests sending Tower on a tour through New South Wales to canvass the squatters to send their wool to Newcastle to be shipped by us thence. I presume he would at the same time endeavour to obtain consignments of wool to you. Of course if he was successful in getting the promise of any wool for shipment, we should arrange with a Newcastle firm to look after it as we have done with Fisher's wool, and at some future date we might locate Tower there as a sort of sub-agency under Sydney.

Tower is an exceedingly agreeable, well-mannered, gentlemanly fellow and would I should think make a capital canvasser among the squatters.

Newcastle is a pushing, busy place and there is little doubt that it will increase in importance, as looking at the map it seems inevitable that it should get a large quantity of wool now shipped from Sydney.

From Newcastle I went over-land to Headington Hill, a fine freehold station of C.B. Fisher's on the Darling Downs. All the way the results of the unfortunate drought were very apparent, except in part of New England, and at Fisher's Station; though as yet they had lost no stock, the paddocks were perfectly bare of feed. I reached this place on the night of the 30th and found all well.

Hart has been pretty hearty lately and Hannay is happy and contented with his position here, and does his work entirely to Hart's satisfaction.

Hannay is a very able manager of the clerks and general office business; perhaps he is a little deficient in pluck and decision when anything unexpected turns up, but he is very careful and will never let us in for a mess. I feel great confidence in him.

Southerden strikes me as rather old and slow of speech and ideas, but Hart as you know is much attached to him and speaks of him as most loyal and devoted: Hannay also considers him a good man.

Hassall the Insurance Clerk and Scott the Salesman also strike me as satisfactory.

The Royal Fire Insurance Co. At our present rate of commissions this barely pays for the large clerical labour it entails. This branch applied for an increase some time back to Salter, the Coy's head agent in Melbourne and he promised to write to London: however nothing more has been heard and Hart is rather disposed to give it up. Could you do anything in London to make them increase our commissions as we have asked them. If they would do this we would then try to get the 'Sun'[975] or some other good fire company on the same terms and work the two together.

British India. We sent you a telegram enquiring how things stood, as it was necessary for us to know what line we should take as to endeavouring to get them a long emigration contract with the Queensland Government (see P.S. to L'pool 46). It was signed by me that you might know I was in Brisbane.

On hearing from you that you had resigned we sent you a long telegram which you may have thought unnecessary, but I was anxious you should know what were the feelings of this branch.

Of course I am quite in the dark as to what actually led to your resigning the Agency but I presume you found Gray Dawes impertinent and impracticable. From all I can learn here the B. India cannot do without us and will have to come back to us; if so they should certainly do so on our terms – that they cease to write insolently, subordinate Hansard and allow us a commission for surplus stores which we sell for them: in fact all our arrangements should be revised and reconsidered. Morehead spoke to me himself and showed me a letter from his partner expressing their determination to abide by our action, and Forrest of Parbury's will also run straight. He is on his way to London and you will no doubt be specially civil to him. These things being so and G.D. & Co. being obliged by their mail contract to continue the service, they appear to me practically at our mercy. Of course there may be some cat in the cupboard and they may have made arrangements but I don't believe it possible. In case it should be *guerra ad anhillo*[976] between us and them, so that you don't expect to come together again, and have definitely ceased to be their Agents, I hope

---

[975] The Sun Fire Office.
[976] *guerra ad anhillo*. *guerra* is legible, but the remainder of the phrase is less so - it looks like *ad anhillo* but that isn't quite right for any language. Gibbs' meaning from context seems to be "War to destruction".

you will cable to us:- 'Refuse' by which this house will understand that until they hear further they are not to allow the use of our wharf to the B.I. boats. This would bring things to a head at once. I have read up several of Gray Dawes letters and they are <u>insufferable</u>. The last mail brought one about our tugs saying that under every petty pretext we run up charges against them in an unreasonable manner. You will see our answer by this mail, which is pretty stiff.

With our wharf accommodation and Moreheads' command of wool there ought to be a very good opening for another line of steamers to run next season against the B.I.. Would the E.&A. be game to charter some big boats and try it? I believe it would pay, and I would dearly like to pay off Gray Dawes for their insolence.

I think G.D.& Co. don't realise the weakness of their position, otherwise it would be almost insane of them to break with us unless they have secured other wharfage.

Arthur's resignation. I enclose a lot of papers about this; I hope you will not consider it necessary to close the Dunedin House. Either Merivale, Keating or Bell could very well go down there - in my opinion it is rather a question of convenience than great importance which is selected; at least, I should be satisfied whichever goes. Sending Bell would be the simplest and give the least trouble, but I see no hurry. Arthur can't expect to leave at a month's notice like a common clerk.

I am off to **Amby** next Monday with Hart, if all goes well.

[Final page missing]

Letter #22 from Vicary Gibbs (Sydney) to his brother Alban

Our Last: 19th May 1884
Your Last: 10th and 25th April 1884
2nd June 1884 - Sydney
No. 22

My dear Alban,

Thanks for your two notes as above. I last wrote to you from Brisbane and on the 28th Hart and I left by steamer for this place which we reached all right.

British India. All I have to say has gone to you in P.S. from Brisbane so I have really nothing to add but am anxiously waiting to hear what you are doing on your side.

I am glad to hear you are going to the Bank of England.

Tobin. I cannot myself understand what you want to pay the price you mention for but as you know I am very *mesquin*[977] on these points.

I hope you had a pleasant stay at the Isle of Wight and that Katie continues to improve.

I do not think my letter to you about New Zealand can have been more lurid than the place deserved. Bell says their P&L a/c[978] reads like a long bad joke, their Gross Credit side not better than a luncheon bar: it is very difficult to judge how far this sort of thing is owing to bad management, and as in any event someone would have to go down for 3 mo. to liquidate it is just as well to let Bell go steadily on there for that time and then make his report. It is obvious that the place could not bear so expensive a man as Bell permanently and indeed it would be a waste to leave him there, he will be wanted in Melbourne; you will see from the enclosures that both Regi and Keating are equally loath to part with him. The recently started Cowan's business will make it a little difficult to shut up in N.Z. On getting to Sydney I telegraphed to Regi to send Bell up to meet us and yesterday afternoon he arrived and immediately began to talk business with me and I was much pleased to see that he has a clear head and good manner and can put things before one very well. I went out for a walk with him yesterday and Saturday afternoon and of course we were jawing about Ceylon, B.I., Winham, Dunedin etc. all the time. It is early days to express an opinion, but I must say he impresses me very favourably; he seems to have picked up a lot about the business. I suspect Bell will probably recommend the closing of the Dunedin House and should he do so I suppose you will have no hesitation in carrying out his recommendation.

Tower had nothing to do with his father calling on you as you will see from the enclosed letter. The Canon is an old man and most naturally wished to see his son. Murray could not spare him for a holiday without inconvenience and Tower very sensibly does not wish to go home if he would injure his prospects by doing so.

Hart and I go to Melbourne on Wednesday and probably Bell with us though it is possible he may go up to Brisbane for a week.

---

[977] *mesquin*. (French) Suspicious, wary.
[978] P&L a/c: Profit and Loss account.

Johnny Gibbs[979]. I have not spoken to Regi but I should think in the course of this year he might very well come out to Melbourne.

The Sydney Business seems to be going on very well indeed and up to the present point contrasts very favourably with last. They will be a long while getting into their new offices, not I presume much before 1st Jan. 1886. I hope the Contractor will be able to carry the job through but he has a great deal of work on hand.

'The Sharpshooter'. I forget what we advanced against this ship but apparently it is very difficult of sale and not worth more than about £3000; it is no use Swyney, the owner, keeping on impossible limits, he had better reduce them or pay us off our advance.

Apparently this is not going to be a very long or interesting letter, but I send you several enclosures from which you will glean all that has been going on.

Winhams business will turn out ill as I have feared for some time; we shall have to advance some more money (of course, properly secured) otherwise we should stand to lose £7000. This seems to be owing almost entirely to the failure in the wheat crop which is about ¼ of what was anticipated. Bell does not seem to think the matter reflects discredit on Meeks, and looks on it more as bad luck than bad judgement. No doubt all the matter has been fully explained to you. Bell has drawn up a clear and intelligible statement of the affair, such as Meeks certainly never could have done.

With kind love to Bride.

I remain your most affectionate brother, Vicary Gibbs.

P.S. Please tell Marion on the arrival of the British India Steamer to enquire for 2 parrots which Captain Smith is bringing home for me and to send them to St. Dunstan's conservatory; if Bride would care for one of them please ask her to take it. I have just heard that **D.L. Brown's** have got the British India Steamers coming to a close, but I have no time to write about it. I do hope you will be able to arrange for a regular line to come to us instead.

---

[979] John Arthur Gibbs (1860-1949), eldest child of Reverend John Lomax Gibbs (Vicary's father's brother) and his wife Isabel Marianne (née Bright; the sister of Regi, Tyndall, and Charles Bright), and therefore Vicary Gibbs' first cousin.

Vicary Gibbs (Brisbane) to George Merivale (Sydney)

On his arrival in Brisbane, Vicary replies briefly to George Merivale in Sydney.

5th May 1884 - Brisbane

My dear George,

Thanks for your two letters of the 29th & 30th April enclosing letter from Arthur at whose conduct I am much annoyed in spite of your excuses. I think he was very wrong considering the substantial improvement which has recently occurred in his position to chuck it up by telegram in that off-hand way. What is the mysterious cause of offence to which Murray alludes in a letter to R.B.? What with this and the B. India farago I should think neither Keats nor I have time for anything much except business.

I suppose by this time Regi will have telegraphed home the news of Arthur's resignation.

Constant rain since I arrived in Brisbane.

Hannay knows your connection Capt. Heath and says he is a good fellow but the girls have a name for being rather brusque.

The London House have telegraphed that they have resigned the B.I. but think it possible they may enter into fresh negotiations with them. I feel that we have the key of the situation and should be firm with these impudent blackguards Gray Dawes.

Yours ever, Vicary Gibbs.

Reginald Bright (Melbourne) to Vicary Gibbs (Brisbane)

Letter from Regi Bright to Vicary in Brisbane, with good news of prospects for the British India Line.

12th May 1884 - Melbourne

My dear Vicary,

I have to answer your letter of the 4th May. Hannay quite right – glad he likes Brisbane, where he had better stay. I shall be sorry to lose him from Melbourne.

British India I shall wire Evans[980][?] that there[981] the Government talk of giving British India an Immigration Contract for 10 years if we recommend it. With this in our pocket it would be easier to come to terms. Of course we must stipulate for a commission for working this.

I doubt the **E & A Coy.** going into the direct Trade with London. Any negotiations with the **Orient Coy.** had better be done in London when the time comes, not here. I will write home fully about it this mail.

Yours truly, Reginald Bright.

Vicary Gibbs (Brisbane) to William Murray

A series of letters all written from Brisbane by Vicary Gibbs. The first went to William Murray in Sydney, and dealt with Mr Arthur's resignation from the Dunedin House, the progress with the new Sydney office, and 'British India'. The second went to Regi Bright in Melbourne, with an update on the Brisbane Wool market and House Accounting comparisons. The short extract from the third letter to Melbourne put Frank Keating in possession of useful information about Queensland shipping. The last two of this group of letters were from Vicary to his friend and colleague Regi Bright back in Melbourne, on the negotiations continuing over the agencies in Gibbs Bright's sights.

19th May 1884 - Brisbane

My dear Mr Murray,

I am much obliged to you for your letter of May 10th and for the various copies of your interesting private correspondence with Reginald and the Melbourne House.

Dunedin. Mr Arthur wrote to me sending copy of his resignation, and I have replied. I am very anxious that he should be prevailed on to stay a reasonable time before leaving us as otherwise we shall have to

---

[980] Possibly "Evans", but almost impossible to read.
[981] "There" being wherever Evans(?) is, presumably.

inconvenience the Melbourne office and throw unnecessary work on Mr Bright by sending Mr Keating to fill the blank if Mr Bell goes to Dunedin.

I quite concur in the suitability of Mr Bell visiting Brisbane and Sydney,- certainly Sydney, before going to Dunedin.

Mr Hannay is doing so well here and is of so much use it would be a pity to uproot him. Bell is just as Scotch[982] as he is for that rôle.

Ledger balance to 31st March. I am much pleased to see this which is very satisfactory. I hope you will be able to arrange with Mr John to complete the first and ground floor of our new office so that we can get into them in 12 mo. It might be worth while to say that we would give a bonus of £100 if they were ready by that date.

Mr Hart and I propose to leave on the 28th by the 'Lyeemoon' for your port and shall therefore soon have the pleasure of seeing you.

I am very sorry to hear there is another bother about Rowans[983] wool-packs. I don't think Rowans can be nice people to do business with.

'Coorang'. I am very glad you have been able to sell her.

British India. We have formally told their Marine Superintendent[984] that we have ceased to be Agents, and elicited from him that he knows of no fresh arrangements. We have also seen our co-agents who express their determination to abide by our action, so thus far everything is satisfactory, and I believe Gray Dawes are in a corner and will have to come back to us.

I am my dear Mr Murray,
Yours very sincerely, Vicary Gibbs.

Vicary Gibbs (Brisbane) to Reginald Bright (Melbourne)

19th May 1884 - Brisbane
My dear Regi,

I have several letters from you to answer, dated 6th, 9th, 12th and 13th May for all of which I am much obliged. I left last Monday morning in Hart's company for Amby and found all going on well there; we had fine

---

[982] The implication being that Scots staff would be preferable in the 'Scottish' Dunedin.
[983] A. and F. Rowan were major wool-producers at the time.
[984] Captain Arthur Agar Hansard.

cold weather during our stay. As you know they have had heavy rain in February and light rains last month, consequently though the country does not look well yet it is very different from some that I have seen - the Darling Downs, for instance. On the whole you must be considered lucky though it is the <u>worst</u> season Amby has experienced for a long while. I should fear your next crop of wool will be rather below the average but Macpherson does not anticipate any very serious falling off. It rained very heavily at Roma and Bendango[985] while we were at Roma but none fell on Amby or Eurella.

I liked Macpherson who struck me as an able, intelligent, very energetic, man. I should fear the risk there would be that you should not keep him very long.

We had a Kangaroo drive,- not as you call it but more like a Scotch deer drive and you will be pleased to hear we had nothing at all interesting.

[The remainder of the letter is too smudged to read all but the occasional word, but seems to deal with the desirability of Gibbs, Bright & Co. entering into the Brisbane wool trade, possibly via an Agency. The latter half of the letter is a report on the Seasonal Accounts.]

Vicary Gibbs (in Brisbane) to Frank Keating

20th May 1884 - Brisbane

My dear Keats,

Thanks for yours of the 6th, 9th and 13th of May. I hear some talk that the B. & I.[986] have been trying to get hold of the gasworks wharf; if they did it would be too small and consignees would hardly be able to take delivery as there is no room for drays. I also hear that the secretary of Q.S.N.[987] is on his way out here from London. I should not be surprised if he arrives with full powers from G.D. & Co.[988] to take in hand both agencies, the

---

[985] Bindango.
[986] Gibbs writes "B. & I." very clearly here but presumably it is just a mistake and he means "B.I." - i.e. British India.
[987] This is hard to read but looks like Q.S.N. - possibly Queensland Steamship Navigation Company, formed in 1861, although that company seems to have ceased trading in 1868 following fierce rivalry between it and the Australasian Steam Navigation Company and the loss of the Queensland Mail Subsidy. In 1885, the Queensland Steam Shipping Company was formed by the British India Steam Navigation Company. In 1887, it was amalgamated with the Australasian Steam Navigation Company to form the Australasian United Steam Navigation Company.
[988] Gray, Dawes and Co.

Q.S.N. & Q.R.M.[989], and set up Hansard or himself or somebody in place of Parburys and G. Marks as however he will neither be able to get wharf or freight. I anticipate he will be like the King of France who marched up a hill with 20,000 men. Forrest and Parbury's people anticipate that there is some game of this kind on, and if so it must be done in defiance of Parbury who is as you know on the direction of the Q.S.N. in London.

This secretary left London after they knew Forrest had left L'pool[?] and Parbury's were never advised that the sec. was coming out but 'count it by cool wind'.

Hart is rather disposed to cable Gray Dawes "What arrangements have you made for berthing your steamers elsewhere"? Of course it would lead to our being their neighbours, but I don't think it will work out as it might tend to make a reconciliation impossible. **[Remainder of letter illegible]**

Vicary Gibbs (Brisbane) to Reginald Bright

20th May 1884 - Brisbane

My dear Regi,

I last wrote to you yesterday and I now enclose copy of mine to Alban describing my interview with Hansard which will interest you. Since then Hart has seen Parbury's and Moreheads who are determined to back us in the matter. I also enclose copy of mine to Arthur and Murray. When you have read these enclosures please send them to Alban by next Orient mail, as they will probably get there quicker than the original which I send by S.S. Dunedin this week.

We must have a talk when I see you about forming Amby South and Bendango into a company. Morehead would be glad to do it as far as Bendango is concerned, and we will try and arrange a definite scheme and put it before London.

Oriental Bank. I asked Hannay to let me send you what Bell had written, as I thought you might like to see it and send it on to AGH[990][?].

---

[989] Queensland Royal Mail?
[990] This letter is particularly badly smudged and barely legible throughout. This seems to be three initials: an A (or possibly W); a G; and either H or M or K. The most likely interpretations, based on the names of people mentioned elsewhere in the diary and letters, are either "AGH" (i.e. Alban George Henry Gibbs, Vicary's brother to whom he writes many letters), or (less likely) "WGM" (William Gilmour Murray). However, in both cases this

I am pleased to think of Hannay, Merivale, Hart ([illegible word in brackets]) each settled in their respective places, and doing so well in them.

I shall have been long enough in Brisbane to get a good idea of the business, and will have to try to describe[?] it, not to you but to Arthur, who may later be working there[?].

[In the][?] same country where you saw so many, I don't suppose we saw 50 marsupials all day, and Willis?/Miller?[Name illegible] 3 kangaroo, and the rabbits. They[?] fell to my gun right and left. We also killed some plains turkey.

We found Chrystal in the train on our way down last Saturday. The young fellows, really drafts from your office apparently, are doing well. Old Donald will be glad to hear his son is steady and useful. Young Day seemed about the sharpest of the crowd.

Hart and I leave here on the 28th for Sydney where we shall probably stay a week then come on to Melbourne from which place he wants to bring back his eldest daughter.

With regard to Dunedin I wish to say that if you fix on Bell - and on the whole I think this would be as good as anything – I really don't see the advantage of Keating going down for three months' interregnum instead of letting Bell be vaccinated,- apart from the loss I mean-, picking up the business from Arthur instead of having it distilled through Keating. Not to mention the inconvenience to us in Melbourne of having K. shipped off, - who knows the stockroom[?] run of the work - to be uprooted by a man, sent somewhere again, would be distasteful just as he gets into it.

At the same time I quite agree with him[?] saying that if Bell goes it would be well he should have something of Melbourne and Sydney for it and if possible[?] Brisbane too, and this House, so if you take my advice you will write to Arthur at once to the effect[?] that he must know what a man occupying his position cannot expect is to leave at a month's notice like a clerk, and that though we have every desire to relieve him as soon as possible, yet we have no-one we can confidently send except Bell whom we wish to visit our other branches before going and therefore we cannot see our way to parting with him before August without detriment to the business etc. etc.

---

would be the only time that Gibbs referred to those people by their initials, so it is also possible that it is someone else altogether (obviously known to both Regi Bright and Vicary Gibbs by those initials without further explanation), or it is an acronym rather than initials (possibly "AGM" for Annual General Meeting, although that wouldn't make much sense in the context).

Then if he kicks and makes a fuss we can, if you think well, send Keating. I am writing to Murray today and will ask him if he writes to Arthur to tell that really[?] he can't expect to dash off at a few days' warning.

After thinking the matter well over I have told Hannay to look at Brisbane as a fixture, at any rate as far as our present ideas[?] are; once he is quite satisfied to remain, and Hart is well pleased that he should.

I tell you frankly I don't like your idea of making a junction with the other wharf owners and throwing our tugs into the boiled[?] pot[?], - [I][?] doubt the former being practicable and consider the latter, the goal[?], a monopoly to my idea[?].

K's thoroughly understood this big business[991], it is very profitable; it would be difficult for anyone to compete with us while[?] we are the "cock o' the hill". We can, K.[?] thought[?], do the business and I am very glad we bought them both[992]. If you don't mind not saying anything to Hart about your idea[993], you can broach it yourself when he comes to Melbourne. I know he won't approve.

British India. I am rather surprised that you should wire home that we can put the immigration 10 years cont.[contract], though I believe that we could have done so but that is a very difficult case. I consider Dawes asking Charles to breakfast a decided case of 'weakening' and hope the London House raises them the limit.

I am racing to catch a mail - have no time for more. I will tell you all I think about this business when we meet.

Greymouth[994] won't do at all in its present form.

The travelling sheep were bothering Amby a lot - 2 or 3 mobs[995], - some of Fisher's dying like flies; all travelled from N.S.W.; one mob lost 1000, between Mitchell[996] and Amby and 400 died in crossing over our run; wherever we were we saw dead and dying sheep.

Yours ever, Vicary Gibbs

---

[991] i.e. The purchase of the Kangaroo Point wharf.
[992] Does this mean both wharfs? Or the warehouse and the wharf?
[993] i.e. The idea of joining with the other wharf owners.
[994] Greymouth: Gibbs visited this town and went down one of the coal mines in the area (in nearby Brunner) on 6th March 1884.
[995] Mob = flock.
[996] Mitchell is only about 14 miles west of Amby - a tiny proportion of the whole journey from New South Wales.

Vicary Gibbs (Brisbane) to Reginald Bright

28th May 1884 - Brisbane

My dear Regi,

Hart and I arrived today after a pleasant passage, and find all well. Chrystal came with us and goes on to Melbourne today.

I found your letter of the 28th awaiting me and I have today telegraphed you in answer "Send Bell". I don't in fact see anything else to be done though I am much worried that Bell should not have had more time to make himself acquainted with our Australian business more thoroughly before going to New Zealand. He will of course see Hart, Murray and myself here and we can have a talk with him on all matters. I am very glad to hear you like Bell and that he seems to have a good knowledge of business. Hannay evidently looks on him as his A1 business man.

Murray is very keen on him going up for a week to Brisbane before leaving and no doubt it would be adviseable if time permitted.

I suppose Bell will be here on Monday or Friday in all probability. I think you might write to Arthur that his successor would arrive by the 1st of July and that we could dispense with his services by the 1st of August.

[Remainder of letter missing]

Vicary Gibbs (Brisbane) to Johnny Gibbs (Liverpool)

Young Johnny Gibbs in Liverpool planned to gain his Australian experience in the coming year. He was the son of the marriage between Reverend John Lomax Gibbs and Isabelle Marianne Bright, still in his early twenties at that time. He and Vicary knew and liked each other, and Vicary's letter was meant as a friendly introduction to the Melbourne House.

20 May 1884[997] - Brisbane

My dear Johnny,

Many thanks for your long and interesting letter. As you imagine I have had plenty to do out here and find my life very comfortable on the whole.

I am sure, whether in Melbourne or Sydney, you will have a very good time whenever you come out. The way you conducted the consignment and purchase was appreciated in Melbourne more especially following as it did on [3 or 4 illegible words].

The L'pool office seems to be in capital order though your Uncle Tyndall must be having hard work running the whole show by himself. There will be I suppose a little less to do now that the Indent business has gone to London; what clerks have gone with it besides the Moellers?

I am not surprised at what you tell me about Coles; all the people on this side fancy "oh if I was in England I could get consignments fast enough"; when they go over, they find their mistake.

Your Uncle Regi was interested to read your letter, particularly the remarks about consignments which he thought very sensible, but we shouldn't like the idea of buying soft goods on adventure account at all. I am very glad you took the trouble to tell me all about the L'pool office as I take a great interest in it and I hope you will do so again from time to time.

If the English manufacturers won't take off the discount, they have to pay duty in Victoria on the whole amount which is aboard; they will simply

---

[997] The date of the letter is illegible, but we know that it must have been written on approximately this date because Gibbs gives the wording of the announcement he plans to send to the Brisbane Courier regarding the Gibbs, Bright & Co. resignation of the Queensland Royal Mail agency, and the announcement appears in the Brisbane Courier on 21 May 1884. The resignation of the agency was sent to Gray, Dawes & Co. on 20 May 1884 according to Gibbs' diary.

stop finances altogether if they don't take the discount off. Remember me to Sam Rathbone if you see him.

I hope all your family are well; mine seem to have been in a wretched condition with typhoid, measles and one thing and another.

Give my very kind regards to Carruthers, Sylvester[?], Wilson and all the rest of our friends in L'pool. I am going north this week overland to Brisbane and I shall probably stop at John's[?] freehold station in the Darling Downs to have a look at it: I suppose it will have suffered a great deal from the fearful drought which thank goodness seems to have broken or be breaking up.

They are putting a new storey on the Melbourne premises, and our specifications are just out inviting tenders for building the grand new House lower down in Pitt St.[998] here.

Old Murray is going to make a great speech of course in favour of the Government running the wharves here, which is his pet scheme.

[Remainder of letter illegible]

---

[998] See the footnote on the diary entry for 23 October 1883, which contains information about the new offices.

Despatch Note for Amby Downs Wool to GB&Co. (Brisbane)

"Hoggetts" (more usually "Hoggets") can refer to either a young sheep, or to the wool from the first shearing of a sheep older than 7 months. It is the best wool that the animal will ever give, being as soft as an unsheared sheep's, but longer. The process of "Combing" removes vegetable matter and short strands from the scoured wool, and aligns the wool fibres in preparation for spinning. "Clothing" (or carding) involves brushing the wool with a mesh of pins to disentangle and clean it.

74. Amby Downs Despatch Note

Gibbs, Bright & Co. (Brisbane) to Antony Gibbs & Sons (London)

11th September 1884 - Brisbane

Amby Accounts

Dear Sirs,

We duly received your favour of 24th July acknowledging receipt of the Amby Accounts for 1883 and enclosing your Acct. current with the proprietors, also copy of letter to Melbourne of 19th August 1883.

It is much to be regretted that we did not get a copy of your letter to the Melbourne House of 17th August '83 which would have enabled us to make up the accounts in accordance with your wishes and thereby saved you much trouble in remaking them.

We have now made the several entries necessary to bring the accounts in the Amby books to agree with your figures

[Several lines missing from the bottom of this page]

[Several lines missing from the top of the next page]

enclose remade copies of our Profit and Loss Account and Balance Sheet, but those have not yet come to hand. We hope to receive them by a subsequent mail.

£775.1.0 due to us for our Balance Sheet is for orders drawn upon us for labour on the station previous to 31st Dec 1883 but which were not paid till 1884. The several accounts representing those orders being charged in accounts of 1883.

Copies of our accounts with the station to 30th June 1883 You say you did not receive but in our private series of 7th August 1883 No. 4 you will find that we mentioned them as being enclosed. In case they have been mislaid we send you copies.

We may mention that we have opened an account in the Amby Ledger for advances made by you on account of the station and at the credit of which the sum of £36,383 . 12 . 9 now stands. Proceeds of wool we presume you will put to credit of this account, advising us and giving us cash dates.

The Capital Account shows an amount at credit of £120,000. This amount according to your instructions we will keep intact neither crediting interest nor profits.

We are, Dear Sirs, Yours very truly,

Gibbs Bright & Co.

Enclosures: Copies of accounts to 30 June 1883.

Angus MacPherson to D. Chrystal

This letter from Angus MacPherson to his colleague Chrystal - both of them key players in the Gibbs Bright wool trade - brings a clearer picture of the life and circumstances of those actually 'on the ground'.

?? October 1884[999]

My dear Sir,

I have to apologise for not writing oftener lately, but the fact is that my eyes have been so bad that I have not been able to write at night, as the season has been such a severe one that I have had no spare time during the day. However, fortunately we have had a little rain at last and the grass will now get a chance to grow, snd our work will be lighter.

Losses Our losses will be very heavy, and if heavy rain had come at first when the sheep were at their worst they would have been still heavier. Of the four thousand aged ewes that we had for sale there is not two thousand left, so we may congratulate ourselves on the fact that we sold so many of them this last season, or else we would have had five or six thousand deaths among them alone. Altogether I reckon that the drought will cost **[several missing words]** four thousand sheep over and above our usual losses, and that we will lose about four hundred head of cattle and from ten to fifteen head of horses. The most of the cattle that have died were old FAT[?] cows that were heavy in calf and when they once got down were far too weak to get up again. Of course this will make a difference

---

[999] We were unable to determine the date of this letter, but it was amongst other letters from the time of Gibbs trip. Certainly, 1880-1886 and 1888-9 were years where Australia was hit by severe drought in many areas. The Queensland area that MacPherson is describing - near Roma, about 300 miles west of Brisbane - was particularly badly hit from 1883-6 and 1888-9.

in numbers of our calves this season, but the cows themselves are not a heavy loss as most of them were from ten to twelve years old.

I wired Melbourne on the 24th saying that we had finished shearing, and that we had 325 bales of wool, also that up to date we had had no more rain, however on the 25th we had a sprinkle, on the 26th or on the 27th one inch and 6 points, and thus we may consider the drought as broken up and our losses at an end. We had a fair clip, the Tourelle ewes cutting 2 lbs and 1/2, all of our clean washed wool; all the bales with the Tourelle wool in them have got a "T" over "EWES" as shown above[a small diagram showing the letters drawn that way], so that's alright.

Weight of Wool We have 115730 lbs nett weight of washed wool, and 15179 lbs nett weight of greasy wool, making a total of 130909 lbs of wool. I drove the rams in their grease, also the balance of the aged ewes, as if we had attempted to wash them I would have killed the lot, they were all very weak.

Carting We were carting all the wool to the Muckadilla[1000] [illegible word] this year as I understood that you wished that done. I do not think there is the slightest chance of us getting a siding where we wanted it.

Euthulla[1001] I am sorry to say that B. Smith will be leaving Euthulla at the beginning of the coming year, the twins[1002] got the management of Durham Downs[1003] cattle station. I have arranged for Bob Owens, the man I have at present at Cornwall[1004] to take his place. The man Owens is a first class man and I think he will get on all right at Euthulla.

I will write you again as soon as possible in answer to other queries in your letter but at present must conclude, and hoping that you have had a good season at Mulwala[1005] and Torrumbarry.

I remain yours faithfully,

Angus McPherson[1006]

[1000] Muckadilla is about 70 miles west of Roma in Queensland.
[1001] Euthulla is about 13 miles north of Roma, Queensland.
[1002] 'The twins' possibly refers to Fred and Robert Dunsmere, cousins of Charles Hill Douglas, mentioned by Gibbs in the diary on 13th May 1884.
[1003] Durham Downs is about 40 miles north-east of Roma in Queensland.
[1004] Cornwall is about 45 miles north-west of Roma, Queensland.
[1005] Mulwala, New South Wales, is about 100 miles east of Torrumbarry Station (which is over the state border in Victoria).
[1006] Angus MacPherson sent a telegram from Echuca, Victoria in February 1884, but by the time of this letter he seems to be working in Queensland in the stations near Roma.

Frank Keating (Melbourne) to Reginald Bright (Sydney)

The final two letters from Frank Keating in Melbourne to Reginald Bright in Sydney, written after Vicary Gibbs had left (first for Ceylon, and then home to England), leave us with the forward-looking plans for business to flourish as best it could in the last years of the 19th century and the testing early years of the 20th.

Gibbs, Bright & Co., Melbourne

12th May 1885 - Melbourne

To: Reginald Bright & Co., Sydney

My dear Bright,

Thanks for your letter received this morning.

Chrystal turned up here today and goes on to Sydney this afternoon. We have got his signature to the promissory notes so those we sent you can now be destroyed. Wentworth like the rest "doesn't see his way to go in for the plough just now".

Can you tell me where Watt's flour report is? They don't seem to know and perhaps it may be among your papers. I am anxious that our flour scheme should not fizzle.

Klingender asks me to tell you that he met Andrew Rowan who said that as it seemed to him that Gillanders were trying to let us in, it would be a good thing for us to come to terms with him and join our forces with his in "slating Gillanders"!

Finck has overbought himself in wheat and having got in a funk has offered us 2000 quarters per 'Hampshire' at 35/- c.f.i.[1007] As Lenders wire us a firm off-market for parcels at 36/-, I got Finck to put the wheat firm in our hands and have offered it to Lenders at 36/3. This transaction will I think go through.

The Railway Department have issued tenders for 1000 buffers and springs to be sent in by June 1st. The sample buffer is one of the lot last

---

[1007] c.f.i. = Cost, Freight, and Insurance (usually written as CIF now).

supplied and as in that case Ibbotson was the successful tenderer we have wired them today asking if they will tender again.

Frasers have sent in their valuations of Spencer Street and Gregory Lane. They put Spencer Street at £10,000 and Gregory Lane at £3,300.

I have an enquiry from Derham and Co. as to 2000 bales of cornsacks August shipment – and have wired Gillanders for an offer. Meanwhile we are making fresh enquiries at the Bank – all previous ones entered in the book have been very satisfactory – but the sum is large, £10,000 or so.

I've half a notion if you approved of running over to Adelaide, just about when Johnnie Gibbs arrives and going up to Silverton[1008] to see about their stacked ore we are advancing on and also whether there are any new accounts worth taking up. The Broken Hill[1009] which is a new company has an enormous find, a lode it is said 4 miles long and carrying rich chlorides. What do you think of the idea? I suppose Bell will be back here before very long.

Yours very sincerely

F. A. Keating

I enclose a letter which came to the club and which the porter handed to me today.

[1008] Although there is a Silverton, South Australia quite close to (about 65 miles south-west of) Adelaide, Keating is probably referring to Silverton, New South Wales (about 330 miles north-east of Adelaide), because that Silverton is only about 16 miles from Broken Hill.
[1009] Broken Hill, New South Wales, is now an isolated mining city. Originally found to be rich in lead-zinc ore (and in fact the world's richest lead-zinc ore body), silver ore was also discovered there in 1883. The "broken hill" which gave the place its name now no longer exists, having been mined away. The company Keating refers to became The Broken Hill Proprietary Company Limited, incorporated in 1885, now the world's largest mining company BHP Billiton.

From Guano to Gold: The Diary and Letters of Vicary Gibbs from 1883-5

Frank Keating (Melbourne) to Reginald Bright (Sydney)

Gibbs, Bright & Co., Melbourne

14th May 1885 - Melbourne

My dear Bright,

I am sending up your letters to Brisbane. W. Reid came in to see me today and I mooted to him an idea which has long been incubating in my brain, namely that he should come to us and undertake the charge of a flour and grain department. It appears that some such idea had also occurred to him, but he hadn't liked to speak of it, and was in fact in negotiation with Allen Glover & Co. about something of the same kind. However he would far rather he says work with us and he has placed himself under firm offer on the following terms. We guarantee him £250 a year and allow him a bonus of say 10% on the net profits of his department, after paying all salaries, expenses etc. The cost of the department would be as following:

W. Reid: **£250**; a town traveller to look after bakers etc.: **£150** (Reid has now with him a man who knows all the bakers and would come at the salary named); and an a/c sales clerk (Reid also could bring this man who is conversant with the flour trade) - his salary would be **£125** a year. In addition to this there would be the cost of a **horse and buggy**, say **£100** a year. A total cost for the Department of **£625** a year.

Reid says that his own a/c's and some others that he has now and can transfer at once will more than cover this outlay while he is absolutely certain that under our wing he can do an enormous and most valuable business. We should have to advance up to but not exceeding 75% of value on consignments and Reid says we could get an average commission of 2½%.

At Sydney it is 3% but we could not get more than 2 ½%. On the other hand more is sold for cash here than in Sydney.

[The only copy we have of the remainder of this letter can be seen, very faintly and in reverse, through the back of another page, so there are many missing sections and some words are conjecture.]

Of course, we should have to exercise the greatest care with our bakers' a/cs. I think this is a chance of which we should at once take advantage. Reid is sure about it and thinks this rare coincidence brings with it a certain amount of business ready made and an intimate practical knowledge of the trade. He can bring the staff we want with him at reasonable salaries and is in a position to commence business for us at once.

It will be necessary for us to set apart some of the Spencer Street premises as a flour store. No doubt if we build at Gregory Lane a store there will be much handier. Reid wants office room for this department. Reid thought of a new way, rather than disturb offices why not utilise the cellar **[Illegible line]** opening into Bond Street and on thinking it over it seems that we can easily give Reid the small glass-panelled room on the 1st floor and have a couple of desks just outside for his staff.

Business could be tried for grain and other cereals as well as flour and bread. Reid says also that he **[Missing words]** deliver[?] **[Missing words]** season[?].

Making all allowance for saving for his **[Missing word]** I feel confident that Reid is very good in this and trust that it will be a most desirable exchange for the wearisome and wasteful machinery department.

As I don't want to keep Reid in suspense longer than I can help it I wish you would kindly wire me your general approval of the scheme and I will then retain Reid definitely, subject to details to be arranged. Personally I am strongly in favour of having him and setting up our department and **[Missing words]**.

Reid says he could steadily save on this as he can earn beyond his £250 **[Missing words]** towards reduction of his debt to us. Just had a telegram from Bell that he leaves Sydney today & will be back here tomorrow.

Yours very sincerely,

F. A. Keating.

From Guano to Gold: The Diary and Letters of Vicary Gibbs from 1883-5

75. Portrait of Vicary Gibbs
Courtesy of Lord Aldenham

Epilogue

The changes in Britain's relationship with India in the mid-19th century were of potential significance to AG&S. Provinces were formed in British India and administered by Provincial Governors who were subject to the Governor-General (or, from 1858, the Viceroy). The maintenance of law and order had been transferred to the British Army, and there was a gradual release of control by the East India Company allowing a small amount of structured Indian promotion in order to prepare the stage for Empire and for local autonomy. In 1858, Queen Victoria was proclaimed Empress and her familiar figure began to appear prominently - often as a dominant sculptured presence reminding her subjects of their benign ruler. Many old 'East India servants' retired to coffee- or tea-growing in Ceylon, or to farming and mining in the Australian and New Zealand colonies, rather than returning to the homes they had left too long ago. Some ex-Indian Army officers found themselves needed as protection for these new colonial settlers, as in the more serious skirmishes of the Land Wars in New Zealand. Wherever the British went they hoped for cheap land and labour and the making of a good living, if not a fortune. Merchants like AG&S also saw their chance to benefit from potential new developments.

As they had found to their cost before, it was not the changes themselves but the timing of them that caused problems for AG&S. Their desire to invest in Ceylon and expand further in Australia and New Zealand was tempered by the economic uncertainties of the period which continued through the 1880s and 90s and up to the turn of the century.

Technological advances were cause for optimism. Local telephone communication had been introduced as early as 1879 in some colonial centres of commerce, and now the international cables being laid across the oceans and continents meant that a Head Office's ability to make rapid contact with their colonial 'outposts' relieved the isolation of its senior management there and allowed for faster decision making. The opening of the Suez Canal, more streamlined ship design, new lightweight marine materials, and more sophisticated propulsion all meant quicker – and therefore more profitable – passage.

But on the downside, these improvements also helped their competitors - some of whom had invested heavily in new innovations such as refrigeration and faster production line techniques. In addition, the older markets for iodine and nitrates declined in the 1880s and reduced AG&S's income from South America. In the next decade, the European demand for Australian products declined too, and there was a steep drop in wool prices, followed by a similar decline in the profitability of the newly-discovered colonial copper and other metals.

Vicary Gibbs, then influential in London, was determined to alter the whole situation. He resolved to reduce the threat to the partners' capital – seen as partly due to some rash investment as well as to over-borrowing throughout the 1880s – and to break the cycle of 'boom and bust' before it became established.

Vicary himself had always been cautious, making decisions based on local experience and advice. Within his business circle he saw himself as a peacemaker and as the family diplomat. In all his letters to colleagues, but particularly when writing to his father or his brother Alban, he trod carefully and made his case tactfully. In one reply to Alban, Vicary was particularly quick to defend Reginald Bright, whose over enthusiasm and occasional rash move he had noted but understood. Pointing to pressure of work in the Melbourne office he said, "There is all the unimportant detail of Liverpool [there] besides a continual amount of anxious and responsible new business cropping up, people incessantly seeing one, besides the noises incident to a shipping office which can hardly be realised by those living in the quiet Bank-like dignity of No.15 [the London House in Bishopsgate]. I can only say I have never worked harder or indeed so hard in my life since I have been in Australia, and I have taken several days' holiday whereas Regi has never been away for a business day since I came; he sticks very closely to work. I am sure you will bear all this in mind whenever you have occasion to complain of any lacks or errors of judgement which must occur when men are working at high pressure." (Good advice from Vicary, and to those in charge of man-management today: exile from the protection of the family's elevated position in the City had given him a closer view of the 'real' world. He might also have added that enthusiasm like Regi's should be valued).

Vicary and the other partners were obliged to make savings in their company budget as it became obvious that their liabilities were beginning to exceed their capital. Destructive rumours began to spread in the City, and at one stage their drafts were even refused by the Hong Kong and Shanghai Bank. It was the general confidence in AG&S's reputation and trust in Vicary's reassurances that persuaded the market that the rumours were malicious and much-exaggerated, and the firm was saved from disaster, climbing steadily back from the edge. However in 1921, when the AG&S boom of the war years was over, their losses on nitrates alone were reported by Kleinworts as being about £660,000. Chilean producers asked for the formation of a London Nitrate Pool to safeguard the market, with Herbert Gibbs as chairman. In a similar situation, Baring Brothers needed all the available financial support of the City to see them through until their eventual nemesis in the 1990s.

Both Herbert and Vicary Gibbs agreed that banking was really a single-minded occupation. Vicary's short time in the House of Commons had taught him, with some humiliation over the Chilean Navy case, that politics too should be unencumbered by other interests. After one failed attempt to return to Parliament he made no further political incursion. He learned from his time in the colonies that expertise in a more limited field could be far more valuable in the long term than too wide a spread of interests. In the early 1900s, there was speculation and great excitement in Western Australia over the Lake View Gold Mine. AG&S were involved in this concession, but left direct control to the experts and played no part in the manipulation of a rush by the mine owners which was intended to stimulate interest without frightening off bona fide investors.

As the 20th century advanced, AG&S began to stabilise their control of the colonial market – if not always at its old level of profitability. The 'Great War' had created a demand for nitrates – used in the manufacture of the explosives both for the static conflict of the trenches and the airborne attacks on civilians of both sides – and for canned meats to help feed the men at the front. The wartime demand encouraged new production techniques, which meant a more reliable – and more profitable – product. The additional revenue made during the war by the Australian Houses' investments in these and other industries persuaded AG&S to risk additional peacetime investment in the supporting infrastructure, whereas previously they had concentrated more on the trade itself.

Grain, wool, gold and other minerals; meat and dairy produce from New Zealand and Australia; sugar, cotton, timber, and many other commodities - some even fabricated and refined in colonial enterprises - were all becoming recognised 'shipping' to Europe. The scene was set for the shortages and subsequent rationing of the Second World War, and for the deaths of some of the courageous merchant seamen, victims of German U-boats.

Passing another World War in which AG&S played their part in the southern hemisphere - as did so many of our old colonies and industries once again - we arrive at a significant change in the structure of the Merchant Bank. Sons of many of those encountered in the diary were lost in the conflicts and were deprived of their moment in which to play this peaceful role with honourable mention; but they have not been forgotten.

The London House wound down its work towards the end of the 20th century when it was to be taken over by the Hong Kong and Shanghai Bank (HSBC). The vaults were cleared, and the banking records of nearly 200 years were shared amongst archives around their world. There were original or copy letters from many members of the family and staff over the whole of that period. Copy letters would often have been made by the original writer, and then further copied by clerks and entered into a copy folder or letter-book; the result is often so badly smudged as to be illegible. Some of those written by Vicary Gibbs during his secondment to the colonial houses can still be seen in archives, while others are still retained by surviving members of the family.

A more recent family member also found himself involved with the Australian end of the business. David Gibbs (1927-2009), a merchant banker, was Chairman of Gibbs, Bright and Co., Property Ltd., until the Parbury Henty Bank took over in 1980s Melbourne. This contemporary member of the Gibbs family had taken their Christian commitment into the business just as Tyntesfield's William Gibbs had done before him. David Gibbs narrowly chose commerce over his 'call' to the Anglican ministry. After Eton and Oxford he became a director of AG&S in London in 1958, having first worked with GB&Co. from 1949 to 1955. By 1968 he had attained the position of Chairman and was fully involved in Australian Fund Management. He also took his enthusiasm for wildlife conservation and the world of the Arts and Music into his busy social schedule, and he contributed effectively - as members of the Gibbs and Bright families have often done - to the life of the vibrant community of Victoria.

With the arrival of the 21st century, and following the death of David Gibbs, another new era has begun. The stage is larger, there are many new players, and the production may well play to a different audience on the other side of the world where its future lies, but we may be sure there are more major rôles to be played and the company may still be recognisable as the one conceived by the cosmopolitan Antony Gibbs of the original Spanish House.

Epilogue

From Guano to Gold: The Diary and Letters of Vicary Gibbs from 1883-5

Index of People

Bold page numbers indicate the location of footnotes.

(

(Captain of the S.S. Shannon), 83
(Chip's younger brother), 258
(F A Woods? Farwoods? Hawoods?), 267
(Manager of Hennewelle), 213
(Secretary of QSN), 333, 334
(Smeb's nephew), 322
(Superintendent of Monarakande Estate), 218
(Tyntesfield coachman), 8, 198
(Unknown surname), Dr., 208, 209
(Unknown surname), Dr. ('City of New York'), 49
(Unknown surname), James, **285**, 298, 305
(Unknown surname), Marion, 329
(Unknown surname), Sophia, 130
(Willis? Miller?), Mr., 335

,

'Count Linseed'. See Edwards, Sir Henry MP
'Dirty Adams'. See Cokayne, George Edward

A

Adamoli, Constance, **155**
Adams, George Edward. See Cokayne, George Edward
Adams, Louisa, 121
Agnew
  Agnes, **251**
  Sir Andrew, **251**
Aitken, Mr., 219
Alban. See Gibbs:Alban George Henry
Albertsohn, Mr. (possibly K. Abbotson?), **136**
Alexander, Captain Ezekiel, **39**
Alfonso XII, King of Spain, **228**
Allen, 268
Allen Glover & Co., 346
Alt & Co., 300
Anderson, Captain (of the Constabulary), 127, 129
Anderson, Mr. (son of the Head of the Orient Co.), 112, 155
Andersons, **275**
André, Major John, **25**
Anglo-South American Bank. See Bank of Tarapaca
Antony. See Gibbs:Antony(?)
Antony Gibbs & Sons, xi, xii, 3, 5, 6, 8, 9, 10, 12, 17, 18, 40, 54, 62, 64, 66, 78, 114, 117, 141, **147**, 149, 222, 223, 224, 226, 229, 234, 241, 273, 293, 295, 297, 349, 350, 351, 352
Arnold
  Matthew, **71**
  Richard Penrose, **71**
Arthur
  George, 248
  Mr., 66, 104, 109, 110, 111, 112, 165, **248**, 281, 282, 304, 305, 306, 307, 327, 330, 331, 334, 335, 336, 337
  Mrs., 111, 304
Arthur Briscoe & Co., **307**
Arthur, John. See Gibbs:John Arthur
Arthur, President Chester A., **28**
Ashbury, Mr. MP, 70
Atkinson, Jane. See Laidley:Mrs. Jane (née Atkinson)
Aunt Mary. See Gibbs:Mary Dorothea
Austen, Jane, 1, 7
Austin, Mr., 46
Australian Frozen Meat Export Co., 65

B

Backhaus
  (daughter), 272
  Mr., 272
Bagot (racehorse). See Malua (racehorse)
Bailey, Miss, 198
Baker
  Miss, 208
  Mrs., 208
Baker, Reverend Shirley Waldemar, **174**, 175, 176
Ballarat, Bishop of. See Thornton:Rev. Dr. Samuel (Bishop of Ballarat)
Balteel, Mr., 248
Bank of England, 8, 227, 328
Bank of London and South America. See Bank of Tarapaca
Bank of Tarapaca, 9

Banks, F., 113, **115**, 117
Baring
  (family), 4
  Colonel Robert, **19**, 20, 22, 23
  Ned, 23, 251
  Tom, **19**, 22, 23, 248
Baring Brothers & Co., 23, 247, 251, 350
Barker's, 286, 287
Barnet, Mr., 45
Bath
  Charles, 76, 77
  Mrs., 77
Beatrice. See Gibbs:Beatrice (née Elton)
Beckett, Edwin, **10**
Bécu, Jeanne (comtesse du Barry), **212**
Beddoe, George, **153**
Bedford, Mr., 208
Bell
  Father Thomas Blizzard, **251**
  Miss (artist), 189
  Miss (artist's sister), 189
Bell and Dangar, 244
Bell, Falkner, **42**
Bell, George Frederick, 105, **157**, 158, 159, 160, 161, 180, 181, 206, 210, 221, 224, 229, 251, 252, 253, 254, **258**, 275, 277, 290, 300, 308, 315, 322, 325, 327, 328, 329, 332, 334, 335, 337, 345
Bell, Mrs. (George Gibbs' nurse), **149**
Bell, Thomas, **42**, 45, 46
Benson, Robert Henry, **19**, 21, 26, 36
Beresford-Hope, Bridget. See Gibbs:Bridget (née Beresford-Hope)
Berkeley, Mr., 127, 128, 129, 132, 133, 138
Berthon-Preston. See Preston, Captain George Berthon
Bethell, Slingsby, **21**, 23
Billings, Frederick H., **31**, 33
Bishop of Ballarat. See Thornton:Rev. Dr. Samuel (Bishop of Ballarat)
Black (Mackinnon neighbours)
  Mr., 98, 99, 100
  Mrs., 99
Black, Dr., **76**, 77
Blackett, James (Jr.), **213**, 214, 215, 217, 218, 219
Blackwood, Arthur, **197**
Blakiston, Mr., 306
Bligh
  Florence Rose (née Morphy), 114, **126**, 131, 132, 134, 137
  Hon. Ivo, **104**, 114, 126, 131, 132, 134, 137
Boko (Tug), 148, **154**, 156, **249**, 282, 288

Bonner, George John, **73**
Bosanquet, Mr., **223**, 224, 229
Bow, McLochlan, & Co., **249**
Bowen, L.J.. See Bowen, Sir Charles
Bowen, Sir Charles, **26**, 35, 36, 44
Bowers, Mr. (of the New York Guardian), 26, 42
Brewers' Company. See Worshipful Company of Brewers
Brien, Mr., 234, 235
Bright
  (family), xii, 91, 352
  Anna Maria Georgiana (née Manners-Sutton), 65
  Catty, 253
  Charles Edward, 21, 57, 58, 61, 64, 65, 67, 68, 69, 70, 72, 73, 74, 76, 78, 84, 85, 86, 87, 245, 247, 248, 252, 253, 254, 255, 256, 258, 262, 263, 264, 268, 276, 277, 278, 282, 283, 284, 285, 291, 293, 305, 308, 309, 310, 311, 319, 325, 336
  Emma Katherine (née Wolley), **202**
  Heywood, **196**
  Mrs. Dick. See Bright:Emma Katherine (née Wolley)
  Reginald, 21, **58**, 61, 63, 64, 65, 67, 68, 69, 70, 71, 72, 73, 74, 76, 78, 84, 85, 86, 87, 88, 89, 91, 92, 102, 103, 104, 109, 111, 127, 138, 139, 140, 141, 143, 159, 160, 161, 163, 164, 182, 183, 184, 186, 189, 191, 193, 194, 195, 196, 197, 198, 199, 200, 201, 202, 204, 205, 206, 223, 228, 245, 247, 251, 252, 253, 254, 255, 256, 258, 262, 270, 290, 291, 292, 300, 307, 308, 310, 315, 319, 321, 322, 328, 329, 330, 331, 332, 334, 337, 338, 344, 346, 350
  Samuel, 63, 64, See Smeb (possibly Samuel Bright)
  Tyndall, **19**, 44, 75, **87**, 191, 242, 246, 254, 255, 274, 276, 279, 288, 289, 291, 293, 298, 309, 310, 322, 323, 338
Bright Bros., 77, 249
Bright(?)
  Antony, 253
Bright, Chrystal & Co., 243
British-India Steam Navigation Company, 104, 155, 156, **256**, 263, 275, 284, 285, 288, 292, 312, 313, 323, 326, 327, 328, 329, 330, 331, 332, **333**, 336
Broad, Mr., 128
Brook, Mr., **219**
Brough, Captain, 78
Brown Brothers & Co., **26**

Index of People

Brown, D.L. & Co., 329
Brown, J. (Newcastle colliery proprietor), 144
Brown, James(?) (of Brown Brothers & Co.), 26
Brown, Mr., 287
Brown, Mr. (of Adelaide), 80
Brownrigg
  Major, **163**
  Mrs, 163
Brown's, 286, 287
Brune, Beatrice, **156**, 200
Brune, Mrs., **98**
Brunel, Isambard Kingdom, 4, 6
Bryans, Rev., 230, 231, 233
Bryce
  (John) Annan, **19**, 29, 35
  Viscount James, **19**, 24, 36
Buckingham
  Molly, 118
  Mr. and Mrs., 118
Buckley, Mr., 192
Bull, Mr., 138
Bunny
  Brice Frederick, **164**
  Maria (née Wulsten), **164**, 188
  Miss (Hilda?), **164**, 183, 187, 192
Bunsen, Baron Georg von, **29**
Burnaby, Colonel Frederick Gustavus, **235**
Burnett, J. P., **209**
Burns, John, **30**, 38, 40, 42, 44, 160
Burston, Mr., 88
Butterfield & Swires, **263**
Butterfield, Mr., 97
Butterworth, Mr., 141
Buxton, Francis William MP, **22**, 24, 36
Bywater, Mr., 287

C

Cadell (Tug). See Francis Cadell (Tug)
Caldecott, Mr., 230, 233
Callender, Mr., 103
Campbell, Donald, **136**, 140, 163, 164, 165, 167, 168, 169, 171, 172, 173, 175, 177, 180, 181, 182, 183, 202, 203, 205
Campbell, Miss, 200
Candler, Samuel Curtis, **74**, 89, 162, 196, 204, 205
Canterbury, Lord. See Manners-Sutton:Henry Charles
Captain of the Ly-ee-mon. See Walker, Captain D.
Captain of the S.S. Wairoa. See Holbeche, Captain E.A.

Carandini, Fanny Helen Hannah. See Morland:Fanny Helen Hannah (née Carandini)
Carlos, Don (Carlos I of Portugal), **226**, 227, 228, 229
Carnegie
  Hon. Charles, **165**, 167, 171, 173, 177, 180, 197
  James (9th Earl of Southesk), **165**
Carrington, Lord, **19**, 22, 23, 24, 25, 29, 35, 36, 37, 44
Carruthers, Mr., 311, 339
Carter, Miss, 202
Cater, Captain, 270, 271
Cates, Frank, **125**, 192
Cave
  Henry, **169**, 170, 248
  Mrs., 169, 170
Chadwick, Miss, 51, 52
Chamberlain, Mr., 218
Chamberlains, (The young), **81**
Chambers, William Knox, **175**, 180
Chapman, Henrietta. See Douglas:Henrietta (née Chapman)
Charnock, Mr., **269**, 278, 279
Chatfield, Captain H.W.H., **180**, 181
Cheyke, Mr., 158
China Traders, 274, 299, 314, 318
Chip, 257, 258, 263
Christison, Robert, **86**
Chrystal
  (Schoolboy son), 96
  David, **68**, 95, 96, 156, 157, 289, 301, 335, 337, 344
  Mrs., 95
Churchward, William B., **172**, 173
Clarke
  A., **42**, 43, 138
  Evelyn, **42**
  Lady Janet Marian (née Snodgrass), 75, 183, 184, 200
  Miss, **67**, 71, 75, 186, 187, 189
  Mrs., 160
  Sir William, 64, 67, **72**, 75, 183, 184, 187, 200, 301
Clayton, T., **104**, **115**, **227**, 321
Clough, E. A., **46**, 51, 52, 55, 56, 87, 160, 192
Clutterbuck, Miss. See Davenport:Mrs. (née Clutterbuck)
Cobb, William B. (Captain of 'The City of New York'), **47**, 49
Coghill, (James Henry?), 24
Coghlan, Captain J. E., **206**, 208
Cokayne, George Edward, 12, **45**, 61, **258**
Coldham, (Walter Timon?), **196**
Coleridge, John Duke, 26

Coles, 305, 338
Compagnie des Messageries Maritimes, 104, **232**, 276, 286, 302, 309, 315
Conil, Mr. (Head of Messageries), 302
Connell, Hogarth & Co., **118**
Conran
  (son), 189
  Lieutenant-Colonel Lewis Charles, **189**
Conran, Captain, 88
Cook
  James, **249**, 262, 278, 292, 307
  Mr., 144, 249
Cooper, Dr., 76, 77
Corner Bros., 26
Cornish
  Mr., 188
  Mrs., 188
Cotton, Caroline. See Le Soeuf:Caroline (née Cotton)
Cotton, Marian. See Ryan:Marian (née Cotton)
Cotton, Mr., 118
Cowan & Co., **59**, 144, 249, 262, 263, 278, 281, 292, 307, 328
Cowan, Jas John, 292
Crace
  Edward Kendall, **106**, 109, 110, 113, 115, 200
  John Gregory, 7, **106**
  Kate Marion (née Mort), **106**
Craig, Captain Hugh, **188**
Crawford, Miss, 121
Crawley
  Charles, **242**
  Herbert, **19**
  John, **19**
  Mary (née Gibbs), 2
  Reverend Charles, **2**
  William S., **19**
Crawley, Mary. See Crawley:Mary (née Gibbs)
Crawley-Boevey, Antony Page, **211**
Crawley-Boevey, Matilda Blanche. See Gibbs:Matilda Blanche (née Crawley-Boevey)
Creswick, Mr., **195**
Croker, Miss, **187**, 200
Cromwell Gold Mine, 305, 306
Crossman
  F.V., **167**, 171
  James Hiscutt, **167**
Crowther
  Mr., 213
  Mrs., 214
Cruickshank
  Miss, 132, 157
  Mr., **51**, 132, 133

Cruikshank
  D.B. (possibly), **126**, 180
  Miss, 126, 133
  Miss (Sister), 126
Cunard (family), 8
Cunard Steamship Company Ltd., 30
Cunningham, Miss, **196**
Curtayne, Mr., 91, 101, 102
Custer, General, 30

D

D (Danson? Dawes?), **275**
D&G Fowlers, **118**
Dalgety & Co., 66, 91, 113, **116**, 144, 145, 269, 324
Dalley, William Bede (Attorney General, NSW), **59**
Danson, Mr., 66, 110, 112, 272, 282, 286, 305, 306
Darling's, 268
Davenport
  Mr.(brother of), 157
  Mrs. (née Clutterbuck), **157**
Davey, Horace QC MP, **19**, 20, 24
Davey, Paxman, and Davey, **285**
Davy, (George Thomas?), **242**
Dawes, Mr. (possibly of Gray Dawes), 284, 285, 286, 336
Day, Mr., 335
Delinage, Mr., 223
Dent, Arnold, **215**, 300
Derham & Co., 345
Dibbs, Sir George Richard (Colonial Treasurer), **59**
Disney
  Anne Eliza, **163**
  Colonel Thomas Robert, **103**, 163
Dixon, Captain, 78
DM. See Mackinnon:Donald
Dobie, Captain, **187**
Donald, Mr., 335
Douglas
  Charles Hill, **21**, 46, 152
  Henrietta (née Chapman), **21**, 46, 49, 50
Dowling, Major, 81
Downall, Reginald Beauchamp, 210, **215**, 217, 218, 222, 224
Dr. Fitz. See FitzGerald:Sir Thomas Naghten
Duff, Mr., 218
Duncan, J., **221**
Dunedin Iron and Woodware Company, 307
Dunn, Mr., 265
Dunn, Rosa. See Lewis:Rosa (née Dunn)
Dunsmere

Index of People

Fred, 152, 153, 343
Robert, 152, 343
Durant, Anna Maria. See Gibbs:Anna Maria (née Durant)
Durston, Mr., 306
Dutch East India Company, 4

E

E&A Company. See Eastern and Australian Steamship Co. Ltd.
E&A Line. See Eastern and Australian Steamship Co. Ltd.
E.. See Gibbs:Edith Caroline
East India Company, 349
Eastern and Australian Steamship Co. Ltd., 140, **188**, **250**, 263, 269, 282, 283, 284, 300, 301, 302, 303, 312, 327, 331
Edith. See Gibbs:Edith Caroline
Edwards, Frederick Lewis, **82**, 83
Edwards, Miss, **209**
Edwards, Sir Henry MP, **22**, 24, 35
Eggert, Mr., 311
Elder, Miss. See Hogg:Mrs. (possibly née Elder)
Elder, Mr., **279**
Elder, Sir Thomas, **81**, 207
Ellis, 254
Elmblad, Madame, **208**
Elton, Beatrice. See Gibbs:Beatrice (née Elton)
Elton, Sir Arthur Hallam, **75**
Evans(?), Mr., **331**
Evans, Gowen Edward, **159**, 183, 186, 187, 190, 195, 197, 198, 199, 200, 209
Evarts, ? (possibly Maxwell, youngest son of William Maxwell), 43
Evarts, William Maxwell, **27**, 29, 30, 33

F

Fairbairn
  George, 65, **93**, 94, 186, 196
  Miss, 93, 184, 196
FAK, F.A.K.. See Keating, Francis Amboor
Fama, Mr., 123
Fannings(?), **264**
Farr, Esther Joanna. See Gibbs:Esther Joanna (née Farr)
Father. See Gibbs:Henry Hucks
Fearon, Low & Co., 300
Fearon, Mr., 300
Fels(?) & Co., 314
Fenwick, Noel, 79, 82, 96

Finch-Hatton, Miss Edith (née Harcourt), 131
Finck, Mr., 344
Finlay, Campbell, **99**, 100, 101, 102
Fisher, Charles Brown, 147, **252**, 254, 301, 308, 309, 325, 336
FitzGerald
  Catherine Naghten (née Higgins), **194**
  Margaret (née Robertson), 74, **194**
  Sir Thomas Naghten, **68**, **74**, 92, **97**, **194**
Fitzgerald, (Sir Robert Uniacke Penrose?), **20**
Floyer, Mr., 73
Forbes, Mr., 46, 47, 49, 50, 51, 52, 110, 160
Ford
  Dr., 71, 103
  Miss, **71**
Forrest, Mr., 326, 334
Forrest, William, **85**, 139, 158
Foster and Martin (photographers), **162**
Francis Cadell (Tug), 148, 249, 282, 298
Francis, Mr., 74
Fraser
  Hon. Captain, **167**, 180
  Mrs., **180**
Fraser & Co., 300, 345
Freeman, Alice. See Meeks:Alice (née Freeman)
French, Miss, 71
Freudenberg, Philipp, 211, **216**, 222, 223, 226, 227, 228, 229
Fuller, Mr., 148
Furnival, Mr., 125
Furse, Miss, 48

G

G.S.H., **153**, **218**
G.S.H. (possibly?). See Hayton, Mr.
Gaukrodger, Mr., 124
George. See Gibbs:George Henry, See Gibbs:George ('poor George')
  Major, 51, 127
  Mr., 242
  Mrs., 51
Gibb, Livingston & Co., 263, 274, 299, 300
Gibbs
  (Alban's wife), 10
  (family), xii, 1, 2, 3, 4, 5, 7, 8, 352
  Alban George Henry, 8, 10, **46**, 59, 66, 68, 71, 75, 78, 84, 94, 95, 101, 102, 104, 110, 111, 113, 137, 143, 148, 150, 152, 155, 158, 181, 222, 224, 232, 234, 235, 241, 245, 246,

359

250, 251, 253, 269, 272, 275, 286, 287, 288, 289, 293, 297, 298, 300, 301, 302, 303, 307, 308, 310, 314, 316, 317, 320, 321, 323, 324, 327, 334, 350
Anna Maria (née Durant), **220**, 228, 235, 236, 239
Anne (née Vicary), 1
Antony (1756–1815), 2, 3, 4, 352
Antony (George Abraham Gibbs' brother), 2
Antony(?), 7, 8, **141**
Beatrice (née Elton), 43, **68**
Bridget (née Beresford-Hope), **309**, **315**, 329
Caroline Blanche, **236**
Catherine Louisa, **312**, **328**
David, 352
Doreen Albinia, 8
Dorothea Barnetta (née Hucks) (1760–1820), 3
Edith Caroline, 8, 9, **71**, 75, **88**, 97, 101, 102, 137, 160, 212, 234
Esther Joanna (née Farr), 1
Francis Lomax, **238**
George ('poor George'), **88**
George (1753–1818), 1, 2, 4
George (1779-1863), 1, 2
George (1873-1931), 8
George Abraham (1718–1794), 1, 2, 3
George Henry, **149**
George Henry (1785–1842), 3, 4, 5, 6, 8
Harriet (née Gibbs), 2
Harriet (née Gibbs) (1786–1865), 3
Henry Hucks, 6, 7, 8, 9, 10, 12, **20**, 23, 26, 27, 64, 65, 71, 84, 93, 94, 101, 102, 104, 112, 143, 148, 153, 167, 239, 242, **291**, 293, 294, 295, 296, 297, 315, 316, 320, 321, 350
Henry Lloyd (probably), 9, **94**, 138, 167, 320
Herbert Cokayne, 9, 12, 18, 72, 75, 78, 84, 86, 88, 94, 96, 97, 104, 137, 142, 160, 220, 224, 228, 231, 232, 234, 235, 236, 237, 238, 239, 252, 256, 275, 292, 298, 313, 315, 316, 320, 350
Isabel Alice, **236**, 238
Janet Louisa (née Merivale), 8
John Arthur, **18**, **285**, **329**, 338, 345
Kenneth Francis, 9, **141**, 142, 158
Lieutenant Colonel Charles, **150**
Louisa Anne (née Adams), 7, 8, 9, **12**, 42, 67, 69, 71, 75, 84, 86, 88, 94, 101, 102, 104, 115, 141, 153, 158, 160, 224, 234, 239, 320
Mary Dorothea, **12**, 114, **121**

Matilda Blanche (née Crawley-Boevey), 7
Mrs. George, 42
Reverend John Lomax, **232**, 235, 236, 238
Salvina (née Hendy), 2
Sir Vicary (1751–1820), 1, 3
Ursula Mary (née Lawley), 8
Vicary, xi, xiii, xvi, 1, 8, 9, 10, 11, 12, 13, 17, 18, 40, 41, **48**, 53, 54, 62, 63, 64, 65, 77, 78, 91, 104, 105, 113, 114, 117, 141, 145, 199, 210, 211, 241, 246, 250, 253, 255, 256, 257, 259, 263, 266, 267, 269, 271, 275, 285, 288, 290, 292, 297, 300, 302, 304, 307, 309, 315, 321, 323, 324, 329, 330, 332, 336, 350,352
Victoria Florence de Burgh (née Long), 8
Walter Antony, 8
William (1790–1875), xiii, 3, 4, 5, 6, 7, 8, 352
Gibbs, Blanche. See Gibbs:Matilda Blanche (née Crawley-Boevey)
Gibbs, Bright & Co., 18, 54, 55, 62, 63, 70, 78, 91, 92, 104, 117, 141, 142, 143, 156, 210, 211, 243, 244, 265, 281, 292, 293, 312, 352
Gibbs, Bright & Co. Property Ltd., 352
Gibbs, Bright, and Gibbs, 4
Gibbs, Via. See Gibbs:Victoria Florence de Burgh (née Long)
Gibson, Mr., 164
Gilchrist Watt, 274
Gill, Mr., 195
Gillanders, Arbuthnot & Co., **261**, 283, 344, 345
Given, Mr., 84, 281, 292, 307
Gladstone, William Ewart, 23, 225, 226, 227
Goodwin, Mr., 152
Gordon, Major-General Charles George, **226**, 227
Gostlings, 307
Grant, President Ulysses S., **27**, 28, 30
Gray, Annie. See Rowe:Mrs.(possibly Annie née Gray)
Gray, Dawes & Co., **154**, 263, 288, 299, 303, 326, 327, 330, 332, **333**, 334
Great Cobar Copper Mining Company Limited, **259**
Green, Molesworth Richard, **69**, 70, 217
Green, Mr. (Colombo), 229
Greenwood, Frederick, **22**
Greig, W.J., 85, 125, 138
Grey, Albert MP, **19**, 20, 22, 24, 26, 38
Griffin, Sir Lepel, **20**, 134

Griffiths, Mr., 141, 144
Grimes, Mrs.. See Bell, Mrs. (George Gibbs' nurse)
Guerabella, Madame. See Ward, Miss Genevieve
Guerbel, Madame La Comtesse De. See Ward, Miss Genevieve
Gurdon, Sir William, **23**, 24, 34, 36
Guzman, Mr., 38

H

H.. See Gibbs:Herbert Cokayne
H.M.S. Heroine, 38
H.M.S. Sappho, 38
H.M.S. Swiftsure, 38
Haddon, Frederick William, **197**
Haddow, Mr. (of Neale & Haddow), 124
Haggett, Mr., 184
Haig, Mr., 131, 132
Haigh Bros., **271**
Hale
  Bishop Matthew Blagden, **154**
  Georgina Theodosia (possibly), **154**
Halford, Mrs.?, 230
Hall, Mr., 90
Hamilton, Mr., 201
Hang(?), 283
Hannay
  (eldest brother), 149
  (father), 148
Hannay (family), 149
Hannay, Percival Ramsford, **61**, 67, 69, 70, 72, 73, 78, 86, 148, 149, 150, 154, 155, 251, 252, 253, 254, 258, 259, 261, 275, 290, 292, 300, 304, 308, 312, 316, 322, 325, 326, 330, 331, 332, 334, 335, 336, 337
Hannen
  (Son of Sir James), 38
  Sir James, **33**, 35, 36, 38
Hansard, Captain Arthur Agar, **150**, 156, 288, 292, 326, **332**, 334
Harcourt, Miss Edith. See Finch-Hatton, Miss Edith (née Harcourt)
Harcourt, Mr., 131
Harper's, 299
Harrison, Dr. Edward, **52**
Harry. See Gibbs:Henry Lloyd (probably)
Hart
  Camilla Rose, 58, **160**, 163
  Fanny Mary. See Tyler:Fanny Mary (née Hart)
  Frederic Hamilton Scott, **56**, 58, 60, 78, 80, 86, 87, 88, 148, 149, 150, 151, 152, 154, 155, 156, 158, 160, 163, 164, 245, 246, 248, 249, 251, 254, 255, 256, 257, 258, 275, 282, 284, 286, 288, 312, 322, 325, 326, 327, 328, 332, 334, 335, 336, 337
  Graham Lloyd, **156**
  Harriet Isabel Blanche (née Horsley), **58**, 148, 149, 150, 153, 154, 155, 156
Hassall, Mr., 326
Hatteraik, Dirk, 69
Hatterod, Mr. and Mrs., 229
Hay, Captain Alexander, **150**
Hayley, A., 47
Hayne, James Charles, **219**, 242, 308
Hayton, Mr., 157
Headley, Mr., 194, 199
Heath
  Baron Robert Amadeus, **156**
  Captain G.P., **156**, 330
Hector, Captain G. N., **206**, 207, 208, 209
Hendy, Salvina. See Gibbs:Salvina (née Hendy)
Henry Bath, 273, 274
Henty, James and Company, **74**
Herbert. See Gibbs:Herbert Cokayne
Heriot, Mr., 234
Higgins, Catherine Naghten. See FitzGerald:Catherine Naghten (née Higgins)
Hill
  Charles Lumley, **85**, 148, 149, 150, 201, 202, 205
  Tom, 85
Hilliard
  (brother), 57
  Mr., 57, 59
Hogg
  Mrs. (possibly née Elder), 217
  William E., **193**, 202, 204, 206, 217
Holbeche, Captain E.A., **165**
Holford, Sir George Lindsay, **22**, 23, 24, 26, 35, 38
Hong Kong and Shanghai Bank (HSBC), xi, 350, 351
Hopcraft, Mr., 309
Horn, Mr., 301
Hornsby, James William, **49**, 50, 55, 160
Horsley, Harriet Isabel Blanche. See Hart:Harriet Isabel Blanche (née Horsley)
Houlton, Mr., 110, 118, 165
Howard Smith, **284**
Howard, Ernest William, **201**
Howard, Mr., 184, 196
Howell, Alfred, **211**, 213, 215, 216, 217, 219, 220, 222, 223, 224, 230, 231, 234, 235

361

Hucks, Dorothea Barnetta, 7, See
  Gibbs:Dorothea Barnetta (née Hucks)
  (1760–1820)
Huskisson, William MP, **34**
Hutchinson, Major General C. S., **21**, 26
Hutton, Miss, 196
Huxley, Thomas Henry, 138

I

Ibbotson, 345
Ind
  Captain, **163**, 195, 200
  Mrs., 163, 195, 198, 200
Ingles. See Inglis, J. O.
Inglis, J. O., **201**
Irvine
  (Richard's son), 24
  Richard, 24, 25
Irvings, 263, 283, 287, 307, 314
Isaacson, Mr., 233

J

Jackson, Miss, 230
Jago, Amelia Durrant. See
  Williams:Amelia Durrant (née Jago)
Jardine, Mr., **211**
Jervois, Sir William Francis Drummond, **132**
Jo. See Lee, Jennie (Actress)
John Arthur. See Gibbs:John Arthur
John Winham & Sons, 105, 264, 265, 266, 267, 268, 287, 291, 293
John(?), Mr., 339
John, Mr., 332
Johnny. See Gibbs:John Arthur
Johnson, President Andrew, 27
Joseph
  Miss, 71
  Mrs., 71
Joseph (Sydney merchant), 69

K

K.. See Keating, Francis Amboor
Keating, Francis Amboor, **58**, 67, **68**, 70, 78, 84, 85, 86, 87, 88, 89, 90, 91, 93, 96, 101, 102, 103, 104, 105, 111, 119, 137, 138, 141, 143, 144, 155, 159, 160, 161, 162, 163, 184, 186, 187, 189, 190, 192, 194, 195, 196, 197, 199, 200, 201, 202, 203, 204, 205, 206, 207, 223, 245, 246, 251, 253, 254, 255, 257, 258, 259, 271, 272, 275, 277, 285, 290, 291, 292, 300, 308, 310, 312, **313**, 314, 315, 316, 319, 327, 328, 330, 332, 333, 335, 336, 345
Keats. See Keating, Francis Amboor
Kelly, Julia Elizabeth. See Mason:Julia
  Elizabeth (née Kelly)
Kelly, Mr., 273, 274
Kennedy, Mr., 127
Kenneth. See Gibbs:Kenneth Francis
Keyser, Mr., 140
King of Tonga. See Tupou, George I
  (King of Tonga)
Kinross, Jane. See Mackinnon:Jane (née
  Kinross)
Klingender, Mr., 344
Knox, Ellen Washington, **206**

L

L., Christopher, 229
L.J. Bowen. See Bowen, Sir Charles
Labouchère, Henry Du Pré, **31**
Laidley
  (eldest son - Shepheard?), 59
  Hon. William George MLC, **57**, 59, 71, 126, 137, 143, **204**
  Mrs. Jane (née Atkinson), 57, 59, 71, 126, 137, 143
  Shepheard Edgecliff, **157**
Laidley, Emily Jane. See Merivale:Mrs.
  Emily Jane (née Laidley)
Laing, Mr., **185**
Lamb, Clemence L.. See Parbury,
  Clemence L. (née Lamb)
Lambert
  Charles, 76, 77
  Mrs., 77
Lamoi, 309
Landers, Mr. (of the Guardian), 43, 44
Langley, Mr., 287
Law, Mr., 221
Lawley
  Eustace, 8
  Lady, 8
  Richard, 8
  Sir Arthur, 8
Lawley, Ursula Mary. See Gibbs:Ursula
  Mary (née Lawley)
Le Brere, Miss. See Knox, Ellen
  Washington
Le Grand (racehorse), 140
Le Patourel, Mr., 82
Le Soeuf
  Caroline (née Cotton), **189**
  Caroline Lilian, **189**
Leach
  Mr., 95
  Mrs., 95
Lee, Barnard, 255

Index of People

Lee, Jennie (Actress), **81**, 206, **207**, 209
Lee, Jenny. See Lee, Jennie (Actress)
Leechman
  G.B., 210, **220**, **221**, 224, 229
  Mrs., 223
Leighton, Mr., 322
Leishman
  Mr., 184, 190
  Mrs., 184, 190, 197
Lenders, 323, 344
Lewis
  Louis Ludwig, **162**, 163, 183, 184, 185, 186, 188, 191, 192, 193, 194, 195, 196, 197, 198, 199, 200, 201, 203, 204, 205, 207
  Rosa (née Dunn), **102**, 162, 163, 164, 183, 184, 186, 187, 188, 190, 191, 192, 193, 194, 195, 196, 197, 198, 199, 200, 201, 202, 203, 204, 205, 207
Lewis, Dr., 132
Liddell, Mr., 38
Lincoln's Inn, 10
Lingen, Mr., 141
Lister
  Mr., 155
  Mrs., 155
Lloyd, Mr., 136
Loch, The Rt Hon Lord (Governor of Victoria), **182**
Locker, Frederick, **187**
London Assurance Co., 296
Long, Heathcote, 20
Long, Mr., 73
Long, Victoria Florence de Burgh. See Gibbs:Victoria Florence de Burgh (née Long)
Lord Macclesfield. See Parker, Lord Thomas Augustus Wolstenholme (6th Earl of Macclesfield)
Lord South Esk. See Carnegie:James (9th Earl of Southesk)
Lord, Mr., 267
Lorimer, John, **118**
Lorimer, Mr., 251
Lorrimer. See Lorimer, John
Lowrey, Mr., 287
Lowther, Mr., **19**
Lucas, Mr. (cricketer), **184**
Luce, Captain, **176**
Lucy, Sir Henry William, **160**
Lyons, Admiral Sir Algernon McLennan, **38**
Lytton, Lord, 20

M

M.. See Mackinnon:Donald
MacEwans, 273
Macinell, Miss, 48
Mack. See Mackinnon:Donald
Mackinnon
  Bill, 97, 98
  Daniel, **89**, 97, 98, 100, 102, 186, 193
  Donald, 41, **42**, 45, 46, 47, 49, 50, 51, 52, 88, 89, 97, 98, 99, 100, 103, 160, 186, 192, 198, 199, 206, 313
  Jane (née Kinross), 97, 98, 100, 102
  Jim, 98
  Kenneth, 98, 100
  Miss (first daughter), 98
  Miss (second daughter), 98, 100
Mackinnon, Sir Lauchlan Charles (Editor of the Melbourne Argus), **69**, 163, 200
Macknickel, Mr., 192
Maclaine, Mr., 201
Maclaren
  (brother of South Sea trip Maclaren), **202**
  H., **167**, 169, 180, 202
  J.H., **167**, 169, 180, 202
Macleod of Macleod, Norman, **20**, 36
MacPherson
  Angus, **151**, 152, 153, 206, 244, **289**, 333, **343**
  Mrs., 151, 153
Macpherson & Marshall, 300
Madame du Barry. See Bécu, Jeanne (comtesse du Barry)
Mair, Major William Gilbert, **167**, 173
Malohi, Wellington Gu Tubou, **176**
Malua (racehorse), **201**, 202
Mann, Mr., 271
Manners-Sutton
  Anna Maria Georgiana. See Bright:Anna Maria Georgiana (née Manners-Sutton)
  Henry Charles, **202**, 277
  J., **276**, 277, 309
Mansfield, His Honour Deputy Judge Edward, **155**
Marie de Gray, Miss. See Knox, Ellen Washington
Marks, G., 334
Marshall, Mr., 43, 44
Martin, Dr. (Gibbs' family doctor), **198**
Martin, Patrick MP, **34**, 38, 43
Martini Henry (racehorse), 69, 140
Maryllan & Harriman, 300
Mason

Julia Elizabeth (née Kelly), **147**
Maurice Charles, **147**
Mason & Barry, 309
Mason Bros. Limited, 299
Matheson, Sir Alexander Perceval (3rd Baronet of Lochalsh), **198**
Maude, Mr., 45
Maxwell, James Riddle, **37**
Maxwell, Mr., 320
Mc. See Mackinnon:Donald
McBride, Doris Eleanor, xiii, 10, 11, 12
McElhone, Thersites, **84**
McEllister, Mr., 265, 266, 267, 278, 287
McGuigan(?), Mr., 271
McIlwraith
   Lady Harriette Ann (née Mosman), **286**
   Sir Thomas, 54, **284**, 285
Mecklenberg
   Duchess Marie of, **226**, 227, 229
   Duke Paul Friedrich of, **226**, 227, 228, 229
Medcalf, Mr., 247, 248
Meeks
   Alice (née Freeman), 77, 78, **82**, 207
   Sir Alfred William, 77, 78, **79**, 80, 81, 82, 88, 105, 118, 207, 252, 264, 265, 266, 267, 269, 277, 278, 279, 286, 287, 299, 302, 313, 324, 329
   Victor, 78, **82**
Menzies, Archibald, **152**
Merivale
   Angel, 8, 104, 137, 143, 263
   George Montague, 53, **56**, 57, 58, 66, **71**, 74, 84, 96, 97, 104, 105, **106**, 107, 109, 110, 111, 112, 114, 116, 117, 118, 119, 120, 123, 125, 132, 137, 140, 141, 143, 144, 157, 158, 164, 203, 204, 205, 248, 249, 251, 253, 254, 261, 262, 273, 274, 289, 290, 292, 304, 310, 312, 315, 324, 327, 330, 335
   Janet Louisa. See Gibbs:Janet Louisa (née Merivale)
   John Lewis, 8
   Mrs. Emily Jane (née Laidley), 8, 57, 71, 84, 104, 114, 125, 137, 143, 144, 157, 158, 263
Messageries Co.. See Compagnie des Messageries Maritimes
Messrs. Joseph Stilling & Co., **269**, 278, 315
Meyer, Captain, **43**, 44
Mignonette (yacht), **190**
Mildmay, Fred, **19**, 23
Miles & Co., 113, **115**, 116, 313
Miller, George, **183**
Milling Co., 268

Milner
   Granville, **20**, 21
   Rt. Hon. Sir Frederic George, **20**
Milo(?), Mr., 270
Milton(?), Mr., 271
Mitchell, Mr., 158
Moeller (family), 338
Money, Eleanor, **198**
Moore, Mr., 283
Morehead
   Boyd Dunlop, 139, **155**, 243, 244, 326, 334
   Mrs., 155
Morehead's, 85, 91, 276, 284, 327, 334
Mores, Marquis de, **31**
Morewood's, 307
Morey
   Mr., 131, 132, 134
   Mrs., 131, 132, **134**
Morgan
   George, 286
   Sir William, **286**
Morgan, J.P., **37**
Morgan's. See William Morgan & Co.
Morland
   Fanny Helen Hannah (née Carandini), **206**, 208, 209
   Sir Henry, **206**
Morphy, Florence Rose. See Bligh:Florence Rose (née Morphy)
Mort, Kate Marion. See Crace:Kate Marion (née Mort)
Mort, Thomas Sutcliffe, 54, 62
Mosman, Harriette Ann. See McIlwraith:Lady Harriette Ann (née Mosman)
Mother. See Gibbs:Louisa Anne (née Adams)
Mumford, Mr., 132
Mun & Dennerd(?), 271
Munckley, Samuel, 1
Murdoch, G. B., **106**, 110, 115, 141
Murdoch, William (Billy) Lloyd, **88**
Murphy, Alec, 93
Murphy, Mr., 148
Murray
   Mrs., 59, 111, 140, 144, 158
   William Gilmour, 53, **56**, 57, 59, 78, 84, 104, 137, 139, 140, 141, 144, 145, 157, 158, 164, 203, 246, 249, 250, 253, 256, 258, 260, 263, 279, 280, 281, 288, 290, 298, 304, 305, 310, 311, 312, 321, 322, 324, 325, 328, 330, 331, 332, 334, 336, 337, 339
Musgrave
   Anthony, **148**, 149, 150, 154, 155, 156

Sir Anthony, **148**

N

Nankivell, (possibly Thomas J., or George), **195**
Neale & Haddow, **124**
Nevill, Lord William, **196**
New Zealand Co., 278
New Zealand Refrigeration Company, 113
Newton, General, 27
Nicholls, Mr., 93, 252, 291, 300
Normanby, Lord, **82**
North China Insurance, 274, 314, 325
North, John, 9
Northcote, Miss, 20
Northern Pacific Railroad. See Northern Pacific Railway
Northern Pacific Railway, 12
Nott, Dr., 81
NPR. See Northern Pacific Railway

O

O'Connell, Lady Eliza Emily, **154**
Ogg(?), Mr., 271
Onslow
  Lady, 29
  Lord, **29**
Orchard, Mr., 218
Orient Steam Navigation Co., 54, 104, 112, 190, 253, 260, 269, 279, 284, 299, 301, 302, 309, 315, 331, 334
Oriental Bank, 324, 334
Ormond, Francis(?), **233**
Osborne, Mr., 201
Osbourne, Mr., 139
Owens, Robert, 343
Oxham
  Mr., 123
  Mrs., 123

P

P&O. See Peninsular and Oriental Steam Navigation Company
Pacific Co., 253, 269, 278, 279
Pacific Fire and Marine Insurance Company, 322
Paget, Mr., 73
Palmer, Mr., 140
Parbury Henty Bank, 352
Parbury Lamb, 91, 284
Parbury, Charles, 334
Parbury, Clemence L. (née Lamb), **204**, 233
Parbury's, 274, 326, 334

Parker, Hon. Edmund William, 113, **116**
Parker, Lord Thomas Augustus Wolstenholme (6th Earl of Macclesfield), 113, **116**
Parkes, Mr., 319
Paxton, Mr., 212, 213
Pearson, Mr. (Sydney House), 260
Pell, Albert, **20**, 25, 29, 34, 36
Peninsular and Oriental Steam Navigation Company, 69, 80, 82, 137, 208, 232, 234, 269
Peto, Mr., 212
Pinder, Rev. North, **318**
Plunkett, Mr., 147
Popham, F.A.L., **180**
Porter, Mr., 211, 212, 213, 229
Portman, Lord, 73
Portman, Mr., 73
Potts, Mrs., **52**
Power
  Miss, **184**
  Mrs., **85**, 163, 184
  Robert, **84**, 163, 184
Presse, Jules, 291, 302
Preston, Captain George Berthon, **206**, **208**, 209
Prim, General Juan, **228**
Princess Marie of Windisch-Graetz. See Mecklenberg:Duchess Marie of
Prior, The. See Gibbs:Henry Hucks
Purver
  Ellen Blanche (née Surridge) (Mrs. McBride's mother), 11
  Frederick George (Mrs. McBride's father), 11

Q

Q.R.M. (Queensland Royal Mail?), 156, **334**
Q.S.N. (Queensland Steam Navigation Company?), **333**, 334
Quakers, The, 4
Queensland National Bank, 210

R

Ramsay, 274, 299
Rathbone JP, Samuel Greg, **21**, 25, 339
Raymond, Mr., **48**, 49, 50, 52, 87
RB, R.B.. See Bright:Reginald
Reader, Lieutenant Colonel H.E., **134**
Rede, Colonel Robert William (Sheriff of Melbourne), **194**, 197
Rede, Mr., 121
Reg, Regi, Regi B., Reginald etc.. See Bright:Reginald
Reginald Bright & Co., 344

Reid, Sir George (Minister for Public Instruction, NSW), **59**
Reid, W., 346
Remnant, Mr., 274
Ribet, Mr., 123
Richards, Mr., 274
Rio Tinto, 309
Ritchie, John Macfarlane, **112**
Roberts, Mr., 154
Robertson
  Miss (two of them), **201**
  Murray (Director of the Chartered Mercantile Bank), 252
  William, **70**, **71**, 101, 139, 140, 191, 205, 206
Robertson, J.M. & Co., 251, 317
Robertson, Margaret. See FitzGerald:Margaret (née Robertson)
Robinson, Augustus Frederick, **193**, 195, 196, 202, 204, 233
Robinson, Charlotte. See Youl:Charlotte (formerly Robinson, née Williams) (?).
Robinson, Sir William Cleaver Francis, **70**, 201
Rogers, (James Edwin) Thorold, **34**
Romanis, Blanche (née Cokayne), **67**, 75
Romilly, Hugh Hastings, 138, **155**
Ronald, Mr., 249
Rowan, A. and F., **332**
Rowan, Andrew, 344
Rowan, Captain Frederic Charles, **161**
Rowe
  Mr.(possibly Charles James), **219**
  Mrs.(possibly Annie née Gray), **201**, 219
Royal Fire Insurance Company, The, 326
Rumbold, Sir Horace, **21**
Russell, Charles MP, **34**, 36, 38, 39, 43
Ryan
  Ada Mary. See Scott:Lady Ada Mary (née Ryan)
  Alice Elfrida (née Sumner), **84**
  Blanche Adelaide, **161**
  Charles, **73**, 76, 105, 106, 160, 161, 189, 190, 195, 206
  Dr. Sir Charles Snodgrass, **84**
  Mabel Hartley, **105**, 106, 129, 132, 133, 161
  Marian (née Cotton), **105**, 129, 132, 133, 160, 161, 189, 190, 191, 196, 206
Ryder, Mr., 127, 128, 129

S

S.S. Almora, 155
S.S. Brindisi, 229, 232, 233
S.S. Caernarvon Castle, **274**
S.S. Carthage, 206
S.S. Catterthun, **250**
S.S. City of New York, 40, 41, **44**, 87, 110, 127, 160
S.S. City of Sydney, 52
S.S. Coorang, 332
S.S. Cuzco, 285
S.S. Dunedin, 113, 334
S.S. Fenstanton, 307
S.S. Gallia, 18, 41, 42, 46, **160**
S.S. Garonne, 293, 299
S.S. Great Britain, 6, 42, 64, 104, 253, 256, 291, 311
S.S. Guthrie, 188
S.S. Holmesdale, 254, 298
S.S. Iberia, 82, 89, 268
S.S. John Elder, 53, 58, **60**, 258
S.S. John O'Gaunt, 86
S.S. Kembla, 144
S.S. Killarney, 296
S.S. Kuiru i Huid(?), 271
S.S. Liguria, 89, 142, **188**
S.S. Lusitania, **190**
S.S. Ly-ee-moon, 156, 332
S.S. Mataura, 113
S.S. Mongolia, 234
S.S. Nelson, 70, 73, **81**, 195
S.S. Normanton, 254
S.S. Protos, 66
S.S. Queen of the Pacific, 37
S.S. Rome, 86, 141, 270, 321
S.S. Rotoruahama, 125, 126
S.S. Shannon, **82**
S.S. Sorata, **76**, 189, 269, 278, 279, 318
S.S. Soukar, 254
S.S. South Australia, 254
S.S. Strathleven, 54, 66
S.S. Tarawera, 105, 108, 134
S.S. Tibre, 226
S.S. Wairarapa, 166, 169, 171, 173, 174, 180
S.S. Wairoa, **164**, 167
S.S. Wanaka, 124
S.S. Wellington, 133
S.S. Winifred, 254, 298
S.S. Yarra, 232, 233
Sackville-West
  Hon. Lionel (2nd Baron Sackville), **33**, 34, 35
  Miss, **35**
Salter, Mr., 326
Samuelson
  Mr. MP, 27
  Mrs., 27
Sandeman, Albert, **150**

Index of People

Sandeman, Mr., 68, 150
Sangsue. See Leechman:G.B.
Saurey, Mr., 287
Scott
  Admiral Lord Sir Charles Montagu Douglas, **76**, 105
  Lady Ada Mary (née Ryan), **76**, 105
Scott, Mr., 326
Scottish Investment Co., 276
Selby, Mr., 96
Sharp, Cecil James, **207**
Sharpshooter (barque), 296, 329
Shaw, Captain, **26**
Shepherd, Tommy, 103
Sheppard, Tommy, 168
Sheridan, General Philip, 28
Shuttleworth, Kay (brother of our friend), **212**
Sillem, Augustus (Charles Herman?), **242**, 279
Silver Cres(cent?), 313
Simon, Mr. (Lawyer), 265
Simpson, Mr., 184
Simpson, Mr. (Sydney House), 259, 260
Sinnatambi (VG's servant), **215**, 218, 219, 221, 222, 229
Sitting Bull, **30**
Smeb (possibly Samuel Bright), **69**, 94, 153, 158
Smith (Brindisi), Mr., 234
Smith (Superintendent of Banagala)
  Mrs., 214
  William(?), **213**, 214
Smith (Tarawera, 18th March 1884). See Tyson, Mr.
Smith, B., 343
Smith, Captain, 155, 329
Smith, Dr., 230, 233
  Mrs., 230, 233
Sniders, J., **207**
Snodgrass
  Janet Marian. See Clarke:Lady Janet Marian (née Snodgrass)
  Miss (sister of Lady Janet Marian Clarke), 75
Snyder. See Sniders, J.
Southerden, Mr., 248, 251, 312, 326
Southerdon, Mr.. See Sutherland, Donald
Spacey, Mr., 85
Spiro, Mr., 138
Stackpoole, Mr., **26**, 27, 37
Steinthal, Rev. Samuel Alfred, **24**
Stephen
  George Milner, **118**
  Sir Alfred, **119**
Sterling, Antoinette, **208**
Stewart, Mr., 119

Still, W.T., **171**, 175
Stillings. See Messrs. Joseph Stilling & Co.
Storey, Mr., 70, 85, 285
Strachan, Mr., **183**, 184, 185, 192, 197, 204, 206
Strahan, Major Sir George Cumine, **70**
Strahan, Mr., 87, 91
Stratford, Mr., 120, 121
Strauss, 246
Strauss, Mr., 274
Strickland, Sir Edward, 82
Strong, Mr., 47
Stuart, Sir Alexander (Premier of New South Wales), **53**, **59**, 60
Stubbs, Edward, 215
Stubbs, Mr., **283**
Studleigh, Mr., 118
Sturgis, Frank K., **37**
Sturgis, Mr., 196
Sugar Company, The, **318**
Sullivan, Aleck, 195
Sullivan, Colonel, 195
Sullivan, Mr., 69, 85, 139, 202
Sumner, Alice Elfrida. See Ryan:Alice Elfrida (née Sumner)
Sun Fire Office, The, **326**
Surridge
  Alfred Alonda (Mrs. McBride's grandfather), 11
  Ephraim (Mrs. McBride's grandfather's brother), 11
Sutherland, Donald, **108**
Swaine, Colonel Leopold V., **235**
Swires (?Butterfield and Swires?), 300
Swyney, Mr., 329
Sylvester(?), Mr., 339
Symonds, Henry Francis, **177**
Syria, **169**

T

Tawhiao (King of the Maoris), 135
Tayler, Commissary General, 221
Taylor
  Mr., 200
  Mrs., 200
Taylor, Mr., 201
Tebbit, Canon. See Tebbut, Rev. Canon
Tebbits, Canon. See Tebbut, Rev. Canon
Tebbut, Rev. Canon, **169**, 176
Tennant, Mr., 103, 299, 300
Terry, Charles Gailey, **118**, 119, 120, 122, 123, 127, 129, 132, 134
Tetley
  Mr,, 224
  Mrs., 224

Thomas, Captain, **188**, 190, 192, 195, 198
Thomas, Flag Lieutenant, 38
Thomas, Mr., 45, 46, 47, 48, 115, 117
Thornton
  Emily, 45
  Rev. Dr. Samuel (Bishop of Ballarat), **45**, 46, 47, 51
Tideman, 250, 299
Tobin?, Mr., 328
Tower
  Canon, 328
  Mr., **144**, 246, 251, 272, 325, 328
Trask, Dr. Ed, 45, 46
Travers
  Mr., 188
  Mrs., 188
Trollope
  Anthony, 8
  Henry Merivale, 8
Trust and Agency Co., **276**, 301, 306, 307
Tupou, George I (King of Tonga), **174**, 176
Turner, Mr., 287
Turner, Mr. (Queensland squatter), 272
Tylecote, Edward Ferdinando Sutton, **67**, **75**, 186, 187, 189
Tyler
  Fanny Mary (née Hart), **160**
  John Chatfield, **21**, 87, 160
Tyndall (family, of Miles, Queensland), 85
Tyndall, John, 138
Tyson, Mr., 127, 128, 129, 131, 308, 309

U

Uncle John. See Gibbs:Reverend John Lomax
Union of Canton, 274, 325
Union Steam Ship Company (of New Zealand), **180**, **315**

V

Vallombrosa, Duke of, 31
Varvill, Elizabeth, xiii
Vernon, Howard, **184**, 194
Vicary
  Anne. See Gibbs:Anne (née Vicary)
  Antony, 1
Villard, Henry, 17, 18, **29**, 39, 40
Vincent
  Colonel Sir Charles Edward Howard, **231**, 233
  Mrs., 231, 233

Vine, Mr. (Shipping Clerk), 60
Voeux, Sir George William des, **102**, 168, 172, 177

W

W. Winham & McEllister, 265, 266
Walcott, Mr., 112, 305
Wales, Prince of, 101, 203
Walker, Captain D., **157**
Walker, Mr., 224, 226
Wallace Bros., **19**
Wallington, Mr., 103, **168**
Walters, Mr., 132, 133
Ward, Lucy Genevieve Theresa. See Ward, Miss Genevieve
Ward, Miss Genevieve, **183**, 184, 194
Wardell
  (Son), **190**
  William Wilkinson, 54, 190, **216**, 247, **280**
Waterhouse, Mr., 278
Waterlow, Sir Sydney, **23**
Watson, Mr., 206
Watt, Mr., **196**, 299, 344
Way, Sir Samuel James, **207**
Weaver, Mr., 51, 52
Webster, Mr., 86
Weigall, Mr., **196**
Wells
  David Ames, **26**, 34, 37
  Mrs., 34
Wentworth, Mr., 344
West
  (daughter). See Sackville-West:Miss
  Hon. Lionel. See Sackville-West:Hon. Lionel (2nd Baron Sackville)
West, Mr., 150
Westbury, Lord, 21
Westby, Mr., 85
Whatman, C.M.C., **173**, 180
White, Captain (Fire Brigade), 42, 43
White, Dr., **221**, **312**
White, Horace, **24**
White, James, 140, **197**, 202
White, Mr. (3), 143
White, Mr. (owner of the Cup winner), **70**
Whiteford, Mr., 219, 220
Wickham, J. D., **52**
Wilcox, Mr., **94**, 230
Wilkie, Dr. David Elliot, **205**
William Morgan & Co., 276, 282, 283, 302
Williams
  Amelia Durrant (née Jago), **111**
  Judge Joshua Strange, **110**, 111
  Miss, 111

Williams, Charlotte. See Youl:Charlotte (formerly Robinson, née Williams) (?).
Wilson Meyer, 42
Wilson, David, **219**
Wilson, Mr. (Adelaide), 278
Wilson, Mr. (Egypt), 233, 234
Wilson, Mr. (Liverpool), 339
Wilson, Mr. (Tauranga), 133
Wilson, Sir John Cracroft, **116**
Wilsons, 263
Winham (Adelaide Merchants), **80**
Winham, Mr., 264, 265, 266, 267, 275, 277, 278, 287, 293, 309, 310, 313, 324, 328, 329
Wittie, Miss, 201
Wolley, Emma Katherine. See Bright:Emma Katherine (née Wolley)
Wolseley, Lord. See Wolseley, Sir Garnet
Wolseley, Sir Garnet, **221**, 235
Worshipful Company of Brewers, **167**
Wright, John T., **167**, 181
Wulsten, Maria. See Bunny:Maria (née Wulsten)

Y

Yonge, Charlotte, 7
Youl
 Charlotte (formerly Robinson, née Williams) (?)., 69
 Dr. Richard, **75**, **196**
 James Arndell (?), **69**
 Miss (daughter of Richard), 75
Young, 275
Yuill, George Skelton (?), **139**, 140, 157, 315

From Guano to Gold: The Diary and Letters of Vicary Gibbs from 1883-5

Index of Locations

(To find names of obscure places, use the Hierarchical List of Locations first). Bold page numbers indicate the location of footnotes.

A

Accademia di Belle Arti (Florence), **238**
Adelaide (South Australia), 73, 76, 77, 78, 79, 81, 82, 84, 86, 87, 88, 104, 105, 118, 120, 141, 184, 208, 252, 264, 265, 268, 270, 271, 274, 275, 276, 277, 278, 279, 282, 283, 286, 291, 293, 297, 302, 309, 310, 311, 313, 314, 315, 319, 345
Adelaide Cathedral. See Cathedral (Adelaide)
Adelaide Club. See Club (Adelaide)
Adelaide Harbour. See Harbour (Adelaide)
Adelaide Office. See Office (Adelaide)
Aden (Yemen), 222, **231**
Agricultural Show (Melbourne), 70
Ahaura (West Coast Region, South Island), 121
Ahaura Magistrate's court. See Magistrate's court (Ahaura)
Ahaura Warden's court. See Warden's court (Ahaura)
Ainsworth (Washington), **35**
Albany (Western Australia), 208
Albury (New South Wales), 159, 164
Aldenham. See Aldenham House (Elstree)
Aldenham Church (Elstree), 13
Aldenham House (Elstree), xiii, 6, 7, 10, 11, 12, 13, 40, 320
Alexandria (Egypt), 231, 233, 234
Amby Crossing (Amby), 151
Amby Downs (Amby), **21**, 63, **68**, 72, 152, 153, 154, 156, 245, 246, 273, 287, 308, 315, 327, 332, 333, 336, 341
Amby South (Amby), 334
Amoy (Fujian Province), **231**
Amsterdam (North Holland), 4
Ancona (Marche Region), 235
Anika paddock, Lara, near Geelong (Melbourne), 93
Apia (Upolu (island)), **172**, 173
Argentina, 11
Armidale (New South Wales), 145
Athenaeum (Melbourne), **197**

Auckland (Auckland Region, North Island), 38, 50, 51, 52, 55, 56, 86, 114, 127, 132, 133, 164, 165, 180, 245, 308
Auckland Club. See Club (Auckland)
Auckland Museum. See Museum (Auckland)
Australia, xi, xii, xvi, 4, 6, 8, 9, 11, 12, 40, 41, 55, 62, 64, 65, 91, 93, 96, 99, 107, 109, 114, 116, 117, 119, 121, 123, 128, 139, 188, 193, 199, 203, 208, 210, 220, 225, 229, 241, 247, 256, 257, 270, 273, 290, 295, 296, 308, 313, 316, 321, 349, 350, 351
Avon River (Christchurch), 116

B

Badlands (Bismarck), 30
Banagala Estate (Moneragala), 213
Barbados, 304, 315
Barnes Hall (Nuwara Eliya), **217**
Basilica di Santa Croce (Florence), **236**
Bata?, **324**
Bath (Somerset), 272
Bay of Islands (Northland Region, North Island), 136
Bealey (Canterbury Region, South Island), 118
Belgrove (Nelson Region, South Island), 124
Bella Union Theatre (San Francisco), 44
Bellasyse Estate (Barbados), 304
Bendango. See Bindango (Queensland)
Berlin (Germany), 227
Bijou Theatre (Melbourne), 103, 206
Billings (Montana), 31
Bindango (Queensland), **153**, **333**, 334
Bishopsgate (London), 297
Bismarck (North Dakota), 30, 31
Bluff, The (Invercargill), 108, **181**
Blundell's School (Tiveton), 4
Boboli Gardens (Florence), 237
Bohemian Club (Melbourne), **71**, 182
Bohemian Club (San Francisco), 44
Bolivia, 5, 6
Bolivia (New South Wales), 146
Bologna (Emilia-Romagna Region), 234, 235, 239

Bombay (Maharashtra), 206, 235, 271
Botanical Gardens (Melbourne), 67, **71**
Botanical Gardens (Sydney), 53, 55, 139
Botanical Gardens (Wellington), 125
Botanical Reserve (Brisbane), 149
Bozeman (Montana), 32
Brindisi (Apulia Region), 232, 234, 235
Brisbane (Queensland), 56, 58, 66, 67, 68, 70, 73, 84, 85, 104, 119, 141, 148, 149, 150, 153, 154, 155, 158, 243, 244, 245, 246, 248, 249, 251, 254, 255, 256, 257, 258, 268, 273, 275, 277, 284, 285, 287, 288, 292, 293, 297, 299, 301, 304, 308, 309, 312, 315, 321, 322, 324, 326, 327, 328, 330, 331, 332, 333, 334, 335, 336, 337, 338, 339, 341, 346
Bristol (Bristol), 1, 4, 5, 7, 62
Broadway (New York), 26
Broken Hill (New South Wales), **345**
Brooklyn (New York), 25
Brooklyn Bridge (New York), **25**
Brunner (Greymouth), **120**
Buller River (Lyell), 123

C

Cadiz (Andalusia), 3
Cairo (Egypt), 233
Calais (Pas-de-Calais), 239
Calcutta (West Bengal), 206, 208, 230, 259, 260, 261, 271, 273, 284
Cambridge (Waikato Region, North Island), 132
Campbell's Cove (Sydney), 55, 92, 142
Camperdown (Victoria), 97, 101, 192
Canterbury Region, South Island (New Zealand), 306
Cape Colony (South Africa), 278
Cape Flattery (Washington), 39
Cape Leeuwin (Western Australia), **208**
Capella Ricardi (Florence), 238
Carlton Club (London), 18
Cascina (Tuscany), 237
Casino (New York), 25
Cathedral (Adelaide), 97
Cathedral (Dunedin), 112
Cathedral (Melbourne), 97
Cathedral (Queenstown), **20**
Caulfield Races (Melbourne), 88, 196, 198
Central Park (New York), 25
Ceylon, xi, 9, 12, 73, 150, 201, 210, 211, 214, 216, 219, 220, 241, 251, 252, 261, 298, 328, 349
Chehalis (Washington), 37
Cheltenham (Gloucestershire), 77

Chennai. See Madras (Tamil Nadu Region)
Chicago (Illinois), 27
Chile, 5, 255
China, 274
Chincha Islands (Peru), 5, 6
Chinese quarter (San Francisco), 43, 44
Christ Church College, Oxford (Oxford), 10, **80**, **138**, **155**
Christchurch (Canterbury Region, South Island), 112, 113, 117, 303, 313
Cinnamon Gardens (Colombo), 222, 227
Circular Quay (Sydney), 54, 55, 91, 246
Circus (Wellington), 125
Clarence District (New South Wales), 247
Cliff House (San Francisco), 43
Clifton (Bristol), **120**, 147
Clifton Hampden (Oxfordshire), 10
Club (Adelaide), 79, 81, 82, 269
Club (Auckland), 133, 165, 166
Club (Brisbane), 148, 149, 150, 154, 156
Club (Christchurch), 113, 115, 116
Club (Colombo), **215**, 221, 222, 223, 226, 228, 229
Club (Dunedin), 109, 110, 111, 112, 115, 181, 304
Club (Honolulu), 47
Club (Kandy), 212
Club (Melbourne), **61**, 67, 68, 69, 70, 72, 74, 76, 85, 86, 87, 88, 89, 91, 101, 103, 136, 159, 160, 161, 162, 163, 182, 183, 184, 186, 187, 188, 189, 190, 191, 192, 193, 194, 195, 197, 198, 199, 200, 201, 202, 205, 217, 257, 286, 304
Club (Sydney), 55, 59, 96, 138, 139, 144
Coal Pit Heath mine (Greymouth), 120
Cobar (New South Wales), 273
Cobden (Victoria), 192
Cobh. See Queenstown (County Cork)
Colac (Victoria), 70, 71, 101
Colombo (Western Province), 210, 211, 213, 215, 217, 219, 220, 229, 230, 251, 259, 270, 271
Columbia River (Washington), 35, 36, 37
Cornwall (Queensland), **343**
Crete (Greek Islands), 235
Cricket ground (Melbourne), 199
Criterion Hotel (Napier), 127
Crow Indian Reservation (Montana), 31
Crows Nest, The (Newcastle), 144
Crushington (West Coast Region, South Island), 122
Cusco (Cusco Region), **85**

Cuzco. See Cusco (Cusco Region)

D

Dambatenna. See Dambatenne Estate (Haputale)
Dambatenne Estate (Haputale), 218
Darling Downs (Queensland), **147**, 325, 333, 339
Darling Harbour (Sydney), 54
Darling Point (Sydney), 137, 139
Dawes Point (Sydney), 92
Devil's Hole (Wairoa), 130
Devon (England), 1, 2, 4, 7
Doteloya Estate (Sabaragamuwa), **214**
Dotyloyan. See Doteloya Estate (Sabaragamuwa)
Double Bay (Sydney), 143
Dunedin (Otago Region, South Island), 86, 104, 108, 109, 113, 116, 117, 157, 161, 165, 167, 180, 221, 272, 274, 275, 281, 282, 293, 296, 297, 304, 305, 306, 307, 312, 314, 325, 327, 328, 331, 332, 335
Duomo (Florence), **236**, 237, 238
Durham Downs (Queensland), **343**

E

Eagle on the Hill (Adelaide), **82**
Eagle Street wharf (Brisbane), 256
Eastern Europe, 4
Echuca (Victoria), **95**, 96, 99, 289
Edinboro'. See Edinburgh (Scotland)
Edinborough. See Edinburgh (Scotland)
Edinburgh (Scotland), 281
Egypt, 9
Ellagala (Central Province), **211**, 213
Elstree (Hertfordshire), 6, 10, 11
England, 5, 9, 10, 41, 65, 77, 78, 114, 174, 183, 187, 198, 215, 224, 225, 226, 227, 233, 241, 245, 274, 282, 293, 295, 296, 305, 307
English Cathedral (Christchurch), 116
Enoggera Reservoir (Brisbane), 154
Erie Railroad (USA), **26**
Esquimalt (British Columbia), **37**
Eton College (Windsor), 1, 9, 19, 113, 116, 132, 138, 150, 158, 162, 165, 209, 225, 230, 352
Eurella Station (Eurella), **21**, 152, 333
Europe, 2, 4, 5, 9, 11, 54, 63, 66, 78, 113, 351
Euthulla (Queensland), **343**
Exeter (Devon), xiii, 1, 2, **202**

F

Fernshaw (Victoria), 89, 90, 91
Fiji, 102, 163, 164, 165, 168, 170, 248
Florence (Tuscany), 235, 236
Foochow. See Fuzhou (Fujian Province)
Foxhill (Nelson Region, South Island), 124
France, 9, 302
Frankfurt (Germany), 188
Frankfurt an der Oder. See Frankfurt (Germany)
Frenchman's Pass (Wellington), 125
Friendly Islands. See Tonga
Frognal (Camden), 8, **112**
Fuzhou (Fujian Province), **103**, 299

G

Gampola(?) (Central Province), **212**
Gate Pa (Tauranga), **133**
Gavdos (Greek Islands), **235**
Geelong (Melbourne), 62, 65, 66, 93, 101, 162, 189
Genoa (Liguria), 155
George Sound (Southland Region, South Island), 107
Germany, 18, 66, 211, 236
Gilmer's Hotel (Greymouth), 120
Glen Esk (Colombo), **222**, **223**
Glen Innes (New South Wales), 145
Glen Ormiston (Finlay's) (Victoria), 101, 102
Glenelg (Adelaide), **207**
Globe gold mine (Reefton), 122
Gloucestershire (England), 77
Gold Creek (Montana), 17
Golden Gate (San Francisco), 39
Good Hope Island. See Niuafo'ou (island) (Tonga)
Government Baths, Ohinemutu (Rotorua), 129
Government House (Melbourne), 67, 76, 200, 257
Government House (Suva), 168
Graham's Hotel, Ohinemutu (Rotorua), 129
Grand Hotel (Colombo), 226, 229
Grand Hotel (Dunedin), 109
Grand Hotel (Melbourne), 183
Great Britain, xii, 4, 5, 12, 66, 78, 211, 349
Great Divide (USA), **34**
Great Western Railway (England), 4
Great Western Railway (Ontario), **26**
Gregory Lane, 345
Grey River (Greymouth), 114, 119, 120

Greymouth (West Coast Region, South Island), 119, 120, 122, **336**
Gunbower Station (Gunbower), **95**

H

Haberdashers' Aske's Boys' School (Boreham Wood), xiv, 11
Hampstead (London), 8
Harbour (Adelaide), 82, 269
Harbour (Pago Pago), **173**
Harbour (Sydney), 55, 91, 92, **136**, 142
Harbour (Vava'u), **174**
Hastings (Hawke's Bay Region, North Island), 127
Hawaiian Hotel (Honolulu), 47
Hawaiian Islands (Hawaii), **46**, 47, 51
Headington Hill (Darling Downs) (Queensland), 325
Heads (Melbourne), 84
Heads (Sydney), 41, 55, 137
Helena (Montana), 32
Hennewelle Estate (Central Province), 213
Hertfordshire (England), 6
Hiragalla Estate (Ceylon), 218
Hobart (Tasmania), **181**
Hoffmans Restaurant (New York), 25
Hokitika (West Coast Region, South Island), **117**, **119**
Holton House (Tacoma), 36
Honolulu (Hawaii), 45, 47, 49, 51
Honoocutua. See Hunukotuwa Estate (Nawalapitiya)
Honookootua. See Hunukotuwa Estate (Nawalapitiya)
Hope Island. See Niuafo'ou (island) (Tonga)
Hope River (Lyell), 123
Hotel Abbat (Alexandria), 234
Hotel Abbat, Alexandria. See Hotel Abbat (Alexandria)
Hotel Grande Bretagne (Florence), 236
Hotel Lafayette (Minnesota), **28**
Hudson River (New York), 25, 37
Humes. See Humes House, Eton College (Windsor)
Humes House, Eton College (Windsor), **167**
Hunukotuwa Estate (Nawalapitiya), **212**, 213

I

India, 4, 20, 187, 208, 231, 349
International Hotel (Apia), 173
Invercargill (Southland Region, South Island), 108, 181

Ireland, 5, 6
Isle of Wight (England), 328
Italy, 4, 5, 9, 232

J

Jamaica, 148, 215
Japan, 160, 300

K

Kalama (Washington), 37
Kandy (Central Province), 211, 212
Kangaroo Point (Brisbane), 104, 143, 256, **268**, 284, 285, 286, 299, 303, 313
Kao Volcano (Kao (island)), **176**
Kew Gardens (Richmond), 11
Khartoum (Khartoum State), 226
Kineton (Victoria), 96
King George Sound (Western Australia), 206, 208, 270
King William Street (Adelaide), 80
King's College (Cambridge), 1
Kingston (Otago Region, South Island), 108
Kobe (Honshu (Island)), 300
Kumara (West Coast Region, South Island), 114, 119

L

La Maison Dorée (Melbourne), 86, 96, 101, 103, 104, 160, 183
Lake Lyndale (Minneapolis), **28**
Lake Minnetonka (Minnesota), 28, 29, 39
Lake Pend Oreille (Idaho), **34**
Lake Rotoruam, Ohinemutu (Rotorua), 129, 257
Lake Taupo (Waikato Region, North Island), 129
Lake View gold mine (Kalgoorlie), 351
Lake Wakatipu (Otago Region, South Island), 108
Lamostotte. See Llaymostatte Estate (Haputale)
Lara, near Geelong (Melbourne), 65, 93
Levuka (Ovalau (Island)), 168, 169
Lillydale (Victoria), 89
Lima (Lima Province), 3, 5
Liverpool (Merseyside), 5, 18, 34, 41, 62, 81, 155, 191, 253, 255, 258, 265, 274, 276, 279, 284, 285, 287, 288, 289, 290, 292, 295, 296, 298, 311, 313, 322, 326, 334, 339
Livingston (Montana), 32
Llaymostatte Estate (Haputale), **218**

Index of Locations

London (Greater London), 3, 4, 5, 7, 8, 9, 12, 13, 18, 44, 54, 64, 99, 113, 114, 117, 118, 131, 133, 231, 232, 234, 239, 251, 252, 255, 259, 260, 263, 267, 269, 273, 274, 276, 279, 287, 292, 307, 322, 326, 331, 333, 334
Low Countries, The, 4
Lower Hutt (Wellington), 125
Lyell (West Coast Region, South Island), 122, 123
Lyttelton (Christchurch), 117

M

Madison Square Theatre (New York), 24
Madras (Tamil Nadu Region), 229
Madrid (Madrid), 3
Magistrate's court (Ahaura), 121
Mago Island (Fiji), **170**
Maha Uva Estate (Central Province), 219
Manchester (Greater Manchester), 24, 252
Mango. See Mago Island (Fiji)
Maori village below Ohinemutu (Rotorua), 129
Marida Yallock (Mackinnon's place) (Victoria), 88, 97, 99, 101
Mariner's Cave (Vava'u), **175**
Marseilles (Provence-Alpes-Côte d'Azur region), 232
Marysville (Victoria), 90
Matale (Central Province), **211**
Medicean Chapel. See Medici Chapel (Florence)
Medici Chapel (Florence), **238**
Melbourne (Victoria), 6, 8, 21, 43, 46, 53, 56, 58, 60, 64, 65, 66, 67, 69, 72, 74, 77, 78, 79, 80, 86, 90, 91, 94, 96, 97, 109, 111, 120, 126, 133, 136, 138, 139, 140, 141, 143, 148, 156, 157, 158, 160, 162, 163, 164, 168, 169, 180, 182, 193, 196, 197, 198, 199, 204, 205, 206, 219, 223, 231, 233, 243, 245, 250, 253, 254, 256, 257, 258, 261, 262, 263, 271, 272, 273, 274, 275, 285, 286, 288, 289, 293, 297, 298, 299, 300, 301, 306, 308, 309, 314, 315, 316, 321, 322, 323, 324, 325, 326, 328, 329, 330, 331, 335, 336, 337, 338, 339, 343, 344, 346, 352
Mexico, 30, 86
Middle Harbour (Sydney), 139
Milford Sound (Southland Region, South Island), 107, 108
Millers Point (Sydney), 55
Mills Buildings (New York), 24

Minneapolis (Minnesota), 27, 28
Minnetonka. See Lake Minnetonka (Minnesota)
Mitchell (Queensland), 153, **336**
Monarakande Estate (Uva Province), **217**, 218
Montana (USA), 32
Moonerackanda. See Monarakande Estate (Uva Province)
Mount Abundance (Queensland), 276
Mount Adams (Washington), 37
Mount Clarence (Western Australia), 208
Mount Eden (Auckland), **51**
Mount Lavinia (Colombo), **221**
Mount Lofty (Adelaide), 82
Mount Macedon (Victoria), 160, 189
Mount Rainier (Washington), **36**, 37
Mount St. Helens (Washington), 37
Mount Tacoma. See Mount Rainier (Washington)
Mrs Macquarie's Chair (Sydney), **56**
Muckadilla (Queensland), **343**
Multnomah Falls (Oregon), 37
Mulwala (New South Wales), **343**
Mumbai. See Bombay (Maharashtra)
Museum (Auckland), 175
Museum (Brisbane), 150
Museum (Christchurch), 117
Museum (Wellington), 125

N

Nagasaki (Kyushu (Island)), 300
Napier (Hawke's Bay Region, North Island), 114, 126, 127
Narbethong (Victoria), 90
Nawalapitiya (Central Province), **212**, 213, 215, 217
Nawalapitya. See Nawalapitiya (Central Province)
Nayabedde(?) (Uva Province), **217**
Neiafu (Vava'u), **175**
Nelson (Nelson Region, South Island), 114, 119, 121, 122, 124
Nelson Creek (West Coast Region, South Island), **121**
Nelson's Creek. See Nelson Creek (West Coast Region, South Island)
New College, Oxford (Oxford), 41, **43**
New England (New South Wales), 145, 325
New Office (Adelaide), 207
New South Wales (Australia), 12, 53, 58, 63, 68, 73, 88, 91, 98, 106, 117, 119, 136, 147, 153, 200, 248, 249, 261, 308, 314, 316, 322, 325, 336
New Swamp (Echuca), **95**, **301**

New York (New York), 18, 24, 25, 26, 29, 42, 43, 55, 64, 73
New Zealand, xi, xii, 8, 9, 10, 11, 12, 26, 46, 52, 54, 62, 103, 107, 113, 114, 117, 118, 120, 121, 123, 129, 134, 138, 139, 173, 181, 192, 210, 245, 257, 258, 275, 281, 282, 295, 301, 304, 306, 307, 309, 312, 313, 314, 316, 328, 337, 349, 351
Newabudde. See Nayabedde(?) (Uva Province)
Newabuddy. See Nayabedde(?) (Uva Province)
Newcastle (Jamaica), 148
Newcastle (New South Wales), 12, 62, 63, 66, 91, 141, 144, 146, 321, 324, 325
Newport (Victoria), 65
Niagara Falls (New York), 26
Niuafo'ou (island) (Tonga), **171**
North Adelaide (Adelaide), 81
North Dakota (USA), 30
North Island (New Zealand), 129
North Point (Sydney), 139
Northern Club (Auckland), **51**, 52, 134, 165, 180, 308
Nu'uanu Pali (Oahu (island)), **47**
Nuwara Eliya (Central Province), **217**, 219
Nymagee (New South Wales), 273

O

Oahu (island) (Hawaii), 47
Oamaru (Otago Region, South Island), 112, 113, 117
Occidental Hotel (Wellington), 125
Office (Adelaide), 77, 79, 80, 82, 207
Office (Brisbane), 105, 141, 148, 149, 150, 154, 156, 335, 341, 342
Office (Colombo), 216, 220, 222, 224, 229
Office (Dunedin), 66, **109**, 117, 181
Office (Liverpool), 18, 19, 338, 350
Office (London), 5, 18, 54, 63, 65, 66, 78, 91, 97, 104, 105, 141, 155, 215, 221, 228, 241, 250, 252, 258, 259, 265, 269, 274, 275, 278, 282, 285, 287, 293, 295, 297, 298, 299, 301, 313, 325, 326, 330, 331, 334, 336, 338, 350, 351, 352
Office (Melbourne), **60**, 68, 71, 74, 76, 84, 85, 88, 89, 101, 105, 152, 159, 160, 182, 186, 189, 190, 201, 202, 204, 205, 206, 224, 250, 331, 332, 341, 344, 346, 350
Office (Sydney), 53, 54, 55, **56**, **57**, 91, 105, 137, 139, 140, 164, 246, **339**

Ohinemutu (Rotorua), **129**, 130
Old Tank Stream (Sydney), 54
Oliphant Tea Estate (Nuwara Eliya), **219**
Opera House (Livingston), 32
Oram's Hotel (Auckland), 134
Oram's Hotel, Auckland. See Oram's Hotel (Auckland)
Orient Office (Sydney), 144
Otago Region, South Island (New Zealand), 306, 307
Otira Gorge (Otira), **119**
Otway Forest (Victoria), **192**
Oxford University (Oxford), 9, 19, 68, 81, 136, 168, 225, 352
Oxfordshire (England), 10

P

Pago Pago (Tutuila (island)), **173**
Palace Hotel (Chicago), 27
Palace Hotel (San Francisco), **39**
Palazzo Pitti (Florence), 237, **238**
Palazzo Vecchio (Florence), 236
Pali. See Nu'uanu Pali (Oahu (island))
Palisades (New York), 25
Paris (Île-de-France Region), 23, 27, 40, 239
Park (Melbourne), 61
Parrearra (Queensland), **259**
Penang Island (Penang Region), 230
Pen-Y-Lan Estate (Dolosbage), 213, 214
Perth (Western Australia), 141
Peru, 3, 5, 91
Petty's Hotel (Sydney), 53, **55**, 109
Piazza Santissima Annunziata (Florence), 238
Picton (Marlborough Region, South Island), **124**
Picture Gallery (Sydney), 53, 139
Pink Terrace (Wairoa), **130**
Pitt Street (Sydney), 54
Pompey's Pillar (Alexandria), 234
Pompey's Pillar, Alexandria. See Pompey's Pillar (Alexandria)
Port Adelaide (Adelaide), 207, 282
Port Chalmers (Dunedin), 109, 113, 117, 181
Port Melbourne. See Sandridge (Melbourne)
Port of Refuge. See Harbour (Vava'u)
Port of Spain (Trinidad), 214
Port Townsend (Washington), 38
Portland (Oregon), 17, 37, 38
Portland Place (Brisbane), 148, 150, 153
Prussia, 4
Public Gallery (Melbourne), 86
Puget Sound (Washington), 37, 39

Pytte House (Exeter), xiii, 1, 2, 3

Q

Quay (New York), 25
Queensland (Australia), 51, 63, 85, 91, 103, 131, 138, 139, 146, 147, 149, 156, 157, 244, 246, 249, 272, 273, 276, 284, 301, 312, 316, 326
Queenstown (County Cork), **20**

R

Racecourse (Melbourne), 68
Randwick race course (Sydney), 140, 142
Red Sea, 232
Reefton (West Coast Region, South Island), 114, **121**, 122
Reeftown. See Reefton (West Coast Region, South Island)
Reservoir (Elstree), 301
Rewa River (Suva), 168
Richmond District (New South Wales), 247
River Mississipi (Mississippi), 27
River Watts (Victoria), 89
River Yarra (Melbourne), 65, 70, 190
Rock Cave Estate (Ceylon), 211, 212
Rockies (USA), 32, 33, 34, 40
Roma (Queensland), 151, 153, 333
Rose Bay (Sydney), 143
Rotorua (Bay of Plenty Region, North Island), 114
Roubaix (Nord-Pas-de-Calais), **252**
Royal Botanical Gardens, Peradeniya (Kandy), 212
Royal Devon and Exeter Hospital (Exeter), 1
Russia, 4

S

Samoa, 171, 172, 174, 179
San Francisco (California), **21**, 36, 38, 39, 40, 43, 46, 52, 86, 88, 94, 110, 115, 160, 192
San Miniato al Monte (Florence), **236**
Sandgate (Brisbane), 150
Sandridge (Melbourne), **182**
Sandwich Islands. See Hawaiian Islands (Hawaii)
Santa Maria Maddalena dei Pazzi (Florence), **236**
Santa Maria Novella (Florence), 237
Santiago (Santiago Metropolitan Region), 5
Seal Rock (San Francisco), 43

Seattle (Washington), 38
Semite Valley. See Yosemite Valley (California)
Silverton (New South Wales), **345**
Sleepy Hollow. See Nelson (Nelson Region, South Island)
Sliding Rock (Apia), 172
Snake River (Washington), 35
South America, 3, 4, 54, 64, 349
South Australia (Australia), 271, 277
South Island (New Zealand), 114
South Yarra (Melbourne), **87**
Southampton (Hampshire), 230
Spain, 2, 3, 4, 5, 228, 309
Spencer Street, 345
Spokane Falls (Spokane), 35
Springfield (Canterbury Region, South Island), 118
Sri Lanka. See Ceylon
St. Albans (Hertfordshire), 10
St. Dunstan's, Regents Park (London), **60**, **85**, 182, 329
St. Kilda (Melbourne), 70, 85, **88**, 102, 202
St. Leonards (Bright's house) (Melbourne), **61**, 67, 68, 72, 84, 87, 91, 94, 104, 127, 182, 190, 196, 197, 205, 245
St. Lucia's RC Cathedral (Colombo), **222**
St. Mark's Church (Florence), 238
St. Paul (Minnesota), 17, 27, 28, 29, 36
Stanthorpe (Queensland), 146
Staten Island (New York), 24
Stewart's Hotel (Kumara), 119
Stock Exchange (New York), 24, 37
Straits of Sunda. See Sunda Strait
Suez (Egypt), 233, 234
Suez Canal (Egypt), 349
Suez harbour (Suez), 232
Sunda Strait, 41, **271**
Supreme Court of Victoria (Melbourne), **198**
Suva (Viti Levu (Island)), 168, 169
Sydney (New South Wales), 8, 41, 53, 54, 55, 62, 63, 65, 66, 67, 69, 73, 77, 78, 80, 83, 84, 91, 92, 104, 106, 109, 110, 114, 124, 125, 136, 140, 141, 142, 143, 144, 145, 156, 158, 164, 174, 180, 186, 191, 197, 204, 205, 216, 245, 246, 248, 249, 250, 251, 253, 254, 255, 256, 257, 258, 259, 260, 262, 272, 275, 277, 279, 280, 281, 282, 283, 285, 288, 290, 294, 296, 297, 298, 299, 301, 304, 305, 309, 310, 314, 316, 318, 320, 321, 323, 324, 325, 327, 328, 329, 332, 335, 338, 344, 346

Sydney Harbour Bridge (Sydney), 55

T

Tacoma (Washington), 37, 38
Tarawera (Hawke's Bay Region, North Island), **128**
Tasman Sea, 66
Taupo (Waikato Region, North Island), 128, 129, 133
Tauranga (Bay of Plenty Region, North Island), 132, 133
Taveuni (Island) (Fiji), **170**
Taviuna. See Taveuni (Island) (Fiji)
Taviuni. See Taveuni (Island) (Fiji)
Tenterfield (New South Wales), 146
Timaru (Canterbury Region, South Island), 112
Tin Can Island. See Niuafo'ou (island) (Tonga)
Tonga, **163**, 174, 178
Tongan Group (Tonga), 174, 176
Tongatabu. See Tongatapu (Tongatapu (island))
Tongatapu (Tongatapu (island)), **177**
Toowoomba ranges (Australia), **151**
Topsham (Exeter), 2
Torrumbarry (Echuca), 95, **289**, 343
Town Hall (Melbourne), 70, 72, 200
Trieste (Friuli-Venezia Giulia Region), 229
Trinidad, 214
Tutuila (island) (Samoa), 173
Tyntesfield (Wraxall), xiii, 5, 6, 7, 8, **198**, 352

U

Uffizi Gallery (Florence), **236**, 237, 238
Underwood Street (Sydney), 54
Union Club (New York), 25
Union Club (San Francisco), 43
Union Club (Sydney), 53, **58**, 138, 140
University (Cambridge), 23, 49, 93, 99
Upolu (island) (Samoa), 172
USA, xi, 4, 9, 12, 18, 40, 64

V

Valparaiso (Valparaiso Region), 5, 21, 296

Vavau. See Vava'u (Tongan Group)
Vava'u (Tongan Group), **174**, 176
Venice (Veneto), 234, 235
Victoria (Australia), 6, 8, 13, 53, 54, 65, 69, 88, 97, 117, 136, 159, 301, 338, 352
Victoria (British Columbia), 36, 37
Victoria Square (Adelaide), 82

W

Wairoa (Hawke's Bay Region, North Island), 129, 130
Wallaroo (South Australia), 259
Warden's court (Ahaura), 121
Wellington (Wellington Region, North Island), 114, 115, 124, 125
West Indies, 168, 260, 318
West Point (New York), 25, 27, 37
Western Australia (Australia), 117, 206, 351
Whakarewarewa (Rotorua), **129**
Williamstown (Melbourne), 76
Windsor Hotel (New York), 24
Winyard Square. See Wynyard Square (Sydney)
Wodonga (Victoria), 159
Woolloomooloo (Sydney), **56**
Wraxall (Somerset), 5, 6
Wynyard Park. See Wynyard Square (Sydney)
Wynyard Square (Sydney), **281**

X

Xiamen. See Amoy (Fujian Province)

Y

Yarra flats (Victoria), 89
Yo Semite Valley. See Yosemite Valley (California)
Yokohama (Honshu (Island)), 300
Yosemite Valley (California), **43**

Z

Zagazig (Egypt), **233**
Zoo (Melbourne), 159

Hierarchical List of Locations

Each entry shows four parts separated by a vertical bar (usually Country, Region, Town, Place). Once the location has been found, use the Index of Locations to locate its occurrence(s) in the text. For example, to find the Club that Gibbs visits in San Francisco without remembering its name, search under USA, California, San Francisco in this list to find "Bohemian Club" or "Union Club", both of which can then be found in the Index of Locations.

I

|||Bata?.
|||Eastern Europe.
|||Europe.
|||Gregory Lane.
|||Low Countries, The.
|||Red Sea.
|||South America.
|||Spencer Street.
|||Sunda Strait.
|||Tasman Sea.

A

Argentina|||.
Australia|||.
Australia|||Toowoomba ranges.
Australia|New South Wales||.
Australia|New South Wales||Clarence District.
Australia|New South Wales||New England.
Australia|New South Wales||Richmond District.
Australia|New South Wales|Albury|.
Australia|New South Wales|Armidale|.
Australia|New South Wales|Bolivia|.
Australia|New South Wales|Broken Hill|.
Australia|New South Wales|Cobar|.
Australia|New South Wales|Glen Innes|.
Australia|New South Wales|Mulwala|.
Australia|New South Wales|Newcastle|.
Australia|New South Wales|Newcastle|Crows Nest, The.
Australia|New South Wales|Nymagee|.
Australia|New South Wales|Silverton|.
Australia|New South Wales|Sydney|.
Australia|New South Wales|Sydney|Botanical Gardens.
Australia|New South Wales|Sydney|Campbell's Cove.
Australia|New South Wales|Sydney|Circular Quay.
Australia|New South Wales|Sydney|Club.
Australia|New South Wales|Sydney|Darling Harbour.
Australia|New South Wales|Sydney|Darling Point.
Australia|New South Wales|Sydney|Dawes Point.
Australia|New South Wales|Sydney|Double Bay.
Australia|New South Wales|Sydney|Harbour.

Australia|New South Wales|Sydney|Heads.
Australia|New South Wales|Sydney|Middle Harbour.
Australia|New South Wales|Sydney|Millers Point.
Australia|New South Wales|Sydney|Mrs Macquarie's Chair.
Australia|New South Wales|Sydney|North Point.
Australia|New South Wales|Sydney|Office.
Australia|New South Wales|Sydney|Old Tank Stream.
Australia|New South Wales|Sydney|Orient Office.
Australia|New South Wales|Sydney|Petty's Hotel.
Australia|New South Wales|Sydney|Picture Gallery.
Australia|New South Wales|Sydney|Pitt Street.
Australia|New South Wales|Sydney|Randwick race course.
Australia|New South Wales|Sydney|Rose Bay.
Australia|New South Wales|Sydney|Sydney Harbour Bridge.
Australia|New South Wales|Sydney|Underwood Street.
Australia|New South Wales|Sydney|Union Club.
Australia|New South Wales|Sydney|Woolloomooloo.
Australia|New South Wales|Sydney|Wynyard Square.
Australia|New South Wales|Tenterfield|.
Australia|Queensland||.
Australia|Queensland||Darling Downs.
Australia|Queensland||Headington Hill (Darling Downs).
Australia|Queensland||Mount Abundance.
Australia|Queensland|Amby|Amby Crossing.
Australia|Queensland|Amby|Amby Downs.
Australia|Queensland|Amby|Amby South.
Australia|Queensland|Bindango|.
Australia|Queensland|Brisbane|.
Australia|Queensland|Brisbane|Botanical Reserve.
Australia|Queensland|Brisbane|Club.
Australia|Queensland|Brisbane|Eagle Street wharf.
Australia|Queensland|Brisbane|Enoggera Reservoir.
Australia|Queensland|Brisbane|Kangaroo Point.
Australia|Queensland|Brisbane|Museum.
Australia|Queensland|Brisbane|Office.
Australia|Queensland|Brisbane|Portland Place.
Australia|Queensland|Brisbane|Sandgate.
Australia|Queensland|Cornwall|.
Australia|Queensland|Durham Downs|.
Australia|Queensland|Eurella|Eurella Station.
Australia|Queensland|Euthulla|.
Australia|Queensland|Mitchell|.
Australia|Queensland|Muckadilla|.
Australia|Queensland|Parrearra|.
Australia|Queensland|Roma|.
Australia|Queensland|Stanthorpe|.
Australia|South Australia||.
Australia|South Australia|Adelaide|.
Australia|South Australia|Adelaide|Cathedral.
Australia|South Australia|Adelaide|Club.
Australia|South Australia|Adelaide|Eagle on the Hill.
Australia|South Australia|Adelaide|Glenelg.
Australia|South Australia|Adelaide|Harbour.
Australia|South Australia|Adelaide|King William Street.
Australia|South Australia|Adelaide|Mount Lofty.
Australia|South Australia|Adelaide|New Office.
Australia|South Australia|Adelaide|North Adelaide.
Australia|South Australia|Adelaide|Office.

Hierarchical List of Locations

Australia|South Australia|Adelaide|Port Adelaide.
Australia|South Australia|Adelaide|Victoria Square.
Australia|South Australia|Wallaroo|.
Australia|Tasmania|Hobart|.
Australia|Victoria||.
Australia|Victoria||Glen Ormiston (Finlay's).
Australia|Victoria||Marida Yallock (Mackinnon's place).
Australia|Victoria||Otway Forest.
Australia|Victoria||River Watts.
Australia|Victoria||Yarra flats.
Australia|Victoria|Camperdown|.
Australia|Victoria|Cobden|.
Australia|Victoria|Colac|.
Australia|Victoria|Echuca|.
Australia|Victoria|Echuca|New Swamp.
Australia|Victoria|Echuca|Torrumbarry.
Australia|Victoria|Fernshaw|.
Australia|Victoria|Gunbower|Gunbower Station.
Australia|Victoria|Kineton|.
Australia|Victoria|Lillydale|.
Australia|Victoria|Marysville|.
Australia|Victoria|Melbourne|.
Australia|Victoria|Melbourne|Agricultural Show.
Australia|Victoria|Melbourne|Anika paddock, Lara, near Geelong.
Australia|Victoria|Melbourne|Athenaeum.
Australia|Victoria|Melbourne|Bijou Theatre.
Australia|Victoria|Melbourne|Bohemian Club.
Australia|Victoria|Melbourne|Botanical Gardens.
Australia|Victoria|Melbourne|Cathedral.
Australia|Victoria|Melbourne|Caulfield Races.
Australia|Victoria|Melbourne|Club.
Australia|Victoria|Melbourne|Cricket ground.
Australia|Victoria|Melbourne|Geelong.
Australia|Victoria|Melbourne|Government House.
Australia|Victoria|Melbourne|Grand Hotel.
Australia|Victoria|Melbourne|Heads.
Australia|Victoria|Melbourne|La Maison Dorée.
Australia|Victoria|Melbourne|Lara, near Geelong.
Australia|Victoria|Melbourne|Office.
Australia|Victoria|Melbourne|Park.
Australia|Victoria|Melbourne|Public Gallery.
Australia|Victoria|Melbourne|Racecourse.
Australia|Victoria|Melbourne|River Yarra.
Australia|Victoria|Melbourne|Sandridge.
Australia|Victoria|Melbourne|South Yarra.
Australia|Victoria|Melbourne|St. Kilda.
Australia|Victoria|Melbourne|St. Leonards (Bright's house).
Australia|Victoria|Melbourne|Supreme Court of Victoria.
Australia|Victoria|Melbourne|Town Hall.
Australia|Victoria|Melbourne|Williamstown.
Australia|Victoria|Melbourne|Zoo.
Australia|Victoria|Mount Macedon|.
Australia|Victoria|Narbethong|.
Australia|Victoria|Newport|.
Australia|Victoria|Wodonga|.
Australia|Western Australia||.
Australia|Western Australia||Cape Leeuwin.
Australia|Western Australia||King George Sound.

Australia|Western Australia||Mount Clarence.
Australia|Western Australia|Albany|.
Australia|Western Australia|Kalgoorlie|Lake View gold mine.
Australia|Western Australia|Perth|.

B

Barbados|||.
Barbados|||Bellasyse Estate.
Bolivia|||.

C

Canada|British Columbia|Esquimalt|.
Canada|British Columbia|Victoria|.
Canada|Ontario||Great Western Railway.
Ceylon|||.
Ceylon|||Hiragalla Estate.
Ceylon|||Rock Cave Estate.
Ceylon|Central Province||Ellagala.
Ceylon|Central Province||Hennewelle Estate.
Ceylon|Central Province||Maha Uva Estate.
Ceylon|Central Province|Dolosbage|Pen-Y-Lan Estate.
Ceylon|Central Province|Gampola(?)|.
Ceylon|Central Province|Kandy|.
Ceylon|Central Province|Kandy|Club.
Ceylon|Central Province|Kandy|Royal Botanical Gardens, Peradeniya.
Ceylon|Central Province|Matale|.
Ceylon|Central Province|Nawalapitiya|.
Ceylon|Central Province|Nawalapitiya|Hunukotuwa Estate.
Ceylon|Central Province|Nuwara Eliya|.
Ceylon|Central Province|Nuwara Eliya|Barnes Hall.
Ceylon|Central Province|Nuwara Eliya|Oliphant Tea Estate.
Ceylon|Sabaragamuwa||Doteloya Estate.
Ceylon|Uva Province||Monarakande Estate.
Ceylon|Uva Province||Nayabedde(?).
Ceylon|Uva Province|Haputale|Dambatenne Estate.
Ceylon|Uva Province|Haputale|Llaymostatte Estate.
Ceylon|Uva Province|Moneragala|Banagala Estate.
Ceylon|Western Province|Colombo|.
Ceylon|Western Province|Colombo|Cinnamon Gardens.
Ceylon|Western Province|Colombo|Club.
Ceylon|Western Province|Colombo|Glen Esk.
Ceylon|Western Province|Colombo|Grand Hotel.
Ceylon|Western Province|Colombo|Mount Lavinia.
Ceylon|Western Province|Colombo|Office.
Ceylon|Western Province|Colombo|St. Lucia's RC Cathedral.
Chile|||.
Chile|Santiago Metropolitan Region|Santiago|.
Chile|Valparaiso Region|Valparaiso|.
China|||.
China|Fujian Province|Amoy|.
China|Fujian Province|Fuzhou|.

E

Egypt|||.
Egypt|||Suez Canal.

Hierarchical List of Locations

Egypt||Alexandria|.
Egypt||Alexandria|Hotel Abbat.
Egypt||Alexandria|Pompey's Pillar.
Egypt||Cairo|.
Egypt||Suez|.
Egypt||Suez|Suez harbour.
Egypt||Zagazig|.
England|||.
England|||Great Western Railway.
England|Berkshire|Windsor|Eton College.
England|Berkshire|Windsor|Humes House, Eton College.
England|Bristol|Bristol|.
England|Bristol|Bristol|Clifton.
England|Cambridgeshire|Cambridge|King's College.
England|Cambridgeshire|Cambridge|University.
England|City of London|London|Bishopsgate.
England|City of London|London|Office.
England|Devon||.
England|Devon|Exeter|.
England|Devon|Exeter|Pytte House.
England|Devon|Exeter|Royal Devon and Exeter Hospital.
England|Devon|Exeter|Topsham.
England|Devon|Tiveton|Blundell's School.
England|Gloucestershire||.
England|Gloucestershire|Cheltenham|.
England|Greater London|Camden|Frognal.
England|Greater London|London|.
England|Greater London|London|Carlton Club.
England|Greater London|London|St. Dunstan's, Regents Park.
England|Greater Manchester|Manchester|.
England|Hampshire|Southampton|.
England|Hertfordshire||.
England|Hertfordshire|Boreham Wood|Haberdashers' Aske's Boys' School.
England|Hertfordshire|Elstree|.
England|Hertfordshire|Elstree|Aldenham Church.
England|Hertfordshire|Elstree|Aldenham House.
England|Hertfordshire|Elstree|Reservoir.
England|Hertfordshire|St. Albans|.
England|Isle of Wight||.
England|London|Hampstead|.
England|Merseyside|Liverpool|.
England|Merseyside|Liverpool|Office.
England|Oxfordshire||.
England|Oxfordshire|Clifton Hampden|.
England|Oxfordshire|Oxford|Christ Church College, Oxford.
England|Oxfordshire|Oxford|New College, Oxford.
England|Oxfordshire|Oxford|Oxford University.
England|Richmond upon Thames|Richmond|Kew Gardens.
England|Somerset|Bath|.
England|Somerset|Wraxall|.
England|Somerset|Wraxall|Tyntesfield.

F

Fiji|||.
Fiji|Mago Island||.
Fiji|Ovalau (Island)|Levuka|.
Fiji|Taveuni (Island)||.

Fiji|Viti Levu (Island)|Suva|.
Fiji|Viti Levu (Island)|Suva|Government House.
Fiji|Viti Levu (Island)|Suva|Rewa River.
France|||.
France|Île-de-France Region|Paris|.
France|Nord-Pas-de-Calais|Roubaix|.
France|Pas-de-Calais|Calais|.
France|Provence-Alpes-Côte d'Azur region|Marseilles|.

G

Germany|||.
Germany||Berlin|.
Germany||Frankfurt|.
Great Britain|||.
Greece|Greek Islands||Gavdos.
Greece|Greek Islands|Crete|.

H

Hawaii|||Hawaiian Islands.
Hawaii|Oahu (island)||.
Hawaii|Oahu (island)||Nu'uanu Pali.

I

India|||.
India|Maharashtra|Bombay|.
India|Tamil Nadu Region|Madras|.
India|West Bengal|Calcutta|.
Ireland|||.
Ireland|County Cork|Queenstown|.
Ireland|County Cork|Queenstown|Cathedral.
Italy|||.
Italy|Apulia Region|Brindisi|.
Italy|Emilia-Romagna Region|Bologna|.
Italy|Friuli-Venezia Giulia Region|Trieste|.
Italy|Liguria|Genoa|.
Italy|Marche Region|Ancona|.
Italy|Tuscany||Cascina.
Italy|Tuscany|Florence|.
Italy|Tuscany|Florence|Accademia di Belle Arti.
Italy|Tuscany|Florence|Basilica di Santa Croce.
Italy|Tuscany|Florence|Boboli Gardens.
Italy|Tuscany|Florence|Capella Ricardi.
Italy|Tuscany|Florence|Duomo.
Italy|Tuscany|Florence|Hotel Grande Bretagne.
Italy|Tuscany|Florence|Medici Chapel.
Italy|Tuscany|Florence|Palazzo Pitti.
Italy|Tuscany|Florence|Palazzo Vecchio.
Italy|Tuscany|Florence|Piazza Santissima Annunziata.
Italy|Tuscany|Florence|San Miniato al Monte.
Italy|Tuscany|Florence|Santa Maria Maddalena dei Pazzi.
Italy|Tuscany|Florence|Santa Maria Novella.
Italy|Tuscany|Florence|St. Mark's Church.
Italy|Tuscany|Florence|Uffizi Gallery.
Italy|Veneto|Venice|.

J

Jamaica|||.
Jamaica||Newcastle|.
Japan|||.
Japan|Honshu (Island)|Kobe|.
Japan|Honshu (Island)|Yokohama|.
Japan|Kyushu (Island)|Nagasaki|.

M

Malaysia|Penang Region||Penang Island.
Mexico|||.

N

Netherlands|North Holland|Amsterdam|.
New Zealand|||.
New Zealand|Auckland Region, North Island|Auckland|.
New Zealand|Auckland Region, North Island|Auckland|Club.
New Zealand|Auckland Region, North Island|Auckland|Mount Eden.
New Zealand|Auckland Region, North Island|Auckland|Museum.
New Zealand|Auckland Region, North Island|Auckland|Northern Club.
New Zealand|Auckland Region, North Island|Auckland|Oram's Hotel.
New Zealand|Bay of Plenty Region, North Island|Rotorua|.
New Zealand|Bay of Plenty Region, North Island|Rotorua|Government Baths, Ohinemutu.
New Zealand|Bay of Plenty Region, North Island|Rotorua|Graham's Hotel, Ohinemutu.
New Zealand|Bay of Plenty Region, North Island|Rotorua|Lake Rotoruam, Ohinemutu.
New Zealand|Bay of Plenty Region, North Island|Rotorua|Maori village below Ohinemutu.
New Zealand|Bay of Plenty Region, North Island|Rotorua|Ohinemutu.
New Zealand|Bay of Plenty Region, North Island|Rotorua|Whakarewarewa.
New Zealand|Bay of Plenty Region, North Island|Tauranga|.
New Zealand|Bay of Plenty Region, North Island|Tauranga|Gate Pa.
New Zealand|Canterbury Region, South Island||.
New Zealand|Canterbury Region, South Island|Bealey|.
New Zealand|Canterbury Region, South Island|Christchurch|.
New Zealand|Canterbury Region, South Island|Christchurch|Avon River.
New Zealand|Canterbury Region, South Island|Christchurch|Club.
New Zealand|Canterbury Region, South Island|Christchurch|English Cathedral.
New Zealand|Canterbury Region, South Island|Christchurch|Lyttelton.
New Zealand|Canterbury Region, South Island|Christchurch|Museum.
New Zealand|Canterbury Region, South Island|Springfield|.
New Zealand|Canterbury Region, South Island|Timaru|.
New Zealand|Hawke's Bay Region, North Island|Hastings|.
New Zealand|Hawke's Bay Region, North Island|Napier|.
New Zealand|Hawke's Bay Region, North Island|Napier|Criterion Hotel.
New Zealand|Hawke's Bay Region, North Island|Tarawera|.
New Zealand|Hawke's Bay Region, North Island|Wairoa|.
New Zealand|Hawke's Bay Region, North Island|Wairoa|Devil's Hole.
New Zealand|Hawke's Bay Region, North Island|Wairoa|Pink Terrace.
New Zealand|Marlborough Region, South Island|Picton|.
New Zealand|Nelson Region, South Island|Belgrove|.
New Zealand|Nelson Region, South Island|Foxhill|.
New Zealand|Nelson Region, South Island|Nelson|.
New Zealand|North Island||.
New Zealand|Northland Region, North Island||Bay of Islands.
New Zealand|Otago Region, South Island||.
New Zealand|Otago Region, South Island||Lake Wakatipu.

New Zealand|Otago Region, South Island|Dunedin|.
New Zealand|Otago Region, South Island|Dunedin|Cathedral.
New Zealand|Otago Region, South Island|Dunedin|Club.
New Zealand|Otago Region, South Island|Dunedin|Grand Hotel.
New Zealand|Otago Region, South Island|Dunedin|Office.
New Zealand|Otago Region, South Island|Dunedin|Port Chalmers.
New Zealand|Otago Region, South Island|Kingston|.
New Zealand|Otago Region, South Island|Oamaru|.
New Zealand|South Island||.
New Zealand|Southland Region, South Island||George Sound.
New Zealand|Southland Region, South Island||Milford Sound.
New Zealand|Southland Region, South Island|Invercargill|.
New Zealand|Southland Region, South Island|Invercargill|Bluff, The.
New Zealand|Waikato Region, North Island||Lake Taupo.
New Zealand|Waikato Region, North Island|Cambridge|.
New Zealand|Waikato Region, North Island|Taupo|.
New Zealand|Wellington Region, North Island|Wellington|.
New Zealand|Wellington Region, North Island|Wellington|Botanical Gardens.
New Zealand|Wellington Region, North Island|Wellington|Circus.
New Zealand|Wellington Region, North Island|Wellington|Frenchman's Pass.
New Zealand|Wellington Region, North Island|Wellington|Lower Hutt.
New Zealand|Wellington Region, North Island|Wellington|Museum.
New Zealand|Wellington Region, North Island|Wellington|Occidental Hotel.
New Zealand|West Coast Region, South Island|Ahaura|.
New Zealand|West Coast Region, South Island|Ahaura|Magistrate's court.
New Zealand|West Coast Region, South Island|Ahaura|Warden's court.
New Zealand|West Coast Region, South Island|Crushington|.
New Zealand|West Coast Region, South Island|Greymouth|.
New Zealand|West Coast Region, South Island|Greymouth|Brunner.
New Zealand|West Coast Region, South Island|Greymouth|Coal Pit Heath mine.
New Zealand|West Coast Region, South Island|Greymouth|Gilmer's Hotel.
New Zealand|West Coast Region, South Island|Greymouth|Grey River.
New Zealand|West Coast Region, South Island|Hokitika|.
New Zealand|West Coast Region, South Island|Kumara|.
New Zealand|West Coast Region, South Island|Kumara|Stewart's Hotel.
New Zealand|West Coast Region, South Island|Lyell|.
New Zealand|West Coast Region, South Island|Lyell|Buller River.
New Zealand|West Coast Region, South Island|Lyell|Hope River.
New Zealand|West Coast Region, South Island|Nelson Creek|.
New Zealand|West Coast Region, South Island|Otira|Otira Gorge.
New Zealand|West Coast Region, South Island|Reefton|.
New Zealand|West Coast Region, South Island|Reefton|Globe gold mine.

P

Peru|||.
Peru|||Chincha Islands.
Peru|Cusco Region|Cusco|.
Peru|Lima Province|Lima|.
Prussia|||.

R

Russia|||.

S

Samoa|||.

Hierarchical List of Locations

Samoa|Tutuila (island)||.
Samoa|Tutuila (island)|Pago Pago|.
Samoa|Tutuila (island)|Pago Pago|Harbour.
Samoa|Upolu (island)||.
Samoa|Upolu (island)|Apia|.
Samoa|Upolu (island)|Apia|International Hotel.
Samoa|Upolu (island)|Apia|Sliding Rock.
Scotland||Edinburgh|.
South Africa|||Cape Colony.
Spain|||.
Spain|Andalusia|Cadiz|.
Spain|Madrid|Madrid|.
Sudan|Khartoum State|Khartoum|.

T

Tonga|||.
Tonga|Kao (island)||Kao Volcano.
Tonga|Niuafo'ou (island)||.
Tonga|Tongan Group||.
Tonga|Tongan Group|Vava'u|.
Tonga|Tongan Group|Vava'u|Harbour.
Tonga|Tongan Group|Vava'u|Mariner's Cave.
Tonga|Tongan Group|Vava'u|Neiafu.
Tonga|Tongatapu (island)|Tongatapu|.
Trinidad|||.
Trinidad||Port of Spain|.

U

USA|||.
USA|||Erie Railroad.
USA|||Great Divide.
USA|||Rockies.
USA|California||Yosemite Valley.
USA|California|San Francisco|.
USA|California|San Francisco|Bella Union Theatre.
USA|California|San Francisco|Bohemian Club.
USA|California|San Francisco|Chinese quarter.
USA|California|San Francisco|Cliff House.
USA|California|San Francisco|Golden Gate.
USA|California|San Francisco|Palace Hotel.
USA|California|San Francisco|Seal Rock.
USA|California|San Francisco|Union Club.
USA|Hawaii|Honolulu|.
USA|Hawaii|Honolulu|Club.
USA|Hawaii|Honolulu|Hawaiian Hotel.
USA|Idaho||Lake Pend Oreille.
USA|Illinois|Chicago|.
USA|Illinois|Chicago|Palace Hotel.
USA|Minnesota||Hotel Lafayette.
USA|Minnesota||Lake Minnetonka.
USA|Minnesota|Minneapolis|.
USA|Minnesota|Minneapolis|Lake Lyndak (UNKNOWN).
USA|Minnesota|St. Paul|.
USA|Mississippi||River Mississipi.
USA|Montana||.
USA|Montana||Crow Indian Reservation.

USA|Montana|Billings|.
USA|Montana|Bozeman|.
USA|Montana|Gold Creek|.
USA|Montana|Helena|.
USA|Montana|Livingston|.
USA|Montana|Livingston|Opera House.
USA|New York||Niagara Falls.
USA|New York|New York|.
USA|New York|New York|Broadway.
USA|New York|New York|Brooklyn.
USA|New York|New York|Brooklyn Bridge.
USA|New York|New York|Casino.
USA|New York|New York|Central Park.
USA|New York|New York|Hoffmans Restaurant.
USA|New York|New York|Hudson River.
USA|New York|New York|Madison Square Theatre.
USA|New York|New York|Mills Buildings.
USA|New York|New York|Palisades.
USA|New York|New York|Quay.
USA|New York|New York|Staten Island.
USA|New York|New York|Stock Exchange.
USA|New York|New York|Union Club.
USA|New York|New York|West Point.
USA|New York|New York|Windsor Hotel.
USA|North Dakota||.
USA|North Dakota|Bismarck|.
USA|North Dakota|Bismarck|Badlands.
USA|Oregon||Multnomah Falls.
USA|Oregon|Portland|.
USA|Washington||Cape Flattery.
USA|Washington||Columbia River.
USA|Washington||Mount Adams.
USA|Washington||Mount Rainier.
USA|Washington||Mount St. Helens.
USA|Washington||Puget Sound.
USA|Washington||Snake River.
USA|Washington|Ainsworth|.
USA|Washington|Chehalis|.
USA|Washington|Kalama|.
USA|Washington|Port Townsend|.
USA|Washington|Seattle|.
USA|Washington|Spokane|Spokane Falls.
USA|Washington|Tacoma|.
USA|Washington|Tacoma|Holton House.

W

West Indies|||.

Y

Yemen||Aden|.

Index of Books

For locating the books or other publications that Gibbs refers to, by publication name or author. Bold page numbers indicate the location of footnotes.

(

(Articles/essays). See Smith, Sir Sydney
(book of poems?). See Harte, Bret
(essays). See Temple, Sir William
(Essays). See Macaulay, Thomas Babington
(German Poetry). See Heine, Heinrich
(light/humorous poems). See Praed, Mackworth
(Memoirs). See Malmesbury, Lord
(supernatural fiction). See Marryatt, Florence
(Targetted humour, letters etc.). See Ward, Artemus (Charles Farrar Browne)
(Unknown author)
   Age, The (Melbourne newspaper), **88**
   Bible, The, 203
   Brisbane Courier, The, 156
   Fortnightly Review, The, **134**
   Illustrated London News, The, **221**
   Illustrated Sydney News, The, 54
   Melbourne Argus, 69, 159, 163, 197, 200
   Quarterly Review, **187**
   St. James's Gazette, **22**
(Unknown book). See Shakespeare, William, See Lever, Charles, See Rabelais, Francois, See Balzac, Honoré de, See Horace

A

Adam Bede. See Eliot, George
Age, The (Melbourne newspaper). See (Unknown author)
All in a Garden Fair. See Bessant, Sir Walter
All Sorts and Conditions of Men. See Besant, Sir Walter
Altiora Peto. See Oliphant, Laurence
Amos Barton. See Eliot, George
Anderson, Hans Christian
   Improvisatore, The, **219**
Austen, Jane
   Mansfield Park, **135**
   Northanger Abbey, **106**, 135
   Persuasion, **106**
Autobiography. See Trollope, Anthony

B

Baker, Henry Barton
   Our Old Actors, **225**
Balzac, Honoré de
   (Unknown book), **88**
   Grandeur et décadence de César Birotteau, **189**, **230**
   La Fille Aux Yeux d'Or, **232**
Belot, Adolph
   La Bouche de Madame X, 21
Belot, Adolphe
   Hélène et Mathilde, 224
Besant, Sir Walter
   All Sorts and Conditions of Men, 95
Besant, Sir Walter and Rice, James
   Chaplain of the Fleet, The, 95
Bessant, Sir Walter
   All in a Garden Fair, **207**
Bible, The. See (Unknown author)
Black, William
   White Wings, **50**
   Yolande – The Story of a Daughter, 47
Blackwood, William
   Blackwood's Edinburgh Magazine, **115**
Blackwood's Edinburgh Magazine. See Blackwood, William
Boyeson, Hjalmar Hjorth
   Daughter of the Philistines, A, 43
Brisbane Courier, The. See (Unknown author)
Bulwer-Lytton, Edward George
   Caxtons, The, **147**
Bunyan. See Froude, James Anthony
Burnett, Frances Hodgson
   Haworths, The, **171**
   Louisiana, 85
   That Lass o' Lowries, 85, 171
   Through One Administration, **85**

C

Carlyle, Thomas
   Critical and Miscellaneous Essays, 83

Oliver Cromwell's Letters and
 Speeches – with Elucidations, **221**
Caxtons, The. See Bulwer-Lytton,
 Edward George
Chaplain of the Fleet, The. See Besant,
 Sir Walter and Rice, James
Charlie Thornhill, or The Dunce of the
 Family. See Clarke, Charles (aka
 Carlos-Clarke, Charles)
Cherbuliez, Victor
 Meta Holdenis, **215**
 Samuel Brohl et Cie, 182, 215
Clarke, Charles (aka Carlos-Clarke,
 Charles)
 Charlie Thornhill, or The Dunce of the
 Family, **179**
Clarke, Marcus
 His Natural Life, 136
Cloister and the Hearth, The. See
 Reade, Charles
Colombier, Marie
 Sarah Barnum, **184**
Court Life Below Stairs, or London
 Under the First Georges 1714-1760.
 See Molloy, J.F.
Cowper, William
 Letters, 149
Crawford, Marion
 Dr. Claudius, 47
Critical and Miscellaneous Essays. See
 Carlyle, Thomas

D

Daudet, Alphonse
 Le Nabab, **185**
 Sappho, **185**
Daughter of the Philistines, A. See
 Boyeson, Hjalmar Hjorth
De Long, George Washington
 Voyage of the Jeanette, The, 94
Diderot and the Encyclopaedists. See
 Morley, John
Die verlorene Handschrift (The Lost
 Manuscript). See Freyatg, Gustav
Dillwyn, Elizabeth Amy
 Jill, **203**
Dr Breen's Practice. See Howells,
 William Dean
Dr Thorne. See Trollope, Anthony
Dr. Claudius. See Crawford, Marion
Dr. Grimshaw's Secret. See Hawthorne,
 Nathaniel
Drummond, Henry
 Natural Law in the Spiritual World,
 208
Dumas, Alexandre (fils)
 Tristan Le Roux, 132

Dutch Republic (History) (1856 onwards
 - 3 volumes). See Motley, J.L.

E

Eliot, George
 Adam Bede, **83**
 Amos Barton, **46**
 Romola, **83**
 Stories from Clerical Life, 106
Epistles. See Horace
Expansion of England. See Seeley,
 Professor John Robert

F

Fadette. See Sand, Georges
Feuillet, Octave
 Monsiuer Camors, **227**
Fielding, Henry
 Tom Jones, **149**
Fille de Fille. See Guérin, Jules
Folies Amoureuses (ed. By E. Rouveyre
 and G. Blond). See Mendès, Catulle
Fortnightly Review, The. See (Unknown
 author)
Frescoes. See Ouida (Marie Louise de la
 Ramée)
Freyatg, Gustav
 Die verlorene Handschrift (The Lost
 Manuscript), **225**
Froude, James Anthony
 Bunyan, 83
 Henry VIII, 73
 Short Studies on Great Subjects, 78

G

Gerard, Dorothea and Emily
 Reata, **21**
Godolphin Arabian, The. See Stephens,
 Brunton
Goldsmith, Oliver
 Vicar of Wakefield, The, 145
Gordon, Adam Lindsay
 How We Beat the Favourite, 96, 102,
 167
 Victorian Poet, The, **156**
Grandeur et décadence de César
 Birotteau. See Balzac, Honoré de
Green, Anna Katharine
 Leavenworth Case, The, **202**
Greville, Henry
 Leaves from the Diary of Henry
 Grenville, 188
Guérin, Jules
 Fille de Fille, **239**

H

Halves. See Payn, James
Harte, Bret
   (book of poems?), 81
Haworths, The. See Burnett, Frances Hodgson
Hawthorne, Nathaniel
   Dr. Grimshaw's Secret, 74
   House of the Seven Gables, The, **39**
   Scarlet Letter, The, 39
   Twice Told Tales, **186**
Heart of Midlothian, The. See Scott, Sir Walter
Heine, Heinrich
   (German Poetry), 100, 205, 207, 208
Hélène et Mathilde. See Belot, Adolphe
Henry VIII. See Froude, James Anthony
Hill, John
   Waters of Marah, The, 74
His Natural Life. See Clarke, Marcus
Histoire de la littérature anglaise. See Taine, Hippolyte Adolphe
Horace
   (Unknown book), 84, 185, 199
   Epistles, 200
House of the Seven Gables, The. See Hawthorne, Nathaniel
How We Beat the Favourite. See Gordon, Adam Lindsay
Howells, William Dean
   Dr Breen's Practice, 107

I

Illustrated London News, The. See (Unknown author)
Illustrated Sydney News, The. See (Unknown author)
Improvisatore, The. See Anderson, Hans Christian
Initials, The. See Tautphoeus, Baroness Jemima Montgomery
Interpreter, The. See Whyte-Melville, G.J.
Is Life Worth Living?. See Mallock, W.H.
Ivanhoe. See Scott, Sir Walter

J

Jill. See Dillwyn, Elizabeth Amy
John Bull et son Ile. See O'Rell, Max

K

Karr, Alphonse
   La Famille Alain, 132
King Lear. See Shakespeare, William
Kingsley, Henry
   No. 17, 151
   Ravenshoe, 153
   Recollections of Geoffrey Hamlyn, The, 153
Klytia (translated from the German by S.F. Corkran). See Taylor, George

L

L'allemagne amoureuse. See Tissot, Victor
La Bouche de Madame X. See Belot, Adolph
La Famille Alain. See Karr, Alphonse
La Fille Aux Yeux d'Or. See Balzac, Honoré de
La Vie. See Maupassant, Alfred de
La Viè de Jésus. See Renan, Joseph Erust
Lady Grizel. See Wingfield, Lewis Strange
Lambert, Charles J. and Mrs. S.
   Voyage of the Wanderer, The, **138**
Lancelot Ward M.P.. See Temple, George
Le Diable Boiteux. See Lesage, Alain René
Le Nabab. See Daudet, Alphonse
Leavenworth Case, The. See Green, Anna Katharine
Leaves from the Diary of Henry Grenville. See Greville, Henry
Lefebyre, Dr. René (pseudonym of Edouard Laboulaye)
   Paris en Amerique, **48**
Les Filles de John Bull. See O'Rell, Max
Les Fortunes de Rongon. See Zola, Emile
Lesage, Alain René
   Le Diable Boiteux, **185**
Letters. See Cowper, William
Lever, Charles
   (Unknown book), **163**
Life and Opinions of Tristram Shandy, Gentleman, The. See Sterne, Laurence
Life of Voltaire, The. See Oliphant, Margaret Oliphant (cousin of Laurence Oliphant)
Little Schoolmaster Mark (A Spiritual Romance), The. See Shorthouse, Joseph Henry
Lost Sir Massingbird. See Payn, James
Louisiana. See Burnett, Frances Hodgson
Lucretia. See Lytton, Lord (E. Bulwer Lytton)

Lytton, Lord (E. Bulwer Lytton)
Lucretia, 44

M

M. or N. Similia Similibus Curantur. See Whyte-Melville, G.J.
Macaulay, Thomas Babington (Essays), **224**
Madame Adam
   Paienne, **46**
Mallock, W.H.
   Is Life Worth Living?, 138
   New Paul & Virginia (or Positivism on an Island), The, **138**
   New Republic, 138
Malmesbury, Lord
   (Memoirs), 224
Malot, Hector
   Sans Famille (Nobody's Boy), **228**, 229
Mansfield Park. See Austen, Jane
Marryatt, Florence
   (supernatural fiction), 80
Matrimony. See Norris, William Edward
Maupassant, Alfred de
   La Vie, 22
McCarthy, Justin
   My Enemy's Daughter, 191
Melbourne Argus. See (Unknown author)
Mendès, Catulle
   Folies Amoureuses (ed. By E. Rouveyre and G. Blond), **224**
Meta Holdenis. See Cherbuliez, Victor
Midsummer Night's Dream, A. See Shakespeare, William
Molloy, J.F.
   Court Life Below Stairs, or London Under the First Georges 1714-1760, **87**
Monsiuer Camors. See Feuillet, Octave
Morley, John
   Diderot and the Encyclopaedists, 101
Motley, J.L.
   Dutch Republic (History) (1856 onwards - 3 volumes), 79
Murger, Louis Henri
   Scènes de la vie de Bohème, 101, **220**
My Enemy's Daughter. See McCarthy, Justin

N

Nais Micoulin. See Zola, Emile
Natural Law in the Spiritual World. See Drummond, Henry
New Paul & Virginia (or Positivism on an Island), The. See Mallock, W.H.
New Republic. See Mallock, W.H.
No New Thing. See Norris, William Edward
No. 17. See Kingsley, Henry
Norris, William Edward
   Matrimony, **60**
   No New Thing, **49**
Northanger Abbey. See Austen, Jane

O

O'Rell, Max
   John Bull et son Ile, **227**
   Les Filles de John Bull, **227**
Old Mortality. See Scott, Sir Walter
Oliphant, Laurence
   Altiora Peto, 32
Oliphant, Margaret Oliphant (cousin of Laurence Oliphant)
   Life of Voltaire, The, **83**
Oliver Cromwell's Letters and Speeches – with Elucidations. See Carlyle, Thomas
Othello. See Shakespeare, William
Ouida (Marie Louise de la Ramée)
   Frescoes, **159**
Our Old Actors. See Baker, Henry Barton

P

Paienne. See Madame Adam
Paris en Amerique. See Lefebyre, Dr. René (pseudonym of Edouard Laboulaye)
Payn, James
   Halves, **208**
   Lost Sir Massingbird, **213**
   Thicker than Water, **193**
Peck, George Wilbur
   Pecks Bad Boy, **45**
Pecks Bad Boy. See Peck, George Wilbur
Persuasion. See Austen, Jane
Praed, Mackworth
   (light/humorous poems), 81

Q

Quarterly Review. See (Unknown author)
Queensland Poet, The. See Stephens, Brunton

R

Rabelais, Francois

Index of Books

(Unknown book), **147**
Ravenshoe. See Kingsley, Henry
Reade, Charles
   Cloister and the Hearth, The, 83
   Readiana (letters), 157
   Woman Hater, A, **117**
Readiana (letters). See Reade, Charles
Reata. See Gerard, Dorothea and Emily
Recollections of Geoffrey Hamlyn, The. See Kingsley, Henry
Renan, Joseph Erust
   La Viè de Jésus, 230
   Sonneniers d'enfance et jeunesse (Recollections of my youth), **224**
Romola. See Eliot, George
Rudder Grange. See Stockton, Frank Richard

S

Samuel Brohl et Cie. See Cherbuliez, Victor
Sand, Georges
   Fadette, 159
Sans Famille (Nobody's Boy). See Malot, Hector
Sappho. See Daudet, Alphonse
Sarah Barnum. See Colombier, Marie
Scarlet Letter, The. See Hawthorne, Nathaniel
Scènes de la vie de Bohème. See Murger, Louis Henri
Scott, Sir Walter
   Heart of Midlothian, The, **83**
   Ivanhoe, **83**
   Old Mortality, **112**, 115
Seeley, Professor John Robert
   Expansion of England, **239**
Shakespeare, William
   (Unknown book), 23, 90, 171, 203
   King Lear, 23
   Midsummer Night's Dream, A, **195**
   Othello, 102
Short Studies on Great Subjects. See Froude, James Anthony
Shorthouse, Joseph Henry
   Little Schoolmaster Mark (A Spiritual Romance), The, 108
Smith, Sir Sydney
   (Articles/essays), **131**
Sonneniers d'enfance et jeunesse (Recollections of my youth). See Renan, Joseph Erust
St. James. See (Unknown author):St. James's Gazette
St. James's Gazette. See (Unknown author)
Stephens, Brunton

Godolphin Arabian, The, 161
Queensland Poet, The, 156
Sterne, Laurence
   Life and Opinions of Tristram Shandy, Gentleman, The, **147**
Stockton, Frank Richard
   Rudder Grange, **185**
Stories from Clerical Life. See Eliot, George

T

Taine, Hippolyte Adolphe
   Histoire de la littérature anglaise, **203**
Taine's history of English Literature. See Taine, Hippolyte Adolphe:Histoire de la littérature anglaise
Tautphoeus, Baroness Jemima Montgomery
   Initials, The, **21**
Taylor, George
   Klytia (translated from the German by S.F. Corkran), **103**
Temple, George
   Lancelot Ward M.P., **203**
Temple, Sir William
   (essays), 149
That Lass o' Lowries. See Burnett, Frances Hodgson
Thicker than Water. See Payn, James
Through One Administration. See Burnett, Frances Hodgson
Tissot, Victor
   L'allemagne amoureuse, 231
Tom Jones. See Fielding, Henry
Tristan Le Roux. See Dumas, Alexandre (fils)
Trollope, Anthony
   Autobiography, 96, 136
   Dr Thorne, 136
Twice Told Tales. See Hawthorne, Nathaniel

V

Vicar of Wakefield, The. See Goldsmith, Oliver
Victorian Poet, The. See Gordon, Adam Lindsay
Voyage of the Jeanette, The. See De Long, George Washington
Voyage of the Wanderer, The. See Lambert, Charles J. and Mrs. S.

W

Ward, Artemus (Charles Farrar Browne)
   (Targetted humour, letters etc.), **224**

Waters of Marah, The. See Hill, John
White Wings. See Black, William
Whyte-Melville, G.J.
   Interpreter, The, 169
   M. or N. Similia Similibus Curantur, **179**
Wingfield, Lewis Strange
   Lady Grizel, **186**
Woman Hater, A. See Reade, Charles

Y

Yolande – The Story of a Daughter. See Black, William

Z

Zola, Emile
   Les Fortunes de Rongon, 185
   Nais Micoulin, 235